Livelihoods, Natural Resources, and Post-Conflict Peacebuilding

Edited by Helen Young and Lisa Goldman

earthscan
from Routledge

First published 2015
by Routledge
2 Park Square, Milton Park, Abingdon, Oxon OX14 4RN

Simultaneously published in the USA and Canada
by Routledge
711 Third Avenue, New York, NY 10017

Routledge is an imprint of the Taylor & Francis Group, an informa business

British Library Cataloguing-in-Publication Data
A catalogue record for this book is available from the British Library

Library of Congress Cataloging-in-Publication Data
Livelihoods, natural resources, and post-conflict peacebuilding / edited by Helen Young and Lisa Goldman.
pages cm. – (Post-conflict peacebuilding and natural resource management); Includes bibliographical references and index.
ISBN 978-1-84971-233-0 (pbk.) – ISBN 978-1-84977-581-6 (ebk)
1. Peace-building–Environmental aspects. 2. Peace-building–Economic aspects. 3. Postwar reconstruction–Environmental aspects. 4. Postwar reconstruction–Economic aspects. 5. Natural resources–Management. I. Young, Helen, 1957– editor of compilation. II. Goldman, Lisa, editor of compilation.
JZ6300.L58 2013
327 .1'72–dc23

2013018249

Typeset in Times and Helvetica
by Graphicraft Limited, Hong Kong

FSC www.fsc.org MIX Paper from responsible sources FSC® C013604

Printed and bound by CPI Group (UK) Ltd, Croydon, CR0 4YY

Table of contents

Appendices

List of figures and tables

FIGURES

TABLES

Preface

Decades of civil wars, international wars, and wars of secession demonstrate the strong relationship between natural resources and armed conflict. Disputes over natural resources and their associated revenues can be among the reasons that people go to war. Diamonds, timber, oil, and even bananas and charcoal can provide sources of financing to sustain conflict. Forests, agricultural crops, and wells are often targeted during conflict. Efforts to negotiate an end to conflict increasingly include natural resources. And conflicts associated with natural resources are both more likely to relapse than non-resource-related conflicts, and to relapse twice as fast.

Immediately after the end of a conflict, a window of opportunity opens for a conflict-affected country and the international community to establish security, rebuild, and consolidate peace—or risk conflict relapse. This window also presents the opportunity to reform the management of natural resources and their revenues in ways that would otherwise be politically difficult to achieve. Capitalizing on this opportunity is particularly critical if natural resources contributed to the onset or financing of conflict—and, if this opportunity is lost, it may never reappear. Moreover, poorly informed policy decisions may become entrenched, locking in a trajectory that serves the interests of a limited few.

Since the end of the Cold War, and particularly since 2000, substantial progress has been made in establishing institutional and policy frameworks to consolidate peacebuilding efforts. In 2005, the United Nations established the Peacebuilding Commission to identify best practices for peacebuilding. The commission is the first body to bring together the UN's humanitarian, security, and development sectors so that they can learn from peacebuilding experiences.

The Peacebuilding Commission has started to recognize the importance of natural resources in post-conflict peacebuilding. In 2009, along with the United Nations Environment Programme, the commission published a pioneering report—*From Conflict to Peacebuilding: The Role of Natural Resources and the Environment*—that framed the basic ways in which natural resources contribute to conflict and can be managed to support peacebuilding. Building on this report, the commission is starting to consider how natural resources can be included within post-conflict planning and programming in Sierra Leone, the Central African Republic, Guinea, and other countries.

Since the establishment of the Peacebuilding Commission, the policies governing post-conflict peacebuilding have evolved rapidly. In his 2009 *Report of the Secretary-General on Peacebuilding in the Immediate Aftermath of Conflict*, UN Secretary-General Ban Ki-moon articulated five priorities for post-conflict peacebuilding, all of which have natural resource dimensions. In his 2010 update to that report, Ban Ki-moon noted the pressing need to improve post-conflict natural resource management to reduce the risk of conflict relapse, and urged "Member States and the United Nations system to make questions of natural resource allocation, ownership and access an integral part of peacebuilding strategies." The Secretary-General's 2012 report on the topic highlighted progress over the previous two years and called on UN entities to more effectively share knowledge and leverage expertise on post-conflict natural resource management. And a 2011 UN report, *Civilian Capacity in the Aftermath of Conflict*, highlighted approaches for mobilizing civil society to support peacebuilding in many realms, including natural resources.

The World Bank has also begun focusing on natural resources: the Bank's 2011 *World Development Report*, for example, placed the prevention of fragility, conflict, and violence at the core of the Bank's development mandate. Drawing on the Bank's experiences around the world, the report focuses on jobs, justice, and security, and highlights the contribution of natural resources to these goals.

Despite growing recognition of the importance of post-conflict natural resource management, there has been no comprehensive examination of how natural resources can support post-conflict peacebuilding. Nor has there been careful consideration of the risks to long-term peace caused by the failure to effectively address natural resources. Practitioners, researchers, and UN bodies have researched specific resources, conflict dynamics, and countries, but have yet to share their findings with each other at a meaningful scale, and limited connections have been drawn between the various strands of inquiry. As a result, the peacebuilding community does not know what works in what circumstances, what does not, or why.

Given the complexity of peacebuilding, practitioners and researchers alike are struggling to articulate good practice. It is increasingly clear that natural resources must be included as a foundational issue; many questions remain, however, regarding opportunities, options, and trade-offs.

Against this backdrop, the Environmental Law Institute, the UN Environment Programme, the University of Tokyo, and McGill University launched a research program designed to examine experiences in post-conflict peacebuilding and natural resource management; to identify lessons from these experiences; and to raise awareness of those lessons among practitioners and scholars. The program has benefited from broad support, with the government of Finland—one of the few donor governments to explicitly recognize the role of natural resources in both conflict and peacebuilding efforts—playing a catalytic role by providing core financing.

The research program has been guided by the collective experiences of the four members of the Steering Committee: as the coordinators of the program and the series editors, we have drawn on our work in more than thirty post-conflict countries. Our experiences—which include leading environmental assessments in Afghanistan, developing forest law in Liberia, supporting land reform in Mozambique, and fostering cooperation around water in Iraq—have led to a shared understanding that natural resource issues rarely receive the political attention they merit. Through this research program and partnership, we hope to catalyze a comprehensive global effort to demonstrate that peacebuilding substantially depends on the transformation of natural assets into peacebuilding benefits—a change that must occur without mortgaging the future or creating new conflict.

Since its inception in 2007, the program has grown dramatically in response to strong interest from practitioners, researchers, and policy makers. Participants in an initial scoping meeting suggested a single edited book consisting of twenty case studies and crosscutting analyses. It soon became clear, however, that the undertaking should reflect a much broader range of experiences, perspectives, and dimensions.

The research program yielded 150 peer-reviewed case studies and analyses written by 225 scholars, practitioners, and decision makers from fifty countries. The case studies and analyses have been assembled into a set of six edited books, each focusing on a specific set of natural resources or an aspect of peacebuilding: high-value natural resources; land; water; resources for livelihoods; assessment and restoration of natural resources; and governance. Examining a broad range of resources, including oil, minerals, land, water, wildlife, livestock, fisheries, forests, and agricultural products, the books document and analyze post-conflict natural resource management successes, failures, and ongoing efforts in sixty conflict-affected countries and territories. In their diversity and number, the books represent the most significant collection to date of experiences, analyses, and lessons in managing natural resources to support post-conflict peacebuilding.

In addition to the six edited books, the partnership has created an overarching book, *Post-Conflict Peacebuilding and Natural Resources: The Promise and the Peril*, which will be published by Cambridge University Press. This book draws on the six edited books to explore the role of natural resources in various peacebuilding activities across the humanitarian, security, and development sectors.

These seven books will be of interest to practitioners, researchers, and policy makers in the security, development, peacebuilding, political, and natural resource communities. They are designed to provide a conceptual framework, assess approaches, distill lessons, and identify specific options and trade-offs for more effectively managing natural resources to support post-conflict peacebuilding.

Natural resources present both opportunities and risks, and postponing their consideration in the peacebuilding process can imperil long-term peace and undermine sustainable development. Experiences from the past sixty years provide many lessons and broad guidance, as well as insight into which approaches are promising and which are problematic.

A number of questions, however, still lack definitive answers. We do not always understand precisely why certain approaches fail or succeed in specific instances, or which of a dozen contextual factors are the most important in determining the success of a peacebuilding effort. Nevertheless, numerous discrete measures related to natural resources can be adopted now to improve the likelihood of long-term peace. By learning from peacebuilding experiences to date, we can avoid repeating the mistakes of the past and break the cycle of conflict that has come to characterize so many countries. We also hope that this undertaking represents a new way to understand and approach peacebuilding.

Carl Bruch
Environmental Law Institute

David Jensen
United Nations Environment Programme

Mikiyasu Nakayama
University of Tokyo

Jon Unruh
McGill University

Foreword
Saving lives, losing livelihoods

Jan Egeland
Secretary General, Norwegian Refugee Council
Former UN Undersecretary-General for Humanitarian Affairs and Emergency Relief Coordinator

We live in an age of uniquely contradictory trends. Fewer lives are being lost to war, conflict, and terror than in previous decades (Human Security Report Project 2010). At the same time, the number of people affected by natural disasters has dramatically increased because vulnerable communities are increasingly exposed to extreme weather events (Vos et al. 2010). Thus, although the number of lives lost has decreased overall, more people are losing livelihoods, as well as their homes and other assets, to natural disasters.

There has been a steady decrease in child mortality worldwide and an increase in life expectancy in all but a handful of the world's 190 nations (World Bank 2011, 2013). But the economic distance between rich and poor nations is more extreme and more visible than ever before. When my great-grandfather was born in Norway, it was a dirt-poor country, and the richest nations were three times richer than the poorest. Now my country is among the very richest in the world—and a hundred times richer than one of the poorest nations.

We should be encouraged that in the post–Cold War era, the international community has become much better at ending wars and limiting conflicts. Accordingly, the number of armed conflicts has decreased over the past twenty years (UCDP 2012a). For conflicts with more than 1,000 casualties per year, the decrease is particularly encouraging: in Africa, for example, the number of larger armed conflicts was three times higher in the late 1990s than it is today, although it is worth noting that local, natural resource–based conflicts increased over this same time span (UCDP 2012b).

Yet during my thirty years of humanitarian, peace, and human rights work, one contradiction has stood out as especially striking: we keep people alive, but we fail to give them a productive life. In many of the developing and conflict-prone countries that I have visited, we end conflicts and save lives like never before, but too often fail to provide the young, the poor, and the vulnerable with the livelihoods they need to lead the lives they deserve. We fail to build the self-sustaining economies that can lift the bottom 2 billion people out of the abject poverty created by strife, exploitation, armed conflict, and disasters.

A SENSE OF INJUSTICE

Many of the world's poorest people have a sense that the system is stacked against them—that their futures will be as bleak as their present. They feel that they will never have access to the livelihoods and careers of those in developed countries. The data that support their sense of injustice are stark.

Today, a handful of individuals possess greater wealth than the total assets of the poorest billion; in fact, these individuals' wealth exceeds the combined gross national product of the least-developed countries. The poorest 40 percent of the world's population possess 5 percent of global income, whereas the richest 20 percent own 75 percent of global income. To make things worse, 80 percent of the world's population lives in countries where income differentials are increasing (UNDP 2007).

Whether these realities make today's world more unjust than previous ages is debatable, but there is one undeniable new factor: more people *perceive* the world as profoundly unjust—because in the interdependent global village of today, more people know of the enormous distance between the top few and the bottom many. In my grandparents' time, it was not well-known how people in other nations lived or how unevenly global wealth was distributed. Today, even in the remotest, poorest, and most chaotic places on the planet, people know that there are extreme differences in quality of life from one society to the next. The young and the restless learn of the great disparities by surfing the internet. Thus, in societies where people still struggle to get a primary education, it is known that elsewhere, the majority of the population receive from fifteen to twenty years of education—including primary and secondary school, and then either university or vocational training. It is known that pets in many rich societies eat better than children in poor societies. Finally, it is known that in some societies, many people receive sophisticated medical treatments over the course of their lives, whereas other societies lack even enough primary health care to prevent death from diarrhea.

Thus, even at a time when most people are seeing substantial progress in their lives, and there is reason for great optimism, there is also cause for great anger, especially concerning the 1.4 billion youngsters who should be in school or entering productive adult lives—but are not. Who can imagine the volcanic sense of injustice building among these unemployed, uneducated, underengaged youth? For them, the playing field is not level, nor are their opportunities equal. And it is in this context that we have seen, in recent years, the rise of radical demagogues who thrive on the pent-up anger of the disenfranchised—demonizing other civilizations, religions, and neighboring regions to foment conflict based on dangerous and inaccurate stereotypes. This book explores the important links between supporting livelihoods and building confidence to achieve a more productive and satisfying future.

LESSONS FROM PEACEBUILDING: THE IMPORTANCE OF SUPPORTING LIVELIHOODS

From my participation in more than ten peace processes as a mediator, facilitator, observer, or donor representative, I have learned that it is difficult to make bitter enemies agree to a peace plan. And as difficult as it is to achieve an agreement, it is even more difficult to implement it (Egeland 2008). Years of intense conflict create a climate of mistrust and suspicion that can be poisonous when trying to reach consensus on the protection of minority populations, the return of refugees, the reintegration of excombatants, the guarantee of human rights, and efforts (such as truth-finding processes) to address past abuses.

Protracted armed conflict, when combined with high-level, internationally mediated peace processes, can create unrealistic expectations of social and economic progress that cannot be achieved within the time frame that is usually set out in the agreed-upon implementation schedules. I have seen from close up—in Palestine after the Oslo I Accord in 1993, in Bosnia after the Dayton Accords, in Guatemala after the 1996 peace deal, and in South Sudan after the 2005 Comprehensive Peace Agreement—that the so-called peace dividend takes more time to realize than expected (Egeland 2008). Instead, the immediate post-war period is usually not one of economic growth but of stagnation and disorder.

One of the greatest challenges to securing a lasting peace is the reintegration of excombatants. To prevent relapse into conflict, it is important to reintegrate former fighters into civilian life; but the cost of doing so is inevitably higher than expected (and much higher than keeping them in uniform). Moreover, many of the programs designed to prepare former combatants for civilian work are unsuited for the local social and cultural context or natural resource base. As a result, they are unable to absorb those who may only know one thing: how to fight.

If we are to build robust and peaceful societies, nothing is more important than creating and sustaining livelihoods. If communities fail to transform natural resources and youthful labor into economic development, and thereby provide sustainable livelihoods, there will always be the threat of more conflict, more strife, and more disasters. This is what I saw, firsthand, as a United Nations Envoy, as a Red Cross official, and as a Norwegian State Secretary visiting Guatemala and El Salvador, Liberia and Côte d'Ivoire, northern Uganda and South Sudan, Mali and Burundi, Bosnia and Kosovo, Nepal and Cambodia. In most of these war-torn societies, peace was and is definitively breaking out. But livelihoods and the wider economic recovery remain extremely fragile. Criminal violence is unacceptably high, and reintegration of former combatants is incomplete. Economic development is slow (and reversible), and unemployment is dangerously high—in part because of conflict-related changes, including population displacement, and the unsustainable use of natural resources and land.

Livelihoods in post-conflict situations often depend on a common natural resource, with multiple and often overlapping rights. And the rules of ownership, as we understand them in developed countries, often do not apply. Relations between farming and pastoralist groups who previously shared local resources may have irrevocably broken down during the conflict—a problem that may not be addressed by a peace agreement between warring factions at a higher level. This was the case in the central highlands of Afghanistan, where ownership and rights of access to pastures used by both Pashtun nomads and settled

Hazara communities have been contested, contributing to protracted conflict over recent decades. Similarly, in the Karimojong Cluster of Kenya and Uganda, continuing conflict and violence have created widespread insecurity, undermining the livelihoods of local pastoralists. It is important for international organizations operating in particular areas to understand that traditional or local dispute resolution practices—not top-down edicts—are often the best means of repairing broken relations.

This book is a valuable contribution to our understanding of the role of livelihoods and natural resources in post-conflict peacebuilding. The chapters analyze how peacebuilding can be achieved beyond ceasefires and demobilization ceremonies. They also show how natural resources, which are often available in abundance in the midst of conflict and poverty, can help build sustainable economies, jobs, homes, and services, instead of becoming a curse that leads to corruption, inequality, and divisiveness. Finally, the chapters demonstrate how we can avoid having hard-won peace accords collapse and new tensions develop, simply because there was no alternative income for those who lived by the gun and no peace dividends for civilians who lived in the cross fire.

MULTILATERAL ACTION AND LIVELIHOODS PROTECTION

As the UN Emergency Relief Coordinator, I saw time and again how effective multilateral action with local and regional partners could bring relief and emergency health care to large communities. Through the UN, we coordinated massive, lifesaving international relief efforts in response to the Indian Ocean tsunami and the Darfur crisis in 2004, the South Asian earthquake in 2005, the Lebanon war in 2006, and humanitarian disasters in the Horn of Africa and Southern Africa. While far too many people lost their lives in these overwhelming emergencies, lives were also saved because multilateral action, building on local capacities, has become so much more effective than in previous generations.

Too often, however, collective humanitarian action still fails after the emergency phase. We fail because the countries participating in multilateral action often lack unity of purpose. We fail, tragically and repeatedly, when the UN and regional organizations are not provided with the needed political will, or the minimum of economic and security resources, from their member states. Ongoing suffering in many conflict-ridden societies, from Somalia to Colombia, and among growing numbers of climate-change victims in developing countries, stems from a lack of coherent peacebuilding efforts, failure to engage in disaster risk reduction, or simply passive neglect among the leading national, regional, and global actors that could have improved the situation.

To succeed, international action must be timely, it must be coherent, and it must include planning for long-term development after the immediate humanitarian crisis is addressed. Back in 2003 and early 2004, I did believe—naively, it now appears—that the growing Darfur crisis would improve when we managed to bring it to the attention of world leaders. This was, after all, no tsunami, earthquake, or forest fire: the violence and the ethnic cleansing were human caused—and, we believed, could be reversed by humans. But the international response was neither united nor coherent (Egeland 2008). There was too little diplomatic, political, security, and developmental investment in preventing the conflict, in stopping the government-sponsored abuse, and in supporting the sustainable livelihoods of both farmers and pastoralists in drylands where changing land use patterns and insecure land tenure had become a source of conflict.

The only early and sizable international operation in Darfur was, again, humanitarian, which succeeded in reaching displaced persons and refugees once a humanitarian ceasefire agreement had been negotiated in April 2004. The scaling-up of humanitarian operations from a tiny presence to one that eventually delivered assistance to more than 3.5 million people—and that, by 2005, had successfully reduced malnutrition and mortality rates—was an unprecedented achievement. However, with the failure of the 2006 Darfur Peace Agreement, the emergency-affected population was left in limbo, largely because even protracted humanitarian aid was insufficient to address the underlying vulnerabilities and build resilient livelihoods.

In addition to increasing understanding of (1) the vital link between natural resources and local livelihoods and (2) the importance of environmental protection for peace and recovery, the Darfur humanitarian operations contributed crucial lessons on the environmental implications of humanitarian action, sensitizing humanitarians worldwide to their environmental footprint (Tearfund 2007; Bromwich 2008). The result was increasingly effective relief efforts, including improved food distribution and emergency health care—which led, in turn, to rapidly dropping mortality rates. At the same time, the effort revealed that humanitarian aid is only a first step in peacebuilding and does not provide the sustainable, long-term programs that are needed to build security, governmental institutions, and livelihoods (Bromwich 2008). Our efforts in Darfur did not stop the atrocities, help refugees to return home, or create security. Nor did they protect or support livelihoods, or provide livelihood alternatives, all of which could have encouraged reconciliation among the various groups that seemed to be locked in competition for scarce water and land. Moreover, the humanitarian initiatives exacerbated the underlying environmental degradation that had led these groups to compete for scarce resources (Tearfund 2007).

Today, there are several times more internally displaced persons, refugees, and destitute victims of the Darfur conflict than there were when we started our work in the winter of 2003–2004. By 2009, the World Food Programme Emergency Operation estimated that 3.8 million, or a clear majority of Darfuris, continued to be food insecure and to rely on food handouts because prolonged displacement and insecurity had deprived them of their livelihoods (WFP 2010). In a drylands environment where the economy and local livelihoods are largely based on agriculture, both sedentary farming and pastoralist livestock production require support in order to ensure more equitable development and peaceful comanagement of natural resources.

CLIMATE CHANGE: REDUCING THE RISK OF NATURAL DISASTERS

A paralysis similar to what we have seen in Darfur is costing lives in the context of a very different global challenge: climate change. If UN member nations had managed to curb greenhouse gas emissions—as they agreed to do at the 1992 Earth Summit, in Rio de Janeiro—there might not have been such a relentless increase in the number of lives devastated by extreme weather events, nor such heightened vulnerability among the 2 billion poorest people on our planet.

Many more people have been displaced by natural disasters than by armed conflicts. Over five years, 144 million people have been forced from their homes, with 83 percent of this displacement triggered by climate- and weather-related hazards such as floods, storms, and wildfires (IDMC 2013). As a result of increasing atmospheric greenhouse gas concentrations and growing societal vulnerability to climatic conditions, extreme weather and climatic events are likely to increase in frequency, magnitude, and consequence—putting peacebuilding and post-conflict development efforts at risk. A society undergoing a tenuous post-conflict recovery is particularly vulnerable to natural disasters. To worsen matters, the two are often related, as in the case of Darfur, which has a long history of drought-related famine and food insecurity linked to climate variability. Approximately 90 percent of current disasters are associated with weather and climatic factors such as strong winds, heavy rain (resulting in floods), absence of rain (resulting in droughts), and very high or very low temperatures (WMO 2011). Climate change has driven up the intensity, frequency, duration, spatial extent, and damage of extreme weather and climatic events (IPCC 2012). Floods and storms alone account for almost three-quarters of recorded disasters (WMO 2011). As a consequence of decades of conflict, poverty, bad governance, and overpopulation, many countries have become so vulnerable that even small natural events can lead to considerable damage and loss of income and jobs. Climate-related events can also substantially limit livelihood options, as well as exhaust the resources societies and communities require to prepare for and respond to future disasters (IPCC 2012). Good preventive action, planning, and preparation can substantially diminish levels of exposure and vulnerability, reducing loss of life and loss of livelihoods. Important steps—such as the implementation of the Hyogo Framework for Action and the Global Framework for Climate Services—are being taken to plan for and counteract extreme climate effects and preserve livelihoods.[1]

In 2005, I presided over the World Conference on Disaster Reduction—held in Kobe, Japan—which endorsed the Hyogo Framework for Action 2005–2015, whose goal is to increase disaster resilience in both communities and nations. The framework is an ambitious plan of action that emphasizes preparedness,

---

[1] For more information on the Hyogo Framework for Action, see www.unisdr.org/we/coordinate/hfa.

awareness, and risk reduction, in order to help build societies that are capable of protecting lives and livelihoods.

Through 2010, I chaired a task force that initiated the development of a global system to provide climate information, predictions, and advice that will protect the lives, livelihoods, and homes of vulnerable people. This task force proposed the Global Framework for Climate Services, which has since been set up and will provide substantial social and economic benefits through contributions to development, disaster risk reduction, and climate change adaptation (WMO 2011).[2] While all countries stand to gain from participation in this framework, our task force believes that priority should be given to climate-vulnerable developing countries (particularly African countries), the least-developed countries, landlocked developing countries, and small island developing states, where livelihoods are most at risk and where climate services are also often weakest.

A number of countries and organizations are collaborating on the Global Risk Identification Programme, led by the United Nations Development Programme, to develop sustainable national risk-information systems that would include comprehensive, multihazard national risk profiles.[3] Climate information is also being increasingly used in routine risk-reduction operations, including preparedness and response efforts undertaken by humanitarian organizations: for example, in parts of Africa that are subject to drought or excessive rainfall, the International Federation of the Red Cross and Red Crescent Societies and the World Food Programme are relying on climate and weather predictions to ensure that supplies and capacities are sufficient to cope with potential climate and weather-related stresses (WMO 2011). Such efforts will enhance post-conflict countries' understanding of the importance of promoting livelihoods that are resilient to climate change.

NETWORKS OF THE LIKE-MINDED

Even though we have failed so far to lift the bottom billions out of poverty, today the world is seeing an unprecedented network of like-minded intergovernmental, governmental, and nongovernmental organizations channeling investments toward livelihoods support, community resilience, and economic redevelopment. National developmental and humanitarian agencies can feed, vaccinate, and provide primary school for children for a couple of dollars a day, even in the most remote crisis areas. But they can be more effective if post-conflict humanitarian assistance is integrated with longer-term reconstruction, including livelihood creation.

Such investment is, dollar for dollar, more cost efficient than anything I know of anywhere in the private or public sector. Local nongovernmental groups

---

[2] For more information on the Global Framework for Climate Services, see www.gfcs-climate.org/content/about-gfcs.

[3] For more information on the Global Risk Identification Programme, see www.undp.org/content/undp/en/home/ourwork/crisispreventionandrecovery/projects_initiatives/global_risk_identificationprogramme/.

working with international agencies can and should speak up more systematically for neglected peoples and communities. In fact, hundreds of humanitarian and human rights organizations are already holding governments in crisis-affected countries accountable for what will be most beneficial to neglected peoples and communities—namely, sustainable and resilient livelihoods.

In the future we must think more strategically, and more locally, about our long-term efforts to sustain livelihoods and make societies resilient to hazards and strife. We must work more closely with local government and civil society to strengthen their capacity for handling crises and exercising good governance. We must find better ways to forge coordination and partnerships locally, nationally, and internationally. Through such collaborative actions, we will be better able to tap local resources and local expertise. Time and again we see, as in recent natural disasters, that more lives are saved in earthquakes, floods, and tsunamis by local groups than by any expensive airborne fire brigade. Similarly, it is usually local and regional actors who make or break peacebuilding efforts, and who should be empowered to create local livelihoods based on local natural resources.

Never before has there been a generation with the resources, the technology, the political mandate, and the knowledge necessary to realize peacebuilding and development worldwide. For us it is a question of will—and, as this book so clearly demonstrates, the will first of all to ask and to learn what works, and what is needed, to create and preserve sustainable livelihoods in countries recovering from conflict.

REFERENCES

Bromwich, B. 2008. Environmental degradation and conflict in Darfur: Implications for peace and recovery. *Humanitarian Exchange* 39:22–28.

Egeland, J. 2008. *A billion lives: Reports from the frontlines of humanity*. New York: Simon and Schuster.

Human Security Report Project. 2010. *Human security report 2009/2010: The causes of peace and the shrinking costs of war*. New York: Oxford University Press. www.hsrgroup.org/human-security-reports/20092010/text.aspx.

IDMC (Internal Displacement Monitoring Centre). 2013. *Global estimates 2012: People displaced by disasters*. Geneva, Switzerland. www.internal-displacement.org/8025708F004BE3B1/(httpInfoFiles)/99E6ED11BB84BB27C1257B6A0035FDC4/$file/global-estimates-2012-may2013.pdf.

IPCC (Intergovernmental Panel on Climate Change). 2012. *Managing the risks of extreme events and disasters to advance climate change adaptation*. Cambridge, UK: Cambridge University Press. http://ipcc-wg2.gov/SREX/images/uploads/SREX-All_FINAL.pdf.

Tearfund. 2007. *Darfur: Relief in a vulnerable environment*. Teddington, UK. www.tearfund.org/webdocs/website/Campaigning/Policy%20and%20research/Relief%20in%20a%20vulnerable%20envirionment%20final.pdf.

UCDP (Uppsala Conflict Data Program). 2012a. Armed conflicts by region, 1946–2011. www.pcr.uu.se/digitalAssets/122/122540_conflict_region_2011.pdf.

———. 2012b. UCDP conflict encyclopedia. www.ucdp.uu.se/database.

UNDP (United Nations Development Programme). 2007. *Human development report 2007/2008—Fighting climate change: Human solidarity in a divided world.* New York. http://hdr.undp.org/en/media/HDR_20072008_EN_Complete.pdf.

Vos, F., J. Rodriguez, R. Below, and D. Guha-Sapir. 2010. *Annual disaster statistical review 2009: The numbers and trends.* Louvain, Belgium: Centre for Research on the Epidemiology of Disasters. www.who.int/hac/techguidance/ems/annual_disaster_statistical_review_2009.pdf.

WFP (World Food Programme). 2010. Sudan EMOP 10760.0: Food assistance to populations affected by conflict; An operation evaluation. Report No. OE/2010/011. http://documents.wfp.org/stellent/groups/public/documents/reports/wfp227202.pdf.

World Bank. 2011. *World development report 2011: Conflict, security, and development.* Washington, D.C.

———. 2013. *World development report 2013: Jobs.* Washington, D.C.

WMO (World Meteorological Organization). 2011. *Climate knowledge for action: A global framework for climate services—Empowering the most vulnerable.* Geneva, Switzerland. www.wmo.int/hlt-gfcs/downloads/HLT_book_full.pdf.

Acknowledgments

This book is the culmination of many years of research. It would not have been possible without the efforts and contributions of many individuals and institutions.

The volume editors are grateful to our managing editor, Peter Whitten, and our manuscript editors, Sandy Chizinsky, Meg Cox, Kit Johnston, and Amanda Morgan, for their peerless editorial assistance. We are also thankful for the support of our assistant managing editors, Whitney Stohr, Annie Brock, and Sarah Wegmueller, who skillfully shepherded the book through the publication process. Nick Bellorini, of Earthscan, provided guidance; Matthew Pritchard, Arthur Green, and Elan Spitzberg created the maps; and Joelle Stallone proofread the manuscript. We are also grateful to our colleagues at Tufts University for their comments and support.

Research and publication assistance was provided by numerous research associates, interns, law clerks, and visiting attorneys at the Environmental Law Institute, including Peter Aldinger, Elliott August, Jonny Beirne, Susan Bokermann, Marion Boulicault, Gwen Brown, Joanna Chan, Sophie Cottle, Ilona Coyle, Lauren Eineker, Akiva Fishman, Marisa Garcia, Sabrina Ghouse, Tristana Giunta, Ayushi Harayan, Katelyn Henmueller, Abbie Kagan, Rachel Kenigsberg, Amber Kim, Tim Kovach, Sonia Ledith, Brett Lingle, Vrinda Manglik, Shanna McClain, Mark McCormick-Goodhart, Brianna Menke, Asma Mian, Emily Norford, Katarina Petursson, Nancy Rachlis, Delphine Robert, Doug Sharp, Sarah Stellberg, Marielle Velander, Philip Womble, Patrick Woolsey, Louise Yeung, and Joel Young.

Peer reviewers were essential to ensuring the rigor of this volume. The editors would like to acknowledge the many professionals and scholars who contributed anonymous peer reviews.

Financial support for the project was provided by the United Nations Environment Programme (UNEP), the government of Finland, the U.S. Agency for International Development, the European Union, the University of Tokyo Graduate School of Frontier Sciences and Alliance for Global Sustainability, the John D. and Catherine T. MacArthur Foundation, the Canadian Social Science and Humanities Research Council, the Philanthropic Collaborative, the Center for Global Partnership of the Japan Foundation, the Ploughshares Fund, the

Compton Foundation, Zonta Club of Tokyo I, the International Union for Conservation of Nature's Commission on Environmental Law, the Nelson Talbott Foundation, the Jacob L. and Lillian Holtzmann Foundation, and an anonymous donor. In-kind support for the project was provided by the Earth Institute of Columbia University, the Environmental Change and Security Project of the Woodrow Wilson International Center for Scholars, the Environmental Law Institute, the Global Infrastructure Fund Research Foundation Japan, the Japan Institute of International Affairs, McGill University, the Peace Research Institute Oslo, UNEP, and the University of Tokyo.

The cover was designed by Nikki Meith. Cover photography is by Boris Heger/Das Fotoarchiv/Still Pictures.

Except as otherwise specifically noted, the maps in this publication use public domain data originating from Natural Earth (2009, www.naturalearthdata.com).

The designations employed and the presentations do not imply the expressions of any opinion whatsoever on the part of UNEP or contributory organizations concerning the legal status of any country, territory, city or area or its authority, or concerning the delimitation of its frontiers or boundaries.

When available, URLs are provided for sources that can be accessed electronically. URLs contained in this book were current at the time of publication.

Managing natural resources for livelihoods: Supporting post-conflict communities

Helen Young and Lisa Goldman

Reestablishing livelihoods is critical to post-conflict redevelopment and peacebuilding. In the wake of violent conflict, there is both an immediate need to address humanitarian concerns, and a longer-term need to rebuild local, regional, and national capacity for development. Promoting production and providing employment, particularly to former combatants, is paramount. Addressing competition and grievances over access to land, water, forests, and other natural resources—the building blocks of livelihoods in many developing countries—is another priority. All of these challenges involve livelihoods, the focus of this book.

Livelihoods provide the means through which people can rebuild their lives and local communities in the aftermath of conflict. Supporting livelihoods thus promotes local, regional, and national stability and is also key to reintegrating excombatants and other vulnerable groups into post-conflict society, thereby reducing the likelihood of future conflict. Moreover, providing viable livelihood strategies for vulnerable populations may prevent or mitigate further conflict by reducing the incentives to join armed groups.

Rehabilitating areas damaged by conflict requires more than simply restoring physical infrastructure and disbanding militant groups; effective redevelopment must also address the human element of conflict by enabling former adversaries to again live side by side, with both a sense of hope for the present and an opportunity to thrive in the future. In addition to meeting basic needs, livelihoods are important to identity: they contribute to self-worth, confidence, and dignity. Finally, livelihoods offer opportunities for interaction between former warring groups—whether through migration, trade, the exchange of labor, or the shared governance and use of natural resources.

Helen Young is research director at the Feinstein International Center and a professor at the Friedman School of Nutrition Science and Policy, both at Tufts University. Lisa Goldman is a senior attorney with the Environmental Law Institute. The authors are grateful to Whitney Stohr for her significant contributions to this introduction.

This introductory chapter contains three principal parts: (1) a description of the nexus between livelihoods, natural resources, and peacebuilding; (2) a review of the objectives and scope of this book; and (3) a brief conclusion.

LIVELIHOODS, NATURAL RESOURCES, AND PEACEBUILDING

According to one widely accepted definition, a livelihood comprises "the capabilities, assets (including both material and social resources) and activities required for a means of living" (Scoones 1998, 5).[1] Violent conflict frequently damages or destroys the natural resources and infrastructure—including local institutions—that support livelihood systems. When traditional livelihoods are no longer accessible or are severely undermined, conflict-affected populations are forced either to adapt their current livelihoods or to adopt new, and often unsustainable, strategies. In such cases, existing local grievances may be exacerbated, contributing to ongoing insecurity and potentially fostering further conflict. Similarly, when members of local communities engage in maladaptive or illicit means of supporting themselves—including joining local armed groups—further insecurity may result.

Following conflict, recovery programs designed to strengthen existing livelihoods can help ensure that communities are more resilient to future conflict. Both the livelihood systems available in a particular geographic area and the process of designing livelihood-related peacebuilding interventions are influenced by a number of factors, including the local ecology; access to physical and social infrastructure; and a combination of social, economic, and political influences. In post-conflict and conflict-prone regions, livelihoods (or the absence or loss of livelihood opportunities) can substantially shape—and be shaped by—conflict resolution and peacebuilding processes. (For an overview of key terms and concepts related to natural resources and post-conflict peacebuilding, see sidebar.)

A significant percentage of the population in many developing countries, including those affected by conflict, depends directly on natural resources for subsistence and livelihoods. In post-conflict countries, 60 to 80 percent of livelihoods rely on agriculture and natural resources (Bruch et al. 2009; USAID 2009). In such settings, conflict often has devastating implications for livelihoods, and for economic well-being in general. On average, conflict leads to production losses of 12 percent and slows agricultural growth by 3 percent per year (Huggins et al. 2006)—troubling statistics, given the significant role agriculture plays in post-conflict countries.

Armed conflict undermines livelihood security. Landmines are often planted in rural areas, threatening life and health, as well as limiting access to farmland, roads, drinking water, and forestry resources. Safely removing millions of unexploded landmines could greatly expand land available for agriculture—by between 88 and 200 percent in Afghanistan, 135 percent in Cambodia, 11 percent in Bosnia and Herzegovina, and 4 percent in Mozambique (Messer, Cohen, and Marchione 2001).

---

[1] This definition draws upon definitions by Chambers and Conway (1992) and others.

Post-conflict peacebuilding and natural resources: Key terms and concepts

Following conflict, peacebuilding actors leverage a country's available assets (including natural resources) to transition from conflict to peace and sustainable development. Peacebuilding actors work at the international, national, and subnational levels and include national and subnational government bodies; United Nations agencies and other international organizations; international and domestic nongovernmental organizations; the private sector; and the media. Each group of peacebuilding actors deploys its own tools, and there are a growing number of tools to integrate the peacebuilding efforts of different types of actors.

A post-conflict period typically begins after a peace agreement or military victory. Because this period is often characterized by intermittent violence and instability, it can be difficult to pinpoint when the post-conflict period ends. For the purposes of this book, the post-conflict period may be said to end when political, security, and economic discourse and actions no longer revolve around armed conflict or the impacts of conflict, but focus instead on standard development objectives. Within the post-conflict period, the first two years are referred to as the *immediate aftermath of conflict* (UNSG 2009), which is followed by a period known as *peace consolidation*.

According to the United Nations, "Peacebuilding involves a range of measures targeted to reduce the risk of lapsing or relapsing into conflict by strengthening national capacities at all levels for conflict management, and to lay the foundations for sustainable peace and development" (UNSG's Policy Committee 2007). In many instances, this means addressing the root causes of the conflict.

There are many challenges to peacebuilding: insecurity, ethnic and political polarization (as well as marginalization), corruption, lack of governmental legitimacy, extensive displacement, and loss of property. To address these and other challenges, peacebuilding actors undertake diverse activities that advance four broad peacebuilding objectives:*

- *Establishing security*, which encompasses basic safety and civilian protection; security sector reform; disarmament, demobilization, and reintegration; and demining.
- *Delivering basic services*, including water, sanitation, waste management, and energy, as well as health care and primary education.
- *Restoring the economy and livelihoods*, which includes repairing and constructing infrastructure and public works.
- *Rebuilding governance and inclusive political processes*, which encompasses dialogue and reconciliation processes, rule of law, dispute resolution, core government functions, transitional justice, and electoral processes.

Although they are sometimes regarded as distinct from peacebuilding, both peacemaking (the negotiation and conclusion of peace agreements) and humanitarian assistance are relevant to peacebuilding, as they can profoundly influence the options for post-conflict programming. Peacemaking and humanitarian assistance are also relevant to this book, in that they often have substantial natural resource dimensions.

Successful peacebuilding is a transformative process in which national and international actors seek to address grievances and proactively lay the foundation for a lasting peace. As part of this process, peacebuilding actors seek to manage the country's assets—as well as whatever international assistance may be available—to ensure security, provide basic services, rebuild the economy and livelihoods, and restore governance. The assets of a post-conflict country include natural resources; infrastructure; and human, social, and financial capital. Natural resources comprise land, water, and other renewable resources, as well as extractive resources such as oil, gas, and minerals. The rest of the book explores the many ways in which natural resources affect post-conflict peacebuilding.

---

* This framework draws substantially from the *Report of the Secretary-General on Peacebuilding in the Immediate Aftermath of Conflict* (UNSG 2009), but the activities have been regrouped and supplemented by activities articulated in USIP and U.S. Army PKSOI (2009); Sphere Project (2004, 2011); UN (2011); UNSG (2010, 2012); and International Dialogue on Peacebuilding and Statebuilding (2011).

Syria, where the agricultural sector has suffered gravely as a result of the civil war,[2] provides a vivid example of the economic and livelihood impacts of conflict. Despite favorable climatic conditions, wheat production has dropped by 40 percent in comparison to pre-crisis levels, and the shrinking supply of labor, physical capital, and arable land has led to diminished harvests for all crops since the conflict began (ACAPS 2013). Similarly, in Wajir District, Kenya, the effects of localized conflict—including livestock raids—have been severe and widespread: the majority of households have experienced reduced access to food (69 percent), trade (63 percent), education (61 percent), and health care (59 percent) (Omosa 2005).

In many instances, livelihood insecurity is both a driver of armed conflict and its result. In the Darfur region of Sudan, for example, 80 percent of the population relies on natural resources for livelihoods (UNDP 2008). In the decades preceding the outbreak of conflict in 2003, national government policies marginalized the Darfuri population socially, politically, and economically. The combination of marginalization, expansion of agriculture, and population growth among Darfuris led to the breakdown of local systems for managing natural resources, and to increased competition for land, water, fodder, and pasture (UNEP 2007). Furthermore, climate variability, including frequent droughts, has exacerbated tensions between farming and herding groups, which have historically shared natural resources. The long-term failure to address the grievances between Darfuri groups—including grievances focused on natural resources—generated localized tribal conflict; when the rebellion erupted in 2003, the dividing lines between those who supported the Darfuri rebels and those who supported the government were clearly drawn.

In the context of Sudan's national conflict, access to natural resources continues to be a crucial issue—particularly for internally displaced persons, many of whom are confined to camps with restricted access to land and other natural resources. Among those who have not been displaced, conflict over natural resources—between pastoralists and farmers, as well as between different pastoralist groups—has continued to undermine livelihoods.

In short, more than a decade of protracted conflict and insecurity has severely weakened livelihoods, forcing conflict-affected populations to adopt coping strategies—many of which are short-term and environmentally unsustainable, and which have actually increased livelihood insecurity for some groups. This growing insecurity is especially harmful to women, for whom the threat of gender-based violence has substantially limited access to natural resources (UNEP et al. 2013).

In 2009, the United Nations Environment Programme reported that at least 40 percent of all intrastate conflicts during the previous sixty years had involved natural resources, and that at least eighteen violent conflicts since 1990 had been fueled by natural resource exploitation (UNEP 2009a). Resolving disputes over

[2] The Syrian civil war began in 2011 and is ongoing as of this writing.

natural resources and strengthening natural resource management are thus essential to peacebuilding. Given the extent to which livelihoods in post-conflict countries depend on access to and use of natural resources, the revitalization or sustainable development of natural resource–based livelihoods is valuable not only for helping to address local vulnerabilities, but also for promoting cooperation between former adversaries. At the same time, however, unsustainable resource use can degrade the natural resource base, exacerbating local tensions and grievances and potentially contributing to ongoing insecurity and recurring conflict.

In the absence of good governance systems and institutions, land, pasture, forests, and other natural resources central to livelihoods are often a source of local conflict, which can present risks to peacebuilding. However, as discussed later in this book, the interconnections between livelihoods, natural resources, and conflict also present opportunities. In Afghanistan, for example, 85 percent of the population engages in natural resource–based livelihoods, including agricultural production, and 53 percent of the rural population lives in poverty (UNEP 2009b). An estimated two-thirds of Afghan households own livestock (Sexton 2012), and as much as 70 percent of the land in Afghanistan is used for grazing or fodder (UNEP 2009b). Chronic drought has significantly affected natural resource–based livelihoods, decreasing wheat production and the price of livestock by as much as 70 percent. This, in turn, has limited farmers' and pastoralists' purchasing power, as well as their ability to generate sufficient income to meet basic needs (Rassul 2010). Under these difficult and complex economic circumstances, it is not surprising that between 28 and 36 percent of local conflicts in Afghanistan are linked directly to land access and use (Sexton 2012). A 2008 survey found that land and water were the greatest sources of local conflict in Afghanistan (Waldman 2008).

In many conflict-affected countries, the lack of statutory recognition of customary rights to land and other natural resources is a key challenge. In Cambodia, approximately 90 percent of the population, most of whom depend on agriculture and agricultural production (IFAD 2007), live in rural areas. As of 2000, more than 8.5 million Cambodians depended on natural resources for their livelihoods, including 7 million who relied on natural resources for subsistence (McKenney and Tola 2002). In 2002, agriculture, forestry, and fisheries made up 30 percent of the nation's gross domestic product (GDP) and supported 77 percent of all livelihoods; agriculture alone accounted for 23 percent of the GDP and 74 percent of livelihoods (McKenney and Tola 2002). As of 2004, however, despite this dependence on land-based resources, as many as 80 percent of rural households lacked statutory title to land, and 20 percent of rural households lacked access to land—a number that was expected to rise by 2 percent annually (WFP 2013). Given these figures, disputes over land ownership and access could very well lead to violent conflict in the future.

By 2050, the world's population is expected to reach 9 billion. Natural resources—both for agricultural production and other livelihoods—will be essential to meeting the needs created by population growth, particularly as resource consumption is expected to intensify as countries undergo rapid economic development. According to the Food and Agriculture Organization of the United Nations, by 2050, demand for agricultural production in ninety-three developing nations will require an annual investment of more than US$200 billion (FAO 2012).

Between 2000 and 2012, agricultural production in Latin America grew by more than 50 percent, including 70 percent in Brazil alone; by more than 40 percent in sub-Saharan Africa, Eastern Europe, and Central Asia; and by 54 percent in the world's least developed countries (FAO 2012). Despite this progress, however, demographic and economic factors will continue to increase pressure on the finite natural resource base, fueling competition over access to and use of natural resources.[3] At the same time, the projected consequences of global change highlight the importance of wider recognition (and harnessing) of the strong links between natural resources and livelihood needs, in order to address disputes over resource access and use and to develop peacebuilding strategies. The resulting strategies will need to take into account not only the capacity of natural resources to support the basic needs of growing populations, but the role that these resources may play in future conflict.

The interconnections between livelihoods, natural resources, and conflict provide a valuable opportunity to enhance peacebuilding initiatives during the post-conflict period over both the short and the long term. Understanding these linkages is an important first step in resolving natural resource disputes, so as to promote cooperative management, equitable access, and sustainable natural resource use. Supporting sustainable, natural resource–based livelihoods is one means of addressing the connections between a lack of livelihood opportunities and conflict.

ORGANIZATION OF THE BOOK

This book focuses on the opportunities and challenges of using natural resource–based livelihoods as a potential peacebuilding tool. The chapters examine livelihood-related peacebuilding initiatives in over twenty post-conflict countries and territories (see map on page XX). The case studies and analyses were written by more than thirty practitioners, scholars, and other experts from governmental entities, academic institutions, private enterprises, and nonprofit organizations around the world.

The book is organized into three parts: (1) "Natural Resources, Livelihoods, and Conflict: Reflections on Peacebuilding"; (2) "Innovative Livelihood Approaches in Post-Conflict Settings"; and (3) "The Institutional and Policy Context." The chapters examine the use of natural resource–based livelihoods as a platform for promoting peacebuilding on a broader scale. In particular, the case studies present lessons from context-specific scenarios—some successful, some

---

[3] For an overview of the literature on conflicts driven by competition over dwindling natural resources, see Webersik and Levy (2015).

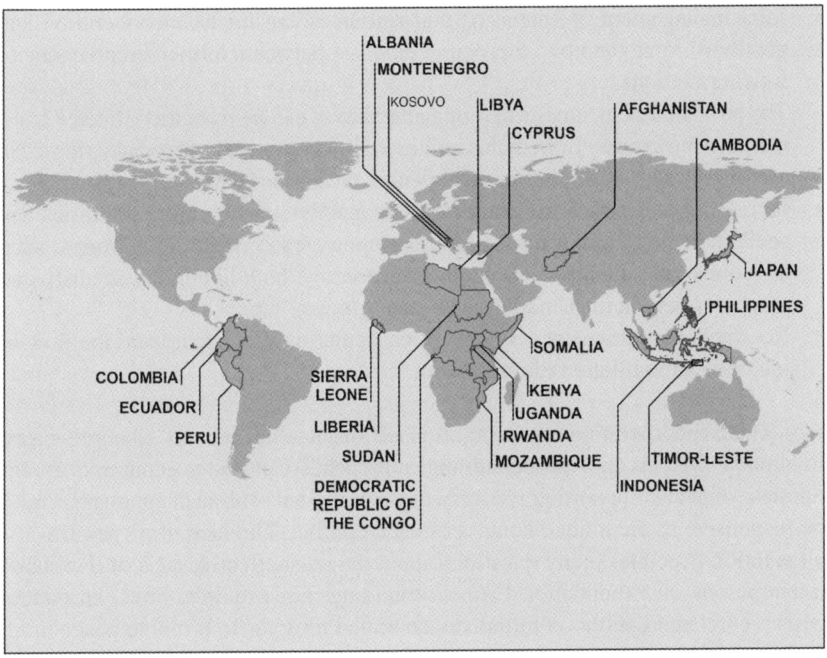

Post-conflict and conflict-affected countries and territories from which lessons have been drawn in this book, either through case studies or broader thematic analyses
Note: UN member states are set in bold.

unsuccessful—in which attempts were made to integrate natural resource–based livelihood approaches into a peacebuilding framework. The book concludes with a comprehensive, global, and forward-looking analysis of the lessons learned from the various experiences presented in the chapters.

Natural resources, livelihoods, and conflict: Reflections on peacebuilding

The link between natural resources, livelihoods, and conflict creates an extraordinary opportunity to develop sustainable livelihood systems that support broader peacebuilding objectives. The benefits of livelihood initiatives undertaken during the post-conflict period include the following:

- Supporting natural resource–dependent livelihoods—including restoring local access to natural resources—can foster and strengthen relationships between former adversaries.
- Strengthening governance institutions and improving natural resource management can help to resolve disputes, promote equitable access to natural resources, and support sustainable economic opportunity and redevelopment.

- Joint management of shared natural resources can increase cooperation and goodwill—and thereby improve relations—between former combatants or warring factions.
- The provision of income-generating alternatives can help conflict-affected communities move away from maladaptive livelihood strategies (especially those that are linked with intimidation or violence, or that destroy natural resources).
- Increasing economic, educational, and capacity-enhancing opportunities and social standing among previously disempowered demographic groups, such as women and unemployed youth, can improve both livelihood security and empowerment among members of such groups.
- Reestablishing financial services (in particular, microfinance) and the flow of income can facilitate redevelopment.

Thus, incorporating the promotion of sustainable, natural resource–based livelihood systems into peacebuilding approaches can foster economic opportunities while also supporting recovery in general. That said, such approaches must be responsive to the unique context of each conflict. The lack of a one-size-fits-all solution generates many questions about the most effective uses of livelihood interventions as a foundation for peacebuilding. For example, how can natural resource–related livelihood initiatives be scaled up so as to promote peacebuilding more broadly? How can livelihood interventions reduce underlying conflict drivers, and thereby sustain livelihood security and peacebuilding? Can natural resource–based livelihood systems be rebuilt in ways that minimize the potential for conflict relapse? What kinds of livelihood approaches are best suited to resolving natural resource–related disputes and enhancing political, economic, and social stability? Finally, how can livelihood initiatives address the natural resource–dependent economic needs of displaced populations without increasing competition, and thereby fueling conflict, with nondisplaced populations?

Through case studies from Afghanistan, Cambodia, Kenya and Uganda, and the Aceh territory of Indonesia, part 1 of this book offers insight into these challenges.

Innovative livelihood approaches in post-conflict settings

The types of livelihoods that develop and take hold vary considerably among post-conflict countries, territories, and regions. Thus, natural resource–based livelihood initiatives must take into consideration the varying geographic, economic, political, and social factors that influence livelihood systems—including, for example, local infrastructure, the type and availability of natural resources, and cultural restrictions on who can engage in various livelihood activities.

Because the uniqueness of local circumstances may make it difficult to reproduce the successful outcomes of livelihood initiatives implemented elsewhere, there is a continuing need to develop innovative approaches that address specific local needs and concerns. In keeping with this goal, a number of conflict-affected countries and their peacebuilding partners have developed or adapted creative approaches to rebuilding natural resource–related livelihoods. The case studies in part 2 of this book highlight a number of such initiatives, including transboundary and cross-border natural resource management in Albania, Montenegro, and Kosovo, as well as in Rwanda, Uganda, and the Democratic Republic of the Congo; and other innovative projects implemented in Afghanistan, Colombia, Indonesia, Mozambique, and Sierra Leone.

Institutional and policy context

Rebuilding institutional capacity and natural resource governance is central to post-conflict recovery. Because most livelihood initiatives require a degree of political stability and a governance system that supports the sound management of the natural resource base, it is critical to ensure that institutions and policies developed or reformed during the post-conflict period support the sustainable use of natural resources for livelihoods.

Part 3 of this book explores the ways in which institutional and policy reform can enhance natural resource management and livelihoods and promote peacebuilding on a broader scale. Case studies from Afghanistan, Cambodia, Somalia, the Philippines, and post–World War II Japan examine challenges, opportunities, and lessons from the institutional and policy perspective.

LIVELIHOODS AND PEACEBUILDING: LOOKING FORWARD

The post-conflict period provides a unique window of opportunity to promote peacebuilding by addressing the underlying causes of conflict; establishing the conditions for a lasting peace; and facilitating consensus on a new economic, political, and social vision for the future. In many cases, natural resources represent a source of conflict; as such, they also represent an opportunity. Although unresolved disputes over natural resources can spark conflict or fuel ongoing conflict, successfully addressing such disputes—including through equitable and sustainable natural resource management—can advance peacebuilding. Revitalizing the natural resource base can also restore livelihoods, providing visible peace dividends that will highlight and reinforce the value of peace. The case studies in this book reaffirm the linkages between livelihoods, natural resources, conflict, and peacebuilding, and provide a strong argument for using livelihood approaches as a platform for broader-scale peacebuilding initiatives.

Livelihood interventions are most effective in strengthening peacebuilding when they are developed and implemented as early as possible—building on humanitarian livelihood interventions implemented during conflict. Competition and other tensions over natural resources can provoke conflict, exacerbate existing grievances, or fuel ongoing conflict. Given that many communities, especially in poor and rural regions, depend on natural resources for their livelihoods, livelihood initiatives must be incorporated into the peacebuilding process from the outset in order to resolve any remaining natural resource–based disputes. Otherwise, as the recovery period progresses, it can become much more difficult to incorporate sound natural resource management and sustainable livelihood initiatives into the redevelopment framework.

Faced with potential conflict scenarios, peacebuilding actors must bear in mind the lessons from past conflicts and post-conflict recovery, in order to ensure that peacebuilding initiatives reflect an understanding of the causes, consequences, and opportunities associated with conflict. Through case studies and analyses, this book advances current knowledge of the connections between livelihoods, natural resources, conflict, and peacebuilding; examines innovative livelihood programs that promote both peacebuilding and sustainable natural resource management; and illustrates how institutional and policy reform can help support sustainable livelihoods and peacebuilding more broadly. While livelihood approaches are often overlooked as a peacebuilding tool, this book demonstrates how sustainable natural resource management can facilitate peacebuilding and strengthen community redevelopment by providing economic opportunity, promoting social equity, and, most importantly, giving despairing populations hope for a brighter future.

REFERENCES

ACAPS (Assessment Capacities Project). 2013. *Impact of the conflict on Syrian economy and livelihoods*. Syria Needs Analysis Project. www.mapaction.org/component/mapcat/download/2960.html?fmt=pdf.

Bruch, C., D. Jensen, M. Nakayama, J. Unruh, R. Gruby, and R. Wolfarth. 2009. Post-conflict peacebuilding and natural resources. *Yearbook of International Environmental Law* 19:58–96.

Chambers, R., and G. R. Conway. 1992. Sustainable rural livelihoods: Practical concepts for the 21st century. Discussion Paper No. 296. Brighton, UK: Institute of Development Studies.

FAO (Food and Agriculture Organization of the United Nations). 2012. *The state of food and agriculture 2012: Investing in agriculture for a better future*. Rome. www.fao.org/docrep/017/i3028e/i3028e.pdf.

Huggins, C., M. Chenje, J. Mohamed-Katerere, and F. Attere. 2006. Environment for peace and regional cooperation. In *Africa environment outlook 2: Our environment, our wealth*. Nairobi, Kenya: United Nations Environment Programme. www.unep.org/dewa/africa/docs/en/AEO2_Our_Environ_Our_Wealth.pdf.

IFAD (International Fund for Agricultural Development). 2007. Enabling the rural poor to overcome poverty in Cambodia. Rome. www.ifad.org/operations/projects/regions/pi/factsheets/kh.pdf.

International Dialogue on Peacebuilding and Statebuilding. 2011. A new deal for engagement in fragile states. www.oecd.org/dataoecd/35/50/49151944.pdf.

McKenney, B., and P. Tola. 2002. Natural resources and rural livelihoods in Cambodia: A baseline assessment. Working Paper No. 23. Phnom Penh: Cambodia Development Resource Institute. www.cdri.org.kh/webdata/download/wp/wp23e.pdf.

Messer, E., M. J. Cohen, and T. Marchione. 2001. Conflict: A cause and effect of hunger. *ECSP Report* 7:1–16. www.wilsoncenter.org/sites/default/files/ECSP7-featurearticles-1.pdf.

Omosa, E. K. 2005. The impact of water conflicts on pastoral livelihoods: The case of Wajir District in Kenya. Winnipeg, Canada: International Institute for Sustainable Development. www.iisd.org/sites/default/files/pdf/2005/security_pastoral_water_impacts.pdf.

Rassul, K. 2010. *Fractured relationships: Understanding conflict between nomadic and settled communities in Wardak's pastureland.* Kabul, Afghanistan: Cooperation for Peace and Unity. www.operationspaix.net/DATA/DOCUMENT/6699~v~Fractured_Relationships__Understanding_Conflict_between_Nomadic_and_Settled_Communities_in_Wardaks_Pastureland.pdf.

Scoones, I. 1998. Sustainable rural livelihoods: A framework for analysis. IDS Working Paper No. 72. Brighton, UK: Institute of Development Studies, University of Sussex. www.ids.ac.uk/files/dmfile/Wp72.pdf.

Sexton, R. 2012. *Natural resources and conflict in Afghanistan: Seven case studies; Major trends and implications for the transition.* Kabul: Afghanistan Watch. www.watchafghanistan.org/files/Natural_Resources_and_Conflict_in_Afghanistan/Natural_Resources_and_Conflict_in_Afghanistan_Full_Report_English.pdf.

Sphere Project. 2004. *Humanitarian charter and minimum standards in disaster response.* Geneva, Switzerland. http://ocw.jhsph.edu/courses/refugeehealthcare/PDFs/SphereProjectHandbook.pdf.

———. 2011. *Humanitarian charter and minimum standards in humanitarian response.* Geneva, Switzerland. www.sphereproject.org/resources/download-publications/?search=1&keywords=&language=English&category=22.

UN (United Nations). 2011. *Civilian capacity in the aftermath of conflict: Independent report of the Senior Advisory Group.* A/65/747–S/2011/85. New York. www.civcapreview.org/LinkClick.aspx?fileticket=JGZvOw7Ch3U%3D&tabid=3746&language=en-US.

UNDP (United Nations Development Programme). 2008. Enhancing livelihood opportunities and building social capital for new livelihoods strategies in Darfur. www.sd.undp.org/content/dam/sudan/docs/project_docs/cp8%20Darfur%20Livelihood%20ProDoc.pdf.

UNEP (United Nations Environment Programme). 2007. *Sudan: Post-conflict environmental assessment.* Nairobi, Kenya. http://postconflict.unep.ch/publications/UNEP_Sudan.pdf.

———. 2009a. *From conflict to peacebuilding: The role of natural resources and the environment.* Nairobi, Kenya. http://postconflict.unep.ch/publications/pcdmb_policy_01.pdf.

———. 2009b. *Recommended strategy for conflict resolution of competing high pasture claims of settled and nomadic communities in Afghanistan.* Kabul, Afghanistan. http://postconflict.unep.ch/publications/afg_tech/theme_01/afg_rangeland_EN.pdf.

UNEP (United Nations Environment Programme), United Nations Entity for Gender Equality and the Empowerment of Women, United Nations Peacebuilding Support Office, and United Nations Development Programme. 2013. *Women and natural resources: Unlocking the peacebuilding potential.* Nairobi, Kenya. www.undp.org/content/dam/undp/library/crisis%20prevention/WomenNaturalResourcesPBreport2013.pdf.

UNSG (United Nations Secretary-General). 2009. *Report of the Secretary-General on peacebuilding in the immediate aftermath of conflict.* A/63/881–S/2009/304. June 11. New York. www.unrol.org/files/pbf_090611_sg.pdf.

———. 2010. *Progress report of the Secretary-General on peacebuilding in the immediate aftermath of conflict.* A/64/866–S/2010/386. July 16 (reissued on August 19 for technical reasons). New York.

———. 2012. *Peacebuilding in the aftermath of conflict: Report of the Secretary-General.* A/67/499–S/2012/746. October 8. New York.

UNSG's (United Nations Secretary-General's) Policy Committee. 2007. Conceptual basis for peacebuilding for the UN system. May. New York.

USAID (United States Agency for International Development). 2009. *A guide to economic growth in post-conflict countries.* Washington, D.C. pdf.usaid.gov/pdf _docs/PNADO408 .pdf.

USIP (United States Institute of Peace) and U.S. Army PKSOI (United States Army Peacekeeping and Stability Operations Institute). 2009. *Guiding principles for stabilization and reconstruction.* Washington, D.C.: Endowment of the United States Institute of Peace.

Waldman, M. 2008. Community peacebuilding in Afghanistan: The case for a national strategy. Oxford, UK: Oxfam International. www.comw.org/warreport/fulltext/0802waldman .pdf.

Webersik, C., and M. Levy. 2015. Reducing the risk of conflict recurrence: The relevance of natural resource management. In *Governance, natural resources, and post-conflict peacebuilding*, ed. C. Bruch, C. Muffett, and S. S. Nichols. London: Earthscan.

WFP (World Food Programme). 2013. Livelihoods. www.foodsecurityatlas.org/khm/ country/access/livelihoods.

PART 1

Natural resources, livelihoods, and conflict: Reflections on peacebuilding

Introduction

A livelihood can be defined as "the capabilities, assets (including both material and social resources) and activities required for a means of living"; a sustainable livelihood is one that "can cope with and recover from stresses and shocks, maintain or enhance its capabilities and assets" without damaging the natural resource base (Scoones 1998, 5). Livelihoods are profoundly affected by conflict. Not only does conflict often destroy the natural resources and infrastructure on which many livelihoods depend, but it also displaces significant portions of the population and undermines the institutions that are critical to a formal economy—including those of law, governance, trade, and finance. For example, when local tenure systems governing access to land, water, or pastures break down, the resulting conflicts over natural resource access or use may become violent.

Loss of livelihoods can also prolong conflict: individuals seeking survival, restitution, or revenge may join armed or criminal groups, or engage in illicit livelihoods linked to the conflict economy. Conflict-affected populations have little choice but to adapt their livelihood strategies to the realities of armed conflict: for example, they may avoid areas where there are landmines—and thereby lose access to resources essential to livelihoods—or they may participate in unregulated (and often illegal) artisanal mining. Finally, conflict-affected populations may participate in unsustainable or otherwise problematic exploitation of the natural resource base, or may turn to livelihoods that fuel ongoing conflict—by, for example, growing opium poppy (as in Afghanistan); growing coca (as in Colombia); or engaging in looting (as in Sudan and Bosnia) (USAID 2005).

Incorporating livelihood initiatives into peacebuilding can restore equitable access to crucial natural resources, rebuild communities, forge cooperation, and support peace consolidation. By the same token, failure to address the lack of viable livelihood opportunities can contribute to protracted or recurring conflict. Part 1 of this book explores the role of livelihoods in conflict and peacebuilding, both from a theoretical perspective and through experiences from Afghanistan, East Africa, Indonesia, and Cambodia.

Livelihoods are often central to social identity—and social identity, in turn, can affect post-conflict peacebuilding, particularly where social identity has played a critical role in the conflict. Nevertheless, the connections between social identity, natural resources, and peacebuilding are too often ignored. In "Social Identity, Natural Resources, and Peacebuilding," Arthur Green examines these connections, and addresses the symbolic role of natural resources in racial, ethnic, and social tensions. From a constructivist perspective, to which Green subscribes, identity is a social construct, and therefore subject to change. Whereas current approaches to identity-based conflict tend to focus on establishing territorial boundaries or dividing resources between social groups, Green argues for more creative solutions, such as reframing social identities in ways designed to prevent conflict recurrence, increase recognition of the social value of livelihoods, and strengthen group rights.

The role that natural resources play in racial, ethnic, and social tensions between and among groups is a recurring theme throughout Green's chapter. Social identity as an element of natural resource-based conflicts and post-conflict peacebuilding emerges as an important theme in several other chapters as well, including "Resolving Natural Resource Conflicts to Help Prevent War: A Case from Afghanistan," Liz Alden Wily's analysis of conflict between Pashtun nomads and settled Hazara communities in Afghanistan's central highlands. Similarly, in "Swords into Plowshares? Accessing Natural Resources and Securing Agricultural Livelihoods in Rural Afghanistan," Alan Roe notes that conflict over access to natural resources—particularly water for irrigation—has increased tension and led to violence between villages of different ethnicities and historical alliances.

Roe's chapter also explores the importance of addressing rural livelihoods during the peacebuilding process. Although conflict and violent insurgency tend to be concentrated in remote, rural areas where livelihoods rely primarily on agricultural production, current agricultural policies focus on the river valleys, where high-value agricultural exports flourish and there is ready access both to irrigation resources and regional markets. To promote long-term political stability, Roe recommends implementing agricultural policies that improve livelihood security by addressing the needs of the rural poor. This would include recognizing the comparative advantages of diverse types of agricultural systems (such as semi-irrigated highland farming, rainfed farming, and nomadic pastoralism), and supporting investment in these various practices.

In many post-conflict situations, the unregulated exploitation of natural resources associated with the conflict economy extends into the post-conflict period, devastating traditional resource-based livelihoods. In "Forest Resources in Cambodia's Transition to Peace: Lessons for Peacebuilding," Srey Chanthy and Jim Schweithelm consider the long-term effects of Cambodia's civil war on forest communities, as well as the long-term effects of the unregulated timber harvesting that occurred in the wake of the conflict. Because regulatory capacity is essential to protect the rights and livelihoods of forest communities, Srey and Schweithelm recommend an immediate post-conflict focus on rebuilding the capacity of environmental and resource-related institutions as a means of promoting lasting peace and ensuring sustainable management of the natural resource base.

Similar challenges confront forest-dependent communities in post-conflict situations around the world, particularly those in remote rural regions that depend on the equitable and sustainable management of natural resources. In "Post-Tsunami Aceh: Successful Peacemaking, Uncertain Peacebuilding," Michael Renner explores the history of the conflict in Aceh, highlighting the policies of the national government that excluded the province from the economic benefits and livelihood opportunities associated with the region's natural wealth, particularly in the forest sector, and ultimately led to a twenty-nine-year conflict and attempted secession. Although a 2005 memorandum of understanding (MOU) formally ended the conflict and granted Aceh 70 percent of all revenues from its natural resources, translating natural resource rights into tangible benefits for poor Acehnese remains a challenge. Many former combatants remain unemployed, and poverty rates in Aceh are high; these factors, along with persistent economic instability, threaten both peacebuilding (because the reintegration of former combatants is critical to preventing recurring violence) and environmental sustainability (because many former combatants have turned to illegal logging as an alternative livelihood).

In situations where conflict-affected communities rely on natural resources for livelihood security, peacebuilding solutions must address the livelihood needs of poor and vulnerable populations and ensure the equitable distribution of development assistance. In "Manufacturing Peace in 'No Man's Land': Livestock and Access to Natural Resources in the Karimojong Cluster of Kenya and Uganda," Jeremy Lind analyzes the traditions of natural resource use by pastoralists in the Karimojong Cluster, a region spanning the remote borderlands of northwestern Kenya and northeastern Uganda. Livestock raiding and banditry are common throughout the region, creating a violent and insecure environment that threatens the livelihoods of pastoralists. Moreover, postcolonial development initiatives have severely limited livelihood opportunities in the region. Noting that economic development could help reduce conflict, as long as such development is consistent with cultural norms and practices, Lind argues that peacebuilding must focus on poor and vulnerable populations, addressing structural inequality and underdevelopment in rural areas while creating and supporting sustainable livelihoods.

Inequality in development assistance and peacebuilding efforts can also affect rights of access to natural resources, including farmland. Land access is essential, for example, to the livelihoods of various ethnic groups in Afghanistan—where, largely as the result of inequitable access to pastureland and the government's failure to recognize customary land rights, competition between the Hazara tribes and Pashtun nomads (known as Kuchis) has been a source of recurring violence for generations, creating a roadblock to peace consolidation. In "Resolving Natural Resource Conflicts to Help Prevent War: A Case from Afghanistan," Liz Alden Wily explores innovative efforts to address the persistent conflict between agropastoralist and pastoralist ethnic groups in the central highlands. To resolve land-based conflict and promote lasting peace, Alden Wily recommends establishing a framework that would allocate each group sufficient rights of access to maintain livelihoods. Ultimately, Alden Wily suggests that the best means of resolving conflicts over landownership and access rights is through local mediation designed to lead to community-specific agreements. The success of such efforts will depend, however, on establishing trust among the participants, and confidence that the negotiations will yield an equitable solution that supports local livelihoods.

The six chapters in part 1 demonstrate a strong correlation between livelihood creation, natural resources, and peacebuilding. Taken together, they offer a number of overarching lessons for livelihood interventions in post-conflict situations. Because livelihoods contribute to a sense of social identity and community purpose at the same time that they provide income-generating opportunities, creating and supporting sustainable livelihoods during and immediately after conflict is critical to fostering and maintaining peace. It is therefore essential for the international community to support transnational, national, and local efforts to rebuild and strengthen natural resource management during the post-conflict period, both to promote the recovery of natural resource–based livelihoods for all affected groups and to help prevent overexploitation of resources. Most important, the post-conflict period offers tremendous opportunities to develop and implement innovative peacebuilding initiatives that will promote sustainable livelihoods and support the consolidation of peace.

REFERENCES

Scoones, I. 1998. Sustainable rural livelihoods: A framework for analysis. IDS Working Paper No. 72. Brighton, UK: Institute of Development Studies, University of Sussex. www.ids.ac.uk/files/dmfile/Wp72.pdf.

USAID (United States Agency for International Development). 2005. *Livelihoods and conflict: A toolkit for intervention.* Washington, D.C. http://commdev.org/livelihoods-and-conflict-toolkit-intervention.

Social identity, natural resources, and peacebuilding

Arthur Green

What do coca growers marching in Colombia, communities struggling over property rights in Timor-Leste, and Somali clans disputing charcoal rents have in common? These diverse struggles are all examples of failures to adequately consider social identity in post-conflict natural resource management (PCNRM). This chapter examines how links between social identity, natural resources, and armed conflicts affect peacebuilding and PCNRM. It outlines ways in which social identities are mobilized in conflicts in which resources have political and cultural values. It argues that, contrary to popular perceptions of ancient identities locked in conflicts, social identities are flexibly constructed and linked to natural resources through both individual actor decisions and elite manipulation of political discourses. In conclusion, it proposes a framework for understanding how links between social identities and natural resources may influence PCNRM and, ultimately, peacebuilding processes.

Natural resources are often affected by armed conflict and implicated in conditions that lengthen or intensify armed conflicts (Le Billon 2007). One of the central challenges of PCNRM is identifying how links between natural resources and conflict dynamics continue to impact natural resource management in post-conflict situations. These links affect the ways in which PCNRM programs can define and distribute rights to access, own, or otherwise use and profit from natural resources. Failure to manage these links may lead to both unsustainable resource extraction and renewed or continued violence. For example, successful sanctions on "blood diamonds" show that understanding how the economic rents of natural resources are linked to armed conflict is not only important for sustainable resource management but sometimes critical for peacebuilding and for disrupting incentives and opportunities to pursue violence (Le Billon 2008).

Many studies have examined how the management of economically valuable natural resources influences the onset and duration of armed conflict and can

---

Arthur Green is the chair of the Department of Geography and Earth & Environmental Science at Okanagan College in British Columbia, Canada.

positively or negatively affect peacebuilding (Collier and Hoeffler 1998, 2004, 2005; Ross 2004; Weinstein 2007). These studies indicate the critical role that natural resource rents can play in rebel recruitment, rebuilding of national economies, and other processes. Yet natural resources are important for more than just their economic value. They can play potent symbolic roles in ethnonational discourses, be deeply embedded in local social relations, and be framed in identity-based claims that serve strategic political interests. Despite ample evidence indicating the central role of social identity in conflicts over everything from territory to oil and coca plants, little attention has been directed toward understanding how the cultural and political values of natural resources must be managed in PCNRM. Indeed, there is no analytical framework for understanding how the construction and mobilization of social identities (or the cultural and political values linked to natural resources) impact PCNRM. As a result, PCNRM strategies may often fail to include practical steps for managing the complex links between natural resources, social identity issues, and conflict.

This chapter's focus on social identity is not intended as a rejection of the importance of research on economic values and resource rents in PCNRM. On the contrary, the construction of social identities during armed conflict often involves economic incentives and opportunities for both elites and ordinary people (Fearon and Laitin 2000; Caselli and Coleman 2006). This chapter attempts to broaden existing analytical lenses to include ways that political, cultural, and economic values interact and ultimately affect the ways that social identities connect to natural resources and influence PCNRM.

There are many competing definitions for the terms used in this chapter. Terms such as *natural resources*, *peacebuilding*, *conflict*, and *social identity* are plagued by conceptual debates.[1] It is beyond the scope of this chapter to offer a defense of all the specific concepts used in the chapter. Indeed, future studies should use alternative conceptualizations of these terms in order to examine different theoretical and practical foundations for exploring the nexus of social identity, natural resources, and peacebuilding. Surely, different basic concepts may produce alternative interpretations and conclusions.

The following sections review literature that links social identity and natural resources to armed conflicts, outline four ways that links between social identity and natural resources affect PCNRM and peacebuilding processes, suggest policy options for situations in which social identity concerns are critical to successful PCNRM, and suggest avenues for future research.

---

[1] Stathis Kalyvas recognizes that violence, conflict, and war are often confounded in popular and scholarly accounts even though they express concepts that must necessarily be analytically different (Kalyvas 2006). He notes that the literature on armed conflict—and civil war in particular—suffers from lack of conceptual clarity. This lack of clarity is evident with other terms as well. There is also considerable confusion over terminology in the field of conflict studies, with well over a hundred different ways of classifying types of conflict (Ramsbotham, Woodhouse, and Miall 2005).

SOCIAL IDENTITY AND NATURAL RESOURCES IN ARMED CONFLICT

An elaboration of links between social identity, natural resources, and peacebuilding requires first examining theories linking social identity, natural resources, and armed conflict. Examination of PCNRM programs' successes and failures in taking these links into account must consider not only post-conflict situations but also situations in which armed conflicts might have ended sooner, or not relapsed into violence, if such links had been considered.

Social identities and armed conflict

There is well-developed literature on the links between social identities and armed conflict.[2] Much of this literature focuses on ethnicity or ethnic conflict (Nagel 1994; Gurr and Harff 1994; Gurr 2000; Eriksen 2001; Toft 2003); yet ethnicity is only one type of identity. The ways in which different authors and disciplinary approaches define social identity influences how they describe the links between social identity and armed conflict. It is necessary to consider both the broad literature on social identity development and the more narrowly framed work on ethnic conflict to understand how social identities have been linked to armed conflict.

Approaches to social identity can be located on a continuum between two stances: primordialism and constructivism. Primordialist approaches conceptualize social identity as a fixed collection of traits that are genetically inherited (in the strong sense of primordialism) or determined by cultural narratives and social structures (in the weak sense of primordialism). Primordialist approaches are both essentialistic and deterministic in their understanding of identity as a stable aspect of group and individual psychology (Gurr and Harff 1994; Gurr 2000). Samuel Huntington's well-known work on the clash of civilizations is a modern example of how a primordialist perspective frames some conflicts as the inevitable result of irresolvable, ancient prejudices and predicts people's behaviors along lines of historical identity categories (Huntington 1997). On the other hand, constructivist approaches argue that identity is not fixed and recognize the complex ways in which social identity and collective action are simultaneously constructed through social psychological framing, context, and discourse (Bowen 1996; Kaufman, Elliott, and Shmueli 2003). Constructivist approaches look more at contextual factors and actors' decisions concerning overlapping social roles, the framing of discourses, and historical experiences. In other words, constructivist approaches accept the idea that social identity is historically constructed, multifaceted, and contextually dependent (Gardner 2003). Examples of constructivist

[2] See, for example, Huntington (1997); Fearon and Laitin (2000); and Kaufman, Elliott, and Shmueli (2003).

approaches to identity include Anthony Smith's perennialism (Smith 1998), political opportunity theory (Meyer 2004), social identity theory (Hogg, Terry, and White 1995), and social movement theory (Tilly 2003).

The choice of a primordialist or constructivist viewpoint influences understanding of how social identity relates to natural resources, armed conflict, and peacebuilding. For example, a primordialist would see the link between identity and homeland territories as a fixed relation. Not only would the relation be fixed, but it would determine the types of possible interactions between identity groups with competing claims for the same homeland and would inevitably lead to conflict. On the other hand, a constructivist would argue that violent conflicts are not inevitable but the result of strategic interests and political discourses linking identity to territorial or resource claims. For example, claims by Greece advocating for the return of portions of the southern Balkans to Greece and the flexible links between identities and livelihoods in Darfur show how territory or resource claims are often manipulated or contextually framed as social identity claims (Peckham 2000; Young et al. 2009). These cases move beyond an understanding of identity as a fixed personal attribute to reveal how different contexts bring forth different sorts of identity frames (Gardner 2003). The concept of identity frames illustrates the different ways people understand themselves with respect to others, a specific context, or a specific conflict. Where a primordialist approach envisages inevitable conflict between fixed identities, a constructivist approach encourages a search for ways to reprioritize these flexible identity frames in order to find possible avenues for peacebuilding (for example, deemphasizing some identity claims while creating new identity frames by emphasizing the benefits of shared user rights or pointing to common interests in maintaining resources).

In this chapter, the definition of *social identity* is based on social identity theory—a constructivist approach that emphasizes ways that both structural factors and individual actor decisions play a role in framing and choosing identities (Hogg, Terry, and White 1995). The emphasis of social identity theory is less on how intragroup roles interact and more on how categories (or frames) are formed through intergroup interaction. This approach is useful for moving beyond simply finding identities in conflict to finding out how identities are constructed as categories, interact with each other, and are linked to natural resources in conflicts. Rogers Brubaker and Frederick Cooper identify some key conceptual distinctions that need to be made when investigating how types of social identity are constructed (Brubaker and Cooper 2000). First, does social identity refer to relational or categorical modes of identification? Second, does the act of identification come from an external source or through self-identification? Brubaker and Cooper recognize that the divisions between relational and categorical modes of identification, and between externally imposed identification and self-identification, are not always clear but can be analytically useful. For example, identification by positioning in a relational web (such as kinship, friendship, or business ties) may sometimes overlap with identification through categorical attributes (such as race, ethnicity, language, or citizenship), but these represent two very different modes of identification. Likewise, an externally imposed identity (such as legal citizenship) can be incompatible with self-identification. For example, the Belgian identity cards issued in Rwanda in 1933 rigidly classified residents of Rwanda into ethnic categories of Hutu or Tutsi and denied the mixed heritage and self-identification of many residents. Identification could not allow for anything other than what was specified on the residents' identity cards.

These distinctions can be important for understanding the different phenomena described as social identity in cases involving natural resources and armed conflict. The social identity formed through externally imposed categories (for example, by the colonial state) is analytically different from and plays a different social role than the relational modes of self-identification that are so important in defining incentives in recruitment processes and armed conflict dynamics. Indeed, the social identities discussed in peacebuilding processes commonly involve categorical modes of self-identification and external identification relevant to establishing political negotiation positions or to gaining access to resources or post-conflict aid.

For example, in exploring how economic rents from natural resources are used to recruit soldiers for rebel groups, Jeremy Weinstein examines how young men develop identities tied to rebel groups through relational modes of self-identification (Weinstein 2007). Such dynamics are also evident in places like Darfur, where identities often considered to be ancient labels for ethnic groups or tribes actually have a more fluid and permeable nature in which political alliances, ecology, and livelihood strategies cause individuals or groups to adopt new identities based on context-dependent opportunities (Young et al. 2009). On the other hand, categorical modes of identification are also powerful social organizing tools. For example, the designation of recipients of aid and the timing of aid was affected by ways in which conflict refugees and disaster refugees in post-tsunami Aceh, Indonesia, were categorized by external organizations or through self-identification (Burke and Afnan 2005). Another example of categorical modes of identification can be found in the negotiations leading to the Permanent Court of Arbitration's redrawing of the borders for historical land claims in the Abyei region of Sudan. These negotiations arguably used an understanding of identity based on externally and internally imposed categories that bore little resemblance to the actual historical character of communities and kinship networks in the region.[3]

Natural resources and armed conflict

The literature linking natural resources to armed conflict has mushroomed since the 1990s. As potential sources of plunder or spoils of war, natural resource access and ownership have long been recognized as conditions that sometimes lead to armed conflicts (Galeano 1973; Dyer 1985; Yergin 1991; André and Platteau 1998).

---

[3] For a more detailed discussion of the Abyei conflict, see Salman (2013).

The control of natural resources has also long been recognized as critical for financing, recruitment, and military strategy (Dyer 1985; Yergin 1991). Yet since the 1990s, an increasing interest in the ways that competition for control over natural resources might contribute to armed conflict at several social scales has led to rich debates over causal pathways and the links between types of armed conflicts and types of resources (Homer-Dixon 1994; Gleditsch 1998; Le Billon 2001; Peluso and Watts 2001).

Several issues in this field have gained attention in the popular media. One such issue is the resource-scarcity-versus-resource-abundance debate, wherein arguments that resource scarcity triggers armed conflict in several ways have been criticized by authors who point to the way that petroleum and other examples of resource abundance better predict and explain interstate and intrastate armed conflicts (Homer-Dixon 1999; Peluso and Watts 2001). Popular interest in global environmental change and its potentially dramatic impact on human societies has inspired a large body of research and some misguided popular speculation on the potential for future resource wars caused by environmental degradation, scarcity, and migration (Nordås and Gleditsch 2007; Dyer 2008).

One influential model of the links between resources and armed conflict is the greed-and-grievances model (Collier and Hoeffler 1998, 2004, 2005). The gist of this model is that high-value natural resources provide incentives (for greedy rebel leaders) or opportunities (for rebel groups) that encourage armed conflict and undermine peacebuilding (Aspinall 2007). This model has inspired much theoretical work on how the characteristics of resources affect both rebel group formation and conflict types, and it has driven policy approaches that focus on intervening in resource commodity chains to stop rebel financing and build peace in places such as Liberia and Afghanistan (Ross 2004; Le Billon 2008). But this model has also been criticized by scholars who emphasize that natural resources affect a wider range of economic, political, and cultural factors (Ballentine and Sherman 2003; Ross 2003, 2004; Fearon 2005). For example, an abundance of a high-value resource like petroleum has been shown to destabilize governments by causing macroeconomic instability, to undermine the state's ability to govern dissenting groups, to lead the state to adopt policies that encourage opposition groups to use violence, and to encourage competition over state control when state control becomes equivalent to control of high-value resources (Humphreys 2005). Macartan Humphreys discusses how, in the case of Chad, violent conflict was not maintained through resource rents; rather, alternative revenues were raised in advance to fight for control of the Chadian state and the future oil revenue that would come with control of the state.

While the symbolic value of resources (especially territorial resources) is often recognized as an important factor in conflict escalation, duration, and intractability (Kahler and Walter 2006), popular models like the greed-and-grievances model tend to focus on the economic value of resources as the main causal and limiting factor in the escalation and duration of violence. While the model is useful for understanding many groups engaged in modern conflicts, and responsible for policy prescriptions that undermine rebel financing and capacity to wage war, it does not do much to explain the escalation and duration of armed conflicts over resources that have little economic value. It is also inadequate for explaining the ways in which armed conflicts over identity resources (such as sacred forests, fishing rights, and homelands) and locally valuable livelihood resources occur and become intractable.

Links between social identities, natural resources, and armed conflict

Cultural or political values associated with land, sacred forests, fisheries, water, and other natural resources play a role in ethnonational discourses, livelihood struggles, and religious narratives, and link to many identity frames. Of course, these links between social identity and natural resources exist outside the realm of armed conflict as well. Rather than reviewing the extensive literature on social identity and natural resources, this section focuses on some ways in which the links of social identities to natural resources influence armed conflict.

Theories of armed conflict often undertheorize the complex links between social identities and natural resources (Ballentine and Sherman 2003; Ross 2003; Aspinall 2007). The relationship between identity and resources involves at least four links to armed conflicts. These links are not isolated, and one or more may be found within any one conflict:

1. Identity claims involving ownership of or privileged access (symbolic or material) to resources can lead to armed conflict.
2. Identity can influence claims of inequitable distribution of resource rents and thus lead to grievances and armed conflict.
3. Identities are used by both elites and ordinary people to mobilize collective action in conflicts over natural resources.
4. Identity framing facilitates conflict over natural resources.

The first link includes identity conflicts over the historic use or symbolic value of resources. For example, narratives that influence the legal alienation of Arab lands in Israel draw from historical claims to the land (Forman and Kedar 2004). The second link is represented in several center-periphery relationships in which rents from high-value natural resources located in peripheral regions are captured by urban elites or states and not equitably distributed to populations in these peripheral regions that often bear the environmental and social costs of resource extraction. In situations in which center or periphery groups can be linked to identity frames (like ethnic groups), identity often becomes one of the primary frames through which claims to equitable distribution are pursued. For example, Mohamed Suliman's study and work by the International Crisis Group on the dynamics of the Nuba and Baggara land conflict in Sudan's South Kordofan state indicate how identity has been shaped by center-periphery relations and conflict dynamics (Suliman 1999; International Crisis Group 2008). Munzoul Assal and Suliman argue that the state escalated the conflict and that the conflict itself has heightened the collective sense of a Nuba identity (Assal 2006; Suliman 1999).

> Before the onset of violent conflict in the Nuba Mountains, the diverse Nuba people were fully aware only of their clan affiliations. They neither perceived themselves as a Nuba nation nor actively sought to be one. Their relations with their Arab neighbours, the Hawazma and Misiriya, were tolerable. They exchanged goods and services, and intermarriage was an acceptable practice especially among Arabs and Muslim Nuba. At the beginning of the conflict, many Nuba even sided with the government, because they perceived the conflict to be a political discord, rather than an ethnic or economic strife. . . .
>
> Most violent conflicts are over material resources—actual or perceived. However, with the passage of time, ethnic, cultural, and religious affiliations seem to undergo transformation from abstract ideological categories into concrete social forces. In a wider sense, they themselves become contestable material social resources and, hence, possible objects of group strife and violent conflict (Suliman 1999, 219).

The third link is one often presented in Paul Collier and Anke Hoeffler's line of research (greed and grievances), wherein greedy political entrepreneurs create or manipulate existing local identities in order to profit from new political and social arrangements or continuing conflict (Collier and Hoeffler 2004, 2005). Case studies of Rwanda have sometimes cited the underlying land conflict as a source of tension and indicated the role of political entrepreneurs in using this tension to drive the genocidal conflict (Percival and Homer-Dixon 1996; André and Platteau 1998). Other authors see perceived grievances against a perceived community as one of the main ways in which identity becomes a primary mobilizing frame for conflict. Daniel Robinson's study of the role of natural gas and oil extraction in mobilizing collective identity and legitimizing violence in Aceh, Indonesia, illustrates such a causal chain, from natural resource extraction to political manipulation, identity grievances, and conflict (Robinson 1998).

Examining whether the construction of ethnicity (as a type of identity) raises the likelihood of armed conflict, James Fearon and David Laitin propose three pathways through which identity is constructed: (1) through the logic of cultural discourses, (2) through elites' strategic manipulation of identity categories or relational networks, and (3) through strategic action by ordinary people to maintain specific group boundaries and rights (Fearon and Laitin 2000). Using case studies from Sudan, Sri Lanka, Ireland, Rwanda, and the Balkans, they suggest that in many armed conflicts, so-called ethnic or identity-based violence is actually a mask for strategic actions by elites or ordinary individuals. This seems to indicate that cultural and political values are best understood as ways to mobilize groups during armed conflicts in order to achieve strategic gains in resources or power, which supports the concept of rational economic agency described in the greed-and-grievances model.

The fourth link is subtly different from the third in that it argues that a specific type of identity frame must be present prior to political manipulation and mobilization in armed conflict, rather than assuming that political manipulation can mobilize any identity frame for armed conflict. For example, Edward Aspinall argues that collective grievances and legitimization of violence in Aceh could not have occurred without a specific type of preexisting identity frame:

> Rather than seeing natural resource grievances as a source of conflict, or as a catalyst or accelerant for the crystallization of identity, I emphasize that it was the evolving framework of Acehnese identity that provided a prism through which natural resource exploitation was interpreted in grievance terms. Put more bluntly, one might say that without the identity framework there would have been no grievances, at least no politically salient ones. Instead, natural resource exploitation in Aceh may have been viewed as unfair and irritating, but also as banal and unavoidable, as it arguably was in other provinces. In this view, grievances should not be seen as trigger factors, antecedent to the discourses that motivate violence. Grievances are instead integral to the ideological frameworks though which the social world, including notions like "justice" and "fairness," are constructed and understood (Aspinall 2007, 957).

Despite arguments between scholars prioritizing different causal mechanisms, identity and natural resource conflicts are not mutually exclusive themes in the study of conflict. Natural resources are linked in several ways to social identities in armed conflicts. The ways in which social identities are mobilized in resource conflicts affect how links between social identities and natural resources might positively or negatively affect PCNRM.

SOCIAL IDENTITY IN POST-CONFLICT NATURAL RESOURCE MANAGEMENT

Although literature often refers to the role of social groups in PCNRM and peacebuilding, theoretical links are rarely drawn between natural resources, identity, and peacebuilding. Several cases illustrate how failure to consider such links may undermine both theoretical understanding and practical applications of PCNRM and peacebuilding.

One example is the conflict between coca growers and livelihood projects in Colombia (Rojas 2003). In the Apurímac and Ene River Valley in 2002, coca growers (*cocaleros*) rallied against "zero coca" alternative-livelihood projects supported by international nongovernmental organizations (NGOs). Opposing these international livelihood projects, participants in a peasant rally asserted their cultural right to produce and grow coca by chewing and displaying coca leaves as part of an array of ethnic symbols that included traditional clothing and the Tawantinsuyu (Inca) flag. They rejected externally imposed programs to replace coca cultivation and, soon after, they forced CARE to leave the region, displaying their willingness to forgo foreign aid programs in order to continue engaging in coca production. An obvious question in this case is whether, if coca had no economic value, its cultivation would have been so energetically defended as a cultural right. Nonetheless, this example shows how cultural, political, and economic values can become united in an identity-based discourse.

Another example of the failure of PCNRM to consider complicated ways in which social identity issues interlink to natural resources can be drawn from the Acehnese separatist movement in Indonesia. John McCarthy argues that the grievances concerning the Indonesian government's failure to adequately distribute rents from gas and oil reserves in Aceh were not the primary cause of conflict in Aceh. Rather, the state-managed resource exploitation had a demonstration effect that exemplified other grievances and provided a rallying point that encouraged a solidification of the Acehnese identity as an aggrieved and exploited community (McCarthy 2007). He argues that this demonstration effect is one of the primary ways in which institutionalized prejudices that limit economic opportunity intermix with social identity to result in political violence. He identifies other examples of how resource exploitation resulted in identity-based grievances and ethnic violence in the cases of the Ogoni people in the Niger delta region of Nigeria; the separatist war involving the Rio Tinto Panguna mine in Papua New Guinea; and violent conflicts involving the Freeport-McMoRan mining company, the government of Indonesia, and the Free Papua Movement (Organisasi Papua Merdeka) in the Indonesian province of West Papua (formerly West Irian Jaya). While all these situations illustrate the role of natural resources in conflict escalation, they also illustrate the failure to adequately manage resources or reframe resource demands during negotiations that occurred during pauses in the violence. Reframing of demands away from strict ethnonational identity claims on resource rents and toward comanagement, as is now being pursued in Aceh, could have helped transform these armed conflicts into stable post-conflict situations.

Charcoal production in Somalia might also be considered an example of the impacts that a failure to consider identity can have on the success of PCNRM and peacebuilding.[4] Charcoal trade provides income for producers, traders, retailers, and wholesalers in the Somali informal economy. Yet production reduces local wood supplies and has severe ecological impacts on local communities that do not benefit from the trade. These communities often organize themselves by clan to demand their share of profits. However, clan affiliation in Somalia does not reflect simple or essentialist tribal formations; it expresses a complex relational mode of identification that changes according to context and opportunity. According to this case study, some clans resort to violence in order to claim charcoal profits and thus undermine political stability in the region. One approach to this problem is to seek ways for clans to access an equitable amount of profits from charcoal. A more nuanced approach to social identity might identify how clan membership is simply an organizing principle and how efforts to restore environmental

---

[4] For a more detailed discussion of charcoal production in Somalia, see Christian Webersik and Alec Crawford, "Commerce in the Chaos: Bananas, Charcoal, Fisheries, and Conflict in Somalia," in this book.

resources or to provide alternative livelihoods to selected geographic areas may be more effective than engaging in identity-based negotiations.

While attention to identity framing and the cultural and political values of natural resources seems essential to PCNRM, there are several reasons why it is under recognized in theory and practice. For example, PCNRM projects necessarily have a time-limited, practical focus that emphasizes economic recovery. This may cause important cultural and political dynamics to be overlooked (Bush and Opp 1999; Paris 2004). Social identity might also be undertheorized in the PCNRM literature because recent theoretical work relies heavily on the greed-and-grievances model of conflict and tends to downplay identity claims based on cultural and political values as simple grievances resulting from political manipulation.

Conflicts of interests and conflicts of values

As mentioned above, taking either a primordial or constructivist approach to social identity can influence the understanding of the role natural resources play in both armed conflict and peacebuilding. While the primordial approach provides a limited understanding of conflict and thus options for peacebuilding, the constructivist approach allows for an examination of whether an armed conflict involving resources is a conflict of interests or a conflict of values, and what the appropriate steps for natural resource management would be in each case.

While the line between a conflict of interests and a conflict of values is fuzzy (Aubert 1963); understanding the distinction between the two types of conflict can guide the selection of appropriate approaches to peacebuilding. It is easiest to explain the distinction through an example. In Cameroon, Nyem-Nyem farmers need access to lowlands for nonirrigated agriculture; Mbororo herders need access to these same areas for seasonal pastures for their cattle (Green 2005). To the extent that access and use of these areas is a conflict of interests, it might be resolved through arrangements that specify the time, space, and scope of usage and access rights. However, if Nyem-Nyem farmers define their ownership of the land by their ability to exclude Mbororo herders from it, then any access or usage rights granted to the Mbororo will be seen by the Nyem-Nyem as infringing on their property rights (Green 2005). This latter scenario is an example of a non-negotiable conflict of values. A conflict of values is thus of a different magnitude than a conflict of interests; it is characteristic of identity conflicts and protracted social conflicts in which negotiation often fails to resolve conflicting political or cultural claims that may not have any underlying economic rationale.

If identities are believed to be primordial, one might expect to encounter nonnegotiable conflicts of values that cannot and will never be resolved. If identities are believed to be socially constructed and dependent on context, one can search for creative solutions even to difficult conflicts of values. Addressing identity concerns, but deemphasizing categorical identities in favor of relational identities, may be a better way to approach resource conflicts than simply dividing resources among identity groups, especially when such divisions are impossible. Solutions that focus on constructed identities might attempt to change the primacy of identity frames, search for a common ground in procedural justice (which is concerned with process) rather than substantive justice (which is concerned with outcomes), or expand the focus of peacebuilding beyond the limits of formal negotiations between belligerent groups to informal mechanisms for building cooperation between interest groups. For example, Joane Nagel argued that the idea that there is a clash of civilizations (conflict of values) in the Middle East based on historical communities obfuscates a real understanding of the historical extent and variations of these communities and the conflicts between them (Nagel 1994). This misperception of a clash of civilizations portrays conflicts of interests as conflicts of values, and it conceals ways in which foundations for meaningful peacebuilding can be laid:

> To assert that ethnicity is socially constructed is not to deny the historical basis of ethnic conflict and mobilization. . . . For instance, to argue that the Arab-Israeli conflict is simply historical antagonism, built on centuries of distrust and contention, asserts a certain truth, but it answers no questions about regional or historical variations in the bases or extent of the conflict, or about the processes through which it might be ameliorated. In fact, scholars have asserted that both Israeli and Palestinian ethnic identities are themselves fairly recent constructions, arising out of the geopolitics of World War II and the Cold War . . . (Nagel 1994, 13).

Links between social identity and post-conflict natural resource management

Social identities affect and are affected by conflict over natural resources in at least four ways that should be taken into account when establishing PCNRM programs. Two of these links are primarily related to conflicts of interests, and two are related to conflicts of values.

1. Resources can be at the center of conflicts between groups that have mobilized according to historic identity frames or in which group affiliations have become defined in reference to the resource conflict (conflict of interests).
2. Social identities can be the main way in which people organize resources in the absence of a centralized territorial authority (conflict of interests).
3. Resources can have such strong cultural or political meaning to identity groups that any limits to their use or ownership would threaten a group's identity (conflict of values).
4. Winning or losing in itself can take on a symbolic significance, even when resource ownership or access is of marginal importance (conflict of values).

The first of these four links occurs in situations in which identity groups are mobilized to fight over a resource that has little symbolic significance. For example, diamonds partially funded armed conflicts in the late 1990s over political power in Liberia and Sierra Leone and enriched political elites in the process (Le Billon 2008). In this situation, the cultural significance of the diamonds was less important than the control of revenue streams. If an alternative lucrative, lootable resource became available (for example, if there was a sudden price spike for sapphires), there would be little hesitation to abandon diamonds in pursuit of alternative revenue streams. In these cases, eliminating revenue streams (through sanctions or other direct interventions) and providing alternative livelihoods are often the most practical ways to undermine capacities to wage war and thus to initiate peacebuilding. This link is also manifested in other situations where peacebuilding through decentralization of governance (and thus of resource control) can actually exacerbate identity conflict by stirring up "historic grievances concerning intergroup domination and horizontal inequalities" (Diprose and Ukiwo 2008, 26).

The second link involves the ways in which communities manage resources in the absence of, or in resistance to, a centralized legal state order. Jon D. Unruh, for example, examines how the existence of multiple legal and normative orders influences land tenure regimes in post-conflict situations and how these competing orders can be conceived as communities of interest or identity and affect the peace process (Unruh 2003). Unruh's work illustrates how inadequate understanding of identity groups and their claims to property, inadequate recognition of their need and right to use alternative types of evidence (for example, community testimony rather than statutory titles), and inadequate recognition of their ability to manage resources undermine post-conflict efforts to create and enforce state-administered land administration systems.

For example, in Timor-Leste, centralized land administration is complicated by many overlapping land claims and conflicting practices regarding land management. Indigenous communities throughout the country have claims to communal and private lands, and they define and manage rights in ways different from the state. Timor-Leste has also been exposed to several waves of colonization (Portuguese, Japanese, and Indonesian) that imposed legal systems over and sometimes co-opted or became parts of local customs. Many refugees, absentee land owners, and current residents of Timor-Leste make claims using documents from these different legal systems. Moreover, the country's legacy of forced internal migrations, the destruction of land administration documents in the 1999 post-referendum period, and the subsequent creation of urban refugee communities have also contributed to the confusion surrounding land claims. In response to this confusion, local communities often established informal agreements regarding land access that drew from previous local customs and sometimes became another layer of confusing claims that state and international officials could not easily penetrate (Fitzpatrick 2002). Several interest or identity groups can be identified either on a relational or categorical basis in this setting: urban and rural refugees, expatriated landholders with Portuguese or Indonesian documents, holders of parish certificates of residence, current residents without paperwork, landholders with rights under traditional custom, and others. PCNRM as it relates to land in Timor-Leste has been severely hindered by the political manipulation of elites, confusion over legal frameworks, and conflicting land tenure regimes (Fitzpatrick 2002).

In Timor-Leste, international and national land administration specialists have made considerable efforts to design systems that take into account different types of evidence, provide data in formats that leave boundaries somewhat negotiable, and incorporate just processes for making property claims and negotiating disputes over property. However, the failure of policy and law to adequately recognize different identity groups has frustrated the realization of a clear legal framework for recognizing land and property claims for more than a decade since independence. For example, the 2009 draft land law prioritized statutory claims over all other claims and failed to recognize the importance of communal and informal identity groups' claims to land.[5] Particularly problematic were cases wherein formal title had been issued or deed certified under the Indonesian or Portuguese legal system; the draft land law prioritized these types of paper evidence over local claims based on continued use or adverse possession (the principle under which legal title is awarded to people who occupy or use land for a duration of time during which they do not possess legal title). Recognition of adverse possession can give local communities formal ownership of property they have traditionally managed or used. The draft law impacted both traditional communities and more recent interest groups, such as internally displaced persons who based property claims in urban areas on continued occupation and use of land since independence or since the 2006 violence. These issues led then president José Ramos-Horta to reject the proposed land law in 2012 on the basis of its deleterious impacts on communal groups' property claims. As of 2013, the draft land law is undergoing revisions that incorporate greater recognition of communal title and of adverse possession, yet the draft law illustrates the failure to adequately consider interest and identity group claims and forms of evidence. Indeed, interest group claims often overlap with and develop into identity claims as group identities come to be defined or mobilized around property disputes. While interest and identity groups in Timor-Leste are clearly influenced by the cultural and economic value of land, the land law's recognition (or nonrecognition) of specific interest groups can result in collective mobilization and additional political values being assigned to resources.[6]

The third link involves the symbolic significance of resources. A resource may have conflicting cultural or political significances for different identity groups. Pauliina Raento and Cameron J. Watson reveal the way that particular places in the landscape in the Basque region of Europe, like the town of Gernika (Guernica), have not only economic and livelihood value but also serve as focal points for articulation of cultural values and national identities for separatist movements like Basque Homeland and Freedom (Euskadi Ta Askatasuna) (Raento and Watson

[5] The 2009 draft land law is formally known as the Special Regime for the Determination of Ownership of Immovable Property.

[6] For an analysis of post-conflict land management in Timor-Leste, see Miyazawa (2013).

2000). As evident in Zimbabwe, division of land or provision of alternative land is in some cases unacceptable to groups whose identity is bound to certain places (Moore 2005). Demands by refugees forced to flee during the war in Bosnia and Herzegovina to return to their earlier homes reflect both the need for material recovery and the social and psychological value of certain places (Mikelic, Schoen, and Benschop 2005). The settler dilemma in Israel also reflects different identity groups' conflicting values regarding land (Kedar 2003; Forman and Kedar 2004). This link is often involved in conflicts of values, though these conflicts of values are not inevitable or unmanageable once the dynamics driving them are analyzed.

Elite manipulation and internal group dynamics sometimes bring about a sudden increase in the political or cultural value of natural resources or territories. For example, an area surrounding the 1,100-year-old Hindu temple Preah Vihear on the Thai and Cambodian border has been contested since at least the nineteenth century. As French forces left Cambodia in 1954, Thai forces occupied the temple. Violent skirmishes ensued, and Cambodian protest against the Thai presence led to the case being heard in the International Court of Justice, which ruled in 1962 on the legitimacy of territorial claims to the area.[7]

The court focused, not on cultural or historical claims, but on the technicalities of a border demarcation survey conducted by the French in 1907 in order to fulfill boundary settlements made in the Treaty of 13 February 1904 between Siam and Indo-China.[8] Another important criterion for the court was the way Thailand treated the resulting treaty and the Annex I map of the Dângrêk mountain range, where Preah Vihear is located. Although Thailand never approved the map, its actions in the years between 1907 and 1954 had seemed to respect the placement of Preah Vihear in Cambodia, so in 1962 the International Court of Justice awarded the temple site to Cambodia.

In July 2008, Thai forces once again moved into the area around the temple (Parry 2008). This move seems to have been influenced by tensions between Cambodia and Thailand regarding a controversial Thai political figure, deposed prime minister Thaksin Shinawatra. Since his election in December 2007, Thai prime minister Samak Sundaravej had been under pressure from protesters who accused his government of connections with Thaksin. There was speculation that the July 2008 invasion and ongoing presence of Thai troops at the temple was the result of these pressures and may have been a military test of the convictions of Samak's government. When Cambodia invited Thaksin to be an economic advisor in late 2009, Thailand withdrew its ambassador to Cambodia. Also in 2009, the Administrative Court of Thailand declared unconstitutional a joint

---

[7] International Court of Justice, Case Concerning the Temple of Preah Vihear (Cambodia v. Thailand), Merits, Judgment, 1962, 6.

[8] The formal title of the treaty is the Convention between France and Siam Modifying the Stipulations of the Treaty of 3 October 1893 Concerning the Territories and the Other Agreements. It was signed in Paris on February 13, 1904.

Thai-Cambodian communiqué supporting Cambodia's bid to list Preah Vihear Temple as a UNESCO World Heritage site.

In the case of Preah Vihear, elite manipulation and internal group dynamics periodically increase the cultural and political value of the temple and its grounds. These cultural and political values were not fixed, but changed according to the way politicians used identity to frame conflict over the temple and used the conflict itself to advance domestic political strategies. In some ways, the ambiguity of sovereign claims over Preah Vihear serves as a strategic political resource for gaining nationalist support in the domestic politics of Thailand and Cambodia. Several periods of violence have been followed by friendly concessions during negotiations (such as allowing visitation without visas or passports and not requiring cultural relics taken from the temple to be returned). Yet the International Court of Justice decision in 1962 and subsequent approaches to the problem have focused on absolutist claims to territorial sovereignty rather than ways in which shared territorial status in the region might end the violence surrounding claims to the land.

Preah Vihear is not only an example of the cultural and political values invested in a contested resource and the role of political manipulation in conflicts of values, it has become an example of the fourth link listed above: Victory now means more to Thai and Cambodian identity than the temple itself. The act of winning or losing this conflict has taken on symbolic value. Victory itself has become a new source of political value, whether or not the resource itself is economically valuable.

In another example of this fourth link, the Permanent Court of Arbitration's redrawing of the border in the Abyei region of Sudan in 2009 took on symbolic significance for the Ngok Dinka that went beyond their material interest in the allocation of the region's rich petroleum fields.

> Redrawing the borders of the region, the ruling gives the north uncontested rights to rich oil deposits like the Heglig oil field, which had previously been placed within Abyei.
>
> But the decision leaves at least one oil field in Abyei and gives a symbolic victory to the Ngok Dinka, affirming their claims to the heartland of the fertile region.
>
> "Who controls Abyei has taken on a symbolic importance beyond the traditional tensions over oil," said Colin Thomas-Jensen . . . (Otterman 2009).

The Permanent Court of Arbitration ruling resulted in an unequal division of the oil riches but recognized both the territory's significance to the Ngok Dinka (a type-three link) and the importance of avoiding defeat to both parties (a type-four link).

In addition to the four links just described, the dynamics and identity categories relevant to larger conflicts can often spill over into smaller disputes over resources and into PCNRM projects that do not seem to be related to the central problems of the larger conflict. For example, land administration programs in Aceh from 2005 to 2008 did not adequately recognize separatist identity issues and how these issues affected the legitimacy of the Indonesian state in the separatist region or the appropriate timing and location of development programs (Green 2013). The shadow of identity conflict can be cast over resources not directly involved in armed conflict. Where existing frames for cooperation and legitimacy do not exist and cannot be created, community participation—especially in land use decisions—may not be forthcoming (Kaufman and Smith 1999).

POLICY OPTIONS

Because the four links described above may occur in any combination in a conflict or post-conflict situation, there can be no single recipe for PCNRM policy. To be effective, policies must recognize that social identity plays a key role in PCNRM, and that it is not inherited but constructed (either categorically or relationally), defined either externally or internally, and results from a framing process. Where a conflict of interests exists between groups, economic incentives can often contribute to peacebuilding; however, conflicts of values are more difficult to address and require either more intense reframing away from conflict identities or strategies for partial recognition. PCNRM policy options are described in more detail in tables 1 and 2.

Table 1. Conflict of interests: Policy options for post-conflict natural resource management that consider social identity

Social identity–natural resource link	*Possible policy responses*
Natural resources are at the center of conflicts between groups that have mobilized according to historic identity frames or defined themselves in reference to the natural resource conflict.	1. Interrupt capture of high-value resource commodity chains, and provide alternative livelihoods. 2. Interrupt relational or categorical modes of identification with narratives from alternative historical periods or interest frames.
Social identities are the main way in which people organize natural resources in the absence of a centralized territorial authority.	1. Seek state recognition of group property rights.[a] 2. Implement community-based natural resource management with appropriate legal frameworks. 3. Recognize the authority of identity groups or assign authority to them. 4. Seek state-led reorganization of property rights, where it is possible to equitably implement such programs in accordance with existing rights and obligations.

[a] This can be done by advocating for land administration systems and legal frameworks capable of recognizing communal and individual titles and developing social tenure domain models. A social tenure domain model is a type of land administration system that uses alternative representational formats (for example, a point instead of a polygon) to represent property ownership in situations where strictly defined, parcel-based land administration does not correlate to actual (and often informal) rights and responsibilities on the ground. Social tenure domain models represent an effort to develop pro-poor, flexible land administration systems that move beyond the limitations of current concepts of private property (Lemmen 2010).

Table 2. Conflict of values: Policy options for post-conflict natural resource management that consider social identity

Social identity–natural resource link	*Possible policy responses*
Natural resources have symbolic cultural or political meaning that may make it impossible for competing identity groups to share them.	1. Disaggregate the demands of groups to see if separate rights, timing, locations, or other variables can be negotiated according to identity group.[a] 2. Reframe identity beyond categorical modes of identification using references to alternative historical periods or interest frames.
Winning or losing takes on a symbolic significance even if the natural resources themselves are of marginal importance.	1. Disaggregate the demands of groups to see if separate rights, timing, locations, or other variables can be negotiated according to identity group.[a] 2. Seek agreement on procedural justice standard—for example, referral to the International Court of Justice or Permanent Court of Arbitration. 3. Reframe identity beyond categorical modes of identification using references to alternative historical periods or interest frames.

[a] This approach may reveal that there is no real conflict of values, or it may at least clarify what the conflict of values is about.

CONCLUSION

The links between social identity and natural resources in armed conflicts affect the strategies that can be used for PCNRM. There are four key ways in which identities are constructed in reference to armed conflicts involving resources, and four ways in which social identity and natural resources are linked in PCNRM. The four PCNRM links and the policy responses identified in this chapter provide the beginning of an analytical framework for understanding connections between natural resources, social identity, and peacebuilding. Applying this framework may provide insights into ways to manage resources for peacebuilding in situations that have been considered intractable. While current policy responses frequently focus on fixed social identities, permanent territorial boundaries, and ways to equitably divide resources between identity or interest groups, alternative approaches that engage with constructivist understandings of social identity may provide opportunities for creative solutions. These creative solutions might involve reframing identities in order to disrupt incentives to violence, searching for ways to recognize group rights, establishing procedural justice standards for negotiation, or disaggregating group demands into negotiable subsets. Further work in this area might focus on which resources commonly accrue high symbolic value and how these resources can be managed. Further research is also needed to examine how alternative definitions of social identity and different forms of violent conflict at different social and political scales might change the links and thus foundations of the analytical framework identified in this chapter.

REFERENCES

André, C., and J. P. Platteau. 1998. Land relations under unbearable stress: Rwanda caught in the Malthusian trap. *Journal of Economic Behavior & Organization* 34 (1): 1–47.

Aspinall, E. 2007. The construction of grievance: Natural resources and identity in a separatist conflict. *Journal of Conflict Resolution* 51 (6): 950–972.

Assal, M. A. M. 2006. Sudan: Identity and conflict over natural resources. *Development* 49:101–105.

Aubert, V. 1963. Competition and dissensus: Two types of conflict and of conflict resolution. *Journal of Conflict Resolution* 7 (1): 26–42.

Ballentine, K., and J. Sherman, ed. 2003. *The political economy of armed conflict: Beyond greed and grievance*. Boulder, CO: Lynne Rienner.

Bowen, J. R. 1996. The myth of global ethnic conflict. *Journal of Democracy* 7 (4): 3–14.

Brubaker, R., and F. Cooper. 2000. Beyond "identity." *Theory and Society* 29 (1): 1–47.

Burke, A., and Afnan. 2005. Aceh, reconstruction in a conflict environment: Views from civil society, donors, and NGOs. Jakarta, Indonesia: Decentralization Support Facility; Banda Aceh, Indonesia: Aceh Multi-donor Redevelopment Office.

Bush, K., and R. Opp. 1999. Peace and conflict impact assessment. In *Cultivating peace: Conflict and collaboration in natural resource management*, ed. D. Buckles. Ottawa, Canada: International Development Research Center; Washington, D.C.: World Bank Institute.

Caselli, F., and W. J. Coleman II. 2006. On the theory of ethnic conflict. Working Paper No. 12125. Cambridge, MA: National Bureau of Economic Research.

Collier, P., and A. Hoeffler. 1998. On economic causes of civil war. *Oxford Economic Papers* 50 (4): 563–573.

———. 2004. Greed and grievance in civil war. *Oxford Economic Papers* 56 (4): 563–595.

———. 2005. Resource rents, governance, and conflict. *Journal of Conflict Resolution* 49 (4): 625–633.

Diprose, R., and U. Ukiwo. 2008. Decentralisation and conflict management in Indonesia and Nigeria. Working Paper No. 49. Oxford, UK: Centre for Research on Inequality, Human Security and Ethnicity, University of Oxford.

Dyer, G. 1985. *War*. Homewood, IL: Dorsey Press.

———. 2008. *Climate wars*. Melbourne, Australia: Scribe Publications.

Eriksen, T. H. 2001. Ethnic identity, national identity and intergroup conflict: The significance of personal experiences. In *Social identity, intergroup conflict, and conflict reduction*, ed. R. D. Ashmore, L. J. Jussim, and D. Wilder. Oxford, UK: Oxford University Press.

Fearon, J. D. 2005. Primary commodity exports and civil war. *Journal of Conflict Resolution* 49 (4): 483–507.

Fearon, J. D., and D. D. Laitin. 2000. Violence and the social construction of ethnic identity. *International Organization* 54 (4): 845–877.

Fitzpatrick, D. 2002. *Land claims in East Timor*. Canberra, Australia: Asia Pacific Press.

Forman, G., and A. S. Kedar. 2004. From Arab land to Israel lands: The legal dispossession of the Palestinians displaced by Israel in the wake of 1948. *Environment and Planning D: Society and Space* 22 (6): 809–830.

Galeano, E. H. 1973. *Open veins of Latin America: Five centuries of the pillage of a continent*. New York: Monthly Review Press.

Gardner, R. 2003. Identity frames. *Beyond intractability*, June.

Gleditsch, N. P. 1998. Armed conflict and the environment: A critique of the literature. *Journal of Peace Research* 35 (3): 381–400.

Green, A. 2005. Ethnic and geographic distribution of natural resource management strategies in the Tchabal Mbabo region of Cameroon. Raleigh, NC: Department of Forestry and Environmental Resources, North Carolina State University.

———. 2013. Title wave: Land tenure and peacebuilding in Aceh. In *Land and post-conflict peacebuilding*, ed. J. Unruh and R. C. Williams. London: Earthscan.

Gurr, T. R. 2000. Ethnic warfare on the wane. *Foreign Affairs* 79 (3): 52–64.

Gurr, T. R., and B. Harff. 1994. *Ethnic conflict in world politics*. Boulder, CO: Westview Press.

Hogg, M. A., D. J. Terry, and K. M. White. 1995. A tale of two theories: A critical comparison of identity theory with social identity theory. *Social Psychology Quarterly* 58 (4): 255–269.

Homer-Dixon, T. F. 1994. Environmental scarcities and violent conflict: Evidence from cases. *International Security* 19 (1): 5–40.

———. 1999. *Environment, scarcity, and violence*. Princeton, NJ: Princeton University Press.

Humphreys, M. 2005. Natural resources, conflict, and conflict resolution: Uncovering the mechanisms. *Journal of Conflict Resolution* 49 (4): 508–537.

Huntington, S. P. 1997. *The clash of civilizations and the remaking of world order*. New York: Touchstone.

International Crisis Group. 2008. Sudan's Southern Kordofan problem: The next Darfur? Africa Report No. 145. Khartoum, Sudan.

Kahler, M., and B. F. Walter. 2006. *Territoriality and conflict in an era of globalization*. Cambridge, UK: Cambridge University Press.

Kalyvas, S. N. 2006. *The logic of violence in civil war*. Cambridge, UK: Cambridge University Press.

Kaufman, S., M. Elliott, and D. Shmueli. 2003. Frames, framing and reframing. *Beyond intractability*, September.

Kaufman, S., and J. Smith. 1999. Framing and reframing in land use change conflicts. *Journal of Architectural & Planning Research* 16 (2): 164–180.

Kedar, A. S. 2003. On the legal geography of ethnocratic settler states: Notes towards a research agenda. In *Law and geography: Current legal issues*, vol. 5, ed. J. Holder and C. Harrison. Oxford, UK: Oxford University Press.

Le Billon, P. 2001. The political ecology of war: Natural resources and armed conflicts. *Political Geography* 20 (5): 561.

———. 2007. Geographies of war: Perspectives on "resource wars." *Geography Compass* 1 (2): 163–182.

———. 2008. Diamond wars? Conflict diamonds and geographies of resource wars. *Annals of the Association of American Geographers* 98 (2): 345–372.

Lemmen, C. 2010. *The social tenure domain model: A pro-poor land tool*. FIG Report No. 52. Copenhagen, Denmark: International Federation of Surveyors, Global Land Tool Network, and United Nations Human Settlements Programme.

McCarthy, J. F. 2007. The demonstration effect: Natural resources, ethnonationalism and the Aceh conflict. *Singapore Journal of Tropical Geography* 28 (3): 314–333.

Meyer, D. S. 2004. Protest and political opportunities. *Annual Review of Sociology* 30: 125–145.

Mikelic, V., T. Schoen, and M. Benschop. 2005. *Housing and property rights: Bosnia and Herzegovina, Croatia and Serbia and Montenegro.* Ed. P. Nelsson. Nairobi, Kenya: United Nations Human Settlements Programme.

Miyazawa, N. 2013. Customary law and community-based natural resource management in post-conflict Timor-Leste. In *Land and post-conflict peacebuilding*, ed. J. Unruh and R. C. Williams. London: Earthscan.

Moore, D. S. 2005. *Suffering for territory: Race, place, and power in Zimbabwe*. Durham, NC: Duke University Press.

Nagel, J. 1994. Constructing ethnicity: Creating and recreating ethnic identity and culture. *Social Problems* 41 (1): 152–176.

Nordås, R., and N. P. Gleditsch. 2007. Climate change and conflict. *Political Geography* 26 (6): 627–638.

Otterman, S. 2009. Court redraws disputed area in Sudan. *New York Times*, July 22. www.nytimes.com/2009/07/23/world/africa/23sudan.html.

Paris, R. 2004. *At war's end: Building peace after civil conflict.* Cambridge, UK: Cambridge University Press.

Parry, R. L. 2008. Thailand and Cambodia teeter on edge of conflict at cliff-top temple. Times online, July 19.

Peckham, R. S. 2000. Map mania: Nationalism and the politics of place in Greece, 1870–1922. *Political Geography* 19 (1): 77–95.

Peluso, N. L., and M. Watts. 2001. *Violent environments.* Ithaca, NY: Cornell University Press.

Percival, V., and T. Homer-Dixon. 1996. Environmental scarcity and violent conflict: The case of Rwanda. *Journal of Environment Development* 5 (3): 270–291.

Raento, P., and C. J. Watson. 2000. Gernika, Guernica, *Guernica*? Contested meanings of a Basque place. *Political Geography* 19 (6): 707–736.

Ramsbotham, O., T. Woodhouse, and H. Miall. 2005. *Contemporary conflict resolution: The prevention, management and transformation of deadly conflicts*. 2nd ed. Cambridge, UK: Polity Press.

Robinson, G. 1998. *Rawan* is as *Rawan* does: The origins of disorder in new order Aceh. *Indonesia* 66:127–157.

Rojas, I. 2003. The push for zero coca: Democratic transition and counter-narcotics policy in Peru. *Drug War Monitor* 2 (1): 1–22.

Ross, M. 2003. Oil, drugs, and diamonds: The varying roles of natural resources in civil war. In *The political economy of armed conflict: Beyond greed and grievance*, ed. K. Ballentine and J. Sherman. Boulder, CO: Lynne Rienner.

Ross, M. L. 2004. What do we know about natural resources and civil war? *Journal of Peace Research* 41 (3): 337–356.

Salman, S. M. A. 2013. The Abyei territorial dispute between North and South Sudan: Why has its resolution proven difficult? In *Land and post-conflict peacebuilding*, ed. J. Unruh and R. C. Williams. London: Earthscan.

Smith, A. D. 1998. *Nationalism and modernism: A critical survey of recent theories of nations and nationalism*. London: Routledge.

Suliman, M. 1999. The Nuba Mountains of Sudan: Resource access, violent conflict, and identity. In *Cultivating peace: Conflict and collaboration in natural resource management*, ed. D. Buckles. Ottawa, Canada: International Development Research Center; Washington, D.C.: World Bank Institute.

Tilly, C. 2003. *The politics of collective violence*. Cambridge, UK: Cambridge University Press.

Toft, M. D. 2003. *The geography of ethnic violence: Identity, interests, and the indivisibility of territory*. Princeton, NJ: Princeton University Press.

Unruh, J. D. 2003. Land tenure and legal pluralism in the peace process. *Peace & Change* 28:348–373.

Weinstein, J. M. 2007. *Inside rebellion: The politics of insurgent violence*. Cambridge, UK: Cambridge University Press.

Yergin, D. 1991. *The prize: The epic quest for oil, money, and power*. New York: Simon and Schuster.

Young, H., A. M. Osman, A. M. Abusin, M. Asher, and O. Egemi. 2009. *Livelihoods, power and choice: The vulnerability of the Northern Rizaygat, Darfur, Sudan*. Medford, MA: Feinstein International Center, Tufts University.

Swords into plowshares? Accessing natural resources and securing agricultural livelihoods in rural Afghanistan

Alan Roe

Field experience in Afghanistan emphasizes the importance of understanding rural livelihood security when planning for peace within the broader context of natural resources and agro-ecological landscapes. Achieving secure and sustainable rural livelihoods in the context of such landscapes is a prerequisite to achieving social and political stability in outlying (and often volatile) areas and, therefore, it is important for the Afghan government and its supporters to recognize sustainable rural livelihoods as a distinct goal within the overarching objective of economic growth.

This chapter examines experiences in promoting access to natural resources in rural Afghanistan and the implications for agricultural livelihoods. The first sections of the chapter outline field research conducted in Afghanistan between 2005 and 2009, introduce the context of political and agricultural instability in Afghanistan, and discuss the emergence of a market-oriented agricultural and natural resource management policy. The chapter then draws on the results of the 2005–2009 research to examine the status and attributes of different farming systems, making particular reference to inclusion and exclusion in access to natural resources, and provides evidence of the potentially destabilizing impact of inequitable access to natural resources across different systems of land use. Finally, the chapter highlights lessons that may guide future efforts to strengthen peacebuilding through agricultural policy reform in Afghanistan and other post-conflict situations.

THE RESEARCH (2005–2009)

Data informing this study were collected under the auspices of two natural resource management research projects conducted between 2005 and 2009 across several provinces and districts in Afghanistan.

Alan Roe is a research leader with the National Field Research Centre for Environmental Conservation in Oman and an adjunct research fellow at the School for Environmental Research, Charles Darwin University; he previously served as senior research manager for natural resource management at the Afghanistan Research and Evaluation Unit (AREU).

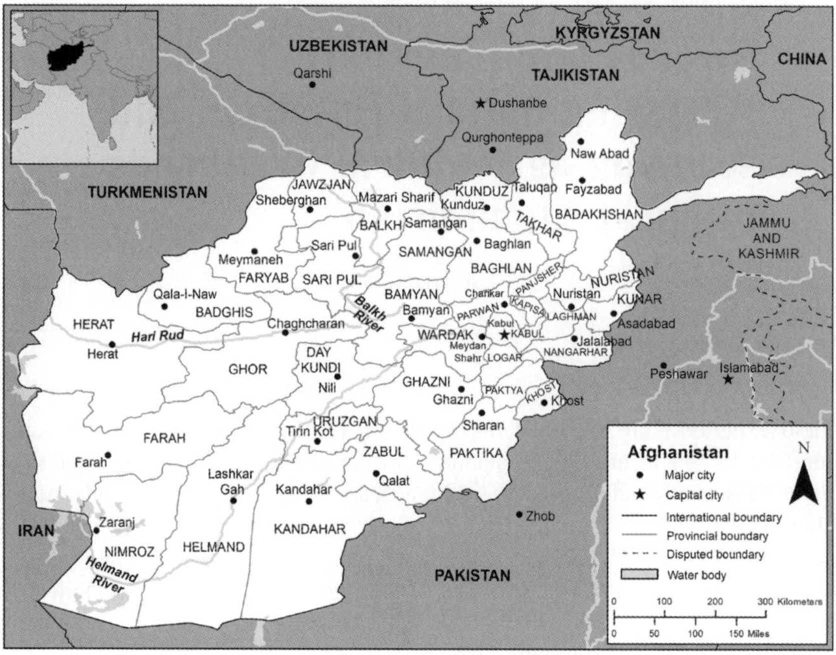

The first research project took an integrated farming systems approach to understanding natural resource management, agricultural production, and rural livelihoods within socioeconomic and biophysical contexts.[1] This approach recognizes that farm decision makers extract benefits across a range of scales and values and make trade-offs between multiple, competing objectives both on the farm and off (Collinson 2000). The research utilized diverse methods, including a longitudinal seasonal farm survey across several provinces,[2] in-depth case studies to examine specific issues, physical measurements of resource conditions, and on-farm experimental research. Comparative studies encompassed a range of different land uses and production systems, including uses and systems employed by nomadic pastoral groups (see figure 1 for land uses in Afghanistan).

The second research project investigated rural conflicts over natural resources and methods for resolving these conflicts. This research involved constructing a typology of natural resource conflicts in Afghanistan, identifying representative

1 This applied, thematic research into water management, the opium economy, and livestock was conducted by a consortium of institutions led by the AREU, with funding from the European Commission.

2 Surveys were taken in the following provinces: Badakhshan, Balkh, Ghazni, Ghor, Herat, Kunduz, and Nangarhar.

conflicts, and piloting formal and informal conflict resolution processes within nomadic and sedentary rural communities in the Afghan provinces of Baghlan, Herat, Kunduz, Panjshir, and Parwan (Deschamps and Roe 2009).[3]

These two coordinated research activities produced a wealth of data regarding natural resource management, farming systems, and wider livelihood strategies at district and subregional levels across Afghanistan, which afforded researchers the rare opportunity to adopt an integrated landscape-scale analysis of the processes and conditions shaping livelihood strategies and farming decisions in rural Afghanistan (see sidebar) (Pijanowski et al. 2010).

In recognition of local heterogeneity and complexity, the research focused on identifying patterns in relationships between natural resource conditions and access, social and political factors, institutions, and livelihood outcomes (Frost et al. 2006; Wu 2006). In particular, application of an integrated landscape approach helped address some of the inadequacies and limitations of largely thematic and sectoral studies previously used to inform Afghan agricultural development policy. A good example of this integrated approach were studies that investigated the dynamics of the opium economy over time across a range of social, political, economic, and agro-ecological conditions and spatial locations (Pain 2006; Mansfield 2008).

These research projects were designed and initiated at a time when the Afghan government and its international backers were struggling to develop an effective and licit agricultural economy to bring stability and prosperity to rural Afghanistan and counter the spread of an illicit opium poppy economy.

Reports and publications

The Natural Resource Management team at the Afghanistan Research and Evaluation Unit (AREU) produced over twenty studies and research reports between 2005 and 2009, authored by more than ten different researchers. Many of these studies and reports (all available online at www.areu.org.af) are cited in this chapter, including the following:

Deschamps, C., and A. Roe. 2009. *Land conflict in Afghanistan: Building capacity to address vulnerability*. Issues Paper Series No. 43. Kabul: AREU.

Flaming, L., and A. Roe. 2009. *Water management, livestock and the opium economy: Opportunities for pro-poor agricultural growth.* Synthesis Paper Series No. 44. Kabul: AREU.

Roe, A. 2008. *Water management, livestock and the opium economy: Natural resources management, farming systems and rural livelihoods*. Synthesis Paper Series No. 97. Kabul: AREU.

Roe, A. 2009b. *Water management, livestock and the opium economy: Challenges and opportunities for strengthening licit agricultural livelihoods.* Synthesis Paper Series No. 80. Kabul: AREU.

Rout, B. 2008. *How the water flows: A typology of irrigation systems in Afghanistan.* Issues Paper Series. Kabul: AREU.

Wegerich, K. 2009. *Water strategy meets local reality*. Issues Paper Series No. 67. Kabul: AREU.

---

[3] The AREU's Capacity Building to Address Land Conflict and Vulnerability project was supported by funding from the World Bank.

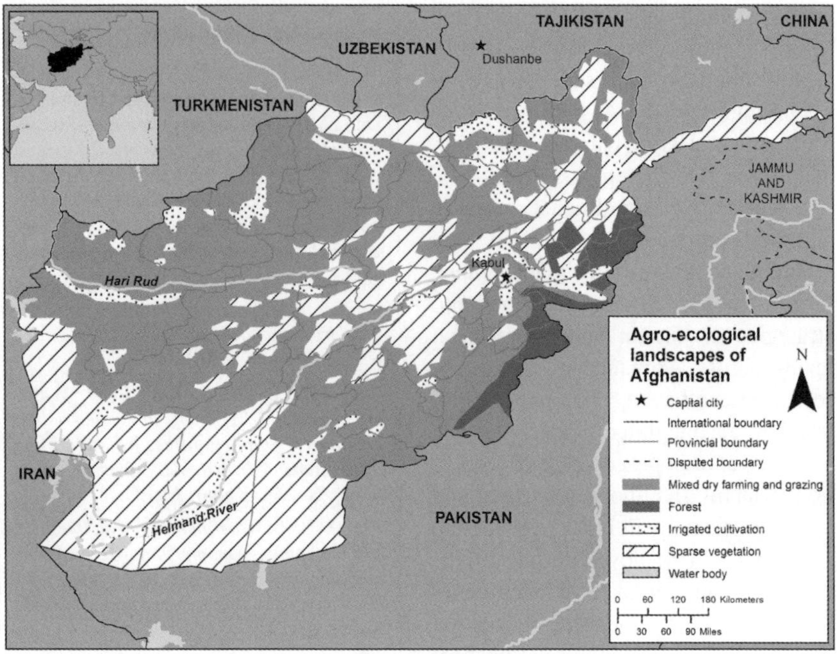

Figure 1. Agro-ecological landscapes of Afghanistan
Source: Roe (2009b).

A LEGACY OF INSTABILITY

Until 1978, Afghanistan not only produced enough food for its own needs but also exported a considerable volume of agricultural products, notably livestock and dried fruits. Historically, agriculture had been the largest and most important sector of the Afghan economy, with a high proportion of the population pursuing livelihoods in agriculture and related activities (FAO 1997a).

Following the Soviet invasion in 1989, political instability and episodic conflict severely disrupted Afghanistan's long-established system of natural resource management and the country's agricultural economy, the negative effects of which were exacerbated by a subsequent severe and prolonged period of drought (1998–2002) (MIWRE 2004). Over the course of the turbulent 1980s and 1990s, and over the course of the drought years, significant numbers of internal and cross-border rural populations were displaced, resulting in widespread abandonment of land and agricultural infrastructure. Similarly, traditional market chains for agricultural products were disrupted or collapsed completely.

Variations in agricultural sector

The impact of these disruptions on the agricultural sector was more nuanced than the donor and development community initially recognized. Although data from this period are known to be inaccurate, the variation reflected in the data sets illustrates the economic instability of this period and reveals how different parts of Afghanistan's agricultural economy responded to years of conflict and drought.

For example, data derived from the *Afghanistan Statistical Yearbook* indicate that, after losing a significant proportion of irrigated land during the initial Soviet invasion, Afghan farmers were slowly able to rebuild their capacity to irrigate lands throughout the 1990s, or at least until the 1998–2002 drought (CSO 2006). Similarly, populations of fast-breeding sheep and goats increased after the initial Soviet invasion, until drought decimated the remaining herds. By contrast, cereals production seems to have been relatively resilient through the years of conflict (food crops were prioritized), and although production declined sharply during the drought, it had recovered to the point that, by 2005, cereals production exceeded pre-Soviet levels. Similarly, the cattle population (used primarily to supply food products for domestic consumption) remained relatively stable during the conflict and drought period, and, since then, has experienced steady growth.

Consequences of sporadic disruptions and population growth

Over the past thirty years, sporadic disruptions to natural resource management systems—made worse by oscillations in agricultural productivity and rapid population growth—significantly decreased political stability and livelihood security in rural Afghanistan. While statistics indicate diversity and complexity in how different parts of the Afghan agricultural economy responded to the instability created by conflict and drought in recent decades, changes in natural resource conditions and agricultural productivity over this period must also be considered in the context of a rapidly growing population. The county's population is expected to double in thirty years (Population Institute 2011; Reuters 2011). This section examines how political instability, when combined with rapid population growth, can exacerbate already tense situations and lead to further conflict over access to, and the use of, land and other natural resources.

First, a decrease in per capita agricultural production has caused food deficits throughout Afghanistan. Even in a good agricultural year, such as 2005, the country faced a 10 percent deficit in cereals demand compared to domestic cereals production (FAO 2006). As local production fell below consumer demand from 2000 through 2005, there was a growing trend toward importation of many domestically produced foods (see table 1). In 2008, deficits in local food production contributed to rising prices for food staples, which triggered political instability and food riots in Afghanistan's major cities.

Second, while political turmoil, institutional weakness, disrupted markets, and physical insecurity have adversely affected many types of agricultural production in Afghanistan, under these same conditions, illicit cultivation and marketing of opium has thrived. According to available data, the amount of Afghan land area currently used for opium poppy cultivation steadily increased over the past

Table 1. Value of Afghanistan's annual food imports, 2000–2005 (in thousands US$)

	2000	*2001*	*2002*	*2003*	*2004*	*2005*
Wheat	5,533	17,700	96,008	47,529	49,119	85,539
Rice	0	0	0	17,480	18,005	29,096
Beef	0	0	0	20	2,023	5,049
Milk powder	80	482	4,132	3,004	3,823	9,149

Source: CSO (2006).

decade, reaching 193,000 hectares in 2007 at the peak of opium production (UNODC 2009). In 2006, the United Nations estimated that over 12 percent of the Afghan population was in some manner involved in opium cultivation (UNODC 2006).[4]

MARKET-ORIENTED STRATEGY FOLLOWING THE TALIBAN'S FALL AND THE BONN AGREEMENT

After the fall of the Taliban regime in 2001, the Bonn Agreement established the Transitional Islamic State of Afghanistan, at which time the international community committed to support new governance structures, initially through the National Development Framework and, later, through the Afghanistan National Development Strategy (ANDS). The goal of the ANDS included achievement of "pro-poor growth"—economic growth benefiting the poor more than the nonpoor as a means to share the benefits of development across the nation's entire population (IROA 2008b, 27).

This planning process highlighted agriculture as an engine for economic growth and recovery. Under the ANDS process, the Afghan Ministry of Agriculture and Animal Husbandry (later renamed the Ministry of Agriculture, Irrigation and Livestock, or MAIL) became a focus for extensive international technical assistance, which led to development of the Agriculture Master Plan. This master plan shaped the direction of agricultural and rural development policy in Afghanistan, including through the ANDS Agriculture and Rural Development (ARD) Sector Strategy (IROA 2008a).

Despite the stated national objective of achieving pro-poor growth, Afghan agricultural development policy in the post-conflict redevelopment period initially emphasized fostering market chains for high-value agricultural products. For example, the ARD Sector Strategy downplayed the role of subsistence agriculture in favor of large-scale commercial production. The strategy explicitly advocated targeting development initiatives in agriculture and rural development zones with high commercial potential around the cities of Herat, Kabul, Kandahar, Kunduz, and Mazari Sharif. Specifically, the ARD Sector Strategy argued that:

---

[4] For analyses of opium production, control efforts, and post-conflict peacebuilding in Afghanistan, see Catarious and Russell (2012) and Pain (2012).

> The advantage of promoting large scale commercial agriculture is that it is led by investors and entrepreneurs who bring substantial resources and market linkages and who are well positioned to: (1) identify profitable opportunities; (2) expand access to quality inputs, technologies and markets; (3) lower costs through volume purchase; (4) lower risk through production contracts; (5) extend credit and extension services; (6) facilitate growth of local allied industries; and (7) provide quality control services (IROA 2008a, 29).

With this strategy in mind, MAIL and its international supporters promoted a range of initiatives to stimulate growth in high-value horticultural production, primarily orchard fruit, vegetables, and industrial crops such as flax and cotton, along with fodder crops and improved livestock production. These crops were considered suitable for a growing export market (including India) and, therefore, most likely to attract foreign investment in the country's growth.

The first years of the Transitional Islamic State were a time of optimism in Afghanistan, which was reflected in the relative stability and security across most of the country (Cordesman 2009). However, sporadic acts of resistance to the new, internationally sponsored government increased; by 2007, the number of monthly insurgency incidents had grown more than tenfold (see figure 2). The activity of the Taliban and other antigovernment elements first escalated in the southern and eastern parts of the country, and by mid-2007, the level of insecurity in the outlying districts of Helmand, Khost, Kunar, Nangarhar, Paktika, and Uruzgan had risen to such a degree that the UN categorized these districts as "hostile environments." Since then, violence and insecurity has spread into other formerly secure parts of the country, including previously stable provinces in western and northern Afghanistan.

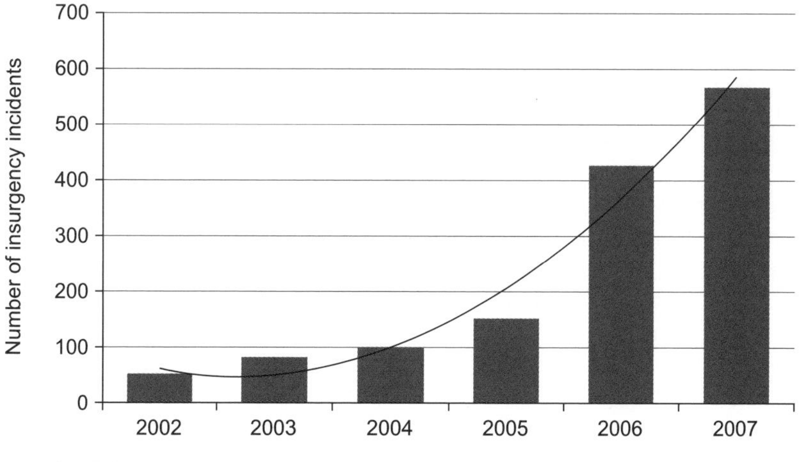

Figure 2. Mean monthly insurgency incidents in Afghanistan, 2002–2007
Sources: Cordesman (2008, 2009).

Many commentators have provided nuanced political and ethnicity-related interpretations of the drivers of the insurgency, and some have suggested links between the insurgency and the country's extensive opium economy (Rubin 2013; UN Country Team in Afghanistan 2013). Few analysts have considered, however, how distribution and management of natural resources and other associated rural livelihood options may have contributed to instability. The following analysis addresses this gap, highlighting some of the risks associated with an economic growth-driven agenda for agricultural development and concluding that an important prerequisite to enhancing political stability may be agricultural policy that improves rural livelihood security.

AGRICULTURAL-BASED LIVELIHOOD ADAPTATION AND CONFLICT DUE TO UNEQUAL RESOURCE ACCESS IN AFGHANISTAN

In many regions of Afghanistan, farming and livestock rearing are economically difficult livelihood options, made worse by—and in turn sometimes exacerbating —patterns of conflict and instability. Given the overall lack of alternative opportunities, however, agricultural production remains a predominant source of income for many Afghans, particularly those residing in rural communities. Agriculturalists utilize a variety of farming systems based on the availability of and access to water resources, and the geographic distance of farmed land from irrigation infrastructure. The following sections examine how disparities in access to natural resources that affect agricultural output can increase competition and conflict in vulnerable, rural communities.

Landscapes, farming systems, and livelihoods

Afghanistan is a rugged and mountainous country covering approximately 65 million hectares, 8 million of which are under cultivation (FAO 1997b). Eighty percent of Afghanistan's crop output relies on irrigation, although in an average year, less than half of the country's agricultural land receives irrigation. The most intensively cultivated and settled areas are located on Afghanistan's alluvial plains and in river valleys, where water from mountain snowmelt can be diverted for crop irrigation. Biannual cropping is possible in river valley regions where conditions—such as reliable summer water flows—are sufficient to support numerous crop seasons. Other regions lacking access to irrigation systems utilize a rainfed system of agricultural production, which typically produces low yields.

After extensively reviewing and comparing farming (agricultural and livelihood) systems across eight Afghan provinces, researchers specializing in water management, the opium economy, and livestock arranged the farming systems under consideration in the following categories: irrigated farming, semi-irrigated farming, rainfed farming, and nomadic pastoralism. While these categorizations risk oversimplifying complex and overlapping farming strategies (both on- and off-farm), they facilitate preliminary comparisons between natural resource access and livelihood outcomes at the landscape level. Subsequent comparative studies, however, reveal important differences between these systems with regard to rural livelihood security and opportunities (see table 2).

Irrigated farming in river valleys

Among the farming systems in Afghanistan, the systems associated with irrigated river valley lands tend to receive the most regular and stable water supplies (through canal systems) and, as a consequence, are able to grow a diverse range of crops. In some areas, these include high-value cash and industrial crops. Road networks and major settlements located in these irrigated river valleys also provide relatively direct access to markets at comparatively low costs in terms of transactions. Farmers in river valleys can also grow fodder crops to feed the families' milk cows, which provide their families with milk. Other livestock, including sheep and goats, graze on seasonal pastures considered common property, but because valley farmers do not have ready access to these pastures, they tend to raise few of these livestock. In terms of livelihoods, however, not only can river valley farmers potentially grow high-value agricultural products and relatively easily take these products to market, they also have ready means to supplement on-farm production income by hiring themselves out as off-farm waged labor in neighboring towns.

Management of irrigation systems in river valleys. Management of irrigation systems in Afghan river valleys usually involves conveying water over long distances and through primary canals that traverse land owned by several communities. Accordingly, management of irrigation water can be highly political and therefore challenging, particularly in the summer months when river flows diminish and water becomes increasingly scarce. Traditionally, Afghan river valley communities practiced sophisticated water management to address challenges associated with water flow and access. Within these traditional and institutionalized systems, landownership carries with it associated water entitlements, and hierarchies of community-elected water masters (*mirabs*) represent the interests of irrigators at the primary and secondary canal levels.

In practice, systemic inequities in access to water resources exist between communities at the head and tail of irrigation canals. These inequities are due in part to inefficiencies in the hydraulic performance of canal infrastructure. Importantly, however, these inequities also reflect asymmetries in power, wealth, and influence among the communities involved, and often relate to ethnic or political affiliations. By virtue of their position, upstream irrigators can and do exceed their allotted water entitlements to the detriment of those downstream. In rural Afghanistan, water-intensive horticulture, as well as cultivation of sugarcane, cotton, and other high-value summer crops, tend to be clustered in the upper and middle reaches of the canal systems. A study of irrigated farming from

Table 2. Comparison between mean production and livelihood attributes of households practicing different farming systems in Afghanistan

	Cultivated area (ha)	*Irrigation water supply*	*Annual crop diversity*	*Sheep/ goats*	*Cattle*	*Household nutrition*	*Household assets*	*Number off-farm incomes*	*Mean incomes value (US$)*
Irrigated farming (n = 252)									
Mean	1.78	57.72	8.44	3.57	1.68	78.64	3.64	1.86	1183.89
Std.dev	2.39	14.534	2.69	9.10	1.63	23.38	2.91	1.22	1555.91
Semi-irrigated farming (n = 106)									
Mean	0.65	39.32	5.57	5.87	0.58	85.66	2.11	1.57	926.00
Std.dev	0.92	9.04	1.39	9.69	1.03	21.94	2.47	1.01	1027.12
Rainfed farming (n = 58)									
Mean	3.58	Not applicable	3.75	14.36	2.34	61.00	1.74	2.00	488.87
Std.dev	3.12		0.50	17.03	2.43	17.23	3.37	1.35	523.70
Nomadic pastoralism (n = 25)									
Mean	Not applicable			45.88	0.76	82.12	1.96	Not available	
Std.dev				40.04	1.14	16.51	1.60		

Source: Roe (2008).

Notes: Irrigation water supply: Farmer assessment of the extent to which their farm irrigation water requirements are met, expressed as a percentage.
Annual crop diversity: Number of different types of crops cultivated annually.
Cultivated area: Cultivated area in hectares (ha).
Sheep/goats: Number of sheep and goats owned.
Cattle: Number of cattle owned.
Household nutrition: An arbitrary value calculated by weekly consumption of different food types within the household.
Household assets: An arbitrary value describing household ownership of nonessential and luxury items (proxy for disposable income).
Number of off-farm incomes: Number of off-farm incomes received by household (irrespective of monetary value).
Mean incomes value (US$): Total annual income (sum of all off-farm waged incomes).
n: Number of households.

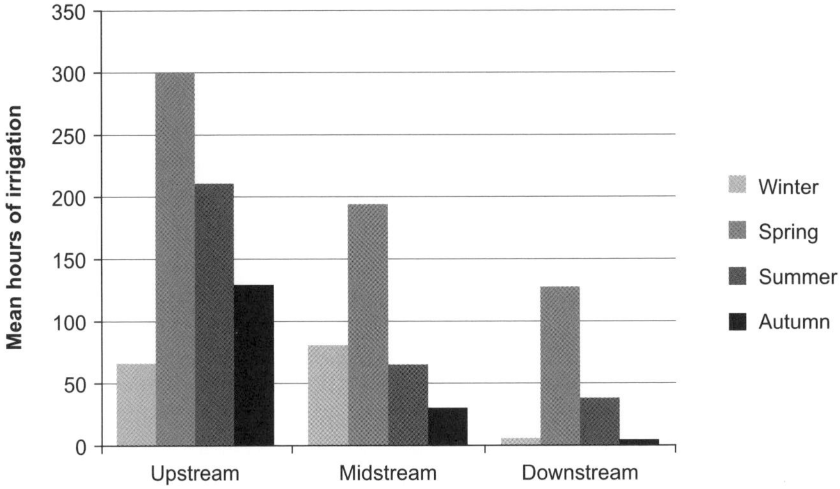

Figure 3. Mean monthly hours of irrigation by farm position in Afghan irrigation systems, 2006–2007
Source: Roe (2009a).
Note: Data from surveying 171 households.

2006 to 2007 indicates that upstream farms received more than twice the mean hours of irrigation flow than comparably sized farms downstream (Roe 2009a) (see figure 3).

Downstream sites have significantly lower mean irrigated wheat yields per hectare, even at higher seed and fertilizer application rates (Roe 2009a). In addition, records indicate that downstream farmers shoulder a much higher burden of irrigation maintenance labor, with direct implications for their opportunity to engage in off-farm waged labor.

Owing to the demand for irrigated land (and the prospect of good farm returns), between 25 and 30 percent of all farmland in Afghan river valleys is worked under a sharecropping arrangement (whereby landowners grant sharecroppers access to use agricultural lands in exchange for an agreed percentage of the harvested crop). As demonstrated by data from Balkh and Kunduz provinces, sharecropped lands tend to be in the middle and lower reaches of irrigation systems and, therefore, carry higher attendant risks than lands in the upper reaches of the canal system. Yet, even land sited along the lower reaches is attractive to farmers who own no land or who are seeking to acquire additional land under subordinate rights. These lands can potentially sustain diverse cropping (including higher-value crops), given sufficient irrigation flows. Sharecropping as a form of tenure is more common in Afghanistan's irrigated river valleys than elsewhere in the country, but the terms of agreement are also less favorable to the sharecropper due to vast disparities in the ultimate division of the harvest between sharecropper and landowner (Roe 2009a).

Preliminary overview. Farmers in Afghanistan's irrigated river valleys enjoy a relatively high level of livelihood security. Despite land scarcity and a low level of cultivated area per capita (given dense clusters of settlement), the soil in these valleys is generally fertile and annual fluctuations in irrigation water supply are often predictable. Cropping is sufficient, on average, to provide more than 50 percent of the food that families require. In these valleys, on average, approximately 60 percent (by monetary value) of the food consumed each week by farming families is produced on-farm, with the remainder purchased at market (Roe 2009a). Farmers in these comparatively populous river valleys have easy access to nearby markets and greater opportunity to engage in off-farm labor for supplementary wages. From 2005 to 2006, river valley households earned a mean off-farm income of close to US$100 per month, an income significantly above the national mean.

However, irrigated river valley farming involves large, structural inequities in resource access—in terms of both land access and water usage. In some districts, gradients of wealth, opportunity, and livelihood security are evident along the canal systems; the farther upstream one goes, for example, the more high-value, irrigation-intensive crops are grown. High levels of sharecropping in the middle and lower sections of these systems indicate that a high proportion of revenue is directed back into the hands of upstream or absentee landowners, further exacerbating wealth, opportunity, and livelihood security inequity (Roe 2009b).

Semi-irrigated highland farming

Higher up in river catchments, in foothills overlooking river valleys, Afghan farmers in remote villages cultivate small plots of land irrigated by intermittent springs, streams, or *karez*—man-made, subterranean canals that draw water from hillside springs and carry it where needed. Here, water scarcity is a constant limitation, and irrigable land areas are often extremely small. Consequently, crop diversity is much lower than in the river valleys, and very little marketable surplus is, or can be, produced. Farmers are often far from regional markets and lack easy access to off-farm wage-earning labor opportunities. Lacking irrigable land for fodder crops, these farmers keep relatively few cows. They do raise other livestock, however. With better access to grazing rangelands and pastures than in river valleys, farmers with access to open hill slopes can maintain relatively high numbers of sheep and goats.

Although the rate of discharge from springs and karez can be high during snowmelt, this rate slows considerably during summer months, and flow can even cease. Consequently, in highland farming systems, there is only one season for cultivation. Also, given the small scale of irrigation infrastructure (canals may only be a few hundred meters in length), there is little difference between the amount of water received on plots at the heads of canals and those at the tail end. Such small-scale infrastructure means that irrigation water moves throughout farming systems in a single village. As a result, upland villages do not normally have specialized governing institutions for water management; rather, village councils of elders typically reach decisions and direct actions on behalf of the village. Therefore, while irrigation water resources tend to be scarcer in highland farming systems than in river valleys, the management of these resources tends to be more equitable.

The small size of irrigated plots in highland farming systems also means that households are generally not self-sufficient in food production. On average, only 45 percent (by monetary value) of food consumed by these households is produced on-farm. Access to labor opportunities is likewise poor, and there are high rates of labor-based migration to other provinces and neighboring countries (RECCA IV 2010). Despite this outward migration, mean off-farm waged incomes among highland farming households remain lower than those recorded among river valley farming households. Also contributing to livelihood insecurity among highland farmers is the remoteness and high elevation of villages and the severity of winter snows, which can cut villages off from the nearest markets for several months each year.

In some districts in central and eastern Afghanistan, highland communities with limited irrigation water and very small irrigable land area (which heightens the need for cash income for food purchases) have become deeply engaged in opium poppy cultivation. Opium poppy is one of the few viable crops available given the lack of alternative resources, and its cultivation can help secure access to scarce land resources and, thus, reduce exposure to risk. In the case of opium poppy cultivation, remoteness from lowland population centers, markets, and law enforcement agencies is an advantage rather than a disadvantage to these households.

Rainfed farming

Across many parts of Afghanistan, outside of river valleys, remotely scattered settlements practice marginal rainfed farming on elevated tablelands (plateaus), on hill slopes, and on lower-elevation plains. Here, unlike agriculture in irrigated or semi-irrigated areas, cultivation is not limited by land scarcity but, rather, by the labor required to prepare and harvest large areas of land. The crops are primarily wheat and barley (cereals) sown in expectation of winter rains. While yields are highly variable between years, they tend to be low. Cultivation of these cereal crops provides food staples for households. Households also gather straw to feed livestock in winter.

Livestock production is a primary source of monetary income for farmers in rainfed systems. In spring, given good access to surrounding pasturelands, and in summer, given the possibility of grazing herds on residues from cereal harvests, farmers in this system are able to produce large flocks of sheep and goats to take to market. The sale of these herds at market not only generates income but also buffers farm households against financial impacts of drought and other risks. In good years, livestock numbers rise, although this capital growth can easily be absorbed or exceeded by forced sales during drought years when crops fail. Although cattle are found most typically in rainfed areas, they are not valuable dairy cows but rather plowing oxen.

Due to their often remote locations, rainfed farming communities tend to have poor access to commodity and labor markets. These communities engage in a high level of waged employment, but it tends to be low-paid temporary work helping with local harvests. Due to the relative abundance of available land, sharecropping agreements are rare, and when such agreements are made, the terms tend to favor cultivators, not landowners. However, access to other lands, such as common-property pastures, is essential for sheep and goat herds that constitute the primary marketable production output of this farming system.

Rainfed farming households also have the poorest diet (corresponding to household nutrition in table 2) of any of the rural farming production systems in Afghanistan; however, they also report the highest level of food self-sufficiency (Roe 2009a). Given the predominate cultivation of cereal crops, their diets are dominated by carbohydrates, supplemented by dairy products (mostly from sheep and goats). Few quantities of additional food are purchased at market, so consumption of fresh fruits and vegetables is low. As mentioned earlier, these households have regular access to off-farm employment, but it is nearly always temporary and primarily agricultural (assisting other farmers), as a consequence of which these households receive significantly less off-farm income than other farming household types (a mean of US$40 per month) (Roe 2008). Low cash income as well as geographic isolation helps explain why these rainfed farming households generally lack the means to diversify and improve their dietary intake.

In sum, rainfed cultivation is associated with high risks of many different kinds, including potential nutritional deficiency, not only due to the vagaries of the Afghan climate and precipitation but also due to extremely low crop diversity. For these communities, a sequence of bad agricultural years can have disastrous effects (as was the case during the 1998–2002 droughts). Although sheep and goat herds can buffer the risk and uncertainty of rainfed farming, these communities regularly engage in livestock sales during years of environmental stress when livestock prices are depressed, which amounts to a risk-averse strategy that limits the potential for economic growth.

Nomadic pastoralism

Of all the farming systems in Afghanistan, nomadic pastoralism most reflects market supply. Aside from processed milk products, nomadic pastoralists generally consume very little of what their livestock produce, relying instead on cash sales from large herds of sheep and goats to purchase food staples. Seasonal mobility offers distinct advantages over most sedentary farming systems in accessing markets; migration routes encompass markets where nomadic pastoralists sell their livestock products, seek opportunities for waged labor, and purchase necessary food stocks and other items.

Afghan pastoralists have traditionally managed their flocks in the mild lowlands during the winter, and then migrated to common-property (open-access) central highland pastures in the spring. While pastoralists continue this lifestyle of transhumance, it is practiced in a modified form today, with tribal groups occasionally opting to camp during the summer months on the outskirts of Kabul. From there, they can access waged labor to supplement income from livestock sales.

The main risk factor associated with nomadic pastoralism in Afghanistan is dependence on access to common-property pasturelands. Pastoralist sheep and goat production is based on a low-input, low-output strategy, in which pastoralists attempt to minimize costs by accessing free or cheap grazing lands during the spring and early summer months (Fitzherbert 2007). Given growing population pressures and the weakening of environmental governance regimes in many parts of the country, nomadic pastoralists' traditional rights of access to common-property pastures face growing opposition (Alden Wily 2004). Conflicting rights of access to pastures and grazing land can lead to violent conflict between pastoralists and settled communities.[5]

Natural resources and farming systems overview

Natural resources (and the social and political mechanisms underpinning natural resource management) support a range of agricultural livelihood strategies across rural Afghanistan. While some Afghan landscapes support rural, agricultural livelihoods where high levels of market engagement are possible, other agriculture-based livelihoods remain more marginalized and subject to high risk and insecurity.

Studies conducted in Afghanistan from 2005–2007 characterize fundamental patterns of resource management, farming behavior, and livelihood security. Analysis of these patterns highlighted a range of natural resource, agricultural, and off-farm factors underlying rural livelihood security, economic opportunity, and sustainability. These factors include the type, tenure status, and condition of local natural resources and the types and functions of informal institutions that govern access to natural resources. Another important predictor of livelihood security is access to markets for a variety of needs, such as to sell farm products, purchase food, and obtain credit, as well as to gain opportunities for waged labor. On- and off-farm diversification is important in terms of both risk aversion and wealth accumulation (Grace and Pain 2004).

---

[5] For a more detailed discussion on pastureland conflicts in Afghanistan's central highlands, see Liz Alden Wily, "Resolving Natural Resource Conflicts to Help Prevent War: A Case from Afghanistan," in this book.

DRIVERS OF LIVELIHOOD INSECURITY AND RURAL INSTABILITY

Afghanistan has a long history of insecurity, which fuels conflict. In the absence of physical and economic security, disputes over existing and available natural resources exacerbate local tensions and can lead to violent conflict. The following sections explore the factors that drive livelihood instability and conflict in different Afghan contexts.

Resource access, scarcity, and drivers of instability

Internationally, associations between poverty, vulnerability, and chronic conflict have been widely documented. Many commentators have suggested that poverty and lack of opportunity are primary predictors of civil conflict in fragile states (Collier and Hoeffler 1998; Hegre et al. 2001). Further, it has been postulated that "vulnerability to poverty and vulnerability to violence" influence the probability that individual households will participate in, or support, armed groups (Justino 2009, 5).

Others argue that poverty itself is not particularly destabilizing but rather the prevalence of horizontal inequalities, such as the perceived or actual biases in a given society that impact the distribution of assets, opportunities, power, and influence (Zaur 2006; Stewart 2008). This dynamic has been noted in agricultural societies where certain segments of society are or have been disadvantaged by geographic location, dysfunctional or biased markets, and exploitation by well-organized and powerful interests controlling access to key resources. Under these circumstances, individuals may be driven to migrate, confront the status quo, or assume other extreme coping strategies (de Soysa and Gleditsch 1999), which may hinder agricultural recovery and the transition to stability (Longley et al. 2007).

As elucidated thus far, the study of natural resource management in Afghanistan has provided evidence of resource scarcity and associated livelihood vulnerability. In some cases, this has contributed to armed conflict, banditry, and even opposition to local authorities (Deschamps and Roe 2009). The following subsections provide examples of natural resource conditions and conflict over access to natural resources that have precipitated rural unrest.

Water management and localized conflict in river valleys

Structural inequities in irrigation water supply in Afghanistan can contribute to instability and increase the potential for localized conflict. A study of the Khalazai Canal in Parwan Province revealed that overextraction of water by villages of one ethnicity at the inlet of the canal led to chronic water scarcity for villages primarily made up of another ethnicity at the tail end of the canal (Deschamps and Roe 2009). As a result, 600 families were displaced and whole villages abandoned as downstream livelihoods became untenable during the drought of 2006. Likewise, there is evidence from the Hari Rud river system that water stress has intermittently flared into violence and bloodshed between upstream and downstream irrigators in Herat Province (Lee 2007). During the 2006 drought, some downstream farmers reported receiving as little as fifteen minutes of irrigation flow over a two-month period, which led to a widespread collapse of cropping systems on the lower Hari Rud. Conflicts over water access were further exacerbated by historical alliances held by the two groups during the civil war. Earlier studies have described similar situations in the Balkh River Basin (Lee 2003).

This research indicates that conflict over irrigation water access and usage in river valleys is, or often has been, intensified not only by drought but also other drivers of rural conflict and insecurity, such as differences in ethnicity and, in the case of Afghanistan, opium poppy cultivation. Structural inequities that affect access to water resources may also serve as precipitants or multipliers of rural conflict. Indeed, many disputes between communities along irrigation systems can persist at low levels of intensity for many years before igniting due to catalytic incidents, such as drought or ethnic or political friction. It does not help that local authorities and policy makers tend to overlook existing, low-level disputes until the disputes erupt into overt violence.

Resource scarcity and emergent conflict in Afghanistan's highlands

In the semi-irrigated, highlands farming systems in Afghanistan, absolute resource scarcity often drives local instability and conflict. In some villages on the upper slopes of the Spin Ghar Range in Nangarhar Province, the mean cultivated area can be as low as 0.001 hectares per person, making it extremely difficult for farming households to achieve livelihood security through licit agriculture alone. Accordingly, households engaged in farming in these resource-scarce areas heavily depend on opium poppy cultivation and labor out-migration to offset risks. In 2006, in the face of a Nangarhar provincial ban on opium poppy cultivation and lack of easy recourse to off-farm wages (other than as paid fighters with armed insurgency groups), members of the Khogiani and Shinwari tribes united to oppose the ban, confronting the authorities with a show of force. Immediately, security conditions began to deteriorate, not only in the Spin Ghar region, but throughout the highlands (Mansfield 2008). Analyses also have attributed the rise of banditry and physical insecurity in 2006 across outlying districts of the Ghor Province to drought-related stresses so great that natural resources could no longer sustain remote farming populations (WFP 2001). In the absence of livelihood alternatives, coping strategies in the highlands and other remote areas included affiliation with criminally or politically motivated armed groups.

Experiences from the Laghman and Nangarhar provincial highlands show that competition over scarce natural resources is an ongoing precipitant of conflict (Koehler 2005). The tiny landholdings associated with semi-irrigated farming systems in the highlands are the result not only of baseline resource scarcity but also of inheritance mechanisms that increasingly fragment landholdings through successive generations. Given the scarcity and high value of irrigable land in the highlands of Afghanistan, little land is open for sale, so growing families must constantly compete to acquire access to land in other ways or, alternatively, move away. In 2005, a survey of twenty-five highlands community disputes revealed that thirteen stemmed from disputes over land and water, and all but two disputes resulted in violence (Koehler 2005).

High-risk rainfed farming and competition for grazing land

In most respects, farmers of rainfed land are more vulnerable to production risks and livelihood insecurity than farmers of semi-irrigated land. Heavily dependent on cereals cultivation for their domestic food consumption, rainfed farming households are among the first to be adversely affected by drought, and profoundly so. In recent years, rainfed farming communities in the remote western and central parts of Afghanistan have been so severely impacted by winter food shortages (and growing population pressures) that they often appropriate and plow pasturelands for cultivation. Anecdotal evidence also suggests that wealthy and powerful landowners sometimes seize large areas of pasturelands in an effort to accumulate and maximize their wealth through landownership (Deschamps and Roe 2009; Unruh and Shalaby 2012).

While it is difficult to assess precisely how many common-property pastures in Afghanistan have been converted for cultivation, a 2003 national survey found that community leaders in 45 percent of all districts reported losses of grazing land (National Surveillance System and Vulnerability Analysis Unit 2003). In addition, between 1999 and 2003, Dasht-e Laili (common-property grazing land in Jawzjan Province) alone lost 15,600 hectares to plowing and cultivation (Favre 2003). Conversion of range or pasturelands formerly used as a common-property resources for livestock grazing seems to have occurred on a large scale, bringing appropriators into direct conflict with migratory livestock herders.

In some parts of the central highlands, competition between migratory livestock herders and other land users over access to pastures has escalated into open conflict. In 2008, armed clashes in the Behsud area of Nangarhar Province resulted in the deaths of dozens of people, displaced thousands more from their homes, and revived national tensions between the ethnic Hazaras and Pashtuns. Since then, conflict over land use has escalated into a significant threat to national stability (Alden Wily 2004).

Comprehensive review of data on land conflicts in Afghanistan indicates that disputes over access to common-property resources are among the most severe, intractable, and enduring land conflicts in Afghanistan (Deschamps and Roe 2009; Alden Wily 2004). While informal institutions and traditional governance systems may be effective in managing internal community disputes over private property, they provide little opportunity for recourse when disputes involve common property and actors who do not share a common set of customary rules and regulations (Roe 2008).

Livelihood vulnerability associated with agricultural production in marginal, resource-scarce areas has the potential to undermine rural stability and peace-building efforts outside of Afghanistan's main river valleys and population centers. Consequently, the oft-cited military adage about Afghanistan—"where the road ends, the insurgency begins"[6]—may hold currency for framing political and policy choices regarding agricultural and rural development. Specifically, it raises questions as to whether policy makers should focus agricultural development investments on sites and industries with maximum potential to drive national goals for economic growth, or whether they should they look beyond "where the road ends" to consider the potential risks of such a market-driven program.

Driving economic growth and fostering rural stability: What the evidence shows

Field experience highlights three key risks associated with market-driven models for agricultural development in Afghanistan, such as those proposed in the 2005 MAIL Agriculture Master Plan and the 2008 ARD Sector Strategy.

First, it is clear that through implementation of the master plan and sector strategy, opportunities for growth in horticultural production would primarily benefit farmers with preferential access to irrigation water, as most horticultural crops require intensive irrigation. Thus, economic growth in Afghanistan's river valleys would be clustered in areas already comparatively prosperous, namely the upstream parts of preexisting irrigation canals. Even where sufficient irrigation flow permits high-value horticulture downstream of the best irrigated lands (for example, in the middle ranges of canal systems), the high incidence of sharecropping recorded in these middle ranges means that a significant proportion of the benefits would be directed back to wealthy landowners.

Second, assuming that planned agribusiness growth would focus solely in populated river valleys, it is likely that households in isolated outlying districts would not share the same level of access to employment opportunities, as is already the case.

Third, Afghan agricultural policies have given little recognition to the value of farm production to household consumption, which implies that this is not an economic value per se but rather an irrational use (in economic terms) of farm resources.

Following from these observations, policy focused on maximizing agricultural sector growth carries with it the risk (at least initially) of exacerbating preexisting differences in wealth between relatively prosperous farming communities and those that are most vulnerable and resource insecure (Roe 2009b). From a purely economic perspective, the wisdom of stimulating growth in the nation's most

---

[6] See, for example, U.S. Senate (2008).

productive agricultural subsectors and regions is unquestionable. From a political perspective, stimulating growth in river valleys and regional centers also makes good sense because the majority of the rural population lives there, and therefore stands to benefit from such growth. Important to this equation, however, is the fact that the central government in Kabul and its international backers face a growing insurgency and diminished influence in remote rural districts. Therefore, policies that further disadvantage farming communities in outlying areas constitute a high-risk strategy that carries with it the potential to further fuel volatility, chronic insecurity, disaffection, and an entrenched, illicit opium economy.

Clearly, the goal of fostering a market-driven, competitive rural economy must be balanced with the need to build a stable rural society as a prerequisite to sustainable growth of the rural economy. The question is how to achieve this. What does the evidence suggest in terms of how to achieve a stable rural society and sustainable growth of the rural economy? Specifically, how can agricultural policies contribute to peacebuilding—to the forging of swords into plowshares—in Afghanistan?

STRENGTHENING PEACEBUILDING THROUGH AGRICULTURAL POLICY: FUTURE DIRECTIONS

While many factors contribute to ongoing political conflict in Afghanistan, resource conditions and disputes over access and use of natural resources can increase insecurity in already volatile regions and exacerbate underlying tensions. In Afghanistan, outlying, natural resource–insecure areas tend to be in or near chronically unstable insurgency strongholds. This is due primarily to the remoteness of communities from centers of governance and the relative inaccessibility of security forces. Even if no causal relationship could be shown between natural resource scarcity, livelihood insecurity, and cycles of conflict and confrontation, there are nevertheless obvious political (if not economic) reasons to target these areas with initiatives designed to mitigate local vulnerability. In this context, agricultural policies that address this vulnerability can contribute to rural stability. Many of the studies conducted in Afghanistan (and cited earlier in this chapter) suggest ways in which this could be done as a means to lend weight to rural conciliation and state building.

Need for more evidence-based policy making. The Afghan government should engage in a greater degree of evidence-based policy making that is sensitive to the heterogeneity of the country's agro-ecology and farming systems. If utilized, this approach could lead to more pragmatic trade-offs between goals rooted in ideology and goals rooted in what is needed on the ground.[7] This kind of decision

[7] For challenges in advancing evidence-based policy making in Afghanistan, see Belinda Bowling and Asif Zaidi, "Developing Capacity for Natural Resource Management in Afghanistan: Process, Challenges, and Lessons Learned by UNEP," in this book.

making clearly requires a sophisticated appreciation of farming behaviors, determination of the types of natural resources available to farming households, and an understanding of the social and political contexts in which these households make decisions. Afghanistan already benefits from mechanisms such as the National Surveillance System, which has been highly effective in directing aid assistance to relieve short-term food security crises. However, more location-specific information is needed to inform future policy development, including how farming systems function and how the various farming systems present in Afghanistan affect livelihood outcomes.

Need for policies that facilitate greater equality in natural resource access. Access to natural resources and livelihood opportunities in Afghanistan is characterized by systemic inequities. While these inequities may be a consequence of local geography and agro-ecology, they are nonetheless often affected by asymmetric power relationships and the function of customary gateway institutions, such as the mirab system. Policies that facilitate greater equality in resource access are needed to create an environment that enables widespread participation in agricultural sector growth (and, more generally, in state building). A number of projects have piloted techniques to improve community management of land and water resources, and have since found traction among Afghan policy makers (Deschamps and Roe 2009; Stanfield et al. 2013).

Comparative advantages among farming systems. The fact that farming systems in Afghanistan are heterogeneous and have distinct advantages is in some ways beneficial as it creates an opportunity for policy making that fosters diverse agricultural production and market chains, each tailored to different production environments and natural resource conditions. For example, while there is little opportunity for rainfed farming communities to participate in production of high-value horticultural crops for export, there is a high potential for them to engage in an industry built around supplying weaned lambs and sheep to irrigated farms for finishing on agricultural by-products. Equally, the opportunity cost of directing labor from semi-irrigated farms to off-farm wage-earning opportunities is comparatively low.

By investigating different farming systems and identifying their respective comparative advantages, decision makers can offer genuinely pro-poor opportunities to mitigate poverty and other vulnerabilities in marginal areas. It is particularly important that planners and decision makers avoid concentrating agricultural initiatives, services, and facilities in populated river valleys, as in the past.

Further, agricultural policy in Afghanistan (and elsewhere) must place greater value on strengthening the whole of farming systems, not just market chains for agricultural products. In particular, agricultural policy must enhance and diversify farm livelihood security by improving access to off-farm incomes or by supporting farm production for domestic consumption. Studies in Afghanistan have shown that subsistence agriculture focused on production of food crops for household consumption can represent an economically efficient allocation of household resources when household monetary savings on food purchases equal or exceed the value of income that could be earned from commercial crops or other sources of income. This situation is common in remote areas with poor market access and a good example of how important it is for development planners and decision makers to take a broader view of how agricultural livelihoods are constructed.

POSTSCRIPT

MAIL's National Agricultural Development Framework (released in April 2009) places significantly greater focus on the need to improve natural resources access. While the policy still identifies middle-scale farmers as "the backbone for sustainable growth in agriculture" (MAIL 2009, 19), the new framework also incorporates a bottom-up approach to agricultural development, citing the need for more equitable distribution of the benefits arising from growth in agriculture. The policy also places less emphasis on prioritizing agricultural development in agro-ecologically favorable areas, focusing more on specific commitments to tailor opportunities for the resource-poor nomads and others across all agro-ecological zones, including populations in the remote highlands and rainfed farming areas.

In an environment of escalating insurgency, this aspirational policy reform reflects a new understanding by the Afghan government and its international supporters that they are more likely to establish a market-driven agricultural economy by adopting a more measured approach during the transitional period. By tempering economic growth with initiatives targeting structural vulnerability and livelihood insecurity, the framework may offer a more effective approach to restoring peace and stability in rural Afghanistan.

REFERENCES

Alden Wily, L. 2004. *Looking for peace in the pastures: Rural land relations in Afghanistan*. Issues Paper Series. Kabul: Afghanistan Research and Evaluation Unit.

Catarious, D. M., Jr., and A. Russell. 2012. Counternarcotics efforts and Afghan poppy farmers: Finding the right approach. In *High-value natural resources and post-conflict peacebuilding*, ed. P. Lujala and S. A. Rustad. London: Earthscan.

Collier, P., and A. Hoeffler. 1998. On economic causes of civil war. *Oxford Economic Papers* 50 (4): 563–573.

Collinson, M. 2000. *A history of farming systems research*. Wallingford, UK: Food and Agriculture Organization of the United Nations / Centre for Agriculture and Biosciences International.

Cordesman, A. H. 2008. *Losing the Afghan-Pakistan war? The rising threat*. Washington, D.C.: Center for Strategic and International Studies. http://csis.org/files/media/csis/pubs/081021_afghanthreat.pdf.

———. 2009. The Afghanistan-Pakistan war: The rising intensity of conflict 2001–2007. Washington, D.C.: Center for Strategic and International Studies. http://csis.org/files/090701_rising_intensity_conflict_2001-2007.pdf.

CSO (Central Statistics Office, Islamic Republic of Afghanistan). 2006. *Afghanistan statistical yearbook*. Kabul.

Deschamps, C., and A. Roe. 2009. *Land conflict in Afghanistan: Building capacity to address vulnerability*. Issues Paper Series No. 43. Kabul: Afghanistan Research and Evaluation Unit.

de Soysa, I., and N. P. Gleditsch. 1999. *To cultivate peace: Agriculture in a world of conflict*. Oslo, Norway: Peace Research Institute Oslo.

FAO (Food and Agriculture Organization of the United Nations). 1997a. *Afghanistan agricultural strategy*. Rome.

———. 1997b. Afghanistan. AQUASTAT database. www.fao.org/nr/water/aquastat/countries_regions/afghanistan/index.stm.

———. 2006. Afghanistan's agricultural prospects for the year ahead. July 17. http://reliefweb.int/report/afghanistan/afghanistans-agricultural-prospects-year-ahead.

Favre, R. 2003. Grazing land encroachment: Joint helicopter mission to Dasht-e Laili, March 25–27. Kabul, Afghanistan: Food and Agriculture Organization of the United Nations.

Fitzherbert, A. 2007 *Water management, livestock and the opium economy: Livestock feeds and products*. Case Study Series No. 58. Kabul: Afghanistan Research and Evaluation Unit.

Flaming, L., and A. Roe. 2009. *Water management, livestock and the opium economy: Opportunities for pro-poor agricultural growth*. Synthesis Paper Series No. 44. Kabul: Afghanistan Research and Evaluation Unit.

Frost, P., B. Campbell, G. Medina, and L. Usongo. 2006. Landscape-scale approaches for integrated natural resources management in tropical forest landscapes. *Ecology and Society* 11 (2): 30. www.ecologyandsociety.org/vol11/iss2/art30/.

Grace, J., and A. Pain. 2004. *Rethinking rural livelihoods in Afghanistan*. Synthesis Paper Series. Kabul: Afghanistan Research and Evaluation Unit. www.areu.org.af/Uploads/EditionPdfs/424E-Rethinking%20Rural%20Livelihoods%20SP.pdf.

Hegre, H., J. Ellingsen, S. Gates, and N. P. Gleditsch. 2001. Toward a democratic civil peace? Democracy, political change, and civil war, 1816–1992. *American Political Science Review* 95 (1): 33–48.

IROA (Islamic Republic of Afghanistan). 2008a. Agriculture and rural development sector strategy: Afghanistan National Development Strategy. Kabul: Ministry of Agriculture Irrigation and Livestock.

———. 2008b. *Afghanistan National Development Strategy 1387–1391 (2008–2013): A strategy for security, governance, economic growth and poverty reduction*. Kabul: Afghanistan National Development Strategy Secretariat. www.undp.org.af/publications/KeyDocuments/ANDS_Full_Eng.pdf.

Justino, P. 2009. *Poverty and violent conflict: A micro level perspective on the causes and duration of warfare*. MICRON Research Working Paper No. 6. Brighton, UK: Institute of Development Studies. www.microconflict.eu/publications/RWP6_PJ.pdf.

Koehler, J. 2005. *Conflict processing and the opium poppy economy in Afghanistan*. Jalalabad, Afghanistan: GIZ (Deutsche Gesellschaft für Internationale Zusammenarbeit) Project for Alternative Livelihoods in Afghanistan.

Lee, J. 2003. *Water resource management in the Balkh Ab River and Hazhda Nahr canal network: From crisis to collapse*. Kabul, Afghanistan: Central Asian Free Exchange.

———. 2007. *Water management, livestock and the opium economy: The performance of community water management*. Case Study Series. Kabul: Afghanistan Research and Evaluation Unit.

Longley, C., I. Christopolos, T. Slaymaker, and S. Meseka. 2007. Rural recovery in fragile states: Agricultural support in countries emerging from conflict. *Natural Resource Perspectives*, No. 105. London: Overseas Development Institute.

MAIL (Ministry of Agriculture Irrigation and Livestock, Islamic Republic of Afghanistan). 2009. Economic Regeneration Programme (ER). Kabul. http://mail.gov.af/Content/Media/Documents/EconomicRegenerationProgrammeDocumentfinal2Apr092392012152836718553325325.pdf.

Mansfield, D. 2008. *Water management, livestock and the opium economy—Resurgence and reduction: Explanations for changing levels in opium poppy cultivation in Nangarhar and Ghor in 2006–07*. Case Study Series. Kabul: Afghanistan Research and Evaluation Unit. www.areu.org.af/Uploads/EditionPdfs/810E-Resurgence%20and%20Reduction-CS-print.pdf.pdf.

MIWRE (Ministry of Irrigation, Water Resources and the Environment, Islamic Republic of Afghanistan). 2004. *Emergency drought assessment in 12 vulnerable southern provinces*. Kabul.

National Surveillance System and Vulnerability Analysis Unit. 2003. *National risk and vulnerability assessment*. Kabul, Afghanistan: Ministry of Rural Rehabilitation and Development.

Pain, A. 2006. *Water management, livestock and the opium economy: Opium cultivation in Kunduz and Balkh*. Case Study Series. Kabul: Afghanistan Research and Evaluation Unit.

———. 2012. The Janus nature of opium poppy: A view from the field. In *High-value natural resources and post-conflict peacebuilding*, ed. P. Lujala and S. A. Rustad. London: Earthscan.

Pijanowski, B., L. Iverson, C. Drew, H. Bulley, J. Rhemtulla, M. Wimberly, A. Bartsch, and J. Peng. 2010. Addressing the interplay of poverty and the ecology of landscapes: A grand challenge topic for landscape ecologists? *Landscape Ecology* 25 (1): 5–16.

Population Institute. 2011. From 6 billion to 7 billion: How population growth is changing and challenging our world. www.populationinstitute.org/external/files/reports/from-6b-to-7b.pdf.

RECCA IV (Fourth Regional Economic Cooperation Conference on Afghanistan). 2010. Working group paper on economic development: Labor migration. http://mfa.gov.af/Content/files/LABOR%20MIGRATION.pdf.

Reuters. 2011. Afghanistan fights population growth with birth control. August 23. www.reuters.com/article/2011/08/23/us-afghanistan-birthcontrol-idUSTRE77M4MU20110823.

Roe, A. 2008. *Water management, livestock and the opium economy: Natural resources management, farming systems and rural livelihoods*. Synthesis Paper Series No. 97. Kabul: Afghanistan Research and Evaluation Unit.

———. 2009a. *Applied thematic research into water management, livestock and the opium economy: Findings from the first year of farm and household monitoring*. Case Study Series. Kabul: Afghanistan Research and Evaluation Unit. www.areu.org.af/Uploads/EditionPdfs/917E-Household%20Monitoring-CS-print.pdf.pdf.

———. 2009b. *Water management, livestock and the opium economy: Challenges and opportunities for strengthening licit agricultural livelihoods*. Synthesis Paper Series

No. 80. Kabul: Afghanistan Research and Evaluation Unit. www.areu.org.af/Uploads/EditionPdfs/920E-Strengthening%20Licit%20Agricultural%20Livelihoods-SP-web.pdf.

Rout, B. 2008. *How the water flows: A typology of irrigation systems in Afghanistan.* Issues Paper Series. Kabul: Afghanistan Research and Evaluation Unit.

Rubin, B. R. 2013. *Afghanistan from the Cold War through the war on terror.* New York: Oxford University Press.

Stanfield, J. D., J. Brick Murtazashvili, M. Y. Safar, and A. Salam. 2013. Community documentation of land tenure and its contribution to state building in Afghanistan. In *Land and post-conflict peacebuilding*, ed. J. Unruh and R. C. Williams. London: Earthscan.

Stewart, F., ed. 2008. *Horizontal inequalities and conflict: Understanding group violence in multi-ethnic societies.* Basingstoke, UK: Palgrave Macmillan.

UN (United Nations) Country Team in Afghanistan. 2013. *Natural resource management and peacebuilding in Afghanistan.* Nairobi, Kenya: United Nations Environment Programme. www.unep.org/disastersandconflicts/portals/155/countries/Afghanistan/pdf/UNEP_Afghanistan_NRM.pdf.

UNODC (United Nations Office on Drugs and Crime). 2006. *Afghanistan opium survey.* Vienna, Austria.

———. 2009. Afghan opium production in significant decline. September 2. www.unodc.org/unodc/en/frontpage/2009/September/afghan-opium-production-in-significant--decline.html.

Unruh, J., and M. Shalaby. 2012. Road infrastructure reconstruction as a peacebuilding priority in Afghanistan: Negative implications for land rights. In *Assessing and restoring natural resources in post-conflict peacebuilding*, ed. D. Jensen and S. Lonergan. London: Earthscan.

U.S. (United States) Senate. 2008. Afghanistan: A plan to turn the tide? Hearing before the Committee on Foreign Relations, United States Senate. Hearing No. 110-609. Washington, D.C.: United States Government Printing Office. www.gpo.gov/fdsys/pkg/CHRG-110shrg45330/html/CHRG-110shrg45330.htm.

Wegerich, K. 2009. *Water strategy meets local reality.* Issues Paper Series No. 67. Kabul: Afghanistan Research and Evaluation Unit.

WFP (World Food Programme). 2001. WFP Afghanistan update on humanitarian situation No. 22. http://reliefweb.int/report/afghanistan/wfp-afghanistan-update-humanitarian-situation-no-22.

Wu, J. 2006. Landscape ecology, cross disciplinarity and sustainability science. *Landscape Ecology* 21 (1): 1–4.

Zaur, I. 2006. Agriculture and conflict: A conceptual framework for development. Unpublished Master's thesis, Tufts University. On file with author.

Forest resources in Cambodia's transition to peace: Lessons for peacebuilding

Srey Chanthy and Jim Schweithelm

Cambodia underwent more than a decade of civil conflict following the end of the Viet Nam War. The Khmer Rouge regime, which took power in 1975, forced much of the population to perform heavy labor and carried out targeted violence against ethnic minorities. After the Khmer Rouge government collapsed in 1979, all Cambodian warring factions agreed to begin negotiating a peace settlement. Years of negotiations in Jakarta, Indonesia, and Paris, France, culminated in 1991 in the Paris Agreements signed by all combatant groups, all major world powers, and many other United Nations member countries.[1] The accords requested the United Nations Security Council (UNSC) to assist with the rehabilitation and reconstruction of Cambodia. Administered by the United Nations Transitional Authority in Cambodia (UNTAC), UN interventions included organizing free and fair national elections, administering the country in the interim, and rehabilitating and developing the country. These goals were to be pursued by disarming all Cambodian warring factions, restoring peace and political and social stability, building democracy and a free market economy, promoting respect for human

---

Srey Chanthy is an independent consultant focusing on agriculture and land reform issues. Jim Schweithelm is the principal of Forest Mountain Consulting in Burlington, Vermont, specializing in issues related to forests and climate change in Asia.

The authors wish to acknowledge support by the U.S. Agency for International Development for their earlier analysis of forest resource conflict in Cambodia (Schweithelm and Srey 2004). Srey Chanthy participated in the events described in this chapter as a member of the initial peace mission, as a United Nations Transitional Authority in Cambodia staff member, and later, in the 1990s, as an employee of the Cambodian Ministry of Agriculture, Forestry, and Fisheries. He also survived imprisonment by the Khmer Rouge.

1 The Paris Agreements are formally known as the Agreements on a Comprehensive Political Settlement of the Cambodia Conflict and were signed in Paris on October 23, 1991. For the complete text of the four agreements—the Final Act of the Paris Conference on Cambodia; the Agreement on a Comprehensive Political Settlement of the Cambodia Conflict; the Agreement Concerning the Sovereignty, Independence, Territorial Integrity and Inviolability, Neutrality and National Unity of Cambodia; and the Declaration on the Rehabilitation and Reconstruction of Cambodia—see www.un.org/en/peacekeeping/missions/past/unamicbackgr.html.

rights, and ensuring respect for and recognition of Cambodia's territorial integrity and sovereignty.

Despite efforts by the international community, the civil war caused substantial harm to the country's forests and the people who depend on them. This chapter explores the challenges UNTAC and the interim government faced and the lessons that can be drawn from the experience for future peacebuilding efforts by the international community. It begins by presenting the impacts on Cambodia's forests and forest users during the transitional period ushered in by the peace accords. It then presents a brief history of forest management in Cambodia leading up to the forest-related events of the 1990s. The chapter revisits the treatment of forests in Cambodia during the country's transition to peace, with an eye to extracting lessons from the experience. The last section considers how these lessons might be applied in other post-conflict countries with significant forest resources.

FOREST RESOURCES IN CAMBODIA'S TRANSITION TO PEACE

UNTAC administered Cambodia from 1991 to 1993 under the provisions of the peace accords, providing the international community with a key role in shaping the peacebuilding process in a country that was slowly emerging from two decades of armed conflict.

During this period, UNTAC and the interim government, the Supreme National Council (SNC), faced many peacebuilding-related challenges, including providing public security amid continuing conflict,[2] preparing for a general election, repatriating displaced people, and providing humanitarian assistance. They also faced the formidable task of stimulating economic recovery and generating government revenues. UNTAC and the donor community recognized that Cambodia's commercially valuable forest resources could provide a means to quickly create economic activity in the shattered economy and generate revenues for the new government.

However, the SNC first needed to control the rampant illegal exploitation of these resources, which threatened both the forests themselves and the ability of the country and the government to benefit from them. In January 1993, the SNC imposed moratoria on round log and sawn wood exports as a temporary solution, allowing for time to assess existing forest resources, which had not been inventoried since the conflict began, and to develop forest management policies and procedures. UNTAC was mandated to monitor enforcement of these moratoria, but its efforts failed to slow the illegal flow of wood out of the country (UNSC 1992). While UNTAC invested US$407 million to train Cambodians in economic development (UN n.d.), none of this training was devoted to forest management or administration.

---

[2] Despite the peace accords, the civil war continued, with Khmer Rouge elements ambushing UNTAC personnel, Khmer civilians, and other factions.

What actually happened to Cambodia's forests after the 1993 general election was quite different from what ordinary Cambodians and the international community might have envisioned. In 1994, the newly elected Royal Government of Cambodia gave authority over timber exports to the Ministry of National Defense to generate revenues to fight the Khmer Rouge forces that still controlled the northwest part of the country (McKenney and Tola 2002). The government also gave the Ministry of National Defense control over sizable areas of forestland for a planned demobilization program. In 1995, despite ongoing talks with key donors over how to effectively manage Cambodia's forests to support economic growth, the government issued timber concessions covering 6.4 million hectares (35 percent of the nation's total land area) to international firms and political allies of senior officials (Global Witness 2002). These concessions were awarded despite the weakness or absence of forest management laws, institutions, and data. Those who lived in and depended on the forests were not consulted in the process of awarding or managing the concessions (see figure 1 for Cambodia's heavily forested provinces).

During the second half of the 1990s, Global Witness documented concessionaires, military forces, and illegal loggers harvesting Cambodian timber far in excess of sustainable levels, with no management plans in place and with techniques that significantly reduced timber yields and caused serious ecological

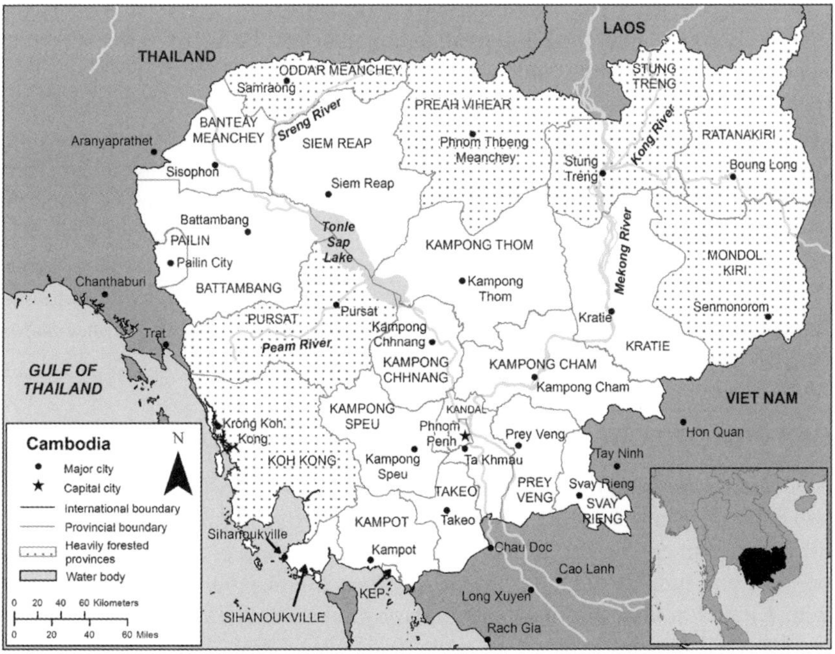

Figure 1. Heavily forested provinces in Cambodia
Source: Schweithelm and Srey (2004).

damage (Global Witness 1996–2002). Royalties were paid on only a small fraction of the harvested timber, greatly reducing projected government revenues. Much of the profits leaked across international borders in the form of either wood or money, diminishing the potential for Cambodia to benefit from employment and domestic investment. Funds generated by illegal logging fueled corruption, reinforcing a system of political patronage that retarded the growth of democratic institutions and undermined the faith of Cambodians in their government. In addition, the Cambodian armed forces used funds from the sale of illegal timber and other illegal ventures to operate semi-independently of civilian oversight.

Forest communities paid a high price for this period of "anarchic logging," as the Cambodian government later referred to it. Many communities lost important livelihood assets such as land for shifting agriculture; financially and culturally valuable nontimber forest products, notably resin; and subsistence resources such as food items and building materials. Yet even as the forests were being logged past the point of commercial viability, the government was reestablishing security in the countryside, giving forestland value that it did not have during the armed conflict. The government quickly took advantage of this opportunity to award agricultural concessions for lands located within timber concessions. The resulting forest conversion displaced communities and eliminated their access to forest resources. Since even degraded forest provides some livelihood resources compared to plantations, this de facto loss of traditional forest resource property rights caused even greater hardship than had logging.

Numerous cases were reported during the late 1990s of serious conflict between concessionaires and communities over control of forest resources, including physical intimidation and the use of deadly force by military and other government security forces working for the concessionaires (Schweithelm and Srey 2004). It has been estimated that as many as 1.7 million people (12 percent of Cambodia's population) may have been affected by such conflict since the end of the UNTAC administration, based on an analysis of people's physical proximity to timber concessions or demonstrated dependence on forest resources (Schweithelm and Srey 2006). Land conflicts are currently increasing as additional forestland is being awarded for agricultural plantations or mining concessions, or is subject to land grabbing by land speculators.

HISTORY OF FOREST MANAGEMENT IN CAMBODIA

The forest management events of the 1990s are rooted in Cambodia's colonial and early post-independence history. Historically, forests have belonged legally to the government, helped support rural livelihoods, and constituted a source of political and military funding. In 1863, a French delegation concluded a treaty with King Norodom offering him military protection in return for timber concessions and mineral exploration rights (Chandler 1993). The ensuing colonial administration introduced land reform in 1884 (Delvert 1961; Tichit 1981), which included some forest governance provisions. The first Forestry Law for Cambodia was adopted in the 1930s, which first permitted commercial logging by local businessmen.[3] Throughout the colonial period, forest-dwelling people had free de facto access to forest resources, as they always had. After independence in 1953, the Royal Government under King Sihanouk continued this policy. A U.S. Agency for International Development–funded forest inventory conducted from 1958 to 1960 indicated that 73 percent of Cambodia was covered by forest, and identified specific areas for timber production, conservation, or conversion to agriculture (Tichit 1981).

Cambodia slid ever more deeply into civil war during Cambodia's Khmer Republic period of 1970–1975, a time when both the government's armed forces and the opposing Khmer Rouge fighters harvested timber to support their operations. During the subsequent rule of the Khmer Rouge (1975–1979), private rights to land and forest resources were not recognized. Anyone caught harvesting forest resources was subject to severe punishment, including death. When the Khmer Rouge regime fell in 1979, it was replaced by a Vietnamese-backed government that morphed into the SNC of the UNTAC period. Two successive constitutions in the 1980s confirmed state ownership of land and forests, while allowing limited forest use by rural people. Meanwhile, the civil war between the Cambodian government (supported by its Vietnamese ally) and the Khmer Rouge continued throughout the 1980s and well into the 1990s. Both sides sold large quantities of timber during this time to traders from Thailand and Viet Nam to fund their respective military operations (Global Witness 1997).

FOREST MANAGEMENT LESSONS FROM CAMBODIA'S TRANSITION TO PEACE

Cambodia's civil war was atypical in terms of its duration, political complexity, and the barbarity of the Khmer Rouge's four-year rule. Yet the forest management failures and consequences described above are possible in any forest-rich country emerging from a period of armed conflict severe enough to destroy forest governance institutions and capacity. In the case of Cambodia, the two years of international administration under UNTAC provided an opportunity, even if brief and under difficult circumstances, for the international community to assist the Cambodian transitional government in developing an interim framework and action plan for forest management. This would have provided a concrete basis for donor assistance in the crucial two years after the 1993 election, when the forest-related dialogue between the government and donors was largely unproductive (ARD, Inc. 1998). During this period, both legal and illegal logging activities were almost completely unregulated. The heated dialogue between the government and donors culminated in an impasse, in which Global Witness, which had been appointed by the government to serve as Cambodia's independent

[3] Arrêté du 21 mars 1930, fixant le régime forestier de l'Indochine.

forest monitor, was expelled from the country and categorized diplomatically as persona non grata, and the World Bank–funded Forest Management and Conservation Project was closed down prematurely. Once the government began issuing timber concessions in 1995, the opportunity to proactively guide forest management was lost—and the task of the international community then shifted to trying to limit the negative impacts of virtually unregulated timber harvesting on a grand scale.

Despite this missed opportunity, the World Bank and other donors and international organizations successfully engaged the government on forest sector issues after the concessions were awarded. Donor pressure led to the creation of the National Steering Committee on Forest Policy and four technical assistance projects to guide what had become a sector reform process: Forest Policy Reform, Forest Concession Management, Log Monitoring and Enforcement, and Forestry Law. Completed in 1998, these projects produced comprehensive recommendations for legal, institutional, and technical reform of the forestry sector, including the adoption of community forest management (ARD, Inc. 1998). Pressure from donors, international nongovernmental organizations (NGOs), and Cambodian civil society organizations mounted during the late 1990s, and forest policy took a prominent position on the agenda of the donor community's annual Cambodia Consultative Group meetings. Partly in response to this pressure, Cambodia's prime minister announced a broad crackdown on illegal logging in 1999, including the establishment of the Forest Crimes Monitoring Unit and appointment of the NGO Global Witness as an independent monitor reporting to the Council of Ministers and the donor community. In 2002, the prime minister announced a total moratorium on logging in Cambodia, although illegal logging and forest conversion to plantation agriculture continues to the present. Also in 2002, the Cambodian parliament enacted the Law on Forestry that incorporated many of the features recommended in 1998, including provisions for community management of forests. By 2009, 401 community forestry sites covering 380,587 hectares had been established, and an additional 2 million hectares of forestland are to be allocated for community forestry between 2010 and 2029 (Royal Government of Cambodia 2010).

The events described above must be viewed in the context of the exceptional challenges encountered in developing and implementing an effective and equitable framework of forest governance in post-UNTAC Cambodia. First, the new government was politically divided and faced difficult peacebuilding and national reconciliation tasks after years of bitter warfare that continued as government forces fought the Khmer Rouge for control of the northwestern part of the country into the late 1990s. Both Khmer Rouge commanders and government armed forces essentially controlled some portions of the country and extracted natural resources to maintain their forces. Full peace and stability was not achieved until 2001.

Second, during its rule, the Khmer Rouge effectively destroyed most government institutions and killed many Cambodians possessing technical, legal, and administrative skills. Faced with these serious shortcomings, the new government focused on establishing core governance functions, ending armed conflict, reconciling the various factions, and ensuring its own survival. Global Witness has asserted that revenues from timber concessions fueled corruption among senior government officials and were used to buy the support of autonomous military units (Global Witness 1996).

While the government of Cambodia eventually adopted many of the elements of a forest governance framework proposed by donors, serious and largely irreversible economic, social, governance, and environmental damage had already taken place. It is clear that the international community's intensive efforts to assist Cambodia to improve forest governance and management in the late 1990s should have been initiated earlier, during the UNTAC administration, in coordination with the declared logging moratoria. However, it is not clear whether that would have prevented the anarchic logging that later ensued. Significant technical assistance, financial support, and possibly international sanctions on timber exports would have been required to achieve a positive outcome.

The experience in Liberia a decade later indicates that a positive outcome for forest management is possible in the transition from armed conflict to peace. Like Cambodia, Liberia is a forest-rich country that suffered under a brutal regime that financed armed conflict through the sale of natural resources—in Liberia's case, diamonds as well as timber. In July 2003, the UNSC imposed sanctions on the export of Liberian round logs and timber (UNSC 2003). By December of that year, the UN had already developed a program to reform the forest sector, identifying specific tasks needed and the international organizations responsible for undertaking them. This program was implemented expeditiously and ultimately successfully—resulting in passage of a comprehensive new forest law and regulations—with the support of the new Liberian government, the Liberian people, and a broad range of donor organizations (Altman, Nichols, and Woods 2012).

Despite the similarities, it should be noted that forest sector reform in Liberia was less challenging than in Cambodia for several reasons. In Liberia, the institutions of forest management had not been completely destroyed; armed warfare had ended; the moratorium was easier to enforce because logs were shipped by sea from specific, easily monitored ports; and the post-conflict government fully supported forest sector reform, including the concept of vesting forest management rights in local communities.

Cambodia's experience with forest sector reform highlights important lessons for other forest-rich countries, especially when contrasted with the case of Liberia:

- In forest-rich countries with large forest-dependent rural populations, forest management in the transition to peace is an important part of the peacebuilding process—socially, economically, and politically.
- Timber is an ideal conflict resource because it is financially valuable and relatively easy to harvest and sell. Mismanagement of forest resources is, therefore, very likely to occur in the transition to peace without countervailing

political will on the part of host governments, awareness and participation of forest dwellers, and encouragement and financial and technical support from the international community.

- Forest governance institutions must comprise an integral part of the national governance structure to ensure sustainability.
- Timing is critical. A concrete forest management action plan and the means to implement it are needed early in the peacebuilding process to avoid the rapid depletion of forest resources.
- Community and individual rights to forest resources and land must be established early in the peacebuilding process to reduce conflict and protect livelihoods.
- Financial and other incentives may be required to achieve buy-in from the government, communities, and other key forest stakeholder groups, which may include security forces and armed groups. Enforceable legal sanctions on the international sale of timber and wood products may also be required at the outset.

APPLYING LESSONS FROM CAMBODIA TO FUTURE PEACEBUILDING EFFORTS

The events that took place in Cambodia in the 1990s raise difficult questions. The newly elected government had an electoral mandate to govern, but it was operating amidst continuing armed conflict in an underdeveloped political environment without meaningful judicial and civil society oversight. In countries emerging from conflict under similar circumstances, does the international community have a responsibility to protect the rights and livelihoods of forest communities that are severely affected by irresponsible forest management, or to prevent an important national economic resource from being squandered? Did UNTAC fulfill its mission in this regard? Or was it too narrowly focused on holding an election, rather than on creating a foundation for governance and national economic development? Tropical forests are now viewed as global resources based on their carbon sequestration value, raising a question about the right or responsibility of the international community to protect these forests during transitions from war to peace. The actions of the international community to build forest governance capacity in Liberia indicate that attitudes are changing. As a practical matter, the international community and the private sector now have legal and technical tools to reduce the international trade in conflict and illegal timber that did not exist in the early 1990s.

Assuming that the international community is responsible for taking an active role in forest management during peacebuilding, the practical actions described below are needed to prepare to meet this challenge. How these procedures and methods are applied will need to be context specific. The teams that further develop the procedures and methods and apply them on the ground will need appropriate technical skills as well as prior experience or training in transitional environments. The overall political and security situation will need to be assessed to determine how much progress is feasible. In most cases, the process of developing a forest governance framework will be incremental, starting with a basic system that becomes more elaborate as more information and stakeholder input become available. It should be noted that some forest stakeholder groups may be difficult to engage in planning and implementation; forest communities, for example, may be difficult to access due to security concerns, and relevant civil society groups may not yet have formed. It will be essential, however, to integrate these stakeholder groups into the planning process as the forest governance framework is refined.

Practical actions that could prove useful to improving forest management during post-conflict peacebuilding include the following:

- Development of procedures and templates designed to support forest stakeholders in rapidly creating forest management frameworks and action plans that address basic policies, property and use rights, resource inventory and allocation, and procedures for timber harvest and royalty payments.
- Deployment of teams of experts skilled in key aspects of rapid forest sector assessment, including remote sensing and spatial planning, community and stakeholder engagement, forest governance, forest management, community forestry, land tenure and property rights, and forest industries.
- Development of standard approaches for supporting transitional and newly elected governments in forest management, including short- and long-term staff training.
- Identification of likely sources of donor funding for both short-term needs and longer-term support.

REFERENCES

Altman, S. L., S. S. Nichols, and J. T. Woods. 2012. Leveraging high-value natural resources to restore the rule of law: The role of the Liberia Forest Initiative in Liberia's transition to stability. In *High-value natural resources and post-conflict peacebuilding*, ed. P. Lujala and S. A. Rustad. London: Earthscan.

ARD, Inc. 1998. Forest policy transition paper for Cambodia. Phnom Penh, Cambodia.

Chandler, D. P. 1993. *A history of Cambodia*. 2nd ed. Bangkok, Thailand: Silkworm Books.

Delvert, J. 1961. *Le paysan Cambodgien*. Paris: Mouton Publishers.

Global Witness. 1995. *Forests, famine, and war: The key to Cambodia's future*. London.

———. 1996. *Corruption, war, and forest policy: The unsustainable exploitation of Cambodia's forests*. London.

———. 1997. *Just desserts for Cambodia? Deforestation and the co-prime minister's legacy to the country*. London.

———. 1998. *Going places: Cambodia's future on the move*. London.

———. 1999a. *Crackdown or pause: A chance for forestry reform in Cambodia?* London.

———. 1999b. *The untouchables: Forest crimes and the concessionaires—can Cambodia afford to keep them?* London.

———. 2000. *Chainsaws speak louder than words*. London.

———. 2001. *The credibility gap—and the need to bridge it: Increasing the pace of forestry reform*. London.

———. 2002. *Deforestation without limits: How the Cambodian government failed to tackle the untouchables*. London.

McKenney, B., and P. Tola. 2002. Natural resources and rural livelihoods in Cambodia: A baseline assessment. Working Paper No. 23. Phnom Penh: Cambodia Development Resource Institute. www.cdri.org.kh/webdata/download/wp/wp23e.pdf.

Schweithelm, J., and C. Srey. 2004. Cambodia: An assessment of forest conflict at the community level. Washington, D.C.: United States Agency for International Development.

———. 2006. Cambodia: The human impact of forest conflict. Washington, D.C.: United States Agency for International Development.

Royal Government of Cambodia. 2010. National Forest Programme 2010–2029. www.twgfe.org/Docs/Plans/NFP%20Strategic%20and%20Implementation%20English.pdf.

Tichit, L. 1981. *L'agriculture au Cambodge*. Agence de Coopération Culturelle et Technique.

UN (United Nations). n.d. A vote for peace. Bangkok, Thailand: Sriboon Printing Industry.

UNSC (United Nations Security Council). 1992. Resolution 792. S/RES/792 (1992). November 30. New York.

———. 2003. Resolution 1478. S/RES/1478 (2003). May 6. New York.

Post-tsunami Aceh: Successful peacemaking, uncertain peacebuilding

Michael Renner

In August 2005, the government of Indonesia and the Free Aceh Movement (Gerakan Aceh Merdeka, or GAM) signed a memorandum of understanding (MOU) that ended the Aceh Province's twenty-nine-year struggle to secede.[1] Unlike several earlier, failed attempts, the MOU addressed key underlying reasons for the conflict, including governance of natural resources. Despite this success, critical tasks lie ahead to ensure that peacebuilding can continue.

The December 2004 tsunami that killed close to 170,000 Acehnese played a catalyzing role in paving the way for the successful peace negotiations and eventual accord (Merikallio 2006). During his election campaign, Susilo Bambang Yudhoyono, who became Indonesia's president in October 2004, had promised to end the Aceh conflict. But it is unclear how successful he would have been absent the toll from the tsunami, for it triggered tremendous acts of humanitarian goodwill by Indonesians across the country, altered the political dynamics underlying the conflict, and drew in unprecedented amounts of international aid and numbers of aid workers, journalists, and peace monitoring personnel (Renner and Chafe 2007). From the beginning, the European Union (EU)–led Aceh Monitoring Mission (AMM) monitored the response and peace efforts, and its mandate did not change after deployment.

After briefly referencing the origins of the Aceh conflict, including the key role natural resource exploitation has played in Acehnese grievances, this chapter outlines key provisions of the 2005 MOU and discusses the emergence of local conflicts since the signing of the accord. The chapter explores possible factors behind these conflicts, including the ongoing political transformation in Aceh toward democratic governance; disparities in levels of Indonesian and international assistance provided to Acehnese communities adversely affected by conflict

---

Michael Renner is a senior researcher at the Worldwatch Institute and is a senior advisor to the Institute for Environmental Security.

[1] The MOU is formally known as the Memorandum of Understanding between the Government of the Republic of Indonesia and the Free Aceh Movement. It was signed on August 15, 2005, in Helsinki, Finland.

as well as by the tsunami; difficulties with reintegration of GAM fighters; and challenges in providing assistance to noncombatants, including the displaced. In the years following the peace agreement, worries mounted that high unemployment (slightly above 9 percent in 2009) and the lack of long-term, sustainable livelihood opportunities could undermine the peacebuilding process. The chapter concludes by exploring how these challenges—along with Aceh's ongoing struggles with resource governance, particularly illegal logging—are being addressed and discusses possible solutions.

BACKGROUND

Indonesia has abundant natural resources and is rich in biodiversity. For centuries, populations with access have exploited the country's natural resources. The desire to utilize these resources has led to prolonged and violent conflicts such as that between the government of Indonesia and the people of the Aceh region.

Natural resource exploitation and its contribution to the conflict

When Indonesia gained its independence in 1949, the Acehnese people allowed their territory to become part of the new nation but came to regret the decision in light of subsequent, excessive central government control and unfulfilled promises for regional autonomy. In the years to follow, the benefits of exploitation of the province's vast natural resources (forests and timber, particularly, in the early years) largely failed to accrue to the Acehnese people. Rather, these resources were exploited by companies connected to the regime in Jakarta (the capital of Indonesia, on the island of Java), and this served as an enduring focal point of local resentment against the central government.

Over the course of President Suharto's thirty-one-year dictatorship (1967–1998), revenues from commercial oil and natural gas exploitation ventures (as well as logging ventures) mostly benefited multinational companies, such as ExxonMobil, and people connected to the Suharto regime. These Javanese elites were resented by the Acehnese as outsiders. For example, in 1971, significant oil and natural gas deposits were discovered in North Aceh (close to Lhokseumawe and Lhoksukon). The national government–owned Pertamina entered into a joint venture with ExxonMobil to construct what was then the world's largest refinery (Waizenegger and Hyndman 2010), yet the central government refused to share more than 5 percent of the profits from this and other oil and natural gas projects with Aceh's provincial government (McCulloch 2005).

Under Suharto, 75 percent of Aceh's total land area was given over to logging and plantation concessions (Fan 2006). After first claiming the land as a state "forest zone," the central government then granted rights to exploit the zone to individuals and companies with close connections to the regime (McCarthy 2002). Extensive logging subsequently reduced forest reserves in certain parts of Aceh by more than 60 percent (Fan 2006).

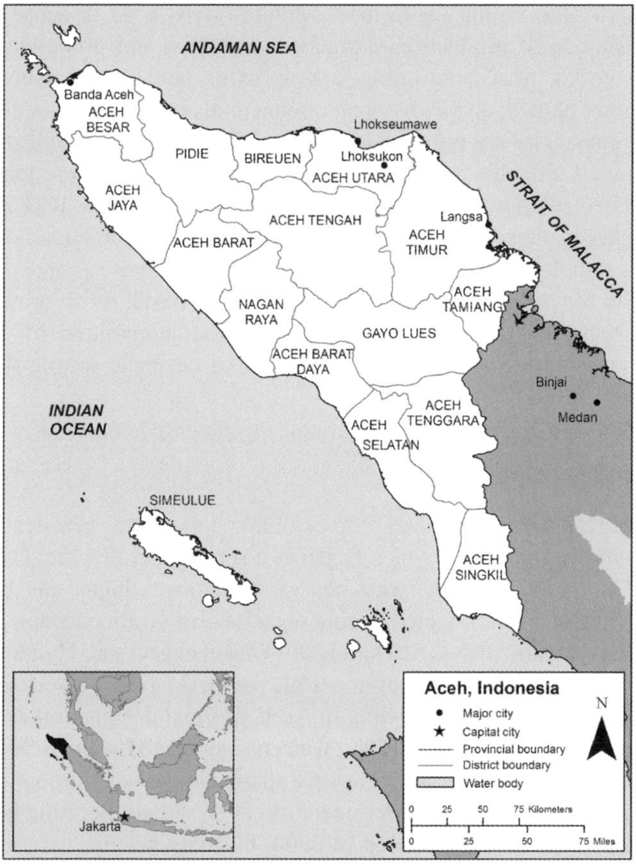

Even as Aceh's natural resources were contributing to national economic growth, the Acehnese people were not prospering. As John F. McCarthy observed in 2002, local entrepreneurs who lacked political connections found it difficult to procure concessions from the Indonesian Department of Forestry (McCarthy 2002). McCarthy noted that even securing permission locally required procuring a number of permits through a process that could be both lengthy and expensive. At a time when poverty was on the wane elsewhere in Indonesia, in Aceh, it was on the rise and, in fact, rose by 239 percent between 1980 and 2002 (Brown 2005).

Throughout this period, the Indonesian military engaged in legal and illegal businesses in order to supplement its budget, which was widely perceived as inadequate. These businesses included illegal logging in Aceh and other Indonesian provinces, production and sale of drugs, and illicit collection of travel and protection fees (McCulloch 2003, 2005). As Lesley McCulloch explained in 2003, under Suharto, the military's business ventures were wide in scope, including "monopolising local production, extraction, transport and processing of some natural resources; price controlling; appropriating land for themselves and on behalf of other parties; and many other commercial activities" (McCulloch 2003, 12). These businesses not only funded military operations but enriched individual officers as well. For this and other reasons, military leaders were long opposed to a negotiated solution to the Aceh conflict (McCulloch 2005; ICG 2001).

In light of these numerous resource exploitation practices—on top of Suharto's generally poor governance—a group of Acehnese founded the GAM in 1976 with the express goal of seceding from Indonesia. As an armed struggle got under way, the severe human rights violations committed by Indonesian security forces further strengthened the Acehnese desire to secede (McCulloch 2005; Schulze 2004).

From conflict to peace

Initially, the Indonesian Military Forces (Tentara Nasional Indonesia, or TNI) easily suppressed the GAM, which began as a small guerrilla unit. The TNI then committed numerous human rights abuses, including killings and beatings of Acehnese civilians, which fueled Acehnese nationalist sentiments and galvanized more citizens to join the GAM's forces (Waizenegger and Hyndman 2010). Although largely outnumbered by the TNI, the GAM posed a serious threat to government control of Aceh, leading to Aceh's formal designation as a Military Operations Zone from 1989 to 1998 (Waizenegger and Hyndman 2010).

President Suharto's resignation in 1998 spurred hopes that the conflict between the GAM and the Indonesian government might be settled. Fighting between the TNI and the GAM was suspended in 2000, but only briefly; it resumed when the new president, Abdurrahman Wahid, withdrew an offer to allow a referendum vote on the matter of independence for Aceh. Wahid's successor, Megawati Sukarnopturi, went on to sign a special autonomy law in 2001 (Law No. 18 of 2001),[2] which, if implemented, would have given Aceh the right to implement sharia law (Islamic law), as well as realize a greater share of natural resource revenues, among other things (McCulloch 2005). The bill granted Aceh 70 percent of natural resource revenues. Meanwhile, peace negotiations in December 2002 yielded a temporary agreement to cease hostilities, but in May 2003, final negotiations failed, and President Sukarnopturi immediately declared martial law in Aceh (Waizenegger and Hyndman 2010).

At this point, the TNI commenced major military operations in Aceh, and the renewal of violence resulted in the deaths of thousands and the displacement of at least 125,000 more Acehnese (NRC 2004). In 2004, the GAM began to run low on weapons, and approximately one-quarter of its soldiers were killed (Nessen

[2] Special Autonomy Law on Nanggroe Aceh Darussalam (NAD), Law No. 18 of 2001, www.kbri-canberra.org.au/s_issues/aceh/aceh_specautonomy.htm.

2006). Forced into a defensive position, some GAM commanders began to consider how to end the conflict, particularly after the TNI captured thousands of suspected mid-level GAM officials (Pan 2005).

The election of General Susilo Bambang Yudhoyono to the presidency in September 2004 made resolution of the conflict seem possible because, while serving as a minister in President Megawati's government, General Yudhoyono had worked directly on the Aceh conflict, and, during his election campaign, had made serious offers of amnesty to the GAM on the condition that it settle for autonomy rather than insist on independence (Waizenegger and Hyndman 2010). Barely two months into his presidency and four days before the tsunami struck, the two sides agreed in secret negotiations to conduct formal peace talks (Merikallio 2006).

With this potential foundation for peace in place, on December 26, 2004, an earthquake in the Indian Ocean triggered a tsunami that killed 167,000 Acehnese and displaced 500,000 more.[3] In the wake of such a calamity, on August 15, 2005, the GAM and Indonesia's leaders came to the table to sign the MOU that brought an end to their long conflict.

THE 2005 MEMORANDUM OF UNDERSTANDING

The 2005 MOU covered a range of critical issues and key Acehnese grievances. These included disarmament and demobilization of GAM fighters, withdrawal of an agreed number of government soldiers and policemen from Aceh, amnesty for GAM members and release of political prisoners, establishment of a Human Rights Court and a Commission for Truth and Reconciliation, reintegration of combatants, political reforms to facilitate the formation of local parties and democratic elections for a provincial governor and legislature, and greater local control over Aceh's ample natural resources (see table 1). From September 2005 to December 2006, implementation of the peace agreement was closely supervised by the EU–led AMM (Feith 2006).

The MOU's natural resource–related provisions are not extensive. The section detailing economic agreements (para. 1.3.3) gives Aceh jurisdiction over all "living natural resources" in the sea surrounding Aceh. The most important section detailing natural resource agreements (para. 1.3.4) entitles Aceh to 70 percent of all revenues from its land and territorial sea-based natural resources—present and future—including any hydrocarbon deposits. Finally, another section of the MOU (para. 3.2.5) requires the government to provide suitable farmland, jobs, and other compensation to excombatants, pardoned political prisoners, and civilians significantly affected by the conflict.

---

[3] The 9.1 magnitude earthquake struck off the coast of northern Sumatra, and the resulting tsunami caused the deaths of an estimated 227,898 people in fourteen countries and displaced an additional 1.7 million people (BBC 2005; USGS 2004).

Table 1. Selected provisions of the 2005 Memorandum of Understanding between the Government of the Republic of Indonesia and the Free Aceh Movement

Issue	*Provision*
Disarmament	GAM to demobilize its 3,000 fighters and relinquish 840 weapons.
Demobilization	Government forces to be reduced to 14,700 soldiers and 9,100 policemen.
Amnesty	GAM members to receive amnesty; political prisoners to be released.
Human rights	A Human Rights Court and a Commission for Truth and Reconciliation to be established.
Reintegration	Former combatants, pardoned prisoners, and affected civilians to receive farmland, jobs, and other compensation.
Political participation	Free and fair elections to be held for Aceh governor and legislature; government to facilitate the establishment of local political parties by amending the national election law.
Economy	Aceh entitled to 70 percent of its natural resource revenues.

Note: GAM is the Gerakan Aceh Merdeka, or the Free Aceh Movement.

By the time the violence between the GAM and the central government ended in late 2005, after nearly three decades of conflict and oppression, at least 15,000 people (and possibly twice that number) had died; some 120,000 to 150,000 people had been displaced; and many homes as well as schools, clinics, and other public infrastructure had been destroyed (Merikallio 2006; Eschenbächer 2005; Barron 2008).

Overall, the peacemaking that followed the signing of the MOU was successful, despite a few drawbacks. For example, it took longer than expected to mount gubernatorial elections in Aceh; some of the MOU's provisions were significantly weakened by the Indonesian parliament; and important human rights institutions (specifically, a Human Rights Court and a Commission for Truth and Reconciliation) were not implemented (Perlez 2006). Still, the political and human rights situation in Aceh is incomparably better than during the conflict, and this improvement has bolstered Acehnese confidence against a relapse to conflict.

When the EU withdrew the AMM at the end of 2006, it was too early for the comfort of many Acehnese who felt an international presence protected them against further human rights abuses. The EU simply did not want to get drawn into an open-ended peacebuilding process (and the Indonesian government, concerned about the implications for its sovereignty, would have been reluctant to agree to a longer-term mandate). Yet the question has arisen as to whether a follow-up mission to monitor and assist the longer-term process of peacebuilding, reintegration, political transformation, and natural resource management in Aceh might not be in the mutual interests of the Acehnese, Indonesia, and international partners.

POST-PEACE CONFLICTS

When conflict between the GAM and the central government ended, Aceh nonetheless experienced a flare up of local disputes that began around November 2005. As figure 1 indicates, these disputes peaked in late 2008, and the vast

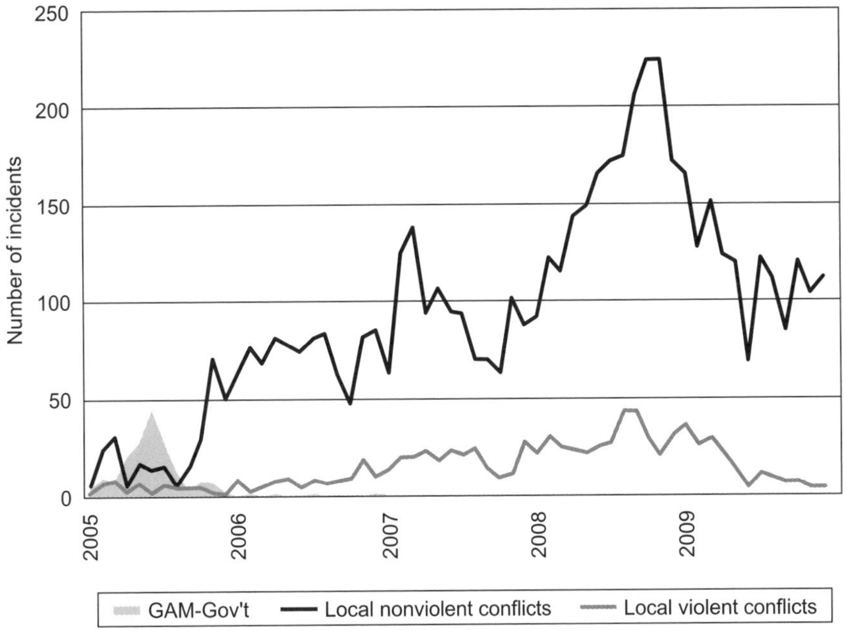

Figure 1. Incidents of conflict in Aceh, January 2005 to December 2009
Sources: CPCRS (2009a, 2009b); World Bank/DSF (2005–2009).
Notes: Some data points are rough estimates derived from summary graphs.
GAM is the Gerakan Aceh Merdeka, or the Free Aceh Movement.

majority were nonviolent. These local conflicts had a variety of causes, including score-settling between the GAM and anti-GAM forces, the splintering of the GAM itself, election-related disputes, discontentment over uneven assistance and compensation provided to those affected by the conflict and the tsunami, and disputes over local lands and natural resources (World Bank/DSF 2005–2009).

By mid-2009, political developments in Aceh had helped consolidate the peace. Although Aceh's legislative (parliament and district) elections in April 2009 were marred by violence, the party formed by former GAM rebels—Partai Aceh—won handily (CPCRS 2009a).

Beyond the GAM's successful transformation into a political force, President Yudhoyono decisively won reelection in 2009, including 93 percent of the votes in Aceh—in large part due to his pro-peace and pro-poor policies, and his informal alliance with Partai Aceh. However, as the Center for Peace and Conflict Resolution Studies noted in a 2009 Aceh Peace Monitoring Update, maintaining an inclusive political coalition in Aceh may turn out to be challenging, given the ongoing need for governance reform and reduction of tensions around sensitive issues (CPCRS 2009b). For example, the relationship between Aceh's Governor Irwandi Yusuf and the parliament has been at times strained due to differences around certain issues, including parliamentary passage in 2009 of the Qanun Jinayat, a sharia-based criminal code, which the governor refused to sign.

Wealth inequalities in post-conflict, post-tsunami Aceh

Certain provisions of the MOU, the lack of sufficient implementation funding and unevenness in funding distribution, and the nature of tsunami-driven aid together created a society of haves and have-nots in Aceh. For example, as discussed further below, a number of excombatants and GAM-associated Acehnese remained unemployed and increasingly disillusioned years after the signing of the MOU. Further, the dearth of livelihoods support drove excombatants toward illegal activities, including unlicensed timber harvesting. Despite generous post-tsunami assistance, some Acehnese fared much more poorly than others. Statements by some donors about "building the province back better" also raised expectations that subsequently were not met.

The 2004 tsunami triggered one of the world's most generous humanitarian aid responses to date, yet not everyone benefited equally. Despite a six-fold increase over the past decade in aid flows to Aceh as well as in provincial revenues, more Acehnese live in poverty now than during the conflict, and this could easily imperil the consolidation of peace. When the conflict was under way, the poverty rate rose from approximately 10 percent in 1996 to 20 percent in 1999 and 28.4 percent in 2004 (Sukma 2004; World Bank 2006a; Barron 2008). Aceh was the only Indonesian province where poverty continued to rise after 2000, making it one of the poorest provinces, despite its abundant natural resources. By 2005, rural poverty in Aceh stood at 36.2 percent (Barron 2008). In 2006, with Aceh's overall unemployment rate at 12 percent, 75 percent of Acehnese polled agreed that such joblessness (and inflation) had made life more difficult since the 2005 signing of the peace agreement (Barron 2008; Diani 2006).

Another key factor in wealth inequalities is that the Indonesian government provided post-conflict assistance (based loosely on the provisions of the MOU) of only US$230 million—a figure for post-conflict assistance that is dwarfed by post-tsunami assistance of US$7.7 billion (Barron 2008; Masyrafah and McKeon 2008). Unsurprisingly, due to the limited funds and the amount of devastation caused by such a prolonged conflict and the tsunami, infrastructure rebuilding in post-conflict Aceh proceeded much more slowly, and poverty there has remained much higher. Inequalities in aid led to significant tensions on the ground, with rising numbers of disputes, including violence. Even among conflict-affected groups—former combatants, displaced people, and other civilian victims—aid has been uneven (Barron 2008).

International experts agree that in post-conflict situations, successful reintegration of excombatants is a crucial factor in determining whether peace, once achieved, will be stable (World Bank/DSF 2006). However, in the case of Aceh, limited funding to implement the MOU and weaknesses in some of the MOU's provisions have resulted in incomplete reintegration of GAM fighters. For example, the MOU provided greater economic peace dividends to former GAM elites than to the average GAM soldier. It also provides reintegration assistance to only 3,000 combatants, when the number of those in need of such aid far exceeds that level (Bakhtiar 2005). In addition, political disputes, bureaucratic delays, and corruption have slowed distribution of reintegration assistance (ICG 2006).

The combination of such factors has resulted in a large group of former GAM members unable to find work. In 2006 and again in 2007, the World Bank found that nearly 75 percent of GAM members remained unemployed (World Bank/DSF 2006; World Bank 2006b). World Bank surveys also found that 50 percent of all GAM excombatants had experienced damage to or loss of their homes during the conflict, and another 25 percent had experienced such damage or loss due to the tsunami. While excombatants who own land have fared reasonably well in the post-conflict, post-tsunami era, others have no land, no capital, and little access to skills training and jobs (World Bank/DSF 2006; World Bank 2006b).

Some attempts have been made to expand the scope of reintegration assistance. In February 2006, the Aceh Reintegration Agency (Badan Reintegrasi Aceh) agreed to extend eligibility for reintegration assistance to more than 20,000 persons, including GAM members and supporters who did not engage in the fighting, former political prisoners, anti-GAM militias, and others (Beeck 2007). Several other assistance projects are currently under way in the region, including the Strengthening Sustainable Peace and Development in Aceh project led by the United Nations Development Programme (UNDP), which seeks to promote peacebuilding by providing sustainable livelihoods assistance to marginalized groups and communities in the province (UNDP 2008). According to that project, unemployment rates among excombatants remain high (UNDP 2008). Many former GAM members, particularly female excombatants, have yet to receive the reintegration assistance for which they are ostensibly eligible.

Illegal and exploitative livelihood strategies on the rise

The lack of employment opportunities for former GAM fighters raised a new set of issues, with respect to Aceh's forest resources. Finding themselves in dire economic straits since the cessation of conflict, some excombatants have taken to armed robbery and extortion (World Bank/DSF 2005–2009), and some have resorted to illegal logging of Aceh's forests—a practice that has generally been on the rise following the tsunami as well as the end of the conflict (Large 2008). According to Greenomics Indonesia, more than 200,000 hectares of forest have been illegally logged in Aceh (Simamora 2009).

Illegal logging in Aceh offers a means of quick financial gain to anyone able to engage in it, including unemployed excombatants. Post-tsunami reconstruction created a substantial demand for timber, one that far exceeded the allowable cut in Aceh (ICG 2007). Also, areas once off limits due to pervasive violence are now more accessible. As a province with vast forest resources, high demand for timber, high unemployment, systemic corruption, and weak governance, Aceh has proven to be an ideal location for extensive illegal logging (ICG

2007). Soon after the MOU was signed, leaders of the Komite Peralihan Aceh, which grew informally out of GAM to represent GAM excombatants, claimed they could do little to prevent their men from engaging in illegal logging until reintegration efforts could provide viable livelihoods (ICG 2007).

ADDRESSING ONGOING CHALLENGES

A key driver in Aceh's quest for independence was its desire for control over revenues derived from its natural resources. The MOU addressed a number of Aceh's natural resource–based concerns, but as Judith Large observed in 2008, in the post-conflict years and as a result of decentralization and special autonomy, Aceh started to become "one of the most corrupt rather than one of the richest provinces in Indonesia" (Large 2008, 65). Greater governmental accountability and transparency and better law enforcement is viewed as critical to long-term peace and stability.

Another challenge is how to reduce the lure of illegal exploitation of lucrative natural resources. One approach is to develop Aceh's economy more broadly to provide other jobs and incomes. By and large, however, donors and aid groups have not yet taken their assistance in this direction (Barron 2008).

The Aceh peace agreement succeeded in ending the conflict between the province and the central government. But in some ways, the issues still at stake have simply been transferred to a new level within the province. This has partly resulted from a less-than-complete peacemaking process, as new grievances emerge and the larger problem of illegal resource exploitation generally characteristic of Indonesia continues.

In the end, lingering economic problems, including unemployment and illegal logging, are generating new dynamics that could threaten the peacebuilding process if left unaddressed. In addition, despite a 2007 provincial ban against illegal logging, such activity has increasingly contributed to flooding, landslides, and biodiversity loss, all of which only further undermine legitimate livelihoods, especially in agriculture (Renner 2007).

POSSIBLE SOLUTIONS

Efforts to improve natural resource management might be pursued in the context of the cooperative EU-Indonesia Forest Law Enforcement, Governance and Trade Support Project, which is designed to help government, civil society, and the Indonesian timber industry tackle illegal logging through sustainable forest management principles, good governance, capacity building, harmonization and enforcement of relevant laws, and timber certification (EU 2009).

Another potential pathway to resolving forest management issues may lie within a concept intended to combat climate change commonly known as REDD—Reducing Emissions from Deforestation and Degradation. In principle, REDD could be a partial solution to forest degradation and a way to promote climate stabilization in Aceh (with proper governance and monitoring). Aceh Governor Yusuf has been at the forefront of efforts to sell forest carbon credits to investors under REDD, as a portion of the funds would flow to local communities and encourage them to develop livelihoods other than illegal logging.

However, in Aceh and elsewhere in the world, questions about REDD schemes, such as how to ensure proper accounting for carbon storage and how to guarantee that forests are indeed preserved, still abound. Of equal concern is that potentially large inflows of money could encourage corrupt practices instead of benefiting local communities, especially if local land tenure is insecure, as is often the case in Aceh (IDLO 2009).

These concerns point to a conclusion that is as relevant to REDD schemes as to the ongoing political evolution and stabilization of Aceh: it is necessary to build state institutions that are capable of providing services in an even-handed, competent manner; that are efficient and transparent in their workings; and that are accountable to the public in terms of decisions and outcomes.

CONCLUSION

It is always tempting to draw from specific cases broader lessons that may apply to other countries or regions emerging from conflict. On the one hand, Aceh's experience is tragically unique, for the province has suffered through a rare combination of violent conflict and a major natural disaster. While this particular combination played a key role in helping to bring about the goodwill and political conditions needed to end the conflict, Aceh's emerging lessons can still be applied to other post-conflict situations.

Aceh's peace agreement directly addressed the political arrangements needed to bring about a transition to peace for Aceh Province, beyond the decommissioning of weapons and the withdrawal of government troops. For the Acehnese, the agreement opened the door to a new political system that promised much greater self-determination and the expectation that inequitable exploitation of their resources by outsiders would come to an end. For Indonesia, it provided assurance that Aceh would not break away as possibly the first in a series of provincial dominoes.

Massive post-tsunami aid certainly facilitated this transition by providing new economic opportunities for at least some Acehnese. The different degrees to which aid has been provided for post-disaster purposes on the one hand, and for post-conflict needs on the other, has raised the risk of creating longer-term schisms and grievances among different population groups, communities, and others that might contain the seeds of future conflict. This is particularly true when discrepancies in short-term humanitarian aid are not remedied through longer-term reconstruction and peacebuilding efforts. The way to avoid or minimize such difficulties is to ensure strong local participation in reconstruction activities from the very beginning; something that—across the world—is often merely an afterthought.

REFERENCES

Bakhtiar, A. 2005. Interview by the author of Free Aceh Movement (GAM) delegate to the Helsinki peace negotiations. December 21.

Barron, P. 2008. Managing the resources for peace: Reconstruction and peacebuilding in Aceh. *Accord*, No. 20:58–61.

BBC. 2005. At-a-glance: Countries hit. December 22. http://news.bbc.co.uk/2/hi/4126019.stm.

Beeck, C. 2007. Nach den gouverneurswahlen in Aceh. BICC Focus Paper No. 3. Bonn, Germany: Bonn International Center for Conversion.

Brown, G. 2005. Horizontal inequalities, ethnic separatism, and violent conflict: The case of Aceh, Indonesia. Human Development Report. New York: United Nations Development Programme.

CPCRS (Center for Peace and Conflict Resolution Studies). 2009a. Aceh peace monitoring update, 1 March–30 June 2009. Banda Aceh, Indonesia: Syiah Kuala University.

———. 2009b. Aceh peace monitoring update, 1 July–31 August 2009. Banda Aceh, Indonesia: Syiah Kuala University.

Diani, H. 2006. Acehnese unsure peace will last: Poll. *Jakarta Post*, March 31.

Eschenbächer, J-H., ed. 2005. *Internal displacement: Global overview of trends and developments in 2004*. Geneva, Switzerland: Norwegian Refugee Council.

EU (European Union). 2009. FLEGT voluntary partnership agreements: Ensuring legal timber trade and strengthening forest governance—Indonesia. www.euflegtefi.int/portal/home/vpa_countries/in_asia/indonesia/.

Fan, L. 2006. The struggle for land rights in post-tsunami and post-conflict Aceh, Indonesia. Paper presented to the World Bank, November.

Feith, P. 2006. The Aceh monitoring mission experience. Paper presented at the "Beyond the Tsunami from Recovery to Peace" seminar. Jakarta, Indonesia, May 3. www.aceh-mm.org/download/English/The%20AMM%20Experience.pdf.

ICG (International Crisis Group). 2001. Indonesia: Natural resources and law enforcement. Asia Report No. 29. Jakarta, Indonesia, and Brussels, Belgium.

———. 2006. Aceh's local elections: The role of the Free Aceh Movement (GAM). Asia Briefing No. 27. Jakarta, Indonesia, and Brussels, Belgium.

———. 2007. Aceh: Post-conflict complications. Asia Report No. 139. Jakarta, Indonesia, and Brussels, Belgium. www.crisisgroup.org/~/media/Files/asia/south-east-asia/indonesia/139_aceh_post_conflict_complications.pdf.

IDLO (International Development Law Organization). 2009. Avoiding deforestation in Aceh, Indonesia: Land, natural resource rights and local communities project. End-of-Phase Report, Phase I: October 2008–May 2009. Rome.

Large, J. 2008. The challenge of hidden economies and predation for profit. *Accord* 2008 (20): 64–65.

Masyrafah, H., and J. M. J. A. McKeon. 2008. Post-tsunami aid effectiveness in Aceh: Proliferation and coordination in reconstruction. Wolfensohn Center for Development Working Paper No. 6. Washington, D.C.: Brookings Institution. www.brookings.edu/~/media/research/files/papers/2008/11/aceh%20aid%20masyrafah/11_aceh_aid_masyrafah.pdf.

McCarthy, J. F. 2002. Turning in circles: District governance, illegal logging, and environmental decline in Sumatra, Indonesia. *Society and Natural Resources* 15 (10): 867–886.

McCulloch, L. 2003. Greed: The silent force of the conflict in Aceh. Paper presented to the Asian Studies Association of Australia.

———. 2005. *Aceh: Then and now*. London: Minority Rights Group International.

Merikallio, K. 2006. *Making peace: Ahtisaari and Aceh*. Porvoo, Finland: WS Bookwell Oy.

Nessen, W. 2006. Sentiments made visible: The rise and reason of Aceh's national liberation movement. In *Verandah of violence: The background to the Aceh problem*, ed. A. Reid. Seattle: University of Washington Press.

NRC (Norwegian Refugee Council). 2004. Prior to tsunami, at least 125,000 people had been displaced since May 2003 by the conflict. Geneva, Switzerland.

Pan, E. 2005. Interview with Sidney Jones on Aceh peace agreement. Council on Foreign Relations. www.cfr.org/indonesia/interview-sidney-jones-aceh-peace-agreement/p8790.

Perlez, J. 2006. Aceh says Indonesia law falls far short on autonomy. *International Herald Tribune*, July 12.

Renner, M. 2007. Aceh governor imposes logging ban. Washington, D.C.: Worldwatch Institute. www.worldwatch.org/node/5179.

Renner, M., and Z. Chafe. 2007. *Beyond disasters. Creating opportunities for peace*. Washington, D.C.: Worldwatch Institute.

Schulze, K. E. 2004. The Free Aceh Movement (GAM): Anatomy of a separatist organization. Policy Studies No. 2. Washington, D.C.: East-West Center.

Simamora, A. P. 2009. During its restoration, Aceh lost forests worth $550m a year in carbon trade. *Jakarta Post*, August 13.

Sukma, R. 2004. Security operations in Aceh: Goals, consequences and lessons. Policy Studies No. 3. Washington, D.C.: East-West Center.

UNDP (United Nations Development Programme). 2008. UNDP Strengthening Sustainable Peace and Development in Aceh (SSPDA). Jakarta, Indonesia. www.undp.or.id/factsheets/2008/ACEH%20Strengthening%20Sustainable%20Peace%20and%20Development.pdf.

USGS (United States Geological Survey). 2004. Magnitude 9.1—Off the west coast of northern Sumatra. December 26. http://earthquake.usgs.gov/earthquakes/eqinthenews/2004/us2004slav/#summary.

Waizenegger, A., and J. Hyndman. 2010. Two solitudes: Post-tsunami and post-conflict Aceh. *Disasters* 34 (3): 787–808.

World Bank. 2006a. *Aceh public expenditure analysis: Spending for reconstruction and poverty reduction*. Washington, D.C.

———. 2006b. Brief—The Aceh peace agreement: How far have we come? Washington, D.C.

World Bank/DSF (World Bank/Decentralization Support Facility). 2006. *GAM reintegration needs assessment: Enhancing peace through community-level development planning*. Banda Aceh and Jakarta, Indonesia.

———. 2005–2009. Aceh conflict monitoring update. Various report editions, August 2005–February 2009. www.conflictanddevelopment.org/index.php?option=com_content&view=article&id=153%3Aaceh-conflict-monitoring-update&catid=11&Itemid=16&lang=en.

Manufacturing peace in "no man's land": Livestock and access to natural resources in the Karimojong Cluster of Kenya and Uganda

Jeremy Lind

Livestock raiding and banditry in a context of generalized and chronic insecurity have seriously undermined the livelihoods of nomadic pastoralists in the Karimojong Cluster that straddles the remote borderlands of northwestern Kenya and northeastern Uganda—known as the Turkana and Karamoja regions, respectively. Since the 1990s, various aid and donor agencies have worked through local civil society to facilitate conflict resolution, including through negotiation of grazing agreements, as a way to improve relations between herders there. The impact of various peacebuilding initiatives has been fairly negligible, however, in large measure due to the inherently limited ability of local reconciliation efforts to address deeper and wider historical and structural drivers of conflict in the region. This chapter assesses the effectiveness of efforts to manufacture peace in the Karimojong Cluster while also examining the role of natural resources in both conflict and in peacebuilding.

After outlining the author's research in the Turkana region in Kenya, the chapter broadly introduces the situation of armed conflict in the Karimojong Cluster and describes its impact on livelihoods in the region. The second section examines the dynamics of this armed conflict and local peacebuilding efforts to end it. The third section critically examines factors affecting the outcomes of these peacebuilding efforts. The chapter ends with lessons learned and other conclusions, including a discussion of future prospects for peacebuilding in the region against the backdrop of regional and national economic development initiatives.

THE RESEARCH

From 2003 to 2007, the author conducted field research in Turkana County on the Kenyan side of the Karimojong Cluster (including ten months in southern

---

Jeremy Lind is a research fellow at the Institute of Development Studies at the University of Sussex, where his research focuses on livelihood dynamics in conflict areas and the relationship between population vulnerability and violence in northeast Africa.

Turkana County). Over the course of his research, the author spent a significant amount of time in pastoralist encampments, market centers, the district administrative center, and farming settlements. The author conducted a mixed quantitative and qualitative survey with over one hundred Turkana households as well as interviews with Turkana's most prominent civil society and aid agency peace promoters and local opinion leaders, including elders, women's leaders, youth, head teachers, local councilors, and business persons. In addition, the author reviewed relevant scholarly and gray literatures and conducted follow-up interviews with nongovernmental organization (NGO) staff in Nairobi, Kenya.

INTRODUCTION TO THE CONFLICT, IMPACTS ON LIVELIHOODS, AND RECONCILIATION EFFORTS

The agropastoralist communities located in the Karimojong Cluster have long engaged in violent conflict over access to, and control of, local resources that support their pastoralist lifestyle. Before British colonization (1916–1962) of the region, local populations often raided and stole livestock. The frequency of regional conflict has continued to escalate in recent years, making governance in the region increasingly difficult for local and national authorities. Regional insecurity and violence has led to livestock losses as well as the loss of human life, has threatened sustainable livelihoods of pastoralist communities, and has spurred the international and NGO community to pursue peacebuilding and conflict resolution in the area.

Background

Organized livestock raiding and individualized theft of livestock have long been commonplace in the Karimojong Cluster, a remote and sparsely populated dryland region with several names, including Karamojong, that stretches from northeastern Uganda and southeastern South Sudan across the Turkana region of northwestern Kenya and into the southwestern corner of Ethiopia (see figure 1). It has been estimated that over 10,000 people from the Turkana tribe were killed during livestock raids from 1991 to 1994 alone (McCabe 2004). Because conflict in the Karimojong Cluster has substantial humanitarian consequences, it has received intermittent attention by international news media.[1] Although the entire Karimojong Cluster has been embroiled in conflict at one point or another, the Kenyan and Ugandan sections have received the most attention in terms of peacebuilding, hence the focus on these areas in this chapter.

Prior to British colonial rule, relations between pastoralist societies in the region were characterized by "reciprocal raiding," which, arguably, worked against escalation of hostilities into wider conflict (Lamphear 1994). Livestock raiding served an important redistributive function by transferring animals across social

[1] See, for example, BBC News Online (2006); *Economist* (1999); and *Independent* (2005).

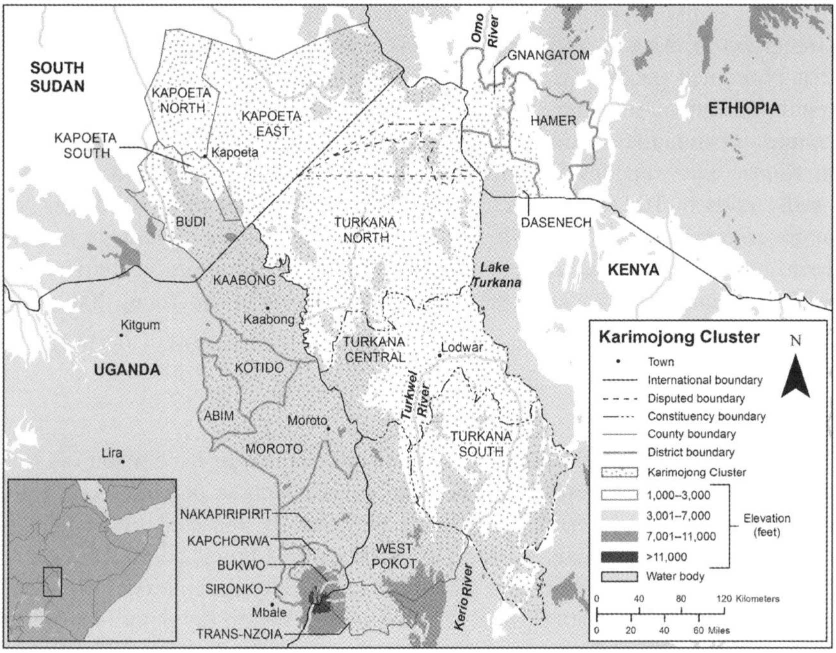

Figure 1. Karimojong Cluster

boundaries in situations of need, such as during drought or when young men sought animals to pay as bride price (Lind 2007). Since then, chronic conflict in the Karimojong Cluster and perceptions of a trend toward worsening violence have caused international agencies engaged in aid policy and programming in the region to shift their activities from development assistance to peacebuilding. Further, on the Ugandan side of the Karimojong Cluster, domestic political pressure has been applied to end raiding by Karimojong pastoralists on their neighbors in Uganda, which earlier, in the 1980s, resulted in heavy losses of livestock and human life (Stites et al. 2007).

There are differing perspectives of conflict dynamics in the region. A popular explanation is that growing scarcity of important natural resources for supporting livestock has caused pastoralists to move over longer distances, thereby bringing them into conflict with each other over access to water, pasture, and browsing opportunities. This view holds sway in news media representations of conflict in the region.[2] Implicitly, this view has also influenced aid interventions to establish a conflict early warning system in the region.

A different view is that the nature of raiding has been transformed from a reciprocal, rule-governed practice into a predatory activity to procure large

[2] For example, Gettleman (2009).

quantities of livestock for sale in the lucrative urban meat markets of East Africa (Hendrickson, Armon, and Mearns 1998). Jan Kamenju and colleagues claim that prominent people have financed livestock raids in the North Rift Valley region of Kenya, including transport of the stolen animals by lorry to down-country urban markets (Kamenju, Singo, and Wairagu 2003). The popular media in Kenya have supported this perspective, reporting suspected links between deadly raids in Turkana and neighboring areas of the Karimojong Cluster and large, criminal syndicates (*Daily Nation* 1999). The problem is thought to have been exacerbated by the influx of small arms from elsewhere in the Horn of Africa, beginning in the early 1980s (Gray 2000; Mirzeler and Young 2000; Pike 2004; and Mkutu 2006).

Effect on livelihoods

The weakening of customary pastoralist institutions to manage conflict, as well as the failure of the Ugandan and Kenyan governments to provide security for herding groups in the Karimojong Cluster, has severely impacted the livelihoods of the region's predominantly pastoralist inhabitants. Chronic conflict has led to the loss of livestock assets across all sections of society, regardless of economic status. For many households, herd size has diminished to the point of material insignificance; as a consequence, livestock transfers have decreased and, with that, the means to build a livelihood safety net. Further, the circulation of stolen animals through legitimate livestock exchanges—a technique favored by stock thieves as a way to dispose of contraband animals—has compromised the smooth functioning of commercial exchanges based on trust.

In addition, armed violence has impeded the movement of livestock to key grazing environments. Due to interference by raiders equipped with small arms, Turkana pastoralists in Kenya have felt insecure in moving their herds to distant pastures in the uplands bordering Karamoja in Uganda, and West Pokot, Kenya, to such an extent that George Monbiot, a well-known British journalist, has labeled these uplands "no man's lands" (Monbiot 1994). For the Turkana, the long-term impact has been displacement to the bottom of the ecological gradient—the drier, less fertile Turkana lowlands—and, as a consequence, they have had to shift the composition of their herds, from cattle to more drought-tolerant, less valuable livestock, such as goats (Lind and Eriksen 2006).

In sum, loss of assets and conflict-induced displacement from key natural resources have rendered the Karimojong Cluster pastoralists far less able to manage the consequences of the ecological uncertainty and variability that is entirely normal in the region.

Reconciliation efforts

Against this backdrop, beginning in the late 1990s, various international aid and donor agencies decided to support various local-level reconciliation efforts, primarily by supporting dialogue as a way to build confidence and better social relations between neighboring pastoralist groups regarding access and use of natural resources for supporting livestock herds. Local male elders, local herdswomen, and young men who engage in raiding ("warriors") were all encouraged to participate in the dialogue—and in the negotiation of agreements—with the goal of creating a culture of peace that relied less on "outside" administrative responses. These efforts subsequently helped foster the growth of an elaborate institutional landscape of local peace committees whose role has been to prevent conflict alongside official state responses, the latter of which have included forced disarmament, tracking and recovery of stolen livestock, and punitive actions against raiders (Knighton 2003; Stites et al. 2007; and Stites and Akabwai 2009).

As background, it should be noted that these official state responses, primarily by Ugandan administrative, security, and police personnel, have been carried out in an environment of mutual hostility and mistrust between the state and pastoralist societies and, indeed, some pastoralists view the state itself as a "raider" (Knighton 2003). By contrast, on the Kenyan side, beyond periodic crackdowns by security personnel on communities that are thought to be raiding instigators, the national government has failed to muster anything resembling a robust security response, choosing, instead, to provide tepid and largely symbolic support primarily to peacebuilding NGOs.

While localized peacebuilding efforts in the Karimojong Cluster have clearly been important as an adjunct to state security responses to armed conflict (as in Uganda) or to lack of state security responses (as in Kenya) and for initiating reconciliation within and among neighboring pastoralist societies, the impacts of peacebuilding efforts have been limited. This chapter explores and critically assesses why this has been the case, the role of natural resources in the conflict, and deeper and wider historical and structural factors affecting prospects for peace.

CONFLICT DYNAMICS AND PEACEBUILDING EFFORTS IN THE KARIMOJONG CLUSTER

Chronic conflict in the Karimojong Cluster and its detrimental impacts on pastoralist livelihoods have given rise to a multitude of localized reconciliation efforts, the primary focus of which has been to improve relations between neighboring pastoralist groups. Further, other complementary actions have been taken to improve pastoralist livelihoods, such as extension of community-based animal health care and promotion of irrigated agriculture as an alternative to livestock production. Preventing conflict over natural resources has been an ancillary objective to promoting broader peace between groups, for it has been hoped that broader peace would permit greater mobility and flexibility in access to and use of resources across a wider geographic area.

Why, then, have these peace initiatives been limited in their effectiveness? In exploring this in detail, this chapter considers the social and ecological dynamics of pastoralism and conflict in the Karimojong Cluster, with a focus on the Turkana pastoralists of northwest Kenya.

Making a living in an uncertain environment

Precolonial-era livestock raiding in the Karimojong Cluster was enmeshed in strategies for managing uncertainty in a nonequilibrium ecological setting. Such strategies included raiding neighboring herds as a way, for example, to recover losses due to drought or an epidemic of animal disease. As an ecological setting that lacks equilibrium by nature, the Karimojong Cluster is dominated by dry rangelands broken by hills and mountains that support a mix of scrub, hilltop forests, and natural springs. As a particular setting within the Karimojong Cluster, the Turkana lowland ranges constitutes one of the driest environments in the Horn of Africa in which pastoralism is practiced, and uncertainty and low predictability of rainfall are the norm. Years of severe drought occur at roughly three- to five-year intervals, with severe adverse effects on rangeland vegetation and livestock health (Little, Dyson-Hudson, and McCabe 1999).

Under these difficult conditions, the Turkana developed a system of pastoralism centered on mobility and flexibility as a means to sustain their livestock. Customarily, Turkana herders would split their multispecies herds on the basis of their varying feeding and water requirements and then move these split herds over long distances to maximize use of key patches of food and water resources. Thus, the adaptability of Turkana pastoralism depended not only on mobilization of herds to access resources but also on flexibility of movement across the highland-lowland ecological gradient that stretches between the higher elevation areas of West Pokot (to the south of Turkana) and of Uganda to the expansive, low plains of Turkanaland itself.

Social ties between the Turkana and their neighbors helped the Turkana negotiate access to resources in Pokot and sites on the Ugandan side of the border. Considerable environmental variation favored development of specialized production systems and, correspondingly, group identities. In the dynamic lie of the land, a multiethnic social order based on "eco-niche specialization" took root (Goldsmith 1997). As Neil W. Sobania has elucidated, the structure of these pastoralist societies was comparatively loose and adaptable; that is, different groups adapted to particular ecological niches by developing particular production strategies and techniques for generating livelihoods from their particular place in the land. Sobania has shown further how the adaptations of neighboring groups to the peculiarities of separate but complementary ecological niches enabled them to establish bond-friendships across societal boundaries (Sobania 1990). In turn, as Richard D. Waller has explained, these bond-friendships proved critical in binding these pastoralist societies together within the context of a wider regional resource system (Waller 1999). Good relations between the Turkana and their neighbors were then maintained through intermarriage, trade and exchange relationships, negotiated resource-use agreements, and reciprocal livestock transfers.

Dynamics and impacts of contemporary conflict in the region

The main type of contemporary conflict in the Karimojong Cluster has been cross-border attacks on neighboring pastoralist societies by organized parties of up to several hundred men intending to raid livestock. However, Elizabeth Stites and colleagues have noted changes in the nature of conflict in the Karamoja region of northeastern Uganda in direct response to disarmament campaigns against Karimojong herders by the Uganda People's Defense Forces (UPDF); although the number of large, organized raids has decreased in Karamoja, the number of raids by smaller bands of men (unsanctioned in their actions by traditional leaders) has increased (Stites et al. 2007). In addition, the goal of these smaller raids is to steal livestock for individual gain by barter or sale. Further, other criminal activity, such as attacks on and acts of theft against village settlements, including by young men within the society, has grown worse as individuals strive to cope with the weakening of livelihoods they can no longer defend due to their disarmament.

Women have been disproportionately affected by these trends. Stites and Darlington Akabwai have reported attacks on women by raiders and bandits on the Ugandan side of the Karimojong Cluster, particularly when women are in remote areas collecting natural resources for food and shelter to compensate for the lack of access to the pastoralists' normal livelihood asset—their livestock—because it is confined in military kraals (Stites and Akabwai 2009).[3] A similar trend of attacks has been apparent in Turkana, including against women gatherers in the bush. There, *ngoroko* (small bands of thieves) have not only taken increasingly to attacking these women but also isolated homesteads and vehicles plying desolate roads (Buchanan-Smith and Lind 2005).

Questioning links between natural resource scarcity and conflict in the region

Importantly, there is neither a simple, direct link of causation between scarce natural resources and conflict in the region nor, indeed, any singular reason for the region's chronic, armed violence. High levels of uncertainty and variability in rainfall and natural resource scarcities are normal ecological features of the Karimojong Cluster. These ecological features have largely defined past and present pastoralist social relations. That is to say that, regardless of variability in their shared climate, the social relations of pastoralists in the region historically has been and continues to alternate between open hostility and cooperation. Another important clarification is that scarcity of natural resources in the region does not necessarily indicate a trend of deteriorating ecological conditions and, thus, a possible cause of conflict.

---

[3] A kraal is a confinement required by the Ugandan military to protect the livestock of pastoralists who have been disarmed.

These caveats are particularly critical to consider when assessing the efficacy of peace interventions and certain media and aid organization representations of and discourses about conflict in the region as being the result of desperate acts by impoverished herders attempting through violence to claim scarce resources in an increasingly degraded environment. Many Turkana explain that violence follows the movements of livestock, emphasizing that acquisition of livestock is the primary motive for armed violence, not the desire to capture key resources, such as grazing sites (Lind 2007). In addition, emphasis on drought-induced resource scarcities as an explanation of conflict has the potential to divert attention from other historical and structural factors that may play a role in encouraging activities such as raiding, as well as from governmental failures to control the security situation (Cullis and Pacey 1992). Indeed, the failure of states to provide timely and appropriate security for pastoralists has been common across the region.

Historical and structural contexts

Acknowledging deep and wide historical and structural contexts is critical to understanding the causes of conflict and patterns of livelihood vulnerability in the region, and, thus, to understanding the limitations of local peacebuilding efforts. As explained above, customary institutions, including flexible boundaries and social fluidity, served as important adjuncts to herding strategies and helped to minimize conflict between pastoralist societies in precolonial times. However, these institutions were weakened by the process of state building in East Africa. This process included use of military force against pastoralist societies to pacify them (Lamphear 1992); punitive confiscation of livestock that destroyed livelihoods; prohibitions on barter and trade between pastoralists; commoditization rather than the traditional exchange, loan, or barter of livestock (Dietz 1993; Fratkin 1991; Little 1985; Zaal and Dietz 1999); and imposition of state practices of control, such as restrictions on livestock movements for a wide range of reasons (Sobania 1990; Waller 1999), the result of which was the creation of fixed, territorially defined ethnic units and more rigid social relations, with detrimental consequences for pastoralist management of ecological uncertainty and resource scarcities.

Some of these detrimental state-building practices continue to this day. In Uganda, the disarmament campaign started in 2006 has involved forced kraaling of pastoralist livestock at sites adjacent to military barracks (essentially military kraals). Establishing these kraals was one way the UPDF responded to the failure of its earlier disarmament operation, conducted in Karamoja in 2001 and early 2002. That operation had worsened insecurity when the communities the UPDF had disarmed sought to rearm themselves in the face of continued threats against them—including the threat of theft from individual bandits as well as livestock raids by pastoralists in neighboring countries that had not been disarmed (Stites et al. 2007). The latest operation, whereby livestock is confined in the shadow of military barracks and therefore assumed to be secure, has created its own problems, however. Notably, under this latest exercise, military officials decide the movements of livestock, even though they lack the herding expertise to make informed decisions on when and where to move the animals. In addition, livestock diseases spread more easily in confined spaces. Also, it has been difficult for members of herding units to access their livestock, either for sale or to get milk to feed vulnerable household members (Stites and Akabwai 2009).

Ultimately, pastoralist conflict and vulnerability in the region today are rooted in deeper and wider historical and structural processes that degraded customary pastoralist institutions (institutions such as reciprocal resource-use agreements, intermarriage, and mutually beneficial trade and exchange). The way in which the Ugandan military has increased its role in responding to livestock raids has marginalized elders who traditionally played important roles in peacebuilding between different groups (Stites and Akabwai 2009). In the past, customary pastoralist institutions encouraged more flexible access to key natural resources across borders and wider herd movements by promoting cross-border bonding, thus strengthening pastoralists' capacities to manage the consequences of droughts and lengthy dry seasons. Arguably, then, the degradation of these customary institutions can be seen as the cause both of conflict and of livelihood vulnerability.

Peacebuilding in an environment of conflict and social violence

Although conflict and a high level of social violence are normal in the Karimojong Cluster—and not symptomatic of ecological changes being driven by climate changes, as some NGOs working in the region and the international media have suggested—peacebuilding became an important activity for aid and donor agencies working in the region. As noted earlier, beginning in the 1990s, many aid agencies began supporting localized peacebuilding initiatives in an effort to rebuild confidence and trust between neighboring pastoralist groups. An important part of these efforts has been the goal of sharing access to natural resources. In Uganda, donors have also advocated that economic development efforts take place alongside disarmament campaigns or, at least, that the sequencing of economic development efforts and disarmament activities be improved. Donors support this tandem approach because disarmament, on its own, could be counterproductive and aggravate tensions (Stites et al. 2007).

Three main sets of peacebuilding activities

Over time, aid and donor agencies have supported three main sets of peacebuilding activities.

Early warning networks. The first main set of peacebuilding activities has involved gathering information useful for early warning of the potential for conflict or reporting actual conflict through two networks—the Famine Early Warning System–Network (FEWS-Net) and the Conflict Early Warning and Response Network (CEWARN)—and use of this information for conflict intervention or amelioration (primarily at the instigation of conflict managers receiving CEWARN reports).

Turkana County is the only part of the Horn of Africa region involved in the regional Intergovernmental Authority on Development's (IGAD's) CEWARN system,[4] which reports information it has gathered about conflicts to NGO and government officials, who then work with local authority figures to defuse conflict situations. Turkana County is also covered by FEWS-Net, a multi-donor and aid agency–sponsored project that assesses food security indicators across the Greater Horn of Africa by gathering information from grassroots sources, such as village chiefs, on agro-ecological conditions, pastoralist herd migration patterns, communal relations, and the potential for armed attacks. FEWS-Net also collects satellite data every ten days and correlates that information with local information to forecast possible conflict.[5] All of this information is then reported up the chain to the national-level FEWS-Net office in Nairobi, Kenya, as well as to CEWARN officials in Addis Ababa, Ethiopia.

CEWARN's specific function is to collate field reports on armed attacks, including livestock losses and human fatalities, and supply that information to conflict managers, who then mobilize to prevent further violence. For example, such mobilization might involve calling a meeting of tribal leaders from both sides, along with area security officials, to negotiate pasture or water sharing agreements. In the end, while the information that FEWS-Net collects is of interest for preventing conflict, it is CEWARN that reports to conflict managers so that action can be taken.

One advantage of this early warning system is that it collects agro-ecological data that can then be used to project the likely movements of herding units and their contact with potentially insecure areas. The weakness of this approach is that it depends on early response from the state—in this particular case, from the Kenyan government—which has not been forthcoming. As noted earlier, chronic insecurity in the Karimojong Cluster is due in part to the failure of the state to provide such a response. If early warnings are to result in early action, that action needs to be by the state, as few other institutions have sufficient legitimacy.

Peace meetings. The second main set of peacebuilding activities by donor-funded aid agencies has been facilitation of peace meetings between elders, youth leaders, and women from competing pastoralist groups, as well as local government and aid agency officials. An inherent strength of this approach is that it establishes new platforms for social bonding between different ethnic and clan groups and,

---

4 IGAD is a regional organization of East African countries dedicated to achieving peace, prosperity, and regional integration.

5 FEWS-Net field officer interviewed by the author, June 2, 2004, Kenya.

thus, provides a basis for dialogue and negotiation on access to natural resources in borderlands and outlying areas.

Such peace meetings were pioneered in the late 1990s by the African Union–Interafrican Bureau for Animal Resources (AU-IBAR), a technical veterinary agency. Before its effort ended in 2003, AU-IBAR used vaccination campaigns in northern Turkana and neighboring areas of southern Sudan (now South Sudan) as an entry point to nurture close ties with traditional leaders, such as elders, seers, and generals, who, heretofore, had mostly been neglected in other development initiatives (Grahn 2005). Initially, in discussions initiated by AU-IBAR, these traditional leaders explained how insecurity was a major constraint on keeping livestock and impeded further implementation of community-based animal health services. Responding, AU-IBAR then organized peace meetings in borderlands and outlying areas and tried to increase participation not only by traditional leaders but by young men involved in raiding.

Distinguishing elements of these peace meetings included that they were cross-border, involved traditional leaders, and promoted the role of women in peacebuilding (Grahn 2005). They also drew on traditional symbols of peace, such as "burying the hatchet," which, in this case, meant burying knives and weapons at a peace meeting, the exchange of traditional stools, and conduct of *alogita a ng'aberu*, a traditional, social ceremony involving women coming together around a common purpose or need. Another traditional symbol employed during the meetings was *epiding*—a pass or path understood as a gateway between neighboring pastoralist groups that often overlaps points of access to key natural resources for herds (Grahn 2005).

AU-IBAR subsequently utilized the concept of epiding to map local institutions that determine access to natural resources in borderlands. For example, epiding was invoked in discussions between the Turkana and neighboring Toposa along the Kenya–South Sudan border to develop plans to manage grazing and water resources during the dry season. The involvement of leaders in evoking epiding was central to the striking of a very localized agreement regarding these resources and communication of this agreement to herding groups on both sides of the border (Grahn 2005).

A peace infrastructure. A third main set of peacebuilding efforts has involved establishing a peace infrastructure to communicate peace messages and inculcate a culture of peace. In recent years, various aid agencies and faith-based organizations have instituted an elaborate peace infrastructure in Turkana consisting of *adakar* (neighborhood) peace and development committees (community peace groups), village peace committees, and area-specific security and border committees. This intricate assemblage was established at a dizzying pace in response to interest by donors in supporting such initiatives and has proliferated into what amounts to "the business of peace" (Eaton 2008, 92). Engagement in such initiatives has involved quite an variety of organizations, including the Intermediate Technology and Development Group, World Vision, SNV (a Netherlands-based international NGO), Veterinarians without Borders–Belgium, the Arid Lands Resource Management Project, the National Council of Churches of Kenya, and the Reformed Church of East Africa, as well as a compendium of community-based organizations.

Like the peace meetings facilitated by AU-IBAR, here too there have been efforts to revive traditional peacebuilding symbols. For example, members of decentralized peace committees have been trained in conflict prevention, management, and resolution in a way designed to raise the profile of such traditional structures as the Ekitoe Angi-kiliok, or the "Elders' Tree."[6]

Village-level committees have the potential advantage of being able to act with unity of purpose in undertaking peacebuilding and policing in their villages.[7] However, this presupposes existence of a single, village-level peacebuilding structure when, in actuality, several overlapping structures often exist under the control of different local leaders, resulting in competition as well as duplication of responsibilities.

A 2003 review by Oxfam–Great Britain of its peace initiatives in Kenya's arid districts found that the possibility of donor funding had led to a number of parallel peacebuilding activities, poor coordination, and tensions between different NGO actors doing peacebuilding work (Oxfam-GB 2003). Later, interviews with the heads of NGO peace projects in Turkanaland revealed a total lack of communication among different peace managers in many cases and a palpable sense of competition and tension between different peace structures (Lind 2007). A few years earlier, Richard Grahn had noted the same and gone on to conclude that the lack of coordination among NGOs was a significant impediment to effective peacebuilding in the Karimojong Cluster. Specifically, he explained that because NGOs operating in the Karimojong Cluster had been unable to agree on a common approach, this had led "to the absurd situation where one location might contain two different peace committees, related to and visited by two different supporting organisations" (Grahn 2005, 18).

Subsequently, although the Turkana District Peace and Development Committee (later renamed *Riam Riam*) was established to coordinate the various peacebuilding activities in the district, it came to be regarded with some suspicion by many Turkana (as revealed in interviews) as just another structure competing for donor funding (Lind 2007). This dovetails with Dave Eaton's finding that many inhabitants of the Karimojong Cluster have come to view peacebuilding efforts by NGOs as irrelevant, which, he has argued, may explain the cynicism, corruption, and incompetence among many of the local organizations working on peacebuilding (Eaton 2008).

---

[6] Chair of the Turkana Peace and Development Organization interviewed by the author, 2004, Kenya.

[7] Community peace worker with World Vision interviewed by the author, 2003, Kenya.

Implications of peacebuilding efforts

While the various peacebuilding initiatives discussed above have generated new insights into contemporary constraints on pastoralist livelihoods in the Karimojong Cluster, little has changed in fundamental patterns of armed violence centered on livestock raiding. In addition to critiques outlined above, in reviewing the impact of AU-IBAR's peacebuilding efforts, Grahn has concluded that they were "broad and shallow, with effective sensitisation of communities but limited impact on root causes" (Grahn 2005, 17). Yet another assessment of peace meetings facilitated by AU-IBAR found they had failed to substantially reduce levels of conflict and violence, build trust, or reestablish security in key grazing and farming environments (CAPE Unit 2004).

Despite these various peacebuilding efforts, agricultural lands in the riparian zones of southern Turkana straddling the Turkwel and Kerio Rivers have been abandoned due to the continuing threat of armed attacks; borderland villagers and pastoralists have continued to restrict livestock movements and livelihood activities to tending farm plots and engaging in trade in market centers; and none of the grazing agreements facilitated by AU-IBAR have lasted, due to incomplete or weak participation by community leaders, youth, local authorities, and state security authorities. In fact, an AU-IBAR-facilitated agreement for the sharing of resources in south Turkana broke down when raiders took livestock from one of the kraal leaders key to the negotiations (Grahn 2005).

FACTORS AFFECTING PEACEBUILDING SUCCESS

Many factors have played a role in the limited effectiveness of peacebuilding efforts in the Karimojong Cluster. These include the structural framing of conflict dynamics in the region, the region's physical geography and nonequilibrium setting, limited grassroots support for largely aid-driven initiatives, and a lack of a clear end to the conflict.

Structural framing of conflict dynamics in the region

Fundamentally, the limited effectiveness of peacebuilding efforts in the Karimojong Cluster relates to the structural framing of conflict dynamics in the region and the lack of regional and national interventions to address historical causes underlying vulnerability and violence. As noted earlier, according to many astute observers and analysts, in these borderlands, state-building processes resulted in deterioration of customary structures for promoting social ties across ecological and group-identity boundaries. Loss of these social ties, which provided for flexibility and mobility in precolonial times, has, in postcolonial times, resulted in pastoralists becoming confined or ghettoized in tribal territories that completely lack association with the human and ecological requirements of pastoralism.

An evaluation of lessons learned from AU-IBAR's peacebuilding work found that such local-level approaches were not sufficient to have more than a limited impact on structural changes and other proximate root causes of conflict in the region (Grahn 2005). While local-level peacebuilding work in the Karimojong Cluster has correctly focused on providing platforms for cross-border dialogue as a way to build trust between groups, this has not altered a historical legacy of underdevelopment and lack of public investment and, also, of inappropriate development interventions (such as encouraging pastoralists to become full-time farmers) that have served only to worsen pastoralists' vulnerability, including through erosion of assets and heightened levels of poverty (Broch-Due and Storas 1983; Hogg 1987). The efficacy of localized peacebuilding initiatives has also been circumscribed by the continued failure of state security operations targeting pastoralists, most notably disarmament campaigns conducted by the Ugandan military targeting Karimojong herders.

Another problem has been the predominant view that conflict dynamics in the Karimojong Cluster center on competition for scarce natural resources in an increasingly degraded environment, for this has justified local-level reconciliation efforts that tend not to address underlying structural dynamics. While local peacebuilding efforts have been important for facilitating dialogue and negotiation to expand access to natural resources, these local approaches have tended to address only manifestations of chronic conflict. In the absence of complementary regional and national efforts around the rule of law, such efforts cannot meaningfully address underlying structural dynamics that have long framed armed violence in the region (Lind and Eriksen 2006). As noted earlier, these underlying structural dynamics include historical underdevelopment and marginalization of pastoralist areas. In addition, although notable progress has been made in generating early warning information on possible outbreaks of armed violence, early responses have been lacking.

Regional geography and nonequilibrium

Another factor affecting the success of peacebuilding efforts in the Karimojong Cluster is the region's physical geography, which covers an expanse of territory stretching across the frontiers of four nation-states (Ethiopia, Kenya, South Sudan, and Uganda). Within the borders of Kenya, Turkana County alone covers an area of a size roughly equivalent to Sierra Leone. Thus, implementation of peacebuilding activities by NGOs and local civil society groups based primarily in the region's large administrative centers and permanent settlements has been patchy at best, particularly given a lack of coordination among these groups, as previously noted.

Related to the region's physical geography is the region's nonequilibrium setting, meaning, in this case, a setting of ecological uncertainty and variability. As Grahn has noted, although "peace meetings, dialogues and crusades all seemed to be having some sort of impact . . . many of the achievements made seemed eventually to falter due to the unremitting harshness of the environment and the situation would gradually slip backwards" (Grahn 2005, 17). As explicated earlier, the adaptability of the region's pastoralists to their environment has been based on managing conditions of ecological uncertainty and variability, including through a variety of interactions that can and do shift over time. Precolonial relations were characterized by reciprocal raiding and transgressive behavior by youth (including livestock raiding for bride price and individualized banditry), as well as by considerable cooperation and mutually beneficial intermarriage and trade. Thus, the breakdown of a grazing agreement negotiated by AU-IBAR following a raid against a key kraal leader was not surprising, for the normal pattern of social interaction between herding groups in the context of a non-equilibrium setting alternates between treating each other as enemies or allies. Ecological uncertainty dictates the need for fluidity in social relations, meaning that, as ecological conditions change, the need for open-ended negotiation and dialogue and the ability to cross boundaries change—all of which make it difficult to reach and enforce a fixed agreement.

Lack of grassroots support

Peacebuilding efforts in the region have been largely driven and supported by donor-supported aid agencies and modeled, in part, on the pioneering efforts of Somali women in the 1990s to reduce levels of armed violence connected to livestock raiding in Kenya's North Eastern Province.[8] The agencies involved in the Karimojong Cluster, including AU-IBAR and Oxfam–Great Britain, have made important contributions to peacebuilding there by learning from and utilizing customary peace symbols and by working with elders, women, and warriors. Also, working alongside civil society organizations, aid agencies have helped establish local peace structures and facilitate local peace meetings. Nonetheless, the legitimacy of these new peace structures has been questioned as structures established to attract donor funds. Viewed at the grassroots level as being initiated by outside actors and under the control of individuals eager to curry favor with larger powers, many of these structures have lacked credibility at the grassroots level and, therefore, have lacked grassroots support (Lind and Eriksen 2006; Eaton 2008).

No clear end to the conflict

Complicating PCNRM in the region is lack of a clear end to the conflict, just as there was no clear beginning. The historical experience of the region's pastoralist societies has been such that entire generations have been socialized in a context of high levels of violence and insecurity. Many in the region have

---

[8] Kenya's North Eastern Province is located outside of the Karimojong Cluster.

never known peace, as envisioned and promoted by aid and donor agencies, nor are they familiar with the notions of peace promoted by NGOs through their efforts.

LESSONS LEARNED

In addressing ongoing conflict in the Karimojong Cluster, the international community has learned fundamental lessons in post-conflict peacebuilding that are relevant to both the Karimojong region and for other post-conflict situations. Crucial peacebuilding considerations include recognizing the limits of local-level reconciliation, identifying what is needed for conflict reduction, and fostering local support of and confidence in peacebuilding efforts.

Limits of local-level reconciliation

Importantly, the shift to peacebuilding by aid programming entities in the Karimojong Cluster has provided support for activities that, it is hoped, will generate greater insights into the nature of conflict there, reasons for continuation of armed violence, and what types of assistance might strengthen livelihoods in such a deeply insecure setting. Notwithstanding these potentially beneficial outcomes, the failure of peacebuilding efforts to broker lasting peace in the Karimojong Cluster serves as a stark reminder of the limits of local-level reconciliation work in a context of structural conflict, generalized insecurity, and absence of the rule of law. Local peacebuilding efforts have been an adjunct to, not a substitute for, the failure of state authorities to provide lasting security for the region's pastoralists. Further, the many initiatives focused on reconciling neighboring groups have tried to address local manifestations of armed violence rather than root causes of conflict.

While localized peacebuilding efforts have been valuable for promoting greater social connectivity that may help people cope with the consequences of conflict and ecological uncertainty, and while promoting dialogue between groups to improve relations governing access to natural resources may lead to a temporary reduction in hostilities, in practice, these efforts have been undermined by continued raiding and banditry, which have their own inner logic and workings that relate to the region's history and social, political, and economic structures. Thus, a fundamental lesson learned from peacebuilding work in the Karimojong Cluster is that its longer-term effectiveness hinges on complementary efforts to address structural inequality and underdevelopment (Lind 2006).

Addressing conflict reduction

The Karimojong region has a long history of violent conflict. Addressing the root causes of conflict and advancing peacebuilding efforts require both improved governance and security, and economic growth of the region.

Needed: Security and rule of law

Another lesson to be drawn from peacebuilding efforts in the Karimojong Cluster concerns the implicit understanding of pastoralist conflict that has informed most conflict-reduction approaches in the region. Resolving conflict is not exclusively—or even foremost—about reconciling neighboring pastoralist groups that are fighting over scarce resources. As Eaton has explained, "at the end of the dry season, they [pastoralists in the region] often are faced with the choice of sharing what little grazing and water remains, or fighting to defend their resources against a well-armed opponent with nothing to lose. The choice is obvious, and only in rare circumstances will a destitute ethnic group be denied access to scarce resources" (Eaton 2008, 101). Thus, ultimately, it is unhelpful to treat the conflict as being tied to a local set of circumstances or, alternatively, as a sociocultural phenomenon requiring intervention to instill more peaceful behavior. Rather, reducing conflict in the region involves the need to establish security and the rule of law in the region, which is only a distant possibility despite the current fixation by national governments (as well as regional organizations such as IGAD and the Common Market for Eastern and Southern Africa) on regional economic integration as a mechanism for reducing conflict across the Horn of Africa, including in the Karimojong Cluster (Healy et al. 2009; Moller 2009).

Needed: Economic transformation specific to the region

While conflict reduction in the Karimojong Cluster could very well be assisted by an economic transformation, that transformation must be specific to the region, including the fact of its remoteness from large markets and centers of political power. To reduce conflict in the Karimojong Cluster, economic transformation needs to be about creating sustainable livelihoods for those who live there because once they lose their herds, they have few other opportunities to productively sustain themselves and their families. Hand in hand with this is the need to encourage social connectivity among the various herding groups across the many borders that divide the Karimojong Cluster in order to reestablish greater mobility, more flexible access to resources, and growth in trade and exchange relations through which these herding groups can acquire the means to restore their livelihoods or, at least, to cope with ecological uncertainty and variability.

The breakdown of grazing agreements facilitated by AU-IBAR in the Karimojong Cluster showed the difficulty of implementing fixed agreements for sharing natural resources in nonequilibrium environments. Fluidity in precolonial pastoralist social relations was determined by flexibility and mobility in accessing the widest range possible of the resources needed to live with uncertainty. Reciprocal grazing agreements—an important part of pastoralist social relations in the past—were constantly renegotiated and also often failed when ecological conditions changed. In nonequilibrium rangeland contexts, it is crucial to encourage the strongest possible social and economic ties among different livelihood groups, for this can serve as a means of building the confidence and trust needed to ease negotiating access to natural resources, even as ecological conditions change. In short, encouraging open dialogue might very well be more effective than negotiating a set agreement when it comes to sharing natural resources in nonequilibrium environments.

Local acceptance and support of peacebuilding efforts

A number of competing factors influence the success of peacebuilding efforts in the Karimojong Cluster. This section discusses some of the most notable factors that raise doubts and concerns—including the inadequate use of confidence-building measures—regarding the potential to achieve prolonged peace in the region.

Many factors raise doubts and concerns

Another lesson learned from peacebuilding efforts in the Karimojong Cluster is that the success of such efforts depends on unequivocal local acceptance and support, and this has been lacking—with no clearer evidence than that the region remains insecure; no clear transition to peace is in sight; and raiding continues unabated, sustained by long-standing factors. As noted earlier, many peacebuilding initiatives in the region have been externally driven. On the positive side, some peacebuilding groups have used traditional peace symbols and prioritized involvement by traditional leaders and women (rather than by local administrative officials, many of whom are regarded by local people as unimportant to the process), and this has broadened participation in peace efforts. However, the proliferation of such initiatives over a relatively short period of time and coordination failures among the various aid agencies involved have raised doubts and concerns, which have reduced local support. Competition for donor support also raised doubts and concerns.

Insufficient use of confidence-building measures

Acceptance and support of peacebuilding work has been further compromised because local-level confidence in such efforts has not been sufficiently built. Failing to adequately engage pastoralist communities prior to engaging in reconciliation efforts has hampered promoters of peace from both local civil society and outside aid agencies. Aid and government agencies have struggled to communicate their notions of peace in an environment where conflict is routine and a normal feature of pastoralist social relations, implying that agencies must articulate their intentions earlier in the process and find better ways to explain their efforts—ways that more deeply take into consideration the experiences and perceptions of pastoralist communities and their approaches to coping with chronic insecurity.

CONCLUSIONS AND NEXT STEPS

Transitions to peace do not happen in a vacuum or in isolation from deeper and wider historical and structural factors. In the case of the Karimojong Cluster, efforts to promote peace have been hampered by the deeply embedded nature of armed violence in the region and by the failure of state governments to articulate policies and act in ways that protect pastoralists and promote their livelihoods.

Economic integration as a peacebuilding concept

Addressing the livelihood concerns of pastoralists in the Karimojong Cluster, including reducing conflict, will become more important as this region becomes more integrated into regional and national economies. As briefly noted earlier, national governments (and regional organizations) in the Horn of Africa are seeking to increase ways in which regional areas, including the drylands of the Karimojong Cluster, can contribute to national and cross-border economic development, such as by supporting increased livestock production for export to the Arabian Peninsula. Other concepts include developing commercial agricultural plantations along permanent rivers as well as water- and wind-powered sources to generate electricity for national power grids. Indeed, economic integration across the region is the latest peacebuilding concept, with the thought that such economic integration will raise the opportunity cost of engaging in conflict (Healy et al. 2009). Yet, the same supportive, integrative ties between pastoralist societies in the Karimojong Cluster that have eased social and economic adaptation across borders (such as through trade and exchange relations) are today working equally well to help conceal and facilitate the transport and sale of stolen livestock.

Security concerns persist

At the regional level, IGAD's conflict early warning system (CEWARN, assisted by FEWS-Net) continues to collect and analyze significant amounts of data on armed violence in and around Turkana, in particular, that should help generate a clearer picture of conflict dynamics in the region. Yet, as noted earlier, there is a lack of effective, early response to such information. On the ground, local police and administrative officials who lack basic communications equipment and transport support are incapable of responding quickly to incidents. Thus, despite the existence of an early warning system and an emergent policy and institutional structure for preventing and responding to conflict, this has not yet been translated into greater protection on the ground.

Uganda

At present, most pastoralists in the Karimojong Cluster continue to rely on their own ways of protecting life and property and to regard the state itself as part of the problem. As Stites and colleagues have explained, the failure of Ugandan authorities to provide security for disarmed communities has dented confidence in that nation state's ability to protect physical safety and household assets (Stites et al. 2007). Thus, communities disarmed by the Ugandan military have rearmed to defend their lives and their livelihoods.

Kenya

On the Kenyan side of the Karimojong Cluster, however, since 2003, the government has taken new and notable steps toward developing an institutional framework for supporting decentralized peacebuilding efforts, primarily in the direction of prevention. First, the National Steering Committee on Conflict Management was established in the Office of the President to institutionalize district peace and development committees, a new status that gave these committees a more official and substantial role in preventing conflict. Today, these committees, as well as district security committees, are still based in towns across the arid and semiarid region of northern Kenya, the former trying to prevent conflict, and the latter trying to respond to violent incidents. In addition, the Kenyan government is considering a policy framework for conflict prevention.

Both the official status of localized peace and development committees in Kenya and a national policy framework for conflict prevention should provide a locus for peacebuilding efforts and incorporation of natural resource management concerns into broader economic development approaches. Further, the Kenyan government's establishment of the Ministry of Northern Kenya and Other Arid Lands in 2008 has been viewed by pastoralist leaders as a sign of a new, political commitment to address both security and development problems in pastoralist areas.

Region's economic development and pastoralist livelihoods

While it has been hoped that the increasing economic importance of drylands to regional and national economic development would occasion new efforts to strengthen pastoralist livelihoods, including by building peace, in practice, thus far, this has not been the case. For example, Ethiopia has continued to build the Gibe III Dam on the Omo River as a source of hydroelectric power, even though the Omo River provides up to 90 percent of the total water flowing into Lake Turkana and is, therefore, an important livelihoods resource for the Turkana people. Despite strong opposition by Turkana civil society and political leaders to the Gibe III Dam, the Kenyan government signed a memorandum of understanding (MOU) in 2006 allowing Kenya to import electricity generated by the project (International Rivers 2011).

Improvement of pastoralist livelihoods?

Although steps have been taken, the development interests of national governments, supported by regional organizations, are still not aligned with objectives to improve livelihoods for the majority of pastoralists in the Karimojong Cluster. Currently, large-scale development schemes involving the drylands are focused first and foremost on contributing to national economic development in a way that will result in wealth creation for pastoralist elites (such as large-scale livestock traders and exporters and others with the status and influence necessary to gain access to coveted lands) and not, necessarily, in a way that will improve the livelihoods of the majority. Thus, considerable hurdles remain to be overcome in the realization of true peace in the Karimojong Cluster.

REFERENCES

BBC News Online. 2006. Cattle raids "kill 38" in Kenya. January 19.

Broch-Due, V., and F. Storas. 1983. The fields of the foe: Amana emoit; Factors constraining agricultural output and farmers capacity for participation—A socio-anthropological case study of household economy among the inhabitants on Katilu irrigation scheme, Turkana, Kenya. Bergen, Norway: Bergen University.

Buchanan-Smith, M., and J. Lind. 2005. Armed violence and poverty in northern Kenya: A case study for the armed violence and poverty initiative. Bradford, UK: Centre for International Cooperation and Security, Department of Peace Studies, University of Bradford.

CAPE Unit (Community Animal Health and Participatory Epidemiology Unit). 2004. *Assessing the impact of conflict management activities in the Karamojong Cluster*. Nairobi, Kenya: African Union–Interafrican Bureau for Animal Resources.

Cullis, A., and A. Pacey. 1992. *A development dialogue: Rainwater harvesting in Turkana*. London: ITDG.

Daily Nation. 1999. Cattle rustling big time business. July 21.

Dietz, T. 1993. The state, the market and the decline of pastoralism: Challenging some myths, with evidence from West Pokot in Kenya and Uganda. In *Conflict and the decline of pastoralism in the Horn of Africa*, ed. J. Markakis and J. Basingstoke. New York: Macmillan.

Eaton, D. 2008. The business of peace: Raiding and peace work along the Kenya-Uganda border (Part I). *African Affairs* 107 (426): 89–110.

Economist. 1999. Kenya's lawless bush. May 13.

Fratkin, E. 1991. *Surviving drought and development: Ariaal pastoralists of northern Kenya*. Boulder, CO: Westview.

Gettleman, J. 2009. Lush land dries up, withering Kenya's hopes. *New York Times*, September 8.

Goldsmith, P. 1997. *Cattle, khat, and guns: Trade, conflict, and security on northern Kenya's highland-lowland interface*. Nairobi, Kenya: Institute of Policy Analysis and Research and United States Agency for International Development Greater Horn of Africa Initiative.

Grahn, R. 2005. Lessons learned from conflict management work in the Karimojong Cluster. Drylands Programme Issues Paper No. 137. London: International Institute for Environment and Development.

Gray, S. J. 2000. A memory of loss: Ecological politics, local history, and the evolution of Karimojong violence. *Human Organization* 59 (4): 401–418.

Healy, S., C. Cramer, D. Styan, and D. Leonard. 2009. *The economics of conflict and integration in the Horn of Africa*. London: Chatham House.

Hendrickson, D., J. Armon, and R. Mearns. 1998. Conflict and vulnerability to famine: Livestock raiding in Turkana, Kenya. Drylands Programme Issues Paper No. 80. London: International Institute for Environment and Development.

Hogg, R. 1987. Settlement, pastoralism and the commons: The ideology and practice of irrigation development in northern Kenya. In *Conservation in Africa: People, policies and practice*, ed. D. Anderson and R. Grove. Cambridge, UK: Cambridge University Press.

Independent. 2005. Kenya army steps in as cattle rustling turns lethal. July 23.

International Rivers. 2011. Ethiopia's Gibe III Dam: Sowing hunger and conflict. www.internationalrivers.org/files/attached-files/gibe3factsheet2011.pdf.

Kamenju, J., M. Singo, and F. Wairagu. 2003. *Terrorized citizens: Profiling small arms and insecurity in the North Rift region of Kenya*. Nairobi, Kenya: Security Research and Information Centre.

Knighton, B. 2003. The state as raider among the Karamojong: "Where there are no guns, they use the threat of guns." *Africa* 73 (3): 427–455.

Lamphear, J. 1992. *The scattering time: Turkana responses to colonial rule*. Oxford, UK: Clarendon.

———. 1994. The evolution of Ateker "new model" armies. In *Ethnicity and conflict in the Horn of Africa*, ed. K. Fukui and J. Markakis. Athens, OH: Ohio University Press.

Lind, J. 2006. Supporting pastoralist livelihoods in Eastern Africa through peace building. *Development* 49:111–115.

———. 2007. Fortune and loss in an environment of violence: Living with chronic instability in south Turkana, Kenya. Unpublished Ph.D. diss., King's College London, University of London.

Lind, J., and S. Eriksen. 2006. The impacts of conflict on household coping strategies: Evidence from Turkana and Kitui districts in Kenya. *Die Erde* 137 (3): 249–270.

Little, M. A., R. Dyson-Hudson, and J. T. McCabe. 1999. Ecology of south Turkana. In *Turkana herders of the dry savanna: Ecology and biobehavioral response of nomads to an uncertain environment*, ed. M. A. Little and P. W. Leslie. Oxford, UK: Oxford University Press.

Little, P. D. 1985. Absentee herd owners and part-time pastoralists: The political economy of resource use in northern Kenya. *Human Ecology* 13 (2): 131–151.

McCabe, J. T. 2004. *Cattle brings us to our enemies: Turkana ecology, politics, and raiding in a disequilibrium system*. Ann Arbor, MI: University of Michigan Press.

Mirzeler, M., and C. Young. 2000. Pastoral politics in the northeast periphery in Uganda: AK-47 as change agent. *Journal of Modern African Studies* 38 (3): 407–429.

Mkutu, K. A. 2006. Small arms and light weapons among pastoral groups in the Kenya-Uganda border area. *African Affairs* 106 (422): 47–70.

Moller, B. 2009. Africa's sub-regional organisations: Seamless web or patchwork? Crisis States Research Center Working Paper No. 56. London, UK: Development Studies Institute, London School of Economics.

Monbiot, G. 1994. *No man's lands: An investigative journey through Kenya and Tanzania*. London: Picador.

Oxfam-GB (Oxfam–Great Britain). 2003. Oxfam GB-funded peace building initiatives in the arid districts of Kenya: Lessons and challenges. Nairobi, Kenya.

Pike, I. L. 2004. The biosocial consequences of life on the run: A case study of Turkana of Kenya. *Human Organization* 63 (2): 221–235.

Sobania, N. W. 1990. Social relations as an aspect of property rights: Northern Kenya in the pre-colonial and colonial periods. In *Property, poverty and people: Changing rights in property and problems of pastoral development*, ed. P. T. W. Baxter and R. Hogg. Manchester, UK: Department of Social Anthropology, University of Manchester, and the International Development Centre.

Stites, E., D. Akabwai, D. Mazurana, and P. Ateyo. 2007. Angering Akuju: Survival and suffering in Karamoja. Medford, MA: Feinstein International Center, Tufts University.

Stites, E., and D. Akabwai. 2009. Changing roles, shifting risks: Livelihood impacts of disarmament in Karamoja, Uganda. Medford, MA: Feinstein International Center, Tufts University.

Waller, R. D. 1999. Pastoral poverty in historical perspective. In *The poor are not us: Poverty and pastoralism in Eastern Africa*, ed. D. Anderson and V. Broch-Due. London: James Currey.

Zaal, F., and T. Dietz. 1999. Of markets, meat, maize and milk: Pastoral commoditization in Kenya. In *The poor are not us: Poverty and pastoralism in Eastern Africa*, ed. D. Anderson and V. Broch-Due. London: James Currey.

Resolving natural resource conflicts to help prevent war: A case from Afghanistan

Liz Alden Wily

History is replete with civil wars driven in part or in full by disputes over rights to natural resources critical to local livelihoods (Richards 2005; Rosset, Patel, and Courville 2006; Pantuliano 2009). A common land grievance in agrarian societies is that governments fail to grant legal recognition of customary land rights as having the force of real property rights (Alden Wily 2008c, 2009). Governments and other authorities have often treated customary lands—particularly unfarmed communal assets such as pastures—as unowned or public and have been predisposed to award them to other-than-customary users, generating serious grievances and conflicts.

For many generations, Afghanistan has witnessed serious conflicts over rights to access pasturelands in general and to those of the central highlands in particular. For some time, the pasturelands of the central highlands have been disputed variously as the property of the Pashtun nomads known as Kuchi and of local, settled Hazara communities who claim the region as their ancient homeland, called Hazarajat. Unresolved, this dispute tends to manifest in violence each spring as Kuchi attempt to reenter Hazarajat for summer grazing. Increased Taliban and Pashtun support of the Kuchi now threatens to bring the conflict onto an open war footing.

This chapter reviews attempts to resolve the pasturelands conflict since the signing of the Bonn Agreement in 2001, which ended the last formal Taliban regime. The chapter has six major parts: (1) a summary outlining the historical origins of the central highlands pastures dispute; (2) a discussion of the official handling of the dispute in recent years, including iterative learning on the ground; (3) an analysis of key lessons learned, lessons that helped in the building of a new strategy and an action plan for resolution; (4) an overview of steps taken in preparation for implementation of the new strategy; (5) a discussion of the strategy's influence on field-level development projects and legislative amendments;

Liz Alden Wily is a land tenure specialist who works as a researcher, practitioner, and independent policy advisor for governments and aid agencies, addressing land and forest tenure issues.

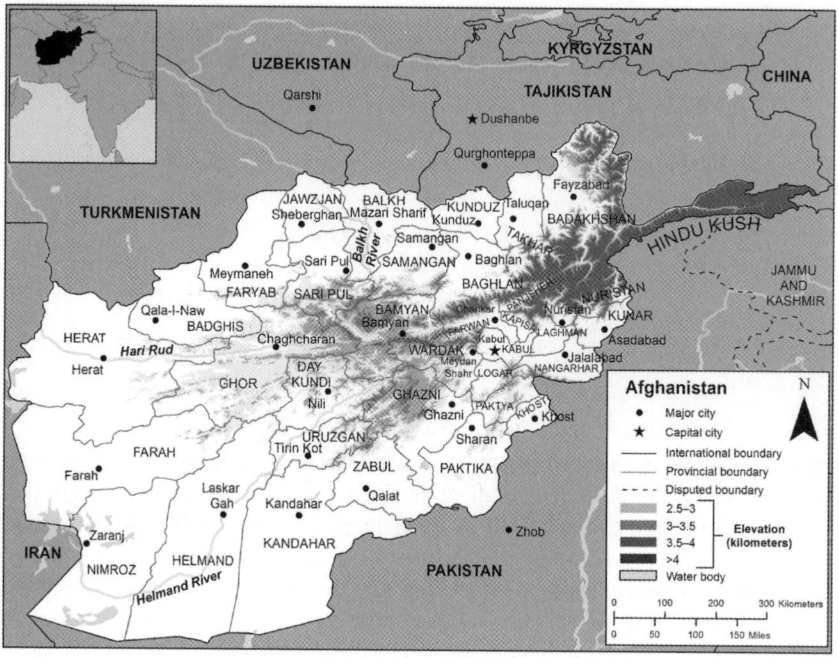

and (6) an examination of the applicability of lessons learned in Afghanistan, including the need to take seriously the contesting of land rights in post-conflict reconstruction.

BACKGROUND

Afghanistan is a high, dry country where only approximately 12 percent of the land is cultivable, including 7 percent rainfed land and 5 percent irrigated land (USAID, n.d.; World Bank 2011). Between 45 and 80 percent of the country is used for pasturing animals (de Weijer 2005), mostly smallstock (small livestock) that provides the wool and mohair needed to make carpets and rugs—the manufacturing of which is an important source of livelihoods for many. Even the poorest benefit from livestock raising, as landless tenants and workers use community pastures to sustain a few smallstock, their only capital asset.

Agrarian dependence on livestock is particularly pronounced in the central highlands, where long, snowy winters prevent production of more than one wheat crop annually. Historically, local Hazara tribes have been agropastoralists who practice transhumance, moving livestock from valleys to alpine grasslands every summer (Gawecki 1980). The high pastures also provide the woody shrubs needed for fuel to keep valley settlements and livestock warm in winter.

Around the turn of the twentieth century, Kuchi nomads began depending on the central highlands for summer pasturing (Glatzer 1981; Pedersen 1994;

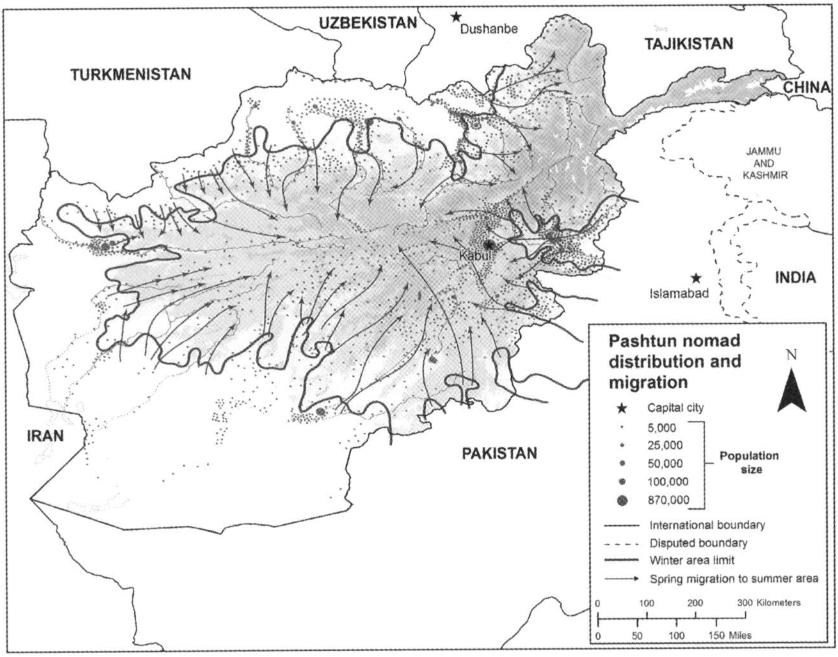

Figure 1. Pashtun nomad distribution and migration
Source: Ferdinand (2006).

Frederiksen 1995; Ferdinand 2006; and de Weijer 2007).[1] Figure 1 illustrates their migration to the central highlands, which begins in spring. The Kuchi travel mainly from the south and east, where a high concentration of Kuchi maintain winter home pastures. While a slightly higher number of Kuchi families migrate today than in the 1970s, a lower proportion of the overall Kuchi population migrates long distances than in the past. Instead, the wealthiest and poorest among them (15 percent) mainly pursue other livelihoods in cities and towns. Another 33 percent migrate only short distances with their livestock (Foschini 2013). Those who continue to carry out long migrations to the central highlands face fierce resistance from local Hazara and generally do not get beyond foothill districts. This is because the Hazara used the turmoil of the civil war years (1978–2001) to recapture their customary ownership and control of the highland pastures, and they now do their utmost to retain the pastures as their exclusive property.

---

[1] There are 2.4 million nomadic people in Afghanistan, just under 7 percent of the total population (de Weijer 2007). Most are Pashtun Kuchi, and the balance are smaller numbers of non-Pashtun Aimaq, Beluch, and Arab pastoralists. Although *Kuchi* means "nomad," it tends to be used to refer only to Pashtun nomads. Spellings of *Kuchi* vary and include *Kochi* and *Koochi*. This is common with spellings in Afghanistan; for example, *Nawur*, referred to later in the chapter, is sometimes spelled *Nawor*.

The roots of the Kuchi and Hazara conflict

For a millenium or more, Hazarajat, the home of loosely aligned Hazara tribes, encompassed most of central Afghanistan, though the territory was much reduced by Pashtun encroachment from the south and the east during the nineteenth century (see figure 2). In the 1880s, Great Britain—fearing that czarist Russian expansion from the north would jeopardize its Indian empire (including what is now Pakistan)—armed the Pashtun emir, Abdur Rahman, and paid him to colonize all areas west and north of Kabul. The result was the establishment of the buffer state of Afghanistan in 1893 (Gregorian 1969; Lee 1996). Although the north fell fairly easily, the highland Hazara were resistant, so the emir armed 30,000 Kuchi to crush them and kill their leaders. As a reward, the British handed over the rich pastures of alpine Hazarajat to Kuchi leaders in 1894, with each entitlement inscribed in vellum deeds (*firman*). The Kuchi were then able to abandon their more characteristic summer migration southward through what is now Pakistan toward present-day India (Ferdinand 2006).

Nomad possession of the pastures was predictably disastrous for settled Hazara, who were now unable to graze animals and were left "without livelihood," in the words of Fayz Mohammad, the emir's own chronicler (Ferdinand 2006). Through 1919, an estimated 100,000 Hazara fled or were killed or imprisoned

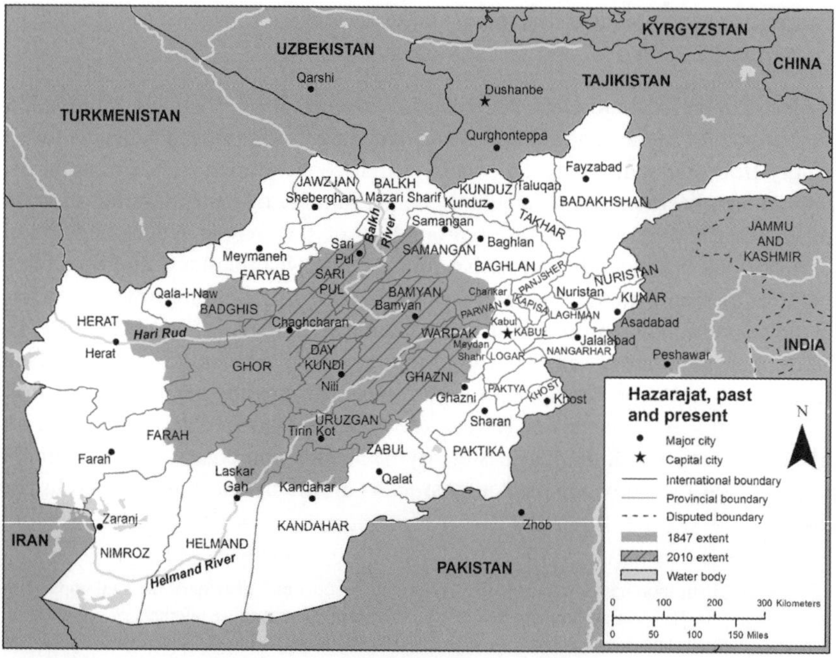

Figure 2. Hazarajat, past and present
Sources: Ferdinand (2006), Mousavi (1998), and author's field experience.

(Mousavi 1998). Respite came in the 1920s under the more benign rule of Emir Amanullah, who stripped the Kuchi of their land deeds and reissued grants that limited them to the highest pastures, reserving lower pastures for local Hazara. This did not make much difference to the Hazara, who still lacked access to the precious alpine pastures essential to livestock keeping. Beginning in the 1930s, Amanullah's successors explicitly favored Pashtun interests over those of the Hazara and other non-Pashtun tribes. Kuchi dominance of the pastures was restored and greatly expanded (Canfield 1986; Pedersen 1994). Livestock numbers soared with the wealth of highland grazing, and some clans abandoned pastoralism altogether in favor of trade and transport businesses and acquisition of whole valleys of scarce farmland from desperately poor and indebted Hazara (Frederiksen 1995; Pedersen 1994). Local grievances were exacerbated as the Hazara often worked as employees or tenant farmers of the Kuchi.

Legal declarations, in 1965 and 1970, that all pasturelands were public land (or state property) under the control of the government changed little, particularly because the laws permitted the government to grant rights of unlimited term to these lands (Alden Wily 2003b). Entitlements continued to be issued, subdivided, and traded (Patterson 2004). The government itself established a number of commercial farming and settlement schemes, absorbing large areas of prime pasture, particularly in the north (Favre 2003).

Civil war (1978–2001)

Festering fury at the suppression of customary land rights at the hands of the Pashtuns quickly surfaced with civil war and the Soviet occupation of 1979–1989. One of the first actions of the Uzbeks in the north was to retake farm and grazing lands that had been forcibly occupied by Pashtun settlers (Male 1982). Armed militias in Hazarajat more slowly resecured control of the pastures that had historically belonged to Hazara, but had been out of their reach since 1894.

Although Kuchi access was almost nonexistent in the 1980s, the Kuchi regained access to some areas with the establishment of Taliban rule (1996–2001). This was especially so in the eastern foothill regions of Nawur and Behsud (in Wardak and Ghazni provinces, respectively), where wealthy Kuchi began to buy yet more farmland from poor Hazara communities, partly to secure associated grazing lands (de Weijer 2007). Access to the heartland Hazarajat province of Bamyan was more limited, except in 1998, when leading Kuchi members of the Taliban terrorized communities in Panjab District (Alden Wily 2004a). For the most part, Hazara in Bamyan Province were firmly in control of the pastures and had enjoyed two decades of autonomous agropastoralism and growth in their livestock numbers. "Without Kuchi, our livelihood has been restored," one Hazara reported.[2]

---

[2] Personal communication with author, 2003.

Problems, beyond those associated with securing access to the pastures, were rampant. For example, the pasture resource—which was already observed as degraded in previous decades (Larsson 1978)—was even more degraded by the end of the Taliban era in December 2001. This resulted in acute shortages of grazing and grasses as well as shrubs to supply winter fodder and household fuel (Alden Wily 2003b). Additionally, conflicts among valleys and villages over customary ownership of high pastures were common, especially in areas where local warlords had taken control during the civil war and Taliban years.

After the fall of the Taliban regime, the reaction of the interim government, led by Hamid Karzai, was simply to restore order to pre–civil war (1978) conditions. Amendments made by the Taliban in 2000 to the Pasture Law of 1970 were dismissed, and firm state control of all pastures actively advocated.

Despite having almost no field staff and having only limited authority outside Kabul, the Ministry of Agriculture determined that only firm government control (and de facto ownership) of the pastures could halt expansion of rainfed farming into pasturelands.[3] The Ministry of Finance was most interested in offering pastures for lease to local and, especially, foreign investors. The Ministry of Tribal and Border Affairs (nicknamed "the Kuchi ministry" and replaced in 2004 by the Department of Kuchi Affairs under the Office of the President) wanted to restore highland pastures to Kuchi control. For all three ministries, the objective was reinforced state ownership and limitation of local access to conditional use rights (Alden Wily 2008b).

There was not much support for this policy outside the Pashtun Kuchi community. The view among many non-Pashtun in the north and Hazara in the central highlands was that they had not fought the long war and liberated themselves and their natural resources from Pashtun domination only to see that domination reinstated. Meanwhile, as Kuchi livestock numbers began to recover from the severe drought of 1999–2001, Kuchi leaders agitated for recognition of Kuchi as the pastures' only true owners. Anxiety grew, particularly among the Hazara (Alden Wily 2003a).

LOOKING FOR A WAY FORWARD (2002–2009)

The positions of international donors were mixed. Initially, leading agencies such as the World Bank, the Asian Development Bank (ADB), and the U.S. Agency for International Development (USAID) assumed that rural tenure issues could be resolved with reinstatement of the titling programs that had been interrupted

---

[3] The ministry responsible for agriculture has had numerous names since 2002: Ministry of Agriculture and Livestock (2002–2004); Ministry of Agriculture and Animal Husbandry (2004–2005); Ministry of Agriculture, Animal Husbandry and Food (2004–2006); Ministry of Agriculture and Irrigation (2006); and Ministry of Agriculture, Irrigation and Livestock (2006–present) (Banzet et al. 2007). In this chapter, *Ministry of Agriculture* refers to the relevant ministry for the time period being discussed.

by the civil war and that, where undertaken, had registered wastelands and pasturelands as government property. Field research conducted by this author and others for the Afghanistan Research and Evaluation Unit (AREU) between 2002 and 2004 concluded otherwise; these researchers argued that reinstatement of titling programs would inflame already vibrant local resistance to either Pashtun or state capture of pastures (Alden Wily 2003b, 2004b; Patterson 2004). Various parties advised that new land tenure principles, including acknowledgment of customary land interests, should be embedded in the new national constitution (Alden Wily 2003a). This recommendation was rejected, as was contrary advice that the new constitution establish pasturelands as government property.[4]

Meanwhile, tensions between Hazara and Kuchi were on the rise. In the spring of 2004, some Hazara were killed as Kuchi nomads attempted to reenter the area with their livestock. Still struggling to resettle some 4 million refugees in the wake of the civil war, the UN High Commissioner for Refugees reported that immense resistance to the return of Pashtun to non-Pashtun areas continued (UNHCR 2004). As pasture-access disputes multiplied in their caseload for assisted mediation, the Norwegian Refugee Council pressed for "the war over pastures" to be addressed (NRC 2004). Increasingly, aid agencies and the Afghan government recognized that continuing to deny customary communal rights to such lands was no longer safe. A new way forward was needed. AREU led the way in advocating an iterative approach to the development of new legal norms for the ownership of pastures and other rural lands that was founded on field research and piloting (Alden Wily 2008b). This was broadly accepted.

Nevertheless, new policies and laws were still being made, largely entrenching the status quo in natural resource ownership. The government launched an interministerial land policy–development process to reevaluate all land and property policies; simultaneously, the Afghan cabinet continued to issue decrees treating pasturelands and other unregistered properties as, in effect, government property.[5] Meanwhile, the United Nations Environment Programme (UNEP), in association with international conservation agencies, worked with the Ministry of Agriculture to produce the Policy and Strategy for Forest and Rangeland Management Sub-Sector in 2006, the new Environment Law in 2007, and a draft Forest Law. While the first of these in particular advocated a community-based approach to forest and pasture management, it made reference to the challenging issue of forest or pasture ownership, thereby implying these would remain the property of government.

---

[4] Only mines and underground resources were recorded as state property (Constitution of Afghanistan, art. 9, 2004).

[5] See, for example, the Decree Limiting Distribution of State Owned Virgin and Barren Lands (No. 99/1381, published June 2003); the Decree for Transfer of Government Property (No. 8/1382, published December 2003); the Presidential Decree on Immovable Property, 2003 (No. 83/1382, published January 2004); and the Decree Amending Article 69 of Land Law of 2000 (published 2006).

Field pilot projects

While new laws were being drafted, the Ministry of Agriculture also began to support practical learning by doing through field projects to guide new legal and policy paradigms of natural resource tenure and governance. The main focus was on the highly contested pastures of Hazarajat. The first initiative followed a 2005 conference with Kuchi leaders, organized by a USAID-funded pastoral program, during which Kuchi moderates indicated a willingness to recognize summer pastures as owned by local communities, as long as these communities guaranteed Kuchi seasonal access (de Weijer 2005). Guidelines for a first field pilot were then drafted with this option in mind (Alden Wily 2005).

Launched in 2006 under the aegis of the Ministry of Agriculture, this first field pilot focused on Nawur Pasture (also known as Nawor), a major locality that had been under dispute for over a century due to its position as a main gateway to the central highlands; its size (600 square kilometers) and largely level terrain; and its water resources, abundant enough to support large herds (de Weijer 2006). The project's first goal was for government and UN representatives, accompanied by technical assistants, to engage local Hazara and Kuchi nomads in discussion about pasture access. This team made good progress until advancing Taliban activity brought discussions to a halt. By then, however, a draft protocol was under consideration by local and nomadic groups. It appeared that while local Hazara were willing to agree that Kuchi should not be deprived of access to highland farms they owned, negotiation of pasture access could not proceed until Hazara communities clarified the boundaries of each village's pasture area and jointly determined which residual areas they would let Kuchi use (de Weijer 2006). As earlier AREU studies had revealed, local Hazara communities were in conflict about pasture rights not only with Kuchi nomads but also among themselves.

This finding reinforced the objectives of a second, larger piloting process subsequently launched in Bamyan Province under the aegis of a community-based pasture management program called SALEH (Sustainable Agricultural Livelihoods in Eastern Hazarajat), which was funded by the Food and Agriculture Organization of the United Nations (FAO) and ran from 2006 to 2008. Its objective was to help Hazara villages to clarify their respective jurisdictions over alpine rangelands and, in the process, to establish regulations to operationally limit the land degradation that was exacerbating intracommunal disputes. The project also was intended to develop a procedure for entrenching local entitlement to these communal properties (Alden Wily 2006b). Shortly afterward, an ADB-funded pilot project outside of Hazarajat took up the latter objective because it found resolving communal tenure issues more pressing than focusing on mechanisms for registering communal properties (Stanfield et al. 2008). Both projects operated in areas free of immediate conflict with nomadic pastoral claimants.

For two years the SALEH project worked with seventy village clusters in three districts and, following resolution of intervillage boundary disputes, brought more than 100,000 hectares of high pasture under working community management and established tested guidelines for the procedure to be applied nationally (Alden Wily 2008a, 2008b). Among other things, the project demonstrated the need to distinguish among near-village pastures that are privately owned by large landlords; larger community pastures extending to uppermost ridges; and a limited number of very large high, remote pastures shared in summer by several valley communities. Assured of their primacy over substantial areas, Hazara were willing, in principle, to allow Kuchi access to some parts of these larger clan assets, albeit on agreed terms. This concept was put into practice only once. In the summer of 2008, 4,000 Pashtun Kuchi nomads moved their livestock into the 3,000-square-kilometer Band-e-Petab Pasture of northern Bamyan Province. It was a special case for several reasons: although these Kuchi were Pashtun, they came from the north and uncommonly, therefore, shared Shiism with the Hazara; they had never claimed to own Band-e-Petab; and they were used to paying grazing fees to Hazara clan leaders. Even so, after Hazara and Kuchi tensions became a national issue later that year, these Kuchi did not attempt to return to Band-e-Petab in 2009 and have not done so since.

Toward new tenure law for pastures

Because the SALEH project was conducted under the aegis of the Ministry of Agriculture, its findings could be and were fed directly to policy-making entities, including the high-level Inter-Ministerial Land Policy Committee (Alden Wily 2006a; Gebremedhin 2007). Although the government subsequently failed to adopt all of SALEH's recommendations, it did issue the National Land Policy in 2007 that, for the first time, allowed community lands to be considered a category of landholding. Specifically, the policy provided for registration of lands held under customary norms to be registered on the basis of documentation that was used customarily and of verbal confirmation by neighboring households or communities. Ownership of pastures was to be defined through community-level procedures such as those developed by the SALEH and ADB projects and laid out as simple guidelines (Alden Wily 2008a; Stanfield et al. 2008).

The SALEH project's findings significantly influenced the strategy of the draft Rangeland Law, written during 2007 and 2008 with technical guidance from UNEP. A main shift that occurred during drafting involved the terminology of ownership of pastures (or rangelands).[6] *Ownership*, in early drafts, was changed to *custodianship*, and the meaning of *custodianship* changed from "ownership" to "lawful possession and long-term management authority." In the law's current iteration, its purpose is "to recognize and formalize the custodianship, management and use rights of communities and other users, to establish a legal framework

6 *Rangeland* and *pasture* or *pastureland* are used interchangeably in documents in Afghanistan.

for bringing all rangelands under community custodianship" and "to define the regulatory, advisory and mediating role of the Government of Afghanistan in relation to pastures" (art. 1).[7]

Although hardly radical, these proposed legal objectives represent a major departure from the paradigms that have prevailed since the promulgation of the Pasture Law in 1970 and that have rendered all pastures a strictly public asset in law, owned and controlled by the government alone, which may dispose of those pastures at will to whom it wills. There is still no acknowledgment that pastures are often the customary property of communities, but at least acknowledgment of the customary possession of and right to control certain pastures is now provided for in the draft law.

The creation of three classes of pastures—private, community, and public—will be practically helpful. Instead of public pastures being the only class of pastures, if the draft law is enacted, the designation "public pastures" will become a residual category, applying only to pastures that "are unable to be categorised as community pastures, due to their long history of established use by communities and nomadic pastoralists who do not reside in the area" (art. 2(12)). And even these pastures will be subject to local community-based management.

Where nomads like Pashtun Kuchi are able to demonstrate a long history of seasonal access to such pastures, the draft law directs that they will receive assistance to negotiate access with local communities. Only when local negotiations and district and provincial mediation fail will Kuchi be able to appeal to a presidentally appointed commission that will decide the matter (art. 22).

Taking stock

That policy makers could draft a rangeland law without it mimicking contested laws and policies of the past suggests that, after many years of debate inside and outside the government, Afghan disputes over pasture rights are well on their way to resolution. However, the situation was and remains more complex than that. Among many Hazara, retention of any traditional pastureland as public property continues to be an alarming proposition, not least because their most valuable pastures are those most likely to be identified as public, and it is those that they most likely would be coerced into sharing with Kuchi. Some Kuchi representatives resent their interests being made secondary, but they also acknowledge that they will regain at least some of their former (pre-1978) access to the central highlands (UNEP 2009). Yet other Kuchi representatives continue to press for recognition of their royal entitlement to high pastures, a call that has now been taken up with violent stridency by one or two powerful clan leaders.

Meanwhile, some officials still find it difficult to envision a future in which the government does not own and control pasturelands. This variously reflects

---

[7] Despite periodic redrafting of the Rangeland Law that continues up to the time of this writing, its purpose has remained the same.

fear of loss of rental opportunities; persistent conservatism within which devolution and democratization in any form struggles to take root; and a conviction that when interethnic contestation occurs, government must take control. These reactions were evident in the process of drafting a clear provision recognizing that many pastures are, by custom and current practice, the customary property of rural communities. In essential ways, the draft Rangeland Law is at odds with the principles laid out in the National Land Policy approved in 2007. Significantly, even with continuing amendments to limit community ownership of pastures, the Rangeland Law has not yet reached parliament. It is now nine years since a new rangeland law was proposed.

Characteristic orthodoxies contribute to the likelihood that the government will recapture its former roles vis-à-vis substantial pastures. These orthodoxies include beliefs that the state is the safest owner and guardian of degradable natural resources; that the state has the personnel and financial means to guard and regulate every pasture; and that the state will not be as vulnerable as it was in the past to rampant self-interest on the part of some officials and politicians. Most important, perhaps, is characteristic discomfort with the notion that collective assets are ownable and registrable as real property.

Such orthodox positions resonate with conservative Afghan officials. For example, in 2009, the Ministry of Justice returned a draft Forest Law to the Ministry of Agriculture because the ministry considered it too radical, even though the draft law shied away from providing for community ownership of forests or any hint that forests could, by custom, be considered already owned and not state property. At most the draft Forest Law provided for communities to be involved in management. A more potent factor strengthening the government's relunctance to surrender rights to communities is the government's wish to be able to freely lease rangelands to investors. Thus, for example, in July 2008, the Law on Managing Land Affairs was amended mainly with this purpose in mind, establishing without doubt that these lands are under the state's authority.[8] This too contradicts the principles laid out in the 2007 National Land Policy.

Worsening conflicts between Hazara and Kuchi

While these contradictions in policy and law stymie change, conflicts between Hazara and Kuchi continue to multiply. Since 2007, Kuchi have taken to raising Taliban flags in incidents that mainly involve the killing of Hazara, the burning of hundreds of Hazara homes, and displacement of thousands of Hazara (*Daily Outlook* 2007, 2008). The spring of 2008 opened badly when a Kuchi member of parliament declared that only Pashtun are true Afghans and owners of pastures. As a consequence, Hazara took to the streets to demand that the Afghan army and coalition forces protect their lands from armed Kuchi invasion (UNAMA

[8] Law on Managing Land Affairs, July 2008, as published in Gazette No. 958.

2008). Hazara also expressed bitterness over the fact that Kuchi remained the only tribal group still exempt from disarmament (*Hazaristan Times* 2008).

In the spring of 2009, Hazara constructed trenches at strategic entry points to the central highlands amid evidence that Taliban were arming Kuchi and rumors of Iranian support for Hazara (Milich 2009; UNAMA 2009). Afghan National Army soldiers and Afghan police forces were deployed to the conflict areas, and a U.S. military mountain unit was positioned in Wardak Province, immediately to the east of the troubled zone. That summer, the U.S. force pursued its own strategy by handing out provisions and water to Kuchi encampments in an effort to discourage Kuchi movement to Hazara front lines and open warfare.

Just the year before, President Karzai had created the Commission for Resolving Land Disputes Involving Kuchis and Settled People, which was technically supported by the United Nations Assistance Mission in Afghanistan (UNAMA). However, by the summer of 2009, the commission's chair acknowledged that no progress had been made despite repeated meetings between high-level Kuchi and Hazara representatives, including Afghanistan's vice president, a Hazara. Escalation of the conflict was only preempted by the onset of winter and the return of Kuchi to their warmer home areas in the south and east of the country. Heightened tensions and the Taliban's involvement in the conflict suggested, however, that open violence would recur the following spring when armed Kuchi would again attempt to enter Hazarajat with their livestock.

TOWARD A NEW APPROACH (2009–2010)

In light of the worsening situation, UNEP took the initiative to help the Ministry of Agriculture adopt a more grassroots approach to resolution of the pasturelands conflict. It funded this author to help the ministry devise a plan of action focusing on the violence-torn eastern entry points to the central highlands. The plan was formally adopted by the ministry, supported by UNAMA and the president's resolution commission, and implemented, starting in 2010 (MAIL 2009; UNEP 2009).

Guided by five parameters and eleven working principles, the plan's central strategic goal was the adoption of a community-based and pasture-specific approach to resolution. Several of the plan's important general features are noted below.

Maximizing opportunity for compromise

The most salient feature was that it was necessary to cease attempts to help top Kuchi and Hazara politicians and leaders agree, given their demonstrated reluctance to be seen as compromisers by their respective ethnic communities. High-level agreements face other challenges as well, including the difficulty of engineering compromises specific enough to fit local needs for practical, workable solutions. For example, blanket decisions were not feasible when it came to whether or not

Kuchi owned the alpine pastures or whether or not they were permitted to use these pastures at a time when population growth, expansion of cultivation into pasturelands, and worsening degradation of remaining pastureland have curtailed even the most modest local Hazara grazing activity. In addition, failure to achieve high-level, national agreement implied to some that the pasture conflict was irresolvable, increasing anxieties and entrenching positions along all-or-nothing lines.

Localization to limit self-seeking and violence

A more localized approach to resolution often allows for the considerable, positive, and useful social familiarity between Hazara and Kuchi to be brought to bear. Not all Hazara-Kuchi relations over the last century have been antagonistic, but more positive relations have been difficult to pursue as long as power brokers on both sides find it advantageous for the dispute to continue or even escalate. These power brokers include Kuchi and Hazara with no historical ties to the areas involved, some of whom have ambitions that are more economic than political. For example, some have used the dispute to secure large swaths of highland pasture for commercial livestock-fattening ventures.

Accordingly, the plan laid out a procedure that enabled only descendants of Kuchi families who could demonstrate a history of long-standing, seasonal use of specific pastures prior to 1978 to be party to negotiations. Included in the procedure was identification of families by Kuchi and Hazara communities alike and vetting of claims against registered Kuchi entitlements and transfers. The process sought to distinguish Kuchi claims that are based solely on acquisition of farmlands in Hazarajat from claims based on specific grants or purchases of pasturelands.

A more localized approach was intended to make it easier to tackle disarmament through deployment of Afghan National Security forces in areas subject to facilitated negotiation, as well as deportation of known provocateurs on both sides. Coalition forces agreed in principle to assist as necessary.

Opening the way for practical and diverse resolution

On-site consultation by disputing parties worked to enable joint Kuchi and Hazara assessments of the condition and scope of the particular pastures in dispute. Technically proficient facilitators were provided. These assessments were preceded by rapid reconnaissance in each main district to broadly rank pasture condition; eliminate pastures that, by location and size, were obviously private or village-adjacent domains; assess local acceptance of renewed Kuchi access; and identify alternative areas (in main districts) for possible redirection of accepted Kuchi claims. Of necessity, alternative districts included inner Hazarajat, to which Kuchi have sought to migrate.

In addition, agreements were reached through and locked into pasture-specific regulations, including measures for rehabilitation, and Kuchi access was conditioned on participation in and compliance with these regulations (as well as other developed and apparent plans and rules).

Distinguishing between what is legal and what is just

The plan's approach aimed to overcome a founding procedural conundrum in the dispute: the Kuchi have held legal entitlements to land estates customarily held by Hazara, but the Hazara have never accepted these grants as rightful. Under these circumstances, most facilitating parties, including the government, have accepted that recourse to legal evidence of Kuchi ownership is insufficient for resolution. While on-site, face-to-face negotiations aimed to limit this deadlock, tangible arrangements were offered in which, for example, the parties could acknowledge local Hazara as the customary owners of the given pasture but also recognize Kuchi claims to the right of viable, seasonal access—a right to be upheld where locational, social, and environmental factors in the area indicate that this is possible. Where agreement on such modifications was not possible—or where environmental and other factors would make Kuchi access impractical—reparation was considered in exchange for a decision by Kuchi clans to surrender past rights.

In addition, practical assistance was provided to Kuchi who wished to settle permanently in their home areas to the east and south. Such voluntary sedentization has been pronounced since the end of the civil war (de Weijer 2007; Milich 2009).

PREPARING FOR IMPLEMENTATION

Expert technical and mediation facilitation is essential to success, along with funding. As a sign of commitment, the government of Afghanistan pledged to use its own budget to cover implementation costs and to engage local and international nongovernmental organizations (NGOs) known to be skilled in peacebuilding and negotiation. In addition, UNEP committed to making senior technical advisers available.

Backup actions included (1) steps to help Kuchi bring their winter pastures in the south and east under community-based jurisdiction and management to address encroachment, not the least of which was by fellow nonpastoral Pashtun seeking to expand poppy production; (2) encouraging the government to move forward with finalization and enactment of the Rangeland Law; (3) building upon the success of pilot cases of local adoption of pasture rehabilitaton as amply launched under the FAO-funded SALEH project; and (4) national programming and funding searches to put community-based pasture management on a wider footing, working in an increasing number of provinces beyond those in the central highlands.

Leading up to the implementation, continued insecurity, uncertain safe access to key areas, and Talibanization of Kuchi pastoralist communities presented complications that overlaid more chronic political turmoil and governance problems. And once implementation was underway, it was still difficult to secure a speedy resolution to the long and bitter contestation between settled and pastoral communities over pasture rights.

Already handicapped by weak rule of law, the government suffers from chronic indecision at all levels when it comes to contentious subjects, and that can put even the smallest achievement at risk. The seminal SALEH pilot project regularly confronted such indecision, which was sometimes compounded by the personal interests of officials. This occurred, for example, when senior regional officials refused to endorse the decisions of local community pasture managers to limit open-ended access by nonlocal livestock owners to heavily degraded pastures for fear that this would limit the officials' own ability to send their large herds of animals to those areas. Nor would the officials follow up on charging lorry owners for taking out large loads of pasture bushes for sale as fuel to urban restaurants, even when it became clear who owned the lorries and when they were given all the details by the community pasture managers (Alden Wily 2008b). Such experiences greatly diminished community will to protect public pastures exposed to these issues, but they also hardened communities' resolve that as many pastures as possible would, one way or another, be recognized as their own communal property.

Of course, local communities are not uniformly steadfast in their handling of natural resource tenure disputes. At times, prior to implementation, inter-village competition—usually aided by the continued influence of former warlords, some of whom hold powerful government positions—thwarted progress. Fortunately, both the SALEH and ADB-funded pilot projects midwived an equal if not greater counterbalancing experience, helping communities to reach some difficult compromises. With its longer time frame, the SALEH project showed that this kind of progress can be sustained and even replicated by neighboring communities enduring comparable conflict and natural resource competition (UNEP 2009).

IMPLEMENTATION AND BEYOND

The various considerations outlined in this chapter were consolidated in a strategy for resolving conflicting claims to high pasturelands (UNEP 2009). After the strategy was delivered to Afghanistan's Office of the President, it was used as a general reference in programming preparation. However, the ambitious, integrated strategy was not implemented as envisioned. The strategy has nonetheless been influential in the design and implementation of field-level development projects in Afghanistan. Recommendations outlined in the plan informed several projects in addressing conflict by promoting community-based dispute resolution, as well as the national program for reintegration of former combatants. In addition, the methodologies and modalities established through the process documented in this chapter to help secure community land rights and the analytical framework to recognize community land claims has influenced related land policies (RRI et al. 2013; Alden Wily 2012, 2013). Three projects illustrate how the ideas and approaches articulated in the strategy have been manifested in the design and implementation of natural resource–related projects in Afghanistan: Solidarités International's community mapping efforts in Bamyan Province; the Afghanistan Pastoral Engagement, Adaptation, and Capacity Enhancement (PEACE) project; and the Afghanistan Peace and Reintegration Programme (APRP).

Using the tested guidelines developed by the SALEH pilot project, which ran from 2006 to 2008, several international and local NGOs have continued to assist rural communities to map and secure high pastures under their jurisdiction. One such example is Solidarités International. Solidarités International has assisted over one hundred villages in Bamyan Province to bring 800 square kilometers of pasturelands under community control (Solidarités International 2013; Alden Wily 2013a).

The PEACE project presented an innovative approach to resolve community-level land conflicts (USAID 2013). PEACE offered a training workshop on conflict resolution and peacebuilding strategies for select Kuchi and Hazara community members. After the training, five leaders from each community were selected to act as so-called "Peace Ambassadors." These peace ambassadors shared their learning with other community members, sought support for peaceful resolutions, and worked with other peace ambassadors to reach their goals (Jacobs et al. 2009). With the help of the peace ambassadors, the project has facilitated resolution of over 2,300 local conflicts (USAID 2013).

The APRP is a UN initiative to reintegrate former combatants back into civilian life. Through the APRP, over 7,000 former combatants have renounced violence, received livelihoods assistance, and undergone reintegration (UNDP n.d.). Reintegration projects, such as vocational training, reforestation, fruit orchards, and irrigation, have provided necessary skills and job opportunities for over 1,000 former insurgents and benefited over 15,000 community members.

Newly proposed amendments to two principal land laws evidence the strategy's impact on national land policies. Enormous strides have been made in the content of the basic land law of Afghanistan, the Land Management Law. Revisions to this long-standing law were proposed in 2012 that introduced, for the first time, community land as a lawful class of landholding (Alden Wily 2012, 2013a).[9] Equally important are the amendments to the Land Expropriation Law being recommended by the Afghan Land Authority (Alden Wily 2013b). Current drafts propose that compensation for the subsistence value of rangelands be paid to communities when their local pastures are lawfully taken for public purposes, including mine developments (Alden Wily 2013b).

---

9 The Ministry of Justice has not yet forwarded, as of March 2014, the proposed changes to parliament.

LESSONS LEARNED

Amid the hard and negative experiences, positive lessons have been learned. Most relate to the utility of adopting community-based approaches to policy and practical natural resource problems, and to the necessity of pursuing—sooner rather than later—an integrated approach to resource conflicts, tenure reform, and environmental and resource governance concerns.

Using experiential learning to move forward

More specifically, the utility of adopting practical piloting as a means to move debates forward in positive and workable directions has been demontrated by the experiences in Afghanistan. Piloting has proved its value in many ways, including the following:

- It has helped to overcome highly charged political and ethnic contestation that has not readily responded to resolution at the national level.
- It has enabled wary or conservative officials to be directly exposed to new possibilities and, when they participate in trial developments themselves, to gain formal ownership of the process.
- It has provided an opportunity to set practical precedents, which can become a force for change.
- It has offered concrete opportunities for at least some communities to have direct input into the development of new approaches to long-standing conflicts. This is critical not only for workability, but also for public ownership of shifting policy and legal paradigms and for improved understanding of the implications of change for local livelihoods.
- It has opened a range of potential routes to resolve standing disputes over natural resources through work with real situations and new sets of actors—not just community leaders, politicians, and officials, but also ordinary people most directly affected by the dispute.
- It has demonstrated repeatedly that ordinary communities have the capacity to compromise and act, helping to overcome deadlocks unresolvable at the national level, when communities are given the incentive and opportunity and when there is an absence of political contraints.
- It urges planners to create community-specific solutions instead of relying on generalized policies and strategies.
- It has afforded opportunities to test and learn from new approaches in what will usually be much-changed circumstances.
- It has enabled national policy makers to acknowledge, capture, and consider diverse circumstances in several parts of the country when they are making decisions.
- It has helped policy makers to view changes in selected areas as models and first cases, especially in matters where incremental implementation will always be the necessary mode of operation.

- It has enabled progress in situations where continued warfare or conflicts elsewhere in the country severely hinder such progress at a more comprehensive, national level.

Although such benefits broadly apply to most contested resource access situations, being able to shift the examination of the issues down to the field level is doubly important in countries like Afghanistan, where the rule of law is weak; where, in the absence of popular ownership, legal dictates are less than meaningful and are subject to manipulation; where people's experience with leading social change is limited; and where, because whole parts of the country are cut off from working governance, self-reliance has enormous potential to thrive, largely out of necessity.

As experienced in Afghanistan, it is not easy for a highly centralized government to eschew the conventional route of developing policies and new legal paradigms in the corridors of power and bureaucracy first. If grounded piloting is to take the lead, characterizing or constructing such projects as learning-by-doing research can be helpful—as was the case with the FAO- and ADB-supported projects. It is also important to place these activities under the aegis of the government.

Of course, reformation of policies and laws continues to be essential, and a lack of experiential learning can greatly handicap the workability and acceptability of new policies and laws. Learning-by-doing approaches are slowly but increasingly proving to be a sound way forward, even in nonconflicted societies such as Tanzania (Alden Wily 2008c). In the case of Afghanistan, if more orthodox intentions had been sustained, the likely result would have been reinstatement of pre-war pastoral policies and yet more death and destruction. It is a subjective but not casually drawn conclusion that opening opportunities through grounded piloting for structural review of old paradigms has done (and will continue to do) much to keep Afghanistan's pastoral conflict from falling into unbridled intertribal warfare.

The need to reach the nub of what is contested

Identifying exactly what needs reform is a complex but necessary process. The Kuchi and Hazara conflict over the pastures has obvious ethnic and religious dimensions that each side continues to use to give identity to and build solidarity around their respective claims. While one cannot discount these dimensions, they cannot be allowed to divert attention from the need to address other underlying and potent drivers of the conflict. Failure to effectively address conflict drivers will result in their rising up again and again as instruments of civil disorder.

It is often the case in agrarian conflicts that reform of the pattern of land relations cannot be avoided. Usually the root conflict has less to do with differences in ethnicity or religion, or even with competing land use systems, and more to do with property rights. Governmental administrations and international advisers often shy away from this recurring lesson. Even if they did not, the reality is that issues of territorial dominion and, more specifically, of customary communal ownership of collective land assets cannot sustainably be manipulated and downgraded at the will of the state. Livelihood relationships with land are too tightly dependent, and convictions around what is "our land" and what are "our rights" too deeply held, to allow lasting subordination to the state's will.

As the many conflicts around indigenous rights in Latin America and especially in Africa illustrate, persistent inattention to chronic dispossession can engender violence and even civil war, especially where reallocation of lost lands is seen as unfair (Pantuliano 2009). On a practical level, as the SALEH project was quick to point out, reluctance to recognize that customary rights amount to ownership removes an opportunity to use the distinction between ownership and access rights as a mechanism through which bitter conflicts between settled and nomadic peoples might be resolved (Alden Wily 2006a).

Helping government understand its role in natural resource conflicts

An associated general lesson is that governments are unwise to dismiss natural resource disputes as merely matters of interethnic or interclass resolve. As is so often the case, the Afghanistan pasture dispute has potent roots in the national policies and laws that the government has pursued. But what government makes, government can unmake. Accordingly, an important potential remedy lies in working closely with government policy makers, including through experiential learning, to expose them to the positive potential of different paradigms.

Certain positions are remarkably common: for example, policy makers often perceive themselves to be best situated as beneficial landlords of lands perceived by one party or another as wrongfully taken. Yet a more modern perception limits government to the role of regulator (Alden Wily 2009). With each passing decade, a shift in paradigms with respect to valuable natural resources becomes more important, and alarmingly so, for the current global land grab is having a deep effect on the natural resource rights of thousands of communities in several Asian states, and of the rural poor in as many as eighteen African economies (Görgen et al. 2009; Unruh and Williams 2013). Nearly every circumstance involves legal but questionably legitimate government ownership of local communal natural resources, including important forest and rangeland resources. Early indications are that yet more natural resource–based conflicts may arise, mainly between people and their governments, as to the legitimacy of the law (Alden Wily 2010). As slow but progressing change in Afghanistan illustrates, the law is not always right, and it may also need to change.

Time is of the essence

This chapter has noted many constraints to progress. In the circumstances that have prevailed in Afghanistan, it is tempting for the government and aid agencies to put pasturelands conflict matters aside until war is over, rule of law is restored, and good governance is achieved. Realistically, that could be a very long-term undertaking, yet failure to act now would ignore the role natural resource conflicts play in misgovernance and in interethnic and political contestation and thereby ignore the potential that resolution of such conflicts has for bringing about sustainable peace. Efforts to resolve Afghanistan's pasturelands conflict are necessary to achieve a sustainable peace, for establishment of clear and fair rights to pastures remains of major concern to virtually all of Afghanistan's rural populations.

In the case of Afghanistan, delay in resolving the pasturelands conflict has proved dangerous so far, but it is hoped it will not be fatal. The government's weak response to date has been unavoidable, in part. Time is required for an administration, particularly one slow to change, to take ownership of such issues while a host of other demands press in. Yet, UN and bilateral agencies have also contributed to delays by investing only low levels of technical and financial assistance toward a solution.

Urgency to act in Afghanistan continues to increase, and action must get under way before Taliban or other insurgents more fully grasp that the pasturelands dispute can be a powerful social problem for them to resolve in ways that could return the country to more widespread and violent warfare. Once again, the power of contested rights to natural resources to engender conflict—both intertribal and between the state and its people—has been demonstrated. And once again, this requires fundamental paradigm changes to remove the thorns that drive contestation, as well as degradation and loss of precious natural resources.

REFERENCES

Alden Wily, L. 2003a. *Land and the constitution*. Kabul: Afghanistan Research and Evaluation Unit.

———. 2003b. *Land rights in crisis: Restoring tenure security in Afghanistan*. Kabul: Afghanistan Research and Evaluation Unit.

———. 2004a. *Land relations in Bamyan Province: Findings from a 15-village case study*. Kabul: Afghanistan Research and Evaluation Unit.

———. 2004b. *Looking for peace on the pastures: Rural land relations in Afghanistan*. Kabul: Afghanistan Research and Evaluation Unit.

———. 2005. *Step-by-step guidelines for facilitating the negotiation of pasture access by settled and nomadic users*. Kabul, Afghanistan: United States Agency for International Development, Rebuilding Agriculture Markets Program.

———. 2006a. *First note on the policy and legal implications of pasture piloting by the SALEH project in Bamyan Province*. Kabul, Afghanistan: Food and Agriculture Organization of the United Nations.

———. 2006b. *A review of pasture ownership and management in Bamyan Province, Afghanistan*. Kabul, Afghanistan: Food and Agriculture Organization of the United Nations.

———. 2008a. *Whose land is it? Commons and conflict states: Why the ownership of the commons matters in making and keeping peace*. Washington, D.C.: Rights and Resources Initiative. www.rightsandresources.org/publication_details.php?publicationID=853.

———. 2008b. *The pasture story: Trying to get it right in Afghanistan—The SALEH experience*. Kabul, Afghanistan: Food and Agriculture Organization of the United Nations.
———. 2008c. *Community based pasture management (CBPM) in Afghanistan: Guidelines for facilitators; Helping communities to bring pastures under conservation management*. Kabul, Afghanistan: Food and Agriculture Organization of the United Nations / Ministry of Agriculture, Irrigation and Livestock, Islamic Republic of Afghanistan.
———. 2009. Tackling land tenure in the emergency to development transition in post-conflict states. In *Uncharted territory: Land, conflict and humanitarian action*, ed. S. Pantuliano. Rugby, Warwickshire, UK: Practical Action Publishing.
———. 2010. Whose land are you giving away, Mr. President? Presentation to World Bank, "Annual Bank Conference on Land Policy and Administration," Washington, D.C., April 26–27.
———. 2012. Land governance at the crossroads: A review of Afghanistan's proposed new Land Management Law. Afghanistan Research and Evaluation Unit Briefing Paper Series, October. www.areu.org.af/Uploads/EditionPdfs/1212E%20Land%20Reform%20I%20BP%20Oct%202012.pdf.
———. 2013a. *Land, people, and the state in Afghanistan: 2002–2012*. Kabul: Afghanistan Research and Evaluation Unit.
———. 2013b. Protecting people's interests? A social analysis of Land Expropriation Law of Afghanistan. July. Unpublished report on file with the author.
Banzet, A., C. Bousquet, B. Boyer, A. de Geoffroy, F. Grünewald, D. Kauffmann, P. Pascal, and N. Rivière. 2007. *Linking relief, rehabilitation and development in Afghanistan to improve aid effectiveness: Main successes and challenges ahead*. Group URD. www.urd.org/IMG/pdf/LRRD_main_successes_challenges_URD.pdf.
Canfield, R. L. 1986. Ethnic, regional and sectarian alignments in Afghanistan. In *The state, religion and ethnic politics: Pakistan, Iran and Afghanistan*, ed. A. Banuazizi and M. Weiner. Syracuse, NY: Syracuse University Press.
Daily Outlook. 2007. Kochis hoist Taliban flag in Behsood. June 24.
———. 2008. Afghanistan's Hazaras protest over pastures. March 31.
de Weijer, F. 2005. Report on proceedings of the "Conference on Afghan Pastoralists (Kuchi)," November 15–17. Kabul, Afghanistan: United States Agency for International Development, Rebuilding Agriculture Markets Program. http://cnrit.tamu.edu/pdfs/AfghanPastorlistConference01.06.pdf.
———. 2006. Status report on the pasture access negotiations in Nawor District. United States Agency for International Development, Rebuilding Agriculture Markets Program.
———. 2007. Afghanistan's *Kuchi* pastoralists: Change and adaptation. *Nomadic Peoples* 11 (1): 9–37.
Favre, R. 2003. Grazing land encroachment: Joint helicopter mission to Dasht-e Laili, March 25–27, 2003. Kabul, Afghanistan: Food and Agriculture Organization of the United Nations.
Ferdinand, K. 2006. *Afghan nomads: Caravans, conflicts and trade in Afghanistan and British India 1800–1980*. Copenhagen, Denmark: Rhodos International Science and Art Publishers.
Foschini, F. 2013. The social wandering of the Afghan Kuchis: Changing patterns, perceptions and politics of an Afghan community. AAN Thematic Report No. 04/2013. Afghanistan Analysts Network. www.afghanistan-analysts.org/wp-content/uploads/2013/11/20131125_FFoschini-Kuchis.pdf.

Frederiksen, B. 1995. *Caravans and trade in Afghanistan: The changing life of the nomadic Nazarbuz*. London: Thames and Hudson.
Gawecki, M. 1980. The Hazara farmers of central Afghanistan: Some historical and contemporary problems. *Ethnologia Polona* 6:163–175.
Gebremedhin, Y. 2007. Land tenure and administration in rural Afghanistan: Legal aspects. Capacity Building for Land Policy and Administration Reform Project, Report No. 7. Kabul, Afghanistan: Asian Development Bank / United Kingdom Department for International Development.
Glatzer, B. 1981. Processes of nomadization in west Afghanistan. In *Contemporary nomadic and pastoral peoples: Asia and the North*, ed. P. C. Salzman. Williamsburg, VA: College of William and Mary.
Görgen, M., B. Rudloff, J. Simons, A. Üllenberg, S. Väth, and Lena Wimmer. 2009. *Foreign direct investment (FDI) in land in developing countries*. Eschborn, Germany: Deutsche Gesellschaft für Technische Zusammenarbeit (GTZ).
Gregorian, V. 1969. *The emergence of modern Afghanistan: Politics of reform and modernization, 1880–1946*. Palo Alto, CA: Stanford University Press.
Hazaristan Times. 2008. Muhaqiq says: Civil war if Kuchis' dispute not resolved. July 10.
Jacobs, M. J., I. Naumovski, C. A. Schloeder, and R. M. Dalili. 2009. Peace ambassadors: An innovative approach to community-level conflict resolution in Afghanistan. Research Brief No. 09-02-PEACE. Davis, CA: Global Livestock Collaborative Research Support Program. http://cnrit.tamu.edu/peace/pdfs/PEACE0902.pdf.
Larsson, J. 1978. *Status of alpine rangelands in central Afghanistan with special reference to the Ajar Valley Wildlife Reserve*. Kabul, Afghanistan: Food and Agriculture Organization of the United Nations.
Lee, J. 1996. *The "ancient supremacy": Bukhara, Afghanistan and the Battle for Balkh, 1731–1901*. New York: Brill Academic Publishing.
MAIL (Ministry of Agriculture, Irrigation and Livestock, Islamic Republic of Afghanistan). 2009. Peace on the pastures: Resolution of conflicts arising from competing claims of settled and nomadic communities to rangelands in Afghanistan. Project concept note. Kabul.
Male, B. 1982. *Revolutionary Afghanistan: A reappraisal*. London: Croom Helm.
Milich, L. 2009. The Behsud conflicts in Afghanistan: A blueprint to avoid further clashes in 2009 and beyond. *Eurasia Critic*, June, 26–33.
Mousavi, S. 1998. *The Hazaras of Afghanistan: An historical, cultural, economic and political study*. Surrey, UK: Curzon.
NRC (Norwegian Refugee Council). 2004. *Report on information and legal advice project: Afghanistan*. Kabul, Afghanistan.
Pantuliano, S., ed. 2009. *Uncharted territory: Land, conflict and humanitarian action*. Rugby, Warwickshire, UK: Practical Action Publishing.
Patterson, M. 2004. The Shiwa Pastures, 1978–2003: Land tenure changes and conflict in northeastern Badakhshan. Kabul: Afghanistan Research and Evaluation Unit.
Pedersen, G. 1994. *Afghan nomads in transition: A century of change among the Zala Khan Khel*. London: Thames and Hudson.
Richards, P., ed. 2005. *No peace, no war: An anthropology of contemporary armed conflicts*. Athens: Ohio University Press.
Rosset, P., R. Patel, and M. Courville, eds. 2006. *Promised land: Competing visions of agrarian reform*. Oakland, CA: Food First Books.
RRI (Rights and Resources Initiative), International Land Coalition, Oxfam, International Union for Conservation of Nature, and HELVETAS Swiss Intercooperation. 2013.

Scaling-up strategies to secure community land and resource rights: An international conference to take stock of current efforts, identify promising strategies, and catalyze new alliances and action; Final report. Conference held at Interlaken, Switzerland, September 19–20. www.rightsandresources.org/documents/files/doc_6495.pdf.

Solidarités International. 2013. Community based pasture management, Yakawlang District, Bamyan Province, Afghanistan 2007–2013. Unpublished report on file with author.

Stanfield, J. D., M. Y. Safar, A. Salam, and Rural Land Administration Project Team. 2008. *Community rangeland administration: Focus on Afghanistan.* Mount Horeb, WI: Terra Institute.

UNAMA (United Nations Assistance Mission in Afghanistan). 2008. Security report. June 23. Kabul.

———. 2009. Security report. July. Kabul.

UNDP (United Nations Development Programme). n.d. Afghanistan Peace and Reintegration Programme (APRP). www.af.undp.org/content/afghanistan/en/home/operations/projects/crisis_prevention_and_recovery/aprp/.

UNEP (United Nations Environment Programme). 2009. *Recommended strategy for conflict resolution of competing high pasture claims of settled and nomadic communities in Afghanistan.* Kabul, Afghanistan. http://postconflict.unep.ch/publications/afg_tech/theme_01/afg_rangeland_EN.pdf.

UNHCR (United Nations High Commissioner for Refugees). 2004. *Data on land ownership and housing of refugees under assisted voluntary repatriation to Afghanistan.* Kabul, Afghanistan.

Unruh, J., and R. C. Williams. 2013. Lesson learned in land tenure and natural resource management in post-conflict societies. In *Land and post-conflict peacebuilding*, ed. J. Unruh and R. C. Williams. London: Earthscan.

USAID (United States Agency for International Development). 2013. Afghanistan Pastoral Engagement, Adaptation, and Capacity Enhancement (PEACE) project. Executive summary. http://cnrit.tamu.edu/peace/pdfs/PEACE_ExecSumm_Final_Report_13_web.pdf.

———. n.d. Afghanistan: USAID country profile; Property rights and resource governance. http://usaidlandtenure.net/sites/default/files/country-profiles/full-reports/USAID_Land_Tenure_Afghanistan_Profile.pdf.

World Bank. 2011. Afghanistan: Priorities for agriculture and rural development. web.worldbank.org/WBSITE/EXTERNAL/COUNTRIES/SOUTHASIAEXT/EXTSAREGTOPAGRI/0,,contentMDK:20273762~menuPK:548212~pagePK:34004173~piPK:34003707~theSitePK:452766,00.html.

PART 2

Innovative livelihood approaches in post-conflict settings

Introduction

Because livelihood issues often lie at the heart of conflict, the failure to address such issues in context-sensitive ways can impede peacebuilding and hinder social and economic development. The structural adjustment programs instituted in Central America in the 1990s, for example, not only ignored the rampant economic inequality underlying the region's extensive history of conflict, but may even have exacerbated post-conflict tensions (Paris 2004).

A number of agencies and organizations have attempted to develop innovative, context-sensitive programs to promote livelihoods after conflict. The seven case studies in part 2 of this book explore these approaches. Although the initiatives vary significantly in scope, context, and geography, they illustrate the importance of fostering sustainable economic growth—not only to generate dividends for national governments and formerly warring parties, but to support communities that have been scarred by conflict and that will serve as the primary sites for the reintegration of excombatants into society.

The post-conflict period offers an opportunity to reorient predominant livelihoods toward greater sustainability—an opportunity that is especially important where disputes over natural resources contributed to the cause or financing of conflict, or where violence occurred in or near important ecosystems. Post-conflict recovery can thus benefit from creative solutions that enable communities to incorporate their natural resource wealth into a sustainable approach to livelihoods that not only generates income but fosters cooperation and reconciliation.

Each chapter in part 2 considers innovative pathways to sustainable, natural resource–based livelihood opportunities in post-conflict situations. The first three chapters describe how transboundary protected areas, including peace parks, can promote peacebuilding by creating and supporting livelihoods, cooperation, and other peacebuilding objectives. Transboundary protected areas are a creative means of linking peacebuilding to conservation and ecotourism, and thereby facilitating cooperation between adversaries and promoting socioeconomic development. In "Transboundary Protected Areas: Opportunities and Challenges," Carol Westrik describes how peace parks and other transboundary protected areas can promote livelihood creation, fostering employment both directly (through the management of such areas) and indirectly (through increased ecotourism). By encouraging former adversaries to cooperatively manage shared natural resources, protected areas not only provide the stability necessary to support viable livelihoods but also encourage sustained peace.

The political will and institutional frameworks needed to establish peace parks are not always present in post-conflict situations, however. In "A Peace Park in the Balkans: Cross-Border Cooperation and Livelihood Creation through Coordinated Environmental Conservation," J. Todd Walters considers a proposed transboundary peace park in Albania, Montenegro, and Kosovo as a means of easing tensions in a conflict-affected region and generating natural resource–related opportunities in conservation and ecotourism. The failure to formally establish the necessary national parks in Albania, Montenegro, and Kosovo has so far prevented the creation of a proposed transboundary park that would include the three national parks. Walters argues, however, that a multitrack approach—in which local officials and residents, nongovernmental organizations, and members of the international community all engage simultaneously—could shift incentive structures, ultimately producing sufficient political support to push officials to formally establish the national parks. The kinds of initiatives Walters describes can also encourage individuals and organizations to work together to create sustainable livelihood opportunities that will enable residents to remain in their communities.

The protection of culturally and biologically important symbols provides yet another means of supporting local livelihoods and building peace in post-conflict situations. In "Mountain Gorilla Ecotourism: Supporting Macroeconomic Growth and Providing Local Livelihoods," Miko Maekawa, Annette Lanjouw, Eugène Rutagarama, and Douglas Sharp explore the livelihood benefits achieved through transboundary management of the mountain gorilla population in a protected area shared by Rwanda, Uganda, and the Democratic Republic of the Congo (DRC). Despite facing various challenges in establishing ecotourism as a viable livelihood option and maintaining sufficient political stability to support the growing industry, Rwanda and Uganda have expanded tourism by developing effective pricing and economic plans for the park, engaging in public outreach, marketing ecotourism nationally and internationally, and gaining the participation and support of the private sector through regulatory reform of the tourism industry. Moreover, the two countries have reinvented their ecotourism sectors while addressing both the conservation needs of the mountain gorilla population and the economic and livelihood needs of local communities. (DRC has yet to achieve the political stability necessary to support a thriving tourism industry.)

The successful disarmament, demobilization, and reintegration (DDR) of former combatants has been identified as one of the most important—if not *the* most important—factor in the success or failure of post-conflict peacebuilding (SIDDR 2006). By providing viable livelihood opportunities to individuals who might otherwise be vulnerable to recruitment into armed groups, peacebuilders can actively engage excombatants and conflict-affected communities in economic redevelopment, thereby increasing the likelihood of successful recovery and lasting peace.

In addition to placing considerable stress on local ecosystems, conflict undermines social cohesion, making it difficult for excombatants to move beyond their wartime roles. In "The Interface between Natural Resources and Disarmament, Demobilization, and Reintegration: Enhancing Human Security in Post-Conflict Situations," Glaucia Boyer and Adrienne M. Stork posit that DDR approaches designed to reintegrate both excombatants and conflict-affected individuals into civilian society can be strengthened through the incorporation of resource-related livelihood opportunities—which, in turn, can increase security in conflict-affected regions. In place of a linear model, in which livelihoods are not addressed until reintegration, the authors argue for a livelihoods-based approach, which includes livelihood support schemes at each phase of the DDR process. Such an approach, centered on access to and management of natural resources, can increase excombatants' incentives to move toward a peace economy. Boyer and Stork offer four case studies—from Afghanistan, Colombia, Indonesia, and Mozambique—in which excombatants used their wartime skills and experiences to develop productive livelihoods that were closely tied to sustainable natural resource management.

Although most DDR programs provide opportunities for excombatants to join new national security forces, additional employment opportunities are still needed. In "From Soldiers to Park Rangers: Post-Conflict Natural Resource Management in Gorongosa National Park," Matthew F. Pritchard explores the DDR process in the aftermath of the civil war in Mozambique. Recognizing the civil war's devastating effects on the park (forces on both sides had hunted game and destroyed park infrastructure), government officials retrained and hired a group of excombatants to act as game wardens and park rangers. The program enabled the excombatants to use the skills they had developed during the civil war, including tracking and spending extended time in the bush, in their new roles as game wardens and park rangers. Although the scope of the program is modest, it demonstrates the potential for integrating natural resource–related livelihoods into DDR programs. National governments looking to adopt this model must promote acceptance of reintegration by working closely with adjacent communities, particularly to ensure ongoing access to natural resources necessary for sustainable livelihoods.

The need for sustainable post-conflict livelihood opportunities is even more acute in countries facing a significant youth bulge. In "Mitigating Conflict in Sierra Leone through Mining Reform and Alternative Livelihoods Programs for Youth," Andrew Keili and Bocar Thiam identify the challenges impeding post-conflict recovery, including a lack of transparency and accountability in mining revenue management, the difficulty of reintegrating excombatants into the labor force, disputes over mining rights, and problematic mining laws and regulations. The chapter's main focus, however, is on the challenge of providing viable livelihood alternatives for artisanal miners and unemployed youth in Sierra Leone.

During the country's protracted civil war, limited livelihood opportunities drove youth into mining camps and urban centers, where many were recruited by armed rebel groups. Today, Sierra Leone's diamonds—long a source of employment and livelihoods—are being exhausted, and the country is beginning to explore other livelihood options. Many of the alternative livelihood programs reviewed by the authors focus on reclaiming mining land for agriculture; others feature microloans, job training, or assistance with developing business plans. The authors conclude that such programs constitute a step in the right direction, but that lack of funding and political commitment risks undermining the programs' success.

Ultimately, no suite of programs can create sustainable post-conflict economic development without the active participation of the private sector. Multitiered value chains that add economic value (and livelihood opportunities), from natural resource extraction through processing and final sale, can facilitate private sector involvement and help countries capitalize more fully on natural resource wealth. Such value chains must be sustainable, however, and should incorporate sound natural resource management practices. In "Linking to Peace: Using BioTrade for Biodiversity Conservation and Peacebuilding in Colombia," Lorena Jaramillo Castro and Adrienne M. Stork examine the BioTrade Initiative, a sustainable value chain program established by the United Nations Conference on Trade and Development (UNCTAD). Although the BioTrade Initiative was not created specifically for use in post-conflict situations, Jaramillo Castro and Stork argue that it could help link DDR and economic development to natural resource management, including biodiversity conservation. A review of several BioTrade Initiative programs in Colombia indicates that they promote conservation and sustainable natural resource use while providing the primary source of income for many local residents. Moreover, because BioTrade Initiative projects require a participatory process, stakeholders have the opportunity to work collaboratively and build partnerships, which helps support broader peacebuilding goals while preserving economic benefits. The authors warn, however, that future BioTrade projects in conflict-affected situations must be sensitive to conflict drivers and directly connected to peacebuilding strategies.

Taken together, the seven chapters in part 2 offer a variety of creative and innovative ways to link post-conflict peacebuilding (including dialogue and co-operation) with livelihoods and sustainable natural resource management. Although the methods described may not succeed in every situation, the chapters provide a useful starting point for policy makers and practitioners. One of the most important lessons is the need to support both excombatants and conflict-affected communities, in order to avoid intensifying existing tensions or creating new rifts.

REFERENCES

Paris, R. 2004. *At war's end: Building peace after civil conflict.* Cambridge, UK: Cambridge University Press.

SIDDR (Stockholm Initiative on Disarmament Demobilisation Reintegration). 2006. Background studies. Stockholm: Swedish Ministry for Foreign Affairs.

Transboundary protected areas: Opportunities and challenges

Carol Westrik

Transboundary protected areas—parcels of land designated for joint protection by neighboring countries—can be important tools for post-conflict peacebuilding and environmental management. The benefits of transboundary protected areas are evidenced by their growth in popularity: in the late 1980s, there were fifty-nine; as of 2012, there were more than 600 (Balkans Peace Park Project n.d.).[1] This chapter discusses three kinds of transboundary protected areas: demilitarized zones (DMZs), World Heritage sites, and peace parks. The focus is primarily on the opportunities and challenges associated with the third category, international peace parks.

DMZs are areas where military activity has been severely restricted or banned altogether in an attempt to avoid further conflict. A DMZ can be formed through a peace treaty or ceasefire agreement; typically, both the respective countries' governments and the United Nations play a role in the establishment of a DMZ. Examples include the UN Buffer Zone in Cyprus; the Sinai Peninsula, between Egypt and Israel; and the DMZ between North Korea and South Korea.

World Heritage sites, which are designated by the United Nations Educational, Scientific and Cultural Organization (UNESCO), must be of "outstanding universal value" and meet one or more of ten criteria (UNESCO World Heritage Centre 2012, 2). Sites that meet criterion (ix), for example, are "outstanding examples representing significant on-going ecological and biological processes in the evolution and development of terrestrial, fresh water, coastal and marine ecosystems and communities of plants and animals"; and sites that meet criterion (x) are "the most important and significant natural habitats for in-situ conservation of biological diversity" (UNESCO World Heritage Centre 2012, 21).[2]

Carol Westrik holds a Ph.D. in post-war reconstruction and development and has her own consultancy as a heritage advisor.

1 See also UNEP (2009).

2 Countries adopted the Convention Concerning the Protection of World Cultural and Natural Heritage in 1972. UNESCO administers the convention, the full text of which is available at http://whc.unesco.org/en/conventiontext/.

Examples include Garamba National Park, in the Democratic Republic of the Congo, and Grand Canyon National Park, in the United States.

Peace parks—transboundary protected areas formed as part of a peace treaty or a multilateral peacetime agreement—symbolize peace and cooperation between nations. Examples include the Waterton-Glacier International Peace Park (UNESCO World Heritage Centre n.d.), which is shared by the United States and Canada, and the Cordillera del Cóndor peace park (IEDS n.d.), which is shared by Ecuador and Peru. The formation of a peace park often involves various parties, including the UN (for example, the United Nations Security Council or the United Nations Environment Programme), stakeholder governments, and nongovernmental organizations (NGOs) such as the International Union for Conservation of Nature (IUCN) or the Global Transboundary Conservation Network.

OPPORTUNITIES FOR PEACEBUILDING

Transboundary protected areas in general, and peace parks in particular, can strengthen post-conflict peacebuilding in several ways: by supporting negotiation and the withdrawal of troops; building trust; fostering economic development; facilitating disarmament, demobilization and reintegration (DDR); providing a neutral meeting place; and attracting international attention to the region. These are considered in turn.

Supporting negotiation and the withdrawal of troops

Transboundary peace parks offer valuable opportunities to promote cross-border cooperation and natural resource management. In the immediate aftermath of conflict, a park can provide a neutral location for meetings and negotiations. The designation of a peace park can also be used to resolve territorial disputes that might otherwise hinder the resolution of armed conflict. For example, even if adversaries would prefer to end a conflict, they may be reluctant to lose land and honor by withdrawing; establishing a neutral park in a contested area can "enable both armies to withdraw under conditions of honor and dignity" (Ali 2002, 318).

The Cordillera del Cóndor peace park demonstrates how protected areas can be used to encourage parties to withdraw armed forces from a contested region. Ecuador and Peru had engaged in border clashes for over 150 years. The Rio Protocol, a peace agreement signed in 1942, ended hostilities for a time, but failed to clearly define the new boundaries of the Cordillera del Cóndor region, leaving room for disagreements that eventually led to armed conflict in 1981 and 1995 (Franco 1997; Ali 2007). Finally, in 1998, the countries signed the Acta Presidencial de Brasilia, which committed them to withdraw from the disputed zone. Although only a relatively small part of the Cordillera del Cóndor region was designated as a protected area—two adjoining parcels on each side of the border—and the political conflict has yet to be completely resolved, a joint committee has been governing the development of the area in accordance with the

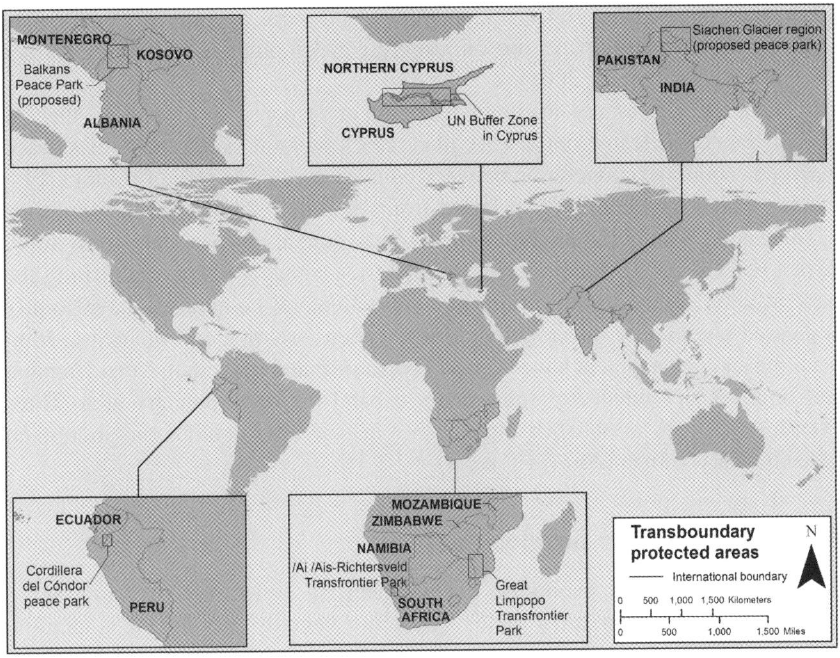

Bi-National Development Plan, and there has been no further armed conflict (Global Transboundary Conservation Network n.d.).

The Siachen Glacier region—a high-alpine area located in the Kashmir territory of India, and the subject of long-standing conflict between India and Pakistan—might benefit from the designation of a peace park (Tallone 2003). Despite an informal ceasefire in 2003 that ended nineteen years of open conflict, military forces remain stationed in the region, and both countries continue to lose forces because of the harsh living conditions. Creating a peace park in the disputed region might help resolve the conflict by allowing both sides to withdraw; in addition to protecting the environment, such a park would save money and lives (Ali 2002).

Building trust

By fostering trust—an essential element in peacebuilding—cooperation helps countries move toward a sustainable solution to conflict. Working together to achieve a common goal, such as the development and management of a peace park, enables former belligerents to learn from each other. Moreover, joint management of a peace park can create a foundation for working through more sensitive issues, such as the original causes of conflict and the presence of continuing tensions. To achieve this level of collaboration, the emphasis must be on shared management and responsibility: no one party should take charge. Acknowledging differences in available resources, authority, and legal systems is also vital to ensuring that all participants are on a more equal footing and avoiding further conflict (Sandwith et al. 2001).

Although it was not in direct result of or response to a conflict, the /Ai /Ais-Richtersveld Transfrontier Park illustrates how joint management of a peace park can encourage cooperation between countries with a history of conflict (PPF n.d.a). In an armed conflict that lasted from 1966 to 1988 and led to more than 8,000 deaths, Namibia (then South West Africa) sought independence from South Africa (UCDP 2013). Namibia and South Africa signed a treaty establishing the park in 2003. Since its inception, numerous bilateral committees have jointly addressed community development, conservation, security, and financing. Joint planning and development have been so cooperative and constructive that Namibia and South Africa intend to significantly expand the transboundary area. Thus, even a peace park established more than a decade after conflict can strengthen transboundary cooperation (PPF n.d.a).

Fostering economic development

Peace parks can spur economic development by generating or encouraging ecotourism—which, in turn, yields economic benefits that create a tangible incentive for former adversaries to maintain peace. In addition to providing direct employment by creating demand for park employees, ecotourism can spur indirect economic growth in nearby areas, in the form of stores and accommodations, along with possible opportunities for local residents to be employed as guides. The income generated should not only improve livelihoods but also encourage local communities to help protect and maintain the park. Local economies may also benefit from increased cross-border movement, which can provide merchants and manufacturers with access to new markets. Finally, relaxed borders may enable pastoralists to reach better land, thus improving regional food security and reducing the potential for pastoral-agricultural conflict (Pavanello 2010).

The proposed Balkans Peace Park provides a prime example of ecotourism opportunities. Situated between Albania, Kosovo, and Montenegro, the park has already created jobs in all three countries and promises to create more. Local residents have assisted with the early stages of park planning—for example, participating in biodiversity studies and water resource management projects. A fully functional park would create opportunities for alpinist organizations, local small businesses, and the local transportation industry, among other entities, thereby contributing significantly to regional stability in a post-conflict area.[3]

The Great Limpopo Transfrontier Park, which is intended to join existing parks in Mozambique, South Africa, and Zimbabwe into a single protected area, offers another example of economic development potential (Siyabona Africa

[3] For more discussion on the Balkans Peace Park, see J. Todd Walters, "A Peace Park in the Balkans: Cross-Border Cooperation and Livelihood Creation through Coordinated Environmental Conservation," in this book.

n.d.). The three existing parks, which include South Africa's Kruger National Park, are popular destinations that have already boosted their respective national economies (PPF n.d.a, n.d.b, n.d.c). Kruger National Park alone attracts almost 1 million visitors a year, generating approximately US$30 million (Saayman and Saayman 2006). The creation of a transboundary protected area is expected to benefit all three countries, bringing more tourists to Zimbabwe and Mozambique and boosting South Africa's considerable tourist appeal by expanding the park area, increasing support for park development and management, and helping to ensure stable and peaceful relations with its neighbors.

Facilitating DDR

Peace parks can support peacebuilding and economic development through the employment of former combatants. The UN approach to DDR is designed to help excombatants reintegrate into civilian life, in part by providing sustainable livelihood opportunities. As the following chapters explore in greater detail, protected areas in general, and peace parks in particular, directly support post-conflict peacebuilding by creating employment opportunities for excombatants—for example, as park rangers or ecotourism guides.

Mozambique and Indonesia both illustrate successful efforts to integrate DDR into the development of protected areas. In 1994, Mozambique's Gorongosa National Park hired seventy-six former combatants to provide much-needed repairs and help reestablish control of the park, which had been occupied by militant groups during the conflict. The excombatants were hired because they knew the locations of landmines and wildlife, and possessed the necessary skills to track and apprehend poachers.[4]

Indonesia's Aceh region, where 70 percent of the forest is under some form of protection, has seen a huge boom in ecotourism since the conflict subsided, in 2005; as of 2008, more than 400 tourism sites had been established. Seeking employees with strong local knowledge, tourism companies hired former rebels who had operated as combatants in the jungles.[5] As in Mozambique, hiring excombatants has helped with reintegration while strengthening the local economy. Because transboundary parks offer similar tourism and employment opportunities, DDR programs can also function at the transboundary level.

Providing a neutral meeting place

The neutral status of transboundary protected areas makes them a useful meeting place for hostile parties, as exemplified by the UN Buffer Zone on the island of

---

[4] For a discussion on this topic, see Matthew F. Pritchard, "From Soldiers to Park Rangers: Post-Conflict Natural Resource Management in Gorongosa National Park," in this book.

[5] For more information on integrating natural resources into DDR frameworks, see Glaucia Boyer and Adrienne M. Stork, "The Interface between Natural Resources and Disarmament, Demobilization, and Reintegration: Enhancing Human Security in Post-Conflict Situations," in this book.

Cyprus. Established as a temporary dividing line in 1964, the zone marks the boundary between the Republic of Cyprus, in the south, and the Turkish Republic of Northern Cyprus, to the north. Since the establishment of the zone, land that was once the scene of conflict became the only neutral meeting place on the island. Over the years, the UN Peacekeeping Force in Cyprus has facilitated meetings between northern and southern communities, as well cooperation on antimosquito programs, mixed farming, and water use—which was necessary because the demarcation line effectively divided the island's water resources (Westrik 2003).

Focusing international attention

Heightened international attention and involvement can help prevent conflict from escalating into violence. World Heritage sites, which can increase both tourism and the involvement of international organizations, are a prime example: areas designated as protected sites under international law benefit from the attention of the UN and other international organizations. And if violence does occur, World Heritage status can assist in obtaining support for the affected area that might otherwise be more difficult to secure.

The DRC provides a good example of the usefulness of World Heritage status. As of this writing, all five World Heritage sites in the DRC were included on the List of World Heritage in Danger, meaning that their "outstanding universal value" was deemed at risk. In 2004, the director-general of the Congolese Institute for Nature Conservation (Institut Congolais pour la Conservation de la Nature, or ICCN) noted that "the prospects for the future lay mainly in the commitment of the Congolese Government to support the conservation of the World Heritage sites" (UNESCO World Heritage Centre 2004, 108). Although the status of the parks has not insulated the sites from the effects of conflict, it has helped draw attention to their needs.

A number of parties—among them UNESCO, ICCN, and several NGOs, including the World Wide Fund for Nature and the Wildlife Conservation Society—have worked together to help protect the DRC sites on the danger list. At the height of the civil war, four of the five sites were in rebel-held territory, and the cooperating organizations were among the only groups in the area capable of providing support (UNESCO World Heritage Centre 2010). Despite having suffered some impacts from the conflict, a number of sites have shown signs of improvement—however fragile—including increased tourism and financial investment (Virunga National Park n.d.).

CHALLENGES FACING PROTECTED AREAS

Although peace parks offer significant opportunities to promote conflict resolution and post-conflict peacebuilding, a number of obstacles must be addressed before such opportunities can be brought to fruition. First and foremost, it is imperative that all fighting factions support the establishment of the park. In practical terms, this requires political goodwill and trust—as well as a durable agreement—between former adversaries. Without a strong framework, a peace park will not serve its intended purpose and could even trigger further conflict.

Once former belligerents have agreed to support the park, they must be given equitable footing with respect to developing and maintaining it. Rosaleen Duffy warns of the potential difficulties that may arise when some partners stand to gain more than others by establishing a park. If the parties feel that they are not receiving fair representation or benefits, the situation could easily devolve into further conflict (Duffy 2007).

Even when initial obstacles are addressed, the parties may disagree about priorities, such as whether to promote economic development at the expense of environmental conservation, or vice versa. Managing tourism so as to maximize both of these objectives can be particularly difficult (Fennell 2008). Areas of disagreement must be addressed carefully, and with full participation of nearby communities, to sustain peaceful relations between all parties.

Although strong and continuous support from external actors can help overcome some of the challenges, such support may be hard to sustain: many aid groups tend to depart after open conflict has ceased. Fortunately, however, two primary resources can provide lasting support: first, NGOs such as IUCN and the Global Transboundary Conservation Network are devoted to sustaining peace parks; second, World Heritage status brings attention from UNESCO even after conflict has ended.

Although the challenges associated with establishing and maintaining peace parks are substantial, they are not insurmountable. The IUCN World Commission on Protected Areas (WCPA) has developed the following guidelines to help ensure that peace parks are developed in an inclusive, sustainable manner (Sandwith et al. 2001):

- Identify and promote common values.
- Involve and benefit local people.
- Obtain and maintain support of decision makers.
- Promote coordinated and cooperative activities.
- Achieve coordinated planning and protected area development.
- Develop cooperative agreements.
- Work toward funding sustainability.
- Monitor and assess progress.
- Deal with tension or armed conflict.

Each of these steps requires a great deal of time and effort, particularly in a post-conflict situation, but the potential payoff is substantial.

CONCLUSION

Protected areas establish a space where natural ecosystems can be revived; when such areas take the form of peace parks, they can also provide a number of additional benefits to peacebuilding. Peace parks must be carefully planned, developed, and maintained, however, to avoid exacerbating existing conflicts or inciting new ones. As more peace parks are developed, they can serve as positive examples of how to promote conservation while supporting local livelihoods, both of which are critical elements in the post-conflict peacebuilding and redevelopment process.

REFERENCES

Ali, A. 2002. A Siachen peace park: The solution to a half-century of international conflict? *Mountain Research Development* 22 (4): 316–319.

Ali, S., ed. 2007. *Peace parks: Conservation and conflict resolution.* Cambridge, MA: MIT Press.

Balkans Peace Park Project. n.d. Leaflet. www.balkanspeacepark.org/docs/uploaded/1298216906-leaflet_2lowres.pdf.

Duffy, R. 2007. Peace parks and global politics: The paradox and challenges of global governance. In *Peace parks: Conservation and conflict resolution*, ed. S. Ali. Cambridge, MA: MIT Press.

Fennell, D. 2008. *Ecotourism.* 3rd ed. New York: Routledge.

Franco, J. 1997. Peru Ecuador border dispute. ICE (Inventory of Conflict and Environment) Case Studies, Case No. 5. www1.american.edu/ted/ice/perecwar.htm.

Global Transboundary Conservation Network. n.d. Cordillera del Condor Transboundary Protected Area. www.tbpa.net/page.php?ndx=59.

IEDS (Institute for Environmental Diplomacy and Security). n.d. Cordillera del Condor—Negotiating a peace park. www.uvm.edu/ieds/node/154.

Pavanello, S. 2010. Working across borders: Harnessing the potential of cross-border activities to improve livelihood security in the Horn of Africa drylands. London: Humanitarian Policy Group.

PPF (Peace Parks Foundation). n.d.a. /Ai /Ais-Richtersveld Transfrontier Park. www.peaceparks.org/story.php?pid=1001&mid=1034.

———. n.d.b. Great Limpopo Transfrontier Park. www.peaceparks.org/tfca.php?pid=19&mid=1005.

———. n.d.c. Peace Parks Foundation. www.peaceparks.nl.

Saayman, M., and A. Saayman. 2006. Estimating the economic contribution of visitor spending in the Kruger National Park to the regional economy. *Journal of Sustainable Tourism* 14 (1): 67–81.

Sandwith, T., C. Shine, L. Hamilton, and D. Sheppard. 2001. *Transboundary protected areas for peace and co-operation.* Best Practice Protected Area Guidelines Series No. 7. Gland, Switzerland: International Union for Conservation of Nature. https://portals.iucn.org/library/efiles/edocs/pag-007.pdf.

Siyabona Africa. n.d. Archive news: Great Limpopo Transfrontier Park. www.nature-reserve.co.za/archive-news-transfrontier-park.html.

Tallone, G. 2003. Siachen peace park: A case study for the valorisation of high mountain ecosystems. Paper presented at the "Transboundary Protected Areas" workshop, 5th World Parks Congress, Durban, South Africa, September 12–13.

UCDP (Uppsala Conflict Data Program). 2013. UCDP conflict encyclopedia: South Africa. www.ucdp.uu.se/gpdatabase/gpcountry.php?id=142&regionSelect=2-Southern_Africa#.

UNEP (United Nations Environment Programme). 2009. *From conflict to peacebuilding: The role of natural resources and the environment.* Nairobi, Kenya. http://postconflict.unep.ch/publications/pcdmb_policy_01.pdf.
UNESCO (United Nations Educational, Scientific and Cultural Organization) World Heritage Centre. 2004. *Promouvoir et préserver le patrimoine congolais: Lier diversité biologique et culturelle.* Proceedings of the conference and workshops, Paris, September 13–17. http://unesdoc.unesco.org/images/0015/001501/150170f.pdf.
———. 2010. World Heritage in the Congo Basin. http://whc.unesco.org/uploads/activities/documents/activity-43-10.pdf.
———. 2012. Operational guidelines for the implementation of the World Heritage Convention. http://whc.unesco.org/archive/opguide12-en.pdf.
———. n.d. Waterton Glacier International Peace Park. http://whc.unesco.org/en/list/354.
Virunga National Park. n.d. About Virunga. www.visitvirunga.org/about-virung/#virungahistory.
Westrik, H. C. 2003. *Reading contested landscape: From buffer zone to peace tool; The case of Cyprus.* Ph.D. diss., University of York.

A peace park in the Balkans: Cross-border cooperation and livelihood creation through coordinated environmental conservation

J. Todd Walters

The peace movement of the 1960s and the growing sophistication of an environmental movement that embraced a scientific, evidence-based approach to advocacy helped pave the way for the development of international peace parks. In the post-apartheid and post-Soviet eras, these parks and their champions have introduced what Nelson Mandela calls "a concept that can be embraced by all" (Peace Park Foundation n.d.). Generations worth of labor have helped shape peace parks into a policy tool that helps resolve border disputes, stimulate cross-border cooperation, and generate opportunities for livelihood creation, particularly with a focus on environmental conservation, sustainable development, ecotourism, and geotourism.

This chapter begins by providing a brief history of international peace parks and highlights their significance in international diplomacy. It continues with an examination of multitrack diplomacy and the use of this approach in the development of a proposal for the Balkans Peace Park, a transboundary park to be shared and jointly managed by Albania, Montenegro, and Kosovo. In addition to transboundary cooperation, the initiative to create a peace park in this region illustrates another benefit of such approaches: the creation of sustainable livelihoods through the needed emphasis on natural resource management. A discussion of lessons learned from the project and the next steps needed for the Balkans Peace Park to be realized conclude the chapter.

THE VALUE OF INTERNATIONAL PEACE PARKS

Nelson Mandela, Ted Turner, and Mikhail Gorbachev have all become champions of a growing global movement to create international peace parks in response to some of the world's most daunting challenges in international diplomacy, environmental conservation, and cross-border cooperation in areas affected by conflict.

J. Todd Walters is the founder and executive director of International Peace Park Expeditions, which runs experiential peacebuilding expeditions, accredited academic expeditions, and professional collaborative mapping initiatives.

The seed for the concept was planted during the U.S. presidency of Theodore Roosevelt and at the beginning of the modern environmental conservation movement in the United States a century ago. In 1910, the United States established Glacier National Park, and over the next two decades Rotary International worked hard to link Glacier National Park to its Canadian counterpart, Waterton National Park, so the transboundary region could be jointly managed from an ecosystem perspective. In 1932, the U.S. Congress and the Parliament of Canada formally dedicated Waterton Glacier International Peace Park, widely recognized as the world's first international peace park (UNESCO and World Heritage Convention n.d.). It symbolizes the peaceful friendship between Canada and the United States and highlights new opportunities for cross-border collaboration.

International peace parks are an idealized conception of a larger conservation initiative—transboundary protected areas (Dudley 2008). The World Commission on Protected Areas (WCPA) of the International Union for Conservation of Nature (IUCN) defines transboundary protected areas as "areas that meet across international borders" and that "provide important opportunities for collaboration between managers and scientists in neighbouring countries." As the WCPA notes, "these areas provide possibilities for promoting biodiversity conservation and sustainable use across politically divided ecosystems, while at the same time encouraging international collaboration in management, the sharing of experience and the sharing of information" (WCPA n.d.).

International peace parks and other transboundary protected areas have similar core areas of focus, from environmental conservation at the ecosystem level to sustainable development requiring cross-border cooperation. Peace parks and transboundary protected areas in general can also help create local livelihoods and shift incentive structures toward conservation as a land use option.

International peace parks are distinguished from other transboundary protected areas, however, by being formally dedicated as a symbol of peace between two or more sovereign nations. Peace parks recognize conservation of not only environmental resources but also cultural and historical resources, and they are consciously utilized as a tool for international diplomacy. Their establishment can be written into treaties that end active conflicts in order to build trust and effective frameworks for interstate and intrastate cooperation after the conflict has ended. The distinction between international peace parks and other transboundary protected areas was elucidated in 2001 by IUCN, which declared that international peace parks are "transboundary protected areas that are formally dedicated to the protection and maintenance of biological diversity, and of natural and associated cultural resources, and to the promotion of peace and co-operation" (Sandwith et al. 2001, 3).

Whether peace parks promote peace or serve as a symbol of peace is the subject of a highly charged debate. According to positive peace theory, it is important to recognize that peace is much more than just the absence of violence; peace includes active cooperation for mutual benefit (Galtung 1996). It follows that conflict is not a prerequisite for peacebuilding; countries that have not been in conflict can still build peace with one another by actively increasing collaboration and by strengthening bonds between individuals, organizations, and government institutions. Peace parks can be created between longtime allies to serve as a physical symbol of their trust and cooperation, as with Waterton-Glacier International Peace Park.[1] They can also be established between active adversaries during times of war and used as a tool to help solve conflicts and end violence, as seen in the territorial dispute between Ecuador and Peru in the Cordillera del Cóndor region (UNEP 2009).

Peace parks can be used as a common goal that adversaries can work together to achieve. They provide what Ken Conca and Geoffrey Dabelko call a "soft entry point" to cooperation (Conca and Dabelko 2002). The creation of peace parks is less politically charged than attempts at military or economic cooperation—as exemplified by the proposed Demilitarized Zone (DMZ) Peace Park between North and South Korea. The proposed Balkans Peace Park would provide a framework for collaboration across historically conflict-affected border areas, as well as for the development of opportunities for post-conflict livelihood creation and the maintenance of traditional cultural heritage. The multilayered transboundary network in Albania, Montenegro, and Kosovo has developed into a movement to formally establish the park.

A MULTITRACK APPROACH TO PEACE PARK ESTABLISHMENT

The Institute for Multi-Track Diplomacy identifies nine different tracks upon which diplomacy and international collaboration take place, all of which enhance and support one another. The traditional Track 1 approach is official government diplomacy. Its core operational approach is policy coordination, and its primary actors are heads of state, ambassadors, and government ministers. The Track 1 approach is fundamentally top-down, which creates a dominant framework for policy coordination through which all stakeholders must operate.

In contrast with the traditional (Track 1-centered) approach to diplomacy, multitrack diplomacy views the process of international peacebuilding "as a living system. It looks at the web of interconnected activities, individuals, institutions, and communities that operate together for a common goal: a world at peace" (Institute for Multi-Track Diplomacy n.d.). At the core of the multitrack approach is recognition of the multiple pathways to peacebuilding and of the interconnectedness between them. The resiliency of the peace process is increased when stakeholders are engaged on multiple levels in ways that are most effective to each, and when bonds are built across borders among many different individuals, organizations, and institutions.

International diplomacy in the post-Westphalian world has broadened in scope dramatically. The secretaries of state, ambassadors, and special envoys of

---

[1] For an analysis of peace parks generally, see Carol Westrik, "Transboundary Protected Areas: Opportunities and Challenges," in this book.

nation-states no longer dominate international diplomacy with the Track 1 approach. Additional tracks to conduct diplomacy between nations have been identified and are being creatively used. A sports-based track thrusts athletes into a diplomatic role, as with the U.S.-China ping-pong diplomacy of the 1970s and U.S.-Iran wrestling matches and wrestler exchanges more recently. A scientific track does the same with scientists, as is most evident in the joint development of the International Space Station and the Intergovernmental Panel on Climate Change, and in the collaboration on scientific experiments that were developed and conducted as a result. An educational track places students and professors in a diplomatic role through exchange programs like Fulbright fellowships and Rhodes scholarships, as well as direct university partnerships across borders.

Multitrack citizen diplomacy allows for multiple layers of society to be engaged simultaneously. This process can continue even when official diplomatic efforts falter or fail. By engaging a wider range of stakeholders, citizen diplomacy can increase the number of connections across borders over time and build a critical mass of individuals and organizations with friends and colleagues on the other side of a border, all of whom may oppose a return to conflict.

The multitrack approach cannot be used by itself to formally establish a peace park; that requires an official declaration from Track 1 diplomatic actors. Though multitrack diplomacy is broad and deep, it is limited when it comes to official actions, particularly concerning issues of sovereignty. The transition from a multitrack collaboration around a peace park proposal to the establishment of an official international peace park requires recognition from actors at the Track 1 level in the form of an official diplomatic declaration—often a memorandum of understanding (MOU) or formal treaty.

THE PROPOSED BALKANS PEACE PARK

A prime example of the use of a multitrack approach is the proposal for the Balkans Peace Park in a part of former Yugoslavia, currently being developed between formerly communist Albania and newly independent Montenegro and Kosovo (see figure 1). Due to the dramatically different relationships that Montenegro and Kosovo have with the former state of Serbia, as well as the role that the United Nations Mission in Kosovo played in building up Kosovo's institutional capacity, the decision for Kosovo and Montenegro to formally recognize each other's sovereignty and independence was fraught with consequences—not least of which was Serbia's expulsion of the Montenegrin ambassador the day after recognition (*Helsinki Bulletin* 2010).

Another dynamic on the national level is the national park structure in each of the three countries. Thethi National Park in Albania lacks the funding and park management to effectively enforce regulations and management principles, and the park boundaries do not extend all the way to the country's borders. Prokletja National Park in Montenegro was created by an act of parliament in 2010, but it has not yet been formally defined or implemented on the ground; locals often call it a "paper park." Bjeshket a Namuna National Park in Kosovo

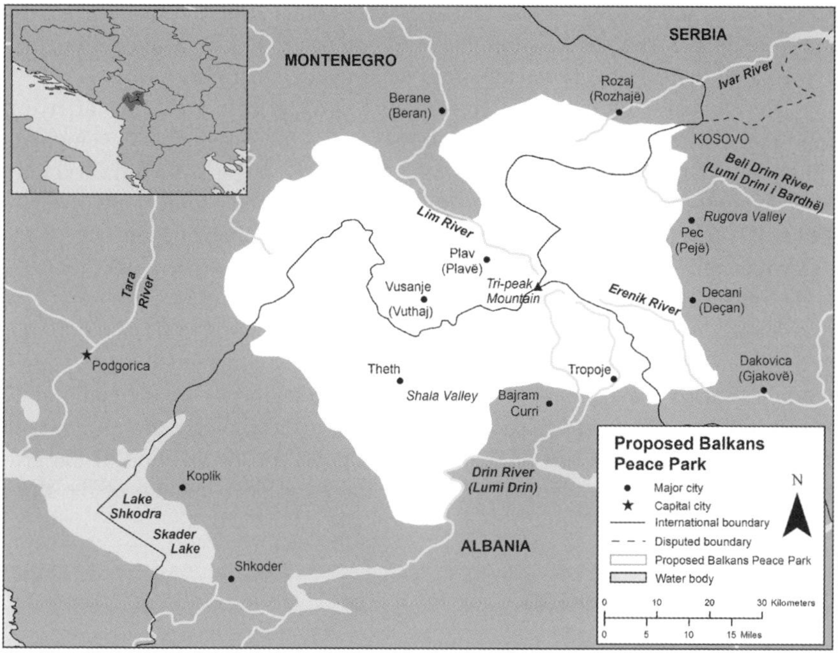

Figure 1. Proposed Balkans Peace Park
Source: B3P (2003).

has not yet been formally dedicated by the Assembly of Kosovo, and it faces significant challenges, such as local opposition to the idea, a lack of local consultation, and a lack of understanding about potential local benefits and not just restrictions. It is impossible to create a functioning international peace park that links the national parks of all three countries until national parks in each country are established and operational.

Such circumstances render a Track 1 approach to formally creating an international peace park extremely challenging. However, it is possible to employ a multitrack approach just below the highest levels of government, where political constraints are not as significant.

The multitrack approach for the proposed Balkans Peace Park has created a collaborative community, comprising mayors of the municipalities where the proposed peace park would be located; government ministries for environment, tourism, and development; international development agencies of foreign countries, including SNV Netherlands Development Organisation (SNV) and German Society for International Cooperation (Deutsche Gesellschaft für Internationale Zusammenarbeit, or GIZ);[2] individuals from the U.S. Peace Corps and the U.S. and British embassies; local nongovernmental organization (NGO) leaders from Albania,

---

[2] GIZ was formerly German Technical Cooperation (Deutsche Gesellschaft für Technische Zusammenarbeit, or GTZ).

Montenegro, and Kosovo, who created a cross-border coalition of local NGOs; and local people who reside within the proposed peace park area and buffer zone, immediately outside the protected areas designated as national parks.

The presence of many different actors and projects yields a variety of opportunities for livelihood creation—from small-scale sustainable development initiatives to large-scale biodiversity surveys, and even larger-scale infrastructure-development projects. The loosely knit coalition of stakeholders involved in the park's development can grow closer over time, capitalizing on one of the under-recognized benefits of collaboration: efficiency and effectiveness increase as the same group of people collaborate together.

A decade after the Balkans Peace Park Project began in 2001, the commitment made—to cooperate across borders on issues of environmental conservation, natural resource management, and sustainable development—by the community of stakeholders still exists (Kennard 2009). These stakeholders are all engaged in working together toward many of the core goals for the creation of the proposed peace park, while supporting the creation and development of the three national parks as well.

CREATING LIVELIHOODS

It is important to create sustainable livelihood opportunities for individuals living in and around a peace park. This can be accomplished through the establishment of incentives for the local population to support and work with other stakeholders in creating and managing the park itself and for sustainable activities that occur around and within the park, as well as the establishment and enforcement of regulations that discourage activities that work against those ends, such as illegal logging, dumping of waste, or poaching.

Peace parks can shift the economic incentive structure away from resource exploitation and toward environmental conservation and cultural heritage preservation by providing livelihood opportunities for local people who may not otherwise have a clear reason to support the creation of a peace park. Residents may work as park rangers, managers, and guides; host tourists in homes or guesthouses; sell food, drinks, supplies, and handicrafts to tourists (from both within and outside the region); or provide transportation to visitors. Peace parks can give people living in and around the park an incentive to remain in their communities instead of relocating to urban centers for employment or turning to environmentally detrimental income-generating activities.

The ongoing development of the proposed Balkans Peace Park has produced jobs that are as diverse as the efforts under way to stimulate cross-border cooperation. Some of these jobs have gone to highly educated citizens of the three countries, including scientific researchers, civil engineers, and resource managers. In cases where local expertise falls short of the need, international experts from universities, development agencies, and NGOs have been brought to the region to contribute their expertise and to work in concert with local experts and other local people.

One ongoing initiative is a transboundary biodiversity survey of the Bjeshket a Namuna–Prokletja mountain ecosystem, one of the areas to be included in the proposed peace park. This effort is being spearheaded under a larger program known as the Dinaric Arc Initiative, a collaboration of many international organizations which began in 2008 (Erg 2010). The Dinaric Arc Initiative has hired local forestry experts, biologists, hydrologists, and botanists for programs to improve local living conditions, focusing on waste management, personal hygiene, and better cooking facilities inside homes in this remote mountain region. Some of the programs are managed by the ministries of cultural heritage of each country, while others are initiatives of international NGOs and development agencies, particularly GIZ (and before it, GTZ). A local NGO in Kosovo, Environmentally Responsible Action group, has already developed a similar program to update the biodiversity information in Kosovo's National Environment Report, which as of 2010 was still using scientific data from the 1970s.

Coordinated water resource management systems at both the local and regional levels address everything from traditional rural irrigation methods to small-scale and major hydroelectric projects (such as a dam on the Drin River), as well as shared cleanup and pollution regulation efforts in Lake Shkodra, on the border between Albania and Montenegro.[3] These projects provide high- and low-skilled jobs in construction, installation, and maintenance for the local population, in addition to short-term volunteer opportunities and nonmonetary benefits including cleaner water and more reliable electricity. The projects also bring people together to work side by side, developing a framework for cooperation that evolves and improves over time. All of these efforts demonstrate how transboundary environmental collaboration can catalyze action on multiple levels, bring together a new community of stakeholders, and generate a critical mass of political will to press for the establishment of a functioning national park system and eventually a linked international peace park through the Track 1 diplomatic process.

Ecotourism is often touted as one of the key forces for generating livelihood opportunities for local populations in and around peace parks, and for helping to shift the incentive structure toward ecosystem-level conservation and cooperation, both domestically and across political borders. In order to move toward conservation and cooperation, stakeholders must shift their activities away from illegal exploitation of forests or game animals and competition for limited, protected resources. Geotourism takes the ecotourism approach one step further. It can be defined as:

> Tourism that sustains or enhances the geographical character of a place—its environment, culture, aesthetics, heritage, and the well-being of its residents.
>
> Geotourism incorporates the concept of sustainable tourism—that destinations should remain unspoiled for future generations—while allowing for ways to protect a place's character. Geotourism also takes a principle from its ecotourism cousin—that tourism revenue should promote conservation—and extends it to culture and history as well, that is, all distinctive assets of a place (National Geographic Center for Sustainable Desitnations n.d.).

[3] Drin River is also known as Lumi Drin, and Lake Shkodra is also known as Skader Laker.

Geotourism and ecotourism both seek to capitalize on an advantage of the multitrack approach: the ability to focus on a region from a strategic-planning perspective and an ecosystem point of view. This is in sharp contrast to the Track 1 approach, which elevates the importance of sovereign boundaries and creates diplomatic challenges that must be negotiated and overcome in order for cross-border cooperation to be stimulated. Focusing on an ecoregion can prompt a powerful shift in perspective for diverse stakeholders whose interests may suddenly align when they view an issue without human-drawn boundaries and sovereignty constraints.

An excellent example of this shift in perspective can be seen with the Jordan River Peace Park and the work done by Friends of the Earth Middle East, an organization comprising and headed by Jordanians, Palestinians, and Israelis. The group has mounted the successful Good Water Makes Good Neighbors campaign to shift public perception away from a focus on sovereign borders and a tragedy-of-the-commons mentality toward one that views the Jordan River and its wetland ecosystem as a critical part of a shared heritage that should be protected for a number of cultural, political, and environmental reasons.[4]

This shift in perspective can foster a whole new realm of opportunities for coordination and cooperation that are not possible under a strict Track 1 approach. In the case of the proposed Balkans Peace Park, ecotourism has helped spur the founding of local small businesses that cater to tourists visiting the region, who often spend time in more than one country. Outdoor-adventure seekers can contact one of the many alpinist organizations founded in the past ten years to book mountain trekking, climbing, white-water rafting, and mountain biking packages. On their expeditions, these tourists can stay at local guesthouses that have adapted traditional cultural notions of hospitality to host paying customers who are eager to contribute to the local economy and spend a night in a traditional stone house; eat traditional dishes made with locally grown, organic ingredients; and sample local wine and raki (spirits distilled from plums and other fruits).

Tourist expeditions have also helped stimulate the local transportation industry because reaching remote mountainous regions is best done with a local driver and a four-wheel-drive vehicle. The demand for souvenirs has begun to revitalize the local handicrafts industry as tourists purchase everything from hand-knit socks and locally woven rugs to woodcarvings and handmade instruments like the *chieftelli*. One goal of the Dinaric Arc Initiative is to link all of these independent initiatives in a comprehensive informational database that tourists can use to plan a cross-boundary adventure vacation (Erg 2010). Another resource developed by the international community is a guide by the United Nations Environment Programme (UNEP) to managing the social and environmental impact of mountain tours, which includes a section on "Local Communities and Livelihood Planning" (UNEP 2007). The guide has proved to be a valuable

[4] For more on the work by Friends of the Earth Middle East, see Mehyar et al. (2014).

resource to businesses. Together, the informational database and guide represent a conscious effort by the international community to ensure that the initiative is locally grounded.

Opportunities for construction laborers, both skilled and unskilled, arise around locally managed sustainable development projects, which can, with the help of stakeholder focus groups, help set priorities for the type of development that should occur. Livelihood opportunities can also be created by conservation initiatives, such as rehabilitation efforts for degraded areas, conservation easements for local landowners, and infrastructure improvements designed to minimize human impacts on the environment. In the proposed Balkans Peace Park, such initiatives have taken the form of an in-progress mountain road–engineering project; improvements in small-scale hydroelectric power generation; and the development of an ecotourism infrastructure of converted guest-houses, GPS-navigable hiking routes with well-marked trails, and a local guide service.

The multitrack approach also enables the coordination of programs across multiple levels: local, regional, national, and international. Jobs may be local or national, and they may be private sector or government based. Two key areas of focus, conservation enforcement and park management, require a significant degree of coordination among workers from each country—including rangers, park managers, conservation biologists, natural resource managers, and guards seeking to prevent illegal poaching and logging. Through coordinated, sustained dialogue, stakeholders can develop a strategic plan for these areas that addresses both livelihood needs and natural resource protection. The Balkans Peace Park Project and the Dutch aid group SNV have been conducting facilitated dialogues, hosting conferences of stakeholders to conduct needs assessments, developing a strategic plan, and generating transboundary collaboration among stakeholders—but many of the livelihood opportunities still exist only in the plan, and not yet in reality.

National park creation and management remains a challenge in the Balkans, primarily due to lack of funding and minimal human resources, as well as unresolved issues such as private landownership within park boundaries and the related challenge of balancing private use with the requirements of park regulations. These issues have been exacerbated by a lack of communication between governments and local people and, in the case of Kosovo, have led to local opposition to the formal creation of the Bjeshket a Namuna National Park. In existing national parks, enforcement of such regulations (particularly with respect to conservation) is negligible, as rangers are local people who intimately understand the survival challenges faced by the local population and are often related through family or tribal ties to those they are expected to police. Hunting is not regulated, and prohibitions against illegal logging are rarely enforced. The few rangers who do work within existing national parks tend to overlook their fellow community members' violations of park regulations. Though many new livelihood opportunities have been created as the idea of a Balkans Peace Park takes shape, viable alternatives have yet to be provided that eliminate the need of communities to rely on the environment for basic necessities.

LESSONS LEARNED

International peace parks possess great potential as a tool for cross-border cooperation for environmental conservation, sustainable development, and livelihood creation—if they are created and managed with the participation of a broad range of stakeholders from all affected countries. It is important to coordinate efforts to develop peace parks at the ecosystem level. Short- and long-term employment opportunities during the proposal stage can help shift incentive structures for local communities toward conservation as a viable land use option and can consolidate public support for the establishment of a peace park. Use of an integrated multitrack approach can increase the chances of success and spur the development of a wide range of related programs, projects, and initiatives on multiple levels.

Timing is critical in the development of an international peace park because a park cannot be created unless the principal state decision makers are ready and the concept is embraced by a critical mass of stakeholders. In the Balkans, the time is not yet ripe to officially create the proposed peace park. Kosovo is struggling to maintain government stability under UN oversight, and it still has significant Track 1 diplomatic issues to work through with Montenegro. Diplomatic ties between Kosovo and Montenegro were not formally established until January 2010, and the repatriation of refugees remains a challenging issue. Bjeshket a Namuna National Park is not yet established in Kosovo, Prokletja National Park exists only on paper in Montenegro, and Thethi National Park in Albania lacks the resources to effectively enforce regulations; until these challenges can be solved, combining the national parks into an international peace park will remain a goal and not a reality. Yet steps in the direction of establishing the park can be taken, and cross-border connections can be built and strengthened while stakeholders prepare for the proper moment to apply pressure at the national level for the formal creation and dedication of the proposed Balkans Peace Park.

CONCLUSION

The world is increasingly acknowledging the value of international peace parks, which serve many different roles in many different circumstances, all of them stimulating cross-border cooperation and building trust and peace among countries, organizations and institutions, and individuals. The proposed Balkans Peace Park illustrates many of the challenges inherent in creating an international peace park, highlights examples of effective measures to overcome some of those challenges, and provides some key lessons that are informing new initiatives to create international peace parks in different regions around the world.

One of the main lessons involves local support and stakeholder involvement. In working to create an international peace park, it is critical to develop locally specific solutions in concert with the local population and with their support. This means involving and effectively coordinating a diverse range of stakeholders on multiple levels and across multiple sectors. During this process, it is important to recognize and acknowledge the power discrepancies among stakeholders, as well as the variety of ways in which different stakeholders can contribute their strengths and resources to address the issues that emerge.

Consistent laws and policies are needed on an ecosystem level. These laws and policies will require collaboration among the countries in terms of implementation and enforcement. Creation of livelihoods as part of an international peace park can shift incentive structures toward conservation and more sustainable uses of land, but only if the economic incentives are sufficient to generate a meaningful and measurable change in behavior, attitude, and income. Finally, a balance should also be maintained between large infrastructure projects and smaller community development projects, and the diverse array of benefits must be distributed in a way that all stakeholders feel is equitable, so no one has an incentive to become a spoiler.

A diverse, multitrack group of stakeholders has continued to work toward the goal of making the proposed Balkans Peace Park a reality. This amalgamation of different individuals, organizations, and institutions is actively working through each challenge of creating the proposed park, is continually building a critical mass of people on the local, regional, national, and international levels who support the vision, and is continuing to prepare the ground for the day when Mandela's "concept that can be embraced by all" reaches the Track 1 leaders who can put pen to paper and make the dream a reality.

REFERENCES

B3P (Balkans Peace Park Project). 2003. The Balkans Peace Park proposal. First International Conference on the Balkans Peace Park, Shkoder, Albania. July.

Conca, K., and G. Dabelko, eds. 2002. *Environmental peacemaking*. Baltimore, MD: Johns Hopkins University Press.

Dudley, N., ed. 2008. *Guidelines for applying protected area management categories*. Gland, Switzerland: International Union for Conservation of Nature and Natural Resources. http://data.iucn.org/dbtw-wpd/edocs/paps-016.pdf.

Erg, B. 2010. Dinaric Arc Initiative to boost transboundary cooperation in the Western Balkans. Gland, Switzerland: International Union for Conservation of Nature. www.iucn.org/about/union/secretariat/offices/iucnmed/?5059/Dinaric-Arc-Initiative-to-boost-transboundary-cooperation-in-the-Western-Balkans.

Galtung, J. 1996. *Peace by peaceful means: Peace and conflict, development and civilization*. London: Sage Publications.

Helsinki Bulletin. 2010. Montenegro: Regime in Podgorica constantly criminalized. Issue No. 59. February.

Institute for Multi-Track Diplomacy. n.d. What is multi-track diplomacy? www.imtd.org/index.php/about/84-about/131-what-is-multi-track-diplomacy.

Kennard, A. 2009. The Balkans Peace Park as a paradigm for transboundary conflict resolution. Conflict and Reconciliation Symposium, Trondheim, Norway, June.

Mehyar, M., N. Al Khateeb, G. Bromberg, and E. Koch-Ya'ari. 2014. Transboundary cooperation in the Lower Jordan River Basin. In *Water and post-conflict peacebuilding*. London: Earthscan.

National Geographic Center for Sustainable Destinations. n.d. About geotourism. http://travel.nationalgeographic.com/travel/sustainable/about_geotourism.html.

Peace Park Foundation. n.d. Words from Dr. Nelson Mandela. www.peaceparks.org.

Sandwith, T., C. Shine, L. S. Hamilton, and D. Sheppard. 2001. *Transboundary protected areas for peace and co-operation*. Best Practice Protected Area Guidelines Series No. 7. Gland, Switzerland: International Union for Conservation of Nature. https://portals.iucn.org/library/efiles/edocs/pag-007.pdf.

UNEP (United Nations Environment Programme). 2007. Tourism and mountains: A practical guide to managing the environmental and social impacts of mountain tours. Nairobi, Kenya.

———. 2009. *From conflict to peacebuilding: The role of natural resources and the environment*. Nairobi, Kenya. http://postconflict.unep.ch/publications/pcdmb_policy_01.pdf.

UNESCO (United Nations Educational, Scientific and Cultural Organization) and World Heritage Convention. n.d. Waterton Glacier International Peace Park. http://whc.unesco.org/en/list/354.

WCPA (World Commission on Protected Areas). n.d. Transboundary protected areas. www.unep-wcmc-apps.org/protected_areas/transboundary/index.html.

Mountain gorilla ecotourism: Supporting macroeconomic growth and providing local livelihoods

Miko Maekawa, Annette Lanjouw, Eugène Rutagarama, and Douglas Sharp

With a population currently hovering around just 880 individuals, the mountain gorilla (*Gorilla beringei beringei*), endemic to two park systems extending across Rwanda, Uganda, and the Democratic Republic of the Congo (DRC), was considered to be dangerously close to extinction even before major conflicts arose in the region during the 1990s. Despite the proximity of hundreds of thousands of refugees, countless rebels, and national armies that pass through and occupy the parks, the mountain gorilla has miraculously survived an extended period of civil war and genocide. With the return to relative peace in Rwanda and Uganda (although not in the DRC), the mountain gorilla has emerged not only as a national symbol for the countries but also as a vehicle for strengthening conservation efforts, national economies, and local livelihoods through gorilla–related ecotourism. Although mountain gorilla ecotourism existed in Central Africa prior to the conflict, important lessons can be learned from experiences in the post-conflict period.

This chapter analyzes how mountain gorilla ecotourism can be used in Africa's Great Lakes region to support macroeconomic growth and provide livelihoods to local populations following a series of conflicts in the region. Although ecotourism will not solve all economic problems, it can play a prominent role in a broader post-conflict development framework. The chapter first details the conflicts in Rwanda, Uganda, and the DRC and provides an overview of the mountain gorilla population to introduce the post-conflict situation in which

---

Miko Maekawa is a lecturer at the Graduate School of Human Sciences at Osaka University and a former staff member of the United Nations Development Programme who has managed a wide range of environmental projects on climate change mitigation, biodiversity conservation, and environmental mainstreaming. Annette Lanjouw is vice president for Strategic Initiatives and the Great Apes Program of the Arcus Foundation. Eugène Rutagarama is director of the International Gorilla Conservation Programme. Douglas Sharp, formerly an intern with the Environmental Law Institute working on post-conflict natural resource management, is a J.D. candidate at Stanford Law School. A subsequently published paper with excerpts and findings from this chapter was published in the *Natural Resources Forum*.

mountain gorilla ecotourism has developed. It then analyzes the various strategies and approaches used by each country to boost ecotourism. The chapter identifies opportunities and challenges for further developing mountain gorilla ecotourism in the Great Lakes region. Finally, it presents policy recommendations and considerations for future ecotourism operations.

REGIONAL CONFLICT HISTORY

The area most critical to mountain gorilla ecotourism lies at the center of the Great Lakes region of Africa—the Virunga Volcanoes region, shared by Rwanda, Uganda, and the DRC. Each of these three countries plays a part in the region's complex history. They share borders and a contiguous park that is segmented into each country's own protected area: Volcanoes National Park (Parc National des Volcans, or PNV) in Rwanda, Virunga National Park (Parc National des Virunga, or PNVi) in the DRC, and Mgahinga Gorilla National Park (MGNP) in Uganda. The shared park contains approximately half of the region's mountain gorilla population. A separate park, Bwindi Impenetrable National Park (BINP) in Uganda, is home to the other half of the mountain gorilla population (see figure 1).

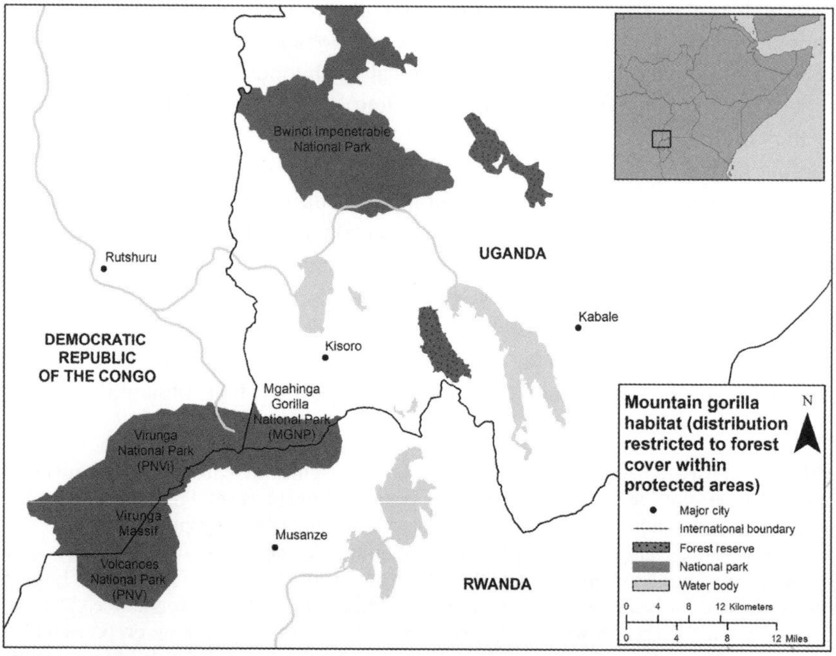

Figure 1. Mountain gorilla habitat
Source: Blomley et al. (2010).

A variety of forces have driven conflict in the region, including ethnic clashes and competition for natural resources. Rwanda's civil war began in 1990, when the Rwandan Patriotic Front attacked from bases in southern Uganda, and lasted through 1994, when Rwandan president Juvénal Habyarimana was assassinated. His death triggered a genocide that killed almost 1 million Tutsis and moderate Hutus in the span of one hundred days. The genocide resulted in a massive shift of 2 million people from their homes, including the Interahamwe—a group of radical Hutus who are believed to have perpetrated the genocide. Most of the displaced people returned to Rwanda within two years, but many Interahamwe remained in the DRC, attacking Rwanda and putting pressure on those managing PNV and its mountain gorilla population (Lanjouw 2003). Rwandan tourism, which had reached a peak of 22,000 visits in 1990, quickly disappeared during the civil war. It recovered fully by 2002, less than a decade after the genocide ended (Nielsen and Spenceley 2010).

Although the majority of Uganda's internal conflict has been generated by the Lord's Resistance Army in the northern part of the country, far from the mountain gorilla parks, Uganda has played a role in the conflict in eastern DRC and the park region. It supported Laurent Kabila in his overthrow of the Mobutu Sese Seko regime in the DRC (then Zaire), hoping Kabila would stop Allied Democratic Forces (ADF) rebels from attacking southwest Uganda from bases within the DRC's PNVi park. Once it became clear that the central DRC government could not contain the ADF, Uganda began supporting other rebel movements, contributing to the instability in the DRC. Uganda and the DRC signed a treaty in 2002 with deadlines for Uganda to remove its troops from the DRC and for the DRC to gain control over its eastern sector, but both failed to keep their promises (Varga, Draman, and Marriott 2002).

Despite this unrest, mountain gorilla ecotourism has grown steadily in Uganda since its formal introduction in 1991. In 1999, Uganda's tourism industry encountered a setback when members of an Interahamwe group based in the DRC killed eight tourists who had come to see the mountain gorillas (BBC 1999). Surprisingly, tourism numbers recovered quickly after a drop immediately following the incident.

The DRC has played a central role in the region's instability. Civil wars in both 1996 and 1998 involved Rwanda and Uganda as allies to remove Zaire's president Mobutu. Rwanda and Uganda became rivals, fighting over natural resources available in eastern DRC (Hammill and Brown 2006). The eastern part of the country, too far away from the central government to be controlled by it, continued to serve as a shelter for 8,000 to 10,000 Interahamwe, including those involved in the 1999 Uganda tourist massacre (Hatfield and Malleret-King 2007).

Instability due to the presence of rebel groups and Rwandan and Ugandan armies discouraged tourism in the DRC until 1999, and since then most tourists have been DRC residents and nongovernmental organization (NGO) staffers working in the DRC. Prior to these conflicts, the DRC had a well-developed mountain gorilla tourism industry, greater than that of either Rwanda or Uganda, but business was devastated by the continued conflict in and around the park (Hatfield and Malleret-King 2007). Concerns about violence and instability in the eastern and northeastern regions of the DRC continue to hinder development of mountain gorilla tourism in the country. For example, the U.S. Department of State has been advising against travel to the DRC because of continued instability and the high risk of violence (U.S. DOS 2013). While some travelers may choose to ignore this warning, it is more likely that they will visit Rwanda or Uganda to see mountain gorillas.

Despite the conflicts noted above, Rwanda, Uganda, and the DRC have collaborated on natural resource management issues, including mountain gorilla protection.[1] The countries' informal transboundary collaboration, facilitated in part by the International Gorilla Conservation Programme, was formalized in 2006 through the Greater Virunga Transboundary Collaboration agreement between Rwanda, Uganda, and the DRC, known as the Transboundary Strategic Plan. An output of eighteen years of collaboration among the countries, the plan provides guidance for managing the transboundary area, with a secretariat to monitor its implementation. Because mountain gorillas cross borders, a crucial aspect of the plan provides for the sharing of revenues among the three countries to prevent tension over the uncontrolled movement of the tourism-generating gorilla population (Refisch and Jenson 2014).

The impacts of mountain gorilla ecotourism are best understood in light of conditions in the communities near the parks. Rwanda, Uganda, and the DRC are among the poorest countries in the world, and population densities surrounding the parks are among the highest in the world—up to 700 people per square kilometer (Plumptre et al. 2004). Over 75 percent of Rwandans live below the international poverty line of US$1.25 per day, and 90 percent of Rwandans rely on subsistence agriculture for survival (Tusabe and Habyalimana 2010; UNDP, REMA, and UNEP 2006). The 1994 genocide cut Rwanda's gross domestic product (GDP) by 50 percent (UNDP, REMA, and UNEP 2006).[2] Ugandans are slightly better off, due mainly to the greater degree of political and economic stability Uganda enjoyed during the late 1990s and early 2000s, but residents still suffer from a shortage of land and resources (Plumptre et al. 2004). The three countries fall among the bottom fifteen countries overall by GDP per capita, although their GDP growth rates are among the highest in the world—indicating the potential for continued growth (World Bank 2012a, 2012b).

---

1 For a detailed discussion of the various aspects of these collaborations, see Refisch and Jenson (2015).

2 For further discussion of Rwanda's post-conflict natural resource management practices, see Sorensen (2015) and Brooke and Matthew (2015).

MOUNTAIN GORILLA POPULATION HISTORY

The mountain gorilla population, split almost evenly between BINP (321 sq km), PNV (160 sq km), PNVi (250 sq km), and MGNP (27 sq km), totals approximately 880 individuals (Gray et al. 2010; Blomley et al. 2010; Hatfield and Malleret-King 2007). This reflects approximately 1.15 percent annual growth from 1989 to 2003 for the shared parks, and approximately 1 percent annual growth for BINP from 1997 to 2006 (McNeilage et al. 2006). The total mountain gorilla population in the Virunga Volcanoes region spanning the three countries has been counted by census eight times since 1970 (Gray et al. 2005, 2010; McNeilage et al. 2006). The 2010 census showed an estimated population of 480 individuals in the region, a 26.3 percent increase in the total population from 380 individuals in the 2003 census (Gray et al. 2005, 2010).

During and after a time of conflict, any growth in the mountain gorilla population should be considered a success (Gray et al. 2005). Only twelve to seventeen mountain gorillas died between 1992 and 2000 due to military activity —approximately 5 percent of the 1989 population (Kalpers et al. 2003). More significant threats came from the local human population, both during and after the conflict period. During the 1990s, pressures to allow refugees to move into the park were enormous, and although such settlement was not allowed, the siting of refugee camps near the parks increased pressures on nearby natural resources. The greatest threats to the mountain gorilla population during this time included habitat loss, direct poaching, indirect poaching, human diseases, and fires (Gray et al. 2005; GEF 2007). Due to the high human population density near the parks and the fact that more than 50 percent of the nearby communities lack agricultural land, there is also great political pressure to free up land within the park for agricultural and charcoal production, which would further reduce the already limited habitat for the mountain gorilla (Gray et al. 2005).

Although many communities around the parks do not eat gorilla meat, direct poaching is still a serious threat, especially from rebel groups living in the park without a source of income or food. More prevalent is indirect poaching, which occurs when traps set for other animals in the park ensnare gorillas and inflict serious and sometimes fatal injury (Plumptre et al. 1997; Hammill and Crawford 2008). Due to the genetic similarity between gorillas and humans, mountain gorillas are also susceptible to many of the illnesses transmitted by humans. Such transmission posed a particular risk during and after the Rwandan genocide, when refugees were moving through the PNV. Currently, tourists are required to remain at least seven meters away from mountain gorillas to minimize this risk. At one point, human-caused fire also posed a significant risk, but this has been reduced since the conflict ended; only four fires were recorded in the Ugandan parks in 2004 (Blomley et al. 2010).

For inhabitants of Rwanda, Uganda, and the DRC, the mountain gorilla has long been considered a national symbol—something to protect and of which to be proud. Many staff at PNV continued to protect the mountain gorilla population during the civil war because of their pride in their national heritage, despite threats to their own safety (Plumptre 2003). This may help explain why so few mountain gorillas were killed during the conflict. According to José Kalpers (a former staff member of the International Gorilla Conservation Programme) and his colleagues, "many of the warring factions have actually shown commitment and invested resources to ensure that the gorillas were not harmed" (Kalpers et al. 2003, 335).

This transformation from a national symbol to a natural resource has been both a benefit and a threat to the mountain gorilla population. In 2007, nine mountain gorillas were killed in the DRC, and the investigation concluded that the killings were perpetrated by people involved in illegal charcoal production within PNVi (Lovgren 2007; Refisch and Jenson 2014). Rwanda had banned the production of charcoal to prevent deforestation in 2004, making the production of charcoal and its subsequent sale to Rwanda very profitable within the DRC. The perpetrators knew that the mountain gorillas were a source of income for the park service and sought to retaliate against the rangers who tried to shut down their illegal charcoal trade (Lovgren 2007).

In order to capitalize on the mountain gorilla population as a natural resource, Rwanda and Uganda (and more recently, the DRC) have each been promoting gorilla-based ecotourism. Such ecotourism is intended to be low-impact, operate on a small scale, and ideally generate funds to conserve the natural resources at issue. Another principle of ecotourism is to provide financial benefits and empowerment for the local population (Sabuhoro 2006). This can create incentives to conserve both the mountain gorilla population and its habitat, because the entire ecotourism experience is focused on viewing the mountain gorilla in its natural environment. Indeed, rebels in the DRC have realized the profitability of using the gorillas for ecotourism (Burnett 2012); rebel leader Laurent Nkunda even began taking tourists to see gorillas in the park to raise funds to support insurgent activities (Refisch and Jenson 2014). Such opportunity may have motivated the rebels to prevent damage to the mountain gorilla population.

MOUNTAIN GORILLA ECOTOURISM

Rwanda and Uganda used similar strategies and approaches to develop a mountain gorilla–based ecotourism industry during the 1990s and 2000s. This section examines three broad aspects of these actions: pricing and market focus, international outreach, and tourism sector reform. Pricing and market focus involves any actions taken with respect to park entrance and gorilla tracking fees. International outreach includes participation in tourism fairs, the use of national and international marketing strategies, and placement of information in media and documentaries. Tourism sector reform includes interactions with the private sector on such matters as privatization, business law, and tax incentives. Rwanda and Uganda have each employed a mix of strategies within these categories, and their efforts provide lessons for supporting macroeconomic growth by developing the ecotourism sector.

The growing ecotourism sector

Market focus is a key distinction between ecotourism and mass tourism. Ecotourism is characterized by a small volume of tourists and by intimate experiences, while mass tourism may entail larger crowds and more impersonal experiences. Mountain gorillas are an ideal subject for ecotourism, as they are relatively scarce, require visitors to exercise caution, and are difficult to locate and view. Ecotourism gives the tourism sector an opportunity to focus on the high-end market, which is much more profitable in terms of revenue per visitor.

Having studied tourism sectors in Kenya and Mauritius and learning that the latter was reaching a higher-end market with lower volumes of visitors, leaders in Rwanda sought to emulate this success (Nielsen and Spenceley 2010). Rwanda and Uganda have both focused on the high-end market by raising gorilla tracking fees on multiple occasions (Uganda Investment Authority 2001; Nielsen and Spenceley 2010). Uganda raised its fee incrementally from US$175 in 1998 to US$500 in 2013 (Adams and Infield 2003; Hatfield and Malleret-King 2007; Uganda Wildlife Authority 2010, 2013). In Rwanda, the fee was US$375 in 2004; by 2012, it had increased to US$750 (RDB 2012). The fee change in Rwanda led to a shift in the income levels of visiting tourists, with more visitors coming from high-income groups and fewer visitors from lower-income groups. An unexpected result was that the average stay per visitor declined, from 4.2 to 3.6 nights (Nielsen and Spenceley 2010). Nevertheless, by capitalizing on this high-end market, the tourism sector in Rwanda is now the country's largest foreign exchange earner, generating projected earnings of US$317 million in 2013 (Butera 2013).

International outreach played a large role in the growth of mountain gorilla ecotourism, especially in the years following the Rwandan genocide. In Rwanda, national marketing was initially conducted to disassociate the word *tourism* from the negative connotation it had held (in a local language, the term means "wandering around aimlessly") (Nielsen and Spenceley 2010). With improved citizen buy-in, Rwanda began marketing internationally with a focus on security. By contracting with marketing agencies abroad, Rwanda was able to generate interest in mountain gorillas, and increase gorilla-based tourism.

Rwanda invested heavily in its participation in tourism industry trade fairs, winning first prize for the best African display at the ITB Berlin tourism fair for three straight years from 2007 through 2009. Exposure at trade fairs increases interest and investment in safaris and other travel packages put together by private companies, which in turn can generate demand from potential tourists around the world. Rwanda has also gained exposure through media features and various documentaries (Nielsen and Spenceley 2010). Features on international media channels, including CNN and the National Geographic Channel, continue to generate demand for mountain gorilla ecotourism and has helped Rwanda maintain consistent visitor numbers despite its significant increases in mountain gorilla tracking fees.

Both Uganda and Rwanda also enacted extensive policy changes to help grow their respective ecotourism sectors. Uganda began in 1992 with its ten-year Tourism Development Master Plan, which focused on community tourism. Similar to ecotourism, but with a focus on learning about Ugandan communities, community tourism helped to grow the official mountain gorilla ecotourism sector, which was established in 1991 (Mehta and Katee 2005). This was followed by the privatization of Ugandan hotels shortly thereafter, with 90 percent being sold to private businesses by 2001 (Uganda Investment Authority 2001). The Rwandan government identified tourism as a development priority in the country's Vision 2020 planning strategy (Spenceley et al. 2010). The Tourism Working Group was established in 2001 to help implement the Vision 2020 strategy, followed by the development of the new Rwanda Tourism Strategy in 2002 (revised in 2007) and the National Tourism Policy in 2006 (revised in 2009) (Nielsen and Spenceley 2010). In 2009, the Rwandan government also approved the Sustainable Tourism Master Plan.

Uganda also offers generous incentives to investors. It permits 100 percent foreign ownership and has one of the lowest nominal corporate tax rates (30 percent) in Africa. This encourages businesses to invest in Uganda, building the infrastructure necessary to support a high-end ecotourism market (Mehta and Katee 2005). In 2003, Uganda revised its policy to further promote regional tourism linkages. The Uganda Tourism Act of 2008 implemented many reforms and incentives to continue to grow the tourism sector, including the reduction or elimination of taxes on many tourism-related expenses (Aboutuganda.com 2007; Nabyama 2008).[3]

Rwanda has implemented similar policies, with tax exemptions for investors who contribute over US$100,000 to a tourism facility and tax-free importation of tourist-transporting airplanes. In addition, Rwanda exempts from taxation secondary goods such as bedroom furnishings and swimming pools for hotels, further incentivizing investment. A crucial part of Rwanda's strategy has been to streamline the legal framework in which businesses operate; for example, it is now possible to register and open a business in one day, for approximately US$43 (Nielsen and Spenceley 2010). By making it easier to form and run a business, Rwanda hopes to increase Rwandan entrepreneurship as well as foreign investment. Economic opportunities around mountain gorilla ecotourism have contributed to the enormous growth around the PNV headquarters in the Kinigi region. In connection with this growth, Rwanda has decentralized much of its control over the park (as well as other parks) and privatized formerly state-owned

[3] For the text of the law, see http://balukusguide.wordpress.com/2012/05/29/uganda-tourism-act-2008/.

hotels. As a result, in 2009, the tourism industry in the PNV region generated approximately US$42.7 million from hotel accommodations, tour excursions, and shopping (Spenceley et al. 2010).

The combination of these strategies has enabled mountain gorilla ecotourism to make a significant contribution to the Rwandan and Ugandan economies. One indicator of the impact is park attendance. Rwanda's park attendance disappeared during the civil war and genocide, and stayed low through the late 1990s. PNV reopened in 1999, and attendance grew from 417 visits that year to approximately 17,000 in 2008 (Nielsen and Spenceley 2010). In the period from 2001–2002 to 2004–2005, attendance at PNV (Rwanda) increased from 2,000 to 9,000 visitors, and at BINP (Uganda) from 3,000 to 5,000. Over that same period, attendance at MGNP (Uganda) remained relatively constant, while at PNVi (DRC), it increased from zero to a few hundred (Hatfield and Malleret-King 2007).

Income from ecotourism

According to a study conducted by the African Wildlife Foundation (AWF) in 2005, gorilla tourism in the three-country region generates approximately US$20.6 million in annual benefits, with 53 percent accruing at the national level, 41 percent at the international level, and 6 percent at the local level (Hatfield 2005). For Rwanda, tourism is the leading source of export revenue (although exports account for a relatively small part of Rwanda's GDP), taking in US$35.7 million in 2006 (Nielsen and Spenceley 2010; Bush 2009)—80 percent of which was generated by tourism in PNV (Sabuhoro 2006). Rwanda's tourism industry continues to grow: by 2012, tourism-related revenues were US$281.8 million, up 17 percent from the year before (Kanyesigye 2013). Visitor spending related to mountain gorilla ecotourism is a significant contributor to tourism revenues in Rwanda. The park-specific revenue (such as fees and entry permits, for example) generated in 2005 by PNV accounted for approximately 0.2 percent of Rwanda's GDP (UNDP, REMA, and UNEP 2006). However, under the new method of gathering tourism statistics introduced in 2008, which covers a wider range of tourists (including both holiday visitors and business travelers) and tourism activities, the sector generated over US$281 million, contributing 3.9 percent of the country's GDP (World Bank 2013). Livelihood creation is a major benefit of the growing ecotourism industry. PNV alone employs over 180 guides, mountain gorilla group trackers, and law enforcement teams such as antipoaching units, and approximately 800 community members are involved in various activities supporting the park (including crop rangers, public-awareness volunteers, and members of conservation teams and porter clubs) (Nielsen and Spenceley 2010). Others are employed by enterprises related to the tourism industry, including hotels and restaurants.

In Uganda, mountain gorilla ecotourism generated approximately US$46 million in economic impact in 2005, and the potential impact is estimated to be as high as US$151 million. Nearly 1,700 person-year jobs were generated by mountain gorilla ecotourism between 1994 and 1999 (Hatfield and Malleret-King 2007). Overall, tourism brought 200,000 visitors to Uganda in 2001, growing to 945,000 arrivals in 2010 (MTWH 2012). This is the equivalent to approximately US$800 million in foreign exchange earnings (Uganda Tourism Board 2010). Studies in Uganda in 2000 and 2007 found that tourist expenditure per mountain gorilla viewing increased 50 percent over that time period—from an estimated US$810 in 2000 to approximately US$1,228 in 2007 (Moyini and Uwimbabazi 2000; Hatfield and Malleret-King 2007).

Because a variety of business strategies were employed, it is difficult to draw a direct connection between a specific strategy and its impact. However, it is clear that higher fees attract a different clientele. Over 30 percent of visitors to Rwanda and Uganda have an annual income of more than US$85,000 per year (Nielsen and Spenceley 2010). Furthermore, over 80 percent of tourists coming to view mountain gorillas have received a university or postgraduate degree, and many are highly interested in conservation activities (Bush 2009). This shift in clientele has resulted in increased revenue, but also shorter stays and a greater demand for high-end customer service and facilities. When prices were raised, customer satisfaction fell—presumably not as a result of a change in services, but because of a change in expectations, as wealthier visitors are accustomed to higher levels of service and amenities (Nielsen and Spenceley 2010).

Although there are some differences between Rwanda's and Uganda's mountain gorilla ecotourism programs, they have the same underlying goals—to align and connect local interests and livelihoods with parks and ecotourism. Because conservation of the mountain gorilla is essential to ecotourism, each strategy—whether revenue sharing, construction of a community-owned lodge, or establishment of an antipoaching society—can play a role in ecotourism as a whole. When ecotourism provides livelihoods to people in post-conflict situations, both natural resource management and peacebuilding become easier.

Ecotourism-related livelihoods

The most direct way in which local people can benefit from mountain gorilla ecotourism is through employment—for example, as park rangers,[4] gorilla trackers, or staff at lodges and restaurants. Jobs can also be generated in businesses that supply food and other goods to park visitors, including souvenirs. For example, approximately 50 percent of mountain gorilla ecotourism–related employment in Uganda is in lodges or tourist shops, with employment in BINP constituting the next largest source of jobs—for a total of roughly 391 full-time jobs, providing approximately US$360,000 worth of income (Hatfield and Malleret-King 2007). Even in the DRC—a country not yet stable enough to benefit from the

[4] For an analysis of use of demobilized excombatants as park rangers, see Matthew F. Pritchard, "From Soldiers to Park Rangers: Post-Conflict Natural Resource Management in Gorongosa National Park," in this book.

full economic impact of mountain gorilla ecotourism—tourism-related industries provide considerable livelihood opportunities to local communities, including approximately 800 people directly employed at PNVi and an additional 54,000 people employed in the tourism sector surrounding the park (GOR 2013). The income generated by these jobs is then spent locally on goods and services, multiplying the wealth within the community.

Conservation trusts are another source of local livelihoods for those living around the parks. In Uganda, funds from the Global Environment Facility and the World Bank were used to create the Mgahinga and Bwindi Impenetrable Forest Conservation Trust in 1994, with proceeds paying for local conservation and development (Blomley et al. 2010; GEF 2007). The trust has focused on three pillars—community development, research and monitoring, and park management (GEF 2007). Since 1996, more than US$4 million has been distributed for community infrastructure projects (Blomley et al. 2010). Over US$800,000 of that total has been used to provide land to the Batwa people, an indigenous group that was removed from Ugandan parks in the early 1990s (Blomley et al. 2010; GEF 2007).

Local communities have also become engaged in mountain gorilla ecotourism by operating community-owned lodges. In Rwanda, the Sabyinyo Silverback Lodge on the edge of PNV, which holds sixteen visitors, is owned entirely by the local community (Nielsen and Spenceley 2010). Representing a joint venture between the Kinigi and Nyange communities (together represented by the Sabyinyo Community Livelihoods Association), the International Gorilla Conservation Programme, AWF, the Rwandan government, and a private-sector ecolodge company (Governors Camps Ltd.), the lodge capitalizes on the high-end market by charging rates from US$500 to US$1,100 per room per night. Governors Camps Ltd., which operates the lodge, contributes US$50 per occupied bed per night back to the community, as well as 7.5 percent of net sales (Nielsen and Spenceley 2010). Revenues given to the community have been used for community-benefiting projects such as road building, provision of water tanks, and support for schools (Martin et al. 2008). The lodge also purchases agricultural products from local producers and permits the sale of local crafts and cultural activities at the lodge. The lodge creates employment and professional development opportunities for local people: forty-five of its staff members (70 percent of the total staff) come from local communities around the park and receive professional tourism and hospitality training during their period of employment (Nielsen and Spenceley 2010; Martin et al. 2008).

Near BINP in Uganda, visitors can stay at the Buhoma Community Campground, which receives approximately 50 percent of all visitors to the park. The campground employs nine people, who each earn an average of US$1,000 per year, and it allocates 25 percent of its revenues to community projects (Hatfield and Malleret-King 2007). A similar lodge built by the Nkuringo Conservation and Development Foundation, with funding from the U.S. Agency for International Development (USAID), is leased to a private company for US$5,000 per year.

The company operates it as a hotel, and local communities receive a bed-night fee of US$30 per person per night (Martin et al. 2008).

Engagement with associations of former poachers has also helped to conserve mountain gorillas and strengthen local livelihoods. In Rwanda, the government created the Iby'Iwacu Village in 2005 with the help of a tour operator (Nielsen and Spenceley 2010). The village, which allows tourists to experience local culture, takes in approximately US$14,000 per year, 40 percent of which goes to expoachers, and 60 percent of which is allocated toward various community projects (Nielsen and Spenceley 2010; Tusabe and Habyalimana 2010). Annual income for these expoachers is approximately US$1,200, which is comparatively higher than other local incomes (Tusabe and Habyalimana 2010). Rwanda has more than twelve expoacher associations and cooperatives, including a 400-member group that volunteers for park conservation (Tusabe and Habyalimana 2010; Nielsen and Spenceley 2010). Although such groups do not directly provide livelihoods to the expoachers, they can encourage expoachers to develop livelihoods that support conservation efforts and do not degrade the park.

Revenue sharing

Revenue sharing has been a major policy initiative in Uganda since 1994 and in Rwanda since 2005 (Adams and Infield 2003; Nielsen and Spenceley 2010). A percentage of the revenue that tourists pay to the Uganda Wildlife Authority and the Tourism and Conservation Department of the Rwanda Development Board (RDB) is allocated to projects that benefit the communities surrounding the parks. Funds are usually spent on schools, water tanks, soil erosion control, health centers, buffalo walls, and roads (Rwanda Focus 2007; Martin et al. 2008; Tusabe and Habyalimana 2010).

Uganda's program, which began in 1994, initially designated 20 percent of mountain gorilla tracking fees for communities, but the amount was quickly reduced to 20 percent of park entry fees (Adams and Infield 2003). This was a significant drop, as park entry fees are considerably lower than mountain gorilla tracking fees (US$15 initially, now US$25 per entry compared with US$500 for tracking). As a result, the amount shared decreased from approximately US$20 per visitor in 1994 to US$2 in 1998 and US$5 in 2002 (Adams and Infield 2003; Martin et al. 2008). To address the drop, a US$10 "gorilla levy" was implemented to raise the amount shared with communities (Martin et al. 2008).

In Rwanda, 5 percent of all tourism revenue from park fees is shared with local communities (Nielsen and Spenceley 2010). Although this is a smaller percentage than in Uganda, it generates a larger amount of funding because it includes both entry fees and mountain gorilla tracking fees. Thus, whereas Uganda shared US$71,500 with local communities in 2006, Rwanda shared over US$200,000 in 2007 (Martin et al. 2008, Tusabe and Habyalimana 2010). Since 2005, US$1,830,000 has been allocated to Rwandan community projects through revenue sharing (RDB 2013a). The RDB invests 40 percent of the total revenue-sharing funds in community enterprises, with the remaining 60 percent funding local infrastructure projects and invested in communities around two other Rwandan parks—Akagera National Park and Nyungwe National Park (IIED n.d.; Rwanda Focus 2009). This shared revenue has supported ten community associations and has paid for the construction of ten primary schools (serving approximately 3,640 students); community water dispensaries; eighty-eight water tanks (each supporting 1,250 people); an eighty-kilometer buffalo wall; health facilities; local tile and brick factories; and beekeeping and agricultural projects such as seed production and storage, agroforestry, and tree planting (RDB 2013b; Nielsen and Spenceley 2010; Rwanda Focus 2007; ORTPN 2008). Some tour companies have also begun returning funds to the community: for example, Rwanda Eco-Tours gives 20 percent of its profits back to local communities for ecotourism development (Rwanda Focus 2009).

One indicator of the impact these benefits have had on local livelihoods is residents' support for parks in Rwanda and Uganda. Local populations around BINP and MGNP in Uganda and PNV in Rwanda "overwhelmingly support" their respective parks, with communities in Uganda identifying ecotourism and income generation as primary benefits of the parks (Plumptre et al. 2004). In contrast, 61 percent of local populations near PNVi in the DRC consider the forest to be "detrimental to their welfare" (Hatfield and Malleret-King 2007, 49).

Although revenue sharing has been successful, communities are not always aware of its impact. In Uganda, fewer than 50 percent of those surveyed around the parks knew about the revenue-sharing scheme (Blomley et al. 2010). In Rwanda residents and park staff were not knowledgeable about the particulars of revenue-sharing arrangements. For example, a study of PNV park officials found that 68 percent of the staff did not know when revenues were disbursed, and nearly 95 percent did not know how the beneficiary projects were chosen. Within the populations surrounding the parks, the vast majority knew about revenue sharing (87 and 97 percent in two districts), but over 90 percent of them did not know how the money was spent, even though the revenue went to many projects in their districts (Sabuhoro 2006). This lack of awareness raises concern because communities are less likely to support mountain gorilla ecotourism if they do not think it will benefit them.

Community benefits from revenue sharing in Uganda have been mistaken for services provided by the government (Plumptre et al. 2004). Also, the benefits from community projects that were meant to directly assist those living around the park were not perceived as going to people in those communities. In Rwanda, over 80 percent of those surveyed in two districts next to the park said they would prefer individual or household benefits over community benefits. This may be partially due to a belief that community benefits do not reach them, although it is possible that communities simply do not realize what the benefits are (Sabuhoro 2006). A related challenge is that while many local residents want to become involved in the shared-revenue distribution process, those same groups are sometimes not yet comfortable making decisions on their own. For example, community-owned lodges are run not by the community, but by a private-sector partner with the relevant expertise (Rutagarama and Martin 2006).

The direct benefits of ecotourism are often distributed in a way that favors those with higher incomes around the park; one study found that only a few of the poorest households benefited at all (Blomley et al. 2010). Many of the poorest communities around the park, including the Batwa in Uganda, live far from centralized tourism hubs and consequently do not experience any tourist traffic or community benefits. Similarly, in Rwanda "the poorest of the poor do not necessarily benefit" from projects funded through revenue sharing (Rwanda Focus 2009). This division is further illustrated by differences in opinion toward the parks: those with higher incomes tend to have more positive attitudes (Blomley et al. 2010). Further, while the revenue-sharing scheme in Rwanda has distributed approximately US$1,830,000 from its inception in 2005 through 2013 (RDB 2013a), when averaged by population, this amount accounts for only US$6 per person, thereby reinforcing the perception that the revenue-sharing scheme and thus the parks do not benefit local communities. For example, although the construction of schools is beneficial to many families, those whose children must stay home to protect crops from park wildlife are unable to take advantage of schooling. This inequality poses a challenge but also an opportunity for improving benefit-sharing policies.

OPPORTUNITIES AND CHALLENGES

Many opportunities exist to increase the contribution of mountain gorilla ecotourism to both economic growth and local livelihoods in Rwanda, Uganda, and the DRC. Prior to the outbreak of violence in the 1990s, tourism in eastern Africa was growing at approximately 8.25 percent annually (Moyini and Uwimbabazi 2000). This pre-conflict growth indicates the potential for future growth in mountain gorilla ecotourism in the post-conflict period. One option to promote growth is to more fully exploit the current infrastructure by maximizing visitor capacity. In 2004 and 2005, visitor numbers reached only 34 percent of their potential (Hatfield and Malleret-King 2007). A second opportunity is to increase revenue by raising fees. When fees were increased in Rwanda from US$375 to US$750, visitor numbers did not change, but revenue increased dramatically (Bush 2009). Fees could potentially be raised even higher to include more high-end tourists.

Mountain gorilla ecotourism can also be integrated into a wider economic development plan. Because the number of tracking permits is fixed, only limited growth can be gained through higher tracking fees. However, shifting to a more upscale tourism model could induce higher visitor spending through longer stays—although this would run against the trend that wealthier visitors enjoy shorter average stays (Nielsen and Spenceley 2010). Measures to counteract this trend and to integrate mountain gorilla ecotourism into longer visits—including visits spanning neighboring countries—could generate greater revenue for the economy and region.

One significant challenge is how to contain revenue leakage to foreign investors or foreign-owned safari operators, which is estimated to be approximately 55 percent of total tourism revenues—a substantial loss (Sandbrook 2010). Despite this loss, however, a sizable portion of revenue is retained in each country and in the area around the parks. Around BINP in Uganda, approximately US$366,000 per year is retained—significantly more than the US$79,900 that is earned from nontourism sources (Sandbrook 2010). Although revenue leakage may simply be a price to pay for the foreign investment driven by Rwanda's and Uganda's governmental policies, its impact could be reduced by a focus on entrepreneurial policies that stimulate the growth of domestic companies that serve the tourism sector.

The DRC has the potential to grow its mountain gorilla ecotourism industry in the same way Uganda and Rwanda have done. Its park, PNVi, harbors seven tourist-habituated mountain gorilla groups (Hatfield and Malleret-King 2007). Despite the serious challenges of insecurity in the area surrounding the park that is still held by rebel combatants, overall stability and security continue to improve in most parts of the country (UNSG 2011). As a result, the DRC's mountain gorilla ecotourism industry was relaunched in early 2009, and international tourists were invited into the country (Virunga National Park 2011).

In 2010, a belated regional joint census of mountain gorillas was conducted (the last one had been undertaken in 2003). The ability to undertake the census is one of the indications of improved security in the Virunga Volcanoes region: census teams could now freely move around the transboundary park to do the counting. Furthermore, new funding sources had emerged to support the census work. In addition to funding from international NGOs working in conservation, such as the International Gorilla Conservation Programme, personal donations were now coming in via the internet, earmarked for specific conservation and community livelihood programs. Through the official home page of PNVi, US$600,000 has been raised since 2006 to fund necessities such as ranger salaries, uniforms, staff training, and care of orphaned mountain gorillas (Virunga National Park n.d.).

Fundraising via the internet has been an effective resource mobilization measure for shoring up the financial resources of the Congolese Institute for Nature Conservation (ICCN), which manages PNVi. Due to limited funding, at times the park rangers did not receive their salaries on schedule and thus lacked basic necessities such as daily food. Greater security, the strengthened capacity of the ICCN, and more stable sources of funding all make the survival of mountain gorillas more likely, and successful ecotourism may ultimately contribute to macroeconomic growth and the development of local livelihoods in the DRC.

Finally, facilitating community involvement in the ecotourism process is a challenge, whether in shared-revenue distribution or in lodge ownership. Not only do community residents often believe that they do not have the expertise necessary to make programming decisions, they often are unsure about how ecotourism processes work. This challenge also presents an opportunity: when local residents are involved, it is possible to use ecotourism revenue to more effectively support local livelihoods. By partnering with local people and growing businesses with them, government officials and others with relevant expertise can provide more long-term development and training to people in local communities.

LESSONS LEARNED

A number of lessons can be learned from experiences with mountain gorilla ecotourism in Rwanda, Uganda, and the DRC, including lessons on how to improve ecotourism's impact on economic growth and local livelihoods, both with respect to mountain gorillas and in post-conflict situations more generally.

Possibly the most obvious but also the most significant lesson is that security and stability are necessary preconditions for an ecotourism industry to develop. Although it is possible to overcome setbacks (such as the massacre in Uganda in 1999), meaningful numbers of tourists will not travel to a region unless they feel comfortable about their safety. The DRC has not yet implemented many of the approaches that have made mountain gorilla ecotourism successful in Rwanda and Uganda, and it cannot do so without first reestablishing security and stability.

A commitment by the government to developing the ecotourism industry is also a necessary condition. In Rwanda and Uganda, business reforms, investment in tourism fairs, and the inclusion of tourism in economic plans all contributed to a massive increase in the number of visitors and to international attention during the post-conflict period. Countries emerging from conflict often do not have the capacity to develop an ecotourism industry, but by enabling the private sector to provide the necessary investment and expertise, they can enable growth such as that experienced in Rwanda and Uganda.

For countries with endemic endangered species that hold interest for tourists, focusing on the high-end tourism market can enable them to charge higher fees for tracking and viewing. Although a high-end market brings additional challenges, such as the need to upgrade facilities and the quality of services, it is a great opportunity to generate revenues from those visitors who are willing to pay the price.

With respect to livelihoods, it is essential to make connections between the mountain gorillas, ecotourism, revenue, development projects, and local populations. In particular, developing revenue-sharing schemes with local input will help ensure that development approaches are well informed and that they build expertise within the target communities. Partnerships with local communities can promote long-term development so that the communities themselves, rather than private corporations, can run the community lodges.

When mountain gorilla–based ecotourism is promoted, tension can arise between boosting macroeconomic growth and providing local livelihoods. Although these two benefits are not mutually exclusive, they are often thought of as such, and Rwanda and Uganda have attempted to balance them through strategies such as revenue sharing. With appropriate planning, a greater share of the benefits and revenues generated by mountain gorilla ecotourism can be retained within local communities—whether as a higher percentage of revenue shared or in the form of job training to enable community members to work in the tourism industry. It is critical to consider this balance and the synergies between macroeconomic growth and livelihoods when examining how ecotourism fits into a country's or region's development plans, especially for those countries seeking to recover from conflict.

REFERENCES

Aboutuganda.com. 2007. New law to boost tourism in Uganda Africa. www.aboutuganda.com/wordpress/blogroll/new-law-to-boost-tourism-in-uganda-africa.html.

Adams, W. M., and M. Infield. 2003. Who is on the gorilla's payroll? Claims on tourist revenue from a Ugandan national park. *World Development* 31 (1): 177–190.

BBC. 1999. World: Africa–Uganda tourists 'butchered.' March 3. http://news.bbc.co.uk/2/hi/africa/289196.stm.

Blomley, T., A. Namara, A. McNeilage, P. Franks, H. Rainer, A. Donaldson, R. Malpas, W. Olupot, J. Baker, C. Sandbrook, et al. 2010. *Development and gorillas? Assessing fifteen years of integrated conservation and development in south-western Uganda.* Natural Resources Issues No. 23. London: International Institute for Environment and Development. www.iied.org/pubs/pdfs/14592IIED.pdf.

Brooke, R., and R. Matthew. 2015. Post-conflict environmental governance: Lessons from Rwanda. In *Governance, natural resources, and post-conflict peacebuilding*, ed. C. Bruch, C. Muffett, and S. S. Nichols. London: Earthscan.

Burnett, J. 2012. Gorillas and guerrillas share the troubled Congo. National Public Radio, September 13. www.npr.org/2012/09/13/161066078/gorillas-and-guerrillas-share-the-troubled-congo.

Bush, G. K. 2009. The economic value of Albertine Rift forests; Applications in policy and programming. Ph.D. thesis, University of Stirling, Scotland, United Kingdom.

Butera, S. 2013. Rwanda's tourism earnings rise on growing East African travel. Bloomberg, May 29. www.bloomberg.com/news/2013-05-29/rwanda-s-tourism-earnings-rise-on-growing-east-african-travel.html.

GEF (Global Environment Facility). 2007. *GEF impact evaluation: Case study; Bwindi Impenetrable National Park and Mgahinga Gorilla National Park Conservation Project.* Impact Evaluation Information Document No. 7. Washington, D.C.: Global Environment Facility Evaluation Office.

GOR (Government of Rwanda). 2013. More than just a name—Communities benefit from gorilla tourism. www.gov.rw/More-than-just-a-name-Communities-benefit-from-gorilla-tourism.

Gray, M., A. McNeilage, K. Fawcett, M. Robbins, B. Ssebide, D. Mbula, and P. Uwingeli. 2005. *Virunga Volcanoes Range mountain gorilla census, 2003.* L'Institut Congolais pour la Conservation de la Nature, Office Rwandais du Tourisme et des Parcs Nationaux, Uganda Wildlife Authority, and International Gorilla Conservation Programme. www.igcp.org/wp-content/themes/igcp/docs/pdf/VVRmountaingorillacensus2003.pdf.

———. 2010. Censusing the mountain gorillas in the Virunga Volcanoes: Complete sweep method versus monitoring. *African Journal of Ecology* 48 (3): 588–599.

Hammill, A., and O. Brown. 2006. *Conserving the peace: Analyzing the links between conservation and conflict in the Albertine Rift*. Winnipeg, Canada: International Institute for Sustainable Development. www.iisd.org/publications/pub.aspx?pno=951.

Hammill, A., and A. Crawford. 2008. *Gorillas in the midst: Assessing the peace and conflict impacts of International Gorilla Conservation Programme (IGCP) activities.* Winnipeg, Canada: International Institute for Sustainable Development. www.iisd.org/pdf/2008/gorillas_in_the_midst.pdf.

Hatfield, R. 2005. Economic value of the Bwindi and Virunga gorilla mountain forests. AWF working paper. African Wildlife Foundation. www.awf.org/sites/default/files/media/Resources/Books%20and%20Papers/Economic_Valuation_Virunga_0.pdf.

Hatfield, R., and D. Malleret-King. 2007. *The economic value of the mountain gorilla protected forests (The Virungas and Bwindi Impenetrable National Forest).* Nairobi, Kenya: International Gorilla Conservation Programme. www.igcp.org/wp-content/themes/igcp/docs/pdf/EconomicValuationVBForests.pdf.

IIED (International Institute for Environment and Development). n.d. The poverty and conservation learning group: Organizations—Rwanda Development Board (RDB). http://povertyandconservation.info/en/org/o0447.

Kalpers, J., E. A. Williamson, M. M. Robbins, A. McNeilage, A. Nzamurambaho, N. Lola, and G. Mugiri. 2003. Gorillas in the crossfire: Population dynamics of the Virunga mountain gorillas over the past three decades. *Oryx* 37 (3): 326–337.

Kanyesigye, F. 2013. Rwanda: The rising revenues of Rwanda's tourism. *New Times*, February 17. http://allafrica.com/stories/201302180130.html.

Lanjouw, A. 2003. Building partnerships in the face of political and armed crisis. In *War and tropical forest: Conservation in areas of armed conflict,* ed. S. V. Price. Binghamton, NY: Food Products Press. www.igcp.org/wp-content/themes/igcp/docs/pdf/conflict_paper.pdf.

Lovgren, S. 2007. Congo gorilla killings fueled by illegal charcoal trade. *National Geographic*, August 16. http://news.nationalgeographic.com/news/2007/08/070816-gorillas-congo.html.

Martin, A., E. Rutagarama, M. Gray, S. Asuma, M. Bana, A. Basabose, and M. Mwine. 2008. *International Gorilla Conservation Programme community conservation: Lessons learned.* Norwich, UK: University of East Anglia. https://ueaeprints.uea.ac.uk/18812/1/RPP5-Martin.pdf.

McNeilage, A., M. M. Robbins, K. Gushanski, M. Gray, and E. Kagoda. 2006. Mountain gorilla census—2006: Bwindi Impenetrable National Park summary report. Institute of Tropical Forest Conservation, Wildlife Conservation Society, Max Planck Institute for Evolutionary Anthropology, International Gorilla Conservation Programme, and Uganda Wildlife Authority. www.igcp.org/wp-content/themes/igcp/docs/pdf/Bwindicensus2006resultssummary.pdf.

Mehta, H., and C. Katee. 2005. *Virunga Massif sustainable tourism development plan: DR Congo, Rwanda and Uganda.* www.igcp.org/wp-content/themes/igcp/docs/pdf/VirungaTourismMasterPlan_%20Final%20Report.pdf.

Moyini, Y., and B. Uwimbabazi. 2000. *Analysis of the economic significance of gorilla tourism in Uganda.* Kampala, Uganda: Environmental Monitoring Associates. www.igcp.org/wp-content/themes/igcp/docs/pdf/MoyiniUganda.pdf.

MTWH (Ministry of Tourism, Wildlife and Heritage, Republic of Uganda). 2012. *Uganda tourism sector situational assessment: Tourism reawakening*. Kampala. http://tourism.go.ug/index.php?option=com_phocadownload&view=category&id=4&Itemid=281.

Nabyama, P. 2008. Tourism sector sniffs more business after passing of bill. *East African Business Week*, March 10. http://allafrica.com/stories/200803101233.html.

Nielsen, H., and A. Spenceley. 2010. The success of tourism in Rwanda—Gorillas and more. http://siteresources.worldbank.org/AFRICAEXT/Resources/258643-1271798012256/Tourism_Rwanda.pdf.

ORTPN (Office Rwandais du Tourisme et des Parcs Nationaux). 2008. The Rwanda Office of Tourism and National Parks announces midterm results. News release. August 5. Kigali.

Plumptre, A. J. 2003. Lessons learned from on-the-ground conservation in Rwanda and the Democratic Republic of the Congo. In *War and tropical forest: Conservation in areas of armed conflict*, ed. S. V. Price. Binghamton, NY: Food Products Press. www.tandfonline.com/doi/abs/10.1300/J091v16n03_04#preview.

Plumptre, A. J., J. B. Bizumuremyi, F. Uwimana, and J. D. Ndaruhebeye. 1997. The effects of the Rwandan civil war on poaching of ungulates in the Parc National des Volcans. *Oryx* 31 (4): 265–273.

Plumptre, A. J., A. Kayitare, H. Rainer, M. Gray, I. Munanura, N. Barakabuye, S. Asuma, M. Sivha, and A. Namara. 2004. The socio-economic status of people living near protected areas in the Central Albertine Rift. *Albertine Rift Technical Reports* 4:1–127.

RDB (Rwanda Development Board). 2012. Press releases. January 27. http://rdb.rw/~new/?id=479.

———. 2013a. Community initiatives. www.rdb.rw/tourism-and-conservation/conservation/community-initiatives.html.

———. 2013b. RDB launched community projects during Kwita Izina Week. www.rdb.rw/news-pages/news-details/article/rdb-launched-community-projects-during-kwita-izina-week.html.

Refisch, J., and J. Jenson. 2015. Transboundary collaboration in the Greater Virunga Landscape: From gorilla conservation to conflict-sensitive transboundary landscape management. In *Governance, natural resources, and post-conflict peacebuilding*, ed. C. Bruch, C. Muffett, and S. S. Nichols. London: Earthscan.

Rutagarama, E., and A. Martin. 2006. Partnerships for protected area conservation in Rwanda. *Geographic Journal* 172 (4): 291–305.

Rwanda Focus. 2007. ORTPN brings Vision 2020 closer for communities around parks. October 28. http://focus.rw/wp/2007/10/ortpn-brings-vision-2020-closer-for-communities-around-parks/.

———. 2009. 'Responsible tourism' benefits tourists and locals. August 5. http://focus.rw/wp/2009/08/responsible-tourism-benefits-tourists-and-locals/.

Sabuhoro, E. 2006. Ecotourism as a potential conservation incentive for local communities around Rwanda's Parc National des Volcans. M.Sc. thesis, University of Kent, Canterbury, United Kingdom.

Sandbrook, C. G. 2010. Putting leakage in its place: The significance of retained tourism revenue in the local context in rural Uganda. *Journal of International Development* 22 (1): 124–136.

Sorensen, L. W. 2015. Using economic evaluation to integrate natural resource management into Rwanda's post-conflict poverty reduction strategy paper. In *Governance, natural resources, and post-conflict peacebuilding*, ed. C. Bruch, C. Muffett, and S. S. Nichols. London: Earthscan.

Spenceley, A., S. Habyalimana, R. Tusabe, and D. Mariza. 2010. Benefits to the poor from gorilla tourism in Rwanda. *Development Southern Africa* 27 (5): 647–662.

Tusabe, R., and S. Habyalimana. 2010. From poachers to park wardens: Revenue sharing scheme as an incentive for environmental protection in Rwanda. *Mountain Forum Bulletin* 10 (1): 91–93.

Uganda Investment Authority. 2001. Tourism sector profile. Kampala. www.ugandainvest.go.ug/index.php/tourism.

Uganda Tourism Board. 2010. Tourism data bank. www.visituganda.com/information-centre/research/files/TourismDATABANK-2001-2009.pdf.

Uganda Wildlife Authority. 2010. Tariffs. Kampala.

———. 2013. Conservation fees/tariffs July 2011–June 2013. www.ugandawildlife.org/pdfs/Tariffs-2011-2013.pdf.

UNDP (United Nations Development Programme), REMA (Rwanda Environment Management Authority), and UNEP (United Nations Environment Programme). 2006. Economic analysis of natural resource management in Rwanda. www.unpei.org/sites/default/files/PDF/Rwanda-Economic-Analysis.pdf.

UNSG (United Nations Secretary-General). 2011. *Report of the Secretary-General on the United Nations Organization Stabilization Mission in the Democratic Republic of the Congo*. S/2011/298. May 12. New York. www.un.org/ga/search/view_doc.asp?symbol=S/2011/298.

U.S. DOS (United States Department of State). 2013. Travel warning: Democratic Republic of the Congo. News release. April 24. http://travel.state.gov/travel/cis_pa_tw/tw/tw_5939.html.

Varga, S., A. Draman, and K. Marriott. 2002. *Conflict risk assessment report: African Great Lakes*. Ottawa, Canada: Norman Paterson School of International Affairs, Carleton University. http://www4.carleton.ca/cifp/app/serve.php/1106.pdf.

Virunga National Park. 2011. Mountain gorillas vs. human disease. April 14. http://gorillacd.org/2011/04/14/mountain-gorillas-vs-human-disease/.

———. n.d. Who we are. http://gorillacd.org/who-we-are/.

World Bank. 2012a. GDP growth (annual %). http://data.worldbank.org/indicator/NY.GDP.MKTP.KD.ZG/countries?order=wbapi_data_value_2012+wbapi_data_value+wbapi_data_value-last&sort=desc.

———. 2012b. GDP per capita (current US$). http://data.worldbank.org/indicator/NY.GDP.PCAP.CD?order=wbapi_data_value_2012+wbapi_data_value+wbapi_data_value-last&sort=asc.

———. 2013. Rwanda. http://data.worldbank.org/country/Rwanda.

The interface between natural resources and disarmament, demobilization, and reintegration: Enhancing human security in post-conflict situations

Glaucia Boyer and Adrienne M. Stork

Sustainable peace is not won by wars or by pressure on warring parties to come to the peace table, but through the arduous and lengthy resolution of the causes of conflict—economic inequality, social exclusion, and political marginalization. Often, at the heart of this peacebuilding process are issues related to the contested control over natural resources or the unfair distribution of revenues from natural resources, which may have been a source of the conflict. Given the sensitivity of these issues, however, they are seldom addressed in negotiations to end a conflict. This may result in a peace process that avoids dealing with the important role that natural resources can have in post-conflict peacebuilding, especially their contribution to the process of reintegration and recovery in the aftermath of conflict.

Disarmament, demobilization, and reintegration (DDR) is a systematic approach, developed over the past twenty years largely by the United Nations, to assist the reintegration of excombatants and those associated with armed forces and groups back into civilian life. DDR is a key part of security and peacebuilding measures; conditions for it are often negotiated as part of the peace agreement. By contributing to improving overall security and assisting excombatants and supporters of armed groups to return to civilian life, DDR helps to lay the groundwork for long-term development to occur. The primary goal of DDR, however, is to deal with the security threat posed by armed forces and groups in the aftermath of conflict and to enable members ultimately to return to civilian life with sustainable livelihoods.

This chapter argues that DDR programs have, for the most part, ignored or underestimated the importance of natural resources as a fundamental element of

---

Glaucia Boyer is a disarmament, demobilization, and reintegration policy specialist in the Bureau for Crisis Prevention and Recovery at the United Nations Development Programme (UNDP) in Geneva, Switzerland, and coleads the Joint Initiative on Linking Reintegration and Natural Resource Management with the United Nations Environment Programme (UNEP). Adrienne M. Stork is an environmental advisor for the United Nations Environment Programme in Haiti, where she works on post-crisis protected areas management renewable energy, livelihoods, and value chain development.

security, recovery, and peacebuilding. Applying the DDR framework, the chapter examines the role that natural resources play in the functioning of armed forces and the livelihoods of their members and associated groups. It identifies the ways in which the incorporation of a natural resource dimension can contribute to more sustainable reintegration of excombatants. Through a review of case studies and literature, the chapter outlines both the opportunities and risks that natural resources present for DDR programs, and provides policy recommendations for addressing the interface between natural resources and DDR, particularly through community-based approaches to economic reintegration.

The first section of the chapter describes the origins of DDR as a systematic framework, now formulated in the UN's Integrated Disarmament, Demobilization and Reintegration Standards (IDDRS), and highlights its strengths and shortcomings in enhancing post-conflict security and stability, with an emphasis on community-based reintegration of excombatants. It also identifies the various ways that natural resources are implicated in conflict and post-conflict situations. The chapter draws upon case studies and the extant literature to illustrate some of the linkages between natural resources and reintegration programs. It concludes with a discussion of the challenges facing DDR planners and offers recommendations for addressing those challenges.

DDR: ORIGINS, COMMUNITY-BASED REINTEGRATION, AND NATURAL RESOURCES

For over twenty years, the UN has been called upon to support the processes of disarming, demobilizing, and reintegrating excombatants in countries emerging from conflict. The first UN-supported DDR program occurred in 1989 as part of the United Nations Observer Group in Central America. Today, DDR is but one element in a complex set of post-conflict operations that seek to deal with the broader issues of security, economic development, human rights, and the rule of law. Its objectives are to increase security and stability during the immediate post-conflict period and to help lay the foundations for enduring peace and long-term development. DDR is a highly politicized and symbolic process, and indeed some would measure the success of a DDR program by the degree to which it sets the tone for the subsequent post-conflict recovery efforts (Harsch 2005; SIDDR 2006).

The changing nature of peacekeeping and post-conflict recovery strategies requires close coordination among several UN departments, agencies, funds, and programs. To overcome what had been an uncoordinated approach and translate the knowledge and lessons learned through twenty years of DDR experience into practical policy guidance, sixteen entities came together in 2005 as the UN Inter-Agency Working Group on DDR to formulate the IDDRS.[1] The IDDRS is a

[1] The organizations involved were the United Nations Department for Peacekeeping Operations, United Nations Department of Political Affairs, United Nations Department of Public Information, International Labour Organization, International Organization

framework of guidelines, policies, and practices to guide DDR programs globally (UNDDR 2006).

Thus, DDR has evolved into a highly organized and systematic approach. The UN recognizes that the primary responsibility for DDR rests with national institutions and that the UN's role is to support the process as a neutral institution. In practice, however, genuine national ownership is difficult to achieve, particularly at the early stages of post-conflict stabilization, when national legitimacy and capacity tend to be weak. Furthermore, national ownership is understood to be broader than exclusive central government ownership, requiring the participation of a wide range of state and nonstate actors at the national, regional, and local levels. This process is often dependent on international political and financial support.[2]

DDR takes place in both UN mission and nonmission contexts, and the roles and responsibilities of national and international actors will differ according to the situation. In mission contexts, such as in Darfur, South Sudan, and Côte d'Ivoire, the UN tends to act as an implementer (the mission implements disarmament and demobilization, while UNDP carries out reintegration, usually through local implementing partners); whereas in nonmission contexts, such as in Comoros, Sri Lanka, and Colombia, the UN plays more of an advisory role, although it may also be called upon to implement various components of the process depending on levels of national capacity.[3]

DDR programs can also be supported by other organizations involved in post-conflict peacebuilding. For example, the International Organization for Migration played a central role in the DDR process in Aceh, Indonesia, and regional organizations such as the Organization of American States have played a role in the Colombian DDR process. DDR is essential to post-conflict peacebuilding and recovery, and is considered by some to be "the heart of [the] transition from war to peace" (Colletta, Kistner, and Wiederhofer 1996, x; UNSG 2000).

---

for Migration, Joint United Nations Programme on HIV/AIDS, Office for Disarmament Affairs, United Nations Office of the High Commissioner for Human Rights, United Nations Children's Fund, United Nations Development Fund for Women, United Nations Development Programme, United Nations High Commissioner for Refugees, United Nations Institute for Disarmament Research, United Nations Population Fund, World Food Programme, and World Health Organization.

2 DDR is often, though not always, a condition of a comprehensive peace agreement and is led by a national commission on DDR in a particular country, with broad support from donors. The most active donors of DDR have historically been the Nordic countries (Denmark, Finland, Norway, and Sweden); members of the European Union (Belgium, Germany, Italy, the Netherlands, and the United Kingdom); Japan; the United States; and multilateral donors such as the World Bank.

3 Support for DDR is also mandated in several UN special political missions, including in Burundi and Guinea Bissau. An integrated DDR unit was also established within the UN Peacekeeping Mission in Haiti, although it was dissolved in 2007.

Community-based reintegration

Disarmament and demobilization are the easiest phases of the process from an operational perspective and can often occur relatively quickly after the signing of a peace agreement. The demobilization phase will often include a reinsertion period of six to twelve months, during which beneficiaries of the DDR process are assisted with their immediate needs, including food, clothing, and transportation to their communities of return. The reinsertion phase may also include participation in labor-intensive, quick-impact projects, such as building roads and schools or repairing infrastructure damaged during the conflict.

Reintegration is by far the most complex and lengthy phase of DDR, and requires a sound understanding of the range of social, political, and economic challenges faced by excombatants, associated groups (which include women and children who have performed a supporting role to the armed group, although they may not have been weapon-carrying combatants), and the communities that receive excombatants in the aftermath of conflict. The IDDRS defines reintegration as "the process by which ex-combatants acquire civilian status and gain sustainable employment and income . . . essentially a social and economic process with an open time-frame, primarily taking place in communities at the local level. It is part of the general development of a country and a national responsibility, and often necessitates long-term external assistance" (UNDDR 2006, 2). Indeed, it is recognized that the success of DDR will ultimately be determined by the sustainability of the reintegration phase (Fusato 2003).

In DDR, sustainable reintegration aims to achieve the effective transition of excombatants and associated groups from military to civilian livelihoods. To facilitate this process without exacerbating or causing new tensions between excombatants and communities, DDR programs must provide support for excombatants, members of associated groups, and members of communities to which the former combatants will be returning (Pouligny 2004). This model of community-based reintegration is endorsed by the policy guidance of the IDDRS, and has been approved and confirmed by all twenty-one members of the UN Inter-Agency Working Group on DDR.[4]

A community-based approach to reintegration allows DDR programs to address multiple needs and security concerns that will affect the success of the DDR process. For example, it provides support to excombatants and associated groups who are considered a security threat in the aftermath of conflict, mainly because these individuals are considered high-risk for recruitment back into armed groups, often lack job skills and education to self-reintegrate into society, and

[4] The United Nations Institute for Training and Research, the Office of the Special Advisor on Africa, the Office of the Special Representative of the Secretary-General for Children and Armed Conflict, the United Nations Peacebuilding Support Office, the United Nations Environment Programme, and the World Bank joined the Inter-Agency Working Group on DDR after the launch of the IDDRS.

are invariably socialized to high levels of violence (Ember and Ember 1994).[5] (See sidebar for community-based reintegration activities.)

A community-based approach implies working with national and local institutions, civil society, and communities so they also contribute to, and benefit from, successful reintegration. Through a community-based approach, DDR programs are better able to avoid the appearance that excombatants and associated groups are being singularly rewarded for their behaviors and activities during the conflict. The perception of such favoritism often causes resentment by receiving communities who are also in need of development assistance (Knight and Ozerdem 2004; Isima 2004).[6] Working through communities is also recognized to support the multiple forms of capital associated with livelihoods,[7] many of which have been degraded or severely disrupted during conflict (USAID 2005).

Community-based reintegration activities

- Create specific training and income-generating opportunities tailored to the needs of ex-combatants and associated groups, while also allowing other groups at risk that confront similar reintegration challenges to benefit from these opportunities.
- Build the capacity of existing training institutions to absorb excombatants and associated groups into their regular vocational training.
- Create employment and business development services for excombatants and associated groups, such as information, counseling, and referral services, and then gradually open these services to other members of the community through business services centers.
- When income-generating opportunities are created for excombatants and associated groups, ensure opportunities are not only based on solid labor market analysis but also improve the lives of community members and the larger local economic recovery.

Source: Adapted from ILO (2007).

Community-based reintegration can also be an important component in broader peacebuilding and "as means for community recovery" (UNPBC 2009, 1). It is important to remember, however, that DDR programs are only one element of activities in post-conflict situations, and that DDR programs are challenged by the inherent complexity of working in such conditions, including the dearth of local institutions and capacities, as well as challenges in coordination among agencies, a lack of financial resources, and the absence of strong political will

---

5 It is also true that many excombatants, and especially women associated with armed forces and groups, do demobilize voluntarily before DDR has begun. In these cases, the UN and partner agencies make special efforts to identify and provide assistance to these individuals as well.

6 This is especially important since cash payments are often used during the disarmament, demobilization, and reinsertion phases of DDR, as well as during reintegration, when excombatants and associated groups are given special access to education and vocational training that may not be available to the community at large.

7 According to the United Kingdom's Department for International Development, there are five types of capital associated with livelihoods: human capital (skills, knowledge, ability, and health); social capital (relationships, memberships, networks, and connectedness); natural capital (natural resources); physical capital (infrastructure, tools, and equipment); and financial capital (financial resources) (DFID 1999).

(SIDDR 2006; Pouligny 2004). Other processes that often occur simultaneously with DDR include security sector reform, transitional justice measures, macroeconomic adjustment policies, judicial reforms, political reforms, and electoral reforms, among others. The importance of funding and timing in the dispersal of funds for DDR programs has also been widely recognized (Spear 2002; UNOWA 2005).

Natural resources, conflict, and DDR

Access to natural resources for livelihoods can be an underlying tension leading up to a conflict between groups, and can influence the duration of the conflict (Weinstein 2005; Ross 2004b). Natural resources also play a significant role at different stages of a conflict (Ross 2004a). Natural resources that are taken illegally and sold on national or international markets can be used to finance the recruitment of combatants, the acquisition of arms, and the daily subsistence and livelihoods of armed forces and groups connected to combatants.

When natural resources are implicated in a conflict, they become a factor in the conflict economy, with far-reaching effects on the livelihoods of populations in the regions. A conflict economy consists of the collective economic exchanges that occur during armed conflict; they often include the extraction and sale of natural resources to finance conflict by either side. Given the way that the economy becomes intertwined with hostilities, the conflict economy inherently implicates the command structure and military livelihoods of armed groups involved in the conflict, as has been seen in the well-known cases of diamonds and timber in Sierra Leone and Liberia, minerals in the Democratic Republic of the Congo (DRC), and timber in Cambodia. In conflict situations, economic opportunities are often available to members of armed forces and groups due to the fact that they carry weapons and can become a dominant factor driving the recruitment of opportunistic individuals in armed forces (Global Witness 2009; ICG 2007; Weinstein 2005). To compound these problems further, the conflict economy often functions in such a way that both armed forces and their associated groups have an incentive to continue fighting (Ohlsson 2000).

Conflict adversely affects the human, social, financial, physical, natural, and political capital of livelihood systems within communities and the broader society, as access to essential livelihood assets is destroyed, becomes restricted, or comes under control by particular groups (USAID 2005). Without a range of livelihood assets, people tend to rely on immediately available resources to survive, often in ways that are not sustainable in the long term—rapid deforestation, extraction of high-value minerals, or shifting patterns of agriculture and grazing that degrade the land and resource base. Conflict can also degrade the traditional local systems of natural resource management, resulting in a loss of indigenous knowledge about livelihood support systems and ecosystems, and it can destroy the social and cultural practices tied to the management of those resources.

THE ROLE OF NATURAL RESOURCES IN DDR

Given the role that natural resources play in conflicts, whether as underlying drivers of conflict itself or as a means for armed groups to fund their activities, it is important that natural resources are incorporated into all phases of DDR programs. Natural resources are often already implicated in the reintegration activities supported by DDR, and control of natural resources is often a security concern in situations where DDR takes place.

Disarmament

Disarmament is an important security measure because it reduces the number of weapons available to those who would continue the conflict. The disarmament phase is vital in building confidence between the government, its own armed forces, irregular armed groups, and communities, and it is a highly symbolic process (often, there is a ceremonial burning or other means to destroy the arms collected, an oft-called "flame of peace"). Disarmament programs carried out within a DDR program can occur in sequence with or simultaneously to other initiatives for disarmament or reduction in small arms and light weapons from individuals other than members of armed forces or groups (such as members of community security programs).

Disarmament is difficult to incentivize and achieve, since weapons are often the means by which combatants make their livelihoods, and combatants may feel vulnerable and uncertain about their ability to support themselves without weapons.[8] DDR programs in the past have offered cash payments for weapons, although this has inadvertently led to the creation of a market for weapons (Isima 2004), and such buyback schemes are no longer endorsed by the UN (UNDDR 2006).[9] Furthermore, where the economic resources of armed forces and their associated groups are derived from the armed exploitation of natural resources, or where arms provide security for livelihood activities, the incentives to disarm may be especially low (IPA 2003).

Many people in rural communities and highly armed societies rely on arms to defend their livestock, land, and other livelihood assets. In Karamoja, in northern Uganda, the government's enforcement of disarmament programs has led to greater insecurity regarding natural resources among rural communities because they must rely on local police to provide safety for their livestock held in kraals, or pens, as they no longer have weapons with which to protect themselves against raiding groups. With their livestock penned, they have been unable to pursue their

---

[8] In the eastern region of the DRC, AK-47s are often referred to as "credit cards." The same has been noted in the Darfur conflict in Sudan.

[9] The IDDRS specifically advises that DDR programs shall "[a]void attaching monetary value to weapons" as a means of encouraging their surrender, to avoid fueling arms flows (UNDDR 2006, 18).

traditional methods of herding, resulting in severe degradation of the land. Coupled with drought and other climatic changes in the area, this restriction has resulted in a loss of livelihood revenue and traditional natural resource management practices in Karamoja (Sites and Akabwai 2009). While the Karamoja disarmament program was not part of a DDR program per se, it highlights the relationship between access to arms and protection of livelihood assets, and shows the unintended consequences on the natural resources upon which those livelihoods depend.

The disarmament in Karamoja also affected gender roles within the region's communities. Due to fragile security, women were displaced from activities they traditionally participated in alongside men, such as managing livestock, and were forced to rely on exploiting natural resources in ways that increased their vulnerability to violence. For example, as women traveled farther into the countryside to harvest firewood and food, they encountered armed rebels who threatened or attacked them. These unintended consequences affected their relationship with the men in the community, who were unable to offer them protection after being disarmed, and who in turn experienced a profound change in their masculine identities. The impact was especially strong for young men, who traditionally relied on livestock for their livelihoods and to acquire the wealth needed for marriage.

While disarmament programs within an overall DDR strategy may differ from the findings in Karamoja, the importance of arms for security and livelihoods should not be underestimated. The Karamoja program offers DDR practitioners many insights into the links between disarmament and livelihoods. The armed pastoralists in the region were not combatants in a conflict, but they do rely on arms as an essential livelihood asset to protect their livestock. They must now shift their livelihood strategies to depend on assets other than arms. The experience in Karamoja serves as an example for DDR practitioners to consider the broader livelihood implications of disarmament activities, as well as the sequencing of DDR program activities.[10]

Further research is necessary to clarify the effects of disarmament on the extraction of natural resources where such resources have played a significant role in funding armed conflict. Carrying a weapon often is of great importance to identity and to livelihoods following conflict (CSRS 2009). The speed at which weapons are taken away in a DDR program requires that livelihoods support and social assistance for these individuals must be available from the outset. Hence, DDR should not be viewed and funded as a linear process (in which disarmament is the first step, followed by demobilization and then reintegration). Instead, DDR should be viewed as concurrent and mutually supportive activities. For example, reintegration facilitates disarmament and demobilization because weapons are more easily collected when excombatants have alternative livelihood opportunities.

---

10 For additional analyses of livestock and peacebuilding in the Turkana Karimojong Cluster, see Jeremy Lind, "Manufacturing Peace in 'No Man's Land': Livestock and Access to Natural Resources in the Karimojong Cluster of Kenya and Uganda," in this book.

Disarmament may also have a negative impact on the physical environment where it is carried out. Disposal of the collected weapons and ammunition poses potential security and environmental risks. Often, the weapons are simply stored in containers until they can be properly dismantled (while subject to being stolen), or are burned in symbolic "flames of peace" ceremonies. While the symbolic importance of such a ceremony should not be underestimated, it is important that the disposal of weapons does not create a source of risk or contamination to the soil, air, and water resources in the area (UNDDA 2002).

Demobilization

The demobilization process takes place with excombatants receiving documentation certifying their transition from military to civilian life. This marks the beginning of severing participants' formal ties with the military command structures and livelihoods to which they have been accustomed (UNDDR 2006). Demobilization may be done with groups of excombatants gathering in camps, barracks, assembly areas, or cantonment sites, although mobile demobilization teams have been used in certain cases. The demobilization phase generally also comprises reinsertion assistance (transitional support to cover the basic needs of excombatants and their families in the form of monetary allowances, food, clothes, shelter, and short-term training and employment) until the reintegration program is operational (UNDDR 2006).

During demobilization and reinsertion, excombatants go through the process of transforming their personal identities—losing their military identity and gaining a civil one. This process is closely tied to their livelihoods, their previous affiliation with armed forces, and their place in the receiving community. While DDR deals with large numbers of people, the personal transformation of each participant is highly dependent on the motivation of each individual and the specific conditions into which that individual is being reintegrated. Where the military livelihoods depended on the extraction of natural resources, it is important that DDR programs acknowledge the particular skills and survival tactics of excombatants. The activities planned for reinsertion (such as quick-impact projects) and reintegration should seek to build upon these skills and support the acquisition of new ones wherever possible, and to encourage the sound management of natural resources to support livelihoods through the education and training programs associated with reintegration.

As excombatants begin to transform their identities through demobilization and reinsertion, culturally appropriate symbols of identity and power are important. It is common practice that reinsertion assistance includes monetary resettlement packages in addition to basic tools and necessities, so that excombatants are not forced to travel back to their communities empty-handed. This process can be especially important for males, as masculine identity is often tied to the ability to possess assets, and some may feel emasculated after turning in their weapons and losing the identity they possessed as part of a combatant group during the conflict (IAWG 2012).

In transitioning from demobilization and reinsertion to reintegration, access to livelihood assets is paramount for both social and economic reasons. In many societies, land and access to livelihood assets such as livestock are extremely important to personal identity, status in society, family relationships, and prospects for marriage.[11] Land is notoriously one of the most difficult aspects of post-conflict resettlement and reintegration, and often becomes a source of conflict in itself. Rights to land and other natural resources are generally left outside a comprehensive peace agreement, to be resolved at a later stage in the peace process. While the omission is mainly due to the urgency with which agreements are signed in order to cease hostilities, it makes it difficult for DDR programs to assist in the rebuilding of livelihoods and provide access to productive livelihood assets in the post-conflict environment.

The reinsertion part of the demobilization phase offers important opportunities for peacebuilding and community reconciliation. Reinsertion is often composed of short-term, labor-intensive, low-skill, quick-impact projects, designed to keep excombatants busy (and thus reduce their threat to overall security), and to provide them with rapid income that could create peace dividends for the surrounding communities, such as infrastructure rehabilitation, sanitation, and demining of agricultural areas. It is through involvement in such projects that excombatants can begin readjusting to a new type of livelihood and begin reconciling with the civilian population.

Infrastructure rehabilitation projects that rely on natural resources and provide community-wide benefits can also serve as a platform for reconciliation between groups and encourage mechanisms for nonviolent conflict resolution, many of which may exist in the traditional culture of the communities. There is also an opportunity to promote the sound management of natural resources in the course of reinsertion projects. This can have far-reaching effects on the sustainability of the livelihoods supported by those resources, as well as greater resilience to environmental change and reduced vulnerability to natural disasters.

Where demobilization camps are used, they can have a significant impact on local natural resources, depending on the size of the camps, their placement, and the provisioning of fuelwood, water, and waste disposal. It is vitally important that economic resources be rechanneled to support the development of the population as a whole, not just the camps.

Finally, demobilization will challenge the command structure of armed forces, as well as their power and political influence, making this aspect of the peace process a disincentive to their participation in DDR programs. In settings where armed forces and combatant groups are undergoing DDR, incentives for the conflict economy to continue are sure to be present. The incentives include the exploitation of natural resources to continue funding leaders of armed groups and other political interests, as well as to support the livelihoods of rank-and-file excombatants and associated groups.

---

11 For additional analyses of identity, natural resources, and post-conflict peacebuilding, see Arthur Green, "Social Identity, Natural Resources, and Peacebuilding," in this book.

Reintegration

Reintegration is by far the most complex, lengthy, and resource-intensive phase of DDR. As such, DDR practitioners and donors must look critically at the impact of funding cycles on program implementation, paying special attention to the planning and implementation of reintegration. To date, reintegration is usually underfunded and lacks the resources to be planned and executed properly, despite its critical role in ensuring that excombatants and associated groups successfully transition to a civilian life and do not take up arms in the future. In addition to adequate funding, reintegration must complement broader ongoing programs for recovery and development in order for DDR to be successful and sustainable. Access to livelihood assets and their sustainable management must be a central focus of any program that seeks to support the objectives of reintegration and longer-term post-conflict recovery and peacebuilding (UNEP 2009).

The overarching goal of reintegration as a part of DDR is to contribute to security and stability through activities that support sustainable livelihoods for returning excombatants, their social integration within families and communities, and their participation in political processes. These activities, which ultimately aim to support peacebuilding and recovery, also lay the groundwork for long-term development processes to take root.

In many areas where economic reintegration programs take place, livelihoods are based on access to natural capital from local resources (such as arable land for agriculture, fisheries, forests, and subsoil minerals) and ecosystem services (such as freshwater provisioning, regeneration of soils, and sanitation). These may be the same resources that exacerbated tensions leading to conflict or financed the activities of armed forces and other groups during conflict.

Reintegration programs have the opportunity to promote the sustainable management of natural resources to help improve the success of the livelihoods at stake and the objectives of the overall DDR program. Promoting the sound management and productivity of natural resources will improve the contribution they make to development and poverty alleviation, both of which are necessary factors for peacebuilding.

Specifically, natural resources can provide both quantitative and qualitative contributions to reintegration. Quantitatively, the management of natural resources creates jobs and employment opportunities, and facilitates the development of a variety of employable and transferable skills in numerous sectors: agriculture, agroforestry, nontimber forest products, forest management, biotrade, fisheries, aquaculture, sanitation, fresh water provisioning, energy generation, ecotourism, protected area management, and restoration, all of which offer public and private opportunities to expand existing economic opportunities (Holmes and Cooper 2005). In addition, the sustainable management of natural resources offers prospects for value chain development, which can support the development and sustainability of business sectors and industries.

Qualitatively, the management of natural resources can ensure the sustainable use of those resources, thus improving or maintaining the health and flow of natural capital and ecosystem services. Many cultures have traditional natural resource management practices and traditional knowledge about their local natural environment that can contribute to sustainable practices when uninterrupted by conflict, and it is important that these practices are supported as part of rebuilding livelihoods. Furthermore, encouraging cooperation over shared resources and ecosystem services can also promote peacebuilding and reconciliation, thus contributing to the objectives of DDR and laying the groundwork for sustainable development.

The sound management of natural resources can also help preserve and protect the ecosystem services that support livelihoods. Ecosystem services are typically divided into four categories—provisioning (such as food, water, and timber), regulating (protection from natural hazards, climate, and disease control), supporting (soil formation, nutrient cycling, and primary plant production), and cultural (spiritual, educational, recreational, and aesthetic values)—and are directly linked to food security and other basic needs (McNeely 2005). The maintenance of ecosystem services is critical to reducing vulnerabilities to disasters and climate change, and to supporting livelihoods dependent on those services.

CASE STUDIES

The cases described in this section demonstrate how natural resource management has been incorporated into reintegration programs in Afghanistan, Colombia, Indonesia, and Mozambique.

Each case is unique to the conflict and setting in which it took place. While these four cases illustrate only some of the ways that natural resources can support economic reintegration programs, they do demonstrate several concrete options available to DDR programs. The cases range across continents, showing that natural resource management could be further integrated into DDR programs in different ways depending on the specific ecological and development context.

DDR programs should always be evaluated on a case-by-case basis. While the assessment methodologies and approaches followed in each case were modeled on the standards set out in the IDDRS, each program had to adapt to the conditions on the ground. The cases do show, however, that there is potential to further integrate natural resource management into DDR programs, and that the benefits from doing so can support the objectives of overall DDR and reintegration, as well as recovery and long-term development.

Afghanistan: Reforestation, conservation, and employment of excombatants

Following decades of conflict, the condition of many of Afghanistan's natural resources has declined to unsustainable levels, making livelihoods difficult to reestablish. Although Afghanistan has always lacked heavy forest cover for geographical and climatic reasons, nearly half of the woodlands that existed in the

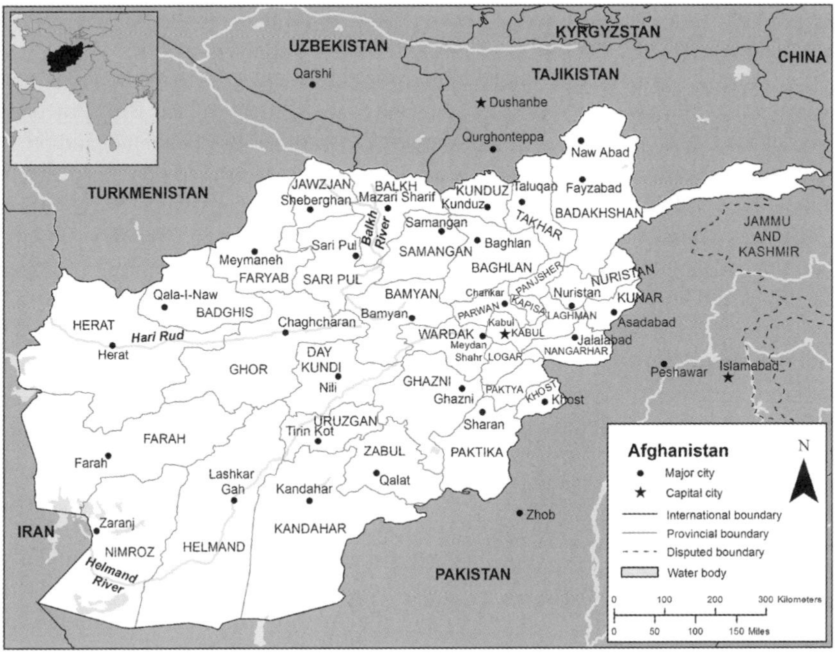

country have been lost since 1991 (Azimi 2007). Only 12 percent of the land in Afghanistan is arable, but 80 percent of the population is dependent on agriculture as the main source of livelihoods (Kelly 2004).

Afghanistan is highly prone to drought, a condition exacerbated by the loss of forest cover. In its post-conflict environmental assessment of Afghanistan, UNEP estimated that the Afghan pistachio woodlands have lost over 50 percent of their natural forest cover, as have other previously forested areas of the country (UNEP 2003). In addition, the majority of irrigation canals and systems, which were responsible for the irrigation of approximately one-third of arable cropland, were destroyed in the conflict with the Soviet Union and later conflicts.

To address the needs of vulnerable populations and to reintegrate former combatants, the government of Afghanistan created the Afghan Conservation Corps (ACC) project, implemented by the United Nations Office for Project Services. Through the ACC, excombatants and vulnerable populations were hired to assist in reforestation work in the pistachio woodlands and the eastern conifer forests. Since its creation in 2003, the ACC has undertaken 350 projects in twenty-three provinces, and generated approximatley 400,000 labor days for vulnerable Afghans (UNDDR 2006). The projects held management and technical training workshops for ministry staff, teachers, and extension workers, and conducted environmental education for villagers and school children. ACC workers have rehabilitated 108 nurseries, restored 32 public parks, planted pistachio seeds on

226 hectares of pistachio woodland in 7 provinces, and planted an average of 150,000 conifer and 350,000 fruit trees each year across the country.[12]

The ACC project was implemented through local governing councils and management structures. According to Wendy MacClinchy of the Best Practices Unit at the UN Department of Peacekeeping Operations, UN personnel and other international participants remained behind the scenes in order to give the projects a local face and voice.[13] Through the ACC, the Women's and Youth Conservation Corps was established for specific projects, such as revitalizing women's gardens, building women's dormitories, beautifying school compounds, planting fruit tree seedlings for future income, and cultivating home nurseries. Additionally, seven training centers have been built in seven provinces, three seed-storage facilities erected, 100 kilometers of irrigation canals rehabilitated in eleven irrigation systems, and 1,000 meters of retaining walls built to stabilize river banks.[14] In Nuristan, a northeastern province with extensive woodland cover that faced threats of illegal logging, conservation of forestry resources through the promotion of traditional Nuristani carpentry has been encouraged, and three projects to implement garbage pickup have helped to collect 1,000 cubic meters of waste.

The establishment of forest management committees (FMCs) by community elders enhanced community capacity and development in seven provinces. The FMCs were supported by the ACC and the Afghan Ministry of Agriculture, Irrigation and Livestock (MAIL), and by 2007 the FMCs had drafted forest protection plans to cover 3,200 hectares of woodlands and established forty full-time guards to protect the pistachio woodlands. Due to increased protection and improved management practices, villagers in the biggest pistachio woodland site, Shareek Yaar, estimated that revenues for their 2006 pistachio harvest had increased by 65 percent.[15]

The ACC project in Afghanistan is a clear example of a livelihoods strategy based upon the restoration of degraded ecosystems. The conflict in Afghanistan affected livelihoods in the pistachio sector, as well as other agricultural sectors harmed by the destruction of irrigation canals and other infrastructure. The conflict also contributed to deforestation and the destruction of productive lands. A focus of the reintegration phase of DDR in Afghanistan is to rebuild these livelihoods and to contribute to the restoration of sustainable ecosystems and ecosystem services.

Colombia: DDR, private-sector engagement, waste management, and organic fertilizer production

Colombia's internal conflict has persisted through various stages for over four decades, resulting in the need to demobilize and reintegrate thousands of

---

12 Simonetta Siligato, UN Office for Project Services official, personal communication with authors, 2009.

13 Wendy MacClinchy, personal communication with authors, May 2009.

14 Siligato, personal communication, 2009.

15 Siligato, personal communication, 2009.

excombatants from both paramilitary and guerrilla groups. As of 2013, 55,800 members of armed groups demobilized in Colombia, 10 percent of whom were women. Reintegration has been supported by individually targeted and community-based approaches through the Colombian High Council for Reintegration (Alta Consejería Presidencial para la Reintegración, or ACR).[16] The program is organized around three pillars: education, psychosocial support, and economic reintegration.

The Colombian DDR program reflects the emphasis in recent years on engaging the private sector in reintegration strategies. Biprocol is a company that produces organic solid and liquid fertilizers by using earthworms to break down plant and animal wastes collected from surrounding communities. Each of

[16] In 2011, ACR became the Colombian Agency for Reintegration (Agencia Colombiana para la Reintegración). For more information about ACR, see www.reintegracion.gov.co/Paginas/InicioACR.aspx#.Uij0JWTXh2I.

the company's ten locations employs approximately thirty demobilized individuals, all of whom are members of Colombia's ACR reintegration program.[17] Some Biprocol projects, such as those in Pereira (west of Bogotá), employ former members of both paramilitaries and guerrilla groups. In several of its locations, Biprocol receives financial support from ACR, as well as from the U.S. Agency for International Development (USAID) and the International Organization for Migration.

In addition to being a profitable business model, the Gonzales family, which operates Biprocol, views it as contributing to sustainable development in Colombia by providing organic fertilizer products that help to rebuild the soil and offer greater productivity to farmers. This contributes to the conservation and preservation of arable land and natural resources, and provides an alternative to harmful petrochemical fertilizers. By producing the fertilizers from animal and plant wastes, the company is offering a free waste disposal alternative to communities that would have to dispose of the organic matter in other ways. Finally, its business model provides alternative livelihoods to excombatants who might otherwise have few opportunities, thereby promoting and supporting the overall peace process in Colombia.

Biprocol demonstrates a strong commitment to encouraging and complementing the psychosocial, educational, and social support for reintegration offered by ACR. Biprocol also supports activities and social events designed to encourage group interaction and participation, such as weekly soccer matches and bring-your-family-to-work events. Employees are also offered a chance to make presentations to groups of colleagues, as well as opportunities to apply the math and business skills that they are learning through the ACR education programs.

Supporting agriculture through DDR allows the issues of livelihoods, identity, and food security to be addressed within reintegration programs. The Biprocol example demonstrates that waste management and fertilizer production can be an entry point for natural resource management within DDR. It further illustrates that a successful private-enterprise model within a DDR program can produce both a marketable product and alternative waste management practices. The organic waste collected is transformed into a useful product with good market value by a process that also supplies jobs to individuals, and avoids waste disposal costs for others.

Colombia is an agriculturally productive society with a growing level of environmental consciousness. There is a healthy domestic market for organic fertilizers, and regional foreign markets could potentially be tapped as well. In areas surrounding Santa Marta, in northern Colombia, coffee and cacao production require intensive amounts of fertilizer, for which Biprocol is a locally derived source. In this model of engaging private enterprise in DDR, demobilized individuals are part of a livelihood strategy in which they are able to build technical

[17] Information on Biprocol is from the company's web site and based partly on the authors' correspondence, in May 2009, with the Gonzales family, which operates the company.

skills, gain business experience, and are seen as contributing to environmental sustainability with a product that improves land and soil conditions—thus contributing to the health of Colombian society as a whole.

Aceh, Indonesia: Employing former combatants as ecotourism guides

Aceh is a region rich in oil, gas, and timber, and competition for these resources was one of the causes of insurgencies in 1953 and again from 1976 to 2005. Historically, the government of Indonesia (GOI) in Jakarta has controlled these resources, with only approximately 0.5 percent of the revenues being returned to Aceh (Beeck n.d.). In the struggle for Aceh's autonomy and independence, the Free Aceh Movement (Gerakan Aceh Merdeka, or GAM) employed both male and female combatants, using guerrilla tactics against the Indonesian military (Tentara Nasional Indonesia, or TNI) that led many combatants to spend great

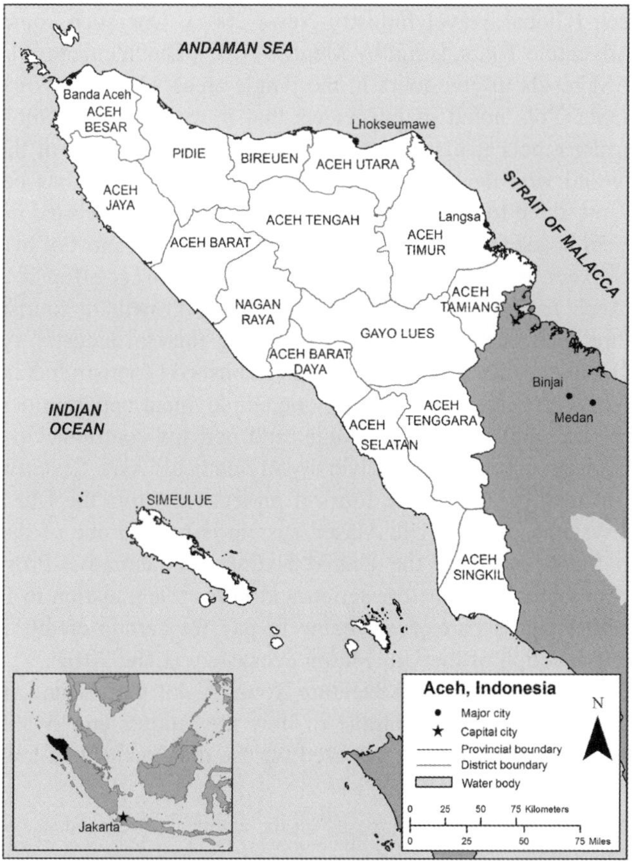

lengths of time deep in Aceh's interior rainforests, developing skills that could later be adapted during their reintegration into civilian life.

As the GOI supplied only 25 percent of TNI's budget, both the national army and GAM supported their struggles financially through cultivation of cannabis, illegal logging, illegal mining, and other activities (Beeck n.d.; Jones 2006). Indonesia has the world's third-largest tropical forest, and its high level of biodiversity was threatened by palm oil production, legal and illegal timber harvesting, and climate change. The deforestation rate in Indonesia is the second-highest in the world, and destruction of the forest and peat moss soils contribute significantly to the country's carbon emissions (Wetlands International 2011).

The tsunami that struck the coast of northern Sumatra in December 2004 devastated Aceh and provided a break in the fighting that led to successful peace negotiations. After nearly twenty-nine years of conflict, the GOI and GAM signed a memorandum of understanding (MOU) in August 2005 that initiated disarmament and established an autonomous government for the province of Aceh.

Since the former GAM combatants know the mountainous terrain of Aceh better than anybody, many have been recruited to work for ecotourism firms around Aceh (Global Travel Industry News 2008). One such company, Aceh Explorer Adventure Tours, is run by Mendel Pols, a Dutch citizen.[18] He employs former GAM rebels to give tours in the jungle areas where they once operated as combatants. Pols noted in interviews that it was very difficult for him to employ former rebels at first, but that once he gained the trust of the ex-GAM community and won the support of former commanders, he has been able to employ twenty-three former combatants as guides. He has invested in the equipment and gear needed for his guides, and in the beginning most of his customers were aid workers living in the region for tsunami recovery efforts.

The Aceh region is experiencing increasing growth in tourism and the infrastructure necessary to support a burgeoning tourism industry. As of 2008, at least 400 tourism sites in Aceh had been established (Tourism Indonesia 2008). If tourism in Aceh succeeds, it can provide employment opportunities to former combatants and conflict-affected people, and perhaps contribute to preserving some of the richest remaining biodiversity in Southeast Asia. Seventy percent of the forest in Aceh is under some form of protection within the Ulu Masen and Leuser ecosystems, and the Ulu Masen system is host to one of the first pilot projects in Indonesia under the United Nations Collaborative Programme on Reducing Emissions from Deforestation and Forest Degradation in Developing Countries (REDD), as part of a scheme to pay for carbon credits in order to support the protection of the Ulu Masen ecosystem (Lang 2010).

Although Aceh Explorer Adventure Tours is not part of an official DDR program, it is a compelling example of how the unique, employable skills of excombatants can be promoted and used for the development of local business

---

18 The Aceh case study is partially based on the authors' correspondence with Mendel Pols in April 2009.

and livelihoods. It is also an example of how the knowledge gained during armed conflict can be used for a productive livelihood afterwards if appropriate opportunities are present. This is especially important considering that most excombatants in DDR often have difficulty finding gainful employment because they are far behind their civilian counterparts in education (UNDDR 2006).

In July 2008 the governor of Aceh released the Aceh Green Strategy, a sustainable development plan that will base the future of Aceh's development on the sustainable use of natural resources and conservation of the area's remarkable biodiversity.[19] Reintegration programs that can support the Aceh Green Strategy are beneficial for the region as a whole, and can complement the broader, long-term development strategy. Ecotourism, as an economic strategy that is based upon conservation principles, is in accordance with the Aceh Green Strategy. Reintegration in Aceh that is based upon the goals of the strategy, including participation in REDD and other carbon credit schemes, can contribute to both environmental sustainability and successful reintegration as part of a long-term development strategy (Zwick 2008).

Mozambique: Employing excombatants in the management of parks

The Rome General Peace Accord in 1992 brought an end to almost twenty years of civil war in Mozambique between the Mozambican National Resistance (Resistência Nacional Moçambicana, or RENAMO) and the government. The post-conflict period has been characterized by the strengthening of institutions for the management of natural resources, as well as the rehabilitation of the wildlife sector and management of protected areas. (In 1994, for example, the government enacted a series of environmental policies, including the Environmental Framework Law, the Land Law, and the Forestry and Wildlife Law.) During the long conflict, natural resources, especially forests and wildlife, had been severely overexploited in some areas, while in other areas forests were able to regenerate. In general, most of the populations of large wild game in Mozambique suffered greatly during the conflict, as did the ecosystems that were easily accessible and exploitable (Hatton, Couto, and Oglethorpe 2001).

The signing of the peace agreement led to the establishment of the United Nations Mission in Mozambique (ONUMOZ), which lasted for two years and was primarily responsible for the disarmament and demobilization of RENAMO and government forces, the organization of national presidential and parliamentary elections, and, in close collaboration with the United Nations High Commissioner for Refugees, the repatriation and resettlement of some 1.3 million refugees returning to Mozambique.

The reintegration component of ONUMOZ was minimal. The mission had a short-term focus, and reintegration was made difficult by the low literacy levels

---

[19] For an analysis of the Aceh Green Strategy and peacebuilding, see Lakhani (2015).

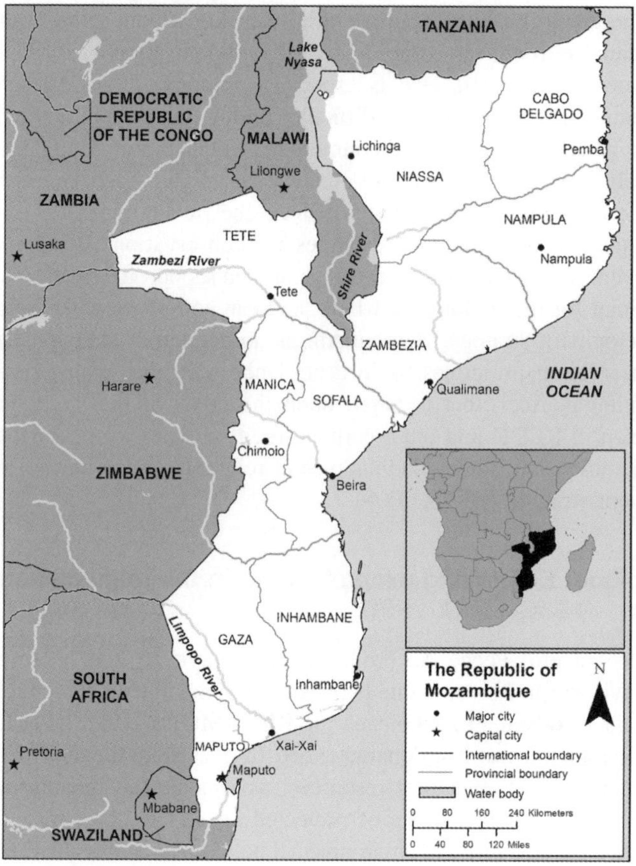

of the excombatants (Schafer 1998). In addition, it was difficult to engage excombatants in rural livelihoods such as agriculture, and many migrated to urban areas after demobilization (Medi 1997). Long-term reintegration was not planned or budgeted for within the Mozambique DDR program, which was at that time conceived as merely a short-term stabilization measure (Levine 2006).

Despite these challenges, some excombatants were employed by the Mozambique National Directorate of Forestry and Wildlife (Direcção Nacional de Florestas e Fauna Bravia, or DNFFB), which was responsible for the management of protected areas in Mozambique until 2001, when that responsibility was transferred to the Ministry of Tourism. The DNFFB employed demobilized combatants to patrol the Gorongosa National Park to control illegal poaching of wild game.[20] To prevent conflict between the teams of guards, former

[20] For a more detailed discussion of the DDR program in Gorongosa National Park, see Matthew F. Pritchard, "From Soldiers to Park Rangers: Post-Conflict Natural Resource Management in Gorongosa National Park," in this book.

members of both sides of the previously warring parties were placed on the same team and were led by a trained wildlife service ranger. Overall, only small numbers of demobilized combatants were employed in the natural resources sector, but those who were employed had highly valued skills and knowledge about the region and the terrain in the park areas, including knowledge of where park authorities could travel safely and avoid landmines (Schafer and Black 2003).

Mozambique's experience is uncommon in that there was little or no focus on supporting long-term reintegration or planning for anything comparable to what today is described in the IDDRS as reintegration. However, since natural resources are so abundant in Mozambique and thus critical to the economic recovery of the country, there were ample opportunities for the management of these resources to incorporate the employment of demobilized individuals. These opportunities focus on several components: development of government jobs in the newly created environmental management agencies, employment opportunities in the management of protected areas, and jobs in the new sectors of tourism and sustainable forestry that emerged after the peace agreement.

INTEGRATING NATURAL RESOURCES AND DDR: CHALLENGES AND RECOMMENDATIONS

Addressing natural resources and livelihoods within a DDR program can be challenging. While some challenges will flow from the particular circumstances of the post-conflict situation in which a program operates, others will arise from three key problems found in any DDR program: funding gaps, lack of an inclusive approach, and the presence of spoilers. Still others may arise from the availability of natural resources and the threat posed by their availability to armed forces and groups.

Within the United Nations, these issues are being taken up by the Inter-Agency Working Group on DDR. Incorporating natural resource management into DDR programs can help to overcome these inherent challenges and support the overall success and sustainability of DDR.

Funding gaps

Implementing DDR remains especially challenging for the international community due to a fragmented funding architecture and a need for more commitment by the international donor community to reintegration programs. The debate continues over how widely to apply financial support for reintegration, and whether the communities where excombatants return should be included as beneficiaries of reintegration programs. (If they were included, additional financial resources would be needed for their programming.) A lack of commitment and funding up front for reintegration programs makes it extremely difficult, if not impossible, to adequately conduct the assessments that are necessary to properly plan reintegration programs. Without proper assessments, it is likely that the role of natural resources in the activities of armed groups and the opportunity that such resources present for reintegration and peacebuilding will continue to be overlooked, especially in funding to support natural resource management in DDR programs.

The lack of funding for reintegration programs also increases the difficulty of linking DDR programs to broader recovery and development initiatives. Reintegration programs provide an opportunity to address the relationship between armed-group activities and natural resources by supporting excombatants, associated groups, and the receiving communities in rebuilding livelihoods. The gains made in this area during reintegration and the contributions of these gains to peacebuilding should continue into long-term development. Funding for reintegration programs and further financial support for the transition to development is essential to achieve these goals.

Links between reintegration and wider recovery initiatives

It is often argued that DDR, while a tool to achieve immediate peace and stability, is effective only when it is also part of a larger, synchronized strategy to achieve long-term peace and stability through community security, security sector reform, and development support. The DDR process will fail if too much pressure is placed on it alone to achieve gains in post-conflict recovery that are better achieved through a coordinated effort among all development and security actors, such as those providing assistance to communities receiving excombatants, working on issues of land tenure and access to land, or addressing the gender dimensions of recovery.

At the same time, it is clear that the opportunities presented by DDR to address security and recovery challenges in the early stages following conflict can have lasting impacts on the security and development outcomes to follow. In Sudan and South Sudan, for example, local conflicts over resources are frequently used to destabilize political agendas. Thus, it is imperative that DDR programs carefully analyze and integrate the linkages between natural resources and security into their planning.

While it is apparent that providing assistance to communities receiving excombatants is an essential part of the reintegration process, how to achieve it is not as clear. At the very time that reintegration programs are being mounted, those communities are likely to also come under pressure from the waves of internally displaced persons and refugees that typically migrate after a conflict ends. Migration provides a further strain on the natural resource base for livelihoods, and a coordinated effort is required to address its impact. Programming needs to more systematically address the issues concerning natural resources that have a direct impact on DDR, including the role of receiving communities, access to and management of land, and gender roles.

Although the importance of land tenure and access to land are recognized by most DDR programs, the means to address them are not always forthcoming.

Land security is extremely important to the restoration of livelihoods and post-conflict peacebuilding, yet is often not addressed within the peace agreement, and may later become a source of conflict due to contradictory regulations or lack thereof.[21] In many countries, land tenure and property rights provide access to productive assets and resources that ensure food security, social status, and sustainable livelihoods. Reintegration programs are inevitably challenged by the problem of access to land for program participants and other returnees, especially where the traditional processes that govern land disputes have been severely disrupted by conflict (Unruh 2001).

Land is an issue for both rural and urban reintegration, and can be a highly symbolic resource for sociopolitical and cultural reasons. Group identity is often inextricably linked to the area from which it originates, thus making redistribution of land and ownership after conflict highly contentious (Unruh 1998). Additionally, there are many competing interests for land resources in the post-conflict context, including the private sector (Pantuliano 2007). DDR programs that seek to promote the access of women to livelihood assets are often particularly challenged by the issue of access to land, as land remains unavailable to women in many areas.[22]

Gender dimensions are critically important to every aspect of the DDR program, from eligibility, to access to benefits, to reintegration support and programming (UNDDR 2006). In many developing countries, women and girls often have the closest ties to natural resources such as agriculture and water, and are responsible for providing the basic resources to feed and clothe families (IFAD 2001). DDR programs integrating the management of natural resources must closely examine ways in which gender roles obstruct access to certain livelihood resources, and promote women's participation in decision making in natural resource management.

Gender roles may shift during the course of conflict, and the changes may have profound effects on the relationships between men and women afterwards. As excombatants and women associated with armed forces change their livelihoods during peacetime, concepts of masculinity and gender roles will invariably need to shift as well. DDR programs should confront these challenges when promoting access to land and other natural resources for women, but currently DDR programs are ill-equipped in terms of guidance to address these issues.

---

21 This is the case for the 2005 Comprehensive Peace Agreement in Sudan, where land issues were left to be decided at a later date, according to a process outlined in the agreement, by the National Land Commission and the Southern Sudan Land Commission (Pantuliano 2007). For a more detailed discussion of land issues between Sudan and South Sudan, see Salman (2013). Land issues have been a source of conflict between refugees and returnees in Rwanda and Uganda as well (Bruce 2007a, 2007b; Rugadya 2009).

22 See, for example, Karuru and Yeung (2015).

Spoilers and security

Control over natural resources is a leverage point for any party to an armed conflict. In many conflicts, access to natural resources, control over extractive resources, and control over the market for these resources lie at the heart of the conflict. Thus, the potential impact of peace spoilers—stakeholders in a DDR process who have vested interests in keeping the status quo, including their access to and control of natural resources, and seek to undermine any aspect of it—must be considered during DDR planning and while conducting assessments.

The private sector, which is important in post-conflict economic development, could also play the role of spoiler. In many post-conflict situations, important aspects of the peacebuilding process are contingent on investments and other forms of support from the private sector. Peacebuilding organizations often rely on the business expertise of those in the private sector when investing in DDR and redevelopment programs. While the private sector has come to fill this essential role in planning for post-conflict recovery, growing private-sector involvement in redevelopment programs also increases opportunities for spoilers who seek either to undermine peacebuilding efforts or utilize redevelopment programs for their own financial gain. To address the use of natural resources in post-conflict peacebuilding, the role of private companies needs to be considered. While the private sector may be abiding by all rules and laws in a particular country, the vulnerability of conflict resources to further exploitation in such weak settings, coupled with their importance for post-conflict peacebuilding and development, make the private sector extremely important for DDR.

* * *

Guidance on these three key issues is needed in the IDDRS in order to ensure that DDR processes foster a more systematic link between natural resources and economic reintegration. Access to renewable and sustainable energy supplies, waste management and sanitation, sustainable food production systems, and fresh water supplies are crucial to supporting livelihoods and reintegration, and can be effectively addressed within DDR programs. Failure to address them may further compromise security and undermine the objectives of such programs. Alternatively, these factors can be addressed in ways that promote livelihoods and form the basis for sustainable recovery in the short and medium term, and development initiatives in the long term.

REFERENCES

Azimi, A. 2007. *Environmental assessment for ADB's programme in Afghanistan*. Asian Development Bank.

Beeck, C. n.d. *Re-paving the road to peace: Analysis of the implementation of DD&R in Aceh Province, Indonesia*. Brief No. 25. Bonn, Germany: Bonn International Center for Conversion. www.bicc.de/uploads/tx_bicctools/brief35.pdf.

Bruce, J. 2007a. *Returnee land access: Lessons from Rwanda*. London: Overseas Development Institute. www.odi.org.uk/sites/odi.org.uk/files/odi-assets/publications-opinion-files/4176.pdf.

———. 2007b. *Drawing a line under the crisis: Reconciling returnee land access and security in post-conflict Rwanda*. London: Overseas Development Institute. www.odi.org.uk/sites/odi.org.uk/files/odi-assets/publications-opinion-files/4174.pdf.

Colletta, N. J., M. Kistner, and I. Wiederhofer. 1996. *The transition from war to peace in sub-Saharan Africa*. Washington, D.C.: World Bank.

CSRS (Center for Stabilization and Reconstruction Studies). 2009. An expansive approach to DDR. Workshop report. Monterey, CA: Naval Postgraduate School.

DFID (Department for International Development, United Kingdom). 1999. Sustainable livelihoods guidance sheets. www.eldis.org/vfile/upload/1/document/0901/section2.pdf.

Ember, C., and M. Ember. 1994. War, socialization and interpersonal violence: A cross-cultural study. *Journal of Conflict Resolution* 38 (4): 620–646.

Fusato, M. 2003. Disarmament, demobilization, and reintegration of excombatants. In *Beyond intractability*, ed. G. Burgess and H. Burgess. Boulder, CO: Conflict Research Consortium, University of Colorado. www.beyondintractability.org/essay/demobilization.

Global Travel Industry News. 2008. Former rebels guide tourists in Aceh. www.eturbonews.com/4867/former-rebels-guide-tourists-aceh.

Global Witness. 2009. *Faced with a gun, what can you do? War and the militarization of mining in eastern Congo*. London.

Harsch, E. 2005. When war ends: Transforming Africa's fighters into builders. *Africa renewal* 19 (3): 14–16.

Hatton, J., M. Couto, and J. Oglethorpe. 2001. *Biodiversity and war: A case study of Mozambique*. Washington, D.C.: Biodiversity Support Program.

Holmes, K., and E. Cooper. 2005. *How community-based natural resource management can benefit the poor*. Washington, D.C.: World Resources Institute. www.wri.org/publication/content/8077.

IAWG (Inter-Agency Working Group on Disarmament, Demobilization and Reintegration). 2012. *Blame it on the war? The gender dimensions of violence in disarmament, demobilization and reintegration*. www.iddrtg.org/wp-content/uploads/2013/05/IAWG-Blame-it-on-the-War-15-June-2012-Final.pdf.

ICG (International Crisis Group). 2007. Aceh: Post-conflict complications. Asia Report No. 139. Jakarta, Indonesia, and Brussels, Belgium. www.crisisgroup.org/~/media/Files/asia/south-east-asia/indonesia/139_aceh_post_conflict_complications.pdf.

IFAD (International Fund for Agricultural Development). 2001. *Rural poverty report 2001: The challenge of ending rural poverty*. Oxford, UK: Oxford University Press.

ILO (International Labour Organization). 2007. *Prevention of child recruitment and reintegration of children associated with armed forces and groups—Strategic framework for addressing the economic gap*. Geneva, Switzerland.

IPA (International Peace Academy). 2003. *Transforming war economies: Challenges for peacemaking and peacebuilding*. Report of the 725th Wilton Park Conference, Wiston House, Sussex, UK, October 27–29.

Isima, J. 2004. Cash payments in disarmament, demobilization and reintegration programs in Africa. *Journal of Security Sector Management* 2 (3): 1–10.

Jones, S. 2006. Relation between logging and conflict in Aceh. Notes from presentation to the Forum on Security, Development and Forest Conflict, hosted by International Crisis Group, Brussels, Belgium, February 8–9.

Karuru, N., and L. H. Yeung. 2015. Integrating gender into post-conflict natural resource management. In *Governance, natural resources, and post-conflict peacebuilding*, ed. C. Bruch, C. Muffett, and S. S. Nichols. London: Earthscan.

Kelly, A. T. 2004. *Securing Afghanistan's future, accomplishments and the way forward: Natural resources sector in recovery*. Manila, Philippines: Asian Development Bank.

Knight, M., and A. Ozerdem. 2004. Guns, camps and cash: Demobilization and reinsertion of former combatants in transitions from war to peace. *Journal of Peace Research* 41 (4): 499–516.

Lakhani, S. 2015. Consolidating peace through Aceh Green. In *Governance, natural resources, and post-conflict peacebuilding*, ed. C. Bruch, C. Muffett, and S. S. Nichols. London: Earthscan.

Lang, C. 2010. Interviews about Ulu Masen, Indonesia: A REDD-labelled protected area. REDD Monitor, January. www.redd-monitor.org/2010/01/20/interviews-about-ulu-masen-indonesia-a-redd-labelled-protected-area.

Levine, D. 2006. *Organizational disruption and change in Mozambique's peace process*. College Park, MD: Center for International and Security Studies, University of Maryland.

McNeely, J. 2005. Biodiversity and security. In *Human and environmental security: An agenda for change*, ed. F. Dodds and T. Pippard. London: Earthscan.

Medi, E. 1997. *Study of vocational rehabilitation, training, and employment programs for persons disabled by the conflict: Mozambique experiences and issues*. Geneva, Switzerland: International Labour Organization.

Ohlsson, L. 2000. *Livelihood conflicts—Linking poverty and environment as causes of conflict*. Stockholm: Environmental Policy Unit, Swedish International Development Cooperation Agency.

Pantuliano, S. 2007. The land question: Sudan's peace nemesis. Humanitarian Policy Group Working Paper. London: Overseas Development Institute.

Pouligny, B. 2004. *The politics and anti-politics of disarmament, demobilization and reintegration programs*. Paris: Centre d'Études et Recherches Internationales.

Ross, M. L. 2004a. How do natural resources influence civil war? Evidence from thirteen cases. *International Organization* 58 (1): 35–67.

———. 2004b. What do we know about natural resources and civil war? *Journal of Peace Research* 41 (3): 337–356.

Rugadya, M. A. 2009. Escalating land conflicts in Uganda: A review of evidence from recent studies and surveys. For the International Republican Institute and the Uganda Round Table Foundation. www.mokoro.co.uk/files/13/file/lria/escalating_Uganda_landconflicts.pdf.

Salman, S. M. A. 2013. The Abyei territorial dispute between North and South Sudan: Why has its resolution proven difficult? In *Land and post-conflict peacebuilding*, ed. J. Unruh and R. C. Williams. London: Earthscan.

Schafer, J. 1998. A baby who does not cry will not be suckled: AMODEG and the reintegration of demobilised soldiers. *Journal of Southern African Studies* 24 (1): 207–222.

Schafer, J., and R. Black. 2003. Conflict, peace, and the history of natural resource management in Sussundenga District, Mozambique. *African Studies Review* 46 (3): 55–81.

SIDDR (Stockholm Initiative on Disarmament Demobilisation Reintegration). 2006. Background studies. Stockholm: Swedish Ministry for Foreign Affairs.

Sites, E., and D. Akabwai. 2009. *Changing roles, shifting risks: Livelihood impacts of disarmament in Karamoja, Uganda.* Medford, MA: Feinstein International Center, Tufts University.

Spear, J. 2002. Demobilization and disarmament: Key implementation issues. In *Ending civil wars: Evaluating implementation of peace agreements*, ed. S. J. Stedman, D. Rothchild, and E. Cousens. Boulder, CO: Lynne Rienner.

Tourism Indonesia. 2008 Aceh tourism agents being trained in Bali. www.tourismindonesia.com/2008/03/aceh-tourism-agents-being-trained-in.html.

UNDDA (United Nations Department for Disarmament Affairs). 2002. *A destruction handbook: Small arms, light weapons, ammunition and explosives*. Geneva, Switzerland: Conventional Arms Branch.

UNDDR (United Nations Disarmament, Demobilization and Reintegration Resource Centre). 2006. *Integrated disarmament, demobilization and reintegration standards.* http://pksoi.army.mil/doctrine_concepts/documents/UN%20Guidelines/IDDRS.pdf.

UNEP (United Nations Environment Programme). 2003. *Afghanistan: Post-conflict environmental assessment.* Geneva, Switzerland. http://postconflict.unep.ch/publications/afghanistanpcajanuary2003.pdf.

———. 2009. *From conflict to peacebuilding: The role of natural resources and the environment.* Nairobi, Kenya. http://postconflict.unep.ch/publications/pcdmb_policy_01.pdf.

UNOWA (United Nations Office for West Africa). 2005. Final communique. Seminar on the challenge of reintegration of excombatants in DDR programs in West Africa, Dakar, Senegal.

UNPBC (United Nations Peacebuilding Commission). 2009. Lessons learned on sustainable reintegration in post-conflict settings. Peacebuilding Commission Working Group on Lessons Learned. New York.

Unruh, J. D. 1998. Land tenure and identity change in post-war Mozambique. *GeoJournal* 46:89–99.

———. 2001. Post-war land dispute resolution: Land tenure and the peace process in Mozambique. *International Journal on World Peace* 18:3–30.

UNSG (United Nations Secretary-General). 2000. The role of the United Nations peacekeeping in disarmament, demobilization and reintegration. Report of the Secretary-General to the Security Council. S/2000/101. February 11. New York.

USAID (United States Agency for International Development). 2005. *Livelihoods and conflict: A toolkit for intervention.* Washington, D.C. http://commdev.org/livelihoods-and-conflict-toolkit-intervention.

Weinstein, J. M. 2005. Resources and the information problem in rebel recruitment. *Journal of Conflict Resolution* 49 (4): 598–624.

Wetlands International. 2011. Peatlands and CO2 emissions. Ede, Netherlands. www.wetlands.org/Whatwedo/PeatlandsandCO2emissions/Aboutpeatlands/tabid/1362/Default.aspx.

Zwick, S. 2008. Painting the town REDD: Merril Lynch inks massive voluntary forest deal. Ecosystem Marketplace, February 8. www.ecosystemmarketplace.com/pages/dynamic/article.page.php?page_id=5584&section=home&eod=1.

From soldiers to park rangers: Post-conflict natural resource management in Gorongosa National Park

Matthew F. Pritchard

The disarmament, demobilization, and reintegration (DDR) of former combatants is essential to post-war peacebuilding. During the post-conflict period, maintaining stability in the short and medium term requires programs that provide employment for combatants rendered jobless by the cessation of hostilities (Colletta, Kostner, and Wiederhofer 1996b; Colletta 1997; Goovaerts, Gasser, and Inbal 2007; Unruh and Bailey 2009). Jobs remove excombatants from the pool of post-war unemployed, facilitate social and economic reintegration, and reduce incentives for individuals to rearm and contribute to the social banditry that can emerge after conflict (Unruh and Bailey 2009). While large-scale employment programs are central to DDR, the traditional jobs designed for former combatants (such as police officers, private security personnel, and members of reformed military units) are often unable to fully absorb the overwhelming number of individuals looking for work following the end of conflict (Colletta, Kostner, and Wiederhofer 1996a; Unruh and Bailey 2009).

Despite a number of innovative alternative employment programs, there is a continued need for sustainable opportunities that pair demobilized combatants with ongoing development initiatives. With the continued need for jobs, a small body of literature has emerged that proposes hiring former combatants in natural resource management positions.[1] While extensive experience designing and implementing DDR programs demonstrates the need to tailor specific projects to the unique sociopolitical, economic, and institutional circumstances of each post-war environment, lessons from one successful effort can often be applied to others.

Specifically, the initial experience of Gorongosa National Park in Mozambique illustrates that excombatants can be effectively deployed as parks and wildlife management personnel. Given the potential for such programs to contribute

---

Matthew F. Pritchard is a doctoral student in the Department of Geography at McGill University.

[1] See, for example, Hatton, Couto, and Oglethorpe (2001); Shambaugh, Oglethorpe, and Ham (2001); Bruch et al. (2009).

simultaneously to DDR and natural resource management following conflict, the United Nations has proposed similar projects for the Democratic Republic of the Congo (DRC), Sudan, and Afghanistan (Hatton, Couto, and Oglethorpe 2001; Shambaugh, Oglethorpe, and Ham 2001; Bruch et al. 2009). In an attempt to highlight the key lessons learned from this project and encourage further research on the potential role of excombatants as parks and wildlife personnel, this chapter provides a preliminary overview of the DDR program in Gorongosa National Park.

Shortly after Mozambique gained independence from Portugal in 1975, conflict erupted between the socialist government of the Liberation Front of Mozambique (Frente de Libertação de Moçambique, or FRELIMO) and the Mozambican National Resistance (Resistência Nacional Moçambicana, or RENAMO), an anticommunist movement supported by the white-minority governments of Rhodesia and South Africa (Vines 1998; Hatton, Couto, and Oglethorpe 2001; Junne and Verkoren 2005). Conflict quickly led to a civil war that lasted from 1977 to 1992. During this period, over 1 million people were killed, damage exceeded US$20 billion, and approximately half of Mozambique's total population was displaced internally or became refugees (Hatton, Couto, and Oglethorpe 2001; Junne and Verkoren 2005).

The establishment of DDR opportunities after the civil war was critical to the peace process. In a small project that was independent of the national DDR programs run by the government of Mozambique and the United Nations, Mozambique's National Directorate of Forestry and Wildlife (Direcção Nacional de Florestas e Fauna Bravia, or DNFFB) hired a small number of former combatants as game guards, anti-poaching personnel, and informants to aid in the reopening of Gorongosa National Park (Hatton, Couto, and Oglethorpe 2001; Unruh and Bailey 2009). Although the number of employees was small and the project constituted only a preliminary attempt to pair DDR with natural resource management, its success demonstrates that employing excombatants can not only mobilize skilled and experienced individuals to reoccupy and manage national parks, but also make a modest but sustainable contribution to the overall DDR process.

While each DDR program must take into account the specific sociopolitical, economic, and institutional dynamics of the particular post-war situation, past experience suggests that former combatants can make an effective contribution to parks and wildlife services once the rehabilitation of protected areas becomes a priority.[2] Beyond generating employment for potential spoilers of the peace process, incorporating excombatants into natural resource management offers a unique opportunity to promote community integration while contributing to post-conflict development.

---

2 This chapter assumes that protected areas will eventually be reopened independent of who is employed as parks and wildlife management personnel. As such, it remains focused on how former combatants can be integrated once priorities for natural resource management are established. Discussion of when and how this should occur is beyond the scope of this chapter.

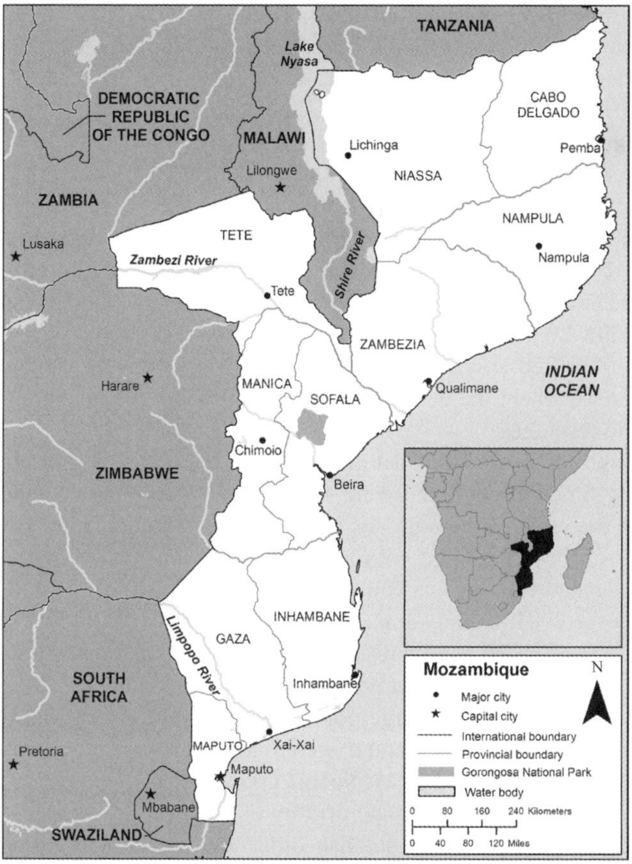

This chapter begins with a brief discussion of the impacts armed conflict has on available natural resources. It proceeds with a historical overview of Gorongosa National Park during Mozambique's civil war, and follows with a preliminary analysis of how and why former combatants were hired as resource management personnel. The chapter then reviews the contextual factors specific to post-conflict Mozambique that helped make the project successful. Finally, the chapter concludes with recommendations for further research and a summary of lessons learned from the Gorongosa National Park project that should be considered when contemplating and designing similar projects in other post-conflict environments.

WAR AND NATURAL RESOURCES

Armed conflict and the initial post-conflict period can have devastating effects on natural resources (Hatton, Couto, and Oglethorpe 2001; Shambaugh, Oglethorpe, and Ham 2001; Schafer and Bell 2002; Dudley et al. 2002; McNeely 2003). Beyond the physical destruction of crops, forests, and protected areas, armed conflicts destabilize local livelihoods and undermine established modes of production by displacing large numbers of people and forcing them to adopt shorter-term coping strategies that often involve uncontrolled resource extraction in the search for food and shelter (Dudley et al. 2002; Unruh and Bailey 2009). As conflict disrupts agricultural production and the delivery of essential services, communities are pressed to find alternative ways to meet basic needs (UNEP and IUCN 2007). Large populations of soldiers and displaced civilians rely on wild game, fruits, and vegetables for their subsistence (Dudley et al. 2003; McNeely 2003; UNEP and IUCN 2007). As internally displaced persons and refugees flee conflict-affected areas, they are often forced onto private landholdings and protected areas, where the demand for food and shelter places extreme pressure on available resources.

Although the majority of natural resources extracted by displaced populations during times of conflict are for subsistence, increasing demand for food, as well as the collapse of regional markets, transportation infrastructure, and commodity chains, combined with a lack of government oversight, can create extensive demand for wild game and illegally harvested goods (Hatton, Couto, and Oglethorpe 2001; Dudley et al. 2002; Austin and Bruch 2003). Furthermore, the scale of uncontrolled natural resource extraction brought on by armed conflict does not end with the cessation of hostilities. Rather, ceasefires, peace agreements, and post-war stability enable large populations to move throughout the country and settle in areas where access and resource extraction were previously restricted by government or rebel forces (McNeely 2003).

Understandably, the immediate priority of post-war governments and international organizations is to reestablish order and maintain stability. As such, management of natural resources and protected areas is often nonexistent or weakened by lack of staff and funding. Although addressing uncontrolled resource extraction is often not a high priority immediately after a conflict, such extraction can cause dramatic reductions in biodiversity, exacerbate existing scarcities, and present a significant threat to local livelihoods in the short, medium, and long term (UNEP and IUCN 2007). Improving the capacity to manage natural resources during and after a conflict is therefore increasingly recognized as a critical element of peacebuilding and livelihoods sustainability for the most vulnerable groups (Bruch et al. 2009).

GORONGOSA NATIONAL PARK

Located in Sofala Province in central Mozambique, Gorongosa was designated as a national park by Portuguese colonial authorities in 1960 (Hatton, Couto, and Oglethorpe 2001). Situated in the southernmost section of the Great African Rift Valley, the park's 5,370 square kilometers of wetland and savannah habitats once supported one of Africa's highest concentrations of large mammals (Hanes

2007). Gorongosa National Park became a world-renowned destination for safari tourism until its development was halted by civil war.

In 1982, DNFFB headquarters at Gorongosa National Park were captured by RENAMO forces. While fighting and displacement precipitated widespread hunting and foraging by combatants and civilians throughout the country, resource extraction in the park was especially severe, as troops were stationed there for long periods of time with relatively little action. From 1982 until the end of the civil war in 1992, Gorongosa National Park was almost continually occupied by government, RENAMO, or South African forces. In addition to large-scale hunting for food and game trophies, park infrastructure was destroyed, and both FRELIMO and RENAMO laid landmines throughout the park (Hatton, Couto, and Oglethorpe 2001).

After fifteen years of conflict, civil war in Mozambique ended on October 4, 1992, when FRELIMO and RENAMO ratified the Rome General Peace Accords. Under the agreement, all combatants were to relocate to predetermined demobilization zones, where they could be disarmed, monitored, and prepared for reinsertion and reintegration into the civilian population. As RENAMO forces withdrew from the park, a large number of internally displaced persons settled inside its boundaries, including in areas that had been inaccessible during the fighting. As a result, resource extraction in the park increased significantly after the civil war. In addition to hunting and foraging for food, people lit fires on the land in and around the park to clear it for agriculture. Hunters mainly targeted small animals for subsistence consumption, as larger game had already been wiped out, and a significant portion of the other resources extracted were for commercial purposes (Hatton, Couto, and Oglethorpe 2001).

Markets in wild game flourished throughout Mozambique. By mid-1994, two years after the official end of the civil war, observers from the International Union for Conservation of Nature (IUCN) estimated that thirty to sixty tons of carcasses were being removed from the park each month (DNFFB 1994; Hatton, Couto, and Oglethorpe 2001). As infrastructure improved throughout the country and landmines were removed from the roads leading to the park, hunters were able to travel greater distances to reach Gorongosa and venture further into the park to extract resources (Hatton, Couto, and Oglethorpe 2001).

As Gorongosa National Park was almost continually occupied by military forces throughout the conflict, researchers were unable to gather data on wildlife until 1992 (Hatton, Couto, and Oglethorpe 2001), by which time Gorongosa's human and natural resources had been decimated. The park suffered massive declines in large-mammal populations, most notably among elephants, buffalo, hippopotami, and wildebeests (table 1). In addition to wiping out the overwhelming majority of megafauna, the civil war also severely reduced the staff available to supervise and maintain all of the parks and protected areas in Mozambique. Of the twenty-eight individuals trained as resource management personnel at Gorongosa's Wildlife Training School (the country's only park management program) before the civil war, only sixteen remained in 1992 to help rebuild

Table 1. Large-mammal populations in Gorongosa National Park before and after Mozambique's civil war

	1968	*1970*	*1979*	*1993*	*1994*
Elephant	2,200	1,900	3,000	4	108
Buffalo	14,000	11,900	18,000	0	0
Hippopotamus	3,000	3,200	4,800	0	0
Wildebeest	5,500	4,900	1,900	7	0
Waterbuck	3,500	2,500	800	200	129
Zebra	3,000	N/D	N/D	7	65
Eland	500	N/D	N/D	0	0
Sable	N/D	N/D	N/D	700	12
Hartebeest	800	N/D	N/D	0	156

Source: Hatton, Couto, and Oglethorpe 2001.
Note: N/D = No data.

Mozambique's entire system of parks, protected areas, and reserves (Hatton, Couto, and Oglethorpe 2001; Shambaugh, Oglethorpe, and Ham 2001).

FORMER COMBATANTS AS GAME GUARDS

Presented with a large number of former combatants, severe declines in animal populations, and the uncontrolled extraction of natural resources from Gorongosa National Park, the DNFFB's priority was to quickly mobilize skilled individuals to reoccupy the park (Hatton, Couto, and Oglethorpe 2001). Reintegrating a modest number of former soldiers and guerrillas was a secondary goal. In other words, the purpose of designating excombatants as game guards in Gorongosa National Park was not to generate large-scale employment opportunities for FRELIMO and RENAMO soldiers. Rather, this project provided a unique opportunity to mobilize highly trained individuals capable of reoccupying the park and monitoring resource extraction while providing stable jobs for a relatively small number of potential spoilers. Given this goal, the following analysis describes the impact that hiring former combatants had on the reopening of the park, as well as the relevance of this DDR project to the specific priorities and challenges of post-war Mozambique.

Despite a severe lack of trained staff, equipment, and support, the DNFFB's first priority following the civil war was to secure and rehabilitate existing park areas in Mozambique (Hatton, Couto, and Oglethorpe 2001). Given the lack of human capital and pressing need to stem the uncontrolled extraction of park resources, in 1994 the DNFFB hired seventy-six former combatants to work as game guards, scouts, and informants in Gorongosa National Park (Hatton, Couto, and Oglethorpe 2001). While these individuals lacked formal conservation training, many of the skills they had developed during combat were highly relevant to the tasks of surveying park resources and controlling poaching. Most importantly, former combatants were able to track animals and poachers within the park, remain self-sufficient in the bush for extended periods, and handle small firearms if required for protection against wildlife and poachers (Hatton, Couto, and Oglethorpe 2001; Unruh and Bailey 2009). Furthermore, as the park had been almost continually occupied by military forces throughout the civil war, many excombatants had firsthand knowledge of the locations of both landmines and wildlife within the park (Hatton, Couto, and Oglethorpe 2001).

In addition to hiring former combatants, the DNFFB also recruited game guards from communities surrounding Gorongosa National Park. Recruits received preliminary training and were organized into scouting teams. Each team was composed of a ranger with pre-war experience, local community members, and individuals from both FRELIMO and RENAMO, in an attempt to support reconciliation and avoid conflict between teams (Hatton, Couto, and Oglethorpe 2001; Unruh and Bailey 2009). Once the teams were ready, the DNFFB entered the park in April 1995 and reestablished the park base at Chitengo. From this camp, located in the southern portion of the park, scouting teams moved through the park along old management roads, setting up temporary camps as they went (Hatton, Couto, and Oglethorpe 2001). By gradually expanding patrol areas out from the camps, these newly formed scouting groups reoccupied the entire park. After eighteen months, the park was under regular management (Hatton, Couto, and Oglethorpe 2001; Unruh and Bailey 2009). Poaching and illegal harvesting were dramatically reduced, and while still low, animal populations stabilized and slowly began to recover (Hatton, Couto, and Oglethorpe 2001).

Although the number of excombatants hired by the DNFFB remained relatively low (compared to the total number of soldiers that required reintegration), hiring these individuals as game guards allowed park services to quickly reestablish a presence, reassert park boundaries, patrol the park, and stabilize the remaining animal populations. While poaching and illegal land clearings continued, occurrences of such activities were dramatically reduced, and wildlife officials were able to initiate one of the largest animal reintroduction programs in history (Hanes 2007). Beyond reoccupying and reasserting park boundaries, the project also provided stable employment for former combatants. While it only served a small number of individuals—seventy-six former combatants out of the 100,000 who needed reintegration—the project demonstrated that former combatants could effectively contribute to natural resource management with very little conflict. Beyond initial squabbling within and between scouting groups, no conflict was reported between excombatants from FRELIMO and RENAMO, or between excombatants and local community members (Hatton, Couto, and Oglethorpe 2001). There were also no reports of the newly appointed game guards using their positions to illegally extract the resources under their protection.

Beyond the basic impacts of reestablishing park boundaries, decreasing poaching, and making a small contribution to the reintegration of former combatants, the project also demonstrated the potential of pairing DDR with other post-war development initiatives. Extensive experience designing and implementing DDR programs in a number of post-war environments has demonstrated the importance of coordinating reintegration with other development priorities, as well as the need for extensive community sensitization (Colletta 1997; UNOSAA 2007). Linking DDR with natural resource management in Gorongosa National Park provided a unique method of targeting both of these goals.

While the original objective of hiring excombatants in Gorongosa was to quickly reestablish control of the park, the project actively engaged individuals in the surrounding communities whose livelihoods depended on the extraction of park resources. Prior to reoccupying Gorongosa National Park, the DNFFB contacted district and provincial administrators, local chiefs, and members of the FRELIMO and RENAMO political parties throughout the area surrounding the park, to discuss the project's goals and to mobilize local support (Hatton, Couto, and Oglethorpe 2001). In addition to building consensus among the groups most affected by the reassertion of park boundaries, project officials invited local communities to play an active role in reopening and monitoring Gorongosa National Park. First, after landmines were cleared, people living in and around the park participated in food-for-work projects to rebuild park infrastructure (Hatton, Couto, and Oglethorpe 2001). Second, in exchange for providing information on illicit activity within the park, and for not hunting or clearing land, local communities were allowed to harvest honey, fish, plant materials for construction, and a number of other goods from within the park (Hatton, Couto, and Oglethorpe 2001). By engaging the communities that rely on park resources for subsistence in the short term post-war period, park personnel established a positive relationship with local residents and helped reduce resistance to the reopening of Gorongosa National Park. Finally, in addition to helping rebuild infrastructure and shifting to more sustainable harvesting, as previously mentioned, local residents were hired, trained, and deployed alongside former combatants as game guards (Hatton, Couto, and Oglethorpe 2001; Shambaugh, Oglethorpe, and Ham 2001; Unruh and Bailey 2009).

Involving local inhabitants in reopening the park helped garner support for the project and allowed the DNFFB to reestablish park boundaries and decrease illegal resource extraction without alienating local inhabitants. Interaction between local residents and former combatants not only decreased the chance that the DNFFB would be seen as privileging the perpetrators of the conflict, but also actively encouraged the mutual reintegration of former combatants and local community members.

In addition to facilitating reintegration, jobs in Gorongosa National Park have proven to be more sustainable than some of the other opportunities offered through national DDR programs, if sustainability is measured by employment opportunities beyond the immediate post-war period as well as by the potential for promotion within the institution. Unlike a number of jobs designed for excombatants in Mozambique, those working for Gorongosa National Park retained their positions beyond the short-term post-war period. Indeed, all seventy-six former combatants initially hired by the DNFFB in 1994 were still working in the park in 1997. Unlike opportunities created for the sole purpose of reintegration of former combatants, the jobs in Gorongosa National Park filled an existing need for personnel.[3]

Beyond the initial need for human capital to reenter and reestablish Gorongosa National Park following the civil war, the continued employment of excombatants as game guards was indirectly supported by the park system's severe lack of training capacity. Fifteen years of conflict had not only reduced the number of experienced personnel available to supervise Mozambique's entire system of protected areas but also destroyed the institutions established to train resource management personnel. Mozambique's only parks and wildlife management training program, Gorongosa's Wildlife Training School, relocated to Maputo in 1981 and later shut down altogether (Hatton, Couto, and Oglethorpe 2001; UNOSAA 2007). Without the ability to educate and deploy new recruits, by the end of the conflict in 1992, there was a complete absence of trained personnel capable of establishing and monitoring the park, with the DNFFB lacking the institutional capacity to train future employees. While this presented a serious challenge to the park system, it offered early post-war employees significant opportunities for upward mobility.

The long-term sustainability of the Gorongosa National Park initiative was enhanced by national policies that emphasized natural resource protection. The opening page of Mozambique's 1997 Law on the Environment emphasized the importance of the relationship between a protected environment and "the socio-economic and cultural development of communities and the preservation of the natural resources that sustain them." Furthermore, the success of pairing DDR with park management in Gorongosa prompted an agreement between the ministries of tourism and defense on "the permanent multiple use of former soldiers in policing the nation's national parks" (Unruh and Bailey 2009, 165). Programs that employ excombatants to reestablish protected areas need not, therefore, be restricted to immediate post-conflict situations, but can be an important source of trained and disciplined personnel in the long term.

Finally, the successful deployment of excombatants in Gorongosa National Park highlights the project's relevance to the unique obstacles of post-war environments. Given the relatively small number of employees and minimal training they required, the DNFFB was able to proceed without extensive policy prescriptions or government mandates. The small scale of the project fostered centralized decision making within the DNFFB and avoided the challenges of working with a large number of participants spread throughout the country in protected areas and multiple communities disparately affected by the conflict.

---

[3] The difference between an existing and a created need for personnel can be seen clearly in the contrast between the Gorongosa experience and that of the Operational Skills Development program, one of the least successful DDR programs in Mozambique, which offered two-month training courses in forty-nine different fields, aimed at graduating skilled and semiskilled workers. Implemented by the International Labour Organization, this program was developed with very little regard to target beneficiaries (Alden 2002). For example, many former combatants were trained as electricians in communities with no electricity.

After an armed conflict, there is often a strong need—and opportunity—for large-scale reform. However, there are also often overwhelming obstacles that can delay, if not completely halt, the development and implementation of government programs. The small scale of the Gorongosa project enabled the DNFFB to peacefully mobilize local community members and former combatants without the need for extensive government debate or new legislation. Support for a national DDR program independent of projects designed and implemented by the international community would have been difficult to garner in 1994, when the government of Mozambique was focused on organizing the first elections since 1975. While the country has since legislated a number of initiatives regarding the protection of parks and the continued employment of former combatants, the success of excombatants as game guards in Gorongosa National Park stemmed directly from its regional specificity and independence from national and international development initiatives.

FACTORS AFFECTING SUCCESS AND POTENTIAL CONSTRAINTS

Going beyond the valuable contributions excombatants have made to securing and reopening Gorongosa National Park, it is important to understand the contextual factors unique to post-war Mozambique that influenced the successful implementation of this project. When thinking of ways to expand on this experience and apply it in other protected areas and post-conflict environments, it is important to acknowledge that several factors particular to post-war Mozambique and Gorongosa National Park contributed to the project's success. Specifically, the successful contribution of former combatants to the reopening of Gorongosa National Park was supported by the nature of both the conflict and ensuing peace in Mozambique, the unprecedented national and international support for DDR programs, the hiring of excombatants who were already settled in local communities, the extensive informal community reconciliation ceremonies, the ability of game guards to begin their work without weapons, and the project's independence from the national DDR framework. After outlining each of these factors, this section concludes with an overview of two key challenges that should be addressed when considering programs that pair excombatants with parks and wildlife management across other post-war environments.

First, the nature of the civil war and ensuing peace in Mozambique supported the successful employment of excombatants as parks and wildlife management personnel. By the time peace talks were initiated in 1990, combatants on both sides not only had become dissociated from the ideological roots of the civil war, but also felt that the respective goals that provoked the conflict were unattainable (Junne and Verkoren 2005). Initially driven by political rather than ethnic factors, by the late 1980s a new group of leaders within RENAMO saw the conflict as unwinnable and began the transition toward peace (Junne and Verkoren 2005). Conflict fatigue in Mozambique was so prevalent that of the 100,000 combatants eligible under the peace agreement to join the new army, only 12,000 volunteered (Junne and Verkoren 2005). Soldiers were so skeptical that anything could be gained by continuing the conflict that they became "willing partners in their own demobilization" and overwhelmingly supported national DDR programs (McMullin 2004, 635).

In addition to extensive conflict fatigue, Mozambique also experienced unparalleled financial backing from the international community for the most comprehensive set of DDR programs to date (McMullin 2004). The need for extensive funding was underlined by the breakdown of peace in Angola, which prompted the United Nations Mission to Mozambique to mobilize US$95 million in donor funding for an extensive series of DDR programs (Alden 2002; McMullin 2004). Most of these funds were dedicated to the Reintegration Support Scheme, a program that transported demobilized soldiers anywhere in the country and provided a fixed salary for two years (Junne and Verkoren 2005; Alden 2002; McMullin 2004), with monthly payments based on their previously held rank that could be collected by presenting a voucher at any branch of the nationwide People's Development Bank (Banco Popular de Desenvolvimento) (Alden 2002).[4] Payments were designed to support former combatants and their families as they returned home or looked for work, and helped ensure that excombatants were not seen as burdens to their new communities (Alden 2002; McMullin 2004; Junne and Verkoren 2005). Not only did this program distribute former combatants throughout the country, but it also supported them as they (re)established social networks in local communities.

As a direct result of the support provided by the Reintegration Support Scheme, the overwhelming majority of excombatants recruited by the DNFFB for Gorongosa National Park in 1994 were already settled and integrated into local communities. As such, when hired by the DNFFB, former combatants were not as likely to be seen as complete outsiders, but rather as new or returned community members with significant familial and economic ties to the area. The two-year lag period between the end of the civil war and initiation of the Gorongosa program significantly reduced the number of obstacles faced by the DNFFB when training and supervising excombatants and local community members.

The successful introduction of former combatants as game guards in the park was also indirectly supported by informal community reconciliation ceremonies (Igreja 2007; Lundin 1998). Like most peace treaties, the Rome accords granted combatants unconditional amnesty. While such agreements are essential to long-term peace, they are often difficult to accept for noncombatants who suffered during the conflict and who must interact with people they see as responsible for that suffering. Reintegration of former combatants not only helps pacify soldiers but also supports local community members who are forced to interact

---

[4] In addition to the Reintegration Support Scheme, DDR initiatives in Mozambique included the Operational Skills Development program, described in footnote 3, and a program of the German Society for Technical Cooperation (Gesellschaft für Technische Zusammenarbeit), which provided US$1,000 to US$5,000 for business enterprises that involved former combatants (Alden 2002).

with those individuals on a daily basis. In Mozambique, informal reconciliation ceremonies helped to make this step palatable. While their specifics differed from one region to the next, the ceremonies generally had three aspects in common: (1) they were designed to help former soldiers overcome their aggressive identities; (2) the community gathered to give thanks for the safe return of the excombatants; and (3) the excombatants were invited to reconcile with the spirits of the dead by asking forgiveness, demonstrating remorse, and making remunerations to family members of the dead. While these ceremonies were not a part of the formal DDR programs, they were an important method of supporting reintegration and reconciliation in many places across Mozambique (Igreja 2007).

The lack of large mammals in Gorongosa National Park following the civil war, along with restrictions on firearms (for poachers and game guards), meant that park and wildlife management personnel were initially able to reoccupy and patrol the park unarmed. This provided the DNFFB with an opportunity to present a more people-friendly approach to scouting without endangering the lives of park employees (Hatton, Couto, and Oglethorpe 2001; Unruh and Bailey 2009). As Mozambique transitioned through the post-war period and the park was gradually repopulated with large mammals, guns slowly became available, and special scouting units within the park received light arms (Hatton, Couto, and Oglethorpe 2001).

Finally, another key component of the successful employment of excombatants as parks and wildlife management personnel in Gorongosa was the speed with which the DNFFB was able to hire employees and reestablish control of the park. Although the new game guards and scouts were not deployed until 1995, once occupied, the park was under regular management within eighteen months. While this may not seem especially quick, it is a relatively short time given the size of the park and the extent of the damage caused during the civil war (Unruh and Bailey 2009). The speed with which the DNFFB was able to transition from initial consultations with surrounding communities to the deployment of game guards was largely due to the project's independence from the national DDR framework, the relatively small number of employees involved, and the independent funding that left decision making in the hands of park authorities. Operating outside the national decision-making framework significantly reduced the institutional lag time that often characterizes new projects.

In addition to the contextual factors that promoted the successful deployment of excombatants as parks and wildlife management personnel, it is also important to acknowledge existing and potential constraints that hinder the implementation of similar programs in other protected areas and post-war contexts. These include (but are not limited to) the need to tailor DDR efforts to widely varying post-conflict situations and the difficulties that can arise in managing excombatants and their relations with local civilians.

- First, to be successful, DDR programs must be adapted to local contexts, be adjusted to existing opportunity structures, and must incorporate the needs of excombatants and their families (Colletta 1997; UNOSAA 2007). The importance of adjusting reintegration programs to meet the divergent needs of former soldiers within and between countries makes it difficult to make general prescriptions about how to design a successful DDR initiative (UNOSAA 2007). However, while programs should be developed in line with specific post-war environments, the need for contextual relevance does not undermine the general opportunities presented by pairing excombatants with parks and wildlife management. Although project design, implementation, and evolution will differ between locations, the general goals of providing stable employment and reducing the uncontrolled extraction of natural resources remain the same.

- The second major constraint to employing former combatants as parks and wildlife management personnel is the fact that these individuals can be difficult to manage and can easily alienate local communities. When former combatants are placed in positions of power, local residents may view them as providing a key public service, but they may also see excombatants as further harming the community by limiting access to park resources (Colletta 1997). Concerns are especially likely to arise where civilians blame excombatants for the conflict and the hardships they experienced during the conflict. Experience from Gorongosa National Park demonstrates that this difficulty can be overcome when surrounding communities are sensitized and actively included in natural resource management. Furthermore, the challenges of managing former combatants are not new. Indeed, the most common jobs offered to excombatants have been as members of police forces, private security teams, and reformed military units (Colletta 1997; Colletta, Kostner, and Wiederhofer 1996a; Unruh and Bailey 2009). As such, the challenges of hiring and managing excombatants in positions of power have been addressed through extensive experience in a number of post-conflict situations, and are not restricted to employment as natural resource management personnel.

When considering these and other challenges associated with employing excombatants in parks and wildlife management, it is important to focus on the unique sociopolitical and economic frameworks that are particular to post-war environments, rather than measuring the challenges against an idealized peaceful situation. The potential risks of hiring excombatants should be weighed not only against the contribution these individuals can make but also against the problems that can arise if they are not offered stable employment and actively included in development priorities (Unruh and Bailey 2009).

LESSONS LEARNED

In light of the key factors and constraints faced when employing former combatants as game guards, this final section provides an overview of the initial lessons learned from the project at Gorongosa National Park. These lessons are discussed in terms of the general opportunities for connection between DDR and natural resources management, and the influence of factors that are specific to Mozambique's experience.

The main lesson drawn from this initial overview is that former combatants can play an important role as parks and wildlife management personnel in post-war environments in a way that minimizes the possibility of future conflict, supports community reintegration, and helps provide the human capital required to reassert control over protected areas. Integrating former combatants into parks and wildlife management can lead to a relatively quick mobilization of personnel while making a modest (in terms of the number of individuals employed) but sustainable contribution to DDR. Furthermore, pairing DDR with parks and wildlife management can help transform excombatants from potential spoilers into active participants in local and national development priorities, while stabilizing natural resource use for local livelihoods beyond the short term.

Beyond the general contributions former combatants can make to natural resource management, this chapter also presents several key ideas to consider when evaluating, designing, and implementing similar initiatives in other post-conflict situations. First, it demonstrates that hiring former combatants will be more effective if initial DDR has already occurred. While any lag in program implementation will likely increase the amount of damage to protected areas, it also allows government agencies to establish conservation priorities, determine institutional capability, and reach out to local communities involved in or affected by resource extraction. Any initial delay also provides time for local residents to transition away from short-term post-war coping strategies—specifically, to reestablish housing and market infrastructure—and therefore reduce their dependence on illegally extracted goods. After excombatants have experienced initial reintegration, it is easier to train and supervise them; local residents are less likely to view the DDR program as privileging the perpetrators of the conflict.

Second, the Gorongosa experience demonstrates the importance of actively involving local communities in reestablishing and maintaining conservation areas. Engaging local residents and acknowledging the significance of natural resources to subsistence livelihoods can increase support for conservation projects while adding to the human capital needed to monitor protected areas. In Gorongosa National Park, local community members helped reassert park boundaries in a number of ways. While the methods for engaging communities will differ from one post-conflict situation to the next, it remains an essential component of hiring and managing former combatants, reducing resource extraction, and supporting local livelihoods.

Third, in areas without large animals or violent poachers, patrolling reestablished boundaries without weapons presents a more community-friendly image without endangering park employees. Although experience from Gorongosa National Park demonstrates the benefit of not arming game guards when they are first deployed, the decision of whether to supply weapons depends heavily on the nature of the conflict and ensuing peace, local perceptions of former combatants, and the need for firearms to protect employees from wildlife and poachers.

Finally, independent funding can play a critical role in supporting natural resource–based DDR programs. Many donors fear that without guaranteed salaries and strong institutional capacity, former combatants employed in parks and wildlife management could exploit the resources under their protection for their own benefit (Bruch et al. 2009). However, this risk is not restricted to former combatants. Providing stable and competitive salaries can reduce incentives for illegal resource extraction and encourage new employees to remain in the program, thus supporting their continued reintegration into surrounding communities. Experience from Gorongosa National Park demonstrates the benefit of providing staff salaries through funding that is independent of the national DDR framework, as this can be more reliable and facilitate more effective decision making by project managers as well as streamlined implementation. The Gorongosa project's independence from the national DDR framework was essential to its flexibility and capacity to guarantee continued support for excombatants and local community members.

CONCLUSION

The DDR of former combatants is essential to establishing and maintaining peace in post-conflict situations. Despite extensive efforts to design and implement DDR programs, the traditional jobs available for excombatants after a war are never able to fully absorb the number of individuals that need work (Colletta, Kostner, and Wiederhofer 1996a; Unruh and Bailey 2009). By drawing on a small but growing body of literature on the importance of natural resources to medium- and long-term recovery in post-conflict countries,[5] DDR programs can further respond to the continued need to provide excombatants with jobs through opportunities created in natural resource management. Where natural resources are essential to reestablishing and maintaining livelihoods damaged during conflict, DDR programs relying on natural resource management can help provide gainful employment for potential spoilers while improving natural resource protection.

In Mozambique, the DDR of former combatants was critical to the peace process. What the individuals hired by the DNFFB lacked in formal conservation training, they made up for with skills invaluable to reducing poaching and other forms of uncontrolled resource extraction. Experience from this project demonstrates that employing former combatants as parks and wildlife management personnel can contribute to a relatively quick mobilization of the human capital needed to reoccupy and supervise protected areas, while making a modest but sustainable contribution to DDR of excombatants and community reintegration. Although specific aspects of project design and implementation differ from one situation to the next, similar initiatives in other post-conflict environments can

---

[5] See, for example, Bruch et al. (2009); Takasu (2008); Unruh and Bailey (2009).

provide stable employment for excombatants while decreasing the illegal exploitation of natural resources and promoting long-term livelihoods.

Given the preliminary nature of this work, the central goal of this chapter has been to demonstrate the opportunities and challenges encountered when employing excombatants as parks and wildlife management personnel, and to initiate a discussion on the potential for designing and implementing similar projects in other post-conflict situations. An overview and analysis of experiences from Gorongosa National Park demonstrates that more research is needed on the role former combatants can play in parks and wildlife management. Most importantly, further research is needed on how DDR programs can promote stable relations between excombatants from opposing sides, as well as between former combatants and local civilians, particularly when the excombatants must enforce park rules and the local civilians have come to depend on park resources for their livelihoods. However, this is less a question of who is patrolling the park and more about the balance between short-term extralegal extraction and long-term development opportunities, as well as the intrinsic importance of environmental protection to sustainable livelihoods.

Finally, further research is needed on the sustainability and scalability of programs that involve excombatants in parks and wildlife management over the short, medium, and long term in different post-conflict situations. Incorporating excombatants into parks and wildlife management presents significant challenges and opportunities for post-war development. Given the need for sustainable jobs for potential spoilers and the importance of natural resources to livelihoods stability, employing excombatants as parks and wildlife personnel presents an important opportunity to pair development priorities and facilitate specific aspects of post-conflict peacebuilding.

REFERENCES

Alden, C. 2002. Making old soldiers fade away: Lessons from the reintegration of demobilized soldiers in Mozambique. *Security Dialogue* 33 (3): 341–356.

Austin, J. E., and C. E. Bruch. 2003. Legal mechanisms for addressing wartime damage to tropical forests. In *War and tropical forests: Conservation in areas of armed conflict*, ed. S. V. Prince. Binghamton, New York: Food Products Press.

Bruch, C., D. Jensen, M. Nakayama, J. Unruh, R. Gruby, and R. Wolfarth. 2009. Post-conflict peacebuilding and natural resources. *Yearbook of International Environmental Law* 19:58–96.

Colletta, N. J. 1997. Demilitarization, demobilization, and the social and economic integration of ex-combatants: Lessons from the World Bank Africa experience. Paper presented at the United States Agency for International Development conference "Promoting Democracy, Human Rights, and Reintegration in Post-conflict Societies," Washington, D.C., October 30–31.

Colletta, N. J., M. Kostner, and I. Wiederhofer. 1996a. Case studies in war-to-peace transition: The demobilization and reintegration of ex-combatants in Ethiopia, Namibia, and Uganda. World Bank Discussion Paper No. 331. Washington, D.C.: World Bank.

———. 1996b. *The transition from war to peace in sub-Saharan Africa*. Washington, D.C.: World Bank.

DNFFB (Direcção Nacional de Florestas e Fauna Bravia). 1994. Gorongosa–Marromeu: Management plan for integrated conservation and development, 1995–1999. Maputo, Mozambique.

Dudley, J. P., J. R. Ginsberg, A. J. Plumptre, J. A. Hart, and L. C. Campos. 2002. Effects of war and civil strife on wildlife and wildlife habitats. *Conservation Biology* 16 (2): 319–329.

Goovaerts, P., M. Gasser, and A. B. Inbal. 2007. Demand driven approaches to livelihood support in post-war contexts. Conflict Prevention and Reconstruction Community-Driven Development Paper No. 29. Washington, D.C.: World Bank / International Labour Office.

Hanes, S. 2007. Greg Carr's big gamble: In a watershed experiment, the Boston entrepreneur is putting $40 million of his own money into a splendid but ravaged park in Mozambique. *Smithsonian* 38 (2): 84–93.

Hatton, J., M. Couto, and J. Oglethorpe. 2001. *Biodiversity and war: A case study of Mozambique*. Washington, D.C.: Biodiversity Support Program.

Igreja, V. 2007. Gamba spirits and the homines aperti: Socio-cultural approaches to deal with legacies of the civil war in Gorongosa, Mozambique. Paper presented at the international conference "Building a Future on Peace and Justice," Nuremburg, Germany, June 25–27.

Junne, G., and W. Verkoren, eds. 2005. *Postconflict development: Meeting new challenges*. London: Lynne Rienner.

Lundin, I. B. 1998. Mechanisms of community reception of demobilised soldiers in Mozambique. *African Review of Political Science* 3 (1): 104–118.

McMullin, J. 2004. Reintegration of combatants: Were the right lessons learned in Mozambique? *International Peacekeeping* 11 (4): 625–643.

McNeely, J. A. 2003. Conserving forest biodiversity in times of violent conflict. *Oryx* 37 (2): 142–152.

Schafer, J., and R. Bell. 2002. The state and community-based natural resource management: The case of the Moribane Forest Reserve, Mozambique. *Journal of Southern African Studies* 28 (2): 401–420.

Shambaugh, J., J. Oglethorpe, and R. Ham. 2001. *The trampled grass: Mitigating the impacts of armed conflict on the environment*. Washington, D.C.: Biodiversity Support Program.

Takasu, Y. 2008. Opening remarks by Ambassador Yukio Takasu, chair of the United Nations Peace Building Commission, at the joint forum "Managing Natural Resources in Post-Conflict Societies: Lessons in Making the Transition to Peace," Columbia University, New York, May 12.

UNEP (United Nations Environment Programme) and IUCN (International Union for Conservation of Nature's Commission on Environmental Law). 2007. Managing natural resources in post-conflict societies: Lessons learned in making the transition to peace. Meeting report. Geneva, Switzerland.

UNOSAA (United Nations Office of the Special Adviser on Africa). 2007. Final report on the Second International Conference On Disarmament, Demobilization, Reintegration and Stability in Africa. Kinshasa, Democratic Republic of the Congo.

Unruh, J., and J. Bailey. 2009. Management of spatially extensive natural resources in postwar contexts: Working with the peace process. *GeoJournal* 74 (2): 159–173.

Vines, A. 1998. Disarmament in Mozambique. *Journal of Southern African Studies* 24 (1): 191–205.

Mitigating conflict in Sierra Leone through mining reform and alternative livelihoods programs for youth

Andrew Keili and Bocar Thiam

Mining has been an important part of Sierra Leone's economy since diamonds were discovered in the 1930s. The promise of economic development offered by diamonds has been tempered by conflict, which has plagued Sierra Leone since the mid-1950s. Decades of bad governance incited widespread and recurring violence, which brought about a decline in the social and economic living standards of the general populace, especially in communities that depend on mining for livelihoods. During the 1990s, violence and unresolved social and economic discontent culminated in civil war (1991–2002), for which diamonds provided a principal source of funding. The growing demand for diamonds impacted mining communities and youth engaged in diamond mining, drawing the country's young population further into conflict as suppliers of conflict resources and as armed insurgents.

Livelihood opportunities in Sierra Leone are severely limited. A large portion of the country's population thus relies on the mining industry as a primary source of income. Over 250,000 people in Sierra Leone engage in artisanal mining for their livelihoods (McMahon and CEMMATS Group 2007). The industry is easy to enter, as it requires only minimally skilled workers, a small capital investment, and no infrastructure development. However, the mining industry and market chain often exploit the miners, who are subject to the vicissitudes of an unfair market system and commonly become indebted to investors (GOSL 2009).

Mining regions are frequently overcrowded, and miners labor under onerous conditions and earn little for their efforts. Dissatisfied with such conditions, many youth engaged in mining choose to abandon their communities. During the civil war, many youth who were unable to find alternative employment, frustrated by the lack of opportunity, and discriminated against by village elders joined rebel groups as armed combatants.

Andrew Keili is executive director of CEMMATS Group Ltd., a leading multidisciplinary engineering, environmental, and project management consultancy in Sierra Leone. Bocar Thiam, a social scientist specializing in natural resource management in sub-Saharan Africa, was chief of party for the Property Rights and Artisanal Diamond Development project—a project funded by the U.S. Agency for International Development, launched in 2007 in the Central African Republic, and expanded to Liberia in 2010 by Associates in Rural Development. This chapter relies, in part, on the authors' experiences in Sierra Leone.

This chapter introduces the diamond-mining trap that pushed Sierra Leonean youth to join rebel groups during the civil war and examines post-conflict efforts to improve national governance of the mining sector. Still, as many youth continue to face unimproved conditions in the mining sector following the end of the civil war, this chapter also examines specific projects undertaken to improve the lives and livelihoods of the country's youth population. It then assesses the success of various schemes to address conflict and insecurity through the development of alternative livelihood opportunities. The chapter concludes by acknowledging the persistent youth issues in post-conflict mining communities, emphasizing the need to prioritize community development programs.

DIAMONDS, YOUTH, AND THE CIVIL WAR

Despite its abundance of mineral resources, Sierra Leone is currently ranked 177 out of 187 countries on the United Nations Development Program's 2012 Human Poverty Index (UNDP 2013). Poverty is pervasive in the country, with approximately three-quarters of the population living below the poverty line and earning less than US$3 per day (Bertelsmann Stiftung 2012).

Diamonds, first discovered in eastern Sierra Leone in the 1930s, play a significant role in the country's economy. Before the onset of civil war, the mineral sector constituted, on average, 20 percent of the country's gross domestic product (GDP), 90 percent of its exports, and 4 percent of revenues (peaking at 8 percent in 1990). Researchers estimate that the mineral sector provides, directly and indirectly, over 250,000 jobs, employing 14 percent of Sierra Leone's labor force (UNEP 2009). It is the second largest employer after subsistence agriculture and is the country's largest foreign exchange earner (McMahon and CEMMATS Group 2007).

This reliance on mining cannot continue indefinitely. The seasonal nature of the work—mining generally happens during the dry season—means that even when the sector is thriving, alternative livelihoods must be developed for the off-season. And the sector is not thriving: artisanal mineral resources are being depleted and are thus becoming harder to mine. Diamonds in particular have become largely inaccessible to artisanal miners, and smuggling and other corrupt practices in the industry are rapidly exhausting the remaining supply. The fluctuating values of mining commodities also influence levels of activity in unpredictable ways.

Government policies and actions exacerbate pressure on the mineral sector by encouraging overcrowding in mining areas. The Ministry of Mines and Mineral Resources grants mining licenses with no restrictions, even when the remaining minerals are below marketable grade (MMRPA 2009).[1] This practice results not

[1] The ministry responsible for mines and mineral resources has had numerous names. In this chapter, *Ministry of Mines and Mineral Resources* refers to the relevant ministry for the time period being discussed. With the passing of the National Minerals Agency Act in March 2012, the Ministry of Mines and Mineral Resources retained responsibility for policy making in the sector, and the newly established National Minerals Agency took on responsibility for policy implementation (MMMR n.d.).

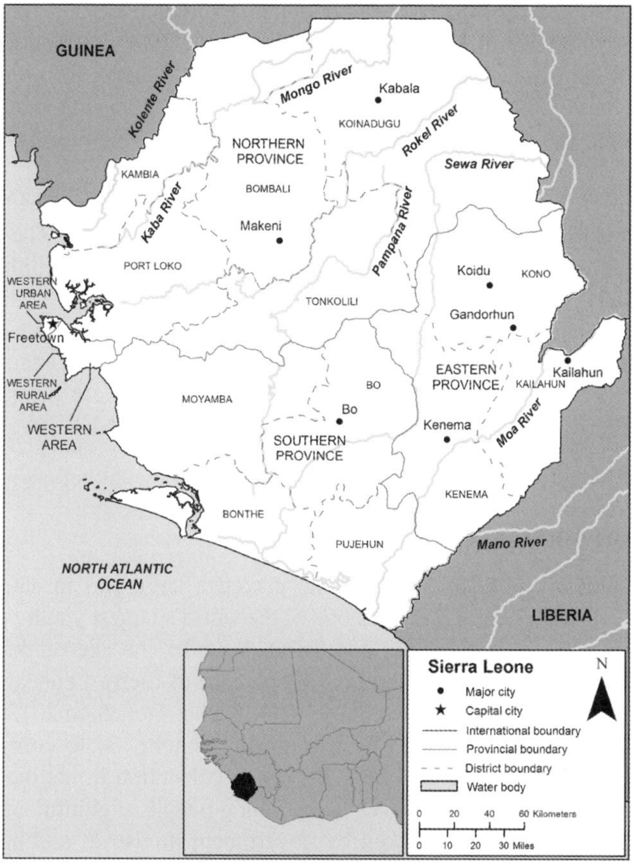

only in wasted effort by the miners, but in wanton environmental damage. A requirement that licenses be withheld could potentially stop new entrants into artisanal mining; however, such a prohibition would succeed only if it were rigidly enforced and if viable alternative livelihoods were made available.

The role of diamonds in the armed conflict

From 1934 to 1956, all discovered diamond deposits were mined exclusively by the Sierra Leone Selection Trust (SLST), a subsidiary of the international diamond mining conglomerate De Beers (Gberie 2005; Abrahamsen and Williams 2005). Following the discovery of more diamond deposits and the corresponding rush to those areas by prospectors, the British colonial government introduced the Alluvial Diamond Mining Scheme in 1956 to prevent illicit mining and diamond smuggling. This scheme allowed artisanal miners to participate in diamond mining for the first time, breaking the monopoly previously enjoyed by SLST. Soon after Siaka Stevens became prime minister of Sierra Leone in 1967, illicit mining, which had previously been contained, exploded. Weak governance and the poor performance of key state institutions in the 1970s opened the door for a variety of companies and individuals to reap huge benefits from the diamond industry (Gberie 2005). Political acquiescence increased tension and led to conflicts, creating problems with security, transparency, and monitoring throughout the country.

Civil war broke out in 1991 when the Revolutionary United Front (RUF) began its insurrection against the government of Sierra Leone. The RUF used diamond funds to sustain its insurgency, and the outbreak attracted the attention of individuals such as Liberian politician Charles Taylor, who was interested in smuggling Sierra Leone's diamonds and laundering the proceeds to fund his own patronage networks (Ojukutu-Macauley and Keili 2008). By 1998, annual diamond exports of between US$25 million and US$125 million were being smuggled through Liberia and used to fund the RUF's war effort (UNEP 2009). Many of the rebels were disaffected or unemployed young men.

The role of youth in the armed conflict

The alienation of youth in Sierra Leone played a large part in catalyzing the country's civil war. Sierra Leone has one of the world's largest youth populations: approximately 60 percent of the population is under the age of thirty (nearly 50 percent is under age 15), and 60 to 70 percent of Sierra Leonean youth are unemployed (SSL and ICF Macro 2009; IRIN 2009c; Trenchard 2013). Employment in Sierra Leone is limited by a stagnant economy, state corruption, and a lack of government accountability. Pervasive corruption limits the growth of a formal private sector and deprives many young people of gainful employment. Employment initiatives undertaken by government ministries and agencies are stifled by a lack of accountability for appropriated funds. The political, social, and economic divide between the poor, unemployed youth and the corrupt and powerful arbiters of the traditional social structure—the chiefdoms—creates friction that has led to increased migration of youth into cities and has prompted them to join rebel groups, such as the RUF (Sommers 2007). Many of those who left their communities as children to join rebel groups, or who were abducted for that purpose, have since returned to their communities having adopted the rebels' behavior and view themselves as independent of pre-war mores and norms.

Prior to the conflict, Sierra Leonean youth were historically alienated from the center of the chiefdoms' political decision making through the customary tradition of deference to elders and by being relegated to low-level tasks (Abdullah 1998). They were excluded from the networks of patronage that provided social security and economic opportunity within their communities and forced to survive in poverty-stricken conditions—either by seeking employment in the saturated diamond pits or by exploiting the illegal possibilities presented by a rebel lifestyle. Isolating the youth demographic contributed to political violence, banditry, hedonism, and brutality as "lumpenised youth are inherently prone to criminal adventurism" given their status as "socially uprooted, chronically impoverished and politically alienated" people (Kandeh 2002, 179).

The government of Sierra Leone now acknowledges that corrupt and oppressive governance in the chiefdoms contributed to the general climate of youth alienation that propelled the nation into conflict (Richards 1995). These factors must therefore be addressed as part of a transition to stability.

INITIATIVES TO ADDRESS POST-CONFLICT CHALLENGES IN THE MINING SECTOR

The international community and the government of Sierra Leone have undertaken several initiatives to encourage transparency and accountability in the management of diamond revenues, the reintegration of excombatants, the allocation of reparations to victims, the reform of laws and regulations related to minerals and the broader environmental sector, and the management of mining rights (Kawamoto 2012). Although these initiatives are related to the complex phenomena that left Sierra Leonean youth with few alternatives to the self-defeating lure of diamond mining, they do not specifically target the alienated youth population (USAID-CEPSL Project 2009).

The Diamond Area Community Development Fund

The first initiative to redirect mining revenues to the support of local communities was established in 2001, before the end of the civil war. The Diamond Area Community Development Fund was designed to redress the inequities of the government's distribution of resources from mining. Roughly 3 percent of the export tax on diamonds was allocated to the fund and used for the development of local mining communities (MMR and MLG 2008). The Ministry of Mines and Mineral Resources, local government officials, local communities, civil society organizations, and nongovernmental organizations (NGOs) are all responsible for monitoring how funds are employed. Although directed to fund infrastructure projects within the various chiefdoms, the funds are often misused (Fischer and Keili 2005; Kawamoto 2012). In April 2011, for example, the government of Sierra Leone raided the Diamond Area Community Development Fund to help pay its national debts.

Reintegration and reparations programs

At the beginning of 2002, a UN-led disarmament, demobilization, and reintegration (DDR) operation disarmed 45,000 rebels, paving the way for national elections in May 2002. The DDR program, which involved compensation and skills training, made progress in meeting the needs of excombatants (UNEP 2009). However, it took almost six more years and additional initiatives at the international level to meaningfully address the needs of those affected by conflict.

In December 2005, United Nations Security Council (UNSC) Resolution 1645 established the UN Peacebuilding Commission to advise countries emerging from conflict and propose integrated strategies to promote post-conflict recovery. The Peacebuilding Commission's role is to focus "attention on the reconstruction and institution-building efforts necessary for recovery from conflict and to support the development of integrated strategies in order to lay the foundation for sustainable development" (UNSC 2005, 2).[2] The United Nations General Assembly and UNSC requested that the UN Secretary-General also establish an independent multi-year, standing peacebuilding fund for post-conflict peacebuilding in Sierra Leone (UNGA 2005; UNSC 2005). As a result, the UN Peacebuilding Fund allocated US$35 million to support the government's ongoing peace consolidation efforts in "youth empowerment and employment, democracy and good governance, justice and security, capacity building of public administration, and support to energy sector" (GOSL 2009, 101).

In December 2007, the government of Sierra Leone and the Peacebuilding Commission adopted a Peacebuilding Cooperation Framework (UN PBC 2007). However, the framework's minimalist wording left the Sierra Leonean government without the necessary enforcement mechanisms to deliver on its commitments to natural resource protection (Lehtonen 2014). Although the framework was intended to provide an outline for priority actions, peacebuilding as a function of natural resource management was a relatively new platform, and the mechanisms for turning priorities into action had yet to be created. This lack of direction led eventually to the creation of the country-owned and -created Agenda for Change,[3] which aimed to restructure Sierra Leone's programmatic priorities and identify the conditions necessary for achieving these priorities. The Agenda for Change aligned with assistance provided by the UN and was also supported by the Peacebuilding Commission as a new core strategy.[4]

In 2008, the UN Peacebuilding Fund allocated US$3 million to a one-year project intended to boost national capacity and implement the recommendations of the Truth and Reconciliation Commission. The government of Sierra Leone subsequently allocated US$246,000 to a reparations program for those affected by the conflict (IRIN 2009a). These funds assisted the government in providing for more than 20,000 victims. A 2011 evaluation confirmed that the reparations were crucial "in providing hope for the population as part of the reconciliation effort" (UN PBF 2011, 10). The UN Peacebuilding Fund also allocated US$4.4 million to fund a reparations unit within the National Commission for Social Action (NaCSA) and a Special Fund for War Victims. The initiatives registered over 32,000 victims (UN PBF n.d.).

---

2 See also UNGA (2005, 2) and Lehtonen (2015).

3 For *An Agenda for Change, Second Poverty Reduction Strategy, 2008–2012*, see GOSL (2009).

4 This collaboration resulted in the publication of a joint programming document titled *Joint Vision for Sierra Leone of the United Nations' Family* (UNIPO-UNCT 2009).

Despite the relative success of the DDR operation for excombatants and reparations funds for those affected by conflict, there was a widespread belief that the perpetrators of violence were being treated better than the victims. Ultimately all of these initiatives were insufficient to meet the wider and more varied needs of young people, as many youth continued to toil in the mines because their basic needs were still not satisfied.

Legal and regulatory reforms

Legal reform has been a central aspect of Sierra Leone's efforts to address environmental, social, fiscal, and accountability challenges related to diamond mining. The government of Sierra Leone has promulgated the Core Mineral Policy and passed the Environmental Protection Agency Act and the Mines and Minerals Act. These laws provide greater clarity to the operation of the mining and environmental sectors.

Core Mineral Policy

Promulgated in 2003, the year after the conflict ended, the Core Mineral Policy was intended to create and enhance an international investor–friendly mining sector, attract private-sector funds, and establish legal and fiscal regulation of all mining operations. The policy claims a free-market approach to ensure the development of best practices in the mining sector and seeks to ensure transparency in all licensing fees, royalties, taxes, and other forms of income from mining (MMR 2003). Thus, it requires that all information related to mining licenses be made available to the public. The policy applies to all mining operations, including artisanal gold and diamond mining, and operations of Sierra Rutile Limited and Koidu Holdings (GOSL and EC 2010).[5]

Although this policy was written in November 2003, there has been little progress in implementation. However, the government has adopted portions of the policy, such as the Kimberley Process Certification Scheme (KPCS), as well as principles of the Extractive Industries Transparency Initiative (EITI).

Environmental Protection Agency Act

The Environmental Protection Agency Act was passed in September 2008 to reverse the trend of natural resource depletion and degradation.[6] The act created

---

[5] Sierra Rutile Limited is one of Sierra Leone's leading mineral sands companies and focuses primarily on the production of rutile, a mineral used to manufacture white pigment. Koidu Holdings, the first commercial entity to invest in the diamond mining sector following the civil war, is a joint venture company operating in Sierra Leone.

[6] Environment Protection Agency Act. Law No. 11 of 2008. www.sierra-leone.org/Laws/2008-11.pdf.

an Environmental Protection Agency as a semiautonomous body to coordinate and monitor all environmental issues within the public and private sectors. It stipulates that all projects involving mineral extraction must carry out environmental and social impact assessments to identify potential effects of mining operations so that mitigating measures can be developed to address them. The act also gives interested parties the ability to comment on the environmental impact assessments.[7]

Mines and Minerals Act

The Mines and Minerals Act, passed in November 2009, was intended to balance the interests of the mining sector, the public, and the government by addressing health and safety standards, environmental protection, and community development.[8] The act strengthens requirements for administrators and mineral rights holders, including mandatory reporting obligations. It also creates a new licensing regime to enhance investments and mineral-sector developments by preventing companies from holding land under license for extended periods of time without using or developing their properties. Finally, the act seeks to balance fiscal benefits in the mining sector by imposing higher royalty rates for precious stones and minerals and distributing these benefits among companies, communities, and the government (MMRPA 2009).

The act promotes local and foreign investment in the mining sector by introducing new provisions for exploration, mine development, and mineral marketing. It includes measures to reduce the harmful effects of mining activities on local communities and the environment by introducing language requiring transparency and accountability, in accordance with international best practice standards (MMRPA 2009).

Although the Mines and Minerals Act has been touted as a decentralized approach to mining management, control under the law is centralized: authority rests solely with the Minister of Mines and Mineral Resources. The minister has used this power to sign mining agreements that have favorable terms for mining companies. For example, a London Mining lease agreement, signed by the minister one day after the enactment of the Mines and Minerals Act, awarded London Mining a lease for a period of twenty-five years, after which it can be renewed for an additional fifteen years. Under the agreement, London Mining can collect scrap metals for resale and export without owing a charge, levy, duty, or royalty to the government of Sierra Leone. The company will also enjoy an 80 percent reduction in income taxes over the first ten years, followed by an additional 80 percent reduction in taxes on other revenue streams for the initial twenty-five-year period of the contract (Gberie 2010).

---

[7] For an analysis of Sierra Leone's Environmental Protection Agency in the country's post-conflict period, see Brown et al. (2012).

[8] Mines and Minerals Act. Law No. 12 of 2009. www.sierra-leone.org/Laws/2009-12.pdf.

The Kimberley Process Certification Scheme

To further promote best practices, Sierra Leone participates in an initiative to reform governance of the diamond industry to meet international standards. The KPCS is an internationally recognized system of rough-diamond certification that is supported by industry self-regulation and is intended to assure diamond buyers that their purchases are not financing conflicts and human rights violations.[9]

Although Sierra Leone is a KPCS participant in good standing, the country has been unable to capture a significant proportion of the legitimate diamond trade. During the civil war, the RUF received up to US$125 million from the diamond trade (Global Witness 2006). The international regulatory system has curtailed illicit smuggling operations, yet estimates suggest that up to 20 percent of the total annual production of diamonds is illegally smuggled out of the country (McConnell 2007).

A 2007 analysis of Sierra Leone's diamond mining sector by a KPCS review team concluded that "although the Kimberley Process seems to be a success in its efforts to stop the flow of conflict diamonds, improved government action is needed to reinforce the KPCS and address illicit trade" (CEMMATS Group 2007). The team also observed that the following were occurring on a regular basis: diamonds were being smuggled into and out of Sierra Leone; exporters, dealers, and financiers were operating without a license; officials were engaging in corrupt practices; and Kimberley Process certificates were being forged, with some of the forgeries involving licensed exporters.

Notwithstanding these concerns, the review team observed that Sierra Leone's recorded diamond exports had grown substantially, which indicated increasing levels of legal compliance. They noted that this uptick was hugely significant in a country whose internal system of controls had been weakened over decades by an asset-stripping dictatorship and then swept away by a highly destructive civil war (CEMMATS Group 2007).

The Extractive Industries Transparency Initiative

Sierra Leone became a candidate for the EITI in February 2008. EITI is an international standard that mandates transparency in extractive industries and includes a requirement that all monetary exchanges be reported. The initiative provides for the creation of a multi-stakeholder group, comprising all appropriate stakeholders, to oversee the EITI process. EITI is expected to improve revenue collection and management; create an attractive investment climate; build trust among the government, communities, and businesses; and provide a forum for discussing broader governance issues (Revenue Watch Institute 2011).

---

9 For analyses of the KPCS, see Grant (2012); Bone (2012); Mitchell (2012); and Wright (2012).

In Sierra Leone, EITI is implemented through a multistakeholder group including mining companies, government agencies, citizen advocacy groups, and the media, and seeks to increase transparency within the mining sector. Information to be disclosed includes tax and fee revenues received from diamond, gold, rutile, and bauxite mining, but does not include payments related to oil extraction or other mineral sources (SLEITI 2010).

The successful implementation of EITI in Sierra Leone will require a significant increase in transparent practices on the part of both the government and private-sector companies, along with a large capacity-building effort to support the initiative.

Management of mining rights

Finally, the United Kingdom's Department for International Development, in conjunction with the United Nations Development Programme (UNDP) and Sierra Leone's Ministry of Mines and Mineral Resources, has introduced land surveys that use computer mapping to identify plot sizes, thereby improving mining transparency. These efforts are, in part, a response to Sierra Leone's history of unregulated mining operations and a mining industry with too few officers and wardens, many of whom are underpaid and lack proper training to provide oversight (Dumbuya and Van der Linde 2012; Revenue Watch Institute n.d.). The land surveys also work to reduce the potential for corruption and conflict when licenses are negotiated (UNDP n.d.; IRIN 2009d).[10]

ALTERNATIVE LIVELIHOOD SCHEMES FOR THE ARTISANAL MINING SECTOR

If Sierra Leone hopes to sustain its progress toward sustainable development and lasting peace, alternatives to employment in the artisanal diamond mining sector must be made available, particularly to the youth demographic.

The reliance on mining for livelihoods is principally due to Sierra Leone's weak local economy, with a limited number of viable, attractive alternatives. Many miners concede that mining would not be their livelihood of choice if they had other feasible options. One reason there are so few livelihood options is that donors rarely offer development assistance to mining communities, so there is not much credit or other support available for nonmining activities in those communities. Hence, artisanal mining will likely decrease when more attractive employment options are made available.

Serious efforts to improve employment options for artisanal miners also are necessary because the diamond supply (especially the alluvial deposit) is nearing exhaustion, making livelihoods diversification an essential development

[10] For a discussion on regulating property rights in the mining sector as a way to stem conflict in the Democratic Republic of the Congo, see Garrett (2015).

priority. Many attempts to directly address this issue have been related to agricultural production. The agricultural sector is critical to Sierra Leone's economy, accounting for approximately 46 percent of the country's GDP and 25 percent of export earnings (Cartier and Bürge 2011). Nearly two-thirds of the country's population depends on agricultural production for livelihood security. Therefore, one opportunity to diversify livelihoods is to support agricultural production of mined-out land.

There is a strong nexus historically between farming and mining and the associated population mobility. Artisanal mining has been viewed as a viable livelihood alternative in predominately agricultural regions, and combining seasonal mining and farming activities is relatively common in rural Sierra Leone. Some Sierra Leoneans believe this link is positive because it allows farmers to reinvest diamond income into their farms; many others are concerned that farm labor is not an effective alternative to mining because of restricted access to land under customary law, lack of opportunities for women, and perceptions among youth laborers that agricultural work is too tedious in relation to the economic benefits. In any case, interest in farming has drastically decreased as youth have been drawn away from agriculture, preferring to pursue employment in the saturated mining market in Sierra Leone as well as in the neighboring countries such as Liberia.

A number of alternative livelihood activities have aimed at providing employment to youth in particular; some of which also involve reclamation of land for environmental rehabilitation and use. The sections that follow discuss four such initiatives in greater detail.

Life After Diamonds

Reclaiming and restoring land once used for mining supports alternative livelihood opportunities, improves living conditions, and promotes redevelopment in post-conflict communities. In many areas of the country, mining has destroyed arable land suitable for agriculture and other uses (DDII 2009). In addition, mining operations divert rivers and streams, diminish potable water supplies, and affect irrigation of food crops. While most mining techniques do not include rehabilitation plans, post-extraction land reclamation is an important step in creating alternative livelihood opportunities in the country's post-diamond future. Taking this into account, the government of Sierra Leone, in 2001, began collecting a land reclamation fee of Le 200,000 (approximately US$67) for every artisanal and small-scale mining lease (200 foot by 200 foot plot) (DDII 2009). The cost of rehabilitating all of the country's mined-out land, however, will likely exceed the fees imposed on mining leases.

In April 2009, One Sky, a Canadian NGO, launched the Life After Diamonds: Land Reclamation for Agriculture and Advocacy pilot initiative with support from the Canadian International Development Agency and individual donors. The project, which targeted 120 rural communities and ran through June 2009, provided support for a community-driven initiative promoting development and sustainable livelihoods diversification among alluvial diamond mining communities in Kono District (in eastern Sierra Leone). Kono has the highest concentration of diamond deposits in the country, as well as extraordinarily high poverty rates and the greatest number of reported incidents of diamond-driven conflict (Wilson 2009). Communities in Kono therefore require special attention in the development and implementation of peacebuilding initiatives and livelihoods diversification programs.

The primary goals of the initiative included sensitizing communities to environment and health issues, strengthening local governance institutions, and empowering citizens to demand land reclamation and restoration. The initiative sought to accomplish these goals by building the capacity of various stakeholders within civil society to promote corporate social responsibility principles within the mining sector, to enhance livelihoods diversification and resilience, and to bolster food security. One Sky also trained community members in value-added agriculture (production techniques and processes that increase the value of agricultural commodities) and market research. To promote local ownership and project sustainability, One Sky partnered with the Conservation Society of Sierra Leone, a national NGO. Through this work, One Sky and the Conservation Society of Sierra Leone engaged local communities in land reclamation to expand productive land and enable agricultural development, while at the same time addressing serious local environmental concerns (DDII 2009).

The Foundation for Environmental Security and Sustainability land reclamation and farming project

The Foundation for Environmental Security and Sustainability (FESS) has been working at three sites in Kono and Kenema districts to provide employment to women and youth through land reclamation activities. By working directly with women and youth, FESS sought to provide alternative livelihood pathways and offer viable and sustainable job opportunities in mining communities. Such alternatives provide women—who generally lack education and access to jobs and skills training—with income-generating opportunities while also increasing stability in vulnerable regions, thus reducing the risk of recurring conflict (FESS n.d.).

In 2007, FESS began its land reclamation work with funding from Tiffany and Company and the U.S. Agency for International Development (USAID). FESS approached the chiefdom authorities, who are custodians of the land, in an effort to reach agreement on the modalities of reclaiming and farming mined-out lands. FESS also organized community workshops that brought together a wide range of community leaders, local NGOs, landowners, women, youth, and others to seek agreement on how the activities would be implemented, how the revenue would be generated and managed, and who would manage the land once the project ended (FESS 2007).

FESS then recruited workers, both men and women, and provided them with land reclamation skills and farming tools. The reclamation activities were carried out exclusively by men because they required heavy manual labor, and the farming activities were conducted by youth and women. When one of the authors conducted a field visit to a FESS site in Kono in 2009, fifty men were working to reclaim the mined-out lands, and twenty-five men and women were farming peanuts and vegetables on the reclaimed lands. The project set a goal of reclaiming fifteen hectares of land every year, for a total of sixty hectares.

Workers at the Kono site engaged in land reclamation activities were paid a stipend of Le8,000 (approximately US$3.39)[11] per day, and each farmer received Le4,500 per day (approximately US$1.92).[12] In addition to this payment, the project provided lunch to workers, with a value equivalent to or greater than the approximately US$2 per day that diggers would receive for artisanal mining (FESS 2007).[13] Produce from the farming activities was sold, and the money was allocated to the chiefdom for community development programs. In other areas, such as Kenema District (in eastern Sierra Leone), where the land belongs to a single family, 75 percent of the revenue went to the chiefdom and 25 percent went to the landowning family.[14]

The COOPI project

COOPI (Cooperazione Internazionale, an Italian NGO) is implementing a program in thirty-two communities in Kono District to help youth from ages fifteen to twenty-five begin farming on community land. The project helps participants grow rice, fruits, and vegetables, and it trains participants to preserve and sell the cassava and fruits they produce. This reinforces the government's efforts to encourage youth to engage in farming (COOPI 2005; IRIN 2009b). A 2008 study of seventy youth involved in COOPI's program found that at the beginning of the project, 60 percent were living below the national poverty line of US$1.25 per day, but that once the project was underway, 90 percent earned between US$2 and $3.50 per day (IRIN 2009b).

---

11 This was the value of Le8,000 on January 1, 2007, while the project was still under way. The value of the leone has declined significantly in recent years.

12 This information was obtained during interviews with FESS personnel during the author's site visit. The field visit took place in May 2009. The author met with Daniel Gbondo, FESS Field Activities Manager, and with both men's and women's groups involved in land reclamation and farming.

13 The stipend offered through the FESS program is generally higher than that available through participation in the artisanal diamond mining industry, which ranges from Le500 to Le8000 per day (in 2010, that represented between US$0.15–US$2.00 per day) (Street Kids International 2010).

14 FESS site visit by author in May 2009.

Youth Reintegration Training and Education for Peace

With the support of the USAID, World Vision Sierra Leone and Management Services International implemented the Youth Reintegration Training and Education for Peace (YRTEP) program in 2000 and 2001 (Hansen et al. 2002).[15] The program—a community-based initiative to help reintegrate conflict-affected youth and excombatants through a six-month training course on a variety of subjects —defined youth broadly to include people in their thirties and forties, including anyone with a living father. The training course was divided into modules that addressed "literacy, numeracy, self-reliance, health, democracy and governance, education for peace, and community-based reconciliation and reintegration" (Hansen et al. 2002, 23), and included over 44,000 participants andfacilitators.

The YRTEP program improved relations between excombatants and conflict-affected youth by training them together in integrated groups (Fauth and Daniels 2001). Activities focusing on introspection, peace, and reconciliation helped encourage enthusiasm and activism within communities and a reduction of violence and "rudeness." The program has also spurred community development through such projects as community gardens, cobbler stands, sewing cooperatives, and road maintenance (Hansen et al. 2002).

Evidence of the program's impacts on livelihoods, literacy, and numeracy is mixed (Fauth and Daniels 2001).[16] Although the program emphasized organizational development and proposal writing, proposals were rarely funded, which left participants frustrated. For example, one community could not find a funder for a series of vocational skills workshops that would have cost only US$100 to implement. A 2002 program evaluation quoted one learning facilitator who commented, "You cannot sensitize people and then have them live in the streets" (Hansen et al. 2002, 30).

Some studies found that YRTEP had a significant effect on livelihoods. A 2001 impact evaluation found that youth were engaging in new activities focused on income and livelihood generation, and that many of them would not have engaged in those activities were it not for YRTEP. For example, 85 percent of surveyed project participants had planted crops, and 77 percent of those reported that they would not have done so if they had not received training through the YRTEP program. Similarly, 40 percent of participants said that they had started

---

15 Seventy-nine percent of participants were between fifteen and thirty-four years of age, and approximately one-fifth were over thirty-five years old. Just two participants were fourteen years of age or younger. Sixty-two percent of the participants were married, and 34 percent were single; only 2 percent were divorced or widowed (Fauth and Daniels 2001).

16 In a 2001 impact study, 98 percent of surveyed YRTEP beneficiaries reported that their literacy had improved, although a project evaluation in 2002 suggested that "the development of the participants' literacy and numeracy was generally very low" (Hansen et al. 2002, 29); see also Fauth and Daniels (2001).

businesses, and 77 percent of these reported that they would not have done so without YRTEP training. Smaller percentages of YRTEP participants had taken on an apprenticeship in a skill or trade (33 percent), enrolled in another training program (28 percent), returned to school (28 percent), or found work (15 percent). Within each of these activities, the majority—sometimes the overwhelming majority—of participants attributed their involvement to the YRTEP training they had received (Fauth and Daniels 2001).

YRTEP's youth learning facilitators received a small stipend to cover some of their expenses as they trained other youth on education and reintegration issues (Hansen et al. 2002). Some learning facilitators pooled their stipends to invest in their communities. One group created a fishing community, another set up a poultry farm, and a third founded an FM radio station so the YRTEP learning mode could reach the entire community over the air.

The reason behind the conflicting findings with respect to YRTEP's impacts on livelihoods and long-term community development is unclear, but additional efforts to support alternative livelihoods and sustainable community development would increase the effectiveness of projects following in the footsteps of this groundbreaking program.

CONTINUING YOUTH ISSUES IN POST-CONFLICT MINING COMMUNITIES

Despite the many initiatives in place to address post-conflict issues in artisanal mining communities, troubles for youth persist.

Following the civil war, youth began migrating to cities, where they participate in the informal economy. The growth of the informal economic sector also rendered many redevelopment strategies, which focused on rural development and formal markets, defunct. Informal economies are often larger and more pervasive than formal markets, and therefore are considered to be a more viable source of income. In cities, men enter the labor force at a young age, but salaried positions in the formal sector are elusive. This can lead to an increase in self-employment—a mainstay of the informal sector—and can drive youth into marginalized areas such as slum quarters and artisanal diamond mining camps as they attempt to boost their status as consumers (Fanthorpe and Maconachie 2010).

The stimulation and possibilities that cities provide also catalyze the rural-to-urban migration of youth. Young people's perception that they can reinvent themselves and will be empowered in cities discourages them from returning to rural settings, where the rite of passage into manhood is often delayed or undermined by power struggles within their village (Sommers 2007). Many village elders control land access and tax the labor of younger men, further exacerbating the vulnerability of youth. Post-conflict reconstruction efforts to maintain political control over the country have focused on chieftaincy and customary law, but rural farmers often wished to remain independent of village rules because they did not trust the elders to manage financial distributions fairly. Many also felt that the corrupt administration of these elders was a direct driver of youth exile and youth involvement in the conflict (Fanthorpe and Maconachie 2010). Indeed, lack of access to land and the absence of inherited land rights continue to present obstacles to programs aimed at improving agricultural opportunities for youth, and are widely cited as root causes of the country's violent history (Cartier and Bürge 2011).

Some youth, in search of employment opportunities, migrate across international borders to work in the Liberian artisanal diamond and gold mining industry. These migratory labor forces—labeled as "diamond boys" in Liberia—are widely known as the most experienced diamond diggers, although they are not well received by many Liberians, who use pejorative words such as "aliens" toward the migratory workers. Some Sierra Leonean miners have also been confronted by immigration authorities in Liberia (PRADD Project 2011).

Struggles in the Kono District illustrate the disorganization and dissatisfaction that continue to cause upheaval between youth and traditional leaders. Seventy-five percent of youth in the district are unemployed (IRIN 2009b). One group—known as the Movement for Concerned Kono Youths—blamed foreigners for the country's devastation and demanded that all foreigners leave the district (Gberie 2002). Subsequent conflict between two youth groups in Kono required the intervention of outside organizations (Gbenda 2003). The youth groups claim to represent the genuine aspirations of the Kono people for the meaningful development of the district, while traditional leaders and others find hope in the return of civil authority to address development challenges. While it is unclear if Kono youth will benefit from existing transition initiatives, there is a clear need to improve communications among the various stakeholders in the Kono District mining sector (CEMMATS Group 2006).

In 2010, a report published by Street Kids International, an NGO supported by the Diamond Development Initiative, analyzed alternative livelihood opportunities for youth in mining communities in eastern Sierra Leone (Street Kids International 2010). Through a workshop and pilot program for youth engaged in the mining industry, Street Kids International analyzed the personal experiences and ambitions of youth and identified a number of obstacles currently undermining alternative livelihood opportunities. For example, the program uncovered a continuous need to provide academic and job training opportunities for youth, especially in areas with low literacy rates, and specifically for girls and young women. Small business pathways should also be encouraged, especially in the small-scale agricultural sector (for example, cocoa, mixed farming, livestock rearing, and honey production) and the urban service sector (for example, taxi service, mechanical service, and vocational trades including textile design, embroidery, and carpentry). Finally, the workshop study indicated that while youth recognize that employment and alternative livelihood creation is a priority of the national government, they are becoming increasingly impatient with the lack of progress and youth consultation in government action.

CONCLUSION

Inadequate employment opportunities in mining, the country's largest industry, coupled with the oppressive governance of community elders, left youth in Sierra Leone with few economic options other than joining rebel forces. Building a sustainable peace in Sierra Leone requires the creation of alternative livelihoods independent of the artisanal mining sector. While credible attempts are being made to create alternative livelihoods in artisanal mining regions, these activities are limited in both impact and scale and are hampered by funding shortages. Additional resources should be invested in the creation of these alternative livelihoods and community development programs.

Continued efforts to strengthen governance and the rule of law in Sierra Leone are also important. Such efforts should include measures to ensure peacebuilding and consolidation, strengthen national security, reform the public sector, enforce an anti-corruption agenda, combat money laundering and financial crime, provide access to justice, improve respect for human rights, and address poverty and youth unemployment. Other important needs include government decentralization, parliamentary and civic oversight, improvements in local governance, and attitudinal change. Conflict management methods that protect stakeholder interests while enabling the development of consensus solutions must continue to be used in artisanal mining regions.

REFERENCES

Abdullah, I. 1998. Bush path to destruction: The origin and character of the Revolutionary United Front/Sierra Leone. *Journal of Modern African Studies* 36 (2): 203–234.

Abrahamsen, R., and M. Williams. 2005. *The globalization of private security: Country report; Sierra Leone*. Aberystwyth, UK: University of Aberystwyth. http://users.aber.ac.uk/rbh/privatesecurity/country%20report-sierra%20leone.pdf.

Bertelsmann Stiftung. 2012. *Sierra Leone country report*. Gutersloh, Germany. www.bti-project.de/fileadmin/Inhalte/reports/2012/pdf/BRI%202012%20Sierra%20Leone.pdf.

Bone, A. 2012. The Kimberley Process Certification Scheme: The primary safeguard for the diamond industry. In *High-value natural resources and post-conflict peacebuilding*, ed. P. Lujala and S. A. Rustad. London: Earthscan.

Brown, O., M. Hauptfleisch, H. Jallow, and P. Tarr. 2012. Environmental assessment as a tool for peacebuilding and development: Initial lessons from capacity building in Sierra Leone. In *Assessing and restoring natural resources in post-conflict peacebuilding*, ed. D. Jensen and S. Lonergan. London: Earthscan.

Cartier, L. E., and M. Bürge. 2011. Agricultural and artisanal goldmining in Sierra Leone: Alternatives to complements? *Journal of International Development* 23:1080–1099. www.academia.edu/1592196/AGRICULTURE_AND_ARTISANAL_GOLD_MINING_IN_SIERRA_LEONE_ALTERNATIVES_OF_COMPLEMENTS.

CEMMATS Group. 2006. *Environmental and social assessment for the mining of ore in Nimikoro, Kono District*. Freetown, Sierra Leone.

———. 2007. *Report on stakeholder analysis, examination of priorities for the mining sector, and review of sector policies for Sierra Leone*. Freetown, Sierra Leone.

COOPI (Cooperazione Internazionale). 2005. Community-based improving of economic, social and environmental security for returnees and host population in 32 communities in Kono District. Milan, Italy. www.coopi.org/en/whatwedo/ouractivities/where-we-work/progetti/659/.

DDII (Diamond Development Initiative International). 2009. Filling in the holes—Policy implications in land rehabilitation: Sierra Leone's artisanal diamond mining challenge. www.ddiglobal.org/contentDocuments/DDI-Policy-Brief-May-2009-en.PDF.

Dumbuya, M., and D. Van der Linde. 2012. Sierra Leone: Government online mining database to increase transparency. IPS-Inter Press Service, January 31. www.ipsnews.net/2012/01/sierra-leone-government-online-mining-database-to-increase-transparency/.

Fanthorpe, R., and R. Maconachie. 2010. Beyond the 'crisis of youth'?: Mining, farming, and civil society in post-war Sierra Leone. *African Affairs* 109 (435): 251–272.

Fauth, G., and B. Daniels. 2001. Impact evaluation: Youth Reintegration Training and Education for Peace (YRTEP) program. Washington, D.C.: Management Systems International.

FESS (Foundation for Environmental Security and Sustainability). 2007. Reclaiming the land after mining: Improving environmental management and mitigating land-use conflicts in alluvial diamond fields in Sierra Leone. Falls Church, VA. www.fess-global.org/Publications/Other/Reclaiming_the_Land_After_Mining.pdf.

———. n.d. Natural resources and conflict: Diamond Development Initiative International (DDII)-sponsored activities in Sierra Leone; Economic diversification and community development in artisanal diamond mining communities in Sierra Leone. www.fess-global.org/DDII-Project.cfm.

Fischer, M., and A. Keili. 2005. *Programmatic environmental assessment for USAID support to small scale artisanal mining activities in Sierra Leone*. Washington, D.C.: International Resources Group and CEMMATS Group.

Garrett, N. 2015. Taming predatory elites in the Democratic Republic of the Congo: Regulation of property rights to adjust incentives and improve economic performance in the mining sector. In *Governance, natural resources, and post-conflict peacebuilding*, ed. C. Bruch, C. Muffett, and S. S. Nichols. London: Earthscan.

Gbenda, T. 2003. Sierra Leone: CCYA moves to avert blood bath in Kono. *Standard Times*, April 11. http://allafrica.com/stories/200304130132.html.

Gberie, L. 2002. Sierra Leone: Peace and diamonds. *Standard Times*, November 22. http://allafrica.com/stories/200211220506.html.

———. 2005. *A dirty war in West Africa: The RUF and the destruction of Sierra Leone*. Bloomington: Indiana University Press.

———. 2010. Sierre Leone: Curse of its riches—again? Tshwane, South Africa: Institute for Security Studies. www.iss.co.za/iss_today.php?ID=1026.

Global Witness. 2006. *The truth about diamonds*. www.globalwitness.org/sites/default/files/import/the_truth_about_diamonds.pdf.

GOSL (Government of Sierra Leone). 2009. *An agenda for change: Second poverty reduction strategy (PRSP II); 2008–2012*. http://unipsil.unmissions.org/portals/unipsil/media/publications/agenda_for_change.pdf.

GOSL (Government of Sierra Leone) and EC (European Commission). 2010. Country strategy paper and national indicative programme for the period 2008–2013. http://ec.europa.eu/development/icenter/repository/scanned_sl_csp10_en.pdf.

Grant, J. A. 2012. The Kimberley Process at ten: Reflections on a decade of efforts to end the trade in conflict diamonds. In *High-value natural resources and post-conflict peacebuilding*, ed. P. Lujala and S. A. Rustad. London: Earthscan.

Hansen, A., J. Nenon, J. Wolf, and M. Sommers. 2002. Final evaluation of the Office of Transition Initiatives' program in Sierra Leone: Final report. Washington, D.C.: CARE, Inc. / Creative Associates International, Inc. http://reliefweb.int/sites/reliefweb.int/files/resources/574F1958F713161485256C8E0053C32F-care-sle-31aug.pdf.

IRIN (Integrated Regional Information Networks). 2009a. Sierra Leone: Compensating war victims. IRIN Humanitarian News and Analysis, December 9. www.irinnews.org/Report/87380/SIERRA-LEONE-Compensating-war-victims.

———. 2009b. Sierra Leone: Diamond miners choose cassava over carats. IRIN Humanitarian News and Analysis, March 16. www.irinnews.org/report.aspx?reportid=83507.

———. 2009c. Sierra Leone: Could youth unemployment derail stability? IRIN Humanitarian News and Analysis, March 3. www.irinnews.org/report/83278/sierra-leone-could-youth-unemployment-derail-stability.

———. 2009d. Sierra Leone: Tap into power of artisanal mining, analysts say. IRIN Humanitarian News and Analysis, July 29. www.irinnews.org/report/85474/sierra-leone-tap-into-power-of-artisanal-mining-analysts-say.

Kandeh, J. D. 2002. Subaltern terror in Sierra Leone. In *Africa in crisis: New challenges and possibilities*, ed. T. Zack-Williams, D. Frost, and A. Thomson. London: Pluto Press.

Kawamoto, K. 2012. Diamonds in war, diamonds for peace: Diamond sector management and kimberlite mining in Sierra Leone. In *High-value natural resources and post-conflict peacebuilding*, ed. P. Lujala and S. A. Rustad. London: Earthscan.

Lehtonen, M. 2015. Peacebuilding through natural resource management: The UN Peacebuilding Commission's first five years. In *Governance, natural resources, and post-conflict peacebuilding*, ed. C. Bruch, C. Muffett, and S. S. Nichols. London: Earthscan.

McConnell, T. 2007. Fighting diamond smuggling in Africa. *Christian Science Monitor*. July 30. www.csmonitor/2007/0730/p07s02-woaf.html.

McMahon, G., and CEMMATS Group. 2007. Mining sector reform in Sierra Leone: A strategic environmental and social assessment. Washington, D.C.: World Bank.

Mitchell, H. 2012. A more formal engagement: A constructive critique of certification as a means of preventing conflict and building peace. In *High-value natural resources and post-conflict peacebuilding*, ed. P. Lujala and S. A. Rustad. London: Earthscan.

MMMR (Ministry of Mines and Mineral Resources, Sierra Leone). n.d. About the National Minerals Agency. www.slminerals.org/index.php/nma.

MMR (Ministry of Mineral Resources, Sierra Leone). 2003. Core mineral policy. Freetown.

MMR (Ministry of Mineral Resources, Sierra Leone) and MLG (Ministry of Local Government, Sierra Leone). 2008. Diamond Area Community Development Fund (DACDF) operational procedures and guidelines. www.slminerals.org/content/images/stories/MMR_Docs/SL%20DACDF%20procedures%20&%20guidelines%20(Nov%202008).pdf.

MMRPA (Ministry of Mineral Resources and Political Affairs, Sierra Leone). 2009. Understanding the Mines and Minerals Act 2009: FAQ. Freetown.

Ojukutu-Macauley, S., and A. Keili. 2008. Citizens, subjects or a dual mandate? Artisanal miners, "supporters" and the resource scramble in Sierra Leone. *Development Southern Africa* 25 (5): 513–530.

PRADD Project (Property Rights and Artisanal Diamond Development Project). 2011. Rich country, poor people: PRA/RRA Report in Grand Cape Mount County.

Revenue Watch Institute. 2011. The Extractive Industries Transparency Initiative (EITI). New York. http://resources.revenuewatch.org/en/backgrounder/extractive-industries-transparency-initiative-eiti.

———. n.d. Sierra Leone: Transparency snapshot. www.revenuewatch.org/countries/africa/sierra-leone/transparency-snapshot.

Richards, P. 1995. Rebellion in Liberia and Sierra Leone: A crisis of youth? In *Conflict in Africa*, ed. O. W. Furley. London: I. B. Tauris.

SLEITI (Sierra Leone Extractive Industries Transparency Initiative). 2010. *First Sierra Leone EITI reconciliation report: Final report*. Freetown. www.sleiti.org/reporting/SLEITI_FIRST_DATA_RECONCILIATION_REPORT.pdf.

Sommers, M. 2007. West Africa's youth unemployment challenge: The case of Guinea, Liberia, Sierra Leone, and Côte d'Ivoire. Vienna, Austria: United Nations Industrial Development Organization.

SSL (Statistics Sierra Leone) and ICF Macro. 2009. *Sierra Leone demographic and health survey 2008*. Calverton, MD. www.measuredhs.com/pubs/pdf/FR225/FR225.pdf.

Street Kids International. 2010. One day I will do something else: Realizing the potential of Sierra Leonean youth. February. http://nmjd.org/publication/one_day_i_will_do_somethingelse.pdf.

Trenchard, T. 2013. Unemployed youth turn to drugs. *IPS News*, January 9. www.ipsnews.net/2013/01/unemployed-youth-turn-to-drugs/.

UNDP (United Nations Development Programme). 2013. Human development report 2013: Explanatory note on 2013 HDR composite indices; Sierra Leone. http://hdr.undp.org/sites/default/files/Country-Profiles/SLE.pdf.

———. n.d. Final report: Implementing mining cadastre system (January 2004–December 2007).

UNEP (United Nations Environment Programme). 2009. *Sierra Leone, environment, conflict and peacebuilding assessment*. Report No. 26141-SL. Geneva, Switzerland.

UNGA (United Nations General Assembly). 2005. Resolution 60/180. A/RES/60/180 (2005). December 30. www.un.org/ga/search/view_doc.asp?symbol=A/RES/60/180.

UNIPO-UNCT (United Nations Integrated Peacebuilding Office, United Nations Country Team). 2009. *Joint vision for Sierra Leone of the United Nations' family*. Freetown, Sierra Leone. ftp.fao.org/TC/CPF/Country%20NMTPF/Sierra%20Leone/UNDAF/UN%20Family%20joint%20vision%20for%20SL.pdf.

UN PBC (United Nations Peacebuilding Commission). 2007. Sierra Leone peacebuilding cooperation framework. PBC/2/SLE/1. December 3. www.refworld.org/docid/47fdfb2f0.html.

UN PBF (United Nations Peacebuilding Fund). 2011. The Peacebuilding Fund: Preventing a relapse into violent conflict; Updates on results and trends. www.unpbf.org/wp-content/uploads/PBF_Brochure_2011.pdf.

———. n.d. Sierra Leone. www.unpbf.org/countries/sierra-leone/.

UNSC (United Nations Security Council). 2005. Resolution 1645. S/RES/1645 (2005). December 20. www.un.org/ga/search/view_doc.asp?symbol=S/RES/1645%20%282005%29.

USAID (United States Agency for International Development). 2009. *Creating an Enabling Policy Environment in Sierra Leone (CEPESL): Final report*. Freetown, Sierra Leone.

Wilson, S. 2009. *Diamonds in Sierra Leone, a resource curse?* Domenico di Fiesole, Italy: European University Institute. http://erd.eui.eu/media/wilson.pdf.

Wright, C. 2012. The Kimberley Process Certification Scheme: A model negotiation? In *High-value natural resources and post-conflict peacebuilding*, ed. P. Lujala and S. A. Rustad. London: Earthscan.

Linking to peace: Using BioTrade for biodiversity conservation and peacebuilding in Colombia

Lorena Jaramillo Castro and Adrienne M. Stork

The creation of sustainable livelihoods for conflict-affected individuals and communities is crucial for a successful post-conflict peacebuilding and recovery process. To ensure a successful recovery, excombatants, associated groups, and conflict-affected communities need to be involved in economically, socially, and environmentally feasible livelihood activities that will continue once external support ends. This requires a reintegration and recovery process that supports peacebuilding objectives and will continue beyond the initial post-conflict intervention.[1] Such a process is especially important in countries where natural resource exploitation played a role in the conflict; research shows that in these cases countries are more likely to relapse into conflict within the first five years following a peace agreement (UNEP 2009). Economic opportunities and

---

Lorena Jaramillo Castro is an economic affairs officer in the Trade, Environment, Climate Change and Sustainable Development Branch of the United Nations Conference on Trade and Development (UNCTAD), working on trade, environment, and sustainable development issues. Adrienne M. Stork is an environmental advisor for the United Nations Environment Programme in Haiti, where she works on post-crisis protected areas management, renewable energy, livelihoods, and value chain development. The opinions expressed in this chapter are those of the authors and are not to be taken as the official views of the UNCTAD secretariat or its member states. The designations and terminology employed are also those of the authors.

1 According to the definitions used by the United Nations Development Programme, the World Bank, and the United Nations Development Group in their *Practical Guide to Multilateral Needs Assessments in Post-Conflict Situations*, the term *post-conflict* refers to the initial two years following the cessation of violence, while the recovery process generally occurs in the first ten years following the end of a conflict (UNDP, World Bank, and UNDG 2004). According to the UN Integrated Disarmament, Demobilization, and Reintegration Standards, *reintegration* is "a social and economic process with an open time-frame, . . . is part of the general development of a country . . . and often necessitates long-term external assistance" (UNDDR 2006, 2). For refugees and internally displaced persons, reintegration is "equated with the achievement of a sustainable return" and is not associated with a time frame (Macrae 1999, 3n2).

benefits are also critical in areas where the lack thereof contributed to the rise in violence.

A value chain approach to supporting post-conflict reintegration and recovery activities provides a means of creating mutually beneficial social and economic relationships among individuals, private entities, government bodies, and communities. It also promotes the generation of employment opportunities in the private sector, which is one of the most challenging aspects of reintegration and recovery programs. The term *value chain* refers to "coordinated relationships between actors who are involved directly and indirectly in a productive activity, with the aim of taking a product or service [such as Amazonian fruits or the natural ingredients for the cosmetic industry] from its supply source and getting it to the customer" (UNCTAD 2009, 3).

Market demand influences how a value chain is developed. There must be a clearly identified market for the chain's products, and those products must have the characteristics and requirements that buyers demand. In addition, participants all along the value chain should be involved in working toward a common goal; this promotes the trust and dialogue that are crucial for peacebuilding, as well as adding economic and employment opportunities at each stage.

Because many countries affected by violent conflict are also highly biodiverse (Hanson et al. 2009), integrating environmental and social considerations into a value chain approach promotes the sustainable management of resources in an economically feasible production system. Furthermore, value chain analyses examine the "horizontal and vertical relationships between different actors in the chain and highlight the power dynamics that influence the ways in which value chains work" (USAID 2008, 12). A value chain approach is therefore an ideal entry point for conflict-sensitive interventions.

Ensuring that economic opportunities presented by a value chain are realized in environmentally and socially sustainable ways is challenging because of the large number of participants in a chain and the variety of environmental and social considerations that need to be taken into account. Especially in a post-conflict recovery environment, poor security, weak governance, or a lack of sufficient infrastructure can pose significant challenges. For example, natural resource–related value chains may be highly corrupted and inefficient where armed groups have usurped control, and conflict may also have detrimental effects on business operations and on the government's capacity for oversight or regulation.

For these reasons, efforts to develop environmentally and socially sustainable value chains that can help to protect natural capital and biodiversity are crucial in countries recovering from conflict, where natural resources are often exploited to restart economic activity and where sufficient environmental and social protection mechanisms may not be in place or may have been substantially weakened during the conflict. Since 2009, such efforts have been undertaken by the United Nations Development Programme (UNDP) and by the BioTrade Initiative of the United Nations Conference on Trade and Development

(UNCTAD);[2] in 2009, UNDP and UNCTAD combined efforts through a pilot project in Aceh, Indonesia.[3]

Although the work in Aceh represents the first program to explicitly engage in BioTrade as a peacebuilding and reintegration tool, prior experience with BioTrade in Colombia can inform those efforts. BioTrade programs were not originally conceived as a tool in peacebuilding processes, but were designed to contribute to biodiversity conservation and poverty alleviation in developing countries. However, experience shows that BioTrade can contribute to reintegration, recovery, and peacebuilding programs.

Through analysis of the BioTrade program implemented in Colombia during the post-conflict period, this chapter examines how such programs can effectively address social equity concerns and integrate natural resource management policies into market-driven value chains to further support long-term economic development. A specific value chain—the Amazonian fruits value chain—is then presented and considered. The chapter proceeds with a discussion of lessons learned from Colombia's experiences in policy making and BioTrade implementation, and concludes with recommendations for integrating BioTrade Initiative programs into the broader peacebuilding and reconciliation framework in conflict-affected areas.

BIODIVERSITY AND RECOVERY IN CONFLICT-AFFECTED AREAS

Between 1950 and 2000—as demonstrated by research published by Thor Hanson and colleagues—two-thirds of Earth's biodiversity hot spot areas had experienced violent conflict (Hanson et al. 2009).[4] In these areas, natural resources provide the sources of livelihoods for the majority of the population; biodiversity-based

---

[2] The term *BioTrade*—as defined by UNCTAD and as used in this chapter—refers to the "collection or production, transformation, and commercialization of goods and services derived from native biodiversity . . . according to criteria of environmental, social, and economical sustainability" (UNCTAD 2007, 1). The sustainability of BioTrade is guaranteed by adherence to principles related to conservation and sustainable use, economic feasibility, generation of sustainable livelihoods, and respect for the rights and culture of all people involved in the chain (UNCTAD 2007).

[3] UNCTAD and UNDP have been working separately on BioTrade and reintegration programs, respectively, for over a decade. In 2009, the two organizations established the UNCTAD-UNDP Joint Initiative on BioTrade and Reintegration. As part of this joint initiative, the pilot project in Aceh was developed with the aim of supporting peacebuilding and reintegration efforts there. The assessment and project-planning phase was completed in 2010, and project activities began in target communities in January 2011.

[4] To qualify as a biodiversity hot spot, a region must meet two strict criteria: it must contain at least 1,500 species of vascular plants, and it must have already lost at least 70 percent of its primary vegetation. The term *hot spot* was coined by Norman Meyers and is described in detail in Mittermeier, Myers, and Mittermeier (2000).

resources are commonly used for shelter, medicine, food, and recreation; and when possible, products derived from such resources are sold in local, national, or international markets for cash income. In addition, such resources are often associated with traditional knowledge that is an important part of social cohesion and cultural connections.

Addressing biodiversity loss is challenging in any area of the world, but in conflict situations the threat of violence, lack of security, disruption of social structures, and weakened governance capacity often make this task even more difficult. In addition, highly valuable species in biodiversity-rich areas can easily be exploited to fuel armed conflict. In other places, biodiversity may become threatened because of the presence of armed groups and efforts to rout them out, especially where they may be using dense forest to protect their bases.

In order to protect biodiversity in conflict-affected areas, it is necessary to align biodiversity conservation objectives with economic recovery efforts. To avoid contributing to the overexploitation of natural resources, recovery and peacebuilding leaders should promote livelihood strategies that help conserve biodiversity, use natural resources for sustainable development purposes, and encourage socially inclusive economic behaviors following the conflict. Because BioTrade works through a value chain approach that builds capacity and encourages sound natural resource management, it represents an effective tool that will help post-conflict recovery practitioners to achieve these goals.

Post-conflict economies depend on natural resources for recovery, and given the environmental degradation that occurs during conflict and the need to ensure a strong peace dividend in the critical first decade following the cessation of hostilities, recovery practitioners need to ensure that sustainability measures are employed. Many conflict-affected areas are high in biodiversity and contain large forests, swamps, and other valuable carbon sinks, which make them especially important for the future of the countries' economies post-2012, when countries with large tracts of tropical forests will be able to take advantage of international financing mechanisms for protecting their forests and other biologically diverse areas.[5] These natural resources can also support the diversification of a region's or country's economy with biodiversity-based, environmentally friendly products.[6]

---

[5] The post-Kyoto climate change negotiations have sought to develop the mechanisms for rewarding developing countries for preserving their carbon stocks, such as forests, wetlands, and agricultural lands, although as of September 2014 countries have yet to agree upon such a mechanism.

[6] The Economics of Ecosystems and Biodiversity study's report for businesses states that by 2050 sustainability-related global business opportunities in natural resources (energy, forestry, food and agriculture, water, and metals) will be in the range of US$2 trillion to US$6 trillion (Bishop 2012). The United Nations Environment Programme's green economy report illustrates the benefits of greening economies for lowering environmental risks, including scarcity of natural resources, and providing development opportunities for the world's poor (UNEP 2011).

However, traditional post-conflict recovery programs have not specifically integrated these concerns into their projects. As the environment, biodiversity, and climate change become larger issues on the international agenda, it will be especially important for post-conflict recovery programs to provide livelihoods support to affected populations and promote peacebuilding in ways that will reinforce the conservation of biodiversity and integrate biodiversity into economic development plans.

THE BIOTRADE INITIATIVE

Launched in 1996, UNCTAD's BioTrade Initiative provides specific financial and technical support that reinforces sound natural resource management, conserves biodiversity, and increases opportunities for economically sustainable trade through value chain development. The initiative contributes to poverty alleviation by creating or strengthening the livelihoods of populations whose economic activities are related to biodiversity. It works through implementing partners in specific countries and in the international arena to build capacity for the successful implementation of BioTrade principles within value chains.

The initiative's efforts further the three objectives of the Convention on Biological Diversity—conservation of biodiversity, sustainable use of its components, and fair and equitable sharing of benefits—while promoting socioeconomic sustainability, compliance with national and international regulations, respect for the rights of people involved in BioTrade activities, and clarity about land tenure and access to natural resources.[7] Together, these objectives constitute the seven principles of the BioTrade Initiative.

Working in accordance with these principles, the BioTrade Initiative develops programs with national, regional, and international partners. This may include strengthening the companies and producers involved, as well as improving the institutional policies and the organizational structure of selected biodiversity-based sectors. The initiative thus requires cooperation, communication, and negotiation among a variety of stakeholders, from government bodies to citizens' groups to the private sector, to ensure that commonly held objectives are met in sustainable and equitable ways. It also requires that practitioners examine key issues that are contentious in post-conflict situations, such as land allocation and resource access, in order to ensure the sustainability of the initiative.

BioTrade programs and activities have been implemented in more than fifteen countries in Asia, Africa, and Latin America (see map on page 6); of these, Colombia, Indonesia, Mozambique, and Uganda have been affected by armed civil conflict. Bolivia, Brazil, Ecuador, Mozambique, Peru, South Africa, and Zimbabwe have also been affected by lower-level internal conflicts over land rights and access to natural resources. All of these countries have high rates of

---

[7] For the text of the Convention on Biological Diversity, see www.cbd.int/convention/text/.

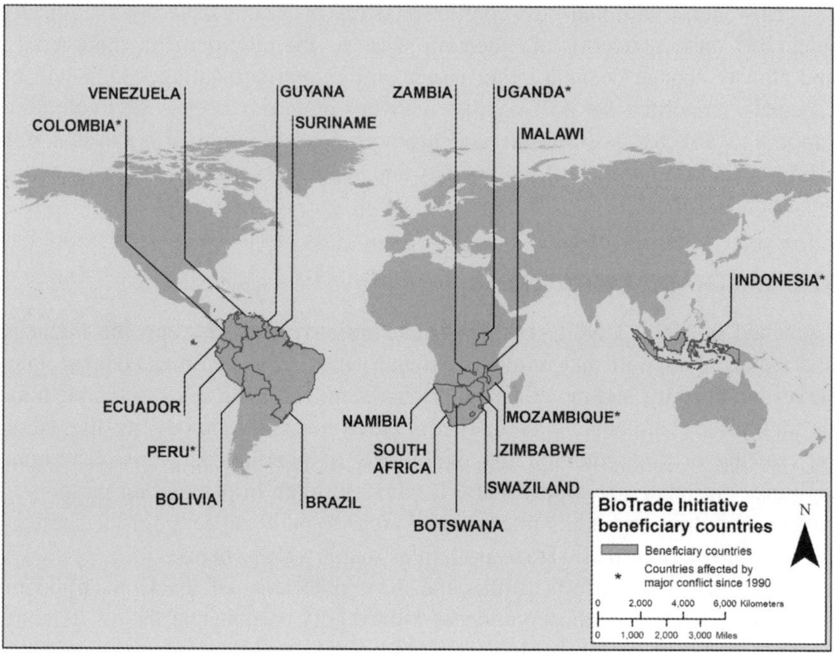

Note: *Major conflict* is a conflict resulting in more than 1,000 battle-related deaths overall (Bruch et al. 2015; UCDP n.d.).

biodiversity and depend on natural resources as one of their primary sources of economic earning. The biodiversity-based sectors currently supported in these countries include flowers and foliage; handicrafts; sustainable tourism; and natural ingredients for the food, cosmetic, pharmaceutical, and fashion industries.

In countries where it has been implemented, BioTrade has been mainstreamed into national and international policy frameworks as well as business practices through linkages with small and medium-sized enterprises (SMEs) and other companies in the Americas and Europe. In addition, an informal network of both South-South and North-South private, public, and academic-sector stakeholders has been established to cooperate and exchange information and experiences related to accessing markets, strengthening value chains, implementing environmentally and socially friendly practices, and developing incentives for biodiversity conservation. BioTrade Initiative activities have been developed primarily in partnership with the Swiss State Secretariat for Economic Affairs.

The effects of BioTrade programs and activities are being documented with the BioTrade Impact Assessment System, which analyzes environmental, socioeconomic, and governance indicators. Initial results showed that, as of 2010, BioTrade programs had benefited more than 30,000 families and have led to the implementation of conservation and sustainable-use practices on over 700,000 hectares of land.

The value chain approach makes support to key sectors possible within the framework of BioTrade programs. The various participants in a value chain—such as producers, processors, distributors, traders, and regulatory and support institutions—begin with the understanding that there is a market demand for the value chain's products and services. They then articulate a joint vision to identify mutual needs, limitations, and strengths and to begin working cooperatively to achieve their goals (UNCTAD 2009). The common goals are defined and agreed upon in a participatory process, and are then translated into sector strategies that promote the sustainable trade of biodiversity-derived products and services.

This approach provides opportunities to also achieve peacebuilding objectives in two principal ways. First, it allows for the integration of producers with processors and market participants so information can flow between various links in the value chain, thereby enhancing communication and transparency among various groups to ensure that economic benefits are realized fairly throughout the process of production. In post-conflict situations, the creation of such linkages provides a neutral platform where a variety of people in the public and private sectors can come together with small landholders and producers to establish common goals and procedures that will provide benefits for all. Such platforms for dialogue also present an opportunity to plan for future activities and to raise other issues relevant to the stakeholders, such as the allocation of resources and relationships to state and local governments.

Ensuring that economic benefits are fairly distributed throughout a value chain is particularly important in post-conflict situations, especially in Colombia. Research by Oeindrila Dube and Juan F. Vargas shows that in labor-intensive economic sectors (such as coffee growing, horticulture, and other agriculture), declines in wages led to higher rates of violence by increasing the likelihood that members of disadvantaged populations will be recruited by or susceptible to the influence of armed groups (Dube and Vargas 2006).

Second, a successful value chain requires that participants are willing to engage in implementation of the strategy by contributing time, energy, and resources, while also sharing responsibility for the associated risks and benefits. Value chain development strategies build on existing capacity and knowledge and promote the coordination of activities and the establishment of partnerships among all participants. Collaborative arrangements can enhance the competitiveness of the chain and facilitate cooperation and coordination among different actors. In post-conflict situations, the creation of new linkages and interdependencies between communities and other value chain participants, such as private sector firms and government agencies, strengthens mutual benefits and understanding, while also providing forums for dialogue.

When value chain participants work independently of one another, they lack relevant information that could improve their functioning. Universities and research organizations may develop studies that are not compatible with the existing productive activities in their region. SMEs may produce and transform plant and animal species without any scientific knowledge of the species' properties, such as regeneration rates, or the species' capacity to add value. For their part, local governments and donors may build processing facilities that are not fully adaptable to the local infrastructure. However, once value chain participants collaboratively define the goals and activities they want to develop as a group, they can begin to build trust and communication, which can foster coherence and synergies between their activities. For example, the SMEs can define—on the basis of their needs—possible research topics to be taken up by universities. Then research institutions, government bodies, and development agencies can fund the recommendations emerging from such research.

The BioTrade Initiative value chain methodology involves five result-oriented steps (see figure 1). These steps enable the bottom-up analysis of existing information on a selected sector or value chain, including its market potential, and they later guide the formulation of specific strategies to support the growth of the sector or chain. The support offered through this methodology, together with its bottom-up approach, ensures that communication and information flow within the value chain, while minimizing miscommunications. Products are thus more likely to meet quality standards, improving market access and overall success.

Five basic elements should be considered in the implementation of the BioTrade Initiative value chain methodology (UNCTAD 2009, 3):

- This is a participatory process in which all actors—both productive and institutional—are involved.
- The support given to value chains involves environmental, social and economic objectives, in accordance with the BioTrade Principles and Criteria, which are analyzed together with the other technological criteria essential to market entry.
- The process focuses on market demand and the sector's potential to enter these markets.
- Strategy development is based on concrete goals for [domestic sales as well as] export and for strengthening the process of entering markets in the short and medium terms.
- This is a flexible process that can be adapted to specific conditions within a country.

Through this methodology and in accordance with the seven BioTrade Initiative principles, projects are planned and implemented with a view toward ensuring maximum social, economic, and ecological sustainability. This approach can be aligned effectively with peacebuilding and recovery programs, which are under extreme pressure to provide employment and income-generating opportunities that will also address social concerns and have a lasting effect on stability, providing a visible peace dividend to conflict-affected populations.

BIOTRADE IN COLOMBIA

Until very recently, BioTrade concepts and methodologies were not integrated explicitly into peacebuilding programs. However, BioTrade has been applied in

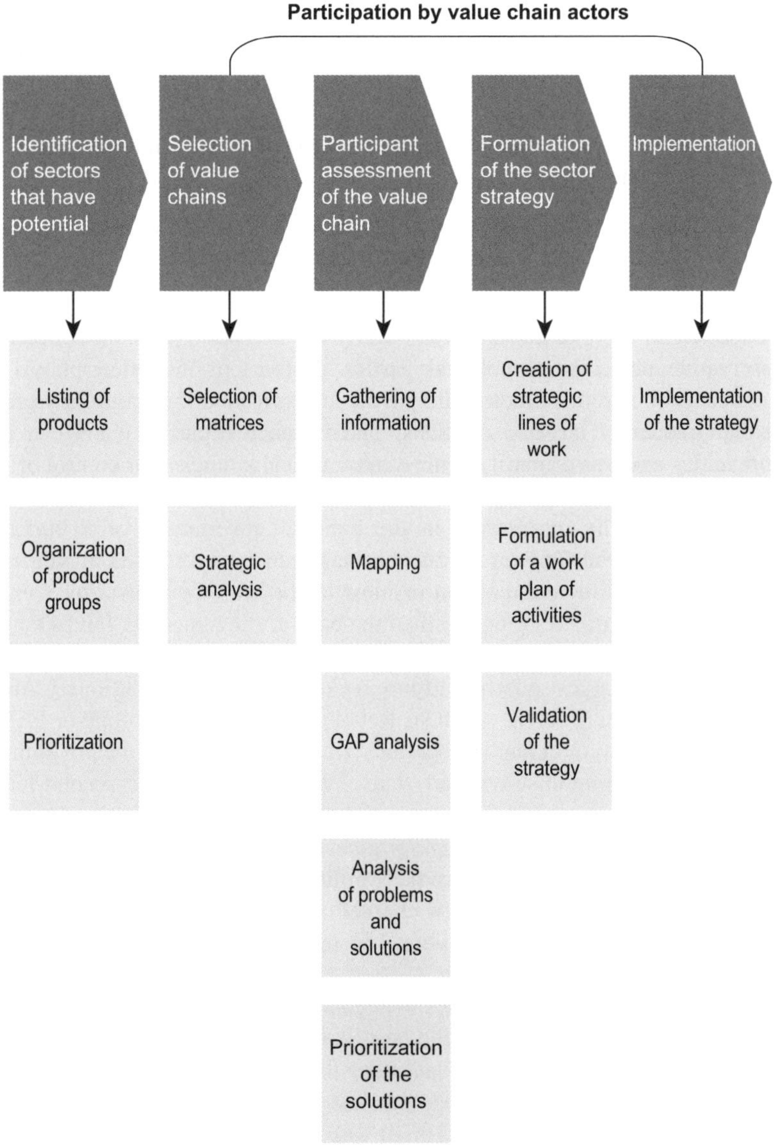

Figure 1. Diagram of the support process for value chains for BioTrade products
Source: Adapted from UNCTAD (2009).

sensitive and highly conflict-affected areas such as the Colombian Amazon, where it has contributed to socioeconomic development.

In Colombia, the national BioTrade program is contributing to the peace process, to the formation of national policies in sustainable rural development, and to the generation of local employment by providing an alternative to the production of illicit crops. The program is also enhancing interinstitutional linkages so as to foster investment, conserve biodiversity, and diversify exports (Pardo Fajardo, Hernández, and Ramos 2000). This section discusses how the Colombian BioTrade program has contributed to peacebuilding and biodiversity conservation objectives in the departments of Amazonas, Caquetá, and Putumayo in southern Colombia's Amazon region.[8]

The civil conflict and natural resources in Colombia

The conflict in Colombia has been ongoing with varying levels of intensity since the cessation, in 1966, of La Violencia—nearly two decades of tensions between the Conservative and Liberal political parties. These tensions often played out through acts of extreme violence that involved insurgent and paramilitary groups and that frequently targeted civilians. The violence occurred mainly in rural communities and was primarily concentrated around struggles for control of land in the rich, coffee-producing regions of the country (Rouvinski and Vasquez Sanchez 2005). The installation in the national government of a bipartisan coalition between the Conservative and Liberal parties in 1957 led to a decrease in violence and the demobilization of most of the armed groups; however, the remnants of these armed groups formed the basis for the guerrilla forces that are still in operation today.

In 1964, the largest guerrilla group in Colombia, the Revolutionary Armed Forces of Colombia (Fuerzas Armadas Revolucionarias de Colombia, or FARC), formed with the aim of defending peasants' rights, overthrowing the government, and forming a communist-agrarian state. Two years later, the second-largest guerrilla group, the National Liberation Army (Ejército de Liberación Nacional, or ELN), was formed. Both groups originated with followers mostly in rural areas and initially targeted government military structures and infrastructure, although over time they have been charged with using the narcotics trade for self-financing and have been implicated in increased targeting of civilians and in attacks on urban areas.

In spite of attempts in the 1980s to negotiate peace accords with the guerrilla groups, the conflict intensified in the late 1990s as the FARC and others sought to capture the political space left vacant by the defeat of the Medellín and Cali drug cartels. The number of kidnappings and acts of extortion also increased in this period. A demilitarized zone (DMZ) was created south of Bogotá as part of peace negotiations between the government and the FARC between 1998 and 2002, but this led to further targeting of urban areas and higher civilian casualties overall. After talks collapsed in 2002, the FARC continued to target urban areas and was pursued by government forces.

Aside from insurgent groups and the national armed forces, the other major actors in the conflict in Colombia are right-wing paramilitary groups, many of

---

[8] Colombia is administratively divided into departments, which are further divided into municipalities.

which were formed by rural elites in response to the guerrilla movements. These paramilitary groups developed to protect large landowners and became a force for promoting the economic interests of large-scale haciendas that grew cash crops and employed rural peasants as wage laborers or sharecroppers (Elhawary 2008).

As the paramilitary groups grew in size and number, they came to include drug traffickers and former members of the national armed forces, as well as combatants recruited by those holding grievances against the guerrilla groups. In 1997, several smaller paramilitary groups joined together to form the United Self-Defense Groups of Colombia (Autodefensas Unidas de Colombia, or AUC), who, in their efforts to combat guerrilla groups, are reported to have increased violence against civilians throughout the 1990s. AUC was placed on the U.S. Department of State's list of foreign terrorist organizations in 2001.

The voluntary demobilization of members of the AUC was negotiated in 2002, and since then some 32,000 former AUC members have been demobilized. Additionally, 18,000 former members of the FARC and ELN have voluntarily demobilized since 2002 (CIDDR 2009). Since 2006, the Colombian High Council for Reintegration (ACR) has managed the demobilization and reintegration process with support from the UNDP, the International Organization for Migration, and various international governments and nongovernmental organizations (NGOs).

The conflict in Colombia escalated during the 1990s due to the expansion of guerrilla and paramilitary activities (Dube and Vargas 2006). Many more people were displaced from their land, and nearly one-third of agricultural land was estimated to be under the control of drug traffickers by the end of that decade (Pettersson 2000). As a result of the violence and consolidation of landownership, the number of internally displaced persons in Colombia since the 1990s has been the highest in the Western Hemisphere and second highest in the world (Moloney 2006).

From 1995 to 1998, 40 percent of all municipalities in Colombia experienced at least one instance of internal displacement, and in nearly 20 percent of those, displacement occurred almost constantly (Rouvinski and Vasquez Sanchez 2005). In addition, since the 1950s, the per capita gross domestic product for rural populations has been roughly half of that for urban populations, although urban poverty has grown with the increasing migration of internally displaced persons to urban areas. Colombia's urban population increased from 57 percent of the total population in 1951 to 74 percent in 1994 (Rouvinski and Vasquez Sanchez 2005).

Despite good overall economic growth rates throughout the 1990s, attributed primarily to booms in the coffee sector and the illegal drug trade (Rouvinski and Vasquez Sanchez 2005), the rural population of Colombia has mostly remained impoverished. This is largely due to the absence of land reform in rural areas and the increasing consolidation of land assets during the waves of violence from the 1950s onward (Pettersson 2000). Colombia has one of the most highly concentrated landownership patterns in the world: 0.4 percent of landowners control 61 percent of rural land. This leaves rural populations, who have little control over their assets, extremely vulnerable to violence and displacement (ABColombia 2010).

The civil violence in Colombia has affected numerous parts of the country over the years, with the most intense violence occurring along the Atlantic coast in the north, where much of the drug trafficking takes place; in the Cauca river valley in the southwest; in the departments of Caquetá and Putumayo along the border with Ecuador; and in the Amazon region in the southeast, where the FARC is still present (ABColombia 2010). Rural development is essential in these areas to strengthen the capacity of municipal administrations to provide essential public services, to promote local development activities, and to help reduce vulnerability to violence from armed groups.

The national Sustainable BioTrade Programme in Colombia

In Colombia, the national Sustainable BioTrade Programme was launched in 1998 as the pioneer BioTrade effort worldwide. It is managed by the Ministry of Environment, Housing and Territorial Development and the National Technical Committee on Biodiversity and Competitiveness. The Alexander von Humboldt Institute for Research on Biological Resources (Humboldt Institute), BioTrade Fund Colombia (Fondo Biocomercio Colombia), Sustainable BioTrade Corporation (Corporación Biocomercio Sostenible), and the Sinchi Amazonic Institute of Scientific Research (Instituto Amazónico de Investigaciones Científicas, also known as the Sinchi Institute) are some of the key entities that are implementing the initiative. Local and regional support comes from authorities such as the regional autonomous corporations and other public, private, and academic partners.

The Sustainable BioTrade Programme in Colombia is benefiting more than 1,850 projects managed by private and community organizations in five sectors (MEHTD 2009; see figure 2): sustainable agriculture systems for medicinal plants, fruits, grains, and other products; nontimber forest products, including fruits, flowers, foliage, fibers, honey, and seeds; wood and guadua (a type of bamboo) products that are sustainably derived from forests; ecotourism; and fauna for food for humans and pets, such as beetles, butterflies, caiman, capybara, frogs, and ornamental fish.

There is potential in national and international markets for Colombian BioTrade producers and SMEs, but the time and resources required to make a value chain successful are substantial. A 2005 national survey of one hundred BioTrade SMEs, micro-SMEs, and community-based organizations found that 20 percent were just forming (they had been in existence less than one year and had acquired infrastructure and equipment), 51 percent were starting production and sales of their goods, 18 percent were consolidating their activities (they had recovered their initial investment and were establishing themselves in their target market), 10 percent were expanding, and 1 percent were in liquidation (Lozada and Gómez 2005). Coordinated work with public, private, and academic stakeholders and development agencies is essential to prevent duplication of effort and to realize a cost-effective intervention that addresses real needs and common goals—features of a value chain approach.

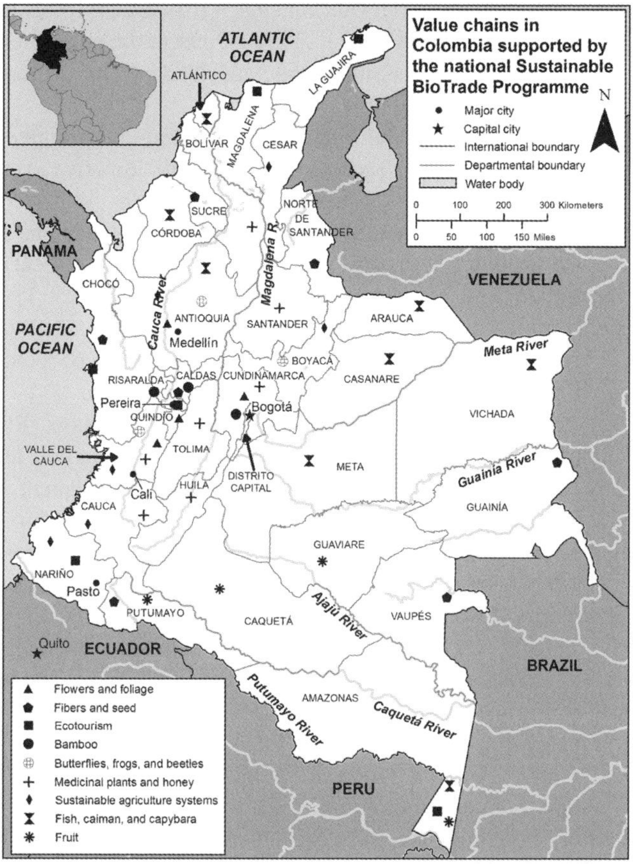

Figure 2. Value chains in Colombia supported by the national Sustainable BioTrade Programme
Source: Gómez and Ortega (2007).

Implementation

In 2006, in the departments of Amazonas, Caquetá, and Putumayo, Humboldt Institute in cooperation with the Corporation for the Sustainable Development of the Southern Amazon (Corporación para el Desarrollo Sostenible del Sur de la Amazonía, or CORPOAMAZONIA)[9] implemented a project to strengthen

[9] CORPOAMAZONIA, headquartered in Putumayo, is a regional autonomous corporation for the departments of Amazonas, Caquetá, and Putumayo. As a regional autonomous corporation, CORPOAMAZONIA is a public entity, responsible by law to manage—within its territory of jurisdiction—the environment and renewable resources, and to foster the sustainable development of the country.

BioTrade business initiatives in the value chains of Amazonian fruits, handicrafts, flowers, and foliage (Arcos Dorado et al. 2009). Other participants included local universities, business support organizations, and NGOs. The project provided support to these initiatives in three phases.

In the first phase, the national Sustainable BioTrade Programme evaluated and analyzed business initiatives according to BioTrade Initiative principles and criteria to identify the initiatives' limitations and strengths with respect to the social, economic, and environmental components of BioTrade. The forty-eight projects involved included not only private initiatives (66 percent), but also initiatives by farmers and indigenous communities (34 percent). These farmer and indigenous community initiatives were based in Putumayo (40 percent), Amazonas (31 percent) and Caquetá (29 percent). Men led 63 percent of the projects, which were primarily small, family-based initiatives.

Business development occurred during the second phase. Practitioners implemented actions to strengthen and incubate business initiatives identified in the first phase, addressing technical, commercial, and management needs. For example, practitioners developed business plans for twenty-seven initiatives, and according to the priorities established in those plans, practitioners received support for equipment purchases, implementation of marketing strategies and commercialization, and acquisition of the required legal permits.

In the third phase, practitioners turned to marketing and commercial strategy, assessing various strategies for regional and international markets and implementing those that were most appropriate for the unique characteristics of the region and the participants. For example, within the native Amazonian fruits chain, a regional identity strategy was developed that included a communication strategy involving a unique logo and the phrase *Amazonia, esencia de vida* (Amazonia, essence of life). Guidelines for the use and management of this brand were finalized by CORPOAMAZONIA, and a consultancy is being implemented to register it as a trademark. Furthermore, the BioTrade Observatory established an online platform where national and regional buyers and sellers of Amazonian products could meet.

Because an enabling policy environment is essential to foster the development of value chains, BioTrade Initiative partners worked with government entities to mainstream the prioritized chains in regional and local development strategies. For example, the regional competitive plan for Caquetá—Caquetá Vision 2032—established that "in the year 2032, the Caquetá region will be integrated into the international trade and will be the most competitive Department in the Colombian Amazon region, through the supply of high-value added goods and services, the consolidation of BioTrade and strengthening of social and human capital" (Regional Competitiveness Commission 2008).[10]

---

[10] Translation provided by Lorena Jaramillo Castro and Adrienne M. Stork, authors of this chapter.

Conflict dynamics in the Amazon region and the impact of BioTrade programs and activities

The Amazon region of Colombia spans the departments of Amazonas, Caquetá, Cauca, Guainía, Guaviare, Meta, Nariño, Putumayo, Vaupés, and Vichada. It has a population of nearly 1 million people, including members of fifty-eight indigenous groups, who represent over 50 percent of the region's population (Bolivar et al. 2008). Reserves of land for the indigenous populations, *resguardos*, cover 20 million hectares of the Colombian Amazon region and are an important contribution to biodiversity conservation in the area (Hammen 2003). Rainforest covers 35 percent of Colombia's land area, making the country one of the most biodiverse in the world (Hungerford 2010).[11]

The Amazon is one of the regions most highly affected by the conflict in Colombia. As one of the primary growing areas for coca, it is also a strategic region for narcotrafficking and antinarcotics activities (Ramirez 2003). The Colombian government has heavily sprayed the departments of Guaviare, Nariño, and Putumayo with herbicides in an effort to halt the cultivation of coca and to regain access to U.S. development funds as part of Plan Colombia (Rouvinski and Vasquez Sanchez 2005).[12] This aerial herbicide spraying has destroyed agricultural crops and sections of forest and has adversely affected the health and economic well-being of the indigenous people who live in these areas and depend on the rainforest for their survival, including the Awa people, who are listed as an endangered group by the United Nations.

The protests against spraying and other responses by the civil society–based Cocaleros Social Movement led to an increased presence in the late 1990s of paramilitary groups that are closely linked with the national army. Violent conflict ensued (Ramirez 2003). High levels of mortality among the civilian population followed as the FARC, the government, and the paramilitaries fought over territorial control and control of the drug trade in rural and urban areas. The results of the conflict include high levels of displacement of indigenous people and the capturing of land, often through violent means, by paramilitaries and guerrilla groups.

Displacement has been higher among indigenous people than for the rest of the population. Although indigenous people constitute only 3.4 percent of the total population in Colombia, they represent 7 percent of those displaced (ABColombia 2010). As a result of disruptions in transport networks, including the blockading of roads, farmers who are involved in the production and sale of

---

11 Colombia hosts many endemic species. It is listed among the ten most biodiverse countries in the world in all main categories; it is number one for amphibians.

12 Plan Colombia—an extensive counternarcotic program developed to respond to the country's rampant drug production and paramilitary violence—was launched in 1999 during the administration of President Andres Pastrana (1998–2002) and backed by international support, including U.S. funding. The program was designed to address human rights violations, bolster democratic institutions, promote economic recovery, and assist internally displaced persons.

BioTrade commodities in the Amazon region often have difficulty delivering goods to markets.[13]

In conflict-affected communities where the BioTrade Initiative has contributed to the development of sustainable livelihoods, social, environmental, and economic benefits are being generated. The funds generated by BioTrade activities in rural communities in Colombia's southern Amazon region represent a high percentage, and sometimes the sole source, of income for many families. In terms of direct employment, 46 percent of the initiatives generated between one and five salaried jobs with benefits. However, only 2 percent of the initiatives generated over one hundred jobs, and 18 percent did not generate any direct employment (Arcos Dorado et al. 2009).

Most of the BioTrade projects in the Amazon region involve agroforestry practices (25 percent) and collection from secondary forests (20 percent). Among the surveyed enterprises, the most common biodiversity-conservation and sustainable-use practices were aimed at the use of raw materials (20 percent), protection of water sources (15 percent), and diversification of crops (13 percent). Other sustainable practices included the creation of live fences and buffer zones, and the enrichment of stubble fields. These initiatives also actively manage their waste in order to prevent pollution of rivers and other water sources and to mitigate the production systems' possible impacts on water (Arcos Dorado et al. 2009).

Overall, the BioTrade activities have strengthened relationships and clarified procedures between suppliers and processing SMEs. The most common practices in this regard include the development of social programs for communities and employees, and policies to promote local employment and good treatment of workers. Other activities that have been implemented include educational and recreational activities, training programs, and hygiene and health programs.

In the case studies below, the authors describe two initiatives—Mukatri, an enterprise in Caquetá, and Pradera Verde Empresa Unipersonal (E.U.) in Putumayo—that worked with Colombia's Sustainable BioTrade Programme and its partners in conflict-sensitive areas. There are also lessons to be learned from unsuccessful projects that Colombia's Sustainable BioTrade Programme and its partners have supported, particularly related to the absence of a market-driven orientation and a lack of competitiveness. These cases demonstrate the need for SMEs to have managerial capacities and the flexibility to address security and market challenges that arise.

CASE STUDIES: AMAZONIAN FRUITS VALUE CHAIN

The Amazonian fruits value chain is the one of the best known in the region because of market interest and the number of operational projects.[14] These projects

---

13 Fondo Biocomercio personnel interviewed by authors, May 2009.

14 Many details in this case study come from personal communication with José Ignacio Muñoz Córdoba, director general at CORPOAMAZONIA, May 23, 2011.

are located in each of southern Colombia's Amazon departments—Caquetá, Putumayo, and Amazonas—as well as in Guainía and Guaviare. The Amazonian fruits value chain spans activities from the production or collection of raw material to industrial processing, commercialization of final products, and transportation to the final consumer. Ten BioTrade enterprises have been identified in the southern Amazon region that involve collection, production, or processing of fruits—three in Caquetá, four in Putumayo, and three in Amazonas. The department of Putumayo generates 78 percent of the total production, followed by Caquetá (19 percent) and Amazonas (3 percent) (Arcos Dorado et al. 2009).

Some of the commonly used fruits are arazá *(Eugenia stipitata)*, asaí *(Euterpe precatoria)*, borojo *(Borojoa patinoi)*, cocona *(Solanum sessiliflorum Dunal)*, copoazú *(Theobroma grandiflorum)*, chontaduro *(Bactris gasipaes)*, seje *(Jessenia bataua Mart.)*, and papayuela *(Carica candemarcensis Hook)*.[15] The fruits are sold fresh or are processed into value-added products such as pulps, sweets, juices, yogurts, snacks, or wines. The value-added products represent a growing business opportunity and a means of generating livelihood alternatives to illicit crop cultivation. For example, in Putumayo, a hectare of coca generates an estimated annual income for farmers in the range of €700 to €1,000 (approximately US$1,000 to US$1,400), whereas the commercialization of value-added products derived from fruits (for example, juices, concentrates, and sweets) may generate an annual income of €1,000 to €2,000 (approximately US$1,400 to US$3,000).[16]

These fresh fruits and value-added products are mainly sold in local markets; however, a few enterprises have also reached the national market by selling through supermarket chains. Other distribution channels include hotels, restaurants, and specialty stores. There are also a few exports to international markets. The top value-added product produced in the region is yogurt, at six tons per month, and the volume of jams made from arazá reaches nearly one ton per month (Arcos Dorado et al. 2009).

Mukatri

Mukatri, whose name means "origin of natural life" in the indigenous Maku dialect, is an associative enterprise created in 2006. Its productive activities are based on sustainable use; fair relationships with producers, suppliers, and clients; and

---

15 The common English names, respectively, are araza, açai, borojó, cocona, cupuaçu, peach-palm, mingucha, and mountain papaya.

16 According to the prevailing exchange rates as of December 2013. Personal communication with Luis Miguel Sanjuan, SALOMAR, May 12, 2011. Sanjuan is a retired military officer who is developing an initiative to support 500 to 1,000 families in Putumayo. He participated in the Vitafoods trade fair with the support of the Osec/ Swiss Import Promotion Programme (an UNCTAD BioTrade partner that provides assistance for SMEs to access European and Swiss markets).

value addition to native fruits as natural ingredients. The enterprise is working in line with BioTrade principles and criteria.[17]

Mukatri is located in the city of Florencia in the department of Caquetá and processes arazá, cocona, and copoazú. Florencia has a high number of displaced persons, and nearly every family there has lost someone to violence. With the expansion of aerial spraying for coca in the area in the mid-2000s, communities in Caquetá have become increasingly isolated (Médecins Sans Frontières n.d.). The spraying and resulting security complications caused development agencies to cease operations in the department. In addition, aggressive activities by the FARC against multinational companies have reduced the presence and support of the private sector in the area (Stubbert 2007). These effects have threatened the livelihoods of poor farmers and have increased the need for business development support such as that promoted by Colombia's Sustainable BioTrade Programme.

Mukatri's product range includes cookies, sweets, and jams; spicy, sweet, and sour sauces; and pulps derived from arazá, cocona, and copoazú. Its unique and differentiated products are certified organic by Biotropico and sold in local and national markets.[18] To ensure sustainability, Mukatri has established a close partnership with its suppliers, which are grouped under the producer consortium Association of Organic Fruit Growers of Caqueta (Asociación de Fruticultores Orgánicos del Caquetá, also known as Ucayali). Mukatri supported the creation of the association and purchases Ucayali's entire yield at a higher-than-market price; with the support of Masawai, an agro-ecological engineering company, Mukatri also provides technical assistance to enhance the quality and productivity of yields.

Three committees have been established to oversee Ucayali's activities and guarantee that they are pursued correctly and transparently. To be a member of Ucayali, producers need to own their own land, they must have been traditionally working with the requested Amazonian fruits for cash income, and the business activity must not pose a threat to their food security. Hence, the system does not encourage the planting of new kinds of crops, but rather the processing of what exists and was previously being wasted. There is only a 5 percent turnover of Ucayali members annually.

Mukatri has established strategic downstream alliances with distributors in order to access national supermarket chains such as Carrefour and EXITO in Bogotá, Medellín, Pereira, and Cali. At the local market, Mukatri has two points of sale, and its products are available in local supermarkets, hotels, restaurants, and transportation hubs (air and terrestrial). Linking producers in the region to larger national and multinational companies is especially important because the

[17] Many details in this case study come from personal communication with Gloria Elsy, Mukatri, on February 4, 2011.

[18] Biotropico—an independent certification body in Colombia—certifies organic produce and livestock, and ensures program compliance by Colombian farmers.

area has been increasingly avoided by the private sector, and the lack of investment has been detrimental to overall business development.

With Mukatri supporting livelihoods in Caquetá, the people involved with the associated value chains are better able to avoid the local conflict dynamics among the FARC, paramilitaries, and government forces. The company does not operate specifically to benefit victims of the conflict, but it does engage vulnerable populations, such as female-headed households, and provides jobs to the unemployed (Mukatri 2009).

The relationship between Mukatri and the producer association, Ucayali, has enhanced trust among participants because the producers are receiving a fair price for their products, as well as nonmonetary benefits (such as capacity building and strengthening of the Ucayali's social structure). It allows the sixty-two local families that are part of Ucayali to earn a stable income while increasing the quality of their products. According to the BioTrade Impact Assessment System, the additional monthly income generated by Ucayali members is approximately US$400 per month, for both male and female producers (UNCTAD 2011).

Mukatri is one example of a business initiative that is working according to BioTrade principles and criteria, and with combined support from a number of organizations, it is becoming a model for the region. The company has fostered an entrepreneurial culture in Caquetá, not only by motivating the creation of complementary businesses but also by serving as a model that can be replicated. For example, Mukatri has created employment opportunities through its store in Florencia, a tourist shop that is becoming a sales point for local products—mainly handicrafts produced by female employees and entrepreneurs. Seven local business initiatives (four in coffee and three in handicrafts) have been launched following Mukatri's model.

Mukatri's business in Caquetá has continued in spite of the worsening security situation there. For example, in December 2009, the governor of Caquetá was kidnapped and murdered by the FARC.

Pradera Verde E.U.

Pradera Verde E.U. is located in the Sibundoy Valley in Putumayo.[19] For over fifteen years, it has been processing Amazonian fruits, particularly papayuela. The company was legally established in 2005, and its products include sweets made from papayuela and sixteen natural flavors of cookies. Papayuela is harvested every fifteen days year-round and is also traditionally used by the local population. Pradera Verde E.U. only uses fruit that would otherwise be wasted.

---

19 Many details in this case study come from personal communication with Pradera Verde E.U. leaders Dario Marín Chavarraiga, director of national sales, on May 23, 2011, and Juan Manuel Marin O. on June 1, 2011, and from the 2011 Pradera Verde E.U. company factsheet, other company documents, and a company video. To view the video, see www.youtube.com/watch?v=l3jddjMpimg.

Therefore, it does not threaten food security, and it promotes the conservation of ecosystems by encouraging farmers to earn income by harvesting fruit that is part of the existing ecosystem rather than by converting forests to other uses.

Currently, 200 families benefit from this initiative as a legal economic activity that represents approximately 20 percent of their family income. Additionally, Pradera Verde E.U. strengthens its producers' capacity in harvesting and post-harvest practices. The long-lasting relationship among all of the participants has fostered trust and collaboration.

Because of the quality of its products—the company has high food-safety standards, and its products contain no preservatives or chemicals—Pradera Verde E.U. has been able to position its products throughout the main supermarket chains in Colombia, in addition to selling them locally.

Pradera Verde E.U. has become a model for business initiatives in the area, motivating entrepreneurship among community members who have replicated the model with business ventures related to aquaculture, dairy production, and fruit processing. The papayuela sweet has become an iconic product from the area, and its success demonstrates that legal activities can be financially viable if producers persevere, maintain transparency, and build good relationships with suppliers and clients. The company has been supported in the development and cofunding of its business plan and in trade fair participation at national and international levels. This has been done with the support of CORPOAMAZONIA within the activities developed under the Colombian Sustainable BioTrade Programme.

The Sibundoy Valley is near the city of Pasto and is well connected to various areas of the country; this proximity and connection facilitates the commercialization and distribution of the final products. Due to its favorable microclimate, the Sibundoy Valley is also an attractive region for agriculturalists from other regions, although it has been used by the AUC paramilitaries and FARC guerrillas for troop movements (Colectivo de Abogados "José Alvear Restrepo" 2005). The close association between narcotraffickers and guerrillas represents a formidable security threat to the Putumayo region and to its young people, who are the most susceptible to recruitment into armed groups. Initiatives such as Pradera Verde E.U. that motivate entrepreneurship and build the capacity of young people are therefore especially needed in this area.

Despite attempts by guerrilla groups to establish a presence in the Sibundoy Valley, efforts by the local population and investment in legal agricultural enterprises have enabled the area to avoid falling under guerrilla control. Violence has still affected these communities adversely, however; the guerrilla groups have assassinated eleven of the most prominent businesspeople in the valley.

LESSONS LEARNED

People in conflict-affected areas need to be involved in income-generating activities so they will be less vulnerable to recruitment into armed groups. This is especially true of youth. Supporting the creation of economically feasible initiatives is essential but also challenging, especially where production and logistics costs are high because of remote locations and limited access to basic infrastructure and services. Such efforts require substantial engagement by public, private, and academic sectors to be effective, particularly where value addition at the local level is needed to guarantee a higher return. Table 1 summarizes the goals, synergies, challenges, and opportunities related to integrating BioTrade projects into post-conflict peacebuilding.

Table 1. Goals, synergies, challenges, and opportunities for integrating BioTrade into peacebuilding

Issue	*BioTrade*	*Post-conflict peacebuilding*
Goals and objectives related to natural resources	• Supports the conservation and sustainable use of biodiversity through trade. • Through its principles and criteria, assesses its own work and that of its beneficiaries toward sustainable development in relation to economic, social, and environmental sustainability. • Engages government representatives, producers, nongovernmental organizations, academia, traders, and others under the common objective of promoting local development by generating initiatives that are socially, economically, and environmentally feasible for excombatants and participating communities.	• Establishes sustainable reintegration options for excombatants, internally displaced persons, and conflict-affected community members. • Recognizes that when conflicts are fueled by disputes over natural resources, relapse into conflict within five years more likely. • Usually is sited in rural areas and is agriculturally based. • Addresses the role of natural resources in supporting livelihoods.
Synergies	• Provide alternative legal livelihoods in areas that are rich in biodiversity and that are affected by conflict dynamics.	
Common challenges	• Must utilize conflict-sensitive approaches that address the specific needs of each group. • Are practiced in conflict areas that often lack infrastructure, are remote, and have limited cooperation among public and private entities; producers tend to be isolated from commercial channels, governance is usually limited, and institutions may be weak. • Have beneficiaries who tend to have high expectations.	
Common opportunities	• Can sustainably generate and commercialize products for niche markets in which price levels reflect the value consumers place on the product or service's special characteristics. • Can provide sustainable livelihood options that support biodiversity conservation and sustainable use. • Promote specialized value chains that have cultural significance and market advantages. • Integrate natural resource management into recovery and reintegration.	

Synergies

The case studies above show that Biotrade, as part of larger initiatives, can contribute to recovery and economic development in conflict-affected areas by increasing the development of products that represent an alternative to illicit crops, by promoting sustainable natural resource management, by supporting the fulfillment of market requirements, by building capacity to create more successful and more competitive products, and by providing opportunities for stronger social cohesion and collaboration.

Opportunities to develop products that represent an alternative to illicit crops play an important role in reducing the vulnerability of farmers and communities to violence associated with narcotrafficking. Such enterprises do not guarantee that farmers will not be pressured to convert land to coca or that they will be able to completely avoid demands by armed groups for involvement and payments, or "taxes." But such opportunities may ensure that the livelihoods that farmers do pursue are more developed, supported, sustainable, and better able to be linked to buyers and markets than they would otherwise be. The products developed through BioTrade are based on local species that are traditionally found in family gardens but not entirely used due to their excess supply; they do not require the introduction of new species or practices that might alter the ecosystem and the current traditions.

In spite of security concerns, sustainable environmental management creates development opportunities in sensitive areas of developing countries. Consumers' consciousness about the environment is growing, as are corporate social and environmental responsibility initiatives. This increases demand for BioTrade products. The origin of such products in conflict-affected areas that are rich in biodiversity and where former combatants are being reintegrated into society can generate an interesting story that motivates consumers who are concerned about environmental and social well-being and about supporting victims of armed conflicts.

Linkages to markets are essential to ensure the feasibility of business initiatives and the generation of social and economic benefits. By helping SMEs and community-based organizations to fulfill specific market requirements, BioTrade programs improve the capacity of the individuals and communities involved in the business to take the necessary steps for the enterprise to achieve viability, to become more competitive, and to generate monetary and nonmonetary benefits for local participants.

The value chain methodology contributes to cohesion and collaboration among participants in conflict-affected areas because it allows for identification of, and agreement on, the needs, concerns, strengths, roles, and responsibilities of all participants in relation to market requirements and demand. It also fosters engagement in activities that enable all interested parties to be involved and informed; this makes dialogue and consensus a possibility. Interested parties normally include government bodies, academia, producers and producer associations, participating communities and their productive initiatives, other SMEs and business associations, NGOs, intergovernmental organizations, and donors.

Although BioTrade value chains will represent only one element of a recovery strategy, including them as part of recovery and reintegration initiatives in post-conflict situations can have many benefits, including an increase in environmentally sustainable development options, support for the growth of local private sectors, and a strategy for local employment.

Challenges

Implementers of BioTrade value chain projects in conflict-affected areas face challenges similar to those faced by their counterparts in areas that are free of armed conflict, such as limited managerial, productive, and processing capacities; disorganization of value chains; limited product competitiveness; lack of access to financial resources and markets; and insufficient policy frameworks.

The main differences for BioTrade projects implemented in conflict-affected areas are the time frame required for implementation, the need for psychological support and conflict sensitivity, the need for collaboration between peacebuilding and BioTrade stakeholders, and the need to minimize the risks associated with stigmatization of business initiatives from conflict-affected areas.

In addition, BioTrade programs can be thwarted by the paternalism that is common in many post-conflict and development situations—where communities and organizations often receive nonreimbursable support for their activities and can become dependent on outside resources. A clear set of rules and responsibilities is therefore essential, and BioTrade activities should be based on a thorough analysis of the existing power relationships and the implications of past conflict. A failure to address these issues can trigger a renewal of conflict, which would negatively affect the development of an enabling environment for business and entrepreneurship.

Post-conflict recovery programs often face the challenge of providing employment and reintegration opportunities to large numbers of people. The BioTrade Initiative and its programs are specifically designed to support community-level engagement in areas of high biodiversity with the development of products for which there is an established market demand. The initiative will always be only one part of a larger recovery program that may engage in value chain development for nonbiodiversity products in additional areas. Once a BioTrade program is established and has a national or local platform and a template for project implementation, it can be scaled up as needed throughout a particular country or region. Regardless of its place in a larger recovery strategy, BioTrade can raise awareness regarding sustainability and conservation among producers, processors, and consumers along a particular value chain, which is essential for long-term sustainable development.

Longer-term support is needed to develop value chains in conflict-sensitive areas than elsewhere because trust, commitment, institutional structures, and skills in management, production, and marketing usually need to be further developed. Support should continue for at least five years and must involve an integral capacity-building program that addresses issues such as management, accounting, production, processing, and commercialization, through both education in business theory and practical training.[20] Additionally, the development of BioTrade companies should be accomplished gradually, as practitioners aim for efficient harmonization between the size of the company and the salaries of managers and employees, and as practitioners consolidate current activities before starting commercialization on a larger scale—from local to national to international.

When designing and implementing development initiatives in conflict-sensitive areas, it is important to integrate vulnerable groups into local businesses and communities, and to expand their employment opportunities. This approach closely aligns with the community-based reintegration approach outlined in the United Nations Integrated Disarmament, Demobilization and Reintegration Standards (UNDDR 2006); it supports the reintegration of excombatants and members of armed groups through community-wide support initiatives that encourage their integration and that address the needs of vulnerable youth and conflict-affected populations collectively. Failure to take a community-based approach in the past has resulted in tensions between the target and nontarget groups of a community or area. Support must also build upon existing capacity within the community by addressing the needs of ongoing business initiatives that are important sites of employment creation and replication.

Opportunities

The BioTrade Initiative program in Colombia and its partners have strengthened post-conflict peacebuilding by providing legal economic alternatives for rural conflict-affected populations that discourage the destruction of natural ecosystems and encourage the sustainable use of biodiversity, while promoting the generation of benefits through each stage of the value chain. The value chain approach provides an opportunity for rural populations to link to markets and to rely on biodiversity-derived products, and it provides an alternative to low-skilled and poorly paid wage labor. By engaging with and supporting the value chains, civil society and local, regional, and national governments have contributed to these positive impacts.

BioTrade provides key economic opportunities for post-conflict regions with high biodiversity. The future of development for such regions will depend highly on each region's ability to effectively and efficiently manage its natural resources and on the ability of SMEs to develop value addition, to access markets, and to equitably distribute the benefits generated. The BioTrade Initiative is a concrete

[20] Dario Marín Chavarraiga, personal communication, May 23, 2011.

approach that helps both the public and the private sector to support these goals. The monetary and nonmonetary gains accrue not only to direct suppliers, but to local communities and to national development through an increase in the number of legal businesses and the creation of incentives for complementary economic activities overall.

RECOMMENDATIONS

The lessons learned from this analysis of BioTrade projects yield several recommendations for the development of BioTrade in post-conflict situations.

First, the selection and support of BioTrade value chains in conflict-affected areas must be market driven and in line with traditional practices and culture in order to guarantee that the products can be sold in the target market. Furthermore, direct financial support in the form of both reimbursable and nonreimbursable funding, including rotation funds, should be considered. Contributors should require in-kind or in-cash engagement from the recipients and should promote the professional and personal development of local participants. Beneficiary organizations must have a solid track record and experience working in the area and with local people. When funding is provided, close monitoring is essential, with concrete indicators and checkpoints that are verified by primary and secondary information sources.

In BioTrade programs that provide capacity building and technical assistance for management, processing, and commercialization in conflict and post-conflict areas should meet several criteria. The participants should understand the potential gains of the initiative as well as the scope of their commitment. They must be committed to the product, to the sustainable use of natural resources, and to participation in trainings, meetings, and decision-making processes. Furthermore, they must understand the importance of fulfilling a commercial partnership and the fact that noncooperation can have negative consequences for the overall sustainability of the initiative and for their own participation in it. For example, if the volume, quality, and delivery-time expectations for a project are not met, the initiative can lose its buyers, be unable to buy necessary raw materials from its producers, and even fail.

Activities should seek to engage excombatants and associated groups in order to demonstrate economic alternatives that can help them maintain their separation from armed groups and allow them to connect with peer groups within their community. In so doing, the program can create an opportunity for demobilized excombatants to be reintegrated into the community and to resume civilian life. At the same time, livelihoods assistance should always be complemented by psychosocial support for participants who have been affected by the conflict and who need help to socially reintegrate into society.

Value chain activities need to be mainstreamed into local and national strategies, contributing to an enabling environment that enhances the development of viable legal local business ventures. Such mainstreaming can contribute to the mobilization of additional support related to technical assistance, applied research, and financial resources. BioTrade projects must be flexible and innovative, and they need to market high-quality and value-added products that are environmentally and socially friendly and that are differentiated from other products, so consumers will value and pay for them.

Finally, the conservation and sustainable use of biodiversity as an element of peacebuilding requires that all participants in the value chain share in its benefits fairly. This not only allows all participants to experience the advantages of being involved in the chain, it also generates trust and transparency among participants.

Practitioners working in post-conflict recovery programs can learn from the experiences of BioTrade in Colombia how to more effectively integrate BioTrade practices into their programs. When they employ BioTrade practices, they can create economic development and employment opportunities that promote sustainable management of natural resources and biodiversity. Such practices are essential for building the foundations for sustainable development as well as for enhancing the private sector and improving market opportunities.

BioTrade should be implemented as part of wider recovery initiatives because it alone cannot provide the volume of employment opportunities typically needed in a post-conflict situation. However, it is an innovative approach that provides ample entry points and demonstrates conflict-sensitivity and inclusiveness through the value chain approach. As an economic recovery option, BioTrade can be especially positive for areas of high biodiversity that require the development of environmentally and socially sensitive business opportunities in order to protect resources for future generations.

REFERENCES

ABColombia. 2010. *Caught in the crossfire: Colombia's indigenous peoples*. London.

Arcos Dorado, A. L., P. A. Lozada Perdomo, D. Mejía González, and J. A. Gómez Díaz. 2009. Análisis de las iniciativas empresariales de biocomercio en el sur de la Amazonía colombiana. Bogotá, Colombia: Alexander von Humboldt Institute for Research on Biological Resources, Corporation for the Sustainable Development of the Southern Amazon, Corporation of Planning and Agricultural Technology Transfer, and University of the Amazon. www.biocomerciosostenible.com/Documentos/BiocomercioEmpresasAmazonas.pdf.

Bishop, J., ed. 2012. *The economics of ecosystems and biodiversity (TEEB) in business and enterprise*. London and New York: Earthscan.

Bolivar, E. E., G. Verschoor, R. Muradian, and G. Ochoa. 2008. *From the Amazon to the supermarket: Innovation and the integration of small-scale Amazonian chilli pepper producers in green markets*. London: International Institute for Environment and Development. http://pubs.iied.org/G03245.html.

Bruch, C., D. Jensen, M. Nakayama, and J. Unruh. 2015. *Post-conflict peacebuilding and natural resources: The promise and the peril*. New York: Cambridge University Press.

CIDDR (International Disarmament, Demobilization and Reintegration Congress). 2009. The Cartagena contribution to disarmament, demobilization, and reintegration. Cartagena, Colombia.

Colectivo de Abogados "José Alvear Restrepo." 2005. Plan Colombia's first two years: An evaluation of human rights in Putumayo, April 2003. June 15. www.colectivodeabogados.org/Reporte-al-Congreso-sobre-Putumayo.

Dube, O., and J. F. Vargas. 2006. *Resource curse in reverse: The coffee crisis and armed conflict in Colombia*. Document No. CEDE 2006-46. Bogotá, Colombia: University of the Andes, Center of Economic Development Studies.

Elhawary, S. 2008. Violent paths to peace?: Rethinking the conflict-development nexus in Colombia. *Colombia Internacional* 67:84–100. http://colombiainternacional.uniandes.edu.co/view.php/308/index.php?id=308.

Gómez, J. A., and C. Ortega. 2007. Biocomercio sostenible: Biodiversidad y desarrollo. Bogotá, Colombia: Alexander von Humboldt Institute for Research on Biological Resources.

Hammen, M. C. 2003. *The indigenous* resguardos *of Colombia: Their contribution to conservation and sustainable forest use*. Gland, Switzerland: International Union for Conservation of Nature.

Hanson, T., T. M. Brooks, G. A. B. da Fonseca, M. Hoffman, J. F. Lamoreux, G. Machlis, C. G. Mittermeier, R. A. Mittermeier, and J. D. Pilgrim. 2009. Warfare in biodiversity hotspots. *Conservation Biology* 23 (3): 578–587.

Hungerford, E. 2010. Sniffing the rainforest. *Diplomat*, March. www.diplomatmagazine.com/issues/2010/march/256-sniffing-the-rainforest-v15-256.html.

Lozada, P., and J. A. Gómez. 2005. Análisis del desarrollo empresarial de 100 iniciativas de biocomercio sostenible en Colombia. Bogotá, Colombia: Alexander von Humboldt Institute for Research on Biological Resources.

Macrae, J. 1999. Aiding peace . . . and war: UNHCR, returnee reintegration and the relief-development debate. UNHCR Working Papers No. 14. Geneva: United Nations High Commisioner for Refugees.

Médecins Sans Frontières. n.d. Caquetá: The enormous difficulties of reaching victims of the conflict. Toronto, Canada. www.msf.ca/focus-countries/colombia/colombia-caqueta.

MEHTD (Ministry of Environment, Housing and Territorial Development, Republic of Colombia). 2009. Report from the Seminario Nacional de Biocomercio Sostenible. Bogotá, Colombia, August 14.

Mittermeier, R. A., N. Myers, and C. G. Mittermeier. 2000. *Hotspots: Earth's biologically richest and most endangered terrestrial ecoregions*. Arlington, VA: Conservation International.

Moloney, A. 2006. Colombia faces worsening internally displaced persons crisis. Fellowship of Reconciliation Colombia Program, November 2. www.forcolombia.org/node/60.

Mukatri. 2009. Plan de negocios: Mukatri de la Amazonia—Fortalecimiento de la planta transformadora de frutales amazónicos. Amsterdam, Netherlands: Business in Development Network.

Pardo Fajardo, M. P., A. M. Hernández, and A. Ramos. 2000. Algunas consideraciones sobre la experiencia de Colombia en materia de protección de los conocimiento tradicionales, acceso y distribución de beneficios y derechos de propiedad intelectual. Paper presented during United Nations Conference on Trade and Development "Expert Meeting on Systems and National Experiences for Protecting Traditional Knowledge, Innovations and Practices," Geneva, Switzerland, October 30–November 1. www.biotrade.org/

ResourcesPublications/Proteccion%20de%20los%20CT%20ADB%20y%20DPI%20-%20experiencia%20de%20Colombia.pdf.

Pettersson, B. 2000. Arable land and internal displacement in Colombia. *Forced Migration Review* 7 (April): 40.

Ramirez, M. C. 2003. The Cocalero social movement of the Amazon region of Colombia. *ReVista: Harvard Review of Latin America*, Spring. www.drclas.harvard.edu/publications/revistaonline/spring-2003/cocalero-social-movement-amazon-region-colombia.

Regional Competitiveness Commission. 2008. Plan Regional de Competitividad: Caquetá Visión 2032. Bogotá, Colombia. www.comisionesregionales.gov.co/descargar.php?id=61312.

Rouvinski, V., and J. Vasquez Sanchez. 2005. The new poor of contemporary Colombia: Armed conflict and impoverishment of internally displaced persons. *Journal of International Development and Cooperation* 11 (1): 69–84.

Stubbert, C. 2007. Left behind in Caquetá. Plan Colombia and Beyond. January 23. www.cipcol.org/?p=333.

UCDP (Uppsala Conflict Data Program). n.d. UCDP database. www.ucdp.uu.se/gpdatabase/search.php.

UNCTAD (United Nations Conference on Trade and Development). 2007. UNCTAD BioTrade Initiative: BioTrade principles and criteria. New York. www.unctad.org/en/docs/ditcted20074_en.pdf.

———. 2009. Guidelines for a methodology to support value chains for BioTrade products: From the selection of products to the development of sector strategies. UNCTAD/DITC/BCC/2008/1. New York: United Nations. www.biotrade.org/ResourcesPublications/unctad_ditc_bcc_2008_1_Eng.pdf.

———. 2011. Developing the baseline of the BioTrade Impact Assessment System in Colombia. Geneva, Switzerland.

UNDDR (United Nations Disarmament, Demobilization and Reintegration Resource Centre). 2006. *Integrated disarmament, demobilization and reintegration standards.* http://pksoi.army.mil/doctrine_concepts/documents/UN%20Guidelines/IDDRS.pdf.

UNDP (United Nations Development Programme), World Bank, and UNDG (United Nations Development Group). 2004. *Practical guide to multilateral needs assessments in post-conflict situations.* New York and Geneva.

UNEP (United Nations Environment Programme). 2009. *From conflict to peacebuilding: The role of natural resources and the environment.* Nairobi, Kenya. http://postconflict.unep.ch/publications/pcdmb_policy_01.pdf.

———. 2011. Towards a green economy: Pathways to sustainable development and poverty eradication. Nairobi, Kenya.

USAID (United States Agency for International Development). 2008. *Conflict-sensitive approaches to value chain development.* Micro Report No. 101. Washington, D.C.

PART 3

The institutional and policy context

Introduction

In the immediate aftermath of conflict, governance institutions that were affected by conflict are rebuilt, and new institutions are established to oversee recovery and develop policy frameworks that can help prevent a relapse to violence. Often, new or rehabilitated governance institutions must address the roots of conflict, including disputes over access to and use of natural resources. Because decisions regarding natural resource management affect livelihoods and economic opportunities for conflict-affected communities, such decisions are central to recovery and the achievement of lasting peace. Thus, policies developed in the post-conflict period must establish an effective framework for resource management and address existing disputes over natural resources, while helping to ensure equitable rights of access to and use of such resources.

The immediate aftermath of conflict provides a crucial opportunity to reform the laws and institutions governing natural resources. The five chapters in part 3 demonstrate how the development and reform of institutions and policies governing natural resources can promote rural livelihoods and strengthen local economies; they also demonstrate the ways in which ineffective institutions and policies can undermine stability, perpetuate unsustainable exploitation of natural resources, and, in some circumstances, contribute to future conflict.

In the immediate post-conflict period, policies that promote sustainable resource management—particularly when those policies are influenced by an occupying force—are often viewed as incompatible with the need to rebuild economic capacity and livelihoods. In "Fisheries Policies and the Problem of Instituting Sustainable Management: The Case of Occupied Japan," Harry N. Scheiber and Benjamin Jones examine programs implemented after World War II that were designed to reestablish Japan's commercial fishing sector.

The Allies believed that strengthening the fisheries sector would provide jobs, generate income, and ensure food security for conflicted-affected populations, but efforts to reform the relevant institutions and policies (in particular, to make the fisheries sector more sustainable) proved difficult to implement in the face of strong production pressure. The chapter highlights the critical importance of integrating sustainable resource management into the policies and institutions governing livelihood-related natural resources. Indeed, sustainable management must be identified and promoted as a policy norm during the initial stages of institutional redevelopment. The failure of the Japanese government and occupying forces to do so in post-war Japan substantially undermined new policies designed to achieve sustainability within the commercial fishing industry.

More recent conflicts, including those in Iraq and Afghanistan, also illustrate the difficulty of rebuilding institutions and policy frameworks in the aftermath of violent conflict—as well as the importance of incorporating sustainable resource management into the redevelopment framework during the initial peacebuilding phase. In "Developing Capacity for Natural Resource Management in Afghanistan: Process, Challenges, and Lessons Learned by UNEP," Belinda Bowling and Asif Zaidi review initiatives implemented in Afghanistan to strengthen environmental governance, which had been devastated by decades of violent conflict. In 2003, following the initial entry of the North Atlantic Treaty Organization and allied forces into Afghanistan, the newly formed Afghan government requested the assistance of the United Nations Environment Programme (UNEP) to reform natural resource policies and practices. Using its *Natural Resources for Peacebuilding and Statebuilding: A Toolkit for Analysis and Programming*, UNEP encouraged a community-based approach to natural resource management and assisted Afghan officials in adopting strategies to resolve disputes over natural resource access. Bowling and Zaidi emphasize that to guarantee the effective implementation of such an environmental framework, environmental policies must be robustly enforced, and overlapping institutional mandates must be clarified.

In their efforts to build and reform institutions and policies governing natural resources, peacebuilding actors must consider approaches that strengthen community resilience to future environmental and social stresses. In "Building Resilience in Rural Livelihood Systems as an Investment in Conflict Prevention," Blake D. Ratner explains how initiatives designed to restore the capacity of resource production systems can be integrated into post-conflict recovery plans, as a means of preventing conflict recurrence. Using Cambodia as an example, Ratner demonstrates the importance of capacity building and effective natural resource management in supporting rural livelihoods and bolstering local economies. To assess the success of recovery programs in post-conflict situations, the author proposes evaluating the extent to which programs address rights of access to natural resources, access to decision-making institutions, and the capacity of governing systems to ensure fair results in the resolution of disputes.

In post-conflict situations where local populations rely heavily on natural resources to provide both basic necessities and livelihood opportunities, recovery programs that rebuild and strengthen local resource management systems can provide entry points for conflict resolution and peacebuilding on a much larger scale. In Mindanao, Philippines, a significant portion of the population relies on agriculture and fisheries for livelihoods and food security; as a result, conflicts on the island have generally revolved around access to land and its accompanying resources.

In "Improving Natural Resource Governance and Building Peace and Stability in Mindanao, Philippines," Cynthia Brady, Oliver Agoncillo, Maria Zita Butardo-Toribio, Buenaventura Dolom, and Casimiro V. Olvida analyze post-conflict efforts to strengthen resource management institutions and policies in Mindanao, following the 1996 peace accord. To promote peacebuilding, the U.S. Agency for International Development (USAID) and its partners have assisted conflict-affected communities to build institutional capacity and improve natural resource management. The authors underscore the benefits of linking environmental governance objectives with broader peacebuilding goals, and identify lessons that may inform the development and implementation of integrated recovery plans in other post-conflict situations. These include bringing peace advocates and excombatants into the resource management process and integrating peacebuilding and conflict-mitigation indicators into resource management frameworks.

In the absence of effective institutions and policies to manage natural resources, products derived from natural resources can be used to finance ongoing conflict. In Somalia, long periods of violent conflict have disrupted traditional livelihood systems and diminished economic opportunities. As a result, even those who are not actively engaged as armed combatants may derive their livelihoods from the conflict economy—and may therefore have a vested interest in propagating the conflict. In "Commerce in the Chaos: Bananas, Charcoal, Fisheries, and Conflict in Somalia," Christian Webersik and Alec Crawford explore how livelihood resources in Somalia—in particular, banana cultivation, charcoal production, and the fishing industry—have supported the country's conflict economy and provided an important source of funding for continuing conflict. At the same time, the authors suggest that the sustainable production and use of these natural resources offers a potential source of nonconflict income, as well as a valuable asset for funding post-conflict recovery. To prevent natural resources from becoming a means of financing conflict, the authors argue that the international community should adopt trade policies that increase transparency in the trade of conflict resources. Most important, peacebuilding should emphasize the creation of alternative livelihood opportunities.

Taken together, the chapters in part 3 examine effective strategies for encouraging economic growth and livelihood creation through institution building, capacity building, and policy development. Transitioning away from a conflict economy often requires considerable policy reform and broad institutional change; it is thus essential to incorporate sustainable natural resource management policies and regulatory authority into broader governance structures. The failure to articulate sustainable approaches and policies during initial recovery may reduce the effectiveness of reform measures to come.

Fisheries policies and the problem of instituting sustainable management: The case of occupied Japan

Harry N. Scheiber and Benjamin Jones

In the aftermath of World War II in the Pacific, a key immediate objective for the Allied occupation of Japan, operating in effect under orders from the U.S. government, was to reconstruct Japan's commercial fisheries. This policy, designed to provide for domestic food supplies during a food crisis at the war's end, comprised an urgent response to a pressing emergency. But beginning only a year after the end of hostilities in 1945, the policy would be significantly broadened to include, by 1949, a comprehensive reform of ownership structure in the coastal fisheries sector. And throughout the occupation, which ended in 1952, the Allied command's cadre of natural resource experts also promoted a vital long-term objective: to promote and (as they naively hoped) to ensure, for future years, marine fisheries sustainability and conservation through a comprehensive reform of Japan's fisheries management policies regarding both coastal and distant-water (high seas) fishing enterprises.

This chapter examines the post-conflict period in Japan following World War II. The first section provides an overview of the occupation command's objectives and associated sustainability goals with respect to Japan's fisheries. The chapter continues by looking back to the Japanese economy preceding the war, including Japan's dependence on fisheries and the maritime lifestyle as an essential component of Japanese culture and economy, and the devastation suffered by the fishing industry during wartime. The third section analyzes the

---

Harry N. Scheiber is the Riesenfeld Chair Professor of Law and History, emeritus, at the School of Law, University of California, Berkeley (UC Berkeley). He is director of the Law of the Sea Institute and is past director of the Sho Sato Program in Japanese and US Law, both in the School of Law, UC Berkeley. Benjamin Jones is an associate in the Global Disputes practice of Jones Day, and is the executive editor of the *World Arbitration and Mediation Review*. This chapter is based heavily upon the archival and other primary sources forming the basis for analysis in Harry N. Scheiber, *Inter-Allied Conflicts and Ocean Law, 1945–53: The Occupation Command's Revival of Japanese Whaling and Marine Fisheries* (Taipei, Taiwan: Institute of European and American Studies, Academia Sinica, 2001).

development and evolution of policies governing fisheries and whaling after the war, and the section following analyzes factors that influenced the direction of these policies and institutional developments. The next two sections of the chapter offer a discussion of the lessons learned from the redevelopment of Japan and the Pacific region during the post-conflict and long-term recovery period, and what can be done differently in future post-conflict situations to promote more sustainable resource-based policy development. The final section of the chapter considers the unintended consequences of the occupation-era fisheries policies and a comparative perspective of the conduct of other states during this period.

SUSTAINABILITY GOALS IN POST-WORLD WAR II JAPAN

The occupation command's objectives with regard to fisheries were pursued within the context of the larger U.S.-led policies for the occupation. One goal was a program to restructure and, later, to rapidly rebuild the Japanese economy—an objective that gained new urgency with the outbreak of the Korean War. Second was a set of efforts to promote the reintegration of Japan into the community of nations, including its participation in the post-war development of multilateral institutions for economic, financial, and resource management coordination.

The occupation initially was intended to be guided on basic policy by the Far Eastern Commission, consisting of representatives of fourteen Allied nations and meeting in Washington, D.C. It was largely ineffective except as a debating forum, however, as the U.S. government and General Douglas MacArthur as Supreme Commander for Allied Powers (SCAP) essentially controlled policies and their implementation. MacArthur blatantly ignored a small body called the Allied Council, which met regularly in Tokyo, essentially rendering it a nullity. The entire bureaucracy of civilian experts and military officers charged with running programs to guide and implement economic reconstruction and social reforms came under the control of MacArthur and the U.S. government. The occupation authority's policies to revive Japan's fisheries—that is, not only policies for rebuilding the coastal and distant-water commercial fisheries but also later programs that were expanded to reintroduce Japan's whaling fleets into the western Pacific and Antarctic regions—achieved full success within four years, at least as measured by the volume of the catch. And there was equal success in the political realm, as the occupation under MacArthur's leadership—and in accord with U.S. foreign policy under President Harry Truman—steered Japan toward the restoration of its full sovereignty at the signing of a peace treaty in 1952.[1]

[1] The peace treaty—formally known as the San Francisco Peace Treaty—signified the end of World War II between Japan and the Allied powers. The treaty was signed by forty-eight nations on September 8, 1951, in San Francisco, California, and entered into force on April 28, 1952. For the complete text of the document, see http://treaties.un.org/doc/Publication/UNTS/Volume%20136/volume-136-I-1832-English.pdf.

The program for the reform of Japan's fisheries management policies, however, had a different outcome. Although not an entire failure, it fell seriously short of its objectives. When national sovereignty was restored in 1952, one of Japan's first diplomatic actions was to sign the International North Pacific Fisheries Convention (INPFC). The convention was a tripartite fisheries management scheme for salmon and several other stocks in the Northeast Pacific, previously exploited by Canada and the United States—an agreement by which scientific determinations of sustainable yield would be honored, with Japan consenting to abstain from fishing for specified species or stocks being fished by the other two powers and determined to be at maximum yield. The convention gave protection to the fishing interests of Canada and the United States, and to that degree it did advance significantly the application of sustainable management practices for salmon and other important fish stocks in the Northeast Pacific. Ironically, under the terms of the agreement, Japan was left free of any treaty-based legal restraints when it turned immediately to full-bore expansion of its distant-water marine fisheries enterprises in all other major ocean fisheries areas of the world. These distant-water fishing efforts thus went forward largely without self-imposed sustainability-oriented controls by Japan and entirely without multilateral regulation for protection of the natural resources that came under exploitation.

The long-term result of the occupation's restoration of Japanese industrialized whaling operations was to enable Japan to contribute to the notorious depletion and endangerment of whale stocks in Antarctic and Pacific waters. This occurred because the occupation had positioned Japan, as a member of the International Whaling Commission (IWC), not only to exert its influence against conservationist measures (as it continues to do today) but also to legitimize its professedly "scientific" whaling activities outside the quotas of the IWC. Japan's aggressive stance on whaling has not softened as decades have passed; and its "scientific" take of whales continues even now.

The implementation of sustainability goals in post-conflict Japan was in key respects unlike other post-conflict situations that are the subject of companion studies in this book. A major difference was that, although the Japanese economy had been decimated by war's end and new pressures on food supply were caused by the return of the defeated armed forces and civilians who had resettled in Japan's imperial colonies, the occupation authority did not have to deal with civil conflict, tribal claims and rivalries, or a threat posed by armed militias or their equivalent. On the contrary, the occupation authority's control of civilian life was comprehensive, strongly administered, and largely accepted by Japan's new political leadership without potentially revolutionary popular resistance. Democratic governance was introduced quickly, under the new 1946 Constitution of Japan, although the authorities did have to cope with significant instability owing to sharp ideological, class-based, and interest-group conflicts—but even these serious tensions were expressed politically and, on the whole, were well contained within the new mechanisms of the political system. Moreover, even

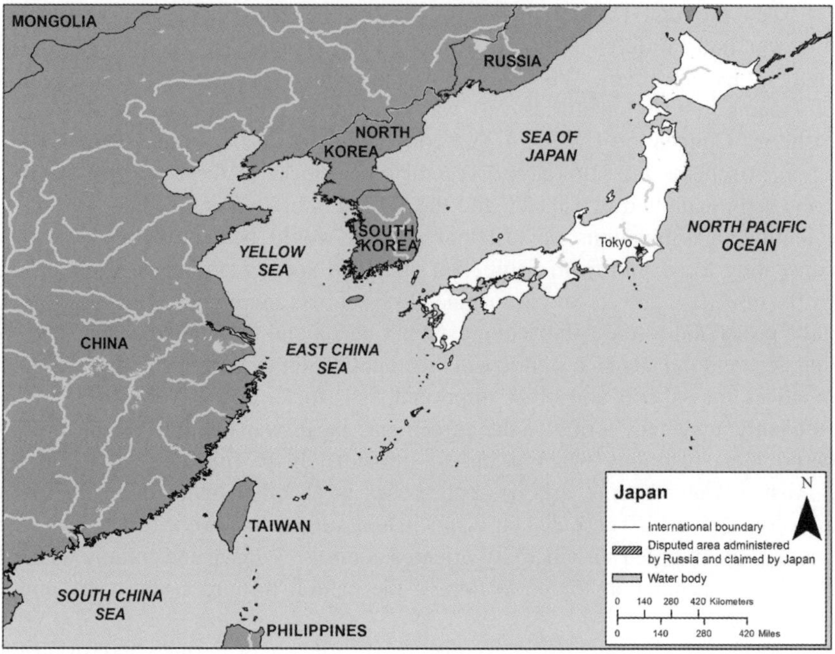

Notes: The Yellow Sea is also known as the West Sea. The Sea of Japan is known as the East Sea (in South Korea) and the East Sea of Korea (in North Korea). In the Philippines, the South China Sea is known as the West Philippine Sea.

though occupation officials steadily yielded an increasing range of authority to the elected Japanese government, MacArthur's headquarters exerted continuous influence through the technique of robust "guidance," in addition to reserving a veto power over high-level policy and the legislative processes in the Diet, Japan's bicameral legislature.

Also distinguishing Japan's situation from others where protracted internal conflict had depleted and degraded natural resources was the fact that the resources in question—the fish and whale stocks—had not been damaged by the conflict; indeed, the diversion of labor and effort to wartime military and naval activities had effectively lessened or eliminated the pressure on the fish and whale stocks. What had to be achieved, and was quickly done, was to restore the capacity to exploit these resources. Whether the exploitation would give priority to the objective of sustainability, or instead would be pursued without regard to long-term sustainability of the resource, was a matter on which the occupation authorities sought to give specific direction. Yet for a variety of reasons, not least being the rapid restoration of Japanese sovereignty over this as well as all other issues of national policy, only a fraction of the sustainability objectives that had initially appeared to constitute a feasible reform program were achieved.

IMPACT OF WORLD WAR II ON JAPAN'S FISHING INDUSTRY

In the years preceding World War II, Japan was the world's leading marine fisheries nation, accounting annually for 20 to 25 percent of the global harvest from ocean waters. The Japanese fishing industry employed more than 1.5 million workers during the 1930s, using more than 350,000 fishing vessels, and was a major source of economic activity in coastal regions. Japan maintained significant coastal fisheries, but it was also a major player in global deepwater fishing as the country's fishing fleets operated in areas that reached into Soviet offshore waters to the north, to many areas in the western Pacific, and off the coasts of Mexico and South America. The fishing fleets had also followed the Japanese military conquests in East Asia, operating intensively in Korean and Chinese coastal waters. The Japanese had been criticized in the 1930s for their aggressive overfishing tactics and disregard for systematic management for sustained yield. Japan also had won notoriety for its unrestrained Antarctic whaling methods, which flouted self-imposed limits adopted by other whaling nations, and for withdrawing in 1941 from the multilateral North Pacific Fur Sealing Convention, which had been in operation since 1911.

Wartime devastation brought low the Japanese fishing industry, with the loss of more than half of the tonnage of the country's deepwater fishing fleet. The remaining fishing vessels and equipment were left largely in poor condition. Moreover, the home population faced severe food shortages in the immediate post-conflict period, and fish was a highly important source of protein for the Japanese consumer. As Supreme Commander, MacArthur began his oversight of the occupation at a moment of extreme uncertainty. The dissolution of the wartime government and the destruction of the fishing fleets posed grave challenges for resource management in the near term. And many of the Allied powers, aggrieved as they were by Japan's aggressive fisheries policies in the pre-war period, urged SCAP to constrain Japanese access to distant waters and to impose upon the defeated power a new (conservationist) paradigm in fisheries management.

The post-conflict resource management picture was complicated, however, by the diversity of actors involved. These actors included not just MacArthur and the SCAP administration operating in Tokyo, but also policy makers in Washington and other Allied nations, as well as their counterparts in the Japanese government. Also influential were the members of the carryover Japanese bureaucracy responsible for regulating the Japanese fishing industry and other leaders within the fishing industry. These various parties approached the post-conflict occupation period with differing expectations and goals, and these goals evolved over time. Their policy differences were complicated further by disparities in power, access to organs of policy reform, and legal status of the various actors.

EVOLUTION OF POST-WAR FISHERIES AND WHALING POLICIES

There were three somewhat overlapping stages of policy with regard to fisheries resources during the occupation years from 1945 to 1952. Initially, from 1945 to 1946, priority was given to alleviating severe protein shortages by reopening coastal fisheries. Hence, SCAP placed priority on the rebuilding of the Japanese fishing fleet, allocating fuel and scarce materials to the construction of both small and large modernized fishing vessels. In 1946, MacArthur also authorized and underwrote the reintroduction of Japanese whaling in Antarctic waters, a move hotly opposed—though in vain—by the other Allied nations. From 1948 onward, moreover, SCAP justified continuing expansion of Japan's distant-water fishing operations on grounds it would enhance the country's export earnings and help relieve the burden of occupation costs for the American taxpayer.

In a second policy phase, climaxing in 1949, SCAP successfully pressed for reforms that would complement the productivity push in fisheries policy. Occupation officials sought to develop a more progressive-minded bureaucracy, including experts in scientific fisheries management, and sponsored new teaching and research facilities. Most dramatically, in 1949 the occupation pushed through a radical democratization of the coastal fishing industry, reversing the centralized system imposed by the militarist regime in the pre-war period. Further SCAP reforms sought to reduce the environmental and cross-border political costs of excessive overfishing in coastal waters by instituting a variety of limitations upon the operation of coastal fishing vessels (these restrictions did not extend, however, to high seas fishing vessels).

The third policy stage, 1950 to 1952, embraced broadening objectives with respect to fisheries activities. One policy goal was to include the fishing industry as part of a larger effort to integrate Japan into the emerging international legal framework for trade, communications, and finance. Also, Japan's fishing industry and bureaucracy were asked to adopt policies that embodied prevailing scientific practices in fisheries management, which focused at that time on the principle of maximum sustained yield.

Japan's integration into international management schemes culminated in the country's accession to the IWC in 1951 and to the terms of the INPFC of 1952—the U.S.-Canadian-Japanese agreement for the Northeast Pacific that required Japan to abstain for a number of years from any fishing in the managed sector for salmon and other specified stocks.

Restoration of the Japanese fishing industry

In the early days of the occupation, SCAP fisheries policy was driven by a need to address vulnerabilities in the Japanese food supply and the unwillingness and incapacity of Allied nations to supply Japan with adequate replacement foodstuffs. Increasing fisheries production was recognized as a vital pillar of the peacebuilding process. Hence in September 1945, MacArthur expanded the fishing zone within which Japanese vessels were authorized to operate, extending the zone out to sea in the western Pacific beyond the strict twelve-mile limitations imposed initially (see figure 1 for Japanese fishing boundaries, after World War II). This zone expansion facilitated a profitable reactivation of larger fishing vessels and created employment for thousands of experienced deepwater fishermen,

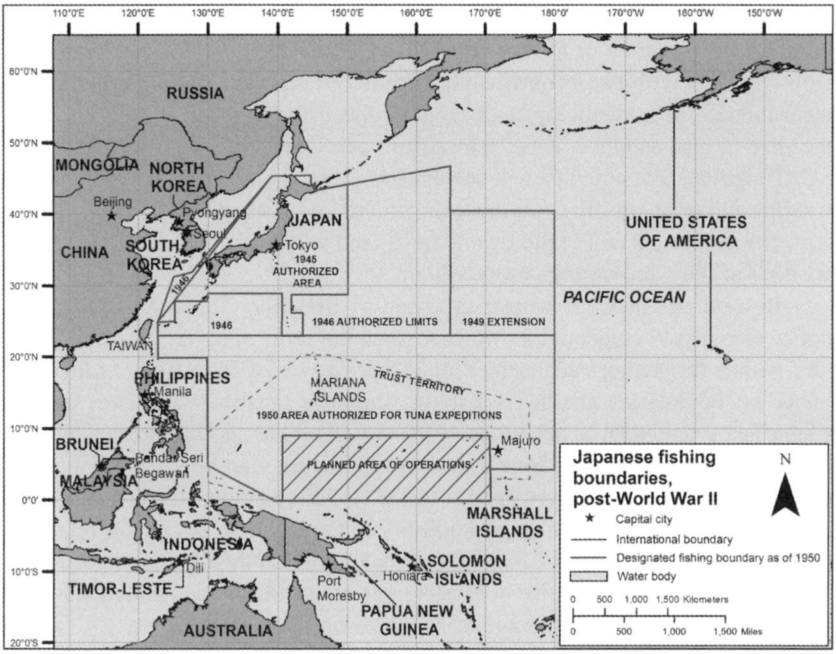

Figure 1. Japanese fishing boundaries, post–World War II

Source: Supreme Commander for Allied Powers files, U.S. National Archives.

Notes: The Trust Territory included a large expanse of territory in the western Pacific Ocean that was administered by the United States as a UN trusteeship following World War II. As the UN-appointed administrator of the area, the United States oversaw activities in the Trust Territory, and under this jurisdiction, monitored and carried out military actions within the Planned Area of Operations. The Planned Area of Operations was the area designated for planned activities of the Supreme Commander for Allied Powers—in this instance, for possible expansion of waters authorized for Japanese fishing operations. The area remained under control of the U.S. Navy, which then was forbidding any operations there by Japanese vessels. Governance of the territory was based on the Code of the Trust Territory established in 1952. Administration of the area by the United States continued until 1986. The United Nations dissolved the Trust Territory in 1990.

many of them returned war veterans. Further expansions of the fishing zone followed, and by 1949 production from the enlarged zone had reached 80 percent of the pre-war Japanese harvest.

The priority given to shipbuilding, including materials allocations by SCAP and preferential loans by the central government, impelled a rise in tonnage of Japan's fishing fleet from 46,000 in 1946 to more than 1 million by 1948. An intentional side benefit of this prioritization was that it strengthened the productive capacity of Japanese shipyards and thus enabled the rebuilding of the Japanese merchant fleet in the late 1940s. At the same time, it frustrated the ambitions of Australia and other Allied nations to have the shipyards dismantled and turned over to them as war reparations. These governments generally favored strict limits on Japanese distant-water fishing and whaling; they were concerned about uncontrolled competition from Japan in the exploitation of their offshore coastal resources as well as high seas fisheries.

General MacArthur and other SCAP officials defended the SCAP whaling program as a matter of justice as well as a key element for reconstruction. However, Allied observers on whaling expeditions reported that Japanese whalers concentrated on maximizing their yield of meat and blubber at the expense of the yield of oils, and they objected to Japan's persistent targeting of young whales. SCAP vigorously asserted its will nonetheless; when the occupation ended, Japan's whaling industry was in a strong competitive position internationally, both in terms of its vessels and skilled work force, and with respect to its assured legal position in the whaling regulatory system.

Beyond the need to withstand criticism from the Allies, SCAP fisheries policy also had to confront its own success in the form of severe resource depletion within the authorized zone. Within three years of the 1946 expansion of SCAP-set boundaries, the heavy fishing efforts by Japanese vessels in the East China Sea resulted in a drastic drop in harvests. Overexploitation of fisheries resources in the authorized zone threatened the future viability of Japan's fishing industry and amplified voices critical of SCAP policy among Japan's neighbors. In the end, SCAP compromised by imposing on the Japanese a policy of relocating fishing away from the East China Sea, where depletion threatened to throw both the fishing industry and marine ecosystem into crisis. SCAP then turned westward and southward to expand the authorized zone on the high seas.

Having achieved its objective of domestic food security, SCAP justified zone expansion as the means for Japan to generate export earnings, providing new dollar revenues for the weakened Japanese economy and in turn reducing the financial burden of the occupation for the American taxpayer. In a shift of policy, high seas tuna fisheries became one of Japan's most lucrative export industries in the later years of the occupation, responding to an extraordinary rise in demand in the American consumer market. SCAP also encouraged the opening of permanent trade offices for Japan in several American cities to expedite the exportation of Japan's fish products and, later, textiles to the United States.

While resource sustainability issues polarized the Allied nations and inflamed the passions of Japan's neighbors, the resurgent fishing industry may have played a substantial role in preventing the outbreak of internal political conflict. Rising fish harvests also counterbalanced black market price pressures on food products. In subsequent stages of SCAP fisheries policy, the production-maximizing attitudes of SCAP officials hardly diminished. Yet the pro-industry voices in SCAP would be partly counterbalanced by the commitment of natural resource experts in the occupation authority to achieve genuine reforms in Japanese fishing law and practice.

Domestic legal reform and the democratization of the coastal fishing industry

While SCAP prioritized economic recovery and support to the fishing industry in the first three years of the occupation, SCAP's civilian experts never formally abandoned the project of fisheries law reform. Indeed, the chief fisheries officer at SCAP, William Herrington, had maintained from the early days of the occupation that fisheries reform was necessary from the perspectives of resource sustainability, long-term health of the Japanese fishing industry, and the goal of normalizing Japan's relations with foreign nations. Occupation officials thus pursued a coordinated policy approach that prioritized both full utilization of the fishing fleet and acceptance of scientific fisheries management by the Japanese government and industry.

Beginning in 1948, this vision for the long-term future of Japanese fisheries became clear, as the SCAP Fisheries Division articulated in public statements its plan for reforms. The essence of the plan was to incorporate into Japanese fisheries policy a model of fisheries management already being applied in certain areas of Northern Europe and the United States—the model that made the concept of maximum sustainable yield (MSY) central to fisheries management. This model required a professionalized fisheries agency that would oversee regulation and coordinate research performed by scientists with training in biology and the dynamics of fish populations. Moreover, this plan involved a corporativist dimension derived from the model that the U.S. State Department was promoting domestically, consisting of a merger of public- and private-sector efforts. That is, fishing industry leaders and fisheries scientists would be jointly involved in developing regulatory programs designed to accomplish MSY—and at the same time to reduce the influence of politicians and nonexpert bureaucrats in the policy process.

While this approach to reform emphasized adoption of best scientific management practices being advocated in Europe and North America, it also had a practical political objective—namely, to advertise to the community of nations that Japan was no longer the predatory fishing power that it was commonly regarded as being. At the same time, a reformed Japanese presence in the waters of the SCAP zone would enhance the chances of gaining support for the readmission of Japan to global ocean fishing, on an equal basis with all other nations. SCAP made no secret of this objective, and occupation officials worked assiduously to promote in Washington the idea that Japan's return to distant-water fishing was a desideratum. In SCAP headquarters, this was seen as a policy imperative, integral to the achievement of occupation objectives.

The post-conflict governance of Japan was a hybrid institutional structure, involving SCAP control working in coordination with a progressively more autonomous civilian government (itself under SCAP tutelage). Occupation authorities faced a significant challenge with regard to the administrative implementation of reforms by the civilian government. This challenge derived in large measure from the remarkable perpetuation of the pre-war bureaucracy, including the great majority of its leadership and nearly all of the bureaucratic rank and file. Left alone by the purges of militarists conducted in the occupation's initial year, the bureaucracy tended to work in its established mode. Its personnel operated within largely the same ideological and administrative parameters as they had done under the militarist regime and even earlier: Japan's civil servants remained largely faithful to established norms and attitudes. In the area of fisheries policy, this meant that the bureaucrats were wed to prioritizing the maximization of production and to the strategic expansion of their high seas fishing industry. They viewed scientific fisheries management principles with great suspicion as being a means for the Allies to quash potential competition from Japan in the high seas fisheries. Late in the occupation years, the bureaucracy in Tokyo seized upon SCAP's promotion of fishing for the generation of export earnings as their opportunity to integrate and coordinate the export-oriented planning, production, and marketing of fisheries products by all major segments of the fisheries and fish-processing industries.

The program for institutional reform was advanced significantly in 1948 by legislation establishing the Fisheries Agency within the Ministry of Agriculture and Forestry, presumably to enhance the influence of professional fisheries managers. But the agency's existence alone could not prevent powerful fishing interests from seeking to obstruct the process of resource policy reform. And without legal reform, even progressive bureaucrats would have little capacity to alter the practices of the Japanese fishing industry.

A more enduring achievement came in the form of the 1949 Fishery Law, passed by the Diet, which restored community fishing rights in coastal communities. The 1949 law created local cooperatives and federations of cooperatives, ending the reign of the pre-war fishing "associations"—organizations dominated by boss control under the influence of the militarist central government and overseeing thousands of tenant-operated fishing units. Consequently, tenant-operated fishing units were virtually eliminated by 1951. The newly established cooperatives were designed to achieve Herrington's goal of advancing democratization of coastal fishing rights. By mid-1950, some 4,721 cooperatives had been formed, with active membership of nearly 750,000 workers and owners. Each member of the cooperative had a single vote regardless of wealth. The law also authorized a flow of government loans to the villages to accelerate the transition toward community organization and to upgrade the coastal fishing fleet and its gear.

The 1949 law also provided for the expansion and development of fisheries research in Japan's national laboratories and universities, a measure seen at SCAP as a crucial prerequisite for training a new generation of scientists and managers devoted to sustainability principles.

Additionally, the 1949 law and complementary legislation enacted in 1950 (the Law for the Prevention of Exhaustion of Marine Resources) tightened the system of licensing for distant-water fishing. These laws vested authority in the Ministry of Agriculture and Forestry to order construction of new fishing vessels. Moreover, the ministry was authorized to order reductions in the size of fishing fleets (including the removal of older vessels from service) in areas where fishing yields were in decline and where it was assumed that dangerous pressure was being exerted upon the fisheries stocks.

SCAP officials pressed hard for these fleet reductions to be implemented. In consequence, Japan did reduce the number of fishing vessels operating in the outer coastal waters, the northern reaches of the East China Sea, and the Sea of Japan (known to South Koreans as the East Sea). Over a two-year period, some 30 percent of the trawling fleet's tonnage was taken out of operation in these areas. The actual result of the new policy, however, was much less than a 30 percent reduction in the intensity and production in trawler fishing, since the vessels retired from service were the oldest and least efficient in the fleet. (This foreshadowed a persistent feature of vessel retirement programs globally in many nations during later years: merely reducing tonnage or number of ships does not in itself guarantee a reduction of yields.) Meanwhile, the policies to scale back the fishing effort in the East China Sea expedited a sharp buildup of Japan's distant-water tuna and salmon fleets, as they took advantage of rich new export opportunities in the American market.

When SCAP officials recognized that monitoring and effective enforcement were essential for the success of any management reforms, they placed an increased focus on enforcement of boundary limits in 1949. Predictably, the bureaucracy proved sluggish in its implementation of the reforms, and the Japanese government failed to provide for effective enforcement of licensing restrictions. Moreover, declining yields and overcrowding of SCAP zone waters encouraged at least some Japanese vessels to slip over zone boundaries, causing serious conflict with the Republic of China (Taiwan) and the Soviet Union; clashes at sea resulted in deaths of Japanese fishermen and confiscation of vessels. Mindful that U.S. strategy for peacebuilding in East Asia could be seriously jeopardized by such incidents at sea, the U.S. Navy dispatched patrols to the East China Sea fishing area and to the areas outside Soviet waters, north of Hokkaido (Japan's second largest island and northernmost prefecture). In sum, when early achievement of the SCAP objective of inspiring the Japanese government to monitor and enforce fishing boundaries proved illusory, it was these naval patrols that restored some measure of orderly fishing operations and avoidance of further conflict at sea.

Concurrently with legal reform, SCAP sent Japanese industry leaders and government officials to consult with scientific experts and fisheries managers in the United States, and in the capacity of observers to international and regional meetings on fisheries policy. The consultations in the United States were explicitly meant to educate Japanese leaders in American principles of scientific fisheries management and corporativist policy processes. SCAP also sought to have the Japanese government send its most progressive-minded resource specialists abroad, in hopes that such international experience would strengthen their prestige at home. Yet even these strategies ran into stiff resistance, both among Allied nations and with the conservative senior Japanese bureaucrats. Allied nations were unsettled by SCAP's efforts to include Japan as an observer and participant in international agency meetings, fearing that inclusion would deprive the Allied powers of a valuable bargaining chip when it came time to conclude a formal peace treaty. Internally, conservative Japanese elites in industry and government were suspicious of the newly appointed experts and administrators, often hampering their operations or even derailing their careers.

Building the international framework for fisheries development

With the outbreak of the Korean War in 1950, the balance of power between SCAP and the Japanese government began to shift heavily in favor of the latter—both because Japan was a staging area for Allied combat operations and because Japan's support was deemed essential for emerging U.S. and Allied security policies in Asia. The government, under Prime Minister Shigeru Yoshida, made effective use of the leverage that it had gained to push for greater autonomy from Allied control. Such assertiveness had a severely detrimental impact on fisheries policy reforms, at the same time that the Japanese industry and its champions in government were escalating their demands for restoration of high seas fishing rights on an equal basis with other nations. Additionally, even the fiercest Allied critics of the Japanese fishing industry, including the Australians and other Commonwealth powers, tempered their opposition as the Korean War accelerated, recognizing the political importance of aligning behind the U.S. position on Japanese economic recovery.

SCAP officials acted decisively in 1951 and 1952 to shape the international legal framework for the restoration of Japanese fishing rights, capitalizing on the political moment to structure Japanese participation in the international fishing arena on drastically better terms than seemed possible at the end of World War II. Moreover, SCAP sought to resolve these issues prior to the 1952 peace conference, recognizing the danger that Allied opposition might pose to the conclusion of the peacebuilding process during multilateral negotiations.

As the occupation went on, two major international developments involving Japanese fisheries policy took place: the 1952 ratification of the tripartite INPFC, and the preparation of Japan to join the IWC, which would enable Japan to become active in the shaping of IWC regulations but also subject to its rules.

Movement toward an early resolution of Japanese distant-water fishing rights began in earnest during the 1951 visit of John Foster Dulles as special U.S. envoy to meet with the Yoshida government about the terms of the prospective peace treaty. The Japanese fishing industry feared efforts (already begun) by Allied nations to write strict limits on Japanese distant-water fishing operations into the peace treaty. Similarly concerned, Japanese government officials promised to adopt stricter regulation of Japanese distant-water fishing for conservationist purposes, if the United States would commit to protection of Japanese fishing rights. Prime Minister Yoshida issued a public letter pledging Japan's voluntary abstention from fishing in other nations' territorial and coastal fishing waters, but specifying explicitly that the promise applied only to fisheries subject to maximum yield exploitation and a conservationist management regime. This letter in turn mirrored the basic structure of the tripartite INPFC draft that was then being circulated for study among the governments of the United States, Canada, and Japan. The thrust of such voluntary abstention was to protect North American Pacific fisheries, as the United States and Canada had conservationist management programs in place in their salmon, halibut, and other fisheries.

The other Allied nations in the Pacific region were unable to benefit from such an abstention by Japan, under the INPFC principles, since they had not previously established conservationist management regimes. Although Yoshida was criticized in Japan for accepting such an abrogation of traditional freedom of the seas and compromise of Japanese fishing interests, in fact the abstention principle left Japan effectively immunized against pressures by other coastal nations (lacking conservation regimes in place) to keep the Japanese fleets out of their offshore fisheries in the period following the peace treaty.

The INPFC was important to the cause of sustainability in international fisheries relations since its terms provided for scientific management evaluated periodically by experts from the three state parties, and because the exclusion of Japan was made contingent on findings that a specific fish stock was not being exploited to the full extent permitted on the MSY principle. (In this sense, the agreement was also important historically because it presaged a key element of the regulatory approach and structure that would be incorporated into the 1958 Geneva Convention on Living Resources of the High Seas, and ultimately in the 1995 UN Fish Stocks Agreement.) While the INPFC commitment to sustainability gave some protection to fish stocks in Northeast Pacific waters, the agreement did little in immediate terms to protect the fishery interests of other nations against the expansionist designs of the Japanese fleets.

One self-proclaimed achievement for SCAP officials was the preparation of Japan to become a signatory to the IWC, which it did in 1951. While the inclusion of Japanese whaling vessels in Antarctic expeditions had done much to galvanize Allied opposition to SCAP reform policy, SCAP officials saw Japan's accession to the IWC as evidence of the success of the occupation authority's reform agenda. SCAP also hailed the inauguration of a Japanese scientific program for the study of whale populations. These ostensible achievements, however, proved but a prelude to lax IWC regulation that accommodated a devastating expansion of intensive Antarctic whaling, including prominently the operations of Japan's whaling fleets.

FACTORS AND CONSTRAINTS AFFECTING OUTCOMES

Post-war fisheries policy reforms in Japan yielded decidedly mixed outcomes. While the Japanese fishing industry exceeded its pre-war strength by the end of the peacebuilding process, when the peace treaty was concluded and the occupation ended in 1952, efforts to implement principles of sustainable resource management in Japanese fisheries were considerably less successful. There are several reasons why these outcomes occurred.

First, SCAP policy efforts in the early years of the occupation were almost exclusively concentrated on rebuilding the Japanese fishing industry for domestic consumption and export trade. If the policy had sought to undertake serious reform efforts earlier in the process, sustainability principles might have been incorporated into all SCAP fisheries policies from the outset. However, even enthusiastic proponents of scientific management based in the SCAP Natural Resources Section had to accept the decision to prioritize Japan's economic recovery. Power disparities between SCAP and the Far Eastern Commission (which from its base in Washington, D.C., found it impossible to restrain or redirect MacArthur and the occupation) as well as asymmetrical power relationships between the United States and the individual Allied governments further limited the range of possible outcomes. The priorities decided upon in the White House, the U.S. cabinet departments, and SCAP headquarters were decisive and virtually beyond effective challenge. Moreover, the main thrust of most Allied objections to SCAP policies was not primarily conservationist; rather, the Allies wanted to slow down Japanese fisheries expansion, with permanent limits placed on the scope of both fishing and whaling activities for many years in the future.

Second, the reformist program dimension of SCAP fisheries policies was troubled by the very success of the initial economic recovery program that had quickly rebuilt capacity of the fleet. The extraordinarily rapid revival of Japan's coastal and distant-water fishing enterprises resulted in a dangerously overheated fishing industry by 1949–1950, and SCAP was faced with a situation that required expansions of the authorized fishing zone, that is, the expansion of Japan's operations in an ever-increasing range of distant waters. Fishing was not merely an important source of protein, but it was regarded by SCAP as a vitally important source of employment in the stressed Japanese economy of the occupation years. Promotion and protection of the fishing industry became a vital element in SCAP's economic reconstruction program and the larger peacebuilding process.

Third, the retention of a conservative bureaucratic elite hamstrung efforts by SCAP officials to enforce vigorously the reform laws, and in particular the regulations for operations at sea. The vision of an industry leadership dedicated to sustainability, working cooperatively with a refashioned bureaucracy composed of progressive, conservation-minded scientific experts, proved to be impossible in the changing political circumstances—especially once the Korean War began and the U.S. government began its determined push in 1949–1950 for an early peace treaty. Consequently, by the time serious conservation initiatives were undertaken that would affect the scope and nature of fisheries policy reform in 1949 and 1950, legal reform objectives and international scientific standards were pitted against a retrenched and fast-growing fishing industry.

The Japanese fishing industry was not monolithic; its several sectors had diverse priorities and interests. Nonetheless, the industry was largely united in exerting its political clout to retain, as much as possible, the traditional model of Japan's fishing policies, which favored expansion of fishing operations and rising production levels. The sustainability goals advocated by the SCAP experts were given lip service but little more, except on the few occasions—such as the retirement of vessels and reduction of fishing effort in the East China Sea—when SCAP headquarters definitively decided on a new or revised policy that the Diet and cabinet had to accept. Such interventions were few in number and, over the entire course of the 1945–1952 period, of much less consequence than the economic support (complemented by a championing of Japan's fishing and whaling ambitions) that SCAP provided to the industry.

CONCLUSION

What can be learned from this experience of a defeated country, with a war-devastated economy, undergoing rehabilitation under control of an occupying power that ruled a mixed industrial-agricultural-fisheries economy and controlled a population that mounted no armed resistance to governance and management of its natural resources?

Several factors account for the obvious uniqueness, as compared to other experiences examined in this book, of the post-conflict situation in Japan. Among the most important factors were the social and cultural norms that colored the responses of the defeated population to the occupation authorities and the authorities' role in declaring the terms of resource management policy, and also the positive advantages of an experienced and administratively skilled Japanese bureaucracy, no matter how conservative the influence it might seek to wield. Of great importance, too, was the political stability resulting from the U.S. decision to retain the emperor while denying his divinity, while dismantling and transforming the hierarchical political and social structure and establishing the institutional and legal basis of a democratic constitutional order. Essential to the enterprise, moreover, were the vast fiscal resources that the United States was willing to invest in recovery policies.

Unlike experiences elsewhere, the post-conflict resource regime under the occupation in Japan was, at least initially, characterized by an effectively enforced command-and-control style. Although, as noted above, a multilateral advisory and policy-setting structure was established by the Allies in 1945, in fact General MacArthur operated with almost exclusive reference to U.S. government instructions on basic policy, and his SCAP headquarters was the locus of decision making at the very nexus of all operational implementation. The SCAP policies embraced the further and more basic objective of defending Japanese interests—in regard to marine fishing and whaling, but also more comprehensively—against the pressures from other Allied nations to reduce American support of rapid economic reconstruction in Japan and the country's participation in the emerging institutional order of the global economy. These pressures from governments that registered basic objections to the occupation strategies were fully defeated by U.S. intransigence until 1950, when the geopolitics in East Asia changed once the Korean War began and U.S. policy became centered on obtaining maximum possible consensus for the peace treaty and its terms.

The experience of Japan in the post-war period was thus highly fact-specific, rooted in a rapidly evolving environment of Cold War geopolitics, and with the United States in the controlling position of guiding policy formation and action by SCAP. The number and importance of such clearly unique elements are a reminder of the perils of seeking to form generalized principles from this complex historical period.

Still, admitting the historically contingent elements of the occupation, there are several lessons that can perhaps be taken from the case of occupied Japan with regard to resource management policy in post-conflict situations.

Balancing long-term objectives against short-term imperatives

It is desirable that economic recovery policies based upon resource exploitation should be explicitly counterweighed by sustainable resource management. Failure by the ruling authority in Japan to articulate from the outset the norms and advantages of resource conservation and sustainable use diminished the effectiveness of reform advocacy at a later time. The obligation to preserve a resource heritage for use by future generations is, no doubt, a "hard sell" in a crisis situation when food and material shortages, let alone a possible breakdown of social order, dominate policy making. Still, the values of resource conservation and the need for scientific management, with explicitly defined sustainability goals, need to be integrated into policy (and highlighted in the rhetoric of leaders and policy makers) in the earliest stage of peacebuilding. As to the specific regulatory approach, clearly defined limits informed by scientifically defensible judgments should be placed upon the allocation of labor and capital of industries that intensively exploit resources, and on the operations of these industries.

The successful 1949 coastal fisheries rights reforms in Japan suggests that where an indigenous tradition exists that reflects commitments to sustainability and conservation, it can be revitalized and incorporated into the overall strategies of the resource management regime. When, however, unregulated resource exploitation is adopted in order to assure short-term political stability, the political gains that advance the peacebuilding process may well involve a long-term cost of environmental degradation and political instability arising from overproduction and possible collapse of the primary industries involved.

The bureaucratic dimension

The existence of an entrenched bureaucracy in a post-conflict country can enhance stability and expedite coordination of resource management policy, but the enduring pre-conflict ideology among civil servants in such a bureaucracy can be an intractable obstacle to reform. The Japanese fisheries bureaucracy revealed in the post-conflict period the same mistrust of any policy for sustainable management of fisheries resources beyond the coastal area that it had manifested in the pre-war period. Mere reorganization of the bureaucracy under the Fisheries Agency, with the installation of a few progressive officials, did not alter the conservative, output-maximizing orientation of the bureaucrats who survived the war and the purge of 1945–1946. This produced serious problems for the implementation and enforcement of legal reforms, and it required frequent interventions by SCAP officials to guide the reform process. Moreover, because of the early focus on economic recovery, the entrenched bureaucracy—having embraced fully the work of promoting revival of the marine fishing sector—was in a position of sufficient political strength to mount significant resistance to later reform efforts. In any post-conflict peacebuilding effort, sensitivity to the possibilities of such hostility to reforms from a carry-over bureaucracy and concern with the internal politics of the civil service is essential. It is presumably advisable to carry forward institutional restructuring at the same time as new substantive policies for resource management are being put in place.

Despite the strength of the post-conflict regime, SCAP officials charged with natural resources administration were unable to achieve more than very attenuated success in selling the Japanese marine fishing industry and government officials on the basics of sustainable fisheries policy and scientific management. Ironically, these officials completely succeeded in restoring the fishing and whaling sectors of Japan to their pre-war areas of activity on the high seas and to pre-war levels of production. Despite efforts at vigilance on the part of SCAP resources officers, the reliance on the civilian government bureaucracy to enforce sustainability policies (however rudimentary) did much to undermine policy goals.

SCAP policies and their outcomes were much more promising with regard to the historic coastal fisheries and fishing communities. Artisanal and near-coastal marine fisheries were subjected to deep structural reforms, dismantling the 1930s' centralized regime that had disenfranchised small operators. Like the land reforms, the substantial restoration of traditional fishers' rights in coastal communities, and the organization of cooperatives, constituted one of the occupation's most celebrated achievements in moving Japan toward a more democratic distribution of economic resources and decision-making authority.

Although occupation officials' efforts to promote sustainable resource management to Japanese industry and bureaucracy were in large measure frustrated by conservative resistance in the government and industry stratagems, a dramatic increase in scientific research capacity was achieved by SCAP during this same period. New and improved fisheries research facilities, strengthening of fisheries sciences education, and mentorship of the newer generation of fisheries management officials were the instruments of some significant change in this regard. The SCAP natural resources officials also believed it essential to bring Japan integrally, and as an equal, into the institutions created as infrastructure for the post-war legal and economic order. This newly instituted infrastructure included the IWC, re-established in 1946; the U.S. government insisted upon the admission of Japan to the IWC to complement the occupation's controversial revival of Japanese industrial whaling in the Antarctic and Pacific waters.

The balance sheet on multilateralism

The advantages and costs of multilateralism need to be assessed in the design of post-conflict interventions. In occupied Japan, SCAP's dominance over the policy-making process gave General MacArthur enormous discretion in prioritizing administrative actions in pursuit of various policy goals, to the detriment of the Allied governments that had a stake in the outcomes of occupation policies. If SCAP had been more concerned in accommodating the interests and demands of the several Allied partners most deeply interested, the imposition of well-designed and strongly administered policies for fisheries sustainability might well have been the result. This is not to deny that authentic multilateralism in administration of post-conflict situations can all too easily have negative effects as well. Indeed, the intransigence of SCAP and the U.S. government in resisting Allied demands for a more restrictive approach to Japanese fisheries expansion reflected the larger policy of resistance by SCAP and the United States to the demands of Australia, New Zealand, the Philippines, and China for a much harsher, thoroughly punitive approach to the treatment of the Japanese population and its economic recovery ambitions in the post-conflict years.

LOOKING BACKWARD ON THE RESULTS

In the time that has passed since the end of military occupation and restoration of full sovereignty in 1952, some unintended consequences have followed. Japan resumed its whaling practices in a manner disruptive to multilateral regulatory efforts—even within the limited constraints of IWC rules—that continues to this day. This is especially so given its industry's notoriously cynical actions under the scientific research exception. Even in the exclusive economic zone (EEZ), the Japanese government has done little to protect whale and dolphin populations, or even its own artisanal tuna fishing industry based in small coastal communities. Japan's policies on high seas fisheries sustainability have consistently resisted effective multilateral cooperation for sustainability or resource conservation, at least until eleventh-hour reversals as the result of intensive international pressures—as happened, for example, with Japan's initial (and long-sustained) opposition to the United Nations efforts that culminated in adoption of the large-driftnet ban and, later, the Fishery Stocks Agreement in the mid-1990s. The same holds true with regard to Japan's extended period of reluctance to become a party to the highly important Western and Central Pacific Fisheries Convention, a multilateral agreement signed in 2000 and designed to control overfishing of Pacific tuna under UN policy for multilateral regulation of high seas fisheries.

Long unreceptive to the most promising efforts at stopping illegal, unreported, and unregulated (IUU) fishing and the transfer at sea to the Tokyo market of illegally harvested fish and whale products, Japan was discovered (and officially admitted) in 2006 to have been complicit in its fleet's drastic overfishing of the southern bluefin tuna, to the point where experts doubt now that the stocks will recover for decades, if ever. None of this is to say that other fishing powers have a clean record with regard to sustainability and respect for enforcement efforts. (On this point, one only has to recall the once-staunch resistance of nations other than Japan to the imposition of a moratorium on whaling; the delay of many years on the part of the European Community nations and bureaucracy to act effectively against IUU fishing and, more generally, the overfishing problem; and, most recently, the refusal of some major European fishing powers to accept a moratorium, or even effective quotas, for protection of the threatened Atlantic tuna). In sum, Japan took full advantage of the benign occupation policies to regain its prominent role in global fishing, and has now taken full advantage of the fragmented, largely ineffective, and in some regards chaotic condition of the international regulatory framework.

From a broader perspective, however, rather than focusing only on Japan's record, one must weigh the almost universal failure of the fishing regimes of the coastal nations, since the signing of the UN Convention on the Law of the Sea, to protect and successfully sustain the most valuable fish stocks within their EEZs. And on the high seas, factors such as the rise in use of flags of convenience in marine fishing, the noncompliance with multilateral regulatory regimes by non-member state flag vessels, and the outright evasion of regulation and control by fishing vessels of any ownership or flag are of fundamental importance as sources of the IUU problem that now plagues so many fishing areas on the world's oceans. Japan has been only one actor among many in the perpetuation of many of these problems, and only one among many in resisting—though in important instances, reversing course to support—effective multilateral solutions.

ADDITIONAL SOURCES

Although the following materials were not cited, they have been listed here since they complement the main source—Harry N. Scheiber, *Inter-Allied Conflicts and Ocean Law, 1945–53: The Occupation Command's Revival of Japanese Whaling and Marine Fisheries* (Taipei, Taiwan: Institute of European and American Studies, Academia Sinica, 2001)—and have contributed to the conceptual development of the chapter.

Cohen, T. 1987. *Remaking Japan: The American occupation as new deal*, ed. T. Passin. New York: Free Press.

Dower, J. 1999. *Embracing defeat: Japan in the wake of World War II*. New York: W. W. Norton.

Scheiber, H. N. 1986. Pacific Ocean resources, science, and law of the sea: Wilbert M. Chapman and the Pacific fisheries, 1935–70. *Ecology Law Quarterly* 13:381–534.

———. 2004. Japan, the North Atlantic Triangle, and the Pacific fisheries: A perspective on the origins of modern ocean law. *San Diego International Law Journal* 6 (1): 27–112.

Scheiber, H. N., K. Mengerink, and Y-H. Song, 2007. Ocean tuna fisheries, East Asian rivalries, and international regulation: Japanese policies and the overcapacity/IUU fishing conundrum. *University of Hawaii Law Review*, 30:97–165.

Scheiber, H. N., and A. Watanabe 2010. Occupation policy and economic planning in postwar Japan. In *Economic planning in the post-1945 period*, ed. E. Aerts and A. S. Milward. Leuven, Belgium: University of Leuven Press.

Developing capacity for natural resource management in Afghanistan: Process, challenges, and lessons learned by UNEP

Belinda Bowling and Asif Zaidi

For several decades, Afghanistan has been crippled by wars, revolution, foreign occupation, and internecine conflicts—all of which have devastated the natural resource base on which the poverty-stricken rural population is highly dependent and shattered the country's environmental governance traditions and institutions. War has resulted in population displacement, returning refugees, internally displaced persons, land degradation, landmines on agricultural land and in irrigation infrastructure, infectious diseases, and underinvestment in sustainable development (UNEP 2003).

In response to the terrorist attacks on September 11, 2001, the United States launched attacks against the Taliban government that had ruled Afghanistan since 1995 and the al Qaeda units operating from the country. By early 2002, the Taliban regime had been removed. After a week of difficult negotiations between various factions, arrangements were in place in the form of the Bonn Agreement that established an interim government headed by Hamid Karzai, opening the doors to significant investment in the country's post-conflict reconstruction and development.

But this tenuous and fragile peace was short-lived, and by the summer of 2005 Afghanistan found itself once again in the midst of a formidable insurgency that threatens to undermine the development activities initiated earlier. By 2005, the Taliban had returned from their sanctuaries after reorganizing and recouping themselves. They were motivated by a desire to end foreign occupation and questioned the legitimacy of the Bonn Agreement. The Taliban adopted guerrilla warfare tactics in both urban and rural areas, with large swaths of rural areas in

---

Until mid-2010, Belinda Bowling was the United Nations Environment Programme (UNEP) country program manager for the Capacity Building and Institutional Development Programme for Environmental Management in Afghanistan, prior to which she was the program's environmental law and international conventions expert. Asif Zaidi is the operations manager of UNEP's Post-Conflict and Disaster Management Branch, prior to which he was UNEP's country program manager in Afghanistan.

southern Afghanistan coming quickly under their control, at least during the hours of darkness. In urban areas, particularly in and around Kabul, Afghanistan's capital, the Taliban increasingly created a state of perpetual vulnerability for the Afghan and foreign troops as well as for the aid community.

In 2003, prior to the Taliban's insurgence and in response to the post-conflict environmental assessment of Afghanistan by the United Nations Environment Programme (UNEP), the government of Afghanistan requested the assistance of UNEP to ensure environmental and natural resource considerations were integrated into the country's development and governance frameworks. With financial support from the European Commission, the government of Finland, and the Global Environment Facility, UNEP began implementing a program to promote institutional and capacity development for environmental management. The program includes institutional development, law, policy, and community-based natural resource management (CBNRM).

Under the Karzai interim administration, a national development framework was designed, and its implementation initiated. The government and its international partners put in place approaches to slow the pace of degradation of the natural resource base, including a nascent environmental governance structure, and appropriate policies, laws, and other tools to enable effective management of the country's natural resource base. At the core of the institutional and regulatory framework is a community-based approach to natural resource management, which is being pilot tested in different parts of the country. The goal is to combine both bottom-up and top-down institutional approaches to develop CBNRM programs on a broad scale, which will help restore the natural resource base, improve rural livelihoods, reduce the number of disputes and conflicts over natural resources, and contribute to peacebuilding. Even as the Taliban insurgency continued, CBNRM projects were being successfully implemented in the central highlands, and in northeastern and western Afghanistan.

This chapter focuses on UNEP's experiences since 2003 in building environmental governance in Afghanistan, namely the development and pilot implementation of a CBNRM policy and regulatory framework, which in Afghanistan must be considered against a backdrop of land tenure insecurity and conflict over access to certain natural resources.

The chapter begins with a brief description of the state of natural resources in Afghanistan. It then looks at Afghanistan's natural resources through a conflict analysis and peacebuilding framework. The next section sketches out the environmental governance architecture, followed by an introduction to the community-based policy and regulatory approach to natural resource management. The chapter then discusses some of the pilot CBNRM efforts and describes some of the obstacles encountered by UNEP in implementing the new approach. The chapter closes with a discussion of lessons learned by UNEP during its operations in Afghanistan and how this experience may inform international response to future conflict scenarios.

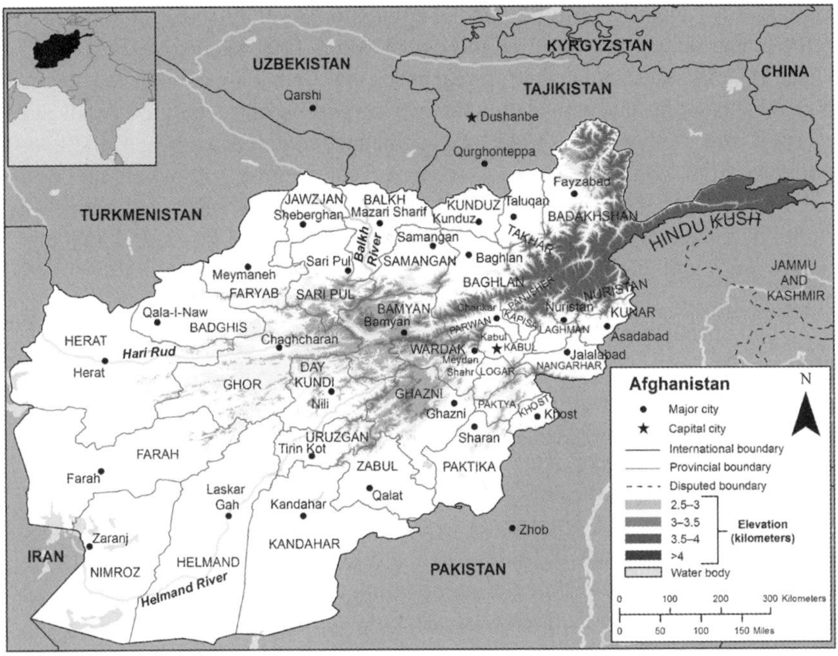

A DAMAGED NATURAL RESOURCE BASE

Afghanistan does not have the rich oil resources of Iraq. But natural resources are critical to the livelihoods and survival of the Afghan people, since the vast majority are farmers and herders who depend on the country's natural resources—water, pastures, forests, and arable land—and the ecosystem services these natural resources provide.

Water is the country's most critical natural resource and key to the health, well-being, and prosperity of the Afghan people (NEPA and UNEP 2008). Because the country has an arid climate, water resources are scarce, especially during drought periods. Mountain ranges, in particular the Hindu Kush range that extends from northern Pakistan to central Afghanistan, serve as "vital 'water towers' for Afghanistan and Central Asia as a whole" (NEPA and UNEP 2008, 11). The availability of, access to, and quality of water—or, especially, its absence—can be a source of conflict or a driving force for migration. Water availability in Afghanistan is affected by the melting of mountain glaciers (due to climate change), severe droughts, and poor management of water resources. Access to water resources has also been affected by war-inflicted damage to large and small irrigation systems and the disruption of existing water supplies.

Pastures, forests, and biodiversity products are also important natural resources for the country's rural population. According to a 2008 report from

Afghanistan's National Environmental Protection Agency (NEPA) and UNEP, "[t]hese natural resources are rightly considered 'the wealth of the poor' in Afghanistan because rural people . . . depend on natural and agricultural ecosystems" to provide pastures and rangelands for grazing and hunting; tangible goods such as crops, fruit, timber, fuel, fodder, and medicine; income, from by-products such as textiles from wool; and services such as erosion control, pollination, and water drainage stability (NEPA and UNEP 2008, 15). Various forces—including war, natural disasters, population growth, and increasing demand for natural resources, such as wool and medicinal plants, at home and in neighboring countries—have led to significant depletion of natural resources.

Land, particularly agricultural land and rangeland, is an equally valued resource. Due to its socioeconomic and geographical conditions and the ongoing conflict, Afghanistan has for decades been severely affected by land degradation, which in turn contributes to increased internal migration, particularly to marginal lands, and causes further stress on ecosystems. While difficult to calculate a numeric value, broad indicators show that the direct and indirect costs of desertification in Afghanistan is colossal and constantly increasing.[1] Additionally, poor agricultural practices are degrading soil fertility; conflict is changing grazing patterns; land claims and drought are affecting traditional grazing patterns; and silting and flooding are damaging irrigation systems (NEPA and UNEP 2008).

The main cause of this somewhat gloomy picture of the state of Afghanistan's natural resource base, and a driver of conflicts over access to natural resources, is the overuse and mismanagement of natural resources that followed the collapse of national and local governance institutions during the conflict period from 1979 to 2002—the long period of conflict after the constitutional government fell in a Marxist revolution, the Soviet Union invaded and occupied the country for ten years, and the Taliban came to power. This institutional collapse led in turn to erosion of the rule of law, disintegration of traditional governance, reduced human capacity to manage natural resources, and unequal access to natural resources.

NATURAL RESOURCES AS A SOURCE OF CONFLICT IN AFGHANISTAN

The guiding framework for UNEP's work in Afghanistan is *Natural Resources for Peacebuilding and Statebuilding: A Toolkit for Analysis and Programming* (the NRP Toolkit) (UNEP 2012). Developed by UNEP and its partner organizations, the NRP Toolkit is designed "as a field level resource to assist practitioners working in peacebuidling and statebuilding contexts in two ways: 1) to diagnose

---

1 Direct costs include loss of associated revenues from forest products; indirect costs include loss of ecological benefits (for example, reduced biodiversity) and key forest functions (such as compromised soil fertility and loss of erosion and flood controls) (NEPA and UNEP 2008).

the linkages between natural resources, land, and violent conflict; and 2) to identify, prioritise, sequence, and monitor natural resource interventions that can support peacebuilding and statebuilding goals" (UNEP 2012, 3). The natural resources that are addressed by the NRP Toolkit are categorized into three classes: "extractive natural resources (such as oil, gas, gold and diamonds), renewable resources (such as water, timber and fisheries), and land" (UNEP 2012, 6).

The NRP Toolkit supports the design and implementation of needs assessment, planning, or programming in a post-conflict situation with various UN-developed tools.[2] Donor agencies, nongovernmental organizations (NGOs), and national actors can also use the NRP Toolkit to inform their own peacebuilding plans, policies, and priorities.

Issues of land tenure and access to natural resources are often the root cause of local disputes in Afghanistan. These disputes present an opportunity for insurgents and antigovernment groups to capitalize on them for their own purposes. A number of studies have shown how local conflicts over natural resources have become flashpoints in the wider conflict.[3]

During the spring of 2008, the Sanayee Development Organization, an Afghan NGO, conducted a field survey in the provinces of Kabul, Ghazni, Logar, and Herat (El Saman 2008). The survey revealed that in rural areas, land and water are the most important causes of local conflict: cultivation of land was mentioned by 78.3 percent of the respondents as a root cause of conflict, water by 70.8 percent, and grazing of animals by 13.3 percent. A 2008 Oxfam survey of 500 people from six provinces also showed that "local disputes are often related to resources, particularly land and water" (Waldman 2008, 3). Oxfam found that this nexus between natural resources and conflict is aggravated by a range of additional factors, such as natural disasters, refugee flows, badly delivered aid, corruption, abuse of power, or the opium trade. A further finding was that in many cases local disputes led to violence, and while the strength and importance of family and tribal affiliations in Afghanistan can be a source of stability, they can also lead to the rapid escalation of disputes. Oxfam concluded that the resulting insecurity not only destroys quality of life and impedes development work but also is exploited by criminal or antigovernment groups and insurgents to strengthen their positions in the wider conflict, beyond the community in question, at regional and national levels.

One local dispute over access to dwindling forest resources is the ongoing armed conflict between the Zambar tribe from Sabari District in Khost Province

---

[2] These tools include, but are not limited to, a conflict analysis, a post-conflict needs assessment (PCNA), an integrated mission planning process, a poverty reduction strategy paper (PRSP), a UN Development Assistance Framework (UNDAF), a post-conflict environmental assessment, and a peacebuilding strategy. For further discussion on UNEP's post-conflict environmental assessment methods and frameworks, including PCNA, PRSP, and UNDAF, see Jensen (2012).

[3] See Adbi et al. (2008); Sexton (2012); and Waldman (2008).

and the Balkhel tribe from Jani Khel District in Paktia Province. The United Nations Assistance Mission in Afghanistan (UNAMA) has documented that the natural resource–related conflict has facilitated penetration of the area by insurgents, which has resulted in the districts in question becoming more unstable (UNAMA 2009).

Increasingly, political bodies (Afghan and foreign, such as the United States and the United Nations) are recognizing that local conflict over access to natural resources can result in local political instability and thereby facilitate insurgent penetration and access at the community level. Viewing local issues of natural resource management through a national-scale peace and security lens adds another dimension of complexity to the problem. For example, certain high-value natural resource products, particularly timber and opium poppy, play pivotal roles in funding the insurgency and increasing insecurity in certain parts of the country (U.S. DOD 2008).[4] According to one source, poppy cultivation finances up to 40 percent of the insurgency in Afghanistan (AFP 2007).

While there have been numerous instances of disputes over access to rangelands all over the country, the most politicized and violent have involved Kuchi nomadic pastoralists, who are of Pashtun ethnicity, and central highlands sedentary communities of the minority Hazara ethnicity.[5] In 2009, UNEP developed the *Recommended Strategy for Conflict Resolution of Competing High Pasture Claims of Settled and Nomadic Communities in Afghanistan* to address the most urgent issues regarding conflicts over access to rangeland resources, especially in the Behsud District of Wardak Province in the foothills of the central highlands (UNEP 2009b). *Recommended Strategy* describes the background of the conflict.

> Tension and incidents throughout the foothill areas increased through the warm seasons of 2005 and 2006, always with the same themes; a dispute of ownership of the pastures and water sources lying immediately beyond village-adjacent paddocks.
>
> In June 2007, arriving Kuchi took the opportunity to raise the Taliban flag in Behsud. . . . In the resulting fracas, thirteen Hazara were killed, tens wounded, hundreds of Hazara homes burnt and thousands forced to flee the area. . . . Only the onset of winter saw Kuchi leave, coinciding with a Presidential Order that they do so.
>
> Spring 2008 opened badly with Hazara marching through Kabul in late March accusing Kuchi of taking their pastures. Hazara MPs [members of parliament] also accused the President of favouring Kuchi in a bid to win votes in the 2009 election. This was followed by declamation by a Kuchi MP that Kuchi alone

---

[4] For more information on the role of opium poppy in Afghanistan, see Catarious and Russell (2012) and Pain (2012).

[5] For a detailed discussion on the conflict between Kuchi nomads and Hazara tribes in Afghanistan's central highlands, see Liz Alden Wily, "Resolving Natural Resource Conflicts to Help Prevent War: A Case from Afghanistan," in this book.

> are true owners of Afghanistan's land and calling other tribes 'immigrants'. Following a walk-out by offended non-Pashtun, Parliament was closed. . . .
>
> President Karzai issued another directive in September 2008 that the Kuchi leave, which again they did given the onset of winter. Karzai also established a *Presidential Commission for Resolving Land Disputes involving Kuchis and Settled People*. . . . Despite immense efforts and meetings with the Hazara and Kuchi leaders, the Commission has been unable to achieve concrete results. . . . During spring and summer 2009 there has been repeated threats by Kuchi and Hazara, a significant amount of alleged arming by both sides, and even some evidence that Hazara have established a front-line of trenches in the Behsud area beyond which no Kuchi will be permitted to pass. ISAF [International Security Assistance Force of the North Atlantic Treaty Organization] forces admit to handing out food to Kuchi moving into Day Mirdad District from the south-east in a bid to discourage them from moving further into Wardak Province. Rumours abound that President Karzai has ordered that Kuchi be paid not to attempt to move into the central highlands to avoid conflicts during the crucial Presidential election year, but these have not been substantiated.
>
> There is little doubt that the Kuchi-Hazara dispute has already reached a dangerous level. Already in 2008 political leaders were voicing concern that civil war could begin in areas which have so far not been directly involved in the fight against Taliban insurgents (UNEP 2009b, 20–21; internal citations omitted).

The strategic document (*Recommended Strategy*) suggests outlining the historical context of the conflict between settled and nomadic people over highland pastures. In doing so, grievances can be identified and expressed, hastening the route to resolution by summarizing lessons from previous experiences in tackling pasture-access disputes. An action plan is then to be proposed, and a road map made for stakeholders to use when addressing grievances over the long term and securing the future sustainability of the natural resource.

The purpose of the *Recommended Strategy* prepared by UNEP is to provide the government, parliament, local communities, and their spokespersons with broad guidelines, as well as specific suggestions, for resolving rangeland-access conflicts. It includes short-, medium- and long-term recommendations and suggested courses of action. Encouragingly, the leadership of the Ministry of Agriculture, Irrigation and Livestock (MAIL) has embraced the recommendations set out in the *Recommended Strategy*, and core funding from the ministry is being utilized to implement the short-term recommendations. A proposal for a national-scale, community-based pasture management program is also under development, which links closely with the new regulatory framework that has been proposed.

A further issue in natural resource management is transboundary management of resources, especially water resources. A real potential exists for conflict (or cooperation) between Afghanistan and Iran and Pakistan over water. Both UNEP and the United Nations Development Programme (UNDP) have implemented transboundary initiatives for the Sistan Wetlands shared by Afghanistan and Iran.[6] The level of success has been mixed; successes at the technical level have been marred by strong resistance at the political level. For example, an attempt led by the Wildlife Conservation Society to establish a peace park in the Pamir mountains some years ago, involving the governments of Afghanistan, Pakistan, Tajikistan and China, ultimately collapsed.

Because of the extreme poverty facing most Afghans, the country's susceptibility to drought and other natural disasters, and the arid nature of much of the country, Afghanistan is highly vulnerable to desertification and the effects of climate change (NEPA 2008). Resulting degradation of the land and natural resource base may fuel ongoing conflict and initiate new conflicts in the years to come.

The UN agencies working in Afghanistan have recognized the critical role that natural resources play in local disputes and conflicts, and made the issue a priority in the UN Development Assistance Framework (UNDAF) for 2010 to 2013 (UN and GOIRA 2010). The goal of the framework was to increase the prominence of natural resources and peacebuilding in the overarching development agenda, especially to a fatigued donor community weary from juggling so many competing and urgent country-level priorities. Among the activities was the study *Natural Resource Management and Peacebuilding in Afghanistan*, which largely draws upon UNEP's field projects in Bamyan Province that started in 2008 (UN Country Team in Afghanistan 2013).

THE NASCENT ENVIRONMENTAL GOVERNANCE ARCHITECTURE

Afghanistan is besieged with wide-ranging problems that demand the attention of the international community: lack of peace and security; a dearth of functioning governance structures; human rights violations and gender inequality; destroyed infrastructure; a flailing and weak economy dependent on illicit poppy revenue; and a population bearing the burden of both extreme poverty and limited social development, ranking 175 out of 185 countries in the 2012 Human Development Index (UNDP 2013). Under such extreme circumstances, environment and natural resource management has had to compete for a place in the post-conflict reconstruction and development agenda.

An emergency *loya jirga* (grand council) held in mid-2002 to determine the structure of the transitional administration of Afghanistan decided that, for the first time in Afghanistan's history, the government mandate should expressly include environmental protection. The mandate was added to the ministry formerly responsible for water and irrigation, which was renamed the Ministry of Irrigation, Water Resources and Environment. However, transitional phases in post-conflict peacebuilding are often characterized by institutional instability, and like a hermit crab looking for the right shell, it took some time before the right institutional

6 For a discussion on transboundary water issues in the Sistan Basin, see Dehgan, Palmer-Moloney, and Mirzaee (2014).

home was found for the new environment mandate. This process was completed in 2005 with the establishment of the National Environmental Protection Agency (NEPA). NEPA's broad mandate is to protect the environmental integrity of Afghanistan and support sustainable development of the country's natural resources by providing effective environmental guidance and management services. The agency, which is an independent entity headed by a director-general who reports directly to the Office of the President, is responsible for policy making, regulation, coordination, monitoring, and awareness raising.

It is important to understand that NEPA is not a line ministry or agency; in regard to natural resource management, that function lies primarily with the MAIL. In one incarnation or another, MAIL has been responsible for natural resource management in Afghanistan for decades. In addition to agriculture, it has the functional mandate to oversee forests, rangelands, biodiversity, wildlife, wetlands, and upper watersheds.[7] As a result, many of its senior personnel have relatively strong (albeit decades-old) technical backgrounds, and long-standing institutional memories. Many officials in the Ministry of Energy and Water, which has responsibility for water resource management, have similar depths of experience. For the senior officials in these line ministries, NEPA is a novel, and sometimes threatening, institutional phenomenon. NEPA has not been as warmly welcomed as one might have hoped by many of the old guard because the new agency has started to occupy some of the policy space that was previously considered the domain of other ministries, like MAIL and the Ministry of Energy and Water. There is a sense that NEPA is encroaching upon the ministries' spheres of influence, thereby threatening the ministries with a loss of stature, funding, and prerogatives.

A national planning process that culminated in July 2008 produced the Afghanistan National Development Strategy (ANDS), which included the development of ministry strategies as well as sector strategies. While in principle this process should have aligned priorities and resolved issues of overlapping mandates, in most instances it did not, as discussed in the following section.

In April 2009, the Minister of Agriculture, Irrigation and Livestock announced a new national agriculture development framework, developed in response to the priority given to the agriculture sector in the ANDS and at the Paris donor conference in June 2008 that followed the release of the ANDS. The framework is based on an "agriculture triangle," consisting of natural resource management at the base, followed by agricultural production and productivity, with economic regeneration at the apex. The framework document states:

---

7 The ministry responsible for agriculture has had numerous names since 2002: Ministry of Agriculture and Livestock (2002–2004); Ministry of Agriculture and Animal Husbandry (2004–2005); Ministry of Agriculture, Animal Husbandry and Food (2004–2006); Ministry of Agriculture and Irrigation (2006); and Ministry of Agriculture, Irrigation and Livestock (2006–present) (Banzet et al. 2007).

> Our forests and grazing land, soil and water resources are each needed for agricultural strength. In some cases we can be satisfied by sustainability, but others demand expanding and then protecting our natural heritage. Deforestation must be reversed, not accepted as a fact of life. Water needs to be better harnessed and more efficiently provided for irrigation. Grazing lands and crop lands can each become more fertile and productive. This [sic], the Natural Resources Management Program (NRM) is the base of the triangle, a foundation for agricultural productivity (MAIL 2009, 3).

REVIVAL OF A COMMUNITY-BASED APPROACH TO NATURAL RESOURCE MANAGEMENT

Afghanistan is a feudal and tribal land; for centuries, communities have been self-governed. Until the latter half of the twentieth century, when the state intervened in conservation, communities governed in a sustainable manner so as to conserve natural resources for the use and enjoyment of both present and future generations. Thus, concepts underlying modern CBNRM are by no means alien to Afghanistan's rural communities. But these traditional practices have been eroded over the last forty years by a variety of factors, including the state's attempt to take control of natural resources in the period preceding the onset of the Soviet war in the late 1970s, as well as the impact of the war itself and the subsequent decades of conflict. The revival of these local traditions is one of the core goals of the community-based approach to natural resource management within the country's policy and regulatory frameworks.

The community-based approach to natural resource management, however, is a significant deviation from past government approaches. Until the endorsement of the new policy, Afghanistan had adopted a centralized and protection-oriented approach to natural resource management—one intended for conservation only, under which the community can use natural resources only with state permission. However, the country has never had a tradition of strong central governance—as the crossroads of Central Asia, it has a history of local tribal governance systems united only symbolically by a monarch. It is no surprise therefore that the paternalistic approach to natural resource management adopted by the state in the 1970s was a resounding failure, leading to a violent and effective tragedy of the commons scenario, which in turn resulted in acute degradation of the natural resource base, compounded by the impacts of three decades of conflict.

The new community-based policy approach was initiated by the Asian Development Bank (ADB) and the Food and Agriculture Organization of the United Nations (FAO), which provided technical support to MAIL to develop the Policy and Strategy for the Forestry and Range Management Sub-sectors, which has been endorsed by the cabinet and is legally binding.[8] CBNRM principles and approaches

[8] Council of Ministers Decision No. 26, 18/11/1384.

that have been so successful in other countries in the region lie at the core of this national policy, which addresses the wildlife sector, forests, and rangeland.

UNEP, which was instrumental in developing Afghanistan's first environment law,[9] has been assisting MAIL to develop new forest and rangeland laws. Other legislation—such as those involving protected areas, wildlife and hunting, and medicinal plants—also reflect the country's environmental policy and are in various stages of development, debate, and promulgation.[10]

All of these legislative instruments contain provisions to promote peacebuilding in the context of natural resource management. The draft rangeland law, for example, contains provisions for conflict resolution that are tailor-made for the ground-level realities of Afghanistan's feudal and tribal society. The draft law codifies the community or tribal council of elders (known as *jirgas* or *shuras*) as the preferred mechanism for community conflict resolution. Only in the event that such customary mechanisms fail is there a need to resort to the more formal court system and related justice mechanisms.

Other measures to encourage genuine community-based management of rangelands and to mitigate further conflict over access include the appointment of local custodians to manage private, community, and public rangelands. Custodians are identified as either owners (for private and community rangelands) or as adjacent communities that hold the strongest social, spatial, and historical rights to the rangeland. Where Kuchi nomads are able to demonstrate a long history of seasonal access to public rangelands, the law requires that their interests be upheld as far as possible and secured strictly through local agreement. Only where local—and then district and provincial—mediation fails, may Kuchi submit claims to a presidentially appointed commission to determine the outcome of a dispute.

PILOTING THE NEW APPROACH

Piloting a CBNRM approach has shown some success, although it is still too early to thoroughly assess the effectiveness of the program. One indication that CBNRM is being accepted on the national level is that MAIL earmarked funding from its core resources for a set of CBNRM projects to be piloted by UNEP.

Most pilot projects have taken place within communities that have already undergone a social mobilization process under the National Solidarity Program, a large-scale rural development program that has been implemented in all thirty-four provinces in Afghanistan and has socially mobilized more than 23,000 communities (MRRD n.d.). Through the program, communities have organized themselves into community development councils, often using the tribal council of elders mechanism referred to previously.

---

9 Environmental Law, Islamic Republic of Afghanistan, Official Gazette No. 912, January 25, 2007.

10 FAO and the Wildlife Conservation Society, among others, have played strong technical roles in the development of these statutory instruments.

On top of this foundation of social organization, technical assistance and seed money from international agencies have stimulated CBNRM projects in Afghanistan. Given the apparent success of UNEP's initial field-level, community-based natural resource projects,[11] additional projects are now under development, which, among other purposes, seek to test and pilot the approaches in the draft forest and rangeland legislation at the community level. A new participatory forest management project being implemented by FAO has a similar purpose.

Other pilot efforts have also fed into the policy and regulatory development framework. One noteworthy effort is a livelihoods project being implemented in the central highlands by FAO, which has assisted several hundred Hazara communities to clarify and entrench collective ownership of rangelands as part of establishing community-based rangeland rehabilitation and management. Resolution of disputes over boundaries and rights of access is the foundation upon which rights of use have been determined by the project partners. Another project—the Afghan Conservation Corps (ACC) implemented by the United Nations Office for Project Services—is a labor-intensive environmental restoration project employing, in particular, women and former combatants. Yet other examples are the successful upper watershed management projects implemented by Mercy Corps in collaboration with the European Commission.

Affected communities have responded positively to the pilot natural resource management approaches contained in the draft CBNRM legislation. Once communities have a sense of ownership (whether recognized by law or not) of the natural resources on which they depend to survive, they will fiercely guard the health of those natural resources.

Traditionally, the government has been seen as an adversary in matters of natural resource management rather than a partner. Now, with the objectives of communities and the government more closely aligned, a spirit of cooperation and trust is being fostered at the local level in these pilot areas. This spirit of cooperation will, in UNEP's view, contribute in the medium- and long-term toward peacebuilding at the community level, and encourage respect for rule of law and increased confidence in the government, as has occurred in the FAO rangeland pilot areas in the central highlands.

OBSTACLES TO IMPLEMENTING THE NEW POLICY APPROACH

In UNEP's view, the primary obstacles to implementing the new community-based policy approach can be grouped into six categories: weak political will, lack of capacity, institutional deadlock, ineffective bureaucratic processes, disputes over land tenure, and security issues.

---

[11] Monitoring and evaluation has been undertaken by UNEP, its donors, and an independent evaluation consultant, as well as the government.

Political will

Generally speaking, the senior management and political leaders of the key environmental and natural resource management institutions—namely MAIL, the Ministry of Energy and Water, and NEPA—are committed to their missions and embrace the big-picture road map needed to conserve the natural resource base and limit natural resource–related local conflicts, as articulated in the new policies adopted by the government. However, some of their colleagues—particularly middle-management policy makers—are skeptical, and remain entrenched in state-directed, protection-oriented, and top-down approaches. In a country facing such enormous institutional and capacity challenges, acceptance of the new decentralized, community-based approach (which necessarily involves the state's relinquishment, at least on paper, of some of its former power) has proceeded slowly, with many members of the old guard within middle management resistant to change.

Technical capacity

Notwithstanding the progress already made, government officials need stronger enforcement machinery to implement new laws and policies. They also need significant investment in human resources, especially at the provincial and district levels. The decades of conflict robbed many Afghans of a basic education in analytical and problem-solving skills. The lack of skills is an enormous obstacle, especially when the government is proposing an entirely new approach to natural resource management, an approach that depends on local skills and initiative.

Mindsets cannot be changed overnight. UNEP has adopted a step-by-step approach that has been successful overall, despite the two-steps-forward, one-step-back modus operandi that is the practical reality experienced by UNEP over the course of eleven years of working closely with government institutions. In August 2010, the European Union (EU), a major donor to UNEP's Afghanistan program, commissioned an independent, third-party, mid-term evaluation of the program, which concluded:

> The programme, now in Phase III (2008 to 2011), is managed by the UNEP Post-Conflict and Disaster Management Branch (PCDMB) with implementing partners including UNEP Regional Resource Centre for Asia and the Pacific (RRC.AP), the UNEP Regional office [*sic*] for Asia and the Pacific (ROAP), UNEP Global Resource Inventory Database and IUCN-The World Conservation Union. Phases I, II and III have been funded by the European Commission, the Government of Finland and the Global Environment Facility (through enabling activities). This has been a rare example of a programme managed in a "step-by step" [*sic*] strategic fashion and as such has been very effective (Delegation of the EU to Afghanistan 2010, 17).

Institutional turf

Vying for turf and power occurs all too often among government agencies and ministries, and bureaucratic infighting has certainly had a negative impact on the progress of Afghanistan's natural resource management.

Afghanistan's first national park, comprising the six stunningly beautiful interlinked high-altitude lakes and travertine dams at Band-e-Amir in the central highlands, should have been legally established in 2007. Due to gridlock between NEPA and MAIL, however, the park was only declared a provisional conservation area (a temporary legal status) in April 2009. Similarly, progress in the irrigation sector, which represents a lifeline for many Afghan farmers, has been delayed due to unresolved mandate disputes between the Ministry of Energy and Water, MAIL, and the Ministry of Rural Rehabilitation and Development, notwithstanding parliamentary approval of a new water law.

Historically, ministries have focused on their narrow sectors. Cooperative governance is a relatively new phenomenon in Afghanistan, as is an institutional culture of managing crosscutting issues like environment in a cooperative manner. This has been one of the hurdles to acceptance of NEPA's new coordinating, policy making, and regulatory role, which has affected the new agency's ability to function as intended. Line ministries like MAIL, the Ministry of Energy and Water, and the Ministry of Urban Development prefer to hold for themselves the environmental aspects of their ministerial prerogatives, and fear that any collaboration with NEPA would result in relinquishing control. In addition, given the nascent nature of NEPA, ministries do not have trust in the technical competence of the agency on such major national issues as transboundary sharing of water resources and the environmental impact of extractive industries. There is an issue of status as well: the line ministries are headed by a minister, whereas NEPA is headed by a director-general, although the director-general is a full member of the cabinet. Thus bureaucratic infighting prevents progress, causes disillusionment among the international partners, and reduces donor confidence in the government's ability to implement its natural resource mandates.

Legislative process

The Ministry of Justice is empowered to make substantive amendments to draft legislation to ensure a law does not conflict with the constitution, sharia law, or existing statutes. In practice, however, the ministry's Legislation Department (or Taqnin) sometimes overreaches its mandate and, in a quest to conserve nineteenth-century Afghan legislative norms, can destroy the spirit and letter of draft laws submitted to it for approval.

The setting of policy is the function of the line ministries, not officials in the Ministry of Justice. Once a policy is set, the officials in the Ministry of Justice must ensure it is implemented, regardless of whether the officials agree with the policy. The draft forest law, developed by MAIL with technical support from

UNEP and FAO, is a case in point. Despite pressure from MAIL and its partners, it took the Taqnin approximately eighteen months to consider the technical draft that reflects the new community-based management policy. Although the Taqnin had been included in all consultation exercises, which were unprecedented in their extent, its officials appeared not to have absorbed the spirit of the new policy approach. In a bid to remove all things foreign from the draft, the Taqnin deleted almost all of the community-based provisions of the law and instead introduced elements of a draft forestry law developed during the Taliban regime. The lawyers in the Taqnin did not recognize that the policy base of this Taliban law is extraction oriented and enshrines a centralized approach to forestry, which is in direct contradiction to the new policy approach endorsed by the Cabinet. The approach of the Taqnin dates back to 1880, when a centralized Afghan state was established, and its role was to be the conservative guardian of the traditional Afghan legislative process.

Land tenure

Land insecurity, in itself a source of conflict in Afghanistan, is also an obstacle to effective implementation of a community-based approach to natural resource management. In many post-conflict countries, land tenure is a complex and multifaceted issue. In a country that saw in the latter half of the twentieth century almost one-quarter of its population displaced and successive political regimes use land as leverage for political patronage and expediency, the issues are all the more acute, particularly in relation to access to natural resources (Newland and Patrick 2001).[12]

Insecurity and weak rule of law

Because portions of Afghanistan are under insurgent control and rule of law remains out of reach for many, the development of new policies and legislation is not necessarily the panacea it might be in more stable countries. Many Afghans resort to traditional justice mechanisms to resolve their disputes, with scant regard for formal justice institutions, and therefore for the principles enshrined in the new policies and legislation (USIP 2009). There are three parallel and overlapping legal systems operating in Afghanistan: customary, Islamic, and statutory. Where or when the state does not have the ability or the writ to enforce statutory law, either customary or Islamic law is applied, depending upon the nature of the case.[13] In terms of natural resources, customary laws are age-old, robust, and well tested. However, given the armed nature of the society and the ongoing

---

[12] For further discussion on post-conflict land tenure issues in Afghanistan, see Batson (2013) and Stanfield et al. (2013).

[13] For an analysis of the role of Islamic land systems in Afghanistan and other post-conflict countries, see Sait (2013).

conflict, justice is not necessarily available to poor and disadvantaged populations through any of the legal systems.

However, in due course, when peace and stability improve, and once successful CBNRM implementation models have been fine-tuned through pilot projects, it is hoped that the number and extent of such national resource–generated conflicts will significantly decrease.

LESSONS LEARNED BY UNEP IN THE DEVELOPMENT OF NATURAL RESOURCE MANAGEMENT CAPACITY

Afghanistan is a unique case. Nonetheless, some of the lessons learned are relevant to other post-conflict countries, particularly those that have been subjected to a long period of conflict and are in geostrategic locations, underdeveloped, land locked, poor, and natural resource dependent.

First, it is important that environmental and natural resource management concerns are integrated into the national planning, reconstruction, and development processes in the immediate post-conflict period. If these concerns are not on the initial agenda, it will be difficult to find an appropriate space at a later point when the agenda is full of competing priorities. To ensure that the concerns do not slip off the agenda, an in-country international partner is needed to champion the environment from the initial stabilization phase well into the final consolidation phase of peacebuilding. It is clear in the case of Afghanistan that had UNEP not taken up this cause, the environment and natural resources would have been excluded almost entirely from the development planning processes that culminated in the ANDS. It is also important that climate change be mainstreamed into a post-conflict development strategy, for the impacts of this global phenomenon on many developing countries are likely to be dire, and likely to contribute to conflict in the future. While considering the environment and natural resources as part of the initial post-conflict agenda, it is useful to apply a conflict analysis framework for natural resource management during the post-conflict intervention phase, to ensure that such considerations are taken into account (UNEP 2009a). In Afghanistan, an independent UNDP-UNEP project funded by the EU has been approved and is ready for implementation in the central highlands.

Another lesson learned from UNEP's experience in Afghanistan is that overlapping government mandates can cause significant obstacles to governance and peacebuilding at the local level. If possible, mandates should be clearly spelled out during the political processes that characterize the transition phase of peacebuilding. If political realities prevent this from occurring, cooperative relationships between the relevant government agencies should be strongly encouraged by international donors and partners. International partners should also support civil service reform, as interventions at this transitional stage can assist in ironing out issues relating to overlapping mandates.

In many post-conflict situations, there is often a dearth of qualified and experienced human resources at the community level. This is especially true in environmental and natural resource management, where the technical and scientific information have evolved quickly in the last few decades, leaving many of those trained in traditional natural resource disciplines, such as hydrology, insufficiently prepared to understand and address problems. In-country natural resource management initiatives are unlikely to succeed unless combined with sustained capacity building.

The third lesson UNEP learned in post-conflict Afghanistan was the importance of developing an effective methodology for natural resource management that is relevant to the context in which it is to be applied. Natural resource management cannot be considered in isolation from the broader political realities of the post-conflict situation. Without consistent and sustained progress in peace and security, and establishment of the rule of law, effective natural resource management and restoration of the natural resource base is unlikely to be achieved. The methodology that seems to work in Afghanistan is a combination of bottom-up and top-down approaches to natural resource management. Ideally, there will be a symbiotic relationship maintained between the two approaches, with each informing the implementation of the other.

The bottom-up approach—consisting of field-level, limited-scale, or pilot CBNRM projects—should be implemented early in the post-conflict period. The sooner local communities see improvement in their lives—including the ability to make decisions regarding natural resources that are essential to their livelihoods and welfare—the more likely they are to support the peacebuilding process and resist a return to conflict. There are often numerous small NGOs and other partners implementing local projects. Ideally, these should all be brought together under one broad policy umbrella in order to maximize impact. In reality, though, this cooperation is difficult to achieve. If possible, natural resource management partners should seek to piggyback their activities on any large-scale rural development programs implemented during the reconstruction phase, such as the National Solidarity Program in Afghanistan. Such a strategy assists in scaling up community-level natural resource management approaches without requiring a vast amount of financial or technical resources, or enormous logistical capability. Another factor to consider is reintegration of former combatants through the creation of job opportunities, including those in natural resource management. This was one of the primary aims of the ACC project implemented by the United Nations Office for Project Services beginning in 2003.

The focus of the top-down approach should be the development of capacity and management tools. In regard to capacity building, the initial focus should be on ensuring that functioning institutions exist, first at the central level and then at the provincial level. Once a functional institution exists, technical capacity needs to be developed. This can be achieved through a number of means—day-to-day mentoring, formal training workshops, country-specific technical manuals and handbooks in local languages, and study visits and trainings abroad. Training is needed not only on broad technical issues but also on how to utilize the institution's management tools, such as laws, standards, policies, databases, and planning instruments.

The combined lessons learned through both bottom-up and top-down approaches should feed into the development of natural resource management policies, laws, and other management instruments, and new policy approaches should be tested in the field on a pilot scale. With each level informing the other, the chances of successfully scaling up pilot activities are significantly increased.

CONCLUSION AND NEXT STEPS

Although significant and positive steps have been taken by the government and its international partners, security and development are still at risk in Afghanistan. The ongoing insurgency and the absence of rule of law in many parts of the country may well thwart all efforts to reverse the destructive trends that threaten the population's livelihoods and survival base. In addition, they may damage the notable progress made in regard to pilot community initiatives, development of environmental governance institutions, strength of natural resource management peacebuilding paradigms, and development of policy and regulatory frameworks.

The government of Afghanistan will need to shepherd its draft laws through the legislative pipelines, including ministerial review, and seek to protect the spirit and integrity of the new laws. Much wider and broader acceptance of the national natural resource management policy is required—including by the parliamentarians who will decide whether or not to enact the new laws and by ministerial officials who review and implement them.

Coordinated piloting of new CBNRM approaches in the field is important. Until the establishment of the Natural Resources Coordination Group in early 2009, there was little coordination and information sharing between the numerous NGOs, UN agencies, and other partners implementing field projects. Coordination is, however, now improving.

The recognition of natural resources as the cornerstone for success in the agriculture sector is a very important milestone. Given current donor interest, it is hoped that additional funding can be secured and allocated toward building the capacity of the natural resource management institutions, including MAIL, the Ministry of Energy and Water, and NEPA, and toward developing an Afghan-specific CBNRM model that can be scaled up by the government in due course. The Minister of Agriculture, Irrigation and Livestock's request for assistance in the development of a national program for community-based pasture management is a positive sign toward this goal.

The peacebuilding and conflict-prevention dimensions of natural resource management need to be explored in more detail in Afghanistan, particularly insofar as these relate or feed into larger-scale political and security concerns. Two encouraging steps in this regard include the goals set forth in Afghanistan's UN Development Assistance Framework for 2010 to 2013 and the field projects analyzed in the EU–funded study *Natural Resource Management and Peacebuilding in Afghanistan*—the latter of which explored the peacebuilding and conflict-prevention dimensions of natural resource management in select parts of the country.

REFERENCES

Adbi, M., S. Tani, N. Osman, S. I. Sadaat, and N. Jan. 2008. *Addressing land-based conflicts in Somaliland and Afghanistan*. Hargeisa, Somaliland: Academy for Peace and Development. www.globalprotectioncluster.org/_assets/files/field_protection_clusters/Somalia/files/HLP%20AoR/local_capacities_for_peace_2008_EN.pdf.

AFP (Agence France-Presse). 2007. Opium funding up to 40 percent of Afghan unrest: US general. October 18. http://afp.google.com/article/ALeqM5iAiVvESOhOSdE7Br-o6IUhcesdJQ.

Batson, D. E. 2013. Snow leopards and cadastres: Rare sightings in post-conflict Afghanistan. In *Land and post-conflict peacebuilding*, ed. J. Unruh and R. C. Williams. London: Earthscan.

Banzet, A., C. Bousquet, B. Boyer, A. de Geoffroy, F. Grünewald, D. Kauffmann, P. Pascal, and N. Rivière. 2007. *Linking relief, rehabilitation and development in Afghanistan to improve aid effectiveness: Main successes and challenges ahead*. Group URD. www.urd.org/IMG/pdf/LRRD_main_successes_challenges_URD.pdf.

Catarious, D. M., Jr., and A. Russell. 2012. Counternarcotics efforts and Afghan poppy farmers: Finding the right approach. In *High-value natural resources and post-conflict peacebuilding*, ed. P. Lujala and S. A. Rustad. London: Earthscan.

Dehgan, A., L. J. Palmer-Moloney, and M. Mirzaee. 2014. Water security and scarcity: Potential destabilization in western Afghanistan and Iranian Sistan and Baluchestan due to transboundary water conflicts. In *Water and post-conflict peacebuilding*, ed. E. Weinthal, J. Troell, and M. Nakayma. London: Earthscan.

Delegation of the EU (European Union) to Afghanistan. 2010. UNEP Capacity Building and *Institutional Development Programme: Phase III; Mid-term evaluation, final report*. On file with the authors.

El Saman, R. 2008. Linking formal and informal conflict resolution mechanisms in Afghanistan: A survey of the people's perspective. Kabul, Afghanistan: Sanayee Development Organization. http://library.fes.de/pdf-files/bueros/kabul/05655.pdf.

Jensen, D. 2012. Evaluating the impact of UNEP's post-conflict environmental assessments. In *Assessing and restoring natural resources in post-conflict peacebuilding*, ed. D. Jensen and S. Lonergan. London: Earthscan.

MAIL (Ministry of Agriculture, Irrigation and Livestock, Islamic Republic of Afghanistan). 2009. Umbrella document for the National Agriculture Development Framework. Kabul.

MRRD (Ministry of Rural Rehabilitation and Development, Islamic Republic of Afghanistan). n.d. National Solidarity Programme. http://nspafghanistan.org/.

NEPA (National Environmental Protection Agency, Islamic Republic of Afghanistan). 2008. National adaptation plan of action for climate change. Kabul.

NEPA (National Environmental Protection Agency, Islamic Republic of Afghanistan) and UNEP (United Nations Environment Programme). 2008. *Afghanistan's environment 2008*. Kabul. http://postconflict.unep.ch/publications/afg_soe_E.pdf.

Newland, K., and E. Patrick. 2001. A nation displaced: The world's largest refugee population. *WorldView* 14 (4).

Pain. A. 2012. The Janus nature of opium poppy: A view from the field. In *High-value natural resources and post-conflict peacebuilding*, ed. P. Lujala and S. A. Rustad. London: Earthscan.

Sait, S. 2013. Unexplored dimensions: Islamic land systems in Afghanistan, Indonesia, Iraq, and Somalia. In *Land and post-conflict peacebuilding*, ed. J. Unruh and R. C. Williams. London: Earthscan.

Sexton, R. 2012. *Natural resources and conflict in Afghanistan: Seven case studies; Major trends and implications for transition*. Kabul: Afghanistan Watch. www.watchafghanistan.org/files/Natural_Resources_and_Conflict_in_Afghanistan/Natural_Resources_and_Conflict_in_Afghanistan_Full_Report_English.pdf.

Stanfield, J. D., J. Brick Murtazashvili, M. Y. Safar, and A. Salam. 2013. Community documentation of land tenure and its contribution to state building in Afghanistan. In *Land and post-conflict peacebuilding*, ed. J. Unruh and R. C. Williams. London: Earthscan.

UN (United Nations) and GOIRA (Government of the Islamic Republic of Afghanistan). 2010. United Nations Development Assistance Framework: In support of the Afghanistan National Development Strategy, 2010–2013. Kabul. www.undp.org.af/publications/KeyDocuments/2011/July/UNDAF%20English.pdf.

UNAMA (United Nations Assistance Mission in Afghanistan). 2009. Weekly briefing report of the Political Affairs Unit. March 30. Gardez, Afghanistan.

UN (United Nations) Country Team in Afghanistan. 2013. *Natural resource management and peacebuilding in Afghanistan*. Nairobi, Kenya: United Nations Environment Programme. www.unep.org/disastersandconflicts/portals/155/countries/Afghanistan/pdf/UNEP_Afghanistan_NRM.pdf.

UNDP (United Nations Development Programme). 2013. *Human development report 2013—The rise of the South: Human progress in a diverse world*. New York. www.undp.org/content/dam/undp/library/corporate/HDR/2013GlobalHDR/English/HDR2013%20Report%20English.pdf.

UNEP (United Nations Environment Programme). 2003. *Post-conflict environmental assessment: Afghanistan*. Nairobi, Kenya. http://postconflict.unep.ch/publications/afghanistanpcajanuary2003.pdf.

UNEP 2009a. *From conflict to peacebuilding: The role of natural resources and the environment*. Nairobi, Kenya. http://postconflict.unep.ch/publications/pcdmb_policy_01.pdf.

———. 2009b. Recommended strategy for conflict resolution of competing high pasture claims of settled and nomadic communities in Afghanistan. Kabul, Afghanistan: United Nations Environment Programme. http://postconflict.unep.ch/publications/afg_tech/theme_01/afg_rangeland_EN.pdf.

———. 2012. Natural resources for peacebuilding and statebuilding: A toolkit for analysis and programming. Unpublished draft. Geneva, Switzerland.

U.S. DOD (United States Department of Defense). 2008. *Report on progress toward security and stability in Afghanistan*. Report to Congress in accordance with the 2008 National Defense Authorization Act (Section 1230, Public Law 110-181). June. Washington, D.C. www.defense.gov/pubs/Report_on_Progress_toward_Security_and_Stability_in_Afghanistan_1230.pdf.

USIP (United States Institute of Peace). 2009. Between the jirga and the judge: Alternative dispute resolution in southeastern Afghanistan. TLO Program Brief No. 1. Washington, D.C. www.usip.org/files/file/jirga_judge.pdf.

Waldman, M. 2008. Community peacebuilding in Afghanistan: The case for a national strategy. Oxford, UK: Oxfam International. www.comw.org/warreport/fulltext/0802waldman.pdf.

Building resilience in rural livelihood systems as an investment in conflict prevention

Blake D. Ratner

Post-conflict reconstruction focuses on restoring the capacity of key sectors of the national economy to meet the basic needs of the population in such areas as food production, transportation, and energy, as well as rebuilding or creating institutions for national and local governance. Planners and advisors engaged in such reconstruction efforts often underestimate the importance of building capacity to manage and adapt to future sources of conflict. Given the high rate of conflict recurrence in post-conflict societies, a critical challenge is finding ways not only to restore production systems but also to strengthen resilience to future stresses and shocks.

Particular attention needs to be placed on rural livelihoods, namely the ability of families to provide for themselves and sustain the rural economy, which in most post-conflict developing countries is heavily reliant on natural resources. A host of technical interventions—from improvements in water productivity in crop agriculture to integrated forestry and farming on sloping lands (agroforestry) to livestock health—can contribute to the productivity of rural livelihoods and strengthen people's ability to cope with future stresses and shocks, whether from natural disasters, climate variability, or civil unrest. But the initial success and especially the longer-term sustainability of such interventions depend on two key enabling factors: rights and governance.

The rights of rural people and governance systems that influence their livelihoods are intimately connected in numerous ways. This chapter highlights these connections and illustrates how they contribute to resilience in rural livelihoods, citing the experience of Cambodia in the years since the conclusion of the United

---

Blake D. Ratner is program leader for governance at the WorldFish Center, a member of the Consultative Group for International Agricultural Research, and served for five years as its regional director in Phnom Penh, Cambodia. Earlier, in 1995, he was a consultant to the World Bank on the design of its first rural development project developed with the post–United Nations Transitional Authority in Cambodia coalition government, focusing on agricultural rehabilitation, and in 1996, he participated in the Bank's first effort to assist with demobilization and reintegration of former combatants in the country.

Nations peacekeeping mission—the UN Transitional Authority in Cambodia (UNTAC)—in 1993.

The rights dimension considers not only rights of access to natural resources (such as land, water, fisheries, and forests), but also protections against abuses (for example, violence and discrimination against women or ethnic minorities) and rights of access to decision making and justice. The governance dimension focuses on the twin challenges of developing systems for equitable decision making across scales (from local to national and regional levels) and across economic sectors. Many of the most difficult cases of strengthening governance for rural livelihoods involve both cross-scale and cross-sectoral dynamics.

This chapter sketches three principles to reorient the design and implementation of livelihood interventions in post-conflict developing countries: (1) strengthen resilience of rural livelihoods as an essential investment toward reducing the risk of future conflict; (2) promote equitable governance to underpin resilience in rural livelihoods; and (3) reinforce rights of poor rural people and marginalized groups as an inseparable complement to improving governance.

The chapter opens with a brief background on official development assistance to Cambodia following the UNTAC peacekeeping mission, and the role of natural resources in post-conflict livelihood rehabilitation. It then examines the links between local rights and broader governance, highlighting examples from the forestry and fisheries sectors. The chapter then outlines the three principles to orient post-conflict livelihood interventions, and it closes with a discussion of some of the challenges to implementing these principles.

CAMBODIA'S TROUBLED PEACE

UNTAC, at the time of its operation (1992–1993), was the most ambitious, multifaceted, and costly UN peacekeeping mission ever mounted. Its tasks included disarming the former warring factions, ensuring law and order, reintegrating soldiers and combatants into civilian life, implementing a multiparty election, establishing institutions of democratic governance, and administering the government before the handover to newly elected authorities.

Measured against such expectations, most analysts deemed the mission a partial success (Brown and Timberman 1998). The Khmer Rouge resistance that had agreed to the peace accord later balked and resumed fighting sporadically through the mid-1990s, but there was no relapse into full civil war. Multiparty elections were institutionalized and to this day continue to be judged as fair, even amid perennial complaints about constraints on access to the media and intimidation of opposition parties. A broad and active nongovernmental organization (NGO) sector has taken root, though human rights organizations and grassroots activists frequently complain of intimidation and occasional violence directed at local leaders. The military successfully integrated former opposition fighters under a single command, but expectations for a withdrawal of military control and influence in natural resource sectors have not been met.

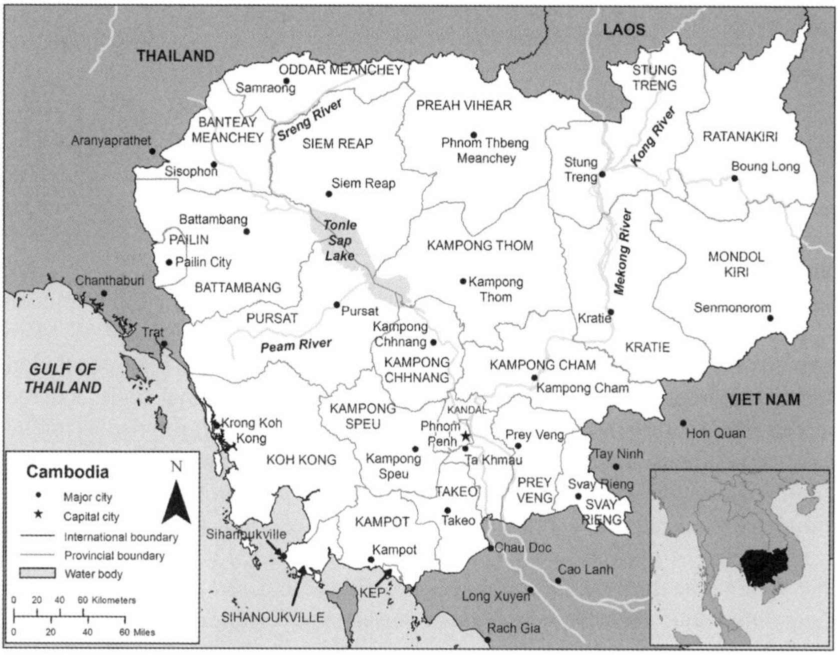

Indeed, the military has remained an active player in a post-conflict era of formally authorized large-scale resource concessions. The legacy of such large-scale commercial resource concessions—combined with a dysfunctional judicial system, the impunity of political and military elites, and the absence of alternative mechanisms for resolving disputes over access to natural resources—has significantly undermined efforts to rehabilitate rural livelihoods in the post-conflict period (Un and So 2009). The end of hostilities enabled a new, more intense phase of natural resource exploitation in the late 1990s and early 2000s, focused especially on forests. Logging operations remained a critical source of revenue for competing political groups, including former opposition factions that had been integrated into the coalition government (Le Billon 2000; Le Billon and Springer 2007). Despite a series of bans on logging and timber exports, commercial exploitation of the country's forest resources continued. The exploitation not only brought serious losses to the environment and local livelihoods but also undermined the significant international investment in promoting institutions of democratic governance in the country (Talbott 1998).

The international community has given significant attention to the links between resource exploitation and the financing of armed conflict. But it has shown less appreciation in the post-conflict period for the role of natural resource management in securing rural livelihoods, or the role of resource conflict in undermining livelihoods. Similarly, during and after the UNTAC years, international organizations focused on building support for human rights, particularly civil and political rights. By contrast, they have been much slower to understand how rights to food and livelihoods link to natural resource management and resource allocation.

LINKING RIGHTS AND RESOURCE GOVERNANCE

Today, the livelihoods of a large portion of Cambodia's rural population are directly affected by ongoing struggles for community rights to access, manage, and derive benefits from natural resources—principally land, water, fisheries, and forests. Such common-property resources are especially important in Cambodia as a source of livelihoods and income for the poor (World Bank 2006). Many proximate factors fuel this resource competition: a steadily growing population; shifts in market demand and increasing integration of regional trade; external shocks related to the global spike in prices of food and fuel; the rise in foreign direct investment in Cambodia's land, mineral, and agro-industrial sectors; and limited alternative livelihood opportunities in rural parts of the country. Yet the most important factors enabling persistent, low-level conflict are (1) a failure to secure rights of the rural poor broadly speaking, and (2) a governance system that systematically frustrates poor people's efforts to assert their rights, leaving them vulnerable when faced with more powerful adversaries making competing resource claims.

To its credit, the Cambodian government's development strategy does recognize the need to address the roots of vulnerability in rural livelihoods, including not only access to natural resources but also food security, health, nutrition, and education. A range of policy and legal reforms in recent years have reinforced the legal basis for community-based management in both forests and fisheries, alongside a more general decentralization and devolution of authority to provincial-, district-, and commune-level development committees. With a combination of technical assistance and finance, the official development aid community contributed substantially to these policy and legal reforms. While far from perfect, this policy and legal framework today includes a plentiful range of safeguards that should, in theory, be accessible to local communities for protecting and strengthening their resource rights.

The key obstacle, therefore, is not the recognition of local rights in policy or law but rather people's capacity to exercise these rights. In the forestry sector, for example, the revised Forestry Law of 2002, the Sub-Decree for Community Forest Management of 2003, and a set of implementing regulations on community forestry from 2006 now offer a clear route to establishing community-based management. Yet they have not erased the underlying dynamics of resource competition, nor have they yet fundamentally shifted the distribution of economic benefits from the forest sector.

Today, most forest-dependent communities throughout the country find themselves in tenuous territory. By law they are guaranteed a range of protections against resource expropriation and a route for formalizing community tenure over forests, but in practice these communities are highly vulnerable, and many are struggling to retain access to resources that are a pillar of their livelihoods (Ratner and Parnell 2011). Often, too, they face companies that have been granted tenure or resource extraction rights through a process that is completely opaque. In many instances, concessions for agro-industrial development or mineral exploration are valued because they offer an indirect route for companies to clear forested areas, or to establish tenure rights to the land itself, often in opposition to the claims of local communities.

The fisheries sector, similarly, has seen a steady strengthening of the legal basis for community management, following a dramatic series of reforms in 2000 and 2001 that reduced the area of commercial fishing lots in favor of community access in inland waters. While the early post-conflict years were characterized by intense competition over fisheries resources and de facto open access in the absence of a legal and institutional framework to replace the commercial lot system (Ratner 2006), this framework has now gradually been strengthened, in particular with the adoption in 2005 of the Sub-Decree on Community Fisheries Management, which provides communities a legal basis to establish authority to manage local fishing grounds.

Whereas in the past most fishing conflicts were local in character and stemmed from competition over fishing activity—between commercial fishing lot concessionaires and small-scale fishers, for instance, or among neighboring fishing villages—conflicts today are increasingly played out at larger scales and stem from intersectoral competition over resources. For example, there is competition over water when flood-recession fish refuges are pumped to irrigate crop agriculture; competition over infrastructure when reservoirs, irrigation systems, and roads block fish migration between Tonle Sap Lake, its tributaries, and the floodplain; and competition over land use when agricultural development schemes convert flooded forest zones to crop agriculture (So et al. 2013). Though community fishery organizations have so far had little voice in the matter, a major threat to the sustainability of inland fisheries is the proposed series of hydropower dams on the Mekong main stem that would alter the flood cycle and jeopardize migratory fish species, which constitute most of the commercial catch (Baran, Starr, and Kura 2007).

As these examples from forestry and fisheries illustrate, defending local livelihoods increasingly means resolving competing resource claims across sectors and scales. Community representatives find it exceedingly difficult to negotiate in such circumstances because they typically do not meet their competitors face-to-face, local authorities are either co-opted or feel disempowered to respond to community grievances involving higher-level decision makers, and the courts have systematically failed to provide impartial dispute resolution (UN 2008). As a result, villagers frequently resort to public protest, at significant personal risk for local community leaders, human rights organizers, and leaders of other domestic civil society organizations that lend support.

Where rights to legal recourse, protection from violence, and participation in public decision making are constrained, it is difficult to defend rights to food, livelihoods, and economic security. Likewise, to the extent that the governance system fails to offer sufficient channels to resolve competing resource claims equitably or hold decision makers publicly accountable for their actions in practice, no amount of legal reform will offer remedy.

It would be unfair to say that official development assistance in post-conflict Cambodia is responsible for these failures in rights and governance, for the country is a sovereign state and the country's current conditions have deep historical roots. Yet the international development community can do better. What lessons, then, should we draw from the experience with post-conflict investments in livelihood security in Cambodia?

POST-CONFLICT LIVELIHOOD INTERVENTIONS AND THE ROOTS OF RESILIENCE: THREE PRINCIPLES FOR ACTION

Three principles should orient the design and implementation of livelihood interventions in post-conflict developing countries:

1. Strengthen resilience of rural livelihoods as an essential investment in reducing the risk of future conflict.
2. Promote equitable governance to underpin resilience in rural livelihoods.
3. Reinforce rights of poor rural people and marginalized groups as a complement to improving governance.

These linkages are examined below.

Strengthen resilience of rural livelihoods to reduce the risk of future conflict

Resilience is defined as the capacity of social-ecological systems to recover from shocks and stresses while retaining key functions (Folke et al. 2005). It applies to the capacity to recover from natural disasters (a shock), long-term trends such as climate variability (a stress), as well as social dynamics including population displacement due to conflict (a shock) or gradually increasing resource competition (a stress). Critically, the social and ecological components of the system are seen as parts of a whole—such that, for example, the capacity of a fishery to provide for the nutritional needs of nearby communities (a key function) depends on the status and productivity of the resource itself, as well as the social institutions that govern who has access to the resource and with what attendant responsibilities.

Livelihood investments should aim to strengthen resilience of rural communities and the resource systems on which they depend. Social-ecological resilience is not a predetermined set of scientific criteria (Anderies, Walker, and Kinzig 2006; Andrew et al. 2007). Rather, it is an organizing principle for describing the parameters of a social-ecological system and engaging in stakeholder-driven deliberation to define locally relevant outcomes. In other words, it is a way of structuring conversations about the future that pays particular attention to risk—both social and ecological—and the capacity to adapt in the face of such risks.

Development interventions seeking improvements in, for instance, the management of forests, fisheries, or water for crop agriculture need to consider not only technical aspects such as economic efficiency or productivity, but also how such interventions contribute to adaptive capacity in the system. Community-based resource management institutions established for one purpose may offer additional benefits as a source of mutual support and resilience in times of stress. A case in point is Nepal, where community forest user groups sustained livelihoods and prevented the further spread of conflict when other elements of the rural economy were disrupted (Sanio and Chapagain 2012).

Promote equitable governance to underpin resilience in rural livelihoods

Much of the research on the institutional aspects of resilience has focused on the characteristics of local resource management institutions that enable self-organization, learning, and adaptation.[1] Less emphasis has been paid to the broader governance frameworks that can encourage or discourage the emergence of such local institutions, and which influence how effectively competing claims on resources can be managed across classes of resource users, across sectors, and across geographic scales.

Several recent contributions to the literature on social-ecological systems have begun to address this gap by proposing desirable characteristics of decision-making structures and processes that support or manage resilience. For example, Louis Lebel and colleagues propose three positive attributes of governance: (1) participation and deliberation in building trust and common understanding about potential courses of collective action, (2) polycentric and multilayered institutions as enablers of decision making that adapt to social and ecological change, and (3) accountability of public authorities in arriving at socially equitable outcomes (Lebel et al. 2006). Critically, each of the three describes attributes of governance in practice—which, as Cambodia's experience highlights, may vary greatly from the descriptions of decision-making or dispute resolution processes provided in policy or law.

Post-conflict development assistance therefore needs to focus early and often on promoting governance systems to identify, prevent, mitigate, and resolve resource conflicts equitably across sectors and scales, and to reinforce social accountability. Often, as has been the case in Cambodia, sectoral investments in agriculture and natural resource management are not linked closely to more cross cutting investments in public sector reform, judicial reform, decentralization,

[1] See, for example, Meinzen-Dick and Pradhan (2015); Berkes (2005).

civil society capacity development, or anticorruption efforts—thus missing opportunities for synergy that could reinforce good governance in practice.

Typically, linking resource management and governance also means engaging with civil society actors, which can push development assistance beyond the comfort zone of technical responses to identified needs and requires a strong appreciation of a country's social and political dynamics. The Philippine Environmental Governance (EcoGov) Project is exceptional in this regard because it focused explicitly on strengthening interagency, cross-sectoral relationships, and created a platform for engaging marginalized groups in joint forest and coastal zone management.[2]

Recognize that improvements to rights and governance are interdependent

In Cambodia, human rights organizations and civil society networks brought resource conflicts into the public spotlight by publicizing cases of villagers who suffered violence and intimidation or who had unwittingly signed over their resource rights to developers. In the fisheries sector, public attention toward violent attacks by armed guards of commercial fishing lots on local fishers in the late 1990s and community mobilization demanding increased access to fishing grounds helped build pressure for subsequent reforms (Ratner 2004, 2006). More recently, human rights organizations have raised the profile of land tenure conflicts and forest access rights. Many conservation and community development organizations, by contrast, have shied away from addressing resource-based conflicts out of a concern for jeopardizing their apolitical status or undermining progress on site-specific projects (Ratner and Parnell 2011).

In designing and implementing post-conflict development assistance, reinforcing local rights should be understood as an essential complement to the work of strengthening equitable systems of governance, as one cannot fully succeed without the other. For poor and marginalized groups whose livelihoods are most at risk when conflict threatens to destabilize rural economies and food production systems, development assistance should focus not only on securing their resource-access rights, but also on associated rights to access information on development planning, to participate in decision making on plans that affect them, to organize and communicate their interests publicly without fear of retribution, and to access justice through the courts and other conflict-resolution channels (WRI 2003).

Violence or the threat of violence against vulnerable or vocal groups needs to be addressed squarely as a fundamental obstacle to improvements in the broader

---

2 For a discussion of the EcoGov Project, see Cynthia Brady, Oliver Agoncillo, Maria Zita Butardo-Toribio, Buenaventura Dolom, and Casimiro V. Olvida, "Improving Natural Resource Governance and Building Peace and Stability in Mindanao, Philippines," in this book.

suite of rights. Similarly, where women and ethnic or religious minorities face systemic barriers to exercising their rights, whether by law or cultural practice, overcoming these barriers should be an explicit goal of development assistance. Sometimes official recognition of such rights can itself be a major component of peacemaking; the Guatemalan peace accords, for example, recognized indigenous mechanisms of dispute resolution as a legitimate system of justice in parallel to the courts (Buvollen 2002). In many instances, overcoming such barriers also entails targeted efforts at building awareness and capacity so that vulnerable groups are better able to exercise their rights in practice.

PUTTING THE PRINCIPLES INTO PRACTICE

If applied consistently, the principles outlined above would lead to fundamental shifts in post-conflict development assistance. Some might argue that there is nothing new here: peacemaking and post-conflict reconstruction efforts already routinely include elements addressing rural livelihoods, public-sector institution building, democratization, and other aspects of governance, and they often include efforts to build the capacity of civil society and buttress the rights of certain marginalized groups as a part of reconciliation efforts. Yet the linkages among such efforts are often weak, and their combined effectiveness is reduced as a result.

Making these links in a sustained way need not depend on the initiative of individual community development organizers, rights advocates, or grassroots leaders alone. Development professionals also have a responsibility to attend to the broader context of governance and rights that conditions the success of more narrowly focused rural livelihood interventions. What are some of the obstacles to achieving this, and how can they be addressed?

One obstacle is a lack of tools to guide investments in natural resource management and livelihood rehabilitation in post-conflict situations. Professionals dispatched from international agencies to plan such investments often have little sense of how the social, cultural, and political dimensions of a country's recent conflict affect current options and risks. Much post-conflict official development assistance remains rooted conceptually in post-World War II reconstruction efforts in Europe, with an emphasis on rebuilding physical infrastructure and reconstituting the institutions of national government. While these goals remain important, today's development professionals typically confront a more nuanced set of challenges caused by tensions at the subnational level, and need to be alert to how decisions about natural resource allocation or access can aggravate inequalities and grievances.

Reviews of experience by the World Bank and United Nations Environment Programme (UNEP) highlight these complexities and offer guidance on how to integrate principles of equity and adaptive capacity when addressing the role of natural resource management in post-conflict assessment and development planning (Ruckstuhl 2009; Conca and Wallace 2012; Jensen 2012). This guidance includes ensuring that livelihood opportunities supported through development investments provide equal access to different socioeconomic groups, investing in community-based management institutions to help rebuild norms of trust and collective action, using independent advisory groups to support project implementation and monitoring, and supporting collaborative knowledge development and learning across diverse groups of resource users (Ruckstuhl 2009).

But tools for assessing the risks and opportunities for natural resource management in war-torn societies remain very basic. The resilience perspective can make a vital contribution to conflict assessment because it focuses on the capacity of social-ecological systems to adapt and reorganize in the face of shocks. This focus would include approaches to better measure vulnerability and to identify governance interventions to minimize social exclusion in natural resource management and use (Adger 2006). It would also provide tools to assess the dynamics of transitions in resource management regimes (Olsson et al. 2006), and guidance drawn from comparative analysis on the factors that influence how resource management institutions reorganize after crises.

A second obstacle is sectoral specialization that tends to divide groups working on different aspects of the linked challenges of improving natural resource management, rebuilding livelihoods, and securing improvements in rights and governance. While technical assistance on legal and institutional reform and capacity building for government agencies may address land and other natural resource issues, it is still relatively rare to find significant official aid investments that link those issues with support to domestic human rights organizations, advocacy groups, and independent media, or that draw systematically on local experiences to generate lessons for national policy. In Cambodia, the Program on Rights and Justice managed by the East-West Institute (and financed by the U.S. Agency for International Development) provides an example of how targeted support to a spectrum of local NGOs and community groups working on human rights protection, land rights, indigenous peoples' rights, forest and water management, and community development can help build linkages that increase the voice and effectiveness of all stakeholders. With such links, these groups have successfully lobbied, for example, for intervention of national policy officials in support of indigenous rights to communal land tenure as recognized by law but frequently ignored in practice (Ratner and Parnell 2011).

Better in-country coordination among international NGOs working, often separately, in support of human rights, rural development, and environmental protection can also improve their effectiveness in both policy dialogue and field-level interventions. Policy dialogue can be facilitated by umbrella organizations, a role played in Cambodia by the NGO Forum, which draws on the expertise of its members to ensure that a consolidated set of analyses and recommendations on development policy and investment priorities—from addressing land conflicts to combating corruption and protecting women's rights—are debated regularly at the high-profile consultative group meeting of major donors. At the local level, site-specific or sector-specific interventions for environmental and natural resource management or conservation too often set up parallel institutional structures rather than investing in local governance (Ribot 2007). Particular attention is needed to ensure that development interventions strengthen the ability of communities to engage with and draw appropriate services from local government, and strengthen the capacity of local government to provide such services in turn.

A third obstacle to linking efforts at livelihood rehabilitation, environmental management, rights, and governance in the post-conflict situation is the interface between development assistance and private investment. As Cambodia's experience demonstrates, a host of well-intentioned efforts aimed at securing land tenure for rural households and communities, piloting and mainstreaming devolution of authority for development planning and natural resource management, and building capacity for an independent judiciary can be quickly undermined by government decisions to grant large-scale private concessions for logging, agro-industry, mining, or hydropower. Not that such schemes are universally unwarranted—some may deliver justifiable benefits—but far too often they circumvent safeguards meant to ensure informed, public deliberation over such weighty development choices.

The pressure on government officials to sign off on investment schemes that undermine local livelihoods can be tremendous. They may have an opportunity for corrupt financial gain. They also face political pressure, imbalances in the information available to them, and investment evaluation processes that typically focus on economic criteria with little assessment of the risks of exacerbating intergroup inequalities and triggering local conflict. The forest sector in Cambodia is a case in point, where a scramble for timber in the mid- and late-1990s caused extreme rates of forest loss. When the World Bank began to engage in forest sector reform, it focused initially on economic efficiency, aiming to improve official revenue capture by tightening regulation of timber harvesting. Gradually, the dialogue among donors broadened, highlighting the role of forest crimes in fueling corruption, spawning violence, and destabilizing rural communities and their livelihoods. The environmental watchdog group Global Witness played a critical role in bringing forward evidence of these links, and the heightened media attention aided the World Bank's efforts to build a broad coalition of donors to advocate for and invest in forest sector reform.

The past two decades have seen important advances in standards set by the World Bank and other major aid agencies for environmental and social safeguards, requirements for public review, and opportunities for civil society engagement in the infrastructure projects the agencies finance directly. But such rules do not apply to private investments in infrastructure or mineral extraction, nor to agricultural land grabs of the sort that toppled the government of Madagascar (Kugelman and Levenstein 2009). One key in anticipating and avoiding the destabilizing outcomes of large-scale private investment in the natural resource sectors is to broaden the dialogue from (largely economic) costs and benefits to encompass an analysis and deliberation over rights and risks. The extended multistakeholder consultation process organized by the World Commission on Dams (2000) produced guidance on such a rights-and-risks approach. It offers essential applications in addressing large-scale investments in other sectors as well, where there is an important need to ask how a range of development options will serve various social goals, and how they will differentially affect the vulnerabilities and opportunities for different social groups.

CONCLUSIONS

The principles offered here are a sketch rather than an action agenda because their main value lies in orienting development practitioners toward a consistent set of questions:

- To what extent are we designing interventions that truly build resilience in the socioecological systems that sustain rural people's livelihoods, as opposed to introducing technical or institutional innovations that will be easily disrupted when conditions change or, worse, that accentuate intergroup inequalities?
- To what extent are we strengthening mechanisms for equitable governance as part and parcel of rural development and environmental management programs?
- To what extent are we reinforcing the ability of poor and marginalized groups not only to participate in development programs but also to exercise their broader social, political, and economic rights?

Periodically reflecting on these questions in the countries where we work, adapting our efforts in response, and sharing the lessons we learn will help foster a shift toward a culture of development assistance more suited to the challenges of post-conflict rehabilitation and conflict prevention.

REFERENCES

Adger, W. N. 2006. Vulnerability. *Global Environmental Change* 16 (3): 268–281.

Anderies, J., B. Walker, and A. Kinzig. 2006. Fifteen weddings and a funeral: Case studies and resilience-based management. *Ecology and Society* 11 (1): 386–397. www.ecologyandsociety.org/vol11/iss1/art21/.

Andrew, N., C. Béne, S. J. Hall, E. H. Allison, S. Heck, and B. D. Ratner. 2007. Diagnosis and management of small-scale fisheries in developing countries. *Fish and Fisheries* 8 (3): 227–240.

Baran, E., P. Starr, and Y. Kura. 2007. Influence of built structures on Tonle Sap fisheries. Phnom Penh: Cambodia National Mekong Committee and WorldFish Center.

Berkes, F. 2005. Commons theory for marine resource management in a complex world. *SENRI Ecological Studies* 67:13–31.

Brown, F. Z., and D. G. Timberman, eds. 1998. *Cambodia and the international community: The quest for peace, development, and democracy*. New York: Asia Society.

Buvollen, H. P. 2002. Identifying cultural and legal barriers to justice in Guatemala. Paper presented at the international workshop "UNDP's Role in Access to Justice," Oslo, Norway, March 3–6.

Conca, K., and J. Wallace. 2012. Environment and peacebuilding in war-torn societies: Lessons from the UN Environment Programme's experience with postconflict assessment. In *Assessing and restoring natural resources in post-conflict peacebuilding*, ed. D. Jensen and S. Lonergan. London: Earthscan.

Folke, C., T. Hahn, P. Olsson, and J. Norberg. 2005. Adaptive governance of social-ecological systems. *Annual Review of Environment and Resources* 30:441–473.

Jensen, D. 2012. Evaluating the impact of UNEP's post-conflict environmental assessments. In *Assessing and restoring natural resources in post-conflict peacebuilding*, ed. D. Jensen and S. Lonergan. London: Earthscan.

Kugelman, M., and S. Levenstein, eds. 2009. *Land grab? The race for the world's farmland.* Washington, D.C.: Woodrow Wilson International Center for Scholars.

Lebel, L., J. M. Anderies, B. Campbell, C. Folke, S. Hatfield-Dodds, T. P. Hughes, and J. Wilson. 2006. Governance and the capacity to manage resilience in regional social-ecological systems. *Ecology and Society* 11 (1): 230–250. www.ecologyandsociety.org/vol11/iss1/art19/.

Le Billon, P. 2000. The political ecology of transition in Cambodia 1989–1999: War, peace and forest exploitation. *Development and Change* 31 (4): 785–805.

Le Billon, P., and S. Springer. 2007. Between war and peace: Violence and accommodation in the Cambodian logging sector. In *Extreme conflict and tropical forests*, ed. W. de Jong, D. Donovan, and K. Abe. Amsterdam: Springer Netherlands.

Meinzen-Dick, R. S., and R. Pradhan. 2015. Legal pluralism in post-conflict environments: Problem or opportunity for natural resource management? In *Governance, natural resources, and post-conflict peacebuilding*, ed. C. Bruch, C. Muffett, and S. S. Nichols. London: Earthscan.

Olsson, P., L. H. Gunderson, S. R. Carpenter, P. Ryan, L. Lebel, C. Folke, and C. S. Holling. 2006. Shooting the rapids: Navigating transitions to adaptive governance of social-ecological systems. *Society and Ecology* 11 (1): 1–21. www.ecologyandsociety.org/vol11/iss1/art18/.

Ratner, B. D. 2004. Environmental rights as a matter of survival. *Human Rights Dialogue* 2 (11): 6–7.

———. 2006. Community management by decree? Lessons from Cambodia's fisheries reform. *Society and Natural Resources* 19 (1): 79–86.

Ratner, B. D., and T. Parnell. 2011. Building coalitions across sectors and scales in Cambodia. In *Forests and people: Property, governance, and human rights*, ed. T. Sikor and J. Stahl. London: Earthscan / Resources for the Future.

Ribot, J. 2007. Representation, citizenship and the public domain in democratic decentralization. *Development* 53 (1): 43–59.

Ruckstuhl, S. 2009. *Renewable natural resources: Practical lessons for conflict-sensitive development.* Washington, D.C.: World Bank.

Sanio, T., and B. Chapagain. 2012. Local peace building and conflict transformation in Nepal through community forestry and forest user groups. In *High-value natural resources and post-conflict peacebuilding*, ed. P. Lujala and S. A. Rustad. London: Earthscan.

So, S., B. D. Ratner, K. Mam, and S. Kim. 2013. Conflict and collective action in Tonle Sap fisheries: Adapting institutions to support community livelihoods. CDRI Working Paper No. 49. Phnom Penh: Cambodia Development Resource Institute.

Talbott, K. 1998. Logging in Cambodia: Politics and plunder. In *Cambodia and the international community: The quest for peace, development, and democracy*, ed. F. Z. Brown and D. G. Timberman. New York: Asia Society.

UN (United Nations). 2008. Report of the Special Representative of the Secretary-General for Human Rights in Cambodia, Yash Ghai. United Nations General Assembly, Human Rights Council, February 29.

Un, K., and S. So. 2009. Politics of natural resource use in Cambodia. *Asian Affairs: An American Review* 36 (3): 123–138.

World Bank. 2006. *Halving poverty by 2015? Poverty assessment 2006*. Report No. 35213-KH. Phnom Penh, Cambodia.

World Commission on Dams. 2000. *Dams and development: A new framework for decision-making*. London: Earthscan.

WRI (World Resources Institute). 2003. *World resources 2002–2004. Decisions for the Earth: Balance, voice, and power.* Washington, D.C.: United Nations Development Programme, United Nations Environment Programme, World Bank, and World Resources Institute.

Improving natural resource governance and building peace and stability in Mindanao, Philippines

Cynthia Brady, Oliver Agoncillo, Maria Zita Butardo-Toribio, Buenaventura Dolom, and Casimiro V. Olvida

The culture of confrontation is gradually being replaced by one of dialogue and negotiation.

—Mayor Wilfredo Asoy, Municipality of Dinas, Zamboanga del Sur, Mindanao

The island of Mindanao has long been contested territory in the Philippines, beginning with Spanish colonization 400 years ago and continuing through the recent decades of conflict between the government of the Republic of the Philippines (GPH) and various rebel groups. For the last forty years, Muslim rebels in Mindanao—the Moro National Liberation Front (MNLF) and the break-away Moro Islamic Liberation Front (MILF)—have been waging a struggle for independence against the government.[1] Although the conflict between these groups and the GPH is often cast in ethnoreligious terms, in reality the unrest in Mindanao has been driven by a mix of injustice and poverty, political and clan rivalries,

---

Cynthia Brady is a senior conflict advisor with the Bureau for Democracy, Conflict and Humanitarian Assistance in the Office of Conflict Management and Mitigation of the U.S. Agency for International Development (USAID). Oliver Agoncillo is team leader of USAID/Philippines' Natural Resources and Biodiversity Program. Maria Zita Butardo-Toribio was a senior policy specialist of the USAID-funded Philippine Environmental Governance (EcoGov) Project. Buenaventura Dolom was forest sector team leader of the EcoGov Project. Casimiro V. Olvida was the uplands and governance specialist for the EcoGov Project. The authors acknowledge the contributions of Ernesto S. Guiang, former chief of party of the EcoGov Project, as well as EcoGov Project consultants Marie Antonette Juinio-Meñez, Maria Fe Portigo, Trina Galido-Isorena, and Edward Iblah Lim. The authors' views expressed in this publication do not necessarily reflect the views of USAID or the U.S. government.

This chapter was initially drafted before the EcoGov Project ended in 2011. The chapter is based on interviews with EcoGov Project personnel, the authors' field experiences, a review of EcoGov Project technical reports and other project materials, and extensive background research about the conflict in Mindanao. The chapter was developed with support from the Center for Global Partnership of the Japan Foundation.

[1] Filipino Muslims, who make up only approximately 5 percent of the total population of the Philippines, are concentrated in the south, central, and western parts of Mindanao (U.S. DOS 2004).

and competition for land and natural resources (Timberman 2003). The heart of the matter for many involved in the conflict has been the struggle for political and economic control over the land and resources necessary to sustain the lives and livelihoods of Mindanaoans.

Following years of negotiation, in 1996 the MNLF signed a final peace agreement with the GPH. Recognizing that an agreement alone would not bring lasting peace to Mindanao, the U.S. Agency for International Development (USAID) provided development assistance in support of the newly created Autonomous Region in Muslim Mindanao (ARMM). This support included investments in natural resource management as well as other sectors. Interventions in natural resource governance were critical to stabilization in post-conflict Mindanao for many reasons—from managing clientelistic politics, to ensuring a revenue base for the new ARMM institutions, to protecting cultural traditions. At the same time, the majority of the population is directly dependent on farming and fishing for their livelihoods and food security.

To increase understanding of the connection between natural resource management and conflict management, this chapter considers ten years of experience from the Philippine Environmental Governance (EcoGov) Project, a project funded by USAID.[2] The EcoGov Project has supported the efforts of local governments and communities in conflict-affected areas in Mindanao to improve the management of forest, coastal, and marine resources. Despite flaws in the 1996 peace agreement and its implementation, as well as the effects of continuing conflict between the GPH and the MILF and other armed groups present in Mindanao today, much can be learned from the experience of supporting improved governance of natural resources as a post-conflict stabilization, peacebuilding, and development tool.

This chapter begins with an explanation of the primary connections between land, natural resources, and conflict in Mindanao. It then provides some brief background on the EcoGov Project, discussing project objectives, implementation sites, and the project methodology and approach. This is followed by an in-depth analysis of two case studies from within the project: coastal resource management in Illana Bay, and forest and forestland management in Maasim in Sarangani Province. Together, these examples highlight the risks associated with sectoral development programs in unstable areas that lack an explicit focus on conflict-sensitive design and implementation. They also highlight key opportunities to effectively harness governance-oriented natural resource management and conservation interventions to proactively support conflict reduction and peacebuilding objectives.

Next the chapter reflects on the critical factors and variables affecting the EcoGov Project that directly influenced peace and security outcomes in Mindanao.

---

2 The EcoGov Project is a joint project of the GPH, through the Department of Environment and Natural Resources, and USAID, through its mission to the Philippines. Development Alternatives, Inc., is the project implementation contractor.

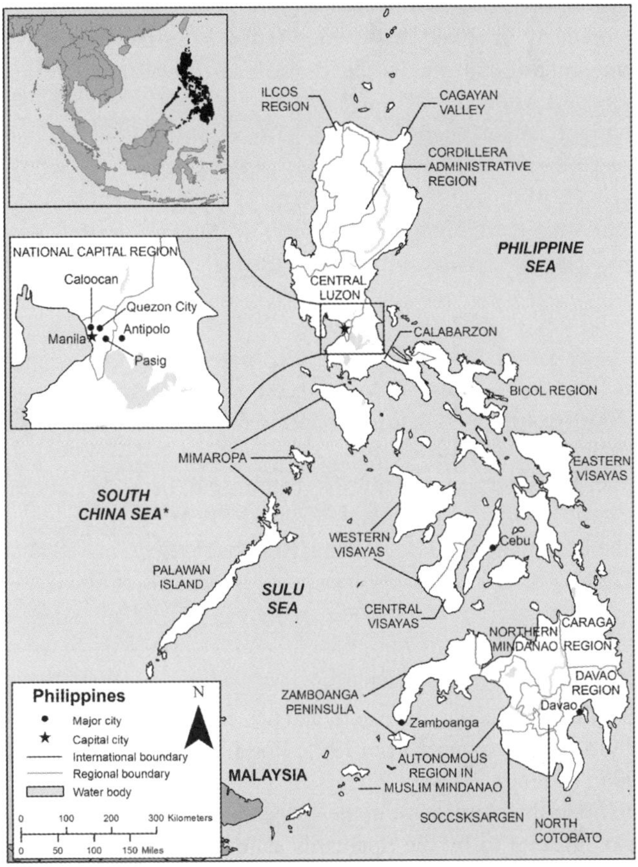

* South China Sea is also known as the West Philippine Sea.

This is followed by consideration of lessons learned from the project regarding the risks of environmental programming and the opportunities it creates for interacting constructively with the economic, social, and political dynamics of instability and conflict. Finally, the chapter concludes with general lessons from the EcoGov Project experience that can inform future efforts designed to connect environmental governance objectives with conflict prevention and stabilization outcomes.

RESOURCE-RELATED CONFLICTS IN MINDANAO

The conflict between the GPH and the Muslim rebel groups (the MNLF and the MILF) stems from the latter's decades-long quest for an independent homeland in the southern Philippines. The unrest has been stoked over time by the local Muslim communities' sense of marginalization from their ancestral land, lack of

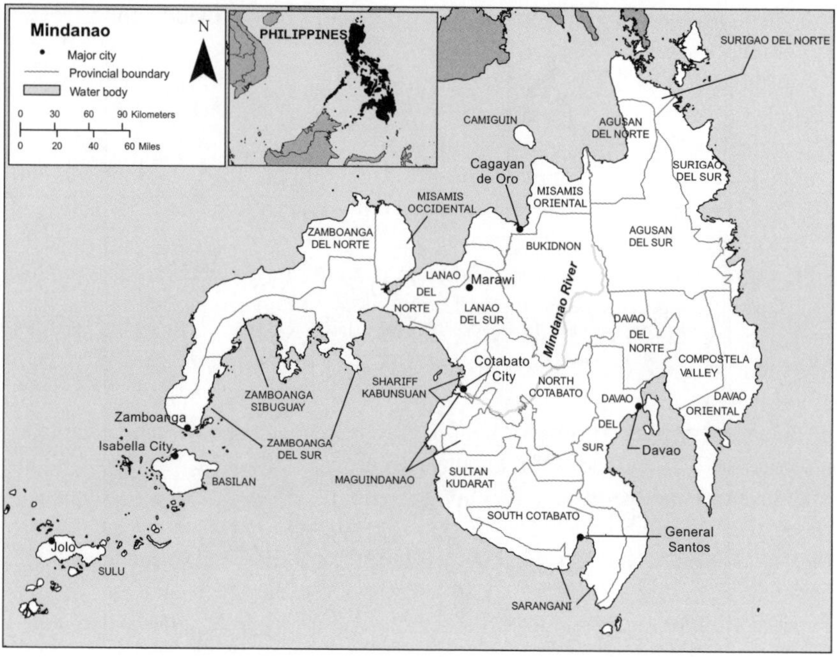

control over natural and economic assets, and perceived loss of political sovereignty and the right to self-governance (Tan 1995; Rodil 2004; Fianza 1994, 1999, 2004; Soriano 2006; Tuminez 2008).

Prior to Spanish colonization in the sixteenth century, the Muslim inhabitants of Mindanao, referred to by the Spaniards as *Moros*, had maintained their own traditional structures of political governance, recognizable territorial boundaries, and clear concepts of ownership and management of land and other resources (Lingga 2007; Quevedo 2003). However, during the Spanish and American colonial regimes (1521–1898 and 1898–1946, respectively), as well as during the post-independence period, various land laws and policies were established that created a new system of land tenure that disregarded customary rights and the traditional local concepts of inheritance rights, community usufruct rights, and the decision-making power of the nobility (*datu* system) (World Bank 2003). By undermining traditional institutions that governed indigenous land practices and entitlement systems (Soriano 2006), the legal changes meant that both Muslims and Lumads (non-Muslim indigenous groups) were increasingly removed from access to power and to decision making over economic resources.

The formation of the MNLF in the late 1960s was largely driven by frustration over centralized government control and government-sponsored settlement in Mindanao of Christians from other parts of the Philippines. The settlement program was perceived by Muslims and Lumads as making unavailable to them the major economic assets in Mindanao. In 1976, the MNLF signed a peace agreement, the Tripoli Agreement, with the GPH that provided for a cease-fire and the framework for the ARMM.

Although an autonomous government was in fact established for the ARMM, this failed to address Muslim grievances sufficiently. Dissatisfied with the state of affairs, the MILF formally split from the MNLF in the early 1980s and advocated a more Islamic identity–based approach to the struggle for independence. The MILF agenda includes establishment of a Bangsamoro homeland,[3] which is to be determined on the basis of traditional land claims (known in Philippine parlance as ancestral domain claims, which include not only land rights but also control over natural resources). The proposed boundaries remain a key point of disagreement between the MILF and MNLF.[4] In 1996, the MNLF signed a final peace agreement with the GPH, which provides that ARMM would have a legislative assembly, executive council, special regional security forces, and an economic and financial system. This agreement is currently under review, but peace talks between the GPH and the MILF continue unresolved today. The most contentious remaining substantive area for negotiation involves the concept of ancestral domain and the associated rights to natural resources.

In addition to the long-standing grievances of the MNLF and the MILF, economic development (for example, plantation development and mining) has contributed more recently to environmental degradation in Mindanao and added to economic displacement. This has caused a proliferation of local grievances in the conflict-affected areas (Umehara and Bautista 2004). Chronic uncertainty due to the sporadic and protracted nature of armed confrontation has also curtailed investment and further exacerbated the effects of poor natural resource management in the conflict-affected areas (World Bank 2003; Soriano 2006). Moreover, the Philippine regulatory regime on the environment and natural resource management suffers from critical weaknesses that affect the Mindanaoan context, including policy ambiguity, overlap of institutions and authorities, poor accommodation of the diversity of cultures, weak enforcement, and unfunded mandates.

---

[3] *Bangsamoro,* or Moroland, describes the ancestral homeland of the Moro people. Bangsamoro was originally home to the Muslim sultanates of Mindanao (such as Sulu and Maguindanao). These sultanates resisted Spanish colonial rule and were therefore not fully integrated with the rest of the islands.

[4] "*Ancestral domain* refers to the Moros' demand for territory that will constitute a Bangsamoro homeland, sufficient control over economic resources in that territory, and a structure of governance that will allow Moros to govern themselves in ways that are consonant with their culture and with minimal interference from Manila" (Tuminez 2005, 2; emphasis added). More precisely, under the Philippines' 1997 Indigenous Peoples Rights Act, the term *ancestral domain* refers to all areas belonging to indigenous cultural communities (ICCs) and indigenous peoples (IPs), including lands, inland waters, coastal areas, and natural resources therein that are, according to the act, "held under a claim of ownership, occupied or possessed by ICCs/IPs, by themselves or through their ancestors, communally or individually since time immemorial, continuously to the present" (IPRA 8371, chap. 2, sec. 3(a)).

Together, these issues hinder effective environmental governance at both the national and local levels. In addition, conflicting interpretations and applications of laws (for example, the Indigenous Peoples Rights Act versus traditional Muslim land tenure concepts) have resulted in many unresolved conflicts over land use and competing land claims in resource-rich Mindanao. Thus, although historical and economic factors, many of which are related to land and natural resources, initially triggered the discontent, issues of power sharing, exclusionary democracy, and poor governance contributed significantly to the intensification of common grievances into collective violence (Soriano 2006).[5]

Ultimately, both the MNLF and MILF peace processes have failed to resolve the deep disunity among a diverse set of stakeholders, including ethnic groups, ideological groups, clans, traditional leaders, and local politicians. The ongoing violence has further aggravated divisions between mixed ethnoreligious communities and magnified local conflicts, such as competition over natural resources and interclan disputes, or *rido* (World Bank 2003).[6] Conflict with the national government has therefore engendered local conflict that must be addressed as well if there is to be sustainable peace in Mindanao.

THE PHILIPPINE ENVIRONMENTAL GOVERNANCE PROJECT

Since December 2001, the EcoGov Project has provided assistance on environment and natural resource management in Mindanao. After the 1996 GPH-MNLF peace agreement, the project was designed as a biodiversity-conservation effort that sought improved local and national environmental governance; improved management of forests and forestlands, coastal areas, and solid waste; and promotion of local government investment in sanitation facilities. Rather than reviewing all EcoGov Project sites,[7] this chapter focuses on project implementation in selected

---

5 Manual E. Valdehueza identifies poor governance as the modern root of conflict in Mindanao (Valdehueza 2009).

6 The concept of *rido*, or feuding, is central to understanding conflict in Mindanao. According to the Asia Foundation's seminal 2007 report (Torres 2007), rido is characterized by sporadic outbursts of retaliatory violence between families, kinship groups, or communities. It may be complicated by a society's sense of honor and shame. Although the triggers of conflict can range from petty offenses like theft and teasing to more serious crimes like murder, land disputes and political rivalries are the most common causes. Rido has wide implications for conflict in Mindanao primarily because of its tendency to become entangled with separatist conflict and other forms of armed violence.

7 The EcoGov Project works with more than 150 local government units in northern Luzon (the northernmost island group), central Visayas, and Mindanao. It works in three conflict-affected provinces in western Mindanao (Basilan, Zamboanga del Sur, and Zamboanga Sibugay) and nine in southern and central Mindanao (Davao del Norte, Davao del Sur, Lanao del Sur, Maguindanao, North Cotabato, Sarangani, Shariff Kabunsuan, South Cotabato, and Sultan Kudarat). Engagement with the local government units is based on demand; priority during the early years of the program was given to conflict-affected areas in Mindanao.

conflict-affected localities in Mindanao where poor governance, resource-based competition, lack of community solidarity, lawlessness, and violence have consistently threatened to undermine not only environmental goals and overall stability in Mindanao, but also the fundamental objectives of the peace agreement.

The EcoGov Project's assistance in these areas coincides with the full continuum of conflict, from the transition and consolidation phases of peacebuilding in relation to the GPH-MNLF conflict, to the ongoing discontent of the MNLF, to the renewed fighting in 2008–2009 and the stalled and then renewed peace talks between the GPH and the MILF.[8] The EcoGov Project experience demonstrates that despite challenging circumstances, improved environmental governance and the implementation processes it employs provide an important entry point for addressing conflict and building peace. By improving natural resource management, the EcoGov Project is helping to address the major economic, political, and sociocultural sources of unrest in Mindanao. Projects have provided opportunities for competing groups (Muslims, Lumads, Christians, rebels, and the GPH) to work together toward a common goal and to find neutral spaces for dialogue, and have offered them a reason to set aside political, ethnic, and economic differences in order to participate constructively and collaboratively in decision making and project implementation.

At the outset, a major challenge for the EcoGov Project was determining how to engage various unorganized and often polarized community stakeholders in the collaborative envisioning, planning, and implementation of natural resource management activities. The project needed to reorient the dominant paradigm of competition and conflict into one of mutual understanding and common objectives, and to create connections between individuals, communities, and government offices at different levels so that the various dimensions of conflict would be addressed sustainably. This was not an easy task.

With respect to institutional interventions, the EcoGov Project assisted local government units (LGUs) and sought to change the attitudes and behaviors of individuals within the LGUs in order to support organizational change. The EcoGov Project's technical assistance focused on developing local government knowledge and organizational capacity to address threats to the environment. It also sought to improve transparency, accountability, and public participation in natural resource management. An intensive information, education, and communication campaign was accompanied by a broader social marketing strategy. Together, the two tracks built a foundation for larger relational change in diverse communities.

Local-level change was reinforced through the enactment of local support ordinances and through the formation and strengthening of local organizations and networks of organizations, as well as local governments. For example, the

[8] Negotiations between the GPH and the MILF broke down in August 2008 as a result of the failure to sign the Memorandum of Agreement on Ancestral Domain but resumed in December 2009.

EcoGov Project used participatory monitoring and evaluation tools that track specific sector improvements and progress in environmental governance, such as the Guided Self-Assessment on the State of Local Environmental Governance, the Marine Protected Area Management Effectiveness Rating, State of the Coast reporting, and an annual forest and forestland tenure assessment, which is part of forest land use planning. One of the governance indicators monitored was the LGUs' adoption of local mechanisms for conflict mitigation. Local stakeholders conducted the assessments and reported on the findings, and this provided a platform for both discussion and problem solving among the stakeholders themselves. The process clearly linked institutional change to public attitudes and perceptions.

The approach taken by the EcoGov Project is consistent with the findings of CDA's Reflecting on Peace Practice Project (RPP) concerning effective peacebuilding strategies.[9] RPP found that two kinds of linkages were particularly critical to influencing "peace writ large" or a broader peace. First, changes sought at the individual or personal level must be connected with action at the institutional or sociopolitical level (that is, individual attitudinal changes must be reinforced by corresponding institutional and structural change to be sustainable). Second, interventions must simultaneously target more people (broad involvement), key people (individuals and groups central to the peace or conflict context), and activities to engage both groups must be strategically linked. While not intentionally designed to apply RPP findings, the EcoGov Project experience in fact reinforces those RPP conclusions about cumulative impact.

Although these strategies, in the case of the EcoGov Project, were employed with environmental and natural resource governance objectives in mind, the processes used in project implementation have contributed both directly and indirectly to peacebuilding efforts in Mindanao. The case studies that follow provide an in-depth examination of these issues.

Case study 1: Coastal resource governance and stabilization

Illana Bay is an important fishing area for four conflict-affected regions in southwestern Mindanao, including the province of Zamboanga del Sur (see figure 1). It is also among the most biodiverse bodies of water in the Philippines. However, it has declined considerably as a resource base over the years, due to factors such as commercial fishpond development (which decimated once-vast mangrove areas and rich fishing habitats), rapid population growth, upland deforestation, unregulated access to coastal and fishery resources, and harmful and illegal fishing methods. In the 1960s and 1970s, at the height of natural resource exploitation in the area, a few wealthy and influential families were the primary beneficiaries of the resources. This caused deep resentment among the local Muslim communities.

---

[9] For further information on CDA and RPP, see www.cdainc.com/cdawww/project_profile.php?pid=RPP&pname=Reflecting%20on%20Peace%20Practice.

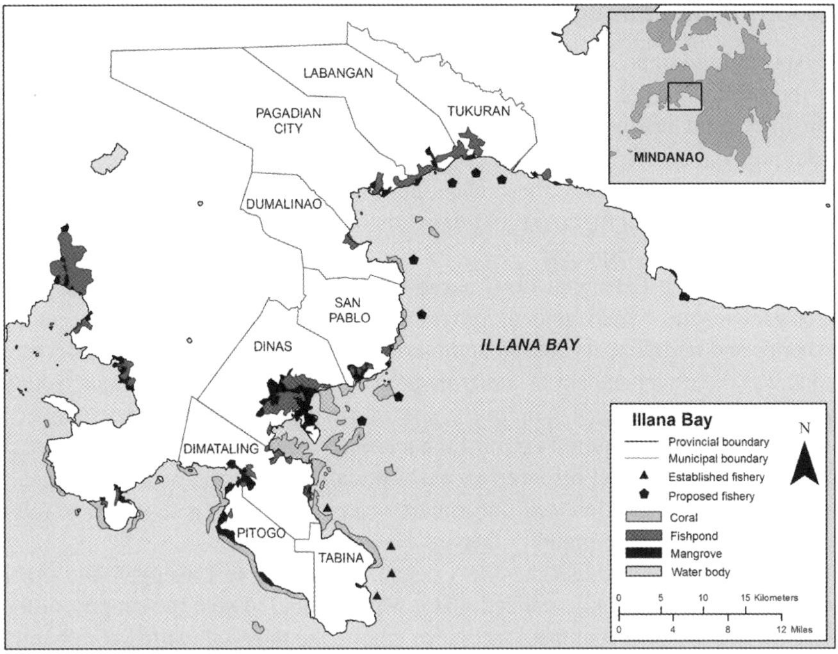

Figure 1. Fisheries of Illana Bay, Mindanao, Philippines
Source: USAID (2004).

Muslim opposition to outsiders' exploitation of resources in what they deemed their homeland became a battle cry of the liberation movement in the 1960s and prevailed until at least the 1980s.

Due to decades of GPH conflict with the MNLF and MILF as well as frequent clashes between warring clans and families, social relations in the area have become strained. There is a low level of trust between the area's diverse inhabitants, who include Muslims, Lumads, Christians, and members of other groups. Decades of conflict have also impeded good governance and economic and social development. As the MNLF has become disillusioned because of the incomplete implementation of the 1996 peace agreement, the MILF has continued to grow in number and influence among Muslim communities in the area.

Faced with increased competition over declining coastal and marine resources, the municipalities of Dimataling, Dinas, Dumalinao, Labangan, Pagadian City, San Pablo, Tabina, and Tukuran and the provincial government of Zamboanga del Sur decided to form the Illana Bay Regional Alliance to conserve, develop, and properly manage their shared coastlines. While the EcoGov Project's assistance to the alliance is primarily directed at improving coastal resource management, it is showing promising results in terms of strengthening social cohesion, improving intercultural understanding, and building collaborative capacity. These linkages are described in the following two examples.

Resolving rido through the establishment of a marine protected area

Labangan is an impoverished municipality along the northern coast of Illana Bay in the province of Zamboanga del Sur. Its population is composed largely of Muslims and Christians. A long and bitter conflict between four clans, arising from political and family differences, has limited development opportunities for the town. For generations, these clans have depended on coastal resources for their livelihoods. Conflict over traditional fishing rights has been one of the most common causes of violence.

In 2004, the Labangan LGU asked the EcoGov Project to help it develop a coastal resource management program to rehabilitate Labangan's degraded fisheries and revitalize its coastal and marine resource base. One of the interventions was the establishment of a marine protected area (MPA) to enhance fishery productivity in Barangay Combo, a site of frequent violent clashes between warring clans. This required establishing a no-take zone that would alter the local community's traditional resource access. Anticipating that this would be a challenge, public consultations and information campaigns were undertaken to raise awareness and gain community buy-in.

As efforts to establish the MPA began, the mayor of Labangan and other local stakeholders quickly realized that it was essential to gain the support of the warring clans, whose members were also among the most influential community leaders and decision makers. The mayor initiated a peacemaking process through the multisectoral and multiethnic Coastal Resource Management Technical Working Group, under the guidance of the local council of elders. The warring clans were engaged in a series of discussions on the importance of establishing mechanisms that would conserve the coastal resource base, which was the main source of livelihoods for the community. After several weeks of dialogue, the leaders of the clans reached a peace accord, which was signed during a public consultation on the establishment of the twenty-two-hectare MPA on May 11, 2006. Over the years, the formerly competing clans continued to work with the rest of the community to implement their coastal resource management plan. The plan included enforcement, monitoring, and rehabilitation of the MPA, as well as information, education, and communication campaigns. This case demonstrates that resource management objectives can best be achieved when local conflict dynamics are recognized and addressed.

The Labangan LGU's technical progress in coastal resource management and process-based progress in enhancing transparency, accountability, and public participation helped improve its credibility. That improvement allowed the LGU to secure international funding to support additional projects, such as raising mudcrabs and shellfish, to promote mangrove-based livelihoods for former MNLF combatants living in Barangay Bulanit. The goal of this project was improved governance of coastal resources, but the outcomes proved to be even more varied and beneficial. Today, the improved livelihood conditions in the area are supporting disarmament, demobilization, and reintegration (DDR) efforts by the GPH in this former MNLF hotbed.

Recruiting former rebels as guardians of the sea

Dinas is another impoverished municipality on Illana Bay. It has a mixed population of Muslims, Christians, and indigenous Subanen. The Christians live mostly in the urbanized areas, and the Muslims predominate along the coast. For generations Dinas enjoyed a wealth of coastal and marine resources, but in the 1970s, when the GPH encouraged aquaculture to increase fish production and exports, 3,000 of its 4,000 hectares of mangrove forests were converted into fishponds. This diminished the breeding grounds for important fish species and decreased the productivity of local fisheries. The gradual breakdown of customary property and user rights left marine and coastal resources under open-access conditions. This, together with population growth and the encroachment of commercial fishers, led to severe degradation of the coastal environment.

As a result of the poverty caused by long periods of conflict and the declining fish catch, more people took part in illegal and destructive fishing practices out of desperation. At the same time peace and security problems, particularly piracy, hindered investment and job creation in the area. With decreasing natural resource–based livelihood options and increasing poverty, grievances expressed along ethnic lines mounted.

In 2000, the vice mayor, Abdulbasit Maulana, suggested establishing a 104-hectare MPA. Community reactions were mixed; in particular, some people felt that an MPA would infringe on their traditional fishing rights. The vice mayor sought buy-in from former rebels by organizing MNLF returnees in the area as members of Bantay Dagat (Sea Guardians). Unfortunately, defending the MPA sometimes involved returning fire and even killing armed intruders. In an area prone to rido, the result was a series of violent clashes between families determined to avenge the deaths of relatives. Out of fear for their own lives, the non-Muslims in the community avoided becoming involved in coastal resource management.

Recognizing the need for a new direction, in 2002 the local government of Dinas requested technical assistance from the EcoGov Project to formulate a new coastal resource management plan. The EcoGov Project's involvement paved the way for an integrated approach. To ensure stakeholder buy-in, one of the EcoGov Project's key strategies was to form a technical working group with diverse ethnic and sectoral composition that would take the lead in formulating and implementing the municipality's coastal resource management plan, thus fostering participatory natural resource management opportunities and practices.[10] The participatory process fostered Muslim-Christian and interclan communication and collaboration. It also imparted a deep sense of local ownership and joint accountability for coastal resources.

Dinas adopted the new coastal resource management plan in 2004, including a zoning framework to rationalize priority use areas and clarify rules on access,

---

[10] Previously, local communities had not been allowed to participate directly in the affairs of the local government, including natural resource management.

thus minimizing resource use conflicts and related occurrences of rido. Positive behavioral changes have since been observed among LGU personnel, residents, and stakeholders who participate in the coastal resource management program. As Mayor Wilfredo Asoy said, "the culture of confrontation is gradually being replaced by one of dialogue and negotiation." As a result, the people of Dinas are reaping the benefits of improved coastal resource governance, such as increased fish catch, additional technical assistance, and foreign and local donor support not only for coastal resource management projects but also for the improvement of water systems and alternative livelihood projects.

Building peace can be risky, and many of these EcoGov Project–supported advances came at a serious cost. Vice Mayor Maulana and four other Bantay Dagat members were killed in July 2005 trying to apprehend illegal fishers from outside the municipality. While setbacks continue to occur due to the still-volatile security conditions in the area, the LGU and community members are determined to face these challenges constructively and to ensure that their coastal and marine resources are protected and sustainably managed.

Case study 2: Transparent and participatory allocation of forests and forestlands

For approximately three decades, the forests of Maasim in Sarangani Province were the site of open conflict and were used as a hiding place by both the MILF and the New People's Army (NPA), the military arm of the Communist Party of the Philippines. In addition, members of the local communities, the MNLF, the MILF, and the NPA all sold illegally harvested logs—to support themselves and, in the case of the rebel groups, allegedly to buy weapons. As a result of this exploitation, the lush forests that had once covered Maasim were rapidly declining. (Figure 2 depicts forest cover in southern Mindanao.)

The mayor of Maasim, Aniceto P. Lopez Jr., realized that in spite of the security challenges, Maasim needed a comprehensive land use policy to help address the pressing problem of forest degradation. In early 2004, he requested technical assistance from the EcoGov Project for forest and forestland management. The subsequent partnership between Maasim municipality and the EcoGov Project led to the drafting of the Maasim Forest Land Use Plan, which was adopted in September 2004 by the Maasim legislative council.

The EcoGov Project's assistance focused on prevention of illegal logging and conversion of tropical forests with the goal of conserving biodiversity. The primary strategy was to incentivize improved forest management for both LGUs and communities by strengthening land tenure rights and ensuring that local communities had equitable access to resources. The first step was to create the Forest Land Use Plan to guide land use and allocation. This step included three components: assessing all tenure holders, whether the holdings were state-granted or customary; defining existing issues, such as declining forest cover and conflicts over resource use in forestlands; and allocating forestland in open-access areas.

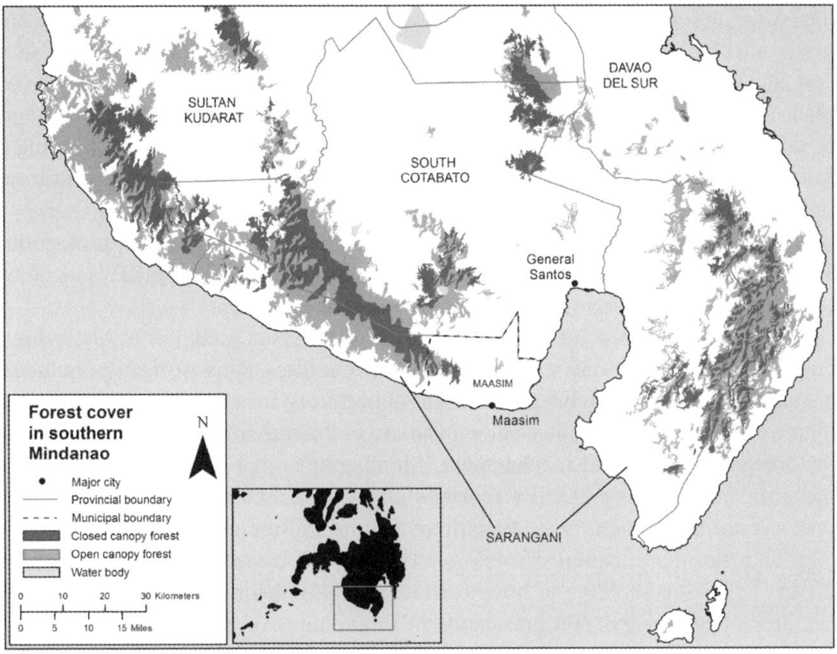

Figure 2. Forest cover in southern Mindanao, Philippines
Source: USAID (2004).

In Maasim, preparation and implementation of the Forest Land Use Plan has had tremendous positive outcomes, including improved land tenure rights, security, and access to forest resources; enhanced participation, transparency, and accountability in forest management; reestablishment of essential public services (such as farm-to-market roads); and public- and private-sector investment. Although the EcoGov Project's intervention was not primarily directed at peacebuilding and conflict mitigation, the program's consistent focus on fostering participation and transparency has contributed to constructive engagement of stakeholders, local confidence building, dispute resolution, and reconciliation. The Forest Land Use Plan addressed some of the most critical sources of grievances in Maasim, including competition over access rights to land and forest resources. Due to improved forest management, the political, social, and economic situation in Maasim has also improved, and the occurrence of local conflicts has thus been reduced.

Building a foundation for peace through forest land use planning

Throughout the development of the Maasim Forest Land Use Plan, the municipal government employed a transparent and participatory process involving a range of key local stakeholders, including leaders and other members of the MNLF, the MILF, and the NPA. A technical working group with representatives of local government, the Department of Environment and Natural Resources (DENR), and local stakeholder groups was created to spearhead the preparation of the plan. Members of this group conducted an information and education campaign in all fifteen *barangays* (villages) situated within the municipality's forestlands. They also enlisted the participation of local communities in resource profiling, mapping, and ground validation. During this period, forest occupancy surveys were undertaken to generate data on issues related to the allocation, protection, and management of the forestlands. Members of the MNLF, MILF, and other rebel groups took part in these community-based activities.

A key component of plan preparation was a situational analysis, which culminated in a three-day workshop with stakeholders. This workshop included a stakeholders' analysis that provided an opportunity for all participants to share their interests, concerns, and ongoing initiatives and other suggestions in relation to forests and forestland management. Members of rebel groups participated in the workshop. Strikingly, MILF representatives brought a perimeter defense map that, according to them, was recognized by the Philippine military. The MILF map and the identification of other areas occupied by rebels provided a better picture to all stakeholders of how to strategically develop the more than 20,000 hectares of open areas and grasslands in the uplands of the municipality while avoiding causing violent conflict.

The experience showed that an inclusive, participatory approach to project implementation can significantly strengthen local resilience and promote peace. Ustadj Hussein Abdulwahab, an MILF municipal leader and the provincial representative of the International Monitoring Team for the GPH-MILF peace talks, said during the workshop, "We are happy that we are part of this workshop. We are thankful that the LGU considered our views and opinions on how to effectively manage our forestlands. We now realize the need to participate in activities like these if we want real change to occur in Maasim."[11]

The preparation and implementation of the Forest Land Use Plan and the stakeholder interactions involved in those processes have built trust between the stakeholders and the local government. As an indicator of this improved relationship, today more people are approaching the municipal government as the first source of assistance before they turn to the National Commission on Indigenous Peoples or the DENR for assistance. The collaborative and participatory decision-making processes also fostered a sense among stakeholders of local ownership

---

[11] Abdulwahab made this statement during the closing ceremony of the workshop. The International Monitoring Team is tasked with monitoring the 2003 ceasefire between the GPH and the MILF. Led by Malaysia, it also has members from Libya, Brunei, Japan, and (since 2010) the EU. In addition to monitoring the ceasefire, the team conducts activities such as providing medical assistance and building schools.

and responsibility for managing shared resources. Community consultations and information campaigns have increased awareness among stakeholders of the need to work together and to overcome ethnic, religious, and political differences in order to effectively manage their forest resources for the common good.

As a result of the collaborative spirit fostered through this activity, local religious organizations (such as the Adventist Church, Islamic religious groups, and the Social Action Center of the Roman Catholic Church) have since worked together on tree planting and other environmental projects under the direction of the municipal government. As an indicator of the sustainability of the attitudinal changes promoted by the EcoGov Project, the circle of stakeholders has expanded and members of the International Monitoring Team joined other peace advocates and environmentalists in a tree planting activity on March 3, 2008, at Maasim's Purok Tabak, Upper Lumasal, inside community-tenured forestland.

Using the Forest Land Use Plan to resolve a land dispute

The situational analysis conducted in Maasim revealed at least seven different land-related conflicts. Resolution of these conflicts was given high priority within the program, since they affected the allocation of forestlands. At the same time, the local government wanted to create a peaceful environment to attract investors. As a result of this confluence of priorities, the local government of Maasim, with guidance from the EcoGov Project, created a multisectoral Municipal Environment and Natural Resources Council to facilitate resolution of land conflicts and perform other functions. The group includes MILF and MNLF representatives.[12]

The first task assigned to the council was the resolution of a twenty-five-year-old land dispute in Barangay Kamanga. The dispute involved the indigenous Fangulo clan and the holders of a 2,000-hectare pasture lease agreement, who are migrant settlers. The pasture lease agreement is a tenure instrument issued by the DENR that allows the holder to use forestland to raise livestock for a period of twenty-five years and is renewable for another twenty-five years.[13]

---

12 Other members of the council include representatives from the LGU, DENR, National Commission on Indigenous Peoples, municipal tribal chieftains, members of the private sector, the Community-Based Forest Management People's Organization, and the Catholic Church.

13 With the exception of vested-right lands and lands covered by ancestral domain and ancestral land titles, practically all forestlands in the Philippines are under the jurisdiction of the state and are administered by the DENR, which issues different types of tenure instruments for forestlands. However, other agencies—such as the National Commission on Indigenous Peoples in the case of ancestral domain lands—can also grant land tenure, which leads to problems when different tenure instruments overlap.

The land dispute arose because the lease area is located inside Fangulo ancestral land. The indigenous group of which the clan is a part enlisted the help of the MNLF and MILF to protect its land against the Christian leaseholders. The hostility worsened when the DENR renewed the pasture lease agreement for another twenty-five years—without coordination with local authorities or, allegedly, with the Fangulo clan—in the same year the National Commission on Indigenous Peoples granted the Fangulo clan's application to have the land in question declared its ancestral land under the Indigenous Peoples Rights Act. As a result of these conflicting claims and the uncoordinated parallel structures supporting them, the dispute festered, and both parties armed themselves to respond.

Several meetings were held in an effort to resolve the dispute, but no progress was achieved. A breakthrough occurred, however, when the EcoGov Project and the local government of Maasim together proposed using the information in the municipality's Forest Land Use Plan as a basis for resolving the disagreement. On the basis of the plan's guidance, the Fangulo clan agreed to allocate approximately 600 hectares from their 2,000-hectare claim to the pasture leaseholders. The agreement was endorsed by both the DENR and the National Commission on Indigenous Peoples. A transparent and participatory forest land use planning process had generated credible information and a plan that was considered legitimate by the stakeholders. The plan has been instrumental in addressing resource conflicts and in promoting peaceful coexistence in the area. More than ten cases of land tenure–related conflicts have been similarly resolved by the Municipal Environment and Natural Resources Council.

KEY FACTORS INFLUENCING PEACEBUILDING AND CONFLICT MITIGATION

The EcoGov Project experience demonstrates the important contribution of environmental governance and natural resources management in fostering lasting peace in conflict-affected areas. A number of key factors affected the success of these efforts.

Capacity and strength of local institutions

Lack of capacity constrained the ability of LGUs and other local agencies to effectively deliver public services or to play the role that was expected of them in terms of natural resource management and conflict mediation. This led to governance-related grievances among the population. Therefore, improving the capacity of LGUs and providing support for (or, when necessary, creating) credible local institutions—such as the Municipal Environment and Natural Resources Council—can fill some of the near-term capacity deficits and help governments be responsive to citizens, thus reducing grievances. If new institutions are developed to meet specific needs, it is important to keep government officials and institutions involved in order to avoid creating competitive or duplicate structures and systems.

Political will

The success of local peacebuilding initiatives hinges on the strong political will of social and institutional leaders. In predominantly Muslim Maasim, although the mayor himself was not a Muslim, his personal involvement, sincerity, and commitment earned him the trust and confidence of the community. Critically, he was also able to persuade various agencies to support agreed-upon actions. In the case of the Illana Bay Regional Alliance, the commitment of member LGUs to pursuing peace is now evident in their willingness to work together to address rido and to negotiate with one another and clarify common rules on coastal resource management, which helps prevent conflict.

Local peace initiatives

When the EcoGov Project was initiated, the peace agreement between the GPH and the MNLF was in effect, but that between the MILF and the GPH was still being negotiated. Although the EcoGov Project's forest management interventions mitigated local conflicts in Maasim, a broader peace was at risk due to the absence of a clear peace agreement recognized by the central command of the MILF. In the absence of a national-level peace agreement, more locally defined zones of peace and development can be established and supported by local stakeholders. When national-level agreements exist, it is important that they be complemented by local plans of action and by monitoring and evaluation systems to ensure that what has been agreed at the national level is properly communicated, implemented, and monitored at the local level.

External support

Following the GPH-MNLF peace agreement and throughout the last decade of sporadic conflict in Mindanao, the development of various public services and infrastructure (such as roads, water systems, school buildings, day care centers, and health services) were assisted by both national and international organizations. External funding, technical assistance, and administrative support are often critical for bridging the immediate gaps in the economy, infrastructure, and basic human and social development services in conflict-affected areas. The presence of the third-party International Monitoring Team has also played a significant role in sustaining the ceasefire between the GPH and the MILF.

Incentives for private investment

The promise of private-sector engagement and economic development can be a motivator for peace. For example, Dole Philippines' contract with local tenure holders to grow pineapple in Maasim provided local employment and helped defuse social tensions that were exacerbated by extreme economic hardship. News about a former NPA rebel earning 100,000 Philippine pesos (US$2,381) in one cropping spread to other barangays and provided encouragement for other rebels and community members to participate in the local government's forestry program rather than engage in conflict. Private investment has thus helped turn a former battleground in Maasim into productive farms that have contributed to the reintegration of former combatants and the premise of which has encouraged active rebels to surrender their firearms in order to pursue peaceful livelihood activities.

Security of project personnel

When the EcoGov Project began work in Maasim, project staff could not enter the upland areas to undertake community consultations because of the volatile conflict situation. To facilitate their entry, field staff had to find local community members who had contacts with MILF and MNLF rebels to vouch for them. As EcoGov and local government staff demonstrated their ongoing commitment to the work and remained both true to their word and consistent with follow-through, their credibility was built; rebel groups were eventually persuaded to join the Forest Land Use Planning Technical Working Group and to participate in the consultations, which enriched the development of stakeholder consensus and a common agenda for action.

LESSONS LEARNED

The EcoGov Project experience has yielded important lessons regarding the potential for environmental and natural resource management programming to contribute to peacebuilding and conflict mitigation, not only during post-conflict stabilization but at any stage of a conflict.

Building on shared interests and concerns

Although competition for use of communal resources often results in degradation of the resource base, cooperation can be forged to promote sustainable use of the same resources for mutual benefit. This is particularly true in western Mindanao, where livelihoods, such as farming and fishing, are primarily resource based. Natural resource management can be a means to highlight common interests and promote shared responsibility among stakeholders and interest groups. Collaborative efforts build trust between parties and foster social resilience.

The "how" versus the "what"

The determining factor in peacebuilding and conflict resolution outcomes is usually not a technical intervention itself but the manner in which it is implemented. For example, when transparency, accountability, and participation are built into natural resource management activities, outcomes such as improved governance, stakeholder empowerment, and reduced grievances often result—especially in areas like Mindanao where local people had felt unable to participate in decision making about economic resources.

To achieve those benefits, it is critical that project implementers have a good understanding of local peace and conflict dynamics and focus on how the project will help enhance social and institutional resilience locally and manage points of tension. For instance, the EcoGov Project consistently sought to engage all key individuals and groups—including the rebel groups (MNLF, MILF, and NPA), Lumads, Muslims, Christians, the military, government agencies, local government, and nongovernmental organizations (NGOs)—in achieving common objectives. Working with only one or a few of these key stakeholders may not have offered the same durable solutions to conflicts in the area at the same time that it could have inadvertently contributed to certain groups' feelings of marginalization. Inclusive approaches are often important.

Under certain circumstances, peacebuilding efforts may need to take an indirect approach. Sometimes introducing terms like *peacebuilding* or *reconciliation* into a conflict context before the moment is ripe can cause tension or provoke a defensive reaction among the parties engaged in or affected by conflict, especially when the conflict resolution objective seems to be imposed from the outside or when parties are not ready to find a solution to their perceived differences—or at least to admit openly that they are ready.[14] In such cases, it may be advisable to describe a program on the basis of sectoral objectives (such as economic growth, biodiversity conservation, or agricultural development) and technical aims (such as improved market access, amount of protected area, or increased crop yields) rather than in terms of conflict-mitigation goals. The process of implementing a conflict-sensitive sectoral program can focus on bringing key parties together to build trust and social cohesion and to increase transparency and accountability while they work toward a common sectoral goal—rather than explicitly on trying to resolve the dynamics driving conflict. An indirect approach may be less threatening to parties entrenched in conflict.

Integration of efforts across different levels of governance

A holistic approach to environmental and natural resource governance can help promote peace and foster stability, but to do so the intervention must tackle the underlying social, cultural, economic, political, and institutional causes and consequences of conflict. For example, investment in physical structures should be complemented by investment in social and institutional structures, which will improve governance. In addition, to achieve a sustainable peace, it is important to enhance or create linkages between positive efforts at all levels—family, community, local, provincial, and national—so that individual efforts are reinforced and strengthened, rather than taking place in a vacuum.

---

[14] See USAID (2009) for a discussion of timing.

Choice of indicators for program monitoring and evaluation

When designing an environmental and natural resource management program in a conflict-affected situation, it is critical to have done an appropriate conflict analysis to inform program design and then to explicitly include peacebuilding and conflict-mitigation indicators in the performance plan in order to trace progress and impact on the conflict situation. If the performance baselines do not take conflict issues into account, then a program's impact on those issues cannot be measured and tracked effectively. There is significant anecdotal evidence to support the argument that EcoGov Project's environmental and natural resource management technical programs helped to mitigate local conflict and had a positive effect on higher-order conflict dynamics; and much has been learned from a retrospective analysis of the program through the lens of peace and security. However, since the EcoGov Project's interventions were not designed in response to identified drivers of conflict or peace (per a conflict assessment) and did not collect data on conflict-specific indicators, there is little empirical evidence to prove their impact or to inform cross-comparisons with respect to conflict mitigation objectives. This hampers the ability to learn from and apply lessons from the EcoGov Project. Moreover, the monitoring and evaluation of these programs did not explicitly include an ongoing assessment of the relationship of the activities to the ever-changing local dynamics of conflict, so there is no systematic record of the intended and unintended consequences of the activities with respect to peace and security over time and during the different phases of the conflict cycle in Mindanao.

Although the EcoGov Project did contribute to improved delivery of public services, it did not attempt to link those improvements to a peace dividend from the 1996 peace agreement or the GPH-MILF peace talks because that was not part of the project objective or its theory of change. As a result, EcoGov Project's ability to promote peace and stability was not maximized, and comprehensive data on natural resources management and conflict—which could have been used to draw valuable lessons for future programming—were not collected. That was a missed opportunity.

Engagement of potential spoilers as well as peace advocates

Strengthening those who promote peace and foster local resilience is a key aspect of peacebuilding, but it is often equally critical to engage stakeholders who have vested interests in perpetuating conflict. In the experience of the EcoGov Project, including both active and former rebels in various activities proved to be critical to mitigating existing conflicts and preventing a return to conflict. Providing potential spoilers an opportunity to engage productively and giving them an active role in peacebuilding and development has helped over time to make them peace advocates rather than spoilers. In order to mitigate conflict it is not enough to reduce grievances; it is also important to constructively engage the individuals or organizations that are otherwise likely to mobilize people toward conflict.

Entry points for conflict resolution

When national entry points for conflict resolution are not available, or when a national political solution might not be workable (for example, when the GPH-MILF peace talks stalled over the ancestral domain issue), it may still be possible to pursue local entry points, such as environmental and natural resource management. As demonstrated by the EcoGov Project, even when national-level peace negotiations are failing, addressing local issues related to natural resources and allocation of benefits from those resources through transparent, accountable, and participatory processes can help resolve immediate conflicts while chipping away at deeper sources of grievance.

Patience and sustained commitment to peacebuilding

Peace agreements alone rarely resolve conflicts, though they may end the violence. Improving the processes and strengthening the institutions needed for effective environmental governance and supporting attitudinal and behavioral change among stakeholders does not happen overnight. Addressing the underlying sources of grievance which fueled conflict and engaging key actors in the process of changing incentives for violence and nonviolence requires time and commitment. Change must be encouraged on many levels, from interpersonal to institutional, and that takes time. There will be setbacks along the way. In the EcoGov Project cases, it often took years for the opposing players to build relationships of trust and then begin working together to resolve conflicts over resource rights and uses. Tending and sustaining the commitment of all relevant actors is critical. In the EcoGov Project experience, elders, former and active rebels, religious leaders, government officials, academics, and members of grassroots associations were all needed to support the gradual process of resolving resource conflicts in their respective areas. The project's success was measured according to specific sectoral benchmarks along the way rather than according to difficult-to-measure effects on overall violence reduction or broad-scale stabilization goals. Displaying progress in terms of staged successes helped sustain donor commitment to the program as well.

CONCLUSION

The EcoGov Project experience shows that governance-oriented interventions in the management of forests, forestlands, and coastal and marine resources can provide a valuable entry point for peacebuilding by directly and indirectly mitigating sources of environment-based conflict, including threats to livelihoods. In Mindanao, the EcoGov Project facilitated confidence building, dispute resolution, and reintegration of former combatants by addressing the central environment-related problems of land tenure security and access to natural resources through transparent and participatory management processes. Technical interventions focused on environmental and natural resource management were implemented in a way that reduced grievances, fostered and strengthened social and institutional resilience, and constructively engaged the key figures who were most capable of mobilizing people for action (whether for conflictive or peaceful purposes) so that problems were less likely to erupt into violent conflict and more likely to be solved through peaceful means.

The international community can constructively engage in fostering peace and development all along the conflict continuum, from conflict prevention to post-conflict stabilization, by providing appropriate and conflict-sensitive technical and logistical assistance in sectors such as natural resource management. Their roles, however, should be those of catalysts, facilitators, and monitors. To achieve a sustainable peace, local stakeholders should actively lead and own the peace process.

REFERENCES

Fianza, M. L. 1994. Indigenous patterns of land ownership and use and the effects of public policy among the Moro people in southern Philippines. *Mindanao Focus*, No. 3.

———. 1999. Conflicting land use and ownership patterns and the Moro problem in southern Philippines. In *Sama-sama: Facets of ethnic relations in Southeast Asia*, ed. M. C. Ferrer. Quezon City: Third World Studies Center, University of the Philippines.

———. 2004. Contesting land and identity in the periphery: The Moro indigenous people of southern Philippines. Paper presented at "The Commons in an Age of Global Transition: Challenges, Risks, and Opportunities," the tenth biennial conference of the International Association for the Study of Common Property, Oaxaca, Mexico, August 9–13. http://dlc.dlib.indiana.edu/dlc/handle/10535/949.

Lingga, A. S. M. 2007. *Conflict in Mindanao: Root causes and status*. Presentation at Asia DCHS regional workshop on "Toward Liberating Democracy: Devolution of Power Matters," Bangkok, Thailand, January 16–17. www.yonip.com/archives/BANGSAMORO/Conflict%2520in%2520Mindanao.pdf.

Quevedo, O. B. 2003. *Injustice: The root of conflict in Mindanao*. Paper delivered at the 27th General Assembly of the Bishops' Businessmen's Conference, Manila, Philippines, July 8. www.cpn.nd.edu/assets/14528/quevedo.doc.

Rodil, B. R. 2004. *The minoritization of the indigenous communities of Mindanao and the Sulu Archipelago*. Davao City, Philippines: Alternate Forum for Research in Mindanao.

Soriano, C. R. 2006. The challenges of relief and rehabilitation assistance in ongoing conflicts: A Mindanao case. *Kasarinlan: Philippine Journal of Third World Studies* 21 (1): 4–33.

Tan, S. K. 1995. The socio-economic dimensions of Moro secessionism. Mindanao Studies Report No. 1. Quezon City: University of the Philippines Center for Integrative and Development Studies.

Timberman, D. G. 2003. Conflict assessment: USAID/Philippines strategy for 2005–2009. Internal document. Washington, D.C.: United States Agency for International Development.

Torres, W. M. III. 2007. Rido: Clan feuding and conflict management in Mindanao. Executive summary. San Francisco, California: The Asia Foundation. http://asiafoundation.org/resources/pdfs/PHridoexecsummary.pdf.

Tuminez, A. S. 2005. Ancestral domain in comparative perspective. Special Report No. 151. Washington, D.C.: United States Institute of Peace.

———. 2008. The past is always present: The Moros of Mindanao and the quest for peace. Working Paper No. 99. Hong Kong: Southeast Asia Research Centre, City University of Hong Kong.

Umehara, H., and G. M. Bautista. 2004. *Communities at the margins: Reflections on social, economic, and environmental change in the Philippines.* Quezon City, Philippines: Ateneo de Manila University Press.

USAID (United States Agency for International Development). 2004. USAID-EcoGov Mindanao Mapping Project and database of local government unit (LGU) partner sites.

———. 2009. *Supporting peace processes: A toolkit for development intervention.* Washington, D.C.

U.S. DOS (United States Department of State). 2004. International religious freedom report. www.state.gov/j/drl/rls/irf/2004/35425.htm.

Valdehueza, M. E. 2009. Roots of modern conflict in Mindanao, bad governance, DILG. *Sun.Star*, January 5.

World Bank. 2003. Social assessment of conflict-affected areas in Mindanao, Philippines. Post Conflict Series No. 1. Washington, D.C.: Environment and Social Development Unit, East Asia and Pacific Region.

ADDITIONAL SOURCES

Although the following materials were not cited, they have been listed because they contributed to the conceptual development of the chapter.

Abinales, P. N. 2000. *Making Mindanao: Cotabato and Davao in the formation of the Philippine nation-state.* Quezon City, Philippines: Ateneo de Manila University Press.

Alejo, A. E. 2000. *Generating energies in Mt. Apo: Cultural politics in a contested environment.* Quezon City, Philippines: Ateneo de Manila University Press.

Bacani, B. R. 2005. The Mindanao peace talks: Another opportunity to resolve the Moro conflict in the Philippines. Special Report No. 131. Washington, D.C.: United States Institute of Peace.

IBRA 9 (Illana Bay Regional Alliance 9). 2004. Fisheries law enforcement plan. Pagadian City, Philippines.

Martin, G. E., and A. S. Tuminez. 2008a. Obstacles to peace in Mindanao ABS-CBN News, August 5. http://rp2.abs-cbnnews.com/views-and-analysis/08/05/08/obstacles-peace-mindanao-eugene-martin-and-astrid-tuminez.

———. 2008b. *Toward peace in the southern Philippines: A summary and assessment of the USIP Facilitation Project, 2003–2007.* Washington, D.C.: United States Institute of Peace. www.usip.org/files/resources/sr202.pdf.

Mindanao State University Naawan Foundation for Science and Technology Development. 2006. *Fisheries profile of Labangan, Zamboanga del Sur.* Naawan, Philippines.

Municipality of Dinas. 2003. *Coastal resource management plan 2004–2013.* Dinas, Philippines.

Municipality of Maasim. 2004. *Maasim forest land use plan 2005–2009.* Maasim, Philippines.

Panolimba, D. S. 2008. A deeper look at the Bangsamoro problem and the armed conflict in Mindanao and its islands. http://barangayrp.wordpress.com/2008/12/04/a-deeper-look-at-the-bangsamoro-problem-and-the-armed-conflict-in-mindanao-and-its-islands/.

Schiavo-Campo, S., and M. Judd. 2005. The Mindanao conflict in the Philippines: Roots, costs, and potential peace dividend. Social Development Papers: Conflict Prevention and Reconstruction Paper No. 24. Washington, D.C.: World Bank. http://internal-displacement.org/8025708F004CE90B/(httpDocuments)/8A4B6AFE92D9BB82802570B700599DA1/$file/WP24_Web.pdf.

Tuminez, A. 2005. Ancestral domain: The key to a more permanent peace in Muslim Mindanao. Current Issues Briefing. Washington, D.C.: United States Institute of Peace.

Vitug-Dañguilan, M. 1993. *The politics of logging: Power from the forest.* Manila: Philippine Center for Investigative Journalism.

Commerce in the chaos: Bananas, charcoal, fisheries, and conflict in Somalia

Christian Webersik and Alec Crawford

> *Some people have suggested that [Somalia] could end up looking like the tribal lands of Afghanistan. Maybe, but there is one saving factor. Unlike Afghanistan, which has opium (and Iraq which has oil), the Horn has little of economic value to fuel a war: its front-line, after all, can barely keep a cow alive.*
>
> *—The Economist*[1]

Despite the *Economist*'s gloomy snapshot of Somalia's prospects, it is wrong to imply that hope for its future lies in a lack of resources of economic value. Over the past two violent decades of Somalia's history, the production and trade of three natural resources central to what remains of the country's economy—bananas, charcoal, and fisheries—have played important roles in funding the Somali conflict. Competing militias have fought one another for control of this production and trade through control of relevant lands, waters, and ports, and used the gains to fund their activities and maintain their power. While this use of bananas, charcoal, and fisheries has contributed to Somali conflict, these resources also represent a potentially important source of nonconflict income that could help the country recover from crisis and, ultimately, strengthen the nascent peacebuilding process. This chapter will examine how, over the course of nearly twenty years, the production and trade of three natural resources has contributed to the ongoing conflict in Somalia and could ultimately contribute to its resolution.

Christian Webersik is an associate professor in the Department of Development Studies at the University of Adger, Norway, and since 2007, has worked as a postdoctoral fellow at the United Nations University–Institute for Advanced Studies. Alec Crawford is an associate with the Environment, Conflict and Peacebuilding Programme at the International Institute for Sustainable Development, and works with the Environmental Cooperation for Peacebuilding Programme at the United Nations Environment Programme.

The background on the links between Somali fisheries, banana production, and trade and conflict discussed in this chapter builds on a paper written for the International Institute for Sustainable Development (Crawford and Brown 2008). Similarly, the end-of-chapter lessons learned and recommendations to international stakeholders reflect observations and recommendations from that paper.

[1] *Economist*, "The Path to Ruin," August 12, 2006.

Built on desk and field-based research on conflict resources in Somalia, this chapter contains four sections. The first and second sections provide background and case studies on the specific links between trade in bananas, charcoal, and fish and conflict in Somalia. The third section outlines broad lessons learned from these case studies, and the fourth section provides recommendations to national and international stakeholders.

BACKGROUND

Since 1969, when the democratically elected president Abdurashid Ali Sharmarke was assassinated and a military regime led by Prime Minister Mohamed Siad Barre seized power and declared Somalia a socialist state, the country has experienced lasting insecurity and violence. War with Ethiopia in the 1970s, followed by civil war in the 1980s, caused the deaths of thousands of Somalis and widespread discontent with national leaders—a legacy Somalia has yet to overcome. The sections that follow examine the cause and consequence of widespread violence and insecurity that have enveloped the country since the collapse of Barre's regime.

Somalia's troubled past and uncertain future

When President Barre fled Mogadishu on the evening of January 26, 1991, the state his regime had supported for twenty-two years effectively collapsed. Falling into the hands of a collection of warlords, Somalia became a country of lawlessness, perpetual civil conflict, and economic ruin. Over the next two years, 280,000 people are estimated to have died from a mix of civil strife, drought, and starvation (Hansch et al. 1994). Other estimates are higher; by some accounts, approximately 400,000 Somalis lost their lives (Bradbury 1994).

Today, Somalia barely exists as a functioning state. Within larger Somalia, Somaliland has declared itself an independent state, and Puntland has declared itself autonomous, although neither has gained international recognition as such.[2] In 2006, the Islamic Courts Union took control of most of the southern part of the country, bringing a degree of peace and stability to Mogadishu not seen for many years. By the end of 2006, however, forces loyal to the alternative and weak transitional government, backed by troops from neighboring Ethiopia, seized control of Mogadishu from the Islamists, and a surge of violence ensued.

In 2012, Somalia's Transitional Federal Government was replaced by the Federal Government of Somalia, and the country passed a new national constitution. Hassan Sheikh Mohamud was elected president, and he has pushed national reconciliation since taking office. Despite this, terrorism and piracy continue

---

[2] Somaliland is located in the northwestern region of Somalia and extends eastward toward Laascaanood. Puntland is located east of Somaliland and extends from the northernmost tip of the Horn of Africa southward into the region of Mudug.

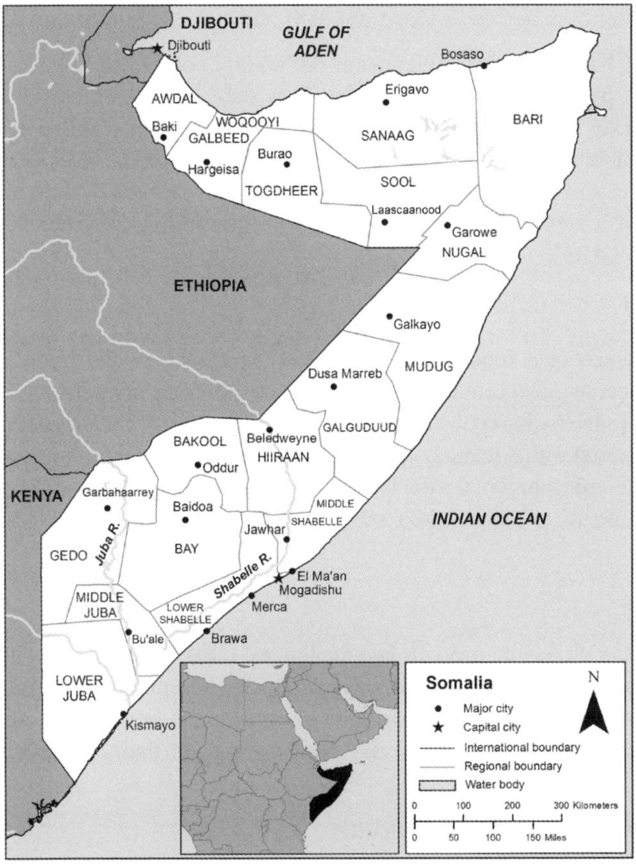

within the state's borders, and the humanitarian situation has remained dire. Thousands died between 2010 and 2012 as a result of drought, civil strife, and a government that is unable to protect its people from starvation (BBC 2011; Ford 2013; IRIN 2011). While the drought and famine has abated, the United Nations estimates that approximately 2.7 million people still require life-saving assistance (Smith-Spark and Elbagir 2013), and widespread violence also remains a persistent threat (Kulish 2013; Straziuso 2012).

Bananas, charcoal, fisheries, and conflict funding

Where monetary resources are lacking, natural resources are often used as a source of conflict funding. In Somalia, the militant groups predominantly responsible for the continuing violence receive funding and support from the production and sale of bananas and charcoal, and the exploitation of the country's fisheries.

Bananas

The use of banana exports as a means of funding conflict in Somalia was made possible in part by a number of factors: how easily the commodity's movement to the market can be obstructed or controlled (the crop's obstructability); the presence of reliable demand markets, including in Europe; weak or nonexistent governance; and the complicity of multinational corporations which, in the 1990s, paid export levies and taxes to warlords and their militias (Webersik 2005).

Charcoal

In the absence of a functioning government, production and trade in charcoal quickly became—and remains—a major pillar of the country's informal economy. As such, trade in charcoal has largely favored powerful businessmen and rival faction leaders while leaving local charcoal-producing communities with little but adverse environmental effects. As a result, local communities have resorted to violent means to protect their interests.

Fisheries

Somalia has rich fishing grounds and the longest coastline in Africa. The country's warlords have exploited Somalia's extensive and unregulated fisheries for profit by issuing false fishing licenses to foreign companies; in doing so, warlords and their militias have been able to raise funds to support their operations.

A new kind of conflict economy

In Somalia, the profits available from bananas, charcoal, and fisheries created a new kind of conflict economy in which trade participants had more interest in maintaining the conflict and continuing to gain from it than in pursuing peace. As David Keen noted when writing of the economic motivations for prolonging war, for Somali warlords, "the aim of war is not necessarily to win it" (Keen 2000, 29).

Livelihoods in Somalia

The long-lasting conflict in Somalia has severely disrupted livelihoods in the country (Le Sage and Majid 2002). Significant variations in social, political, economic, and environmental vulnerability exist among and within Somalia's different clans and social groups, and conflict has often exacerbated these vulnerabilities. Insecurity restricts the livestock grazing mobility of pastoralists, for example, and for riverine farmers, it can result in the depletion of fixed and immobile assets, such as grain stores or land (Le Sage and Majid 2002).

More than two decades of conflict have had a particularly stark impact on the country's livelihood resources. Political resources have disappeared, as governing institutions have collapsed or been made completely ineffectual, and political representation has been replaced by control through violence. Physical resources have been destroyed or degraded; the country's food security has been challenged both by the deterioration of irrigation systems for farming and by increasing difficulties in accessing local markets for livestock and produce. In the absence of effective management mechanisms, natural resources—including forests, fisheries, and farmland—have been systematically exploited and degraded with no concern for sustainability. Financial resources have dried up in the face of rampant inflation, criminality, and a wholly inhospitable investment climate. Social networks have either collapsed through displacement and death or have strengthened along tribal lines across warring factions. Finally, in human resource terms, schools have been destroyed, healthcare systems are failing, and educated populations are leaving the country to live elsewhere.

A different kind of resource-based conflict

How revenues from the banana, charcoal, and fishery sectors have contributed to the perpetuation of the conflict in Somalia differs from how resource revenues have contributed to conflicts in other African countries over the same period. As noted by Sabrina Grosse-Kettler, "In many war economies in sub-Saharan Africa, including the DRC [Democratic Republic of the Congo], Liberia and Sierra Leone, resources such as coltan, diamonds and gold are fuelling the conflict; control and exploitation of local assets means a monopoly on its profit. In Somalia, in contrast, there is no *strategic* resource as such" (Grosse-Kettler 2004, 14).

Somalia's natural wealth may lack strategic value as such. However, its three major natural resources are easily appropriated, as individuals and small groups can easily loot them by harvesting and transporting them to domestic and foreign markets in a way that brings in uncontrolled revenue. This revenue has then been used to perpetuate the conflict in Somalia in the same way revenues from illicit production and trade of coltan, diamonds, and gold have been used to perpetuate conflict in the DRC and revenues from the illicit production and export of diamonds were used to perpetuate conflict in Sierra Leone.

Data challenges

The existence, availability, and reliability of socioeconomic and scientific data in Somalia remain a significant challenge. In collecting socioeconomic, geographical, and historical details about natural resource management in Somalia, the authors had to rely on data generated by aid agencies, international and local NGOs, and (now-defunct) government entities. While these data served as important sources of information, many have yet to be published in the literature.

In addition, given the lack of a functioning government, basic statistical data are missing, and even pre-war data raises questions of accuracy and validity. Further, the quantity and quality of data available in Somalia is subject to bias as relates to secure versus insecure areas and secure versus insecure interview environments.[3]

CASE STUDIES

Natural resource production and exploitation have generated significant funds for militant groups that perpetuate violence. This section examines specific experiences that link banana, charcoal, and fisheries harvesting with conflict in Somalia.

Somali banana production and trade

Somali banana production is concentrated in the Lower Shabelle region in the south of the country, within what remains of the Somali state outside of Somaliland and Puntland. Italian settlers began cultivating bananas in the region in 1919, and, at first, these farmers were in a good export position due to Italian-imposed tariffs on all non-Somali bananas. This guaranteed export market may have had the unintended effect of discouraging competition and investment in the sector (Webersik 2005).

When Somalia declared independence in 1960, Italian settlers began to leave the country. After President Abdirashid Ali Sharmarke was assassinated in 1969, Barre took power and quickly moved to change the structure of the banana sector by nationalizing its production and export trade. Under the 1975 land reform program, he also expropriated unclassified and communal lands for expanding cultivation. Under these changes, production increased at first but then rapidly declined. The amount of land under cultivation and production yields began to drop for a number of reasons, including loss of plantation farming expertise as a result of the Italian settlers' departure; higher levels of soil salinity due to inefficient and poorly maintained drainage systems; and decreased use of fertilizer (Webersik 2005).

In the early 1980s, structural adjustment policies improved the banana sector's outlook. Transportation networks, market links, credit access, and fuel prices all moved in favor of banana producers, and productivity increased. Somalia became East Africa's largest exporter of bananas, with 12,000 hectares dedicated to and 120,000 people employed in the industry (Baars and Riediger 2008). At the same time, privatization of public assets under these structural adjustment

[3] In addition to conducting their own interviews in Kenya and Somalia in 2002, the authors relied on some of the twenty-two interviews conducted in Somalia's Lower Shabelle in 2001 by the Nairobi-based Agency for Cooperation and Research in Development for the purpose of gaining access to information that had been gathered in areas difficult to access, especially south of Mogadishu.

policies bred corruption by permitting insiders and political aides close to Barre to grab land and move to control the banana sector (Webersik 2005). Nonetheless, by the end of 1990, bananas were Somalia's largest agricultural sector after livestock. In that year, the banana sector brought in US$25.6 million in export earnings (30 percent of Somalia's total) (Webersik 2005). Following the outbreak of the civil war, the banana trade came to a standstill but recovered beginning in 1994, at least until 1997. In 1997, due to changes in international trade, devastating floods, and closure of the Mogadishu port, banana production collapsed (Baars and Riediger 2008). In 2009, amid continued instability in Somalia, only 3,000 hectares were dedicated to banana production, and banana exportation no longer constitutes a significant portion of Somali export earnings (*New Agriculturist* 2009).

Conflict and the banana trade

In August 1992, less than two years after Barre had fled the country, Somalia was beset by conflict, and 1.5 million Somalis were close to starvation (Debiel 2003). The food security situation improved somewhat a few months later (by December 1992) when massive food aid interventions caused grain prices to fall below the cost of production (De Waal and Omaar 1993). Even so, by then, important banana production and export companies, including Somalfruit, a private company founded by the De Nadai family in the 1930s (*Il Mondo* 1995), had abandoned their Somali operations entirely due to conflict insecurity, and banana production was suspended.

In southern Somalia, abandoned banana plantations, large-scale farms, and irrigation systems deteriorated or were seized. Local militias took to looting abandoned infrastructure or illegally seizing land and attempting to control irrigation systems. Newcomers, often from the pastoral Haber Gedir clan, expropriated land through violence and without fair compensation but often lacked the skills needed to make the land productive, thus ruining many banana plantations. Farmers took to destroying irrigation systems to prevent losing control and being taxed for their irrigation water.

These local conflicts involving militias, Haber Gedir clansmen, and the local agrarian communities over agricultural lands had a negative effect on the rural populations of Lower Shabelle. Conflict and violence caused families to lose access to their farms, to their irrigation systems, and to work on the old plantations, uprooting a traditional way of life. As the conflict continued, productive lands went fallow, irrigation infrastructure deteriorated further, and a man-made scarcity of land and water resources set in that only served to exacerbate tensions (Webersik 2005).

Profiting from banana production and trade

Despite the ongoing conflict, Somali banana production and exports resumed in 1994 when U.S.-based multinational Dole entered the market via Sombana, Dole's locally based banana production and export subsidiary. This challenged the near monopoly of the sector by the De Nadai family's Somalfruit, which was back in operation and, despite the banana sector's troubles, was said to be worth US$100 million at the time (Webersik 2005).

Warlords learned they could profit from the sector by controlling banana production—and its export. As the UN Panel of Experts on Somalia stated, fighting in Somalia "typically centers on the control of property or income-generating infrastructure, such as harbors, airports, markets, bridges or road junctions that can be 'taxed'" (UNSC 2003c, 6). In particular, the ease with which militias could obstruct a crop from reaching its markets meant that whichever group controlled the points of export could extract significant profits from its trade, given reliable trading partners and export markets. In the case of Somalia's banana crop, the primary traditional exit points were shipping ports in Mogadishu and in the city of Merca, in the Lower Shabelle.

In 1994, General Mohamed Farrah Aideed, the warlord who drove Barre from Mogadishu, clashed with the Hawadle clan for control of Merca's port. When Aideed won control of the port, he was free to tax all bananas leaving from it. When banana exports resumed from the port in 1994, Aideed received US$.05 for every 12.5 kilograms shipped by Sombana, a rate that dropped to US$.04 in 1996, the year Dole suspended its Somali operations (Webersik 2005). Given the volume of banana exports in these years, Aideed's "tax" amounted to an estimated monthly income of US$150,000, which he primarily used to fund his militia's US$40,000 weekly expenses (Norfolk Education and Action for Development Centre 1995). In 1996, heavy fighting broke out in Merca when warlord Osman Hassan Ali Atto demanded a share of Aideed's banana-tax profits (Webersik 2005).

Insecurity leads to chaos and departure

Although Sombana and Somalfruit were competitors, operating in an insecure environment had disadvantaged them both, particularly through financial exploitation by local warlords. In addition to paying Aideed's export tax, both companies found themselves having to pay him or other warlords or militias for security. Aideed charged Sombana cash for protection in the region's riverine areas (Webersik 2005), and both Sombana and Somalfruit reportedly employed militias for securing shipments to ports. At times, these militias even clashed over access to ports (Norfolk Education and Action for Development Centre 1995). In early 1995, shots were fired at Dole's staff lodgings in Mogadishu, fighting broke out between the companies' militias at the city's port, and heavy machine-gun fire was directed at a Dole freighter anchored in the port (Webersik 2005). By late 1996, the high costs of maintaining its militia forced Dole to exit the Somali market altogether (Grosse-Kettler 2004). At the time of Dole's departure, stimulated by competition between Sombana and Somalfruit, banana production had reached 80 percent of pre-conflict production levels (Marchal 1997).

Export markets

In the absence of a functioning government, Somali warlords could continue to profit from the banana trade, but only as long as export markets remained guaranteed. For much of the 1990s, Europe was the principal export market. This began to change in 1997 when a World Trade Organization ruling reduced preferential trade agreements between the European Union (EU) and Somalia. As demand from the EU began to drop due to liberalization of import markets and repeal, in 2006, of EU and the African, Caribbean and Pacific Group of States import quotas, 70 per cent of Somalia's banana trade collapsed (Webersik 2005). Despite donor support for rehabilitation of irrigation infrastructure, as of 2008, banana production in Somalia still had not recovered (Baars and Riediger 2008).

The link between the EU trade and Somali insecurity had previously been drawn by a United Nations Security Council (UNSC) spokesperson, who, in 2004, observed that the "fact that the European Union provides preferential market access to African banana suppliers makes the business quite profitable, which is why there have been recent confrontations to gain control of the area and consequently to monopolize the export market" (UNSC 2004, 26). Even the decline of the banana sector following changes in EU-Somali trade relations did not completely stop the sector and proceeds from the sector from contributing to conflict; clashes for control of the port of Merca in 2003 signaled that warlords were still trying to control trade to export markets, this time to the Middle East (Webersik 2005).

Banana production and trade summary

The banana production and trade that thrived from 1994 to 1997 did not spark the conflict in Somalia nor have these been the driving force in the conflict. However, as Grosse-Kettler has argued, the country's general anarchy has ensured that when "purchasing exports from Somalia, profit goes into private hands and not in official budgets or industrial agencies" (Grosse-Kettler 2004, 14). Typically, the private hands have been those of warlords, and the profits—some of which have come from the banana trade—have been used for the personal enrichment of warlords or reinvested to perpetuate the conflict for greater profit by warlords.

Yet, there is great positive economic potential in the banana trade for Somalia, as Somali bananas are much sought after by the United Arab Emirates and other Middle Eastern countries (Baars and Riediger 2008). Somalia's proximity to Middle Eastern markets, Middle Eastern consumer preferences for Somali bananas, and the Shabelle and Juba rivers' ability to supply irrigation water year-round for banana cultivation all point to one promising foundation for Somalia's eventual economic recovery.

Somali charcoal production and trade

The Somali banana trade's collapse in 1997 flooded the market with a large number of wage laborers who then sought jobs in the country's growing charcoal business. Weak governance, continued exercise of power through violence, and the existence of lucrative export markets (primarily in Saudi Arabia and the Gulf States), as well as a high number of impoverished Somalis willing to work for very little, amounted to an opportunity for predatory elites and warlords to exploit the country's charcoal production and trade. Ahmed Mohamed Ibrahim observed that "[w]hen the banana export collapsed . . . many Somali businessmen started harvesting wood; exploiting the forests. A lot of farm labor was released due to the collapse; and there is a lucrative market in Saudi Arabia" (Ibrahim 2002).

Charcoal production in Somalia is not new; in the colonial era, Italians in Somalia harvested wood for fuel as they established the country's railway service. Since then, production has tended to vary with the season, peaking from December to March when the land is driest, weather conditions are most favorable for harvesting and converting wood to charcoal, and farm labor has been released from other pursuits.

Today, the majority of southern Somalia's charcoal is produced in the riverine zone between the two southern coastal towns of Brawa and Kismayo. The port at Kismayo is the only deep seaport in southern Somalia with proper loading facilities, and that has facilitated export of a substantial percentage of Somali charcoal to foreign markets. While Mogadishu port remained closed from 1991 to 2006 due to militias fighting, much of the charcoal was exported via natural ports, such as El Ma'an north of Mogadishu. The port then reopened under the former Union of Islamic Courts, and today is under the control of the African Union and Somali government (Gatehouse 2013).

Somali "black gold": The business

Traditionally, woodcutters produced charcoal primarily from acacia trees and primarily for local markets for use in the home for cooking. The value chain has changed in the past two decades as charcoal exports have become a more lucrative business (for some) due to increased demand from the Arabian Peninsula and the nature of Somalia's exploitable, lawless market. In recent years, approximately 80 percent of Somali charcoal is exported, largely to Dubai and Saudi Arabia (Mohamed 2012).

Warlords, local militias, and businesspeople have benefited most from the charcoal trade and the country's general lawlessness. Among the main beneficiaries in the not-so-distant past were Mogadishu-based owners of trucks used to transport charcoal and charcoal traders (Gurre 2003). In most of southern Somalia, elites from the Haber Gedir and the Abgal clans dominated the transport sector, and they, in turn, relied on local support and good relations with militia leaders. Even today, on the outskirts of Mogadishu, trucks loaded with charcoal and escorted by young militiamen must pass through numerous roadblocks manned by competing militias looking to wrestle some profit from the trade before the trucks can reach one of many beach ports (IRIN 2006).

Not all businesspeople in Somalia have supported this unregulated trade, as, in the past, it could involve great risk. In 2000, *Somalia Watch* reported that "[t]he Mogadishu charcoal Mafia must pay not only in terms of money but also lives. Militiamen and drivers have been shot at road blocks, and trucks trying to deliver the load to the beach port have sparked off fire-fights and inter-clan conflicts" (*Somalia Watch* 2000).

Although data on some aspects of the situation is lacking, it is clear that charcoal continues to finance militias. For example, Somali pirates hijacked a ship loaded with charcoal outbound from a port controlled by al Shabaab, an Islamic group opposed to the current Transitional Federal Government (Guled 2010). It is no secret that the charcoal export has financially supported the group in control of the important seaports in southern Somalia: Kismayo and Mogadishu ports. In order to cut off al Shabaab from the charcoal trade, the United Nations issued a charcoal ban in 2012 (UNSC 2012). Since then, sacks of charcoal are piling up in places like Kismayo, cutting local businessmen, traders, and laborers off from the lucrative business. Those who are now supporting troops of the African Union Mission in Somalia, such as the Ras Kamboni Brigades, an ethnic Ogadeni clan–based armed group, oppose the sanctions (McConnell 2012). The group's leader, Sheik Ahmed Madobe, an ex-warlord and former Islamist commander, is pursuing the same strategy as al Shabaab, using the charcoal trade for personal gains and ultimately using the trade to finance his armed group.

Historic charcoal costs and margins

The charcoal trade historically has engaged a range of producers, transporters, and other middlemen. Table 1 illustrates who has benefited from charcoal production and trade in the past. The table's data reflect pre-war years, so they may not reflect conditions during the conflict. Nonetheless, it is useful to consider that, in July 1989, the retail margin on charcoal was 14 percent (310 Somali shillings per 100 kilograms (kg) of charcoal) of the official price (2,300 Somali shillings per 100 kg of charcoal) (Soussan 1990). At the time, the exchange rate for the Somali shilling was 181 shillings to US$1. In order to increase this margin and bypass cooperative fees and government taxes, retailers began buying charcoal through informal markets, and the government lacked the resources to intervene.

Table 1. Official charcoal costs and margins in Mogadishu, Somalia, July 1989

Item	*Somali shillings per 100 kilograms of charcoal*
Labor	600
Supervisors	152
Transport	700
Equipment	260
Taxes	15
Cooperatives fees	169
Producer margin	80
Retailer margin	310
Official price	2,300

Source: Soussan (1990).

Moreover, the market price of charcoal was higher than the government's official price, largely due to lack of alternative fuels, which remains the case today. Alternative fuels such as liquid gas and petroleum need to be imported and paid for with foreign exchange, and these funds were—and remain—limited. Given that the wood used for charcoal production is considered a free good in most of Somalia, low producer margins (reported in 1989 to be 80 Somali shillings per 100 kg of charcoal) are unlikely to change. Moreover, the scale of production has shifted from labor-intensive methods of wood harvesting to the use of chainsaws (IRIN 2006).

Charcoal trade and export markets

Beginning in the late 1990s, the Gulf States imposed strict restrictions on their own production of charcoal due to concern over dwindling forest cover. These restrictions did not curtail demand, however, for throughout the Gulf States, charcoal was and remains a principal and preferred fuel source for smoking tobacco, grilling meat, and burning incense. To meet this demand, the Gulf States needed imports, and Somalis, desperately in need of foreign exchange, met that demand. In the face of lax domestic control over charcoal production and trade restrictions due to the general chaos that pervades the country, Somalia became—and remains—a significant source of charcoal exports to the Gulf States (*Somalia Watch* 2000).

Somali charcoal production not exported to the Gulf States is consumed domestically and typically is of lower quality. While total production and consumption figures remain elusive, charcoal remains the main form of fuel used in cooking, both in rural and urban households. As Ibrahim observed, without government oversight, many Somalis have continued "exploiting national forest reserves . . . [in an] informal trade [that] functions like a black market without regulations and no guarantees" (Ibrahim 2002).

Despite domestic demand, Somali traders have had little incentive to provide charcoal to Somalia's domestic market in the face of higher prices overseas. In 2000, the price per sack of charcoal inside Somalia was US$3 to US$4 whereas, in the Gulf, the same size sack (of better quality) sold for approximately US$10 (*Somalia Watch* 2000). In 2003, a Puntland resident confirmed these figures to researcher Ibrahim Gurre, explaining that the export trade is lucrative because "they [traders] do not pay for the trees. They sell a sack of charcoal for approximately US$10 while the cost of production and transport is less than US$3" (Gurre 2003, 51).

In sum, in recent years, a large export market, high export profit margins (due in part to illicit taxation by militias), and the fact that traders do not pay for charcoal's raw material have helped ensure that Somali charcoal production and trade will continue to focus on export markets.

Charcoal exportation has been a clandestine business, managed by the Somali business elite who, in the absence of a functioning government, have maintained

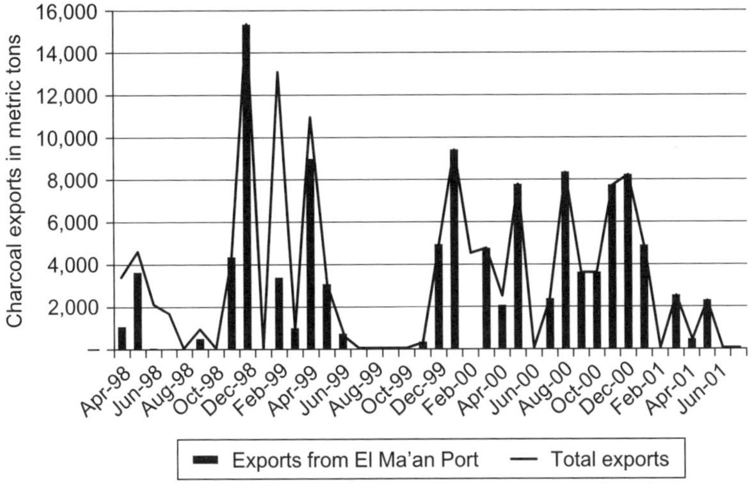

Figure 1. Charcoal exports from southern Somalia, April 1998–July 2001
Source: FSAU–Somalia (2009b).

militias to protect their interests (Webersik 2006). To the point, the collection of illicit taxes at ports and roadblocks on routes linking production to distribution has largely served to guarantee the security of the business elite's interests. For example, the chairman of the Juba Valley Alliance, Bare Aden Shire (also known as Hirale) and his former regional administration imposed a levy of US$0.40 per 100 kg of charcoal bound for export through his territory.[4] Also in 2002, the port authority at El Ma'an, north of Mogadishu, charged US$1,333 per vessel for each ship exceeding 2,000 metric tons capacity and US$333 per vessel for smaller ships (Marchal 2002). In addition, traders had to pay local militias loading and unloading fees of US$0.40 per sack of any commodity, including charcoal, in exchange for security. These security provisions have allowed the port of El Ma'an to dominate the charcoal trade in southern Somalia (see figure 1). Once again, collection of this type of tax by militias in exchange for providing security enabled these militias to maintain their power (Marchal 2002).

Charcoal production

Few of the economic benefits from the production and trade of Somali charcoal have made their way back to the rural laborers and children who collect the wood. In 2002, the daily wage for these laborers was estimated to be US$0.80 (Maykuth 2002), one reason for this being the fairly weak relationship between the riverine farmers of the Digil and Tuni clans, who produce charcoal, and the powerful and

[4] Interviews conducted under the condition of anonymity by the authors in Eldoret, Somalia, on November 21, 2002.

armed Haber Gedir and Abgal subclans of the Hawiye clan, who dominate Mogadishu. Nonetheless, given the country's dire economic situation, for some laborers, just the promise of regular meals has been sufficient.

In southern Somalia, charcoal production has tended to complement other sources of family income and, as such, to help increase families' resilience to external stress. Typically, charcoal production requires little financial capital and only basic skills or knowledge. Most certainly, it buffers poor crop harvests and variable climatic conditions. However, in the absence of a regulatory framework, charcoal production and trade has exploited workers through low wages, has had the potential to destroy the environmental base of workers' livelihoods (for example, when fruit trees are cut down), and has funded ongoing conflict.

Main drivers of Somali charcoal production

According to Laura Linkenback, the main driving factors behind Somali charcoal production are generation of alternative income due to failed harvests, imposition of livestock export bans, devaluation of the Somali shilling, changes in land tenure, lack of or weak governance, rapid urbanization, and the collapse of the banana trade (Linkenback 2001). Many of these factors are described below.

Alternative income

In Somalia, it is typical for one in five harvests to fail. Somalia has experienced a number of droughts in recent decades, and when harvests do fail—as was the case during the inadequate rains of 1999 and 2000—charcoal production tends to increase. In Somalia, most farmers with small holdings are subsistence farmers who must buy grain from others when their own stocks are depleted, and in order to do so, they need an alternative source of income, such as from charcoal production. Drought is not the only threat, however. Major floods in October and November 1997 destroyed most of the irrigated farmland in the Lower Shabelle, freeing labor to engage in charcoal production.

Livestock bans

Bans on importing Somali livestock, imposed by Saudi Arabia and the Gulf States, have also served to stimulate Somali charcoal production. Livestock has long been—and remains—the Somali economy's prime export, constituting some 80 percent of the country's annual export earnings (FSAU–Somalia 2009a). In February 1998, Saudi Arabia imposed an import ban on Somali livestock due to an outbreak among Somali livestock of Rift Valley Fever—a hemorrhagic disease potentially lethal to humans (Steffen, Shirwa, and Addou 1998). Although the ban was lifted in 2009, when it was imposed, there was a lack of foreign currency, Somali households engaged in livestock production were forced to sell livestock at lower margins, and, as a coping strategy, they resorted to charcoal production.

Devaluation of the Somali shilling

Other driving forces behind higher levels of charcoal production in Somalia include devaluation of the Somali shilling and the subsequent need for foreign exchange. As early as 1992, faction leaders began injecting large amounts of counterfeit shillings into the Somali economy (UNSC 2003a). By the end of 2000, the shilling had weakened even further due to the livestock ban. This currency devaluation continues to affect petty traders, farmers of small holdings, and wage laborers in particular, as they have always used the Somali shilling for cash and have no foreign currency savings. When relative fuel prices rise and farmers can no longer afford to hire tractors or buy fuel for their own machinery, the short-term benefits of engaging in charcoal production begin to outweigh the costs of farming and, indeed, help drive such engagement, along with the conflict it engenders.

Changes in land tenure

The Somali charcoal trade has also been linked to issues of land tenure. In the past, rural Somali communities communally managed certain agricultural and pastoral lands, primarily through sophisticated reciprocal access and use-exchange relationships. However, after Somalia's independence, the Barre regime declared these seemingly unowned or customarily held lands to be state lands. Government officials took control of the lands, and then these lands were "liberated" (taken over) by powerful clans from other (central) regions. As a result, urban Somali business elites and militia members ended up owning large areas of previously communally managed farm and pastureland that they then converted to the more profitable enterprise of charcoal production.

Weak governance and lack of regulation

Regulation of the charcoal trade requires an authority that governs production, restricts access, and distributes benefits. Given that the current government of Somalia lacks authority over its territory, Somalia lacks governmental limits on the scale and conditions of charcoal production. In recent years, large quantities of charcoal are still being exported from small beach ports out of the Transitional Federal Government's reach despite attempts at a ban in 2006 by the Islamic Courts Union (IRIN 2006). The United Nations imposed a charcoal ban in 2012, but its effectiveness still remains to be seen.

Collapse of the banana trade

Lastly, the collapse of the banana trade freed labor, which had implications for charcoal production. For some, switching from work in banana production to work in charcoal production was relatively easy, geographically, because lands suited to banana production—fertile lands with patches of forest—are also suited to charcoal production.

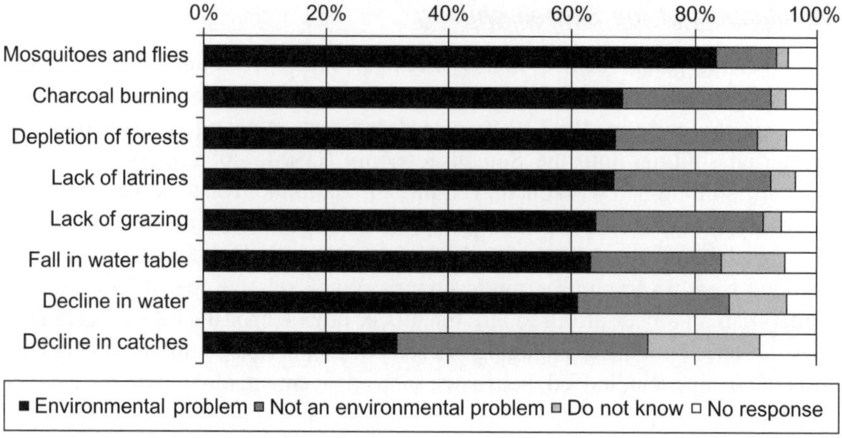

Figure 2. Perception of environmental problems in Somalia, 2002
Source: World Bank and UNDP (2003).

Charcoal and environmental problems

In a 2002 survey by the World Bank and the United Nations Development Programme (UNDP), 68 percent of Somali households identified charcoal burning as an environmental problem, second only to mosquitoes and flies (World Bank and UNDP 2003; see figure 2). Charcoal laborers also suffer. Not only do they gain little from their engagement in the trade, but they also must cope with its environmental consequences, including forest depletion and environmental health issues. Due to a lack of regulatory authority at the local level, unplanned and unregulated exploitation and clearance of forests and woodlands for firewood, crops, and charcoal production is the norm. The result is not only deforestation but, due to forest clearance, the loss of acacia tree fodder for livestock (in Somalia, the acacia species serves both as critical raw material for charcoal production and as a source of livestock fodder). Additionally, riverbanks once protected from development by government regulations are increasingly being cleared for crop and charcoal production (IRIN 2001a), leading to the erosion of nutrient-rich soil and adverse effects on river courses.

Charcoal and conflict factors

Recognizing that the charcoal trade promises high profit margins for retailers (see table 1, above) and the opportunity to earn foreign exchange even while forest clearance leads to sand dune encroachment, loss of fodder for livestock, and erosion of riverbanks, clans local to Somalia's southern coast (Digil and Tuni) have fought with newcomer clans from the central regions (such as the Haber Gedir subclan of the Hawiye clan) for control over the transport, retail, and export business of the charcoal trade (Webersik 2006).

Charcoal and clan affiliations

In an environment where force and political power is essential for engaging in business of any kind, to engage in the charcoal trade in Somalia requires belonging to a powerful clan, such as the Haber Gedir. While affiliation with this clan is particularly advantageous because it largely controls the Somali charcoal trade, as a general matter, clan affiliation has become paramount in the lives of the Somalis. As an agropastoralist explained, "The reason why people support tribalism is that maybe the clan has more weapons or more people. So if you are attacked or killed, somebody else [from the aggressor's side] will be killed in revenge. That is why people are loyal to their clans."[5]

Apart from clan affiliation, in today's Somalia, the use of force (linked to clan affiliation) is what governs the charcoal trade. Coastal clans, such as the Tuni, have little power either to resist the trade or to benefit from it. Somalia's Resource Management and Network reported in 2003 that, "for the local communities concerned with conservation, constant conflicts have erupted between the traders and their contracted laborers who apparently use force to bring down trees for charcoal burning" (Gurre 2003, 48). According to Ibrahim, "Local communities are resisting the practices of the charcoal [production] . . . and there is even evidence that mango trees are being cut down for charcoal production" (Ibrahim 2002). In addition, he noted, "In Brawa, there was conflict between the [local] Tuni and the [nonlocal] Haber Gedir because of the charcoal trade."

At the local level, then, conflict has erupted not only when local communities have resisted destruction of their fruit trees for the charcoal trade but also when local communities have felt they were being excluded from the trade's economic benefits. According to a member of the former Transitional National Government (the predecessor to today's Transitional Federal Government), the Tuni and Haber Gedir clans had clashed specifically and directly over distribution of the benefits of the charcoal trade:

> In Brawa, conflict between the [indigenous] Tuni and the [newcomer] Haber Gedir arose over the cutting of trees [for the production of charcoal]. . . . Regarding the charcoal trade, there was a reported clash between Haber Gedir and Tuni at the beginning of 2002 in Brawa district. The Tuni killed two to three people of the Haber Gedir. In retaliation, two to three villages inhabited by Tuni were burned.[6]

Several other interviewees from the Brawa region have claimed that, since the civil war, newcomer clans there, mostly of the Hawiye clan (which includes the Haber Gedir clan), have monopolized nearly all business sectors, including

---

[5] Agropastoralist interviewed by the Agency for Cooperation and Research in Development on April 14, 2001, in Sablale, Somalia.

[6] Interview with a member of the former Transitional National Government, speaking on the condition of anonymity with the authors, late 2002.

the charcoal trade, with the result that those of different clan backgrounds, such as the Tuni, have not benefited and, in fact, have been driven from their traditional livelihoods.

Local clans seem to have been more concerned about demanding a fair share of the business than in protesting its adverse environmental impacts. "The Tuni want a cut in the charcoal business, currently dominated by the Abgal and Haber Gedir clans. It is not a question of environment but one of money" (IRIN 2001b).

Charcoal production and trade summary

Over the past ten years, trade in charcoal has become more important than ever before. United Nations investigators estimate that the Islamist organization al Shabaab earned, in 2011, approximately US$25 million from the trade (McConnell 2012). In southern Somalia, local communities belonging to militarily weaker clans, such as the Tuni, have tried, primarily for economic reasons, to build resistance to the control of the trade by families belonging to militarily stronger clans, such as the Haber Gedir. In Brawa's rural areas—and elsewhere—local communities and their clans, largely excluded from involvement in the trade at the highest margin levels, have clashed with newcomer clans, and this has led to a number of people being killed. To operate at the retail and export levels is desirable because in Somalia's charcoal trade, the raw material—wood—is mostly considered a free good and, further, the rule of force has undermined traditional ways of managing or restricting abusive land use.

Conflict fish

As the potential for the banana trade to fund Somalia's conflict dried up, those warlords and armed groups interested in perpetuating the conflict for personal enrichment and to fund operations and arms purchases looked to the charcoal trade and to Somalia's rich fishing grounds. Somalia has the longest coastline in Africa and a seasonal upwelling of nutrients that sustains huge numbers of fish, including highly profitable species such as yellowfin and skipjack tuna (UNEP 2005).

Some of the country's most notorious warlords have been funded by commercial fishing off Somalia's coast by virtue of sale of false fishing licenses to foreign fishing interests, including European companies. According to the UN Panel of Experts on Somalia, "All the attempts at managing the Somali fisheries have resulted in a great deal of money—millions [of US dollars] over the past 10 years—being paid into the private hands of faction leaders, allowing for personal enrichment and to some extent the payment and resupply of private militias" (UNSC 2003a, 44). Some of the false fishing permits involved were found to have been typed out on the previous government's letterhead, while others bore the personal seals of warlords (UNSC 2006). According to owners or operators of some of the commercial fishing vessels involved, some vessels negotiate these licenses before entering Somali waters, and some simply make their way to Somali ports hoping to make last-minute arrangements with a local warlord (UNSC 2006).

Commercial interest in Somali fish

A large number of fishing vessels potentially need these conflict-funding licenses. The Food and Agriculture Organization of the United Nations (FAO) estimated that in 2005, 700 foreign-owned vessels from Greece, Italy, and Spain (as well as many other non-European nations) were engaged in unauthorized fishing in Somali waters (FAO 2005). In 2003, the UN Panel of Experts on Somalia referred to Somali waters as a "'free for all' among the world's fishing fleets" (UNSC 2003b, 32), and, in 2006, the UN Monitoring Group on Somalia suggested that, in any one season, some 500 international vessels could be found fishing off of the country's coast (UNSC 2006). In 2001, it was said that the lights from so many ships off some stretches of the Puntland coast resembled the lights of a city at night (Kulmiye 2001).

Over the years that Somalia has lacked a functioning government and, hence, formal authority to issue legal fishing licenses, foreign commercial vessels have caught significant annual tonnages of fish in Somali waters, principally tuna. According to the Marine Resources Assessment Group, from 1992 through 2005, the total reported tuna catch by purse seiners (a specific type of fishing boat) inside the Somali Exclusive Economic Zone (EEZ) amounted to 5–10 percent of the total reported tuna catch in the entire Indian Ocean (MRAG 2005).[7] The total figure for all fish caught in Somali waters (reported and unreported) in these (and subsequent) years is likely to be considerably higher.

A highly lucrative enterprise

Fishing in Somali waters has been highly lucrative. In 2001, Hart Nimrod, an offshoot of a British private military company, estimated that every international purse seiner, long-liner, and trawler plying Somali waters that year caught, on average, some US$2 million worth of tuna per month (Hart Nimrod 2001). This matches an earlier estimate from the Somali Centre for Water and Environment indicating that, in seventy-five days of fishing, each of these commercial vessels can catch up to 420 metric tons of fish worth roughly US$6.3 million (Somali Centre for Water and Environment 1999). That foreign vessels continue to fish

[7] The 1982 United Nations Convention on the Law of the Sea—which Somalia ratified on November 11, 1994—limits coastal states' claim to a territorial sea of twelve nautical miles (nm) in article 3, and establishes an exclusive economic zone (EEZ) of 200 nm in article 57. Within its EEZ, a coastal state has "sovereign rights for the purpose of exploring and exploiting, conserving and managing the natural resource" (art. 56(1)(a)). For the complete text of the convention, see www.un.org/depts/los/convention_agreements/texts/unclos/unclos_e.pdf.

Somali waters despite the need to pay for illegal licenses, not to mention the well-known risk of piracy and kidnapping for ransom, further indicates the trade's highly lucrative value.

Hundreds of foreign vessels fishing in Somali waters in high tuna season (August to November) have caught hundreds of millions of dollars worth—and possibly billions of dollars worth—of skipjack, bigeye, and yellowfin (MRAG 2005). That foreign vessels continue to fish Somali waters despite the need to pay for illegal licenses, not to mention the well-known risk of piracy and kidnapping for ransom, further indicates the trade's highly lucrative value.

Since 1991, Somali warlords have realized millions of dollars from the issuance of illegal fishing licenses. According to a 2006 UN Monitoring Group on Somalia report, a single fishing permit issued by "Jubbaland State" sold for US$80,000 in 2006, and permits for the entire year that year sold for as much as US$150,000 per boat (UNSC 2006). This has generated millions of dollars from 1993 to 2003, much of which was then used to pay private militias and procure arms and ammunition (UNSC 2003c). In 2006, the UN Monitoring Group on Somalia listed fishing licenses and charcoal as the two key revenue generators for what they euphemistically called "local administrations" (that is, warlords) in Lower Juba, Lower Shabelle, and Middle Shabelle (UNSC 2006).

One way fishing licenses have funded warlords is through a company called Africa Fisheries Management (Afmet). In 2003, the UN Panel of Experts on Somalia reported that Afmet fishing licensing profits were funneled into the account of warlord Hussein Ali Ahmed (the "Mayor of Mogadishu"), who then distributed them to five other warlords: Hussein Aideed, Ali Mahdi, Abdullahi Yusuf, Mohamed Abshir, and General Morgan (UNSC 2003b). Despite the fact that these men represented the main opposing factions in Mogadishu, Afmet succeeded in bringing them together to share in licensing revenues. According to the UN Panel of Experts on Somalia, Afmet itself admitted to generating US$600,000 to US$1 million per year in fishing license revenue from 1996 to 1998 and approximately US$300,000 in 2002 (UNSC 2003b).

Warlords operating along the coast can also gain funds through ransom. As has become increasingly apparent, Somali waters are among the world's most dangerous, and should, according to the International Maritime Organization, be considered of significant concern (Kulmiye 2001). In 2003, the UN Panel of Experts on Somalia reported that fishing along the Puntland coast at times resembled naval warfare, with fishing boats typically equipped with heavy anti-aircraft cannons and armed crews (UNSC 2003a).

Fisheries and conflict financing summary

In summary, Somalia's lawlessness and its rich fishing grounds have combined to provide the country's warlords with opportunities to raise funds for their continued war efforts. Significant revenue has been generated through the illegal sale of false fishing licenses, and padded coffers have exacerbated anarchy in and around the country's EEZ, which is increasingly marked by great risks to fishing and shipping vessels and staff from piracy. In 2005 and 2006, the UN Monitoring Group on Somalia recommended that the United Nations Security Council (UNSC) impose sanctions on fish from Somalia (UNSC 2006); however, thus far, the UNSC has not acted on that recommendation. By contrast, if managed properly, for instance by holding public auctions to distribute fishing licenses, Somali fisheries have great potential to foster economic recovery and peace.

LESSONS LEARNED

In Somalia, funds generated through the production and sale of bananas and charcoal and the exploitation of the country's fisheries have been used by militias to purchase arms and perpetuate civil strife. For peace and development to occur, it is necessary to curtail the utilization of conflict resources. This section examines lessons that can be learned from Somalia and applied in other conflict and post-conflict situations struggling with conflict resources.

Trade and conflict

Trade in bananas, charcoal, and fish is not the sole cause of conflict in Somalia; the country's history, its governance structures, the easy availability of small arms, and a host of other factors have all played a role (UNSC 2003a, 2003b). However, as this chapter has shown, in the absence of a formal government and what amounts to an economic free-for-all, warlords backed by arms have profited from wartime production and trade of these resources, with some of the revenue devoted to personal enrichment, and some reinvested to perpetuate the conflict.

Peter D. Little notes that the reason "trade figures so prominently in recent events in Somalia relates to the fact that (1) its economy has always been external and market-oriented, and (2) the current statelessness promotes an excessively open and unrestricted economy" (Little 2003, 3). Political and economic instability in Somalia created an atmosphere in which profits could be made by whomever controlled the economy's access points; it is therefore unsurprising that warlords have fostered that instability to maintain their economic lifelines. With a stable government in place, individuals would not have been able to tax exports for their own gain.

The anarchic conditions that led to this situation in Somalia are unfortunately not unique to Somalia. Other, similar conditions exist elsewhere in Africa and beyond where legal as well as illegal production and trade of natural resources have contributed to perpetuation of conflict and, as a result, the deterioration of livelihoods for civilians caught in the middle. Recent history is rife with examples of this, from diamonds in Sierra Leone and coltan in the DRC to timber in Cambodia.

It would be inaccurate to say that the presence, exploitation, and trade of valuable natural resources are sufficient factors to trigger armed conflict. However, when taken in combination with the strategic and economic interests of warring parties, weak governance, and the generation of significant grievances at the local level based on the losses felt by local communities, trade in natural resources can contribute to violent conflict. Such has been—and remains—the case in Somalia. Alec Crawford and Oli Brown identify two broad lessons that can be drawn from Somalia (Crawford and Brown 2008).

1. "Taxing" the trade in agricultural and marine commodities can raise funds for the onset or perpetuation of conflict.
2. Agricultural and marine commodities, as proxies for key natural resources like land and water, can increase the risk of competition (and conflict) between groups. In the absence of strong governance and law enforcement, this can lead to conflict.

PEACEBUILDING RECOMMENDATIONS TO NATIONAL AND INTERNATIONAL STAKEHOLDERS

From the experiences in Somalia, a number of policy lessons and recommendations can be made to guide national and international stakeholders in addressing future conflict in other regions. These lessons relate to understanding political and socioeconomic factors that influence peacebuilding in post-conflict situations, the importance of raising awareness of the links between natural resources and conflict, and the role that natural resources play in funding conflict.

National stakeholders

Policy makers and agencies involved in peacebuilding in Somalia as national stakeholders need to be informed of the political realities and power relations inside Somalia in order to address the country's key problems of insecurity, poverty, and human suffering. Specifically, such stakeholders should consider the following:

- Any meaningful peacebuilding effort needs to recognize the role of the Somali business class—although somewhat ambiguous—in achieving political stability.
- In order to persuade businesspeople to support the Transitional Federal Government, benefits, such as security and health services, must outweigh incentives to engage in Somalia's conflict economy. Today, automatic weapons have become a means to meet ends in all respects of life, including in the business sector.
- The economic benefits of Somalia's bananas, charcoal, and fish trade must be fairly distributed across all sections of society irrespective of clan, gender, or other social markers.
- Providing alternative livelihoods must be a focus.

International stakeholders

In order to effectively address the role of natural resources in the Somalia conflict, the international peacekeeping and peacebuilding community should consider the following actions:[8]

- The international community, particularly Somalia's major trading partners in Africa, Europe, and the Gulf, should work with and support national policy makers, local stakeholders, and local trading partners to increase the transparency of trade with Somalia to reduce and restrict trade contributions to the conflict. Efforts to do so could include (1) technical and financial support to build the capacity of local law enforcement and strengthen national legal and court systems to reduce illegal harvesting and trade; (2) monitoring key trade and transport hubs; (3) establishing regulated charcoal trading centers similar to those established by the United Nations for conflict minerals in the DRC; and (4) establishing due diligence legislation for international companies operating in or trading with Somalia.
- Neighboring countries and the international community should recognize and support local and national reconciliation efforts already underway to manage natural resources. Thus, for example, only charcoal that is certified and controlled by the African Union and the Somali government could be destined for export trade.
- The international community should support the imposition of effective UN sanctions on Somali bananas, charcoal, and fish, if the domestic sale of and international trade in these resources can be directly linked to financing the Somali conflict. If such sanctions would result in significant economic hardship for the people of Somalia, alternative sanctions, such as travel bans and asset freezes for leadership that would not affect the general population should be used instead. Further, the international community should hold to account any companies found to be operating in contravention of such sanctions (for example, buying false fishing permits).
- The international community should work to ensure that stakeholders and international entities operating in Somalia are made aware of the linkages between the trade in Somali bananas, charcoal, and fish and the conflict. UN agencies within the country should be mandated to help manage these resources in a sustainable way to mitigate the conflict and enforce sanctions, as required.
- The international community should acknowledge the importance of natural resources in Somalia—in particular, bananas, charcoal, and fisheries—for strengthening peacebuilding and economic recovery.
- More broadly, the international community should support the recommendation (by the UK-based organization Global Witness) that the UNSC define conflict resources so that it can identify cases requiring further UNSC action.

---

[8] Adapted from Crawford and Brown (2008).

The definition should include less traditional conflict resources (other than diamonds, coltan, and timber) and address the money flows associated with conflict resources trade.

REFERENCES

Baars, E., and A. Riediger. 2008. *Building the banana chain in Somalia: Support to Agricultural Marketing Services and Access to Markets (SAMSAM) experiences*. Nairobi, Kenya: European Committee for Agricultural Training.

BBC. 2011. Somalia famine: UN warns of 750,000 deaths. BBC News Africa, September 5. www.bbc.co.uk/news/world-africa-14785304.

Bradbury, M. 1994. *The Somali conflict: Prospects for peace: An exploratory report for Oxfam*. Oxford, UK: Oxfam.

Crawford, A., and O. Brown. 2008. *Growing unrest: The links between farmed and fished resources and the risk of conflict*. Winnipeg, Canada: International Institute for Sustainable Development.

Debiel, T. 2003. *UN-Friedensoperationen in Afrika. Weltinnenpolitik und die realität von Bürgerkriegen. Sonderband der stiftung entwicklung und Frieden*. Bonn, Germany: Dietz.

De Waal, A., and R. Omaar. 1993. Famine in Somalia: Letters to the editor. *Lancet* 341 (8858): 1479.

Economist. 2006. The path to ruin—the Horn of Africa. August 12.

FAO (Food and Agriculture Organization of the United Nations). 2005. *Fishery country profile*. Rome.

Ford, L. 2013. Somalia famine in 2010–12 'worst in past 25 years': Nearly 260,000 people died in parts of Somalia between October 2010 and April 2012, including 133,000 children. theguardian.com, May 2. www.guardian.co.uk/global-development/2013/may/02/somalia-famine-worst-25-years.

FSAU–Somalia (Food Security Analysis Unit–Somalia). 2009a. *Livestock in Somalia*. Nairobi, Kenya.

———. 2009b. Monthly reports. Nairobi, Kenya. www.fsnau.org.

Gatehouse, G. 2013. Somalia's fight to harness the power of Mogadishu port. BBC News Africa, May 6. www.bbc.co.uk/news/world-africa-22404123.

Grosse-Kettler, S. 2004. External actors in stateless Somalia: A war economy and its promoters. BICC Paper No. 39. Bonn, Germany: Bonn International Center for Conversion. www.bicc.de/uploads/tx_bicctools/paper39.pdf.

Guled, A. 2010. Somali pirates claim to have hijacked charcoal ship. Reuters, March 17. www.reuters.com/article/idUSTRE62G3T620100317.

Gurre, I. 2003. Deforestation and charcoal burning: Specific case studies from the southern and central regions of Somalia. Case studies presented at the fourth regional workshop on resource-based conflict, Bannano Boarding School, Dubat Village, Gashamo District, Somali Regional State, Ethiopia.

Hansch, S., S. Lillibridge, G. Egeland, C. Teller, and M. Toole. 1994. *Lives lost, lives saved: Excess mortality and the impact of health interventions in the Somalia emergency*. Washington D.C.: Refugee Policy Group.

Hart Nimrod. 2001. Africa's fishing crisis. *African Business*, January.

Ibrahim, A. M. 2002. Interview by authors of Mogadishu-based researcher from the Centre for Research and Dialogue. December 18. Mogadishu, Somalia.

Il Mondo. 1995. Impero somalo. February 27.

IRIN (Integrated Regional Information Networks). 2001a. Without controls, desertification increases. IRIN Humanitarian News and Analysis, June 18. www.irinnews.org/report/22258/somalia-without-controls-desertification-increases.

———. 2001b. Land-mine incidents blamed on charcoal trade. IRIN Humanitarian News and Analysis, July 19. www.irinnews.org/report/23455/somalia-land-mine-incidents-blamed-on-charcoal-trade.

———. 2006. Somalia: Charcoal trade on the rise. IRIN Humanitarian News and Analysis, November 6. www.irinnews.org/report/61489/somalia-charcoal-trade-on-the-rise.

———. 2011. Somalia: Hospitals overwhelmed as bombing death toll rises. IRIN Humanitarian News and Analysis, October 5. www.irinnews.org/report/93896/somalia-hospitals-overwhelmed-as-bombing-death-toll-rises.

Keen, D. 2000. Incentives and disincentives for violence. In *Greed and grievance: Economic agendas in civil wars*, ed. M. R. Berdal and D. Malone. Boulder, CO: Lynne Rienner / International Development Research Centre.

Kulish, N. 2013. Despite exit of militants, violence continues to grip Somali city and raises worries. *New York Times*, July 4. www.nytimes.com/2013/07/05/world/africa/despite-exit-of-militants-violence-continues-to-grip-somali-city-and-raises-worries.html.

Kulmiye, A. J. 2001. Militias or trawlers: Who is the villain? *East African*, July 9.

Le Sage, A., and N. Majid. 2002. The livelihoods gap: Responding to the economic dynamics of vulnerability in Somalia. *Disasters* 26 (1): 10–27.

Linkenback, L. 2001. *Analysis of the socio-economic drivers behind the charcoal trade in Somalia*. Edinburgh, UK: University of Edinburgh.

Little, P. D. 2003. *African issues: Somalia; Economy without state*. Oxford, UK: James Currey; Bloomington: Indiana University Press.

Marchal, R. 1997. *Lower Shabelle region study on governance*. Nairobi, Kenya: United Nations Development Programme Office for Somalia.

———. 2002. *A survey of Mogadishu's economy*. Nairobi, Kenya: European Commission / Somali Unit.

MRAG (Marine Resources Assessment Group). 2005. Review of impacts of illegal, unreported and unregulated fishing on developing countries. London.

Maykuth, A. 2002. Somalia is sacrificing its trees for profit. *Seattle Times*, March 24.

McConnell, T. 2012. Why charcoal may endanger Somalia's best hope for peace. TIME.com, November 12.

Mohamed, A. 2012. Charcoal enterprise of Somalia. Somalia Report, May 2. www.somaliareport.com/index.php/post/3291.

New Agriculturist. 2009. A ripe time for Somali bananas? January. www.new-ag.info/focus/focusItem.php?a=670.

Norfolk Education and Action for Development Centre. 1995. Banana wars in Somalia. *Review of African Political Economy* 22 (64): 274–275.

Smith-Spark, L., and N. Elbagir. 2013. Somalia famine killed close to 260,000 people, report says. CNN, May 2. http://edition.cnn.com/2013/05/02/world/africa/somalia-famine.

Somalia Watch. 2000. Focus on charcoal. www.somaliawatch.org/archiveoct00/001026601.htm.

Somali Centre for Water and Environment. 1999. Local fishermen battle foreign trawlers. www.somwe.com/fishmen.html.

Soussan, J. 1990. *The Government of Somalia Technical Committee for Energy final report on alternative energy sources for urban areas*. London: Overseas Development Administration.

Steffen, P., A. H. Shirwa, and S. I. Addou. 1998. *The livestock embargo by Saudi Arabia: A report on the economic, financial and social impact on Somaliland and Somalia.* Nairobi, Kenya: Famine Early Warning System–Somalia.

Straziuso, J. 2012. Somali's Moadishu loses 'world's most dangerous city' label. Huffington Post, June 13. www.huffingtonpost.com/2012/06/13/somalia-mogadishu-peace_n_1593194.html.

UNEP (United Nations Environment Programme). 2005. *The state of the environment in Somalia: A desk study.* Nairobi, Kenya.

UNSC (United Nations Security Council). 2003a. *Report of the Panel of Experts on Somalia pursuant to Security Council resolution 1425 (2002).* S/2003/223. March 25. New York. www.un.org/ga/search/view_doc.asp?symbol=S/2003/223.

———. 2003b. *Report of the Panel of Experts on Somalia pursuant to Security Council resolution 1474 (2003).* S/2003/1035. November 4. New York. www.undemocracy.com/S-2003-1035.pdf.

———. 2003c. *Report of the UN Expert Panel on Somalia pursuant to Security Council Resolution 1425 (2003).* S/2003/223. March 25. www.securitycouncilreport.org/atf/cf/%7B65BFCF9B-6D27-4E9C-8CD3-CF6E4FF96FF9%7D/SOMALIA%20S2003223.pdf.

———. 2004. *Report of the Monitoring Group on Somalia pursuant to Security Council resolution 1519 (2003).* S/2004/604. August 11. New York. www.undemocracy.com/S-2004-604.pdf.

———. 2006. *Report of the UN Monitoring Group on Somalia.* S/2006/229. May 4. New York. www.undemocracy.com/S-2006-229.pdf.

———. 2012. Resolution 2036. S/RES/2036 (2012). February 22. www.un.org/en/ga/search/view_doc.asp?symbol=S/RES/2036(2012).

Webersik, C. 2005. Fighting for the plenty: The banana trade in southern Somalia. *Oxford Development Studies* 33 (1): 81–97.

———. 2006. Mogadishu: An economy without a state. *Third World Quarterly* 27 (8): 1463–1480.

World Bank and UNDP (United Nations Development Programme). 2003. *Socio-economic survey 2002 Somalia.* Washington, D.C.

PART 4

Lessons learned

Managing natural resources for livelihoods: Helping post-conflict communities survive and thrive

Helen Young and Lisa Goldman

Around the world, natural resources play a significant role in the buildup to, onset of, and continuation of violent conflict. Once peace agreements are signed, natural resources remain critical to peacebuilding, as they can help to ensure that peace is lasting, and that redevelopment is equitable and sustainable. The role of natural resources in promoting peace (or fueling conflict) is often intertwined with the livelihoods of local communities. Thus, a livelihoods lens can improve understanding of how natural resources are linked to conflict, and provide new insights into conflict mitigation and the design and implementation of more targeted and effective peacebuilding approaches.

Because livelihood production systems are often the mainstay of the wider economy and the basis for many social and economic relations, networks, and institutions, natural resources and livelihoods are linked to economic development, as well as to peace and security. Livelihoods not only provide food and income but also contribute significantly to identity, social capital, and personal and social fulfillment.

In many conflict-prone and post-conflict regions, natural resources play a fundamental role in supporting livelihood opportunities for both urban and rural populations, and have a strong impact on community resilience, local security, and long-term sustainability. This is especially true in developing, low-income countries, where natural capital accounts for 26 percent of total national wealth, versus approximately 13 percent in middle-income countries and 2 to 3 percent in developed countries (Lax and Krug 2013; OECD 2008). In many areas, the poorest populations are the most dependent on natural resources for their livelihoods and basic needs, and therefore most vulnerable to shocks that harm the natural resource base or limit or deny access to natural resources (Lax and Krug 2013).

Helen Young is a research director at the Feinstein International Center and a professor at the Friedman School of Nutrition Science and Policy, both at Tufts University. Lisa Goldman is a senior attorney with the Environmental Law Institute.

Local (bottom-up) conflict may develop as a result of rising tensions between livelihood groups, such as farmers and herders (agriculturalists and pastoralists), over access to natural resources. National or international (top-down) conflict—mobilized by political leaders, and involving organized armed forces and large-scale violence—can also be linked to (and affect) natural resources (Keen 2000).[1] In recent conflicts, armed groups have intentionally damaged or destroyed local natural resources and other livelihood-related assets, such as homesteads, land (by laying landmines), irrigation infrastructure, trees, wells, and terracing. Widespread looting of natural resources by militias and military elements (which may be sanctioned by military leaders), or by criminal elements emboldened by the conflict, can lead to further degradation or loss of natural assets that are essential to civilian livelihoods.

Civilians living in conflict-affected regions are often forcibly displaced and may flee across or within national borders to safer areas, or to camps for refugees or internally displaced persons (IDPs). The influx of refugees or IDPs, however, often subjects nearby natural resources to increasing population pressures and potentially uncontrolled natural resource extraction. In many cases, refugees or IDPs are unable to pursue their former livelihoods, as their former access to livelihood assets—such as farms, pastures, fishing grounds, or local businesses—has been lost.

For those who remain behind during conflict, livelihood opportunities are seriously disrupted. To survive conditions marked by insecurity, market distortions, and lack of regulation, households must find ways to cope, which may include seeking alternative livelihood options. In response to the immediate need for food and income, some may engage in maladaptive livelihood strategies—that is, strategies that are harmful to others, to the environment, or both. Illicit ways of earning a living, in turn, may further undermine the natural resource base, perpetuate social inequities and marginalization, and even promote violence or the continuation of conflict.

Following the adoption of a peace agreement, the natural resource base of a country or region can provide opportunities to advance peacebuilding—for example, by addressing lingering tensions over natural resource access and use, or by establishing cooperative management initiatives or institutions that promote natural resource governance, sustainable livelihoods, and benefit sharing. Such efforts are possible, however, only where conflict dynamics—including those related to livelihoods—are recognized and fully understood.

Given the strong connections between livelihoods, natural resources, and conflict, a focus on sustainable livelihoods during the post-conflict period offers opportunities to promote peacebuilding in a much broader sense. As the building blocks of community resilience to a wide range of threats, including conflict,

---

1 This distinction between top-down and bottom-up violence differentiates between conflict mobilized by political leaders and entrepreneurs, whether for political or economic reasons, and violence engaged in by ordinary people, neither of which is necessarily independent of the other (Keen 2000).

livelihoods and natural resources are fundamental to the peacebuilding process. If they are overlooked, important opportunities to promote lasting peace may be lost. Where livelihoods are given priority, however, peacebuilding can promote the sustainable use of natural resources, increase cooperation between opposing groups, provide basic services to the poor and those most in need of resources, create income-generating opportunities for local communities, and enhance both regional security and resilience in the face of recurring shocks and instability.

The chapters that make up this book examine the role of natural resource–based livelihoods in conflict and in post-conflict peacebuilding. Relying on both research and practical experience, the chapters explore and clarify the nexus between livelihoods, natural resources, conflict, and peace. This final chapter offers further analysis of the perspectives on conflict and peacebuilding proposed by the chapters' authors. By closely examining these perspectives and revisiting the case studies, the chapter also identifies key lessons learned from livelihood interventions and livelihood-related peacebuilding initiatives in conflict-prone and post-conflict settings.

The first sections of the chapter lay the groundwork for understanding the nexus between livelihoods, natural resources, and conflict. The chapter begins with an overview of livelihoods and related concepts; in particular, it distinguishes between livelihoods as a means of living (including employment) and the sustainable livelihood approaches currently being applied in conflict and post-conflict settings. The chapter then links the key elements of livelihood systems—assets, strategies, and transforming policies and processes—to concepts of vulnerability, resilience, coping, and adaptation. The third section of the chapter examines the livelihoods–natural resources–conflict nexus more specifically and discusses its relevance to post-conflict peacebuilding.

The chapter's remaining sections proceed with a discussion of effective peacebuilding- and livelihood-related interventions in post-conflict situations. The fourth section focuses on evidenced-based programming; it highlights the importance of building a shared understanding of the issues and examines approaches to apply theory to practice. The section ends by identifying five key elements in the assessment of post-conflict, natural resource–based livelihood initiatives: (1) understanding the historical context—in particular, livelihood- and natural resource–related conflict dynamics; (2) recognizing the impact of climate variability and seasonality on natural resource–based livelihoods; (3) adopting a multilayered analysis of the post-conflict situation, in order to understand the linkages between local tensions and national or transnational conflict; (4) using conflict analysis tools to enhance livelihood-based peacebuilding efforts; and (5) promoting the development and use of new interdisciplinary tools and approaches and expert analysis.

The fifth and sixth sections of the chapter, respectively, consist of (1) a framework for categorizing and analyzing the interventions captured in the case studies, in accordance with their aims and objectives; and (2) a distillation of the lessons learned from the implementation of various livelihood interventions. Both sections include overviews of programming approaches, goals, and results.

The concluding section of the chapter proposes a set of principles to keep in mind when designing and implementing livelihood-based natural resource management projects in countries emerging from conflict.

LIVELIHOOD APPROACHES: TWENTY-FIVE YEARS ON

There is no simple blueprint for talking about livelihoods. One helpful starting point, however, is to distinguish between livelihoods as a means of making a living, and the livelihoods concept that underpins livelihood approaches. With respect to the first meaning, the *Oxford Dictionary of English* defines *livelihood* as "a means of securing the basic necessities of life" (OUP 2010, 1034). This is the basis for Blake Ratner's definition: "the ability of families to provide for themselves and sustain the rural economy"—but Ratner adds an emphasis on rural livelihoods based on natural resources (Ratner 2015*, 327).[2]

The vast majority of rural livelihoods, as well as a high proportion of urban livelihoods, depend on access to natural resources. For example, close to 1.6 billion people (25 percent of the global population) depend on forest resources for their livelihoods, and nearly 540 million people (8 percent of the world's population) rely on fisheries and aquaculture to sustain their livelihoods (UNEP, FAO, and UNFF 2009; FAO 2011, n.d.). The percentage of natural resource–based livelihoods in some regions is even higher: in the Sahel region of Africa, for example, 80 percent of the population relies on natural resources for their livelihoods (UNEP et al. 2011).

While precise estimates for conflict-affected countries are difficult to come by, Somalia and Sudan are known to have the highest number of pastoralist and agropastoralist livestock producers in sub-Saharan Africa (more than 7 million in each) (Rass 2006); in Somalia, pastoralists and agropastoralists account for approximately 80 percent of the population. In Sudan, 52.8 percent of households depend on cultivation and animal husbandry (the two main types of agriculture), and 80 percent of the workforce overall is employed in agriculture (Ahmed 2008).

In the context of international development, *livelihoods* usually refers to the sustainable livelihoods approach—a broader concept that encompasses, for example, livelihood security and livelihood systems. One widely accepted definition of *livelihoods* in this sense is that proffered by Ian Scoones:

> A livelihood comprises the capabilities, assets (including both material and social resources) and activities required for a means of living. A livelihood is sustainable when it can cope with and recover from stresses and shocks, [and] maintain or enhance its capabilities and assets, while not undermining the natural resource base (Scoones 1998, 5).

This definition highlights the key elements of a livelihood system (human capabilities, livelihood assets, and livelihood activities or strategies), while

[2] Citations marked with an asterisk refer to chapters in this book.

emphasizing sustainability—specifically, environmental sustainability, as well as the resilience to cope with and recover from stresses, shocks, and instability.

The Scoones definition builds on earlier work, undertaken in the late 1980s and earlier, that is still highly relevant to post-conflict contexts today. In addition to emphasizing the links between livelihoods and the natural resources on which they depend, this research broadened notions of sustainability to include the net effects and implications for all livelihood groups and systems—a perspective that encompassed social sustainability and equity (Chambers and Conway 1991). Acknowledging the potential effect of one person's livelihood activities on other livelihood systems, both now and in the future (Scoones 1998), is crucial in the context of post-conflict peacebuilding and competition over natural resources.

Before the advent of livelihood approaches, the principal approach to food insecurity was known as the "food-first" approach. In the 1990s, however, Susanna Davies, along with Simon Maxwell and other colleagues, proposed situating food security within the broader context of livelihood security (Davies 1996; Maxwell et al. 1992). This shifted the emphasis from food insecurity (how people fail to feed themselves) to "what people do (e.g. what production systems they are part of and on what terms they participate), where people fit into the local resource management systems, and what kind of flexibility their overall livelihoods provide" (Maxwell et al. 1992, 31). This marked a significant change in outlook and approach. For example, famine early warning systems no longer focused solely on food availability and flows but also began to focus on livelihood issues, including both short-term coping strategies and longer-term adaptations (Buchanan-Smith and Davies 1995).[3]

By the mid- to late 1990s, the focus of development had shifted from economic growth toward sustainability and poverty reduction, which entailed renewed attention to well-being at the individual and household levels. In this context, the sustainable livelihoods approach became the dominant paradigm. Several international organizations adopted such an approach, the most visible promulgation of which was the UK Government White Paper on International Development, released in 1997 (Solesbury 2003).[4]

---

[3] The literature on coping strategies has its roots in research on household strategies for coping with episodes of food insecurity—which has broadened, over the past several decades, to include responses to a wider range of shocks, risks, and hazards. Davies helpfully distinguishes between coping strategies that are temporary responses to sudden food insecurity and adaptive strategies that mark a permanent change in the mix of strategies for accessing food (Davies 1993).

[4] A number of research institutions, agencies, and nongovernmental organizations have adopted livelihood approaches, including CARE, the Food and Agriculture Organization of the United Nations, the International Fund for Agricultural Development, Oxfam, the United Nations Development Group, the United Nations Development Programme, and the United Nations Environment Programme. See Carney et al. (1999); Drinkwater and Rusinow (1999); Hamilton-Peach and Townsley (n.d.); Hoon, Singh, and Wanmali (1997); Morse and McNamara (2013); Solesbury (2003); UNDG (2013); and UNEP (2007).

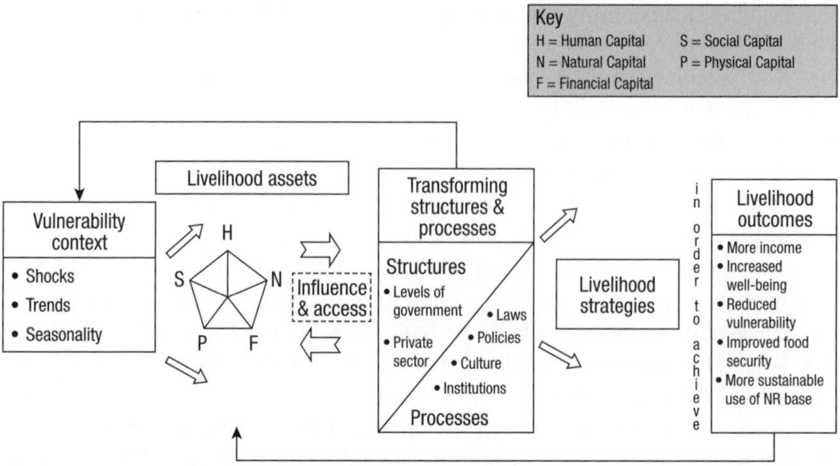

Figure 1. The sustainable livelihoods framework of the Department for International Development, United Kingdom
Source: Adapted from DFID (1999).

The framework shown in figure 1 is that of the United Kingdom's Department for International Development (DFID), and was originally proposed in DFID's sustainable livelihoods guidance sheets (DFID 1999). This framework has since been modified for various contexts, but the core elements remain unchanged. At the household level, those elements are livelihood assets, livelihood strategies, and livelihood outcomes—each of which, in turn, is subject to the influence of a range of institutions, policies, and processes. Among these processes are shocks, trends, and seasonality, which are captured in the figure under the heading of "Vulnerability Context."

Since the mid-1990s, a wide array of national governments, donor countries, development organizations, and research institutions have supported the goal of promoting livelihoods. Livelihood approaches are central to the discourses of development and poverty reduction, and livelihoods analysis has been incorporated into a broad range of other discourses and international strategies—including, for example, those related to disaster risk reduction; climate adaptation; environmental governance; and disarmament, demobilization, and reintegration (DDR).[5]

Livelihood approaches have also been used to link humanitarian programming to developmental approaches (Ross, Maxwell, and Buchanan-Smith 1994). In the late 1980s, following periodic famine and two dry decades across the Sahel, international attention focused on famine prevention, famine early warning,

[5] Ashley and Carney (1999); Ellis and Freeman (2005); UNDP (2005); UNEP et al. (2011); UNEP and UNDP (2013); UNEP (2014).

and protecting and promoting food security and livelihoods. Part of this new imperative included the application of livelihood approaches, particularly where humanitarian crises became protracted, with no end in sight. Such efforts were seen as a means of shifting from short-term emergency interventions designed to save lives to longer-term recovery (Maxwell 1999; Ross, Maxwell, and Buchanan-Smith 1994).

A livelihoods approach to humanitarian crises evolved in the context of rapidly expanding international responses to the complex political realignments—and emergencies—that coincided with the end of the Cold War.[6] These emergencies included Somalia (1992), the Rwandan genocide and the ensuing refugee crisis in the African Great Lakes region (1994), the war in Bosnia and Herzegovina (1992–1995), and the war in Afghanistan (2001–present). While the humanitarian imperative to save lives and prevent suffering took precedence during these crises, one perceived gap in the international response was the lack of broader support for local economies and communities affected by crisis, and for the transition to longer-term recovery and stability.

Such perspectives prompted international organizations working in these new humanitarian settings to make increasing use of livelihood approaches—while simultaneously shifting their focus from adaptation and resilience, viewed in the context of longer-term sustainability, to short-term humanitarian risks and vulnerabilities, viewed in the context of conflict dynamics and their effects on livelihoods (Collinson 2003; Lautze et al. 2003; Le Sage and Majid 2002).[7] For example, Sarah Collinson and her colleagues have proposed a sustainable livelihoods framework for conflict-affected and politically unstable situations that expands on similar earlier frameworks by (1) including a wider range of transforming structures and processes and (2) enlarging the assets portfolio to include political assets (Collinson et al. 2002). In their adaptation of the sustainable livelihoods framework, Sue Lautze and Angela Raven-Roberts take a somewhat different approach by omitting the vulnerability context, arguing that vulnerability is endogenous to livelihood systems in violent (conflict) settings (Lautze and Raven-Roberts 2006). In keeping with this perspective, Lautze and Raven-Roberts categorize livelihood assets as potential liabilities, because they can expose their owners to risk (see figure 2).

Since the mid-2000s, the pendulum has swung back to a focus on resilience, which is viewed as a unifying concept linking humanitarian, early recovery, and development concerns. The notion of resilience is also highly relevant to other

---

6 A complex emergency, as defined by the UN and the Inter-Agency Standing Committee, is "a humanitarian crisis in a country, region, or society where there is a total or considerable breakdown of authority resulting from internal or external conflict and which requires an international response that goes beyond the mandate or capacity of any single agency and/or the ongoing UN country programme" (UN and IASC 2008, 22).

7 See also Baro and Deubel (2006) and Collinson et al. (2002).

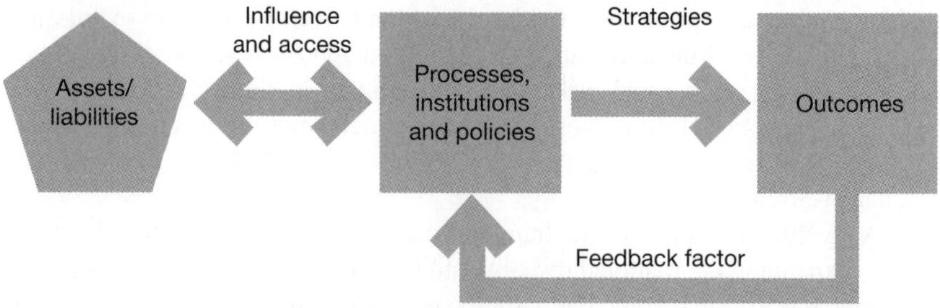

Figure 2. A livelihoods framework adapted for complex humanitarian emergencies
Source: Adapted from Lautze and Raven-Roberts (2006).

international agendas and aid modalities, including disaster risk reduction, climate adaptation and resilience, conflict resilience, and general community resilience (Bahadur, Ibrahim, and Tanner 2010; DFID 2011; Folke 2006). In a project that illustrates the links between resilience and peacebuilding, Cynthia Brady and her colleagues describe how, in post-conflict Mindanao (in the Philippines), collaborative peacebuilding efforts built trust between former adversaries and fostered social and institutional resilience (Brady et al. 2015*).

Livelihood approaches, including the sustainable livelihoods framework, have now been in use for more than twenty-five years (Morse and McNamara 2013). While initially used to promote sustainable development, these approaches have more recently been adapted and applied in a wide range of humanitarian, conflict, and post-conflict settings, in order to protect and support livelihoods, promote sustainability, reduce vulnerability, and strengthen resilience. Increasingly, these livelihood approaches have contributed to peacebuilding even where this was not an explicit goal of the interventions.

LIVELIHOOD SYSTEMS

The way in which livelihoods are framed and interpreted in this book is based on the conceptual framework shown in figure 1, in which livelihood assets, strategies, and outcomes are dynamically linked to vulnerabilities, structures, and processes. In the three subsections that follow, livelihood assets, livelihood strategies, and transforming structures and processes are reviewed in relation to key livelihood concepts, including risk and vulnerability, resilience, coping, and adaptation.

Livelihood assets

Livelihoods are based on a range of assets that a household owns or can access. The livelihood frameworks discussed earlier categorize livelihood assets into five (or sometimes six) types: physical assets, human assets, social assets, financial (and/or economic) assets, and natural resources.[8] Assets can also be viewed in terms of their function—whether, for example, they are used for consumption, production, or income generation; or whether they are convertible, meaning that they can be directly consumed at a later point, or converted into another category of asset. Investing in social relations, for example, can be regarded as a convertible asset, as can savings, and debts that can be called in (Dorward et al. 2001).

Assets need not be owned directly to contribute to livelihoods, and may be accessed through claims and entitlements: for example, social relationships may give rise to opportunities to access assets. In the case of common-property resources, such as rangelands, assets may be shared.

When analyzing the resilience of livelihood systems, it is more useful to consider assets than strategies (which are addressed in the next subsection), since a household's assets more accurately reflect the potential impact of stressors—such as conflict or disaster—on livelihoods.[9] An analysis of livelihood assets also reveals a household's capacity to cope with or survive crisis.

Similarly, at the level of the population group, a deficiency in a particular asset category can seriously undermine livelihoods. In the Darfur region of Sudan, for example, the camel-herding nomads have considerable physical assets in the form of their livestock herds, but the groups' human capital has been weakened by illiteracy and high maternal mortality; moreover, as a result of the Darfur conflict (2003–present), the nomads' relations with other groups have become polarized, weakening their social capital (Young 2009). Among Darfur's agriculturalist populations, forcibly displaced households have not only lost their land—and therefore their principal livelihood asset—but may also have been separated from family members who possess the necessary business skills to generate income. Such losses create profound vulnerabilities that cannot easily be offset by other means. Thus, the Darfur conflict has had a differential impact on livelihood systems, enriching the physical assets of nomads by facilitating

---

[8] Such assets may be defined as follows: (1) *physical assets*: producer goods, including livestock, tools, and equipment; and buildings and basic infrastructure, such as water and sanitation, schools, information and communication technologies, and roads; (2) *human assets*: skills, knowledge, health, ability to work, and the ratio of dependents to productive adults within the household; (3) *social assets*: formal and informal social relationships or resources that can be drawn on in pursuit of livelihoods, including shared norms and values that facilitate cooperation, claims, and exchange; (4) *financial assets*: financial resources, including savings, access to credit and loans, and income from employment, trade, and remittances; (5) *economic assets*: entities that function as stores of value, over which ownership rights are enforced by institutions (individually or collectively), and from which owners may derive economic benefits either by holding them or using them over time; and (6) *natural resources*: environmental resources such as land, rangelands and pastures, water, forests, fisheries, and subterranean resources (such as minerals and oil). (These definitions are adapted from IRP and UNDP-India [2010].)

[9] As discussed later in the chapter, stressors often result in the transfer of assets away from the poor.

their livestock mobility and increasing their access to natural resources (which, prior to the conflict, may have been obstructed by the expansion of farms and the fencing off of pastures), while simultaneously reducing access to cultivable land among those who have been displaced. As long as the asset profile of either group remains skewed, livelihoods will be compromised and grievances will remain—circumstances that threaten to undermine peacebuilding.

Under conflict conditions, control of livelihood assets can shift radically from the perspective of gender and age. For example, in the absence of men, women may shoulder increasing responsibility for household decision making—as was the case in Aceh, Indonesia, where women took on important roles in traditionally male-dominated agricultural sectors, such as aquaculture and fisheries, in order to meet basic household needs (UNEP et al. 2013). While this strategy is practical and often empowering, livelihood security issues can arise when male combatants are demobilized—as occurred in Nicaragua in 1988, when approximately 16,000 women lost their jobs to men returning from the civil war (Karuru and Yeung 2015).

Challenges to traditional gender norms, including those related to natural resource management, can alter notions of masculinity, and may affect relations between men and women in the post-conflict period (Boyer and Stork 2015*). In some cases, shifts in gender roles have been associated with domestic violence and the reinforcement of gender inequalities (UNEP et al. 2013). Given that women and girls often have closer ties to natural resources (through agriculture and horticulture, firewood collection, and domestic water use) and are primarily responsible for household food security—and because men and women often have different conceptions of peace and, in particular, effective natural resource management—gender analysis is crucial to livelihoods in the post-conflict setting (Karuru and Yeung 2015).

Livelihood strategies

Livelihood strategies are what people do to achieve their livelihood objectives and ambitions—that is, the livelihood outcomes that they are seeking. These objectives might include the following:

- Meeting household consumption needs.
- Making investments to maintain or increase income or production, either now or in the future (for example, by purchasing land or tools, or by increasing knowledge, skills, or capacities through education or health care).
- Building social capital (for example, maintaining social relationships and meeting cultural obligations).

Livelihood strategies can also be described as livelihood actions or activities—among practitioners, this description often serves as the starting point for discussing and describing local livelihoods.

In conflict and post-conflict settings, livelihood objectives are often a compromise: a trade-off between competing household needs or, alternatively, between the various risks associated with attempting to meet those needs under difficult conditions. Often, people are willing to face considerable risk to maintain their livelihoods and meet consumption needs, as in the case of displaced women who risk gender-based violence by traveling to their farms for cultivation. In the post-conflict period, returning to one's place of origin is generally a high priority for those who were displaced, and is linked to the resumption of livelihoods. After the war in Bosnia and Herzegovina, returning refugees and IDPs demanded that they be able to return to their original settlements, underscoring the social and psychological value of particular places in connection with livelihoods recovery (Green 2015*). Security—including protection, if required—is a priority and a precondition for sustainable livelihoods.

The chapters in this book illustrate a wide range of livelihood strategies that require access to and use of natural resources, including the following:

- Primary production, including farming, horticulture, pastoralism, and beekeeping (Roe 2015*; Bowling and Zaidi 2015*; Webersik and Crawford 2015*).
- Fisheries (Brady et al. 2015*; Scheiber and Jones 2015*; Webersik and Crawford 2015*).
- Processing, including charcoal making; organic fertilizer production; and the production, in cooperation with the BioTrade Initiative, of value-added products based on biodiversity (Webersik and Crawford 2015*; Jaramillo Castro and Stork 2015*).
- Extraction, including the mining of metals, diamonds, and other minerals (Keili and Thiam 2015*).
- Agroforestry (Renner 2015*; Srey and Schweithelm 2015*; Boyer and Stork 2015*).
- Ecotourism and conservation, including serving as guides, park rangers, and members of patrols tasked with protecting national parks (Maekawa et al. 2015*; Walters 2015*; Pritchard 2015*; Westrik 2015*).
- Rural and urban small businesses, including vocational trades such as textile design, embroidery, carpentry, food processing, and honey production (Keili and Thiam 2015*).
- Trading networks and market chains, including serving as merchants, agents, and middlemen (Webersik and Crawford 2015*).

Most livelihood strategies use or affect natural resources, either directly or indirectly. The majority of the case studies in this book—and indeed the vast majority of livelihoods in post-conflict countries—depend on accessing land and other natural resources. In Viet Nam, for example, over 60 percent of the population relies on agriculture and forest resources for its livelihoods (Lax and Krug 2013); and in Myanmar, 70 percent of the country's 55 million people depend on farming and fishing as their primary livelihood strategies (Talbott, Waugh, and Batson 2013).

The assets and capacities available to a given household influence that household's ability to pursue specific livelihood strategies. The factors referred to in figure 1 as the "Vulnerability Context" and "Transforming Structures and Processes" also wield strong influence. The factors affecting the vulnerability context are dynamic and often seasonal, and have implications for public health, agriculture, and market trends. For example, extreme variability, year to year, in the climatic conditions that affect a major crop raises the risk of an annual hunger gap.

Households often use diversification, intensification, or migration to manage predictable stresses. Diversified livelihood strategies are potentially more sustainable, as one or more strategies may outperform others that are more susceptible to shocks. The case studies support this: as Alan Roe observes, diversification of on- and off-farm income can contribute to both risk reduction and wealth accumulation (Roe 2015*). Examples of intensification include the use of fertilizers or fodder supplements to increase production, or to extend the amount of land under cultivation. Migration includes traveling for work or trade, or moving livestock to access pastoral resources.

In the face of continued stress on livelihoods, households may engage in coping behaviors sequentially, depending on the severity and duration of the threat. Initially, households often cut back on consumption, to protect assets that are essential for livelihoods over the long term. If the situation worsens, households may begin to sell their assets. And, over the long term, large shifts may occur in the number of people practicing a particular coping strategy. In Somalia, for example, after Saudi Arabia imposed a livestock ban on Somali animals to avoid exposure to livestock that may have been infected with Rift Valley Fever, overall market demand for Somali animals dropped, and charcoal production in Somalia increased (Webersik and Crawford 2015*).

Although the phrase *coping strategies* may sound positive, the strategies often entail costs at both the household and community levels. At the household level, for example, reducing the number of meals leads to hunger and malnutrition, and selling assets leads not only to chronic hunger and malnutrition but also to impoverishment. In the wider context, large increases in the number of people practicing a particular coping strategy can devastate the environment: for example, because IDP and refugee settlements generate a massive demand for fuelwood, deforestation often occurs in the areas around such settlements (UNEP 2008). The wider costs of adaptation, and its implications for others, are considered later in this chapter.

Transforming policies, institutions, and processes

The livelihood asset base indicates a household's sensitivity to shocks and stresses and its capacity to respond to them. Adaptive capacity is also influenced, however, by the institutional and policy context, and by wider environmental, economic, and political processes. There are many ways in which policies, institutions, and processes (PIPs) can influence livelihood outcomes, and thereby influence peacebuilding.

The range of influences on local livelihoods—and, by implication, peacebuilding—extends beyond the local community to the regional, national, and international domains. Local production and trade, for example, are affected by local markets—which are, in turn, subject to influences from the wider economy, including links with international trade. Similarly, a drop in local production can affect national and neighboring economies—as occurred when livestock exports from countries affected by Rift Valley Fever were banned, benefiting the export trade of unaffected countries.

The many domains of PIPs are connected through formal and informal institutions and networks, and by governance and policy frameworks that operate at different administrative scales, from the micro to the meso and macro levels. Despite the breadth and diversity across domains and levels, some general observations can be made about the analysis of PIPs and related topics. It is important to keep in mind, however, that any livelihoods analysis should incorporate a review and assessment of stakeholder institutions and the prevailing policy context. To make such efforts more manageable, the objectives of the livelihoods analysis should specify the parameters for reviewing policies and institutions, for example, the sectoral focus, the geographic areas and administrative levels that are of interest, and the historical timeframe.

Relevant topics include the national economy (both domestic and export); markets and trade; and the national, regional, and international policy context. Usually, a policy review will focus on issues pertinent to the specific livelihoods in question. Experience to date shows that local-level livelihoods are not independent from higher-level processes or the prevailing political economy—meaning that connections to national and international policies and processes always exist, and cannot be ignored. The following three subsections review some areas of critical relevance to natural resource–based livelihoods.

Land tenure and natural resource governance

Issues and grievances related to land tenure and other rights of access to natural resources are perhaps the most common challenges that arise in the course of efforts to support livelihoods after conflict. Because land tenure, in particular, may have been historically linked with conflict, it has powerful implications for peacebuilding.

Land tenure can be complicated by legal pluralism—the coexistence of customary laws and institutions with statutory ones.[10] Thus, one common

---

[10] For further analysis of legal pluralism and land management, see Unruh and Williams (2013).

grievance concerns the failure of governments and other authorities to respect customary property rights; in some instances, governments have either claimed state ownership of properties that, under customary law, are owned by other groups, or have awarded property rights held under customary law to entities other than the customary users.[11] Government policies may also affect land use—and, hence, local livelihoods. In Somalia, the shift from customarily held lands to state ownership led to changing patterns of land use: what was once rangelands and pastures or communally managed farmland has now been turned over to charcoal production, which is more profitable (Webersik and Crawford 2015*).

Historically, customary institutions were seen by communities, scholars, and practitioners—as well as by a number of government authorities—as helping to minimize conflict. Among pastoralist societies in the Karamoja region of Uganda, for example, the customary management of natural resources, by means of flexible and permeable boundaries between Kenya, Uganda, Ethiopia, and South Sudan, served as an important adjunct to herding strategies by allowing seasonal cross-border or transboundary migrations. Customary institutions were weakened by the process of state building in East Africa, however, as the authority and responsibilities associated with traditional governance mechanisms were reduced and transferred to a nascent civil and political administration (Lind 2015*).

Shared access to common-property natural resources allows multiple users to benefit from the same area of land at different times of the year and for different purposes. For example, in North Darfur, farmers engage in rainfed agriculture during the cultivation season; meanwhile, during the rainy season, pastoralists move to pastures further north (Osman et al. 2013). At the end of the growing season, pastoralists return to graze their livestock on the crop residues as they travel southward. The relationship between pastoralists and agriculturalists produces a number of mutual benefits: animal manure fertilizes the farmers' fields; the herders' camels help transport produce from fields to farm storage; and farmers and herders exchange animal products and crops. Several trends have undermined this reciprocity, however, including the use of fencing to enclose rangelands, the commercialization of crop residues and manure, and the increasing use of commercial fertilizer and other inputs. These modernizations, in turn, have led to the expansion of rainfed cultivation and an increase in sedentary livestock production, prompting a shift from communally shared land to individual land tenure that has led to increasing tensions, conflict, and polarization between livelihood groups.

---

[11] See, for example, Alden Wily (2015*) and Unruh and Williams (2013). Conflicts between farmers and pastoralists who are also divided by ethnic lines can be found in many other conflict-affected regions—including Darfur, where nomadic Arab pastoralists and settled farming communities are in conflict (Green 2015*).

The economy, markets, and trade

In many post-conflict countries, between 20 and 60 percent of gross domestic product is attributable to the net value added by agriculture—which includes crop cultivation, livestock production, forestry, hunting, and fishing (see table 1).

Table 1. Agricultural value added for countries affected by major armed conflict, 1990–2013

Country	*Agricultural value added as a percentage of gross domestic product (2012)*[a]	*Country*	*Agricultural value added as a percentage of gross domestic product (2012)*[a]
Afghanistan	25	Laos	28
Algeria	9	Lebanon	6
Angola	10	Liberia	39
Azerbaijan	5	Mozambique	30
Bangladesh	18	Nepal	36
Bosnia and Herzegovina	8	Nicaragua	20
Burundi	41	Pakistan	24
Cambodia	37	Peru	7
Central African Republic	54	Philippines	12
Chad	56	Russia	4
Colombia	6	Rwanda	33
Congo, Democratic Republic of the	25[b]	Senegal	17
		Serbia	10
Congo, Republic of	3[c]	Sierra Leone	57[c]
Croatia	5	Sri Lanka	11
El Salvador	12	Sudan	28
Eritrea	15[b]	Tajikistan	27
Ethiopia	49	Thailand	12
Georgia	9	Timor-Leste	17[c]
Guatemala	11	Turkey	9
India	18	Uganda	26
Indonesia	15	United Kingdom	1
Kosovo	14		

Source: World Bank (2014).

Notes:

Major armed conflict is defined as conflict that has resulted in more than 1,000 battle-related deaths overall. This threshold corresponds to the CumInt variable in the Uppsala Conflict Data Program/Peace Research Institute Oslo data (UCDP and PRIO 2013; Themnér and Wallensteen 2013). See also UCDP (2014).

For purposes of this table, agriculture includes forestry, hunting, and fishing, as well as crop cultivation and livestock production.

Data for Guinea-Bissau, Iran, Iraq, Israel, Kuwait, Libya, Myanmar, Palestine, Somalia, South Sudan, Syria, and Yemen are not available.

a. Value added is the net output of a sector after the addition of all outputs and the subtraction of all intermediate inputs. Value added does not reflect deductions for the depreciation of fabricated assets or the depletion or degradation of natural resources.

b. Most recent data are from 2009.

c. Most recent data are from 2011.

Thus, in such settings, economic recovery often depends on agriculture—typically by small, rainfed production systems.

The national value of pastoralist livestock production is often underestimated, in part because of a dearth of data. A study of livestock production in Ethiopia, Kenya, Sudan, and Uganda estimated that their combined livestock business was worth more than US$23 billion in 2009, which was 37 percent higher than official estimates (ICPALD 2013). In East Africa, especially in Somalia and Sudan, pastoralist livestock products have long been an important export; in particular, organically produced desert sheep are prized in the markets of Saudi Arabia and other Middle Eastern countries (AOAD 2009). Such local, often organic production is thus a mainstay of the Somali and Sudanese economies, making exports a key source of local livelihoods (Webersik and Crawford 2015*; UNEP 2013b). In Somalia, livestock exports account, on average, for 80 percent of exports (FAO Somalia 2014).

Market trends are influenced by the regional policy context; Saudi Arabia's 1998 ban on Somali livestock imports is one example. As noted earlier, the ban lowered market demand for pastoralist livestock; as a result, livestock owners were forced to sell livestock at lower margins (Webersik and Crawford 2015*). The livelihood gap created by the drop in livestock exports stimulated Somali charcoal production, in part as a coping strategy. Thus, a major shift in one livelihood system—pastoralism—prompted an increasing number of pastoralists to switch to charcoal production. Similarly, in Darfur, where insecurity has restricted access to preferred rangelands and migration routes, camel-herding nomads have become increasingly sedentary, necessitating a shift in livelihood strategies. Some of those shifts have been maladaptive: for example, nomads have used intimidation and violence as a means of controlling access to natural resources, displacing many rural farmers and destroying the local markets that the nomads depend on to sustain their livelihoods (Young et al. 2009).

Domestic and international policies

The policies of national governments and their neighbors can have wide-ranging effects on natural resource–based livelihoods. The policy, legal, and institutional frameworks that underlie land tenure and natural resource governance, together with the economy, markets, and trade—the focus of the two previous sections—may have developed over a long period of time, and may require reform if post-conflict challenges are to be successfully addressed.

The breadth of the policy domains that potentially impact livelihoods is vast, and the effects may vary in accordance with local conditions. Policy areas that affect natural resource–based livelihoods include the wide array of agricultural policies that support crop and livestock production through extension services and livestock health programs; water and water resource management; land tenure regimes; regulation of production and markets, including taxation; governance and rule of law initiatives that support the protection of rights to natural resources;

and health and education services. In post-conflict settings, additional policy domains may include military conscription, DDR plans, and the lifting of travel and trade restrictions as borders are reopened. For example, trade between eastern Chad and Sudan all but ceased during the conflict between those two countries, which included embargoes. Relations were normalized in 2010—and in early 2013, in anticipation of a particularly good harvest (cereal production in West Darfur State alone was expected to increase by 300 percent) and a surplus of both sorghum and millet, the government of Sudan lifted export bans to neighboring countries, opening the possibility of renewing formal cereal trade with Chad (FEWS-Net 2013).

The Karamoja region of Uganda has a long history of disarmament campaigns that have undermined both livelihood systems and perceptions of peace and security (Stites 2013). For example, the abrupt scaling back of the 2001–2002 disarmament campaign left many communities that had voluntarily disarmed vulnerable to losing their livestock and grain in raids conducted by those who still possessed weapons (Muhereza 2011).[12]

Policies introduced by former warring parties after conflict also influence economic recovery, including natural resource–based livelihoods. During their occupation of post–World War II Japan, for example, the Allies advanced a policy of maximizing natural resource harvesting in order to ensure domestic food security and restore Japan's devastated fishing industry, which was a source of livelihoods for 1.5 million people. The policy met these particular objectives, but it also led to unsustainable fishing and whaling practices, significantly depleting and degrading the whale and fish stocks in Antarctic and Pacific waters (Scheiber and Jones 2015*).

Although policy reform is an important tool of national development, reforms can magnify structural inequities and fuel conflict in post-conflict settings. In his examination of Afghanistan, for example, Roe questions the conventional agricultural development approach—that of maximizing economic growth and returns—arguing that this approach can exacerbate inequality and heighten political tensions (Roe 2015*). In particular, growth-oriented agricultural policies in Afghanistan have targeted areas perceived to be economically productive (such as those with greater access to irrigation water)—thereby marginalizing disadvantaged outlying rural areas, undermining their livelihoods, and aggravating existing tensions. Thus, what is sensible from a macroeconomic perspective may not be good politics.

---

[12] Afghanistan experienced a similar dynamic, in which communities that voluntarily disarmed following the 2001 invasion became vulnerable to those that had not disarmed (Sato 2011). Disarmament efforts in the Karamoja region have also been problematic for other reasons. For example, during the implementation of a subsequent disarmament effort, in 2006, the military was condemned for widespread human rights abuses (Pulitzer Center on Crisis Reporting 2011).

THE NEXUS OF LIVELIHOODS, NATURAL RESOURCES, AND CONFLICT: KEY POINTS FOR POST-CONFLICT PEACEBUILDING

One of the major goals of this book is to improve understanding and analysis of the livelihoods, natural resources, and conflict nexus. This nexus is widely acknowledged as critically important in peacebuilding;[13] until recently, however, it has received little attention. Instead, the literature has explored the links between conflict and livelihoods, and conflict and the environment.

Literature, for example, focusing on the links between conflict and livelihoods addresses, among other topics, the impact of conflict on livelihoods and local responses (Lind and Eriksen 2006; Stites et al. 2005; Young et al. 2005); refugees' pursuit of livelihoods in conflict settings (Jacobsen 2003); and humanitarian protection and local livelihoods (Jaspars and O'Callaghan 2010; Narbeth and McLean 2003). There are also reviews of conflict and violence, power relations, and livelihoods (Collinson 2003; Lautze and Raven-Roberts 2006), more general reviews of livelihoods from a programmatic perspective, and annotated bibliographies (Holland et al. 2002; Longley and Maxwell 2002; Schafer 2002).

In parallel, there has been a growing interest in conflict and the environment—particularly in the links between local-level natural resource conflict and higher-level civil and interstate conflict (Leroy 2009; Ratner et al. 2013; UNEP 2014). Brady and her colleagues have examined the links between local, natural resource–related conflicts and the higher-level national conflict between Philippine government forces and Muslim rebel groups in Mindanao (Brady et al. 2015*). At a global level, the fifth assessment report of the Intergovernmental Panel on Climate Change included a chapter on human security and another on livelihoods and poverty, which examine several livelihood dimensions of human security in the context of local and higher-level conflict, including mobility and migration, and cultural and economic factors (Adger et al. 2014; Olsson et al. 2014).

The dearth of evidence and comprehensive study of the livelihoods, natural resources, and conflict nexus represents a gap not only in the literature but in the tools available for peacebuilding. For peacebuilding to succeed, all actors must fully understand both the broader conflict dynamics and the role of natural resources in promoting sustainable livelihoods and a sustainable peace. Livelihood systems, including livelihood governance and livelihood institutions, play a crucial role in managing natural resources—in particular, by providing mechanisms through which rights can be claimed and disputes resolved nonviolently. The livelihoods, natural resources, and conflict nexus has also been ignored or underestimated in many standard programmatic approaches to building a durable peace after the conclusion of hostilities. Glaucia Boyer and Adrienne M. Stork argue, for example, that most DDR programs have failed to recognize natural resources "as a fundamental element of security, recovery, and peacebuilding" (Boyer and Stork 2015*, 187–188).

---

13 See, for example, Stites (2013), Osman et al. (2013), Engel and Korf (2005), Collinson et al. (2002), UNEP et al. (2011), and IISD (n.d.).

The focus here is on the nexus of livelihoods, natural resources, and conflict; this nexus usually exists, however, in the context of transforming structures and processes—from natural disasters to financial crises, political or demographic shifts, and the threats associated with climate change. (Table 2 lists examples of transforming processes, stresses, and shocks that can affect the livelihoods, natural resources, and conflict nexus.) Often, such transforming structures and processes are intertwined, and may interact synergistically. The challenge for policy makers

Table 2. Examples of national-level transforming processes, stresses, and shocks affecting the nexus of livelihoods, natural resources, and conflict

Natural disasters	• In Aceh, Indonesia, peacebuilding and recovery from the twenty-nine-year separatist conflict were transformed by the 2004 Indian Ocean tsunami, which severely damaged both the customary and statutory land tenure systems (Renner 2015*). • Periods of prolonged drought superimposed on long-standing political tensions or protracted conflict—for example, in Darfur and Sudan—create additional stressors that further erode natural resource–based livelihoods.
Administrative reorganization and new borders (national or subnational)	• A new international border between Sudan and South Sudan has had implications for the citizenship of some groups; control of oil resources; and cross-border livestock migration and trade—all of which have the potential to affect livelihoods and the relations between groups on either side of the border.
Deterioration of local security, including increasing access to small arms	• The transformation of traditional livestock-raiding practices in the Kenyan and Ugandan sections of the Karimojong Cluster from a reciprocal, rule-governed practice into a predatory activity—engaged in to obtain large amounts of livestock to sell in lucrative urban meat markets—was exacerbated by weakened local governments, diminished local security, and the influx of small arms (Lind 2015*).
Demographic trends, including rapid population growth, urbanization, displacement, and return	• The population of Afghanistan has climbed by approximately 70 percent since the mid-1980s, increasing demands on land and other natural resources, affecting agricultural productivity, and degrading the natural resource base (Roe 2015*). • In Sudan, new urban dwellers (often internally displaced persons) have left behind rural livelihoods based on natural resources in exchange for relatively insecure employment or trade, forcing many to adopt marginal, urban-oriented coping strategies (Pantuliano et al. 2011).
Major land reforms, including privatization of communal lands	• In many post-conflict countries—from Colombia to Myanmar to Sierra Leone—governments have aggressively promoted and facilitated foreign investment in agriculture, often leading to charges of land grabbing (Unruh and Williams 2013).
Long-term social and economic marginalization	• In Mindanao, Philippines, historical marginalization has contributed to poverty, local grievances, political rivalries, and natural resource competition (Brady et al. 2015*; Defensor Knack 2013). • In Sudan, growing disparities in wealth and well-being (particularly with respect to health and education) have been linked to a history of political and social marginalization (Young et al. 2005).

is to fully understand the relative importance of—and connections between—these structures and processes.

In Darfur, for example, conflict—and the resulting forced displacement—has undermined livelihoods and created pressures on the environment, including water supplies, cultivable land, and forestry resources. Displacement to urban and peri-urban areas has also led to urban energy deficits, and the increasing demand for firewood from recently urbanized populations carries environmental costs—specifically, deforestation and land degradation. Moreover, firewood collection by IDPs entails high risks of intimidation and violence (Buchanan-Smith et al. 2011; UNEP 2007). At the same time, IDPs and the urban poor cannot afford alternative fuels such as petroleum, kerosene, or liquefied natural gas.

Wide-ranging transformative processes contribute to unique contexts in each post-conflict country; nevertheless, some general patterns are evident, from which clear lessons can be drawn. The two subsections that follow explore the influence of natural resource–based livelihoods on conflict and post-conflict peacebuilding, and the impact of conflict on natural resource–based livelihoods.

Influence of livelihoods on conflict and post-conflict peacebuilding

Livelihoods and related issues affect conflict and post-conflict peacebuilding in a number of ways, including the following:

- Livelihood assets may serve as conflict resources—meaning that they may fuel, prolong, or create incentives for conflict, and thereby exacerbate insecurity.
- Natural resource scarcity and inequitable access to natural resources can fuel conflict, and may be linked to wider political agendas.
- Alienation—in part, as a result of eroding traditional age- and gender-based roles—makes male youth more susceptible to recruitment by militias or the military.
- Identity claims linked to livelihoods can trigger or exacerbate conflict.
- Lack of sustainable livelihood opportunities can undermine the peacebuilding process.

It follows that if these factors are driving conflict at the local level, they can also serve as entry points for peacebuilding.

Livelihood assets as conflict resources

Conflict resources are defined as "natural resources whose systematic exploitation and trade in a context of conflict contribute to, benefit from or result in the commission of serious violations of human rights, violations of international humanitarian law or violations amounting to crimes under international law" (Global Witness 2006, 1). The extraction and exploitation of conflict resources are linked to global and domestic markets, as well as to the domestic conflict economy. The conflict economy may include the illicit extraction and trade of high-value natural resources, such as diamonds, opium, and columbite-tantalite (coltan) by organized networks; the resulting profits may prolong or even fuel the conflict.

In any particular natural resource–related conflict, a number of dynamics may be at play. Two of the chief drivers are (1) competition for economic opportunities related to natural resources (often referred to as the "greed" driver), and (2) social, political, and ideological causes related to natural resources (often referred to as the "grievance" driver). These drivers are not mutually exclusive—and in many cases, both are at work. It is also possible that actors' motivations may change over the course of a conflict—for example, starting with grievance, but quickly moving on to greed.

Michael Ross has proposed that natural resources might lead to armed conflict through four main pathways: (1) effects on economies (such as negative growth and increasing poverty); (2) effects on government (such as corruption, state weakness, and lack of accountability); (3) effects on people living in natural resource–rich regions (such as economic incentives to form a separate state); and (4) effects on rebel movements (such as financing for rebel activities) (Ross 2003). These mechanisms demonstrate elements of both greed and grievance.

Another view, advanced by Paul Collier, suggests that conflicts are more likely to be caused by greed—that is, by economic opportunities and agendas that motivate violent efforts to seize control over high-value natural resources (Collier 2000). Collier also describes the ways in which civil wars create economic opportunities for a minority of actors while destroying them for the majority. In keeping with this perspective, an analysis undertaken shortly after the end of the Cold War highlighted the ways in which post–Cold War civil conflicts had produced a political economy shaped by the power relations between winners and losers, and by the illicit transfer of assets from the weak to the strong (Duffield 1994). In conflict-affected areas controlled by rebels or warlords (including portions of Ethiopia, Liberia, Sierra Leone, Somalia, and Sudan), the emergence of "asset transfer economies"—some of which are linked to international trading networks —has been widely reported (Collinson et al. 2002; Duffield 1994; Keen 2000).

The mechanisms for forcefully transferring assets from losers can range from market pressures to violent appropriation through pillage or looting, which are often justified as a necessary means of supplementing or even replacing the wages of soldiers or officials (Keen 2000). Where commodities are of a lower value but more widely produced and traded, there may be efforts to control the resource trade through the exaction of illegal taxes or the imposition of illegal requirements for licenses. In Somalia, for example, warlords and their militias demanded the payment of levies on banana exports, which were used to directly support their activities and institutions (Webersik and Crawford 2015*). Similarly, Somali militias have gained financing by controlling charcoal exports.

After Somali pirates hijacked a ship loaded with charcoal for export, the United Nations imposed a ban on Somali charcoal exports. Since approximately 80 percent of Somalia's charcoal is exported, the ban severely undermined local businesses and deprived many Somalis of their principal livelihood source. The overall effectiveness of the UN ban has been questioned, however, because illegal exports of charcoal from Somalia have continued—and, by some accounts, increased (Charbonneau 2013).

In an environment in which organized illicit networks control natural resources, a wide range of livelihoods may depend on the perpetuation of conflict. In South Darfur State, Sudan, for example, military and security interests have been linked to the opportunistic—and lucrative—felling of high-value and irreplaceable mahogany forests (UNEP 2008). Meanwhile, militia groups that control other, less valuable forestry resources have engaged in violence and intimidation to prevent others—especially urban IDPs—from collecting firewood. Thus, IDPs who need fuel for cooking are largely dependent on a market controlled by their adversaries (Young et al. 2009).

Some economic activities are actually more profitable under conditions of conflict—and in such cases, those who profit are likely to be a small minority with close ties to powerful interests (Keen 2008). In Somalia, for example, warlords, local militias, and some urban truck owners are among those profiting from the new export trade in charcoal—a trade that also happens to be dominated by certain tribes (Webersik and Crawford 2015*).

Even where large-scale natural resource extraction is not illegally supporting conflict, excessive exploitation is likely to contravene national laws and policies, and contribute directly to deforestation, pollution, land degradation, and widespread erosion—as well as to the loss of livelihoods linked with natural resources. In Sudan, for example, oil development has caused significant environmental and social damage (including forced relocations and water contamination), threatening livelihoods and exacerbating conflict. The construction of roads for oil exploration and production has also hampered livelihoods by altering local hydrology and disrupting irrigation, sparking resentment against oil companies and political leaders; increasing water scarcity offers yet further potential to intensify local conflict (Patey 2012). The rampant illegal exploitation of forest resources in Cambodia is another example: the timber is financially valuable and easy to harvest and sell, but illegal harvesting undermines the livelihoods of large, forest-dependent populations (Srey and Schweithelm 2015*).

Resource scarcity and inequitable access to natural resources

Scarcity has long been put forth as one of the factors fueling competition and conflict over natural resources (Homer-Dixon 1999). Although competition often appears to be the primary cause of local conflict, more complex causal factors are often involved. In many cases, for example, underlying causes include (1) long-term social, political, and economic marginalization of certain groups (sometimes as a result of national policies); and (2) social and economic trends that result in landlessness, displacement, or inequitable access to natural resources—and thereby undermine or destroy livelihoods (Stites 2013).

Structural inequities in access to natural resources can increase competition and fuel local grievances—which, in vulnerable rural communities, may escalate to violent conflict. In Afghanistan, for example, the two most common sources of local conflict are disputes over land and water (Waldman 2008; UNCTA 2013). In his review of natural resource access and livelihood outcomes among four production systems in Afghanistan—irrigated farming, semi-irrigated farming, rainfed farming, and nomadic pastoralism—Roe notes the disparities between the systems: as might be expected, rainfed farming receives less water than irrigated, but there are also disparities within systems. The duration of the irrigation flow to upstream irrigated farms, for example, is more than twice that to comparably sized downstream farms—a disparity that has the potential to trigger violent conflict between upstream and downstream groups. A number of factors have intensified disputes over access to and use of irrigation water in river valleys, including drought, opium poppy cultivation, and ethnic differences (Roe 2015*).

Many researchers now agree that natural resource scarcity is one of several factors that can contribute to conflict, while recognizing that economic, social, and political agendas also play a role (Collinson et al. 2002; Stites 2013). In Mindanao, for example, the heart of the conflict was, for many, "the struggle for political and economic control over the land and resources necessary to sustain the lives and livelihoods of Mindanoans," a perspective that addresses the integration of economic, social, and political factors (Brady et al. 2015*, 342).

Political and economic agendas at various levels are often intertwined: specifically, local competition and conflict over natural resources may be tied to higher-level regional interests, and ultimately to wider national conflicts. For example, in parts of Darfur, a long history of pastoralist-farmer conflict broadly corresponds to wider political allegiances—specifically, to support for either government or rebel forces. Because the two levels of conflict interact, influencing one another, a local conflict between farmers and herders over land, water, or pastures can easily transform into a wider conflict that includes issues of ethnic identity and is linked to the higher-level conflict between the government and the rebels (UNEP 2013a). The lesson for peacebuilding is that the potential interactions between stakeholders at all levels need to be taken into consideration in efforts to foster peace.

Erosion of traditional age- and gender-based roles

Intergenerational relations—including tensions over access to natural resources—can contribute to conflict, and may therefore pose challenges to post-conflict peacebuilding. In Sierra Leone, for example, ancestral lineages traditionally determined who controlled and owned land; as a result, young men who lacked access to land had trouble finding wives, and were more easily recruited by rebels (Keili and Thiam 2015*). Moreover, during the post-conflict period, a number of trends hampered the integration of youth into the post-conflict economy—including rural-to-urban migration; international migration; participation in the informal economy; self-employment in marginalized areas or slums; and widespread unemployment, which created an exceptionally large pool of applicants for any given job. In light of such patterns, Andrew Keili and Bocar Thiam emphasize the importance, in Sierra Leone, of initiatives that target alienated youth, and that focus on education and training (Keili and Thiam 2015*).

Since the mid-1980s, in Karamoja, Uganda, the traditional rites of passage through which young men establish themselves as adult warriors have gradually decayed, alienating male youth from their communities—and particularly from adult men and elders. Instead, young men have increasingly turned to their peers in search of status, support, and recognition as men, undermining the traditional authority of elders (Stites 2013). The role of the Ugandan military in responding to livestock raids has also marginalized elders, who had historically played an important role in maintaining peace between different groups (Stites and Akabwai 2009). The traditional role of male elders in managing natural resources has also diminished: whereas they were once central to the management of access to pastoralist resources (water, pastures, and fodder), they now have no control over the collection, production, sale, or exchange of firewood and wild greens, all of which are increasingly important for subsistence. Finally, as women's roles in natural resource exploitation—and household subsistence—has increased, men's roles have decreased (Stites 2013). In sum, protracted conflict can give rise to dramatic shifts in traditional natural resource management practices, which are likely to have implications for natural resource access, competition, and conflict.

Identity claims precipitating or triggering conflict

In an analysis based on social identity theory, Arthur Green explores the connections between social identity and natural resources, and the ways in which both are connected to conflict and peacebuilding (Green 2015*). Green posits that when group identities are closely linked to natural resources, economic "conflicts of interest" may become intractable "conflicts of values." Green identifies four ways in which the overlaps between identity and natural resources can be related to conflict:

- Identity claims involving ownership of or privileged access to natural resources (either symbolic or material) can drive conflict.
- Identity can influence claims of inequitable distribution of resource rents.
- Identity can be used to mobilize collective action in natural resource conflicts, in order to serve other economic interests.
- Preexisting identity framing can foster conflict over natural resources.[14]

To the extent that a livelihood is a way of life, it contributes to social and cultural identity, which may persist long after the livelihood activity has ceased. Pastoralism, for example, is both a system of livestock production and a cultural identity shared by those who have long since sold their animals. Furthermore,

---

14 Edward Aspinall argues that without the social identity framework, there would be no politically salient grievances (Aspinall 2007).

because pastoralism as a cultural identity cuts across ethnic lines, a focus on the shared interests and values associated with pastoralism has the potential to build unity among ethnically distinct groups, and thereby support peacebuilding.

The Darfur region provides an example of the powerful influence of identity framing on conflict. Since the outbreak of conflict, in 2003, Darfuri identities have been radically and traumatically simplified, creating a misleading "Arab" versus "African" dichotomy (de Waal 2005). By obscuring and depoliticizing the underlying causes of violent conflict (Mamdani 2007), this identity framing further polarized the groups in question. Such divisions, in turn, have reached into the realm of livelihoods, where "Arab groups" are seen as engaging primarily in pastoralism, and "African groups" are seen as engaging primarily in farming. The reality, however, is far more complex: intractable tribal conflicts, including incidents of ethnic cleansing, have increased the incidence and severity of tribal polarization—which in no way mirrors the simple Arab-African divide, and which has clear links to higher-level political interests and actions in Khartoum (UNEP 2013a).

Similarly, in Mindanao, the conflict between Islamic rebel groups and the Philippine government has been framed as a matter of social and religious identity, with inequitable distribution of resources constituting additional causal factors (Brady et al. 2015*). Thus, any effort to address the cause of the conflict requires an understanding of the identity framing, which should feature strongly in peacebuilding efforts.

The coexistence of natural resource conflict and identity framing does not necessarily mean that identity framing is driving the conflict: political or socioeconomic factors may be at work as well, fostering both the conflict and the identity framing. Overestimating the role of identity carries the risk that competing claims or grievances may become entrenched, causing further polarization. Some observers have argued that this has occurred in Darfur, where politicized reporting on the conflict has entrenched identity framing of the issues (Mamdani 2007).

Despite this proviso, evidence does suggest that livelihoods are often the link between social identity and natural resources. In such cases, what is being defended or attacked is not the natural resources as such, but the resources as a livelihood asset—which are crucial for survival, for the development of the wider economy, and for peacebuilding.

Lack of sustainable livelihood opportunities

Disparities at multiple levels can contribute to resentment and grievances, and thereby fuel conflict. In Aceh, Indonesia, the exploitation of natural gas and forestry resources by multinational companies contributed to national wealth—but because benefits did not accrue locally or serve local interests (including through the provision of livelihoods), this resource exploitation contributed to Acehnese grievances, among them resentment toward the central government (Renner

2015*). After the signing of the memorandum of understanding that ended the conflict in 2005, local economic disparities linked to livelihoods (in particular, high unemployment among former rebels, who in some cases were driven to engage in illegal logging) threatened to undermine peacebuilding, as did disparities between the level of assistance directed to tsunami victims and to conflict-affected individuals.

Impact of conflict on livelihoods

Armed conflict has both a systematic (direct) and systemic (indirect) effect on the lives and livelihoods of civilians. Direct impacts include systematic intimidation; rape and other forms of violence; and death. Other direct impacts include forced displacement; the breakup of communities and households; the loss or destruction of livelihood assets; intimidation and gender-based violence; the destruction of infrastructure; and damage to or destruction of social networks, governance, and civil society institutions through the targeted, systematic killing of leaders. The indirect effects of conflict are even wider, and derive primarily from the risks associated with living in a conflict zone.

Conflict destroys livelihood assets or renders them inaccessible, and similarly erodes or destroys long-established livelihood coping mechanisms and the livelihood institutions on which people depend. Even in the face of such massive changes, however, livelihood strategies and local livelihood institutions continue to adapt and evolve (Justino 2009; Young et al. 2005).

Systematic impacts of conflict: Loss of life and livelihoods

Whether local (bottom-up), civil (top-down), or transnational, armed conflict disrupts and destroys lives and livelihoods. In the economic realm, conflict directly impacts local livelihoods through the transfer of assets from the majority of people (losers) to a small minority empowered by the conflict (winners). These systematic transfers are often linked to the top-down agendas of political and military leaders—who may, for example, attempt to persuade young men to join militias by offering them the spoils of war (Keen 2008).

Asset transfers take many forms, including pillage and looting; demanding protection money in return for sparing victims from violence or allowing them limited access to their own land and natural resources; monopolistic control of trade, or of the benefits obtained through aid; exploitation of labor; and taking direct control of land.[15] A number of these activities have implications for the environment and natural resource base, over and above their impact on livelihood assets.

The tactics of war and conflict—including those adopted by organized armies, militias, and others—may result in the deliberate and systematic destruction of the

[15] This list is based on an analysis, by David Keen, of the short-term economic functions of conflict (Keen 2000).

livelihoods of certain groups, or the assets upon which the livelihoods are based. Among the methods used to implement such strategies are intimidation and violence, ethnic cleansing, forced displacement, livestock raiding, and scorched-earth tactics.

Regardless of the type of conflict, deliberate attacks on the means of production and other livelihood assets, including natural resources, are prohibited under international humanitarian law (Stewart 2011; Pejic 2001; Henckaerts 2005).[16] Despite provisions under the Geneva Conventions, other treaties, and customary international law, however, civilians are often in the line of fire: not only do combatants target civilians' livelihood assets, but military commanders have in some cases given combatants license to loot, as a supplement to or substitute for wages. Thus, what would be considered livelihood assets in peacetime potentially become liabilities during conflict, exposing their owners to extreme risks, not only because of their economic value but because of a conflict of interests and clash of identities (Lautze and Raven-Roberts 2006). Predatory livestock raiding in South Sudan and in the Kenyan region of the Karimojong Cluster are examples of vulnerability linked with the ownership of assets—in these cases, cattle (Keen 1994; Hendrickson, Armon, and Mearns 1998).

Forced displacement—when violence, or the threat of it, compels people to leave their homes in search of refuge elsewhere—has serious impacts on livelihoods during and after conflict. In Afghanistan, for example, during the second half of the twentieth century, almost one-quarter of the population was displaced by conflict (Bowling and Zaidi 2015*).

Freedom of movement—strategic mobility—is an essential condition for livelihoods, including those of the displaced. By preventing people from moving safely, insecurity restricts access to farms, rangelands, and other natural resources; constricts market networks; undermines service delivery; interferes with labor migration; and prevents migrant laborers from sending money home to their families. Insecurity, and the resulting restrictions on mobility, is thus one of the most serious constraints on livelihoods—and the main reason why livelihoods fail. In essence, conflict conditions shut down livelihood strategies by limiting mobility and access to livelihood resources and institutions, thus rendering unavailable the vast array of coping strategies that could be used in peacetime.

In wartime, sweeping changes brought about by conflict and insecurity have transformative impacts on local services, social systems, and local governance. Displacement splits families and cuts them off from their wider social systems and support networks. Although their new location may be more secure, displaced people are outsiders: in addition to being separated from family and friends, they

---

16 "It is prohibited to attack, destroy, remove or render useless objects that are indispensable to the survival of the civilian population, such as foodstuffs, agricultural areas for the production of foodstuffs, crops, livestock, drinking water installations and supplies and irrigation works, when the purpose of such action is starvation" (Pejic 2001, 1099).

are often deprived of the support of community networks and institutions. They may also have difficulty obtaining access to health, education, and other basic services.

While the displaced may initially lack leaders or institutions to represent their interests, new leaders, institutions, and forms of governance quickly evolve that are adapted to the new setting. Among the displaced in Darfur, for example, new leaders were elected who were skilled at representing IDPs' humanitarian needs and working closely with the international humanitarian community (Young and Maxwell 2013).

Systemic impacts of conflict: Maladaptation and poor natural resource governance

While the systematic (direct) impacts of violent conflict are plain to see, the indirect, systemic changes brought about by conflict—such as the development of an exploitative conflict economy—are less obvious and more insidious. These indirect impacts involve complex and evolving system dynamics, including interactions and feedback loops between various subsystems. A livelihoods lens helps to discern systemic changes at the local level, revealing the effects of conflict on the different elements of the livelihoods framework.[17]

As noted earlier, conflict can strain positive coping strategies, compelling people to employ strategies that are maladaptive—that is, either illicit or harmful to the lives and livelihoods of others. In particular, maladaptive strategies may undermine the natural resource base, perpetuate inequities and marginalization, and promote continued conflict.

A livelihoods study of Arab camel-herding groups often associated with the Janjaweed militias (which support the government of Sudan's counterinsurgency) found that they had adopted several new livelihood strategies that were deemed maladaptive because of their negative impacts on other groups—in particular, rival ethnic groups that included Fur, Masalit, and Zaghawa farmers, many of whom had a history of tribal conflict with the camel-herding groups and supported the rebels. In an effort to survive under threat of the rebellion undertaken by groups that they regarded as their adversaries, the camel herders had rapidly diversified to include short-term, conflict-related livelihood strategies. In addition to their survival value, these strategies were motivated, in part, by long-held grievances related to the herders' lack of a tribal homeland and land tenure, and their minimal access to health and education services.[18] Although these

---

[17] A participatory livelihoods analysis based on the livelihoods framework shown in figure 2 has been used to explore how conflict differentially affected local livelihood systems in Darfur (Young et al. 2007).

[18] Herders had also suffered substantial livestock losses as a result of a drought in the mid-1980s: distress sales, starvation, and disease led to a 92 percent decrease in the size of the livestock population (Young et al. 2009).

new livelihood strategies provided quick and sizable cash returns, they were often linked with either militarization (membership in militias and armed forces) or intimidation and violence—specifically, controlling the lucrative firewood trade and denying others access to common-property resources (Young et al. 2005).[19]

In the case of the Darfuri camel herders, peacebuilding actors need to understand and address the systemic failures that contributed to the original grievances, including inequitable land tenure regimes and failing natural resource governance. In the short term, the international community's response to the gender-based violence and intimidation perpetrated by Janjaweed militias against IDP women who left their camps to collect firewood is to view rape as a weapon of war and accordingly to promote protection for the women (Gingerich and Leaning 2004). A longer-term solution would also recognize the underlying, livelihood-related rationale for the herders to control access to lucrative natural resources. Such a solution must include improvements to natural resource governance that can ensure sustainable livelihoods for all, including equitable access to resources.

In another example of maladaptive livelihoods, illegal logging in post-conflict Aceh, Indonesia, sparked by high unemployment, constrained the government's ability to assist noncombatants and facilitate the reintegration of former rebels, all of which undermined peacebuilding (Renner 2015*). In the African Great Lakes region, where post-conflict unemployment of excombatants may have resulted in illegal poaching, the solution was to replace maladaptive strategies with adaptive ones: establishing associations of former poachers helped them to develop livelihoods that supported conservation and did not harm protected areas (Maekawa et al. 2015*). In Mozambique, years of conflict had led to dependence on illegally extracted natural resources, which continued as a short-term post-conflict coping strategy. Similarly, in Sierra Leone, a "diamond-mining trap" pushed young men to join rebel groups during the civil war (Keili and Thiam 2015*).

At the local level, maladaptive strategies that harm the livelihoods of others can fuel existing tensions and entrench long-standing grievances, leading to a vicious cycle of expanding violence—particularly in environments characterized by failing natural resource governance, pressure on resources, and manipulation (of all sides) by higher-level interests with their own agendas. Once such feedback loops have been created, the only way out is to break the cycle of conflict.

Conflict has been shown to lower local and national agricultural productivity; causes include the laying of landmines, internal displacement, and limited access to farms (as a consequence of general insecurity). Figure 3 shows the shifting levels of millet cultivation in the Darfur region over several decades. By 2004,

---

[19] Gender-based violence has been used to control access to natural resources in both Darfur and the eastern Democratic Republic of the Congo. See, for example, Hayes and Perks (2012) and Gingerich and Leaning (2004).

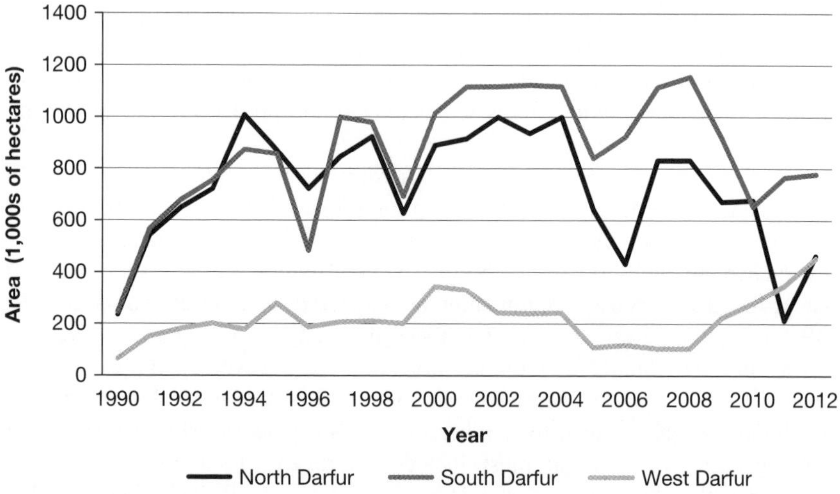

Figure 3. Millet cultivation in Darfur, by state and year
Source: Adapted from Young et al. (2014).

once the conflict in Darfur had taken hold, large numbers of people were displaced and millet cultivation was reduced. By 2007, some recovery had occurred in the states of South Darfur and North Darfur, and by 2012 only West Darfur State had achieved pre-conflict production levels, whereas continued conflict yielded further deterioration in South Darfur. The conflict-caused drops in agricultural productivity led to rising food prices and food insecurity.

In Somalia, productive lands are often left fallow during conflict, undermining livelihood opportunities for local populations (Webersik and Crawford 2015*). In addition, local conflicts often erupt over productive agricultural land, leading to land grabbing and violence. Rural livelihoods have also been compromised by the indirect effects of violent conflict. For example, in 1992, when Somalia was plagued by conflict, major banana production and export companies abandoned their Somali operations because of conflict-related insecurity. These plantations, along with large-scale farms and irrigation systems, deteriorated or were seized by militias or other groups that lacked the skills to manage the land effectively. And in the lower Shabelle region of Somalia, violent conflict caused local populations to lose access to their farms, to their irrigation systems, and to the opportunity to work on former plantations (Webersik and Crawford 2015*).

In the wake of conflict, different factions may remain in control of certain areas, which then become off-limits to certain groups. In Sudan, Chad, and the Central African Republic, for example, pastoralists have been cut off—for years at a time—from their favored seasonal grazing areas (Pantuliano et al. 2009; Young et al. 2009). In Sudan's Darfur region, Arab camel-herding groups were unable to access the rainy-season pastures on the fringes of the Sahara, as this region had been under the control of another ethnic group since 1997 (Young et al.

2009). After lengthy tribal negotiations—which demonstrated the importance of local customary institutions and mechanisms for mediation—the herders regained access in 2010.[20]

Natural resources important to livelihoods—including land, water, and forests—are often used as leverage for political purposes. In Afghanistan, for example, because land offers significant livelihood opportunities, successive regimes have used land to secure political patronage (Bowling and Zaidi 2015*). Similarly, in Darfur, in return for sedentization,[21] the government promised community development, including education, health care, and other basic services, creating a major incentive for Arab camel-herding groups to support the government (Young et al. 2009).

While national policies and statutorily mandated institutions provide the legal framework for rights of access to land and other natural resources, such access often exists, in practice, under conditions of legal pluralism, with local institutions and customary law playing a key role in natural resource management. In such contexts, it is important not only to effectively manage legal pluralism, but also to protect the capacity of both statutory and customary institutions to govern natural resources effectively, including by upholding access rights. Such institutions are central to supporting livelihoods, establishing and maintaining security, and promoting the rule of law.

Conflict—especially conflict over natural resources—can erode or destroy the institutions that allow people to exercise their rights (Ratner 2015*; UNEP 2014), and this loss of capacity and legitimacy can in turn serve as a conflict driver. In Sudan, for example, where traditional authorities lack the capacity to resolve disputes over livestock—in part because they are not aligned with the ruling political party—"villagers resorted to burning pastureland, with considerable damage to the environment, so that the area would not attract pastoralists" (Siddig, El-Harizi, and Prato 2007, 16). Similarly, in the Karimojong Cluster, one of the structural causes of conflict is the degradation of customary pastoralist institutions, such as reciprocal resource-use agreements, intermarriage, and mutually beneficial trade and exchange (Stites 2013; Lind 2015*). Two factors, meanwhile, have seriously undermined livelihoods in the cluster: a severe weakening of the customary institutions that had traditionally been used to manage conflict, and the government's failure to provide security for herding groups.

* * *

The value of a livelihoods lens in a post-conflict setting is that it focuses on the everyday lives of individuals, households, and communities, while recognizing the transforming structures and processes that influence their capacity to survive a crisis, ensure the sustainability of their livelihoods, and maintain

---

[20] Ahmed Sulieman Balah, Nomad Development Council, personal communication, 2013.

[21] The objective of sedentization seems to be the transformation of pastoralists into farmers, and the abandonment of traditional pastoralism (Shazali and Ahmed 1999).

their own livelihoods without harming those of other groups. In many cases, by generating discussions about common interests—including sharing natural resources and building understanding—a livelihoods lens makes it possible to cross barriers between ethnic or livelihood groups that might otherwise seem insurmountable.

EVIDENCE-BASED APPROACHES TO LIVELIHOOD INTERVENTIONS: CHALLENGES, ISSUES, AND LESSONS

Thus far, the chapter has emphasized the nexus of livelihoods, natural resources, and conflict. As noted earlier, understanding this nexus is key to identifying entry points for planning, implementing, and evaluating effective peacebuilding- and livelihood-related interventions. The focus in this section is on an evidence-based approach to livelihood interventions (and related policies) that is designed to generate new information, which can then be shared with different actors at various levels.

The starting point for an evidence-based programming approach is a rigorous assessment and analysis process that is driven by clear objectives; grounded in a recognized conceptual framework (such as the sustainable livelihoods framework discussed earlier); and based on standard practice. Ideally, the assessment should be demand driven, involving several stakeholders with shared interests who have agreed to the goal of promoting peacebuilding through an evidence-based approach. Success in such endeavors requires strong collaboration and commitment from the start; that commitment, in turn, is facilitated by clarifying the roles and interests of all involved.

This section reviews challenges, issues, and lessons associated with the use of evidence-based processes for the development of peacebuilding- and livelihood-related interventions and policies. Such processes are important to the development of integrated approaches to livelihoods recovery—that is, approaches that connect livelihoods to both natural resource management and peacebuilding. Evidence-based approaches are also important to the assessment of the potential environmental and social impacts of interventions, and to the evaluation of projects and programs. Finally, evidence-based processes can be helpful in revealing how and why peace processes unravel, in identifying the motivations of peace spoilers, and in examining other, deeper questions.

Framing of key concepts: Building a shared understanding

How an issue is framed influences how key actors and stakeholders perceive and understand it. Thus, the framing of sustainable livelihoods can make the difference between neglect and attention on the part of decision makers. For example, the notion of supporting livelihoods recovery may gain more traction if the activities are framed as an opportunity to reduce conflict and foster stabilization. Similarly, promoting sustainable natural resource management may have more traction if it is linked to specific economic benefits.[22] And land degradation associated with natural resource extraction may receive high-level political attention only if the resulting economic harm and damage to stability are stressed.

Framing starts with a conceptual framework and the definition of key concepts (such as sustainable livelihoods, resilience, and vulnerability). In part because local and national policy makers, practitioners, and stakeholders may have less access to recent developments, perspectives, and evidence than outsiders, such concepts may have different meanings to different segments of the target audience; it is thus crucial to establish the conceptual framework and definitions from the outset.

With regard to framing, it is important to note that the same concepts may legitimately be assigned different meanings, depending on the disciplinary perspective. Vulnerability, for example, can be framed either as an outcome or a process: the phrase *outcome vulnerability* reflects a scientific framing, whereas *context vulnerability* reflects a human-security framing (O'Brien et al. 2007). In the realm of livelihoods, a focus on outcome vulnerability is associated with quantitative indicators of outcomes—for example, access to food and income, or prevalence of malnutrition. A focus on context vulnerability, in contrast, shifts attention toward the underlying causes of vulnerability (or resilience) in livelihood systems, and lends itself to more qualitative methodologies. Similarly, while outcome vulnerability might favor the household as the unit of analysis, context vulnerability aims to understand the relationships, interconnections, and feedback loops within the system itself. Both approaches can be useful, depending on the aims of the assessment. Because it includes both precise (quantitative) information and more nuanced (qualitative) analysis, a combined quantitative and qualitative approach (also known as a "mixed methods" approach) generates the most comprehensive picture.[23]

There is no blueprint or prototype for analyzing the nexus of livelihoods, natural resources, and peacebuilding, in part because of the wide variation in context—including livelihood systems, use of natural resources, and peacebuilding approaches. Ideally, the analysis that forms a key part of the assessment should be grounded in an explicit conceptual understanding linked to a wider body of theory, as presented in the first part of this chapter. If the assessment objectives are too loosely formulated, they run the risk of generating assorted but largely meaningless data, as there is no frame of reference. However, an explicit conceptual framework—including a theory of change—helps ensure coherence in the planning, design, and implementation of livelihood assessments.[24]

---

[22] See, for example, Sorensen (2015).

[23] The same points—regarding outcome versus context, and qualitative versus quantitative approaches—apply to analyses of resilience.

[24] Increasingly, project design is based on a theory of change—a tool that maps the assumptions or preconditions that are required, at each stage, to bring about the desired outcomes. This approach helps peacebuilding actors better understand the complex and interrelated factors that influence project outcomes. See Coryn et al. (2011).

From theory to practice: Analytical approaches to history, climate variability, and conflict

This chapter addresses both the theoretical debates and the practical considerations associated with the peacebuilding experience, with the ultimate goal of drawing out clear lessons that can be of value to practitioners. This section highlights three elements that are crucial to the success of post-conflict peacebuilding and/or to livelihood initiatives that address both livelihoods and natural resources:

- Taking a historical perspective on the conflict, and being aware of what that history implies for livelihoods and peacebuilding.
- Recognizing the importance of seasonality and climate variability, and their effects on livelihoods, natural resources, and conflict.
- Incorporating conflict analysis into livelihood approaches, in order to understand the reciprocal impacts of livelihoods and conflict.

The section concludes by offering examples of approaches, tools, and technologies that can enable practitioners and other peacebuilding actors to meet the analytical demands of an evidence-based approach.

Historical perspective

Post-conflict settings usually represent a significant shift from the conflict and pre-conflict periods. Liz Alden Wily, Jeremy Lind, and other researchers stress the value of a historical perspective in efforts to understand conflict dynamics and their implications for peacebuilding. Historical perspectives on natural resources, livelihoods, and conflict can be incorporated into the full range of assessment methodologies commonly deployed in conflict-affected countries—including post-conflict environmental assessments, environmental impact assessments, strategic environmental assessments, and post-conflict needs assessments.[25] Alden Wily's examination of the historical origins of the pastures dispute in Afghanistan's central highlands, for example, emphasizes iterative learning on the ground, which is an important principle of qualitative methodologies and is essential both for building a comprehensive understanding of the situation and engaging in deeper analysis (Alden Wily 2015*).

In practical terms, understanding the origins of conflict often means recognizing the effects of political and social marginalization, and the ways in which they may have contributed to poverty, grievances, political rivalries, and natural resource competition—as was the case, for example, in Mindanao (Brady et al. 2015*; Young et al. 2005). Historical analysis should also include the key role that natural resource exploitation can play in local grievances: this was the

[25] See, for example, Bouma (2012), Brown et al. (2012), Jensen (2012), Jensen and Lonergan (2012), and Conca and Wallace (2012).

case, for example, in both Darfur and Aceh, where exploitation led to secessionist movements (Young et al. 2005; Renner 2015*).[26]

Seasonality and climate variability

Seasonality is a crucial dimension of natural resource–based livelihoods: in the agricultural realm, cultivation, livestock production, and horticulture follow distinct cycles. In fact, seasonality even affects mineral extraction: in Sierra Leone, for example, diamond mining is tied to agricultural cycles, because it represents an alternative livelihood strategy (Keili and Thiam 2015*).

Some regions, drylands in particular, are known for their seasonal extremes and interannual climate variability, which can lead to unpredictability in the availability and distribution of water and pastures, and can also determine the success or failure of rainfed harvests. Natural climate variability across geographic areas and over time affects land use patterns, and even small climatic differences yield significant variations in the duration of rainfall, the duration of seasons, and the timing of interannual variability. These differences, in turn, can have a major impact on the viability and production of crops (Ellis and Galvin 1994).

Seasonal climate variability also plays a fundamental role in the selection of livelihood strategies, and may limit livelihood options. For example, in West Africa, a monomodal rainfall pattern favors crop-livestock production, whereas in parts of East Africa, a bimodal rainfall pattern favors more livestock-intensive production methods.

From a policy perspective, crop-livestock production is intimately tied to fundamental interactions between people and ecosystems—which, in turn, are shaped by rainfall patterns and other climatic drivers (such as temperature, humidity, and ambient carbon dioxide concentration). Thus, peacebuilding and development policy cannot ignore climatic influences on production methods. Understanding and being able to project climate impacts on agricultural production and natural ecosystems will enable analysts to infer how land use will respond to future climatic variations, whether they result from natural patterns or are the result of broader climate changes (Luedeling et al. 2014).

Variable environments are those where unpredictability rather than stability is the norm; both the environments themselves and the associated production models are sometimes referred to as "nonequilibrium" (Scoones 1996; Bruch 2008). Pastoralist livestock producers take advantage of such variability, using the mobility of their herds to access the best available pastures for the time of year, while managing stocks of fodder for the hot, dry season before the rains produce new growth. The seasonal and often unpredictable availability of rainfall—and, hence, cultivation and pastures—is a crucial dimension of livelihoods that must

[26] Carol Westrik's overview of peace parks examines their historical development—which, in some cases, includes disagreements over territorial boundaries and other natural resource–related disputes (Westrik 2015*).

be managed strategically to ensure both livelihood security and the sustainability of the natural resource base (AU 2010).

If conflict or insecurity restricts the movements of pastoralist herds, serious consequences may result, including overgrazing, degradation of available pastures, increasing livestock disease, and drops in reproduction rates and in the general quality of the livestock (Young et al. 2009).[27] Participatory rural appraisal tools—including the mapping of livestock migration; the development of seasonal calendars (that show expected seasonal or interannual patterns of production within the agricultural year); and the establishment of historical timelines (that track trends in intra-annual climate variability, such as severe droughts and periods of food insecurity, including famine)—are valuable means of capturing and predicting seasonal variations. In Sudan, Helen Young and her colleagues compared retrospective methods for monitoring land use and livestock migrations (based on semistructured interviews with herders) with real-time monitoring of livestock herds using global positioning system (GPS) tracking devices, complemented by weekly phone interviews with herders (UNEP 2013a). The study revealed the wide range of conflict-avoidance strategies that herders employ in the face of extreme (and potentially violent) tribal conflict. One such strategy—quickly leaving the conflict zone for safer areas, which were often more densely populated or farmed—required the herders to keep their livestock under close control, so as not to damage local farms. Herders also had to negotiate with farmers to ensure that they could stay in the area without creating problems with the host community.

Integrating conflict analysis into livelihood approaches

In the context of livelihood approaches, conflict analysis is essential to improving understanding and informing programming. It can be used, for example, for the following (UNDG 2013; Engel and Korf 2005):

- Identifying the reciprocal impacts of conflict and livelihoods.
- Clarifying and assigning priorities to issues that need to be addressed.
- Identifying the root causes and contributing factors of conflict, in order to determine appropriate responses.
- Clarifying stakeholder motivations, incentives, and relationships, including the willingness and ability to cooperate with other stakeholders.
- Increasing understanding of the links between broader social, political, and economic contexts and natural resource–related conflicts.

Ideally, a conflict analysis includes a political economy analysis, which would reveal how the political and economic processes associated with conflict

[27] For an analysis of incorporating consideration of climate change into post-conflict peacebuilding, see Matthew and Hammill (2012).

have eroded and undermined both local livelihoods and the environment; a political economy analysis is also valuable for informing program design and implementation. Sarah Collinson and her colleagues describe a political economy approach that seeks to understand vulnerability in terms of

> powerlessness rather than simply material need or the failure of basic "entitlements". Vulnerability and power are therefore analyzed as a political and economic process, in terms, for instance, of neglect, exclusion or exploitation, in which a variety of groups and actors play a part. People are most vulnerable when their livelihoods and coping strategies are deliberately blocked or undermined, or if their group identity, political position and/or material circumstances (in some cases their wealth) make them particularly exposed to violence (Collinson et al. 2002, 3; citations omitted).

The tools used in conflict analysis complement those used in political economy analysis. A number of contributors to this book stress the importance of integrating conflict analysis into livelihood approaches and natural resource management initiatives.[28] According to Belinda Bowling and Asif Zaidi, using conflict analysis tools (especially participatory ones) to ensure that conflict dynamics and related considerations are taken into account from the start, by all relevant actors, increases the likelihood that post-conflict natural resource management initiatives will succeed (Bowling and Zaidi 2015*). Based on their work in Mindanao, Brady and her colleagues recommend using conflict analysis to inform project design, and tracing both the project's progress and its impact on the conflict situation; they also advise including peacebuilding and conflict-mitigation indicators in the project performance plan (Brady et al. 2015*). The United Nations Environment Programme (UNEP) also recommends including conflict analysis at the operational planning stage of peacebuilding activities, considering environmental sustainability in planning for relief and recovery operations (to avoid risking future conflict), and integrating environmental and natural resource indicators into peacebuilding strategies (UNEP 2009).

Livelihood approaches can help analyze the connections between administrative levels, and can also help combine local-level (bottom-up) analysis with the regional- and national-level (top-down) analyses of the wider political,

---

[28] Conflict analysis tools include the development of historical timelines for key local and national conflict-related events; identifying and mapping key stakeholders, and tracing changes in their political positions over time; reviewing the relationship between local livelihood groups and other groups connected to the conflict; reviewing the impact of conflict dynamics on livelihood strategies, assets, and key institutions; and reviewing the impacts of livelihood coping strategies (including maladaptive ones) on conflict dynamics. It is important to note that any conflict analysis can provide only a snapshot of the conflict dynamics at play, as the conflict context changes continuously; thus, any analysis needs to be regularly updated and refined (APFO et al. 2004; Mason and Rychard 2005).

economic, and environmental dynamics. Indeed, Collinson advocates such an approach:

> [M]any of the issues and questions of concern to political economy analysis can also be viewed through the lens of livelihoods analysis. The livelihoods approach starts by investigating how individuals, households and communities try to achieve and sustain their livelihoods. Livelihoods analysis is cross-sectoral, and seeks to take into account the totality of economic, political, social and cultural factors affecting people's lives and livelihoods from the local up to the national and international levels. It thus has the potential to complement or be combined with more conventional political economy analysis, which is often approached from the "top down", and frequently fails to connect effectively with the local level (Collinson 2003, 25).

A number of experiences with managing natural resources to support livelihoods in post-conflict settings emphasize the links between local, national, and even transnational conflicts and interests. Alden Wily describes such a case in Afghanistan—where, in 2009, evidence emerged suggesting that "Taliban were arming Kuchi [Pashtun nomads]"; there were also "rumors of Iranian support for Hazara [settled communities]" (Alden Wily 2015*, 126). At the same time, both the national army and local police forces were deployed in the conflict area, and a U.S. military unit was positioned to the east of the area. Various field studies have also explored the many levels of conflict in Darfur (UNEP 2007, 2014; Young et al. 2009).

Analytical approaches, tools, and technologies

A wide range of assessment tools and technologies are available to effectively design and implement projects intended to improve livelihoods and natural resource management in post-conflict situations. While a comprehensive review is beyond the scope of this chapter, it is worth highlighting some of the more widely applied and more innovative approaches.

Where settings are reasonably secure and survey teams have access to local communities or IDP camps, household questionnaires are widely used. Such efforts are often complemented by more qualitative, participatory approaches, such as focus groups and interviews with key informants. When interviews are used, it is crucial to follow the principles of informed consent; moreover, it is important to assess—and minimize—any risks to informants that may accompany the interview process. For example, where being interviewed in public might create risk for interviewees, extreme care must be taken to find a secure and relatively private place to conduct interviews. Gender-sensitive approaches to interviewing are also necessary, both to protect interviewees and to obtain more accurate responses. To the extent possible, interviewees should be drawn from both sexes and should represent a broad range of views, ethnicities, social status, and political affiliations.

Stakeholder analysis, an effective and widely used programming tool, especially where there are multiple land users, involves two steps (DFID 2001):

- Identifying key stakeholder groups—that is, groups whose interest in an initiative differs from that of other groups.
- Analyzing both the perspectives of key stakeholder groups (including their roles, views, and needs), and their relationships with other stakeholder groups.

A stakeholder analysis also involves identifying (1) statutory and customary institutions that are in a position to affect, or to be affected by, an initiative, and (2) individuals holding authority or power, and their links to stakeholder groups.

The wide range of tools for stakeholder analysis includes participatory, qualitative methods such as focus groups, key informant interviews, and surveys based on questionnaires. Where there are many land users whose access and ownership rights exist under conditions of legal pluralism, it is essential to include the interests, rights, and responsibilities of different groups in the mapping exercises and other stakeholder analyses.[29] Young and her colleagues describe a pastoralism stakeholder mapping process that was undertaken for all of Sudan, which then served as the foundation for stakeholder engagement in a subsequent program (Young et al. 2012).

In Mindanao, the Philippine Environmental Governance (EcoGov) Project consistently sought to engage all key individuals and groups in achieving common objectives—including not only those stakeholders who promoted peace and fostered local resilience but those who had vested interests in perpetuating conflict. Accordingly, technical projects addressing natural resources that were important to a range of livelihoods were implemented in a way that "reduced grievances, fostered and strengthened social and institutional resilience, and constructively engaged the key figures who were most capable of mobilizing people for action" (Brady et al. 2015*, 362).

Economic analysis—in particular, of the links between local livelihoods and the national economy—can demonstrate the major contribution of local livelihood systems to wider development, including exports; such information might be overlooked in national statistics, and therefore by policy makers (Behnke 2012). Pastoralists, in particular, have often suffered social, economic, and political marginalization, as well as having been blamed for natural resource conflict, yet the significant contribution of pastoralist livestock production to local and national economies is often underestimated or missed entirely (UNEP 2013b).

---

[29] Stakeholder analysis can help to (1) reveal stakeholders' perspectives, capacity to participate, relative political power, access to information, and institutional means of commanding attention; (2) identify the areas and sources of power and patronage; and (3) determine which stakeholders depend upon which environmental resources and services, and how those stakeholders may be affected by change—or by conflicts, gaps, and overlaps in the roles and functions of other stakeholder groups (DFID 2001).

Thus, analysis of economic contributions can help mitigate negative perceptions of pastoralists.

A number of other approaches to economic and conflict analysis are relevant to local livelihoods and natural resources. Analyses have been undertaken, for example, of the impact of conflict on markets and trade, including livestock, cereals, and cash crops in Darfur (Buchanan-Smith et al. 2012; Buchanan-Smith and Fadul 2008). Commodity-chain analysis can identify power relations, governance structures, and exchange relationships within commercial networks, from primary production to consumption (Collinson et al. 2002). An advantage of this approach is that the analysis spans all levels, from the producer to commercial intermediaries in primary, secondary, and tertiary markets. Moreover, given the sensitivity of information on potential conflict resources, conventional research methods based on structured interviews may not be suitable for investigating who controls the commodity chain at different points. Working with local researchers using qualitative methods, Margie Buchanan-Smith and her colleagues developed a participatory approach for market analysis in Darfur that is based on understanding market trends and the influences on them (Buchanan-Smith, El Tayeb, and Fadul 2013).

Christian Webersik and Alec Crawford describe the challenges of data collection in Somalia, where basic statistical data are missing—and, to the extent that pre-conflict data exist, their accuracy and validity are in question (Webersik and Crawford 2015*). As a result, the authors' analyses relied largely on interviews with staff at aid agencies, local and international nongovernmental organizations, and (now defunct) government entities. Although these sources were important, the authors note that the quantity and quality of data available in Somalia are subject to bias, as the data that are available are obtained from secure (rather than insecure) areas and interview environments.

New interdisciplinary tools

Finally, a wide range of new assessment technologies are being developed and introduced, including remote sensing and spatial planning (Schimmer 2008; Tanik et al. 2008); tracking of cross-border livestock migration through GPS devices (UNEP 2013a); and digital data gathering (DDG) that makes use of smartphones, tablets, and wireless technology to allow rapid data entry, transfer, and analysis.[30]

* * *

Assessments and other analyses are crucial for informing policy processes and designing evidence-based peacebuilding strategies, programs, and projects. The information generated is also crucial to proper monitoring and evaluation of the subsequent impact of interventions.

---

[30] DDG involves the use of handheld devices such as smartphones, tablets, and data pens to record data in the field and transfer information back to a server. It has been used in Chad and Sudan (among other places) by Concern Worldwide (Matturi 2013).

As noted earlier, whenever livelihood-related peacebuilding initiatives are undertaken, there are three key requirements: an understanding of the historical perspective of the conflict, which may include long-standing marginalization of particular groups; a recognition of the implications of seasonality and climate variability on lives and livelihoods; and a grasp of the conflict itself, including interactions between top-down and bottom-up conflict-related processes. Two key challenges remain: (1) establishing a standard set of tools and approaches, based on recognized good practice, for routine application in peacebuilding contexts, and (2) using a meta-analysis or broader review of previous analyses to learn from the collective experience represented therein.

LESSONS FROM POST-CONFLICT EFFORTS TO STRENGTHEN NATURAL RESOURCE–DEPENDENT LIVELIHOODS

Earlier sections of this chapter present an overview of how livelihoods, natural resources, and conflict relate to one another; are explored in the case studies included in this book; and are positioned within the wider literature. This section and the next examine the ways in which various actors are strengthening natural resource–based livelihoods in post-conflict settings, and discuss what these experiences might imply for applying existing livelihood frameworks in such settings, as well as for the post-conflict peacebuilding process.

A broad range of livelihood interventions are in the process of being implemented in countries at various stages of post-conflict peacebuilding and with widely varying histories of conflict. Some of the interventions examined in this book focused specifically on livelihoods or natural resources but had incidental peacebuilding effects, while others focused on peacebuilding but also affected livelihoods or natural resource management. Taken together, the case studies suggest that an intervention in any of these three areas (livelihoods, natural resources, or peacebuilding) is likely to affect the other two, and that at least some of those effects may be positive.

The design of interventions must therefore reflect the interrelated nature of livelihoods, natural resources, and peacebuilding. The three subsections that follow broadly categorize the chapters in this book according to the types of interventions that were undertaken and the primary focus of the initiatives in question (whether livelihoods, natural resources, or peacebuilding), even if the efforts sometimes led to unintended results in other realms. The focus in these subsections is on the rationale for the approaches that drove the interventions, and what the interventions were designed to accomplish. (Chapters that span more than one category are classified according to the primary objective of the intervention.)

Livelihoods: Provision, promotion, and protection

The first category of interventions comprises those case studies in which livelihoods support was a central aim, regardless of whether the interventions supported peacebuilding as well, or existed alongside peacebuilding efforts. The chapters in question focus on markets and trade (conflict economies, value chains, and national economic development); service provision; ecotourism and peace parks; and the rebuilding of livelihoods.

Among the chapters that address markets and trade, some illustrate how a market-driven approach can help strengthen or rebuild livelihoods, while others warn of the risks that such an approach can entail. For example, Lorena Jaramillo Castro and Adrienne M. Stork explore how environmentally and socially sustainable value chains can protect natural capital and biodiversity in countries recovering from conflict (Jaramillo Castro and Stork 2015*). They highlight the BioTrade Initiative, launched by the United Nations Conference on Trade and Development, which has used marketing and commercial strategies targeted to subnational and international markets to strengthen a large number of natural resource–based business initiatives, and thereby develop sustainable livelihoods in Colombia.

Among the potential drawbacks to the market-based approach are those highlighted by Roe, who questions the use of a market-oriented agricultural and natural resource management policy in Afghanistan (Roe 2015*). Roe's concern stems from the fact that maximizing national economic growth (by focusing on areas that already enjoy preferential access to irrigation water) has the potential to exacerbate inequality and sharpen political tensions. To balance the objectives of building a competitive rural economy and a stable rural society—with equal access to livelihood resources, especially irrigation water—Roe recommends the use of evidence-based policy making, the identification of comparative advantages among farming systems, and the development of policies that draw on that identification to facilitate greater equality in natural resource access.

Another illustration of potential constraints on a market-based approach—at least in countries with ongoing conflict—is Somalia, where the trade in bananas, charcoal, and fish has helped drive conflict between local groups and among warlords (Webersik and Crawford 2015*).[31] Webersik and Crawford note that although the country's unrestricted, market-oriented economy holds the potential to support some form of livelihood-based redevelopment, the current lawlessness and the dearth of alternative livelihood options suggest that unsustainable natural resource exploitation will continue to drive conflict for the foreseeable future. Under such circumstances, any market intervention targeting livelihoods would be unavoidably linked to ongoing conflict dynamics, whose complexity may not even be fully understood.

Several chapters focus on ecotourism and peace parks as a means of providing local livelihood opportunities, as well as contributing to economic development more broadly. As discussed by Miko Maekawa and her colleagues, mountain gorilla ecotourism is being used to rebuild local livelihoods in Africa's Great

[31] A United Nations Security Council–mandated monitoring group has estimated that charcoal exports generated millions of dollars in annual revenues for al Shabaab, a militant Islamic group (UNSC 2013).

Lakes region, following a series of armed conflicts (Maekawa et al. 2015*). The market-based approach implemented in the region includes a focus on pricing, international outreach, and reform of the tourism sector. In the former Yugoslavia region, an initiative is under way to establish a transboundary peace park on adjacent lands in Albania, Montenegro, and Kosovo (Walters 2015*). As J. Todd Walters notes, although the park has not yet been established, it holds significant potential to provide ecotourism-related benefits to local populations.

Of the two chapters in this group that focus on direct efforts to rebuild natural resource–based livelihoods following conflict, the first—by Keili and Thiam—surveys a number of alternative livelihood programs for youth in post-conflict Sierra Leone, which were designed to engage and empower young men who are alienated from elders (who were the traditional authorities) and who face limited livelihood prospects, particularly in the diamond sector (Keili and Thiam 2015*). The second chapter, by Harry N. Scheiber and Benjamin Jones, explores the Allied efforts, in post–World War II Japan, to alleviate severe protein shortages, spur economic redevelopment, and restore livelihoods by adopting institutional and policy reforms designed to maximize fisheries production (Scheiber and Jones 2015*). Although the reforms met the goal of supporting local livelihoods, they created significant sustainability concerns.

Natural resource governance and environmental protection

The second category of interventions captured in the case studies focuses on natural resource governance and environmental protection. These interventions are framed in different, often overlapping ways: land and natural resource governance; sustainable management of natural resources; community-based natural resource management (CBNRM); and the building or transformation of natural resource–related institutions and policies. Some chapters profile new environmental governance approaches that were instituted as part of post-conflict peacebuilding efforts, while others examine how a failure to focus on natural resource governance has undermined livelihoods, post-conflict peacebuilding, and sustainable natural resource management.

Several chapters highlight ambitious approaches to strengthening natural resource governance following (and sometimes during) conflict. Bowling and Zaidi examine the new institutional and regulatory framework—rooted in CBNRM—adopted by the interim government in Afghanistan, with the assistance of UNEP (Bowling and Zaidi 2015*). The CBNRM approach was intended to help restore the natural resource base, improve rural livelihoods, reduce the number of disputes and conflicts over natural resources, and contribute to peacebuilding. The approach was pilot tested by UNEP and other international entities in different areas of the country, in order to combine a top-down and bottom-up approach to natural resource governance—that is, (1) to test which top-down measures work (focusing specifically on capacity development and the application of management tools), and which need to be amended, and (2) to identify local approaches that could be scaled up, to inform national policy and practice. The new legal tools that were developed also contained specific provisions to promote peacebuilding in the context of natural resource management.

As Brady and her colleagues recount, in the Philippines, the EcoGov Project sought to strengthen biodiversity conservation by working with local government units on the island of Mindanao, where conflict over land, fisheries, and forests has hindered sustainable natural resource management for community livelihoods (Brady et al. 2015*). The project demonstrated how improved environmental governance can provide an important entry point for addressing conflict and building peace, even where this is not an explicit aim of a given initiative. Among other things, the project helped local governments develop coastal resource management plans, which increased fishery productivity, and a forest land use plan, which strengthened land tenure and access to forest resources.

The remaining chapters in the natural resources category review problems and missed opportunities in natural resource governance following an end to civil conflict. Srey Chanthy and Jim Schweithelm examine the actions of the United Nations Transitional Authority in Cambodia in the early post-conflict peacebuilding years, with a particular focus on forest management, noting the effects of failing to implement sustainable harvesting measures prior to allocating natural resources (Srey and Schweithelm 2015*). In addition to suffering the severe environmental harms brought about by logging (both legal and illegal), forest communities lost important assets—including land, nontimber forest products, foods and food sources, and building materials. These losses were compounded by the subsequent award of agricultural concessions within forested areas.

Taking a broader look at rural livelihood struggles in Cambodia, Blake Ratner notes that the success of post-conflict livelihood interventions depends on two factors: the existence of local rights to natural resources, and a governance system that enables communities to exercise these rights (Ratner 2015*). Michael Renner examines the challenges of natural resource governance following the peace agreement, signed in 2005, that ended a twenty-nine-year secession struggle in Aceh, Indonesia (Renner 2015*). These include a lack of long-term, sustainable livelihood opportunities and difficulties in reintegrating former combatants, who have resorted to widespread illegal logging and other forms of natural resource exploitation.

Peacebuilding

The third category of interventions focuses on peacebuilding and its connection to local livelihoods. One group of chapters examines efforts to build peace between livelihood groups that are competing over natural resources, and to understand how those localized conflicts are connected to higher-level conflicts. A second group analyzes approaches to reintegrating former combatants through the provision of natural resource–based livelihood opportunities. And one chapter discusses how protected areas can help bring divided groups together and indirectly support post-conflict peacebuilding.

The chapters by Jeremy Lind and Liz Alden Wily examine peacebuilding efforts in countries where armed conflict has persisted (particularly at the local level) and is putting pressure on natural resource access for livelihood needs. In a case study focusing on the Kenyan and Ugandan regions of the Karimojong Cluster, Lind examines the dynamics behind persistent livestock raiding and banditry and highlights local peacebuilding efforts to address these conflicts—efforts that have primarily taken the form of confidence-building dialogues between neighboring pastoralist groups (Lind 2015*). The chapter notes, however, that the benefits of local-level reconciliation are limited, as customary pastoralist institutions have weakened over time against a backdrop of structural conflict, generalized insecurity, and the absence of rule of law.

In contrast, Alden Wily highlights the comparative strength of local peacebuilding approaches in Afghanistan, despite weak rule of law and the absence of national governance (Alden Wily 2015*). In her review of efforts to resolve the country's historic pastureland conflicts in the central highlands, Alden Wily stresses the value of a localized approach to resolving conflicts, which can draw on social familiarity between groups. Among the initiatives that Alden Wily describes are field-based pilot projects that brought together Hazara farmers and Kuchi nomads, who negotiated pasture access and developed community-based approaches to natural resource management.

In their chapters, Matthew F. Pritchard and Glaucia Boyer and Adrienne M. Stork examine the use of natural resource–based livelihood opportunities to facilitate DDR (Pritchard 2015*; Boyer and Stork 2015*). Pritchard focuses on the employment of former combatants as game guards in Mozambique's Gorongosa National Park, while Boyer and Stork survey a range of DDR approaches linked to natural resources—including reforestation in Afghanistan, waste management and organic fertilizer production in Colombia, and ecotourism in Aceh. Both chapters highlight the challenges and benefits of using natural resources to meet the livelihood needs of former combatants, in an effort to avert conflict relapse.

The final chapter focused on peacebuilding is Carol Westrik's overview of peace parks. In addition to reviewing their historical development, Westrik notes ways in which the parks can contribute to post-conflict peacebuilding: specifically, by fostering economic development through ecotourism and by providing employment opportunities for former combatants (Westrik 2015*).

*   *   *

Taken together, these three sets of chapters illustrate how interventions addressing livelihoods, natural resources, and post-conflict peacebuilding converge, to varying degrees. All of the interventions profiled in the case studies involve natural resources of one kind or another, whether it is the direct consumption of natural resources (for example, through forestry, pastoralism, or fisheries) or their protection and conservation (for example, through ecotourism) that support local livelihoods. And, depending on both the nature of the conflict and the nature of the resource use, livelihoods interventions and their relationship to peacebuilding initiatives also vary. Where access to natural resources is contested (as in Afghanistan, the Karimojong Cluster, and the Philippines), peacebuilding activities linked to natural resource consumption tend to focus more closely on customary institutional approaches. In contrast, peacebuilding activities that focus on providing employment through natural resource–based jobs tend to rely on market-based efforts to develop alternative livelihoods. Thus, the design of a particular livelihoods intervention should take into account both the type of natural resource and the peacebuilding objectives in question. Even with the most careful of plans, however, situation-specific factors—such as the tsunami in Aceh—can drive interventions in unexpected directions.

Alone or in combination, the three broad categories of intervention presented in this section have been shown to contribute to a variety of outcomes linked to peace, sustainability, and resilience. Their strength lies in their potential synergy: a combined focus on all three response categories provides added value by embracing wider goals, and potentially generating interconnections within complex systems.

LESSONS FROM IMPLEMENTATION

This section turns from the aims of the interventions to the lessons that can be gained from the chapters in this book and from the broader literature. The focus is on experiences with natural resource–based livelihood interventions, as well as on the implications of those experiences for post-conflict peacebuilding. Some of the experiences described were successful; others were not. As a result, the lessons reflect both what seems to have worked, and the obstacles that may be encountered—and potentially overcome.

The lessons have been grouped into four categories: balancing trade-offs, prioritization and sequencing, the role of institutions, and market-based approaches, each of which is discussed in turn.

Balancing trade-offs

One of the most fundamental lessons regarding post-conflict livelihood initiatives concerns the inevitable trade-offs that are required, in light of the political, economic, and cultural context. Among the many factors that can influence decisions about trade-offs are the type and history of the conflict, the natural resources at issue, the content of the peace agreement, and the nature of the post-conflict leadership. The following subsections examine the trade-offs between economic recovery and environmental sustainability; economic recovery and equitable natural resource access and benefit sharing; and DDR programs and local livelihood needs.

Economic recovery and natural resource sustainability

In the immediate aftermath of conflict, it is necessary to balance the need for rapid, large-scale economic redevelopment with the longer-term use of natural resources, including both livelihood uses and ecological purposes. In the absence of adequate policy, legal, and institutional frameworks, the revitalization of natural resource–based harvesting and trade may jeopardize long-term sustainability. In the damaged economy of post–World War II Japan, for example, the revival and expansion of the fisheries sector—through the rebuilding of the fishing fleet, the expansion of authorized fishing zones, and the reintroduction of whaling in the Antarctic—helped alleviate food shortages and create employment. At the same time, efforts to reform the country's fisheries management policies and implement a more sustainable approach to harvesting fell short, partly because the revitalization plan was so successful that fisheries officials became reluctant to implement and enforce policies designed to hold expansion in check (Scheiber and Jones 2015*).

Similarly, peace parks face competing priorities, namely economic development and environmental conservation (Westrik 2015*). Tourism, including ecotourism, can make it difficult to maximize both objectives: although growing numbers of visitors can increase revenues at peace parks and other protected areas, they can also put significant pressure on the natural resources that attracted the visitors in the first place.

Trade-offs between sustainable natural resource use and livelihoods support can also be seen in other natural resource–based activities—such as artisanal mining (which employs large numbers of people but entails significant environmental damage, including toxic air and water emissions) and charcoal production (which bolsters incomes but also contributes to widespread deforestation) (Zulu and Richardson 2012).

In many cases, policies that promote livelihoods redevelopment through the revitalization of natural resource sectors would be more effective if they implemented sustainability measures at the outset; doing so after the fact can be much more challenging.[32] In Cambodia, for example, an overwhelming emphasis on rapid economic development—coupled with widespread corruption and a lack of mechanisms for protecting local rights to natural resources—has led to unchecked mining and logging operations and land grabs for agricultural concessions, all of which have undermined long-term environmental sustainability and livelihoods (Ratner 2015*; Williams 2013). Although a more robust legal framework was eventually enacted, the international community's initial failure to promote legislation that would have helped shape forest policy before the allocation of natural resource concessions had serious consequences (Srey and Schweithelm 2015*). (The issue of when to implement sustainability measures is also discussed later in the chapter, in the section titled "Prioritization and Sequencing.")

[32] For a discussion of the challenges of using strategic environmental assessment for ongoing projects, rather than at the outset, see Bouma (2012).

Economic recovery, equitable benefit sharing, and natural resource access

Research has suggested that economic growth and livelihood security "are not necessarily positively linked or always mutually reinforcing" (Mallett and Slater 2012, 7). Thus, there may be trade-offs between promoting national economic recovery and ensuring equitable natural resource access and benefit sharing. Roe's analysis of potential agricultural interventions in Afghanistan revealed a trade-off between economic recovery, on the one hand, and rural stability and conflict avoidance, on the other (Roe 2015*). Roe also shows how a market-driven approach to agricultural policy reform, which focused on irrigated farming in river valleys, exacerbated unequal access to water in rural Afghanistan. To balance the goal of fostering a competitive rural economy with the need to build a stable rural society, Roe recommends greater emphasis on strengthening farming systems overall, and less focus on the market chains for agricultural products.

DDR, local livelihoods, and natural resource sustainability

Natural resource–related DDR programs also give rise to trade-offs. Given the risk of conflict relapse posed by the reintegration of large numbers of former combatants, programs that seek to employ excombatants in natural resource–related positions (for example, as game wardens, park guides, miners, or farmers) need to attend to competing needs, including community relations, natural resource sustainability, and institutional development.[33]

Experiences in Mozambique's Gorongosa National Park highlight some of the tensions that can arise when DDR programs are implemented (Pritchard 2015*). For example, if local communities are not actively involved in the establishment and management of protected areas, community members may feel alienated from the process and respond by engaging in unsustainable natural resource exploitation; concerns about community involvement also apply to the hiring of excombatants in protected areas. One of the many advantages of active community engagement in DDR-related processes is that it helps ensure that DDR programs do not create the perception that former combatants have an unfair advantage, awarded at the expense of local communities' livelihood needs; community engagement also helps to ensure that excombatants do not alienate local communities.

Another trade-off associated with DDR activities in protected areas is the pressure to act quickly to protect biodiversity resources—such as by hiring excombatants as park wardens before the initial DDR has been completed—versus taking the time to ensure that initial reintegration of excombatants has occurred.

---

[33] For an exploration of the employment of excombatants in industrial coal mining in post-World War II Japan and the challenges of unsustainable natural resource use, see Nakayama (2012).

The latter approach can also afford government agencies time to establish conservation priorities, determine institutional capacity, and reach out to local communities (Pritchard 2015*).

Prioritization and sequencing of interventions

One of the greatest challenges in post-conflict reconstruction is determining how to prioritize and sequence political, social, and economic policies to sustain peace and prevent a return to violence (Timilsina 2007). Prioritization and sequencing inform a broad spectrum of peacebuilding interventions, from policy initiatives to field-based pilot projects and institutional reform. How interventions are prioritized and sequenced helps determine the success of natural resource–based livelihood initiatives. Decisions about prioritizing and sequencing interventions must take a number of factors into consideration: scale (national or local, top-down or bottom-up) and type (policy or pilot initiative); speed (the length of time after the peace agreement that the intervention is implemented); and context (the presence of enabling conditions). The next three subsections consider each of these factors in turn; other prioritization and sequencing options are presented in table 3.

National versus local, policy versus pilot approaches

The initial decision to develop a natural resource–related livelihood initiative at the national or local level (and sometimes at both levels) can lead to divergent outcomes, even with respect to the same country or intervention. Several experiences demonstrate the effectiveness of working at the local level. For example, a review of the EcoGov Project, in the Philippines, emphasizes the value of a locally driven approach that focused on local government units, as well as the critical role of local peace initiatives in the absence of a national-level peace agreement (Brady et al. 2015*). Similarly, with respect to Afghanistan, given the political challenges of addressing land tenure at the national level, Alden Wily stresses the value of a local peacebuilding approach—in this case through the use of local pilot pastureland initiatives (Alden Wily 2015*). Alden Wily also notes that piloting can help overcome national resistance and fear of change, while setting practical precedents and giving communities the opportunity to provide input. With respect to the Gorongosa National Park initiative, the initial success of integrating DDR into the initiative derived, in part, from the fact that a national policy was not required as a precursor, although the subsequent development of national policies emphasizing natural resource protection strengthened the long-term sustainability of the initiative (Pritchard 2015*).

Despite the benefits of working at the community level, purely local approaches do have limitations, and a national approach may be a necessary accompaniment. Lind's chapter on the Karimojong Cluster—a region characterized by structural conflict, general insecurity, and the absence of the rule of

Table 3. Approaches to managing livelihoods in post-conflict situations

	Immediate aftermath	*Peace consolidation*
Livelihood process		
Livelihoods assessment	Identify local livelihood needs and assets in both rural and urban areas, considering the following: • The role of natural resources in contributing to conflict onset. • Impacts of the conflict on livelihoods (including natural resource tenure). • What is necessary to protect and support livelihoods and food security in the short term. • The current status of the natural resource base. • Threats to natural resources posed by seasonal variability and climate change. • Maladaptive coping strategies for livelihoods.	Periodically assess livelihoods. Monitor livelihood interventions. Periodically evaluate the effectiveness of livelihood plans and interventions.
Planning for rebuilding livelihoods	On the basis of livelihoods assessments, develop plans to protect, support, and promote livelihoods in both rural and urban areas. Plans should focus on rebuilding key sources of livelihoods support (such as fisheries, forestry, and agriculture). Develop targeted plans for addressing maladaptive livelihood strategies.	On the basis of the findings from monitoring and evaluation efforts, periodically review plans for supporting livelihoods.
Participatory processes and governance	Ensure the participation of all stakeholders (for example, through local committees that manage natural resource access). Establish community-based mechanisms and capacity to monitor the use of agricultural land, pastures, rangelands, and other natural resources, and to take enforcement action when statutory or customary law is violated. Ensure that participatory measures include women and girls, youth, and other marginalized groups. Include community representatives in the development of natural resource management plans. Facilitate public engagement in peace agreements.	Building on the experiences with participatory processes and governance, consider formalizing these approaches through national laws and policies. Institute channels to allow communities to access decision makers and to access courts to protect their rights to natural resources. Promote public participation in the development and adoption of natural resource laws and policies.

Legal and policy reform	Quickly develop legal safeguards to ensure sustainable resource harvesting. Institute measures to increase transparency and accountability in managing natural resources and their revenues, including measures related to planning, concessions, and payments to the government. Develop measures (including legal pluralism) to address access and tenure issues related to land, forests, and other natural resources essential to livelihoods. Incorporate community-based rights and authority over natural resources into new laws and policies. Where tenure reform (whether for land or other natural resources) is necessary, start a consultative process early, taking account of ethnic, gender, and age differences to assess needs, reform objectives, and options, and to build public support for the process.	Ensure that the legal and policy framework continues to be informed by the experiences of pilot and field-based projects. Review the effectiveness of measures to increase transparency and accountability in the management of natural resources and their revenues; modify laws and institutions, and institute other measures accordingly. Consider ways to more effectively integrate and (where integration is difficult) delineate statutory and customary norms and institutions governing land, forests, and other natural resources essential to livelihoods. Develop measures to ensure shared access to common-property natural resources, being sure to give consideration to age and gender. Building on the consultative process, reform laws and policies governing natural resource tenure (where necessary).
Institution building and reform	Implement institutional reform through capacity building, decentralization of natural resource management, and the hiring of more progressive staff. Minimize jurisdictional conflicts by spelling out governmental mandates clearly. Address tensions between competing groups regarding natural resource use and access through consultative and participatory processes.	Strengthen customary institutions for managing natural resources, while promoting gender balance where possible. Build cooperative relationships between government agencies managing natural resources.
Pilot and field-based projects	Institute pilot projects early on, in order to demonstrate the benefits of peacebuilding, inform the development of national laws and policies, and guide scaled-up interventions. Prioritize efforts to provide young men and women with education and training for livelihoods (including literacy and skills-based training).	Review the effectiveness of pilot projects to determine which should be scaled up. Scale up efforts targeting young men and women.

Table 3. (*Cont'd*)

	Immediate aftermath	***Peace consolidation***
Livelihoods substance		
Maladaptive livelihoods	Strengthen security to support access to basic resources. Explore incentives that will encourage the abandonment of maladaptive strategies.	
Economic recovery	Support efforts to add value through the processing of natural resources. Engage the private sector through natural resource–based initiatives such as the BioTrade Initiative. Promote access to markets by relaxing trade restrictions and improving security. Balance the goal of maximizing agricultural development with the goal of building a more stable rural society.	Improve roads and other infrastructure to allow greater access to markets.
Disarmament, demobilization, and reintegration (DDR)	Analyze the opportunities and risks presented by natural resources in the context of DDR, and develop DDR plans that take the results of this analysis into account. Undertake initial DDR efforts. To support reintegrating excombatants who are taking up or returning to agricultural livelihoods, determine whether there are any barriers to access to land, water, credit, or inputs. Support short-term employment options that will help to rebuild the productive capacity of the natural resource base (for example, through reforestation, rebuilding irrigation structures, or rebuilding roads to transport goods to market).	Using carefully targeted incentives—including a range of services, such as skills-based training and marketing support— promote the reintegration of former combatants into natural resource–based jobs (for example, in agriculture, forestry, fisheries, conservation, and tourism).
Alternative livelihoods	Support local, skills-based training, both (1) to provide alternative livelihoods and (2) build the capacity of local training institutions. Explore the sustainability of local innovation, including opportunties to scale up. Analyze market value chains to address bottlenecks and identify opportunities for added value.	

law—highlights the limits of local-level reconciliation (Lind 2015*). Under conditions such as those that characterize the Karimojong Cluster, local approaches focused only on the manifestation of chronic conflict cannot meaningfully address the underlying structural dynamics, which require complementary efforts at the regional and national levels.

Taken together, the case studies in this book suggest that local approaches may more effectively address contested natural resource access and use by recognizing customary laws and engaging customary institutions—particularly where national governance is weak and political tensions obstruct negotiations at the national level. On the other hand, national approaches may be needed where customary institutions have eroded or where other limits to local approaches exist.

Given the evident advantages of the approach, it is not surprising that successful efforts often engage both the national and local levels. In Afghanistan, combining a top-down approach (focused on building national-level institutional capacity and management tools) with a bottom-up one (focused on limited, field-level pilot projects) maximized the effectiveness of UNEP's legal and institutional reform efforts (Bowling and Zaidi 2015*). In contrast to some of the more limited interventions (such as DDR approaches) examined in the other case studies, this broader strategy succeeded in advancing more comprehensive reforms in Afghanistan, including the development of an environmental governance structure.

Experience suggests that peacebuilding should optimally begin at the local level, in order to inform national processes. This was also the conclusion of a field-based study of livelihoods and vulnerability among pastoralists in Darfur (the Northern Rizaygat), which emphasized the need to begin peace processes at the local level in order to clarify interests and concerns before linking them to higher-level actions and talks (Young et al. 2009). The same conclusion was echoed in other work undertaken by UNEP in Darfur, which focused on rebuilding relationships between livelihood groups and their governing institutions (UNEP 2014).

Early action

A number of arguments support the adoption of measures in the immediate aftermath of conflict to address livelihood coping strategies—in particular, maladaptive strategies that may be harming natural resources. For example, early action helps gain community support and bring rampant (and often illegal or illicit) natural resource harvesting under control, whereas delay can lead to severe natural resource degradation. In Cambodia, for example, the interim government's failure to develop forest management laws, institutions, and data before handing out large-scale timber concessions—and the failure to prohibit the extensive illegal logging that had been under way since the 1990s—drastically reduced timber yields and caused significant ecological damage (Srey and Schweithelm 2015*). Similarly, a case study of Afghanistan suggests that community-based pilot projects in natural resource management should be implemented early in the post-conflict period: the sooner communities experience improvements in their livelihoods, the more likely they are to support the peacebuilding process and resist a return to conflict (Bowling and Zaidi 2015*). The case study also recommends integrating environmental and natural resource management issues into national planning, reconstruction, and development processes during the immediate post-conflict period; otherwise, it will be difficult to raise such issues later, in the face of competing priorities. A corollary point that can be drawn from other experiences (including in the Philippines and the Karimojong Cluster) is that peacebuilding efforts can begin even before peace agreements are signed, including under conditions of protracted conflict.[34]

Failing to act quickly to address livelihood needs can entrench poor natural resource–harvesting practices that may prove difficult to alter later on. Experience with post–World War II fisheries policy in occupied Japan is a reminder of the potential pitfalls of focusing on immediate livelihood needs at the expense of longer-term sustainability (Scheiber and Jones 2015*). This raises the question of how to phase in approaches that can help foster livelihoods recovery in the short term and promote economic development over the long term, without sacrificing the natural resource base. This difficult balance may not be possible in all cases. In Japan, for example, short-term, unsustainable natural resource use was prioritized not only in the fisheries sector but also in the energy sector (Nakayama 2012).

Enabling conditions

Enabling conditions, particularly in the political realm, are often prerequisites for successful natural resource–based livelihood approaches. One examination of post-conflict environments identifies four types of enabling conditions required for economic recovery (Brown, Langer, and Stewart 2008):

- A secure situation.
- An international commitment to help enforce the peace and provide aid for reconstruction and development.
- The capacity of the state to maintain law and order and deliver services.
- The political inclusivity of the state.

Two of the case studies in this book illustrate how these enabling conditions can influence the prioritization and sequencing of livelihood interventions in countries emerging from conflict. In Africa's Great Lakes region, security and stability served as necessary preconditions for the development of mountain gorilla ecotourism (Maekawa et al. 2015*). After peace had been reestablished

[34] See, for example, Buchanan-Smith and Bromwich (2015), Brady et al. (2015*), and Lind (2015*).

in Rwanda and Uganda, both countries were able to successfully revive their ecotourism industries through business reforms, investment in tourism fairs, and the incorporation of tourism into economic plans. In the Democratic Republic of the Congo, however, ongoing instability and insecurity have constrained the adoption of similar measures to boost mountain gorilla ecotourism. In Mozambique, conflict fatigue supported DDR. In addition, extensive international financial support for DDR programs helped lay the groundwork for the successful hiring of former combatants as game guards in Gorongosa National Park, an intervention that supported both livelihoods and post-conflict peacebuilding (Pritchard 2015*).

The role of institutions

In countries emerging from conflict, where institutional capacity has been weakened or destroyed, capacity building is often a core need. Robust institutions governing natural resources can help strengthen livelihoods and peacebuilding; however, when policies are reformed during the post-conflict period, institutions may need to be reformed as well. Institutional resistance to improved natural resource management can undermine both livelihoods and peacebuilding (Mallett and Slater 2012).

The active participation of government and community institutions in natural resource–based livelihood initiatives at the appropriate level—whether national, subnational, or local—is critical for ensuring the sustainability of such initiatives. Such participation can be a challenge, however, where conflict has eroded government and community institutions. An examination of post-conflict forest reform in Cambodia, for example, demonstrates the significant governance challenges posed by the destruction of government institutions during the civil war (Srey and Schweithelm 2015*). With respect to Nepal, where community forest user groups helped sustain livelihoods and prevent conflict after the disruption of the rural economy, Ratner and his colleagues offer a resource rights and governance framework that emphasizes the importance of strong local institutions in supporting rural livelihood resilience (Ratner et al. 2013).

Where entrenched bureaucracies may be corrupt, or wedded to approaches that maximize natural resource exploitation without concern for sustainability, simply engaging with institutions may not be enough. Instead, a number of measures may be required to reform institutions and reduce resistance to new approaches to natural resource management, including capacity building; the introduction of transparency and accountability measures; and the promotion of staff who are less entrenched in previous ways of doing things. In their case study of Japan, Scheiber and Jones note that an entrenched bureaucracy enhanced the stability of the fisheries sector and provided useful assistance with policy coordination; nevertheless, the rigidity of the bureaucracy posed obstacles to policy reform—specifically, a movement away from maximizing production (Scheiber and Jones 2015*). The authors note that, as the result of the Allies' mentoring of a newer generation of fisheries management officials (as well as newer fisheries research facilities and strengthened fisheries sciences), the scientific research capacity of the fisheries sector improved. In Afghanistan, policy makers encountered similar institutional resistance to a decentralized, community-based approach to managing forests, wildlife, and rangelands, particularly within the Ministry of Justice (Bowling and Zaidi 2015*).

On the other hand, informal or community-based institutions have supported post-conflict peacebuilding and redevelopment. In Mindanao, the EcoGov Project engaged local community groups and governance institutions (such as local government units) to support organizational change and increase transparency, accountability, and public participation in natural resource management (Brady et al. 2015*). By engaging various stakeholders in the collaborative envisioning, planning, and implementation of natural resource management initiatives, project staff sought to integrate efforts across different levels of governance (family, community, local, provincial, and national), so that each reinforced the other. Project staff also sought to reorient paradigms of competition and conflict, by focusing instead on mutual understanding and common objectives; those objectives also provided linkages between various levels of natural resource governance. In Mozambique, where informal community reconciliation ceremonies helped facilitate the reintegration component of the DDR initiative undertaken in Gorongosa National Park, customary institutions played a significant role in helping to bring different groups together, preempting potential conflicts over natural resource access in protected areas (Pritchard 2015*).

UNEP's program in Darfur is pioneering a new approach to supporting the recovery of both livelihoods and local governance institutions for natural resources (UNEP 2014). At the core of the program are two related ideas: first, that rebuilding good natural resource governance requires restoring the trust and collaborative relationships that have been destroyed by conflict; and second, that livelihoods can be rebuilt effectively only after trust is reestablished. UNEP's approach focuses on restoring three types of relationships: institution to institution, institution to community, and community to community. UNEP has also developed a framework for assessing and monitoring improvements in the quality of these relationships. The five relationship dimensions addressed in the framework are "Directness (good communication); Commonality (shared purpose); Continuity (time together and a shared history); Multiplexity (mutual understanding and breadth); and Parity (fairness)" (UNEP 2014, 5).

Weakened customary institutions can undermine livelihood access and contribute to conflict. In the Karimojong Cluster, for example, the waning of customary pastoralist institutions that had traditionally helped manage conflict between pastoralist groups led to the loss of livestock assets in the region (Lind 2015*). That this occurred as a result of state building in East Africa illustrates the potentially complex relationship between local and national or regional institutional development. For example, a number of measures undertaken in the name of state control—including the use of military force to subdue pastoralist groups, punitive confiscation of livestock, commoditization of livestock, and prohibitions on barter and trade—intensified ethnic divisions and created more rigid social relations—which, in turn, undermined the customary institutions that pastoralists had historically used to manage ecological uncertainty and natural resource scarcity. In Sierra Leone, control by older chiefs of customary institutions governing access to land led to alienation among young men, which played a major role in precipitating conflict (Keili and Thiam 2015*). Nevertheless, in the context of peacebuilding efforts and when paired with alternative livelihood schemes, customary institutions have the potential to bring together youth and elders.

Institutional reform poses many challenges. Experiences with natural resource management in Japan and Afghanistan, discussed earlier, highlight the need for institutional reform to accompany policy reform, particularly with respect to developing more sustainable approaches to managing natural resources for livelihoods and other purposes. In both countries, tensions arose when policy makers who were wedded to top-down approaches were confronted by new approaches to natural resource management (Scheiber and Jones 2015*; Bowling and Zaidi 2015*).

Problems may also arise when multiple institutions are involved in natural resource management. As Bowling and Zaidi note with regard to Afghanistan, in order to avoid overlapping mandates, which can obstruct local-level governance and peacebuilding, it is essential to clearly delineate governmental mandates during the peacebuilding stage. In his case study of Mozambique, Pritchard attributes some of the success of the Gorongosa DDR initiative to the small scale of the project, which enabled centralized decision making within the National Directorate of Forestry and Wildlife and avoided the need for expansive government mandates (Pritchard 2015*).

Several chapters identify capacity building as a key component of institutional reform. In Afghanistan, Darfur, and elsewhere, natural resource interventions (whether for livelihood purposes or other objectives) are unlikely to succeed without concurrent and sustained capacity-building efforts (Bowling and Zaidi 2015*; UNEP 2014). Experiences implementing natural resource–related DDR efforts in Afghanistan confirm the importance of capacity building, particularly at the community level, where the establishment of forest management committees by community elders strengthened community capacity and development in seven provinces (Boyer and Stork 2015*).

In the Philippines, it was necessary to develop the organizational capacity of local government units to help them address environmental threats, while also improving transparency, accountability, and public participation (Brady et al. 2015*). In Africa's Great Lakes region, the private sector provided critical investment and expertise in countries emerging from conflict, which often lack the capacity to develop an ecotourism industry (Maekawa et al. 2015*). On the other hand, impaired capacity within Mozambique's National Directorate of Forestry and Wildlife actually presented an opportunity for the directorate's DDR initiative: there was a demand for trained park personnel that could be met by drawing on former combatants who needed gainful employment (Pritchard 2015*). The arrangement had the added benefit of offering park employees significant opportunities for upward mobility.

Market-based approaches

Although market-based approaches can support the development of natural resource–based livelihoods in post-conflict countries, experience also suggests that they may, in some cases, undermine equitable natural resource access. Another potential drawback of market-based approaches is that they may offer private-sector entities incentives or opportunities to act as peace spoilers, by seeking to undermine peacebuilding efforts or capitalize on redevelopment programs for financial gain.

Post-conflict Colombia and Sierra Leone are examples of the successful use of market-based efforts. In their case study of Colombia, Jaramillo Castro and Stork describe the Sustainable BioTrade Programme, a market-based initiative that supported local livelihoods, bolstered post-conflict economic recovery, and helped avert further local conflict (Jaramillo Castro and Stork 2015*). And in post-conflict Sierra Leone, small-business development—in particular, small-scale agriculture—nurtured alternative livelihood opportunities and helped support peacebuilding (Keili and Thiam 2015*).

Analyses of opportunities around protected areas have identified the critical role of ecotourism—not only in supporting local communities, but in providing employment for former combatants (for example, as tour guides, park rangers, and hotel and restaurant owners).[35] Maekawa and her colleagues identify concrete ways in which pricing, market development, international outreach, and reform of the tourism sector strengthened mountain gorilla ecotourism and facilitated macroeconomic growth in the Great Lakes region of Africa (Maekawa et al. 2015*). In Colombia, private-sector drivers of livelihoods development include waste management and organic fertilizer production (Boyer and Stork 2015*).

The disadvantages of a market-driven approach are typically associated with the inequitable distribution of benefits—as is the case in Rwanda and Uganda, where the direct benefits of ecotourism (especially jobs) tend to accrue to higher-income communities adjacent to tourism hubs. Although governmental authorities have attempted to address the disparity through revenue sharing, these efforts have been shown to favor wealthier communities, indicating that more must be done to support local livelihoods for poorer communities (Maekawa et al. 2015*). In Cambodia, government decisions to grant large-scale private concessions for logging, industrial agriculture, mining, and hydropower have undermined efforts to bolster local livelihoods by foreclosing community access to natural resources (Ratner 2015*).

---

[35] See, for example, Westrik (2015*), Maekawa et al. (2015*), Boyer and Stork (2015*), and Walters (2015*).

One of the most persuasive illustrations of the potentially harmful effects of market forces is in Somalia, where warlords have appropriated livelihood-based resources, including bananas, charcoal, and fisheries, thereby indirectly facilitating conflict rather than peacebuilding (Webersik and Crawford 2015*). Although these resources lack the strategic value of diamonds or gold, armed groups can still benefit financially from controlling their trade. Thus, natural resources have created a new conflict economy whose participants are more interested in maintaining and profiting from conflict than pursuing peace.

In yet another example of the perverse impacts of market forces in Somalia, the devaluation of the Somali shilling has been driving the unsustainable production of charcoal, as rising fuel prices have turned farmers away from machinery-based agriculture and toward charcoal production. At the same time, the Somalia experience also shows how the power of the markets can be harnessed to correct the perverse incentives that underpin conflict dynamics. For example, when the European Union import demand dropped—as a result of the reduction of preferential trade agreements between the European Union and Somalia, the liberalization of import markets, and the repeal of certain import quotas—70 percent of Somalia's banana trade, which had been captured by warlords, collapsed (Webersik and Crawford 2015*).

CONCLUSION

Supporting the reestablishment of local livelihoods is a fundamental component of post-conflict peacebuilding, particularly in light of the linkages between livelihoods, natural resources, and conflict. The dependence of a large proportion of rural and even urban populations on natural resources means that sustainably managing these resources is essential to economic recovery. Thus, a focus on sustainable livelihoods provides opportunities to promote peace and build community resilience to a wide array of risks, including conflict and environmental degradation.

In considering how to transition from maladaptive to sustainable livelihoods, several core concepts emerge. Successful solutions are based on a participatory approach that incorporates the perspectives of a wide range of stakeholders. In particular, key local and national actors who may exert significant influence over various population groups, or who may be able to initiate new ways of thinking or acting that avoid maladaptive practices, should be drawn into peacebuilding processes. Given that livelihood systems often share or compete with one another for common-property resources, it is critical to broaden the programming lens to consider the implications of a given intervention (or risk) for the livelihoods of all population groups, especially those that depend on seasonal access to natural resources. It is also essential to consider the implications of maladaptive strategies for the livelihoods of future generations.

Livelihoods theory, while important to understanding livelihood dynamics, is insufficient on its own to support the appropriate design of peacebuilding approaches. Purely theoretical approaches risk promoting unrealistic expectations, and fail to address the numerous and complex challenges and exceptional circumstances that present in practice. Instead, theoretical approaches must be informed by best practices that are rooted in messy, complex local realities. By combining theoretical considerations and debates with practical experience, this book highlights issues that deserve particular attention, while contributing to the development of long-term, institutional understanding of the impacts of (and interactions between) peacebuilding and livelihood initiatives.

A livelihoods analysis is the first step in developing an evidence-based approach to livelihood interventions and policies in post-conflict countries. While there is no blueprint for such an analysis, key components include assessments of outcome or process vulnerability, seasonality and climate variability, the conflict (including the political economy), and post-conflict environmental issues and needs. Tools and technologies that can be used in such analyses include local surveys based on household questionnaires, stakeholder analysis and mapping, remote sensing and spatial planning, GPS tracking, and digital data gathering.

Taken together, the case studies in this book illustrate a theory of change that underlies post-conflict livelihood interventions based on sustainable natural resource management. This theory of change consists of three related premises: First, livelihoods are essential to peacebuilding. Second, in most, if not all, developing countries, natural resources are essential to the majority of livelihoods, especially in rural areas. Third, to foster a sustainable peace, natural resources must be managed for the more effective support of livelihoods. Thus, to strengthen peacebuilding and resilience to conflict, practitioners and governments must work at all governance levels and with all stakeholder groups to support, protect, and promote sustainable livelihoods—and the natural resources on which they are based.

In designing livelihood interventions and policies, it is important to balance trade-offs that may arise between national economic recovery on the one hand, and local livelihoods and natural resource sustainability on the other. How to prioritize and sequence interventions is another critical question. Depending on context, it may be desirable to start with a locally based pilot approach that feeds into national-level law or policy—or, conversely, to establish national policy that can provide guidance, structure, and an enabling environment for local interventions. It is also important to act early in the peacebuilding process, in order to address livelihood coping strategies—especially maladaptive ones.

Despite progress in developing natural resource–based livelihood interventions capable of strengthening post-conflict peacebuilding, more work needs to be done, particularly with regard to (1) developing programs to address maladaptive livelihoods, and (2) establishing monitoring and evaluation frameworks that can capture the peacebuilding impact of livelihood programs. Additional experience focused on young males, who play a pronounced role in armed conflict, is also needed. For example, instead of simply providing new livelihoods for excombatants, it is critical to examine both overall sustainability and the differential impacts of particular interventions on various groups. A renewed focus on sustainability and resilience, on examining livelihood challenges from multiple perspectives, and on experiential learning can help inform the future direction of livelihoods, natural resources, and post-conflict peacebuilding.

REFERENCES

Adger, W. N., J. Pulhin, J. Barnett, G. D. Dabelko, G. K. Hovelsrud, M. Levy, U. Oswald Spring, and C. Vogel. 2014. Human security. In *Climate change 2014: Impacts, adaptation, and vulnerability,* ed. H. L. T. A. J. Palutikof. Cambridge, UK: Cambridge University Press. http://ipcc-wg2.gov/AR5/images/uploads/WGIIAR5-Chap12_FGDall.pdf.

Ahmed, N. M. E. 2008. Households depending on agriculture (cultivation and animal husbandry) as a main source of livelihood using 2008 population census data. Paper presented at the Data Dissemination Conference 5th Population Census, Khartoum, Sudan.

Alden Wily, L. 2015. Resolving natural resource conflicts to help prevent war: A case from Afghanistan. In *Livelihoods, natural resources, and post-conflict peacebuilding*, ed. H. Young and L. Goldman. London: Earthscan.

AOAD (Arab Organization for Agricultural Development). 2009. *Arab agricultural statistics yearbook.* Vol. 29. www.aoad.org/Statistical_Yearly_Book_Vol_29.pdf.

APFO (African Peace Forum), Centre for Conflict Resolution, Consortium of Humanitarian Agencies, FEWER, International Alert, and Saferworld. 2004. *Conflict-sensitive approaches to development, humanitarian assistance and peacebuilding: A resource pack.* www.conflictsensitivity.org/publications/conflict-sensitive-approaches-development-humanitarian-assistance-and-peacebuilding-res.

Ashley, C., and D. Carney. 1999. *Sustainable livelihoods: Lessons from early experience.* London: United Kingdom Department for International Development.

Aspinall, E. 2007. The construction of grievance: Natural resources and identity in a separatist conflict. *Journal of Conflict Resolution* 51 (6): 950–972.

AU (African Union). 2010. *Policy framework for pastoralism in Africa: Securing, protecting and improving the lives, livelihoods and rights of pastoralist communities.* Addis Ababa, Ethiopia. http://rea.au.int/en/sites/default/files/Policy%20Framework%20for%20Pastoralism.pdf.

Bahadur, A. V., M. Ibrahim, and T. Tanner. 2010. The resilience renaissance? Unpacking of resilience for tackling climate change and disasters. Strengthening Climate Resilience Discussion Paper No. 1. Brighton, UK: Institute of Development Studies, University of Sussex.

Baro, M., and T. F. Deubel. 2006. Persistent hunger: Perspectives on vulnerability, famine, and food security in sub-Saharan Africa. *Annual Review of Anthropology* 35:521–538.

Behnke, R. 2012. The economics of pastoral livestock production in Sudan. Medford, MA: Feinstein International Center, Tufts University. http://fic.tufts.edu/assets/Briefing-Paper-Economics-of-Pastoral-Livestock1.pdf.

Bouma, G. 2012. Challenges and opportunities for mainstreaming environmental assessment tools in post-conflict settings. In *Assessing and restoring natural resources in post-conflict peacebuilding*, ed. D. Jensen and S. Lonergan. London: Earthscan.

Bowling, B., and A. Zaidi. 2015. Developing capacity for natural resource management in Afghanistan: Process, challenges, and lessons learned by UNEP. In *Livelihoods, natural resources, and post-conflict peacebuilding*, ed. H. Young and L. Goldman. London: Earthscan.

Boyer, G., and A. M. Stork. 2015. The interface between natural resources and disarmament, demobilization, and reintegration: Enhancing human security in post-conflict situations. In *Livelihoods, natural resources, and post-conflict peacebuilding*, ed. H. Young and L. Goldman. London: Earthscan.

Brady, C., O. Agoncillo, M. Z. Butardo-Toribio, B. Dolom, and C. V. Olvida. 2015. Improving natural resource governance and building peace and stability in Mindanao, Philippines. In *Livelihoods, natural resources, and post-conflict peacebuilding*, ed. H. Young and L. Goldman. London: Earthscan.

Brown, G., A. Langer, and F. Stewart. 2008. A typology of post-conflict environments: An overview. CRISE Working Paper No. 53. Oxford, UK: Centre for Research on Inequality, Human Security and Ethnicity, Oxford University. http://economics.ouls.ox.ac.uk/13008/1/workingpaper53.pdf.

Brown, O., M. Hauptfleisch, H. Jallow, and P. Tarr. 2012. Environmental assessment as a tool for peacebuilding and development: Initial lessons from capacity building in Sierra Leone. In *Assessing and restoring natural resources in post-conflict peacebuilding*, ed. D. Jensen and S. Lonergan. London: Earthscan.

Bruch, C. 2008. The end of equilibrium. *Environmental Forum* 25 (5): 30–35.

Buchanan-Smith, M., and B. Bromwich. 2015. Preparing for peace: An analysis of Darfur, Sudan. In *Governance, natural resources, and post-conflict peacebuilding*, ed. C. Bruch, C. Muffett, and S. S. Nichols. London: Earthscan.

Buchanan-Smith, M., and S. Davies. 1995. *Famine early warning and response: The missing link*. London: IT Publications.

Buchanan-Smith, M., Y. El Tayeb, and A. J. A. Fadul. 2013. Understanding trade and markets in a protracted conflict: The case of Darfur. *Humanitarian Exchange*, no. 58:35–37. www.odihpn.org/humanitarian-exchange-magazine/issue-58/understanding-trade-and-markets-in-a-protracted-conflict-the-case-of-darfur.

Buchanan-Smith, M., and A. A. Fadul. 2008. *Adaptation and devastation: The impact of the market on trade and markets in Darfur; Findings of a scoping study*. Medford, MA: Feinstein International Center, Tufts University. http://fic.tufts.edu/assets/Adaptation-and-Devastation-2008.pdf.

Buchanan-Smith, M., A. J. A. Fadul, A. R. Tahir, and Y. Aklilu. 2012. *On the hoof: Livestock trade in Darfur*. Nairobi, Kenya: United Nations Environment Programme. www.un.org/en/events/environmentconflictday/pdf/UNEP_Sudan_Tufts_Darfur_Livestock_2012.pdf.

Buchanan-Smith, M., H. McElhinney, H. Bagadi, M. A. Rahman, A. Dawalbeit, A. Dawalbeit, M. Khalil, and B. E. D. Abdalla. 2011. *City limits: Urbanisation and vulnerability in Sudan; Nyala case study*. London: Humanitarian Policy Group, Overseas Development Institute. www.ircwash.org/sites/default/files/Buchanan-2011-CityNyala.pdf.

Carney, D., M. Drinkwater, T. Rusinow, K. Neefjes, S. Wanmali, and N. Singh. 1999. Livelihood approaches compared: A brief comparison of the livelihood approaches of the UK Department for International Development (DFID), CARE, Oxfam and the United Nations Development Programme (UNDP). London: United Kingdom Department for International Development. www.start.org/Program/advanced_institute3_web/p3_documents_folder/Carney_etal.pdf.

Chambers, R., and G. Conway. 1991. Sustainable rural livelihoods: Practical concepts for the 21st century. IDS Discussion Paper No. 296. Brighton, UK: Institute of Development Studies, University of Sussex.

Charbonneau, L. 2013. Exclusive: U.N. monitors see arms reaching Somalia from Yemen, Iran. Reuters, February 10. www.reuters.com/article/2013/02/10/us-somalia-arms-un-idUSBRE9190E420130210.

Collier, P. 2000. Doing well out of war: An economic perspective. In *Greed and grievance: Economic agendas in civil wars*, ed. M. Berdal and D. M. Malone. Boulder, CO: Lynne Rienner.

Collinson, S., M. Bhatia, M. Evans, R. Fanthorpe, J. Goodhand, and S. Jackson. 2002. Politically informed humanitarian programming: Using a political economy approach. HPN Network Paper No. 41. London: Overseas Development Institute. www.odihpn.org/hpn-resources/network-papers/politically-informed-humanitarian-programming-using-a-political-economy-approach.

Collinson, S. E. 2003. Power, livelihoods and conflict: Case studies in political economy analysis for humanitarian action. HPG Report No. 13. London: Humanitarian Policy Group, Overseas Development Institute.

Conca, K., and J. Wallace. 2012. Environment and peacebuilding in war-torn societies: Lessons from the UN Environment Programme's experience with post-conflict assessment. In *Assessing and restoring natural resources in post-conflict peacebuilding*, ed. D. Jensen and S. Lonergan. London: Earthscan.

Coryn, C. L. S., L. A. Noakes, C. D. Westine, and D. C. Schröter. 2011. A systematic review of theory-driven evaluation practice from 1990 to 2009. *American Journal of Evaluation* 32 (2): 199–226. www.wmich.edu/evalphd/wp-content/uploads/2010/05/A-Systematic-Review-of-Theory-Driven-Evaluation-Practice-from-1990-to-2009.pdf.

Davies, S. 1993. Are coping strategies a cop out? *IDS Bulletin* 24 (4): 60–72.

———. 1996. *Adaptable livelihoods: Coping with food insecurity in the Malian Sahel.* London: Macmillan Press.

Defensor Knack, P. 2013. Legal frameworks and land issues in Muslim Mindanao. In *Land and post-conflict peacebuilding*, ed. J. Unruh and R. C. Williams. London: Earthscan.

de Waal, A. 2005. Who are the Darfurians? Arab and African identities, violence and external engagement. *African Affairs* 104 (415): 181–205. http://afraf.oxfordjournals.org/content/104/415/181.abstract.

DFID (Department for International Development, United Kingdom). 1999. Sustainable livelihoods guidance sheets. London. www.eldis.org/vfile/upload/1/document/0901/section2.pdf.

———. 2001. Sustainable livelihoods guidance sheets. London. www.efls.ca/webresources/DFID_Sustainable_livelihoods_guidance_sheet.pdf.

———. 2011. *Defining disaster resilience: A DFID approach paper*. London.

Dorward, A., S. Anderson, S. Clark, B. Keane, and J. Moguel. 2001. Asset functions and livelihood strategies: A framework for pro-poor analysis, policy and practice. Paper contributed to EAAE seminar on livelihoods and rural poverty. https://cgspace.cgiar.org/bitstream/handle/10568/4163/Asset_Function.pdf?sequence=.

Drinkwater, M., and T. Rusinow. 1999. Application of CARE's livelihoods approach: How the sustainable livelihoods framework has been applied by CARE International. Paper presented at the Natural Resources Advisors' Conference.

Duffield, M. 1994. The political economy of internal war: Asset transfer, complex emergencies and international aid. In *War and hunger: Rethinking international responses to complex emergencies*, ed. J. Macrae and A. Zwi. London: Zed Books / Save the Children Fund.

Ellis, F., and H. A. Freeman, eds. 2005. *Rural livelihoods and poverty reduction policies*. London: Routledge.

Ellis, J., and K. A. Galvin. 1994. Climate patterns and land-use practices in the dry zones of Africa. *BioScience* 44 (5): 340–349.

Engel, A., and B. Korf. 2005. *Negotiation and mediation techniques for natural resource management*. Rome: Food and Agriculture Organization of the United Nations. ftp://ftp.fao.org/docrep/fao/008/a0032e/a0032e00.pdf.

FAO (Food and Agriculture Organization of the United Nations). 2011. Forests and poverty reduction. www.fao.org/forestry/livelihoods/en/.

———. n.d. Fisheries and aquaculture. www.fao.org/docrep/014/am859e/am859e07.pdf.

FAO (Food and Agriculture Organization of the United Nations) Somalia. 2014. Livestock: The mainstay. www.faosomalia.org/livestock.

FEWS-Net (Famine Early Warning Systems Network). 2013. Sudan food security outlook: April to September 2013. http://reliefweb.int/sites/reliefweb.int/files/resources/Sudan%20Food%20Security%20Outlook%20April%20to%20September%202013.pdf.

Folke, C. 2006. Resilience: The emergence of a perspective for social-ecological systems analyses. *Global Environmental Change* 16 (3): 253–267.

Gingerich, T., and J. Leaning. 2004. *The use of rape as a weapon of war in the conflict in Darfur, Sudan*. Boston, MA: Harvard School of Public Health.

Global Witness. 2006. *The sinews of war: Eliminating trade in conflict resources*. www.globalwitness.org/sites/default/files/import/the_sinews_of_war.pdf.

Green, A. 2015. Social identity, natural resources, and peacebuilding. In *Livelihoods, natural resources, and post-conflict peacebuilding*, ed. H. Young and L. Goldman. London: Earthscan.

Hamilton-Peach, J., and P. Townsley. n.d. An IFAD sustainable livelihoods framework. www.ifad.org/sla/framework/index.htm.

Hayes, K., and R. Perks. 2012. Women in the artisanal and small-scale mining sector of the Democratic Republic of the Congo. In *High-value natural resources and post-conflict peacebuilding*, ed. P. Lujala and S. A. Rustad. London: Earthscan.

Henckaerts, J.-M. 2005. Study on customary international humanitarian law: A contribution to the understanding and respect for the rule of law in armed conflict. *International Review of the Red Cross* 87 (857): 175–212. www.icrc.org/eng/resources/documents/publication/p0860.htm.

Hendrickson, D., J. Armon, and R. Mearns. 1998. The changing nature of conflict and famine vulnerability: The case of livestock raiding in Turkana District, Kenya. *Disasters* 22 (3): 185–199.

Holland, D., W. Johnecheck, H. Sida, and H. Young. 2002. Livelihoods and chronic conflict: An annotated bibliography. Working Paper No. 184. London: Overseas Development Institute.

Homer-Dixon, T. 1999. *Environment, scarcity, and violence*. Princeton, NJ: Princeton University Press.

Hoon, P., N. Singh, and S. Wanmali. 1997. Sustainable livelihoods: Concepts, principles, and approaches to indicator development; A draft discussion paper. Paper prepared for the Workshop on Indicators for Sustainable Livelihoods, New York, August. www.academia.edu/3231210/Sustainable_livelihoods_concepts_principles_and_approaches_to_indicator_development_a_draft_discussion_paper.

ICPALD (IGAD [Intergovernmental Authority on Development] Center for Pastoral Areas and Livestock Development). 2013. The contribution of livestock to the economies of

Kenya, Ethiopia, Uganda and Sudan. Policy Brief No. ICPALD8/SCLE/8/2013. Nairobi, Kenya. http://igad.int/attachments/714_The%20Contribution%20of%20Livestock%20to%20the%20Kenya,%20Ethiopia,%20Uganda%20and%20Sudan%20Economy.pdf.

IISD (International Institute for Sustainable Development). n.d. Natural resources, livelihoods and security. www.iisd.org/ecp/es/livelihoods/default.asp.

IRP (International Recovery Platform) and UNDP-India (United Nations Development Programme in India). 2010. *Guidance note on recovery: Livelihood.* Kobe, Japan: International Recovery Platform Secretariat. www.unisdr.org/files/16771_16771guidancenoteonrecoveryliveliho.pdf.

Jacobsen, K. 2003. Livelihoods in conflict: The pursuit of livelihoods by refugees and the impact on the human security of host communities. *International Migration* 40 (5): 95–123.

Jaramillo Castro, L., and A. M. Stork. 2015. Linking to peace: Using BioTrade for biodiversity conservation and peacebuilding in Colombia. In *Livelihoods, natural resources, and post-conflict peacebuilding*, ed. H. Young and L. Goldman. London: Earthscan.

Jaspars, S., and S. O'Callaghan. 2010. Challenging choices: Protection and livelihoods in conflict—Case studies from Darfur, Chechnya, Sri Lanka and the occupied Palestinian territories. HPG Report No. 31. London: Humanitarian Policy Group, Overseas Development Institute.

Jensen, D. 2012. Evaluating the impact of UNEP's post-conflict environmental assessments. In *Assessing and restoring natural resources in post-conflict peacebuilding*, ed. D. Jensen and S. Lonergan. London: Earthscan.

Jensen, D., and S. Lonergan 2012. Natural resources and post-conflict assessment, remediation, restoration, and reconstruction: Lessons and emerging issues. In *Assessing and restoring natural resources in post-conflict peacebuilding*, ed. D. Jensen and S. Lonergan. London: Earthscan.

Justino, P. 2009. Poverty and violent conflict: A micro-level perspective on the causes and duration of warfare. *Journal of Peace Research* 46 (3): 315–333.

Karuru, N., and L. H. Yeung. 2015. Integrating gender into post-conflict natural resource management. In *Governance, natural resources, and post-conflict peacebuilding*, ed. C. Bruch, C. Muffett, and S. S. Nichols. London: Earthscan.

Keen, D. 1994. *The benefits of famine: Political economy of famine and relief in southwestern Sudan, 1983–1989*. Princeton, NJ: Princeton University Press.

———. 2000. Incentives and disincentives for violence. In *Greed and grievance: Economic agendas in civil wars*, ed. M. R. Berdal and D. Malone. Boulder, CO: Lynne Rienner / International Development Research Centre.

———. 2008. *Complex emergencies*. Cambridge, UK: Polity Press.

Keili, A., and B. Thiam. 2015. Mitigating conflict in Sierra Leone through mining reform and alternative livelihoods programs for youth. In *Livelihoods, natural resources, and post-conflict peacebuilding*, ed. H. Young and L. Goldman. London: Earthscan.

Lautze, S., Y. Aklilu, A. Raven-Roberts, H. Young, G. Kebede, and J. Leaning. 2003. Risk and vulnerability in Ethiopia: Learning from the past, responding to the present, preparing for the future. Boston, MA: Feinstein International Famine Center, Tufts University / Inter-University Initiative on Humanitarian Studies and Field Practice. http://fic.tufts.edu/assets/risk_ethiopia.pdf.

Lautze, S., and A. Raven-Roberts. 2006. Violence and complex humanitarian emergencies: Implications for livelihoods models. *Disasters* 30 (4): 383–401.

Lax, J., and J. Krug. 2013. Livelihood assessment: A participatory tool for natural resource dependent communities. Working Paper No. 7. Hamburg, Germany: Thünen-Institut für Weltforstwirtschaft.

Leroy, M., ed. 2009. *Environment and conflict in Africa: Reflections on Darfur*. Addis Ababa, Ethiopia: University for Peace.

Le Sage, A., and N. Majid. 2002. The livelihoods gap: Responding to the economic dynamics of vulnerability in Somalia. *Disasters* 26 (1): 10–27.

Lind, J. 2015. Manufacturing peace in "no man's land": Livestock and access to natural resources in the Karimojong Cluster of Kenya and Uganda. In *Livelihoods, natural resources, and post-conflict peacebuilding*, ed. H. Young and L. Goldman. London: Earthscan.

Lind, J., and S. Eriksen. 2006. The impacts of conflict on household coping strategies: Evidence from Turkana and Kitui districts in Kenya. *Die Erde* 137 (3): 249–270.

Longley, C., and D. Maxwell. 2002. Livelihoods, chronic conflict and humanitarian response: A synthesis of current practice. Working Paper No. 182. London: Overseas Development Institute. www.odi.org/sites/odi.org.uk/files/odi-assets/publications-opinion-files/2991.pdf.

Luedeling, E., R. Kindt, N. I. Huth, and K. Koenig. 2014. Agroforestry systems in a changing climate: Challenges in projecting future performance. *Current Opinion in Environmental Sustainability* 6:1–7.

Maekawa, M., A. Lanjouw, E. Rutagarama, and D. Sharp. 2015. Mountain gorilla ecotourism: Supporting macroeconomic growth and providing local livelihoods. In *Livelihoods, natural resources, and post-conflict peacebuilding*, ed. H. Young and L. Goldman. London: Earthscan.

Mallett, R., and R. Slater. 2012. *Growth and livelihoods in fragile and conflict-affected situations*. Working Paper No. 9. London: Secure Livelihoods Research Consortium.

Mamdani, M. 2007. The politics of naming: Genocide, civil war, insurgency. *London Review of Books* 29 (5): 5–8.

Mason, S., and S. Rychard. 2005. Conflict analysis tools. Bern: Swiss Agency for Development and Cooperation. www.css.ethz.ch/publications/pdfs/Conflict-Analysis-Tools.pdf.

Matthew, R., and A. Hammill. 2012. Peacebuilding and adaptation to climate change. In *Assessing and restoring natural resources in post-conflict peacebuilding*, ed. D. Jensen and S. Lonergan. London: Earthscan.

Matturi, K. 2013. Making real-time M&E a reality through ICT. *Ontrac* 55:2–3. www.intrac.org/data/files/resources/775/ONTRAC-55-New-technologies-in-monitoring-and-evaluation.pdf.

Maxwell, D. 1999. Programmes in chronically vulnerable areas: Challenges and lessons learned. *Disasters* 23 (4): 373–384.

Maxwell, S., and M. Smith, with S. Davies, A. Evans, S. Jaspars, J. Swift, and H. Young. 1992. Household food security: A conceptual review. In *Household food security: Concepts, indicators, measurements; A technical review*, ed. S. Maxwell and T. R. Frankenberger. New York: United Nations Children's Fund; Rome: International Fund for Agricultural Development. www.ifad.org/hfs/tools/hfs/hfspub/hfs.pdf.

Morse, S., and N. McNamara. 2013. *Sustainable livelihoods approach: A critique of theory and practice*. New York: Springer.

Muhereza, F. E. 2011. *An analysis of disarmament experiences in Uganda*. Nairobi, Kenya: Regional Centre on Small Arms. www.recsasec.org/publications/Uganda%20Report.pdf.

Nakayama, M. 2012. Making best use of domestic energy sources: The Priority Production System for coal mining and steel production in post–World War II Japan. In *Assessing and restoring natural resources in post-conflict peacebuilding*, ed. D. Jensen and S. Lonergan. London: Earthscan.

Narbeth, S., and C. McLean. 2003. Livelihoods and protection: Displacement and vulnerable communities in Kismaayo, southern Somalia. HPN Network Paper No. 44. London: Overseas Development Institute.

O'Brien, K., S. Eriksen, L. P. Nygaard, and A. Schjolden. 2007. Why different interpretations of vulnerability matter in climate change discourses. *Climate Policy* 7:73–88.

OECD (Organisation for Economic Co-operation and Development). 2008. *Natural resources and pro-poor growth: The economics and politics*. DAC Guidelines and Reference Series. Paris. www.oecd.org/greengrowth/green-development/42440224.pdf.

Olsson, L., M. Opondo, P. Tschakert, L. Authors, A. Agrawal, S. Eriksen, S. Ma, et al. 2014. Livelihoods and poverty. In *Climate change 2014: Impacts, adaptation, and vulnerability*, ed. C. B. Field, V. R. Barros, D. J. Dokken, K. J. Mach, M. D. Mastrandrea, T. E. Bilir, M. Chatterjee, et al. Draft contribution of Working Group II to the Fifth Assessment Report of the Intergovernmental Panel on Climate Change. Cambridge, UK: Cambridge University Press. http://ipcc-wg2.gov/AR5/images/uploads/WGIIAR5-Chap13_FGDall.pdf.

Osman, A. M. K., H. Young, R. F. Houser, and J. C. Coates. 2013. Agricultural change, land, and violence in protracted political crisis: An examination of Darfur. Boston, MA: Oxfam America.

OUP (Oxford University Press). 2010. *Oxford Dictionary of English*, ed. A. Stevenson. 3rd ed. Oxford, UK.

Pantuliano, S., M. Buchanan-Smith, V. Metcalfe, S. Pavanello, and E. Martin. 2011. *City limits: Urbanisation and vulnerability in Sudan*. London: Humanitarian Policy Group, Overseas Development Institute.

Pantuliano, S., O. Egemi, B. Fadlalla, M. Farah, and M. E. Abdelgador. 2009. Put out to pasture: War, oil and the decline of Misseriyya Humr pastoralism in Sudan. London: Humanitarian Policy Group, Overseas Development Institute. www.odi.org/sites/odi.org.uk/files/odi-assets/publications-opinion-files/4168.pdf.

Patey, L. A. 2012. Lurking beneath the surface: Oil, environmental degradation, and armed conflict in Sudan. In *High-value natural resources and post-conflict peacebuilding*, ed. P. Lujala and S. A. Rustad. London: Earthscan.

Pejic, J. 2001. The right to food in situations of armed conflict: The legal framework. *International Review of the Red Cross* 83 (844): 1097–1109.

Pritchard, M. F. 2015. From soldiers to park rangers: Post-conflict natural resource management in Gorongosa National Park. In *Livelihoods, natural resources, and post-conflict peacebuilding*, ed. H. Young and L. Goldman. London: Earthscan.

Pulitzer Center on Crisis Reporting. 2011. Karamoja: Broken warriors. http://pulitzercenter.org/projects/karamoja-uganda-poverty-violence-disarmament-drought.

Rass, N. 2006. Policies and strategies to address the vulnerability of pastoralists in sub-Saharan Africa. PPLPI Working Paper No. 37. Rome: Pro-Poor Livestock Policy Initiative, Food and Agriculture Organization of the United Nations. www.fao.org/ag/againfo/programmes/en/pplpi/docarc/wp37.pdf.

Ratner, B. D. 2015. Building resilience in rural livelihood systems as an investment in conflict prevention. In *Livelihoods, natural resources, and post-conflict peacebuilding*, ed. H. Young and L. Goldman. London: Earthscan.

Ratner, B. D., R. Meinzen-Dick, C. May, and E. Haglund. 2013. Resource conflict, collective action, and resilience: An analytical framework. *International Journal of the Commons* 7 (1): 183–208.

Renner, M. 2015. Post-tsunami Aceh: Successful peacemaking, uncertain peacebuilding. In *Livelihoods, natural resources, and post-conflict peacebuilding*, ed. H. Young and L. Goldman. London: Earthscan.

Roe, A. 2015. Swords into plowshares? Accessing natural resources and securing agricultural livelihoods in rural Afghanistan. In *Livelihoods, natural resources, and post-conflict peacebuilding*, ed. H. Young and L. Goldman. London: Earthscan.

Ross, J., S. Maxwell, and M. Buchanan-Smith. 1994. Linking relief and development. Report on a workshop titled "Linking Relief and Development," Institute of Development Studies, University of Sussex, March 28–29. Brighton, UK: Institute of Development Studies, University of Sussex. www.ids.ac.uk/files/dmfile/DP344.pdf.

Ross, M. 2003. Oil, drugs, and diamonds: The varying roles of natural resources in civil war. In *The political economy of armed conflict: Beyond greed and grievance*, ed. K. Ballentine and J. Sherman. Boulder, CO: Lynne Rienner.

Sato, M. 2011. Disarmament, demobilization, reintegration, and natural resources in Afghanistan. In *Harnessing natural resources for peacebuilding: Lessons from U.S. and Japanese assistance*, ed. C. Bruch, M. Nakayama, and I. Coyle. Washington, D.C.: Environmental Law Institute.

Schafer, J. 2002. Supporting livelihoods in situations of chronic political instability: Overview of conceptual issues. Working Paper No. 183. London: Overseas Development Institute. www.odi.org/sites/odi.org.uk/files/odi-assets/publications-opinion-files/2686.pdf.

Scheiber, H. N., and B. Jones. 2015. Fisheries policies and the problem of instituting sustainable management: The case of occupied Japan. In *Livelihoods, natural resources, and post-conflict peacebuilding*, ed. H. Young and L. Goldman. London: Earthscan.

Schimmer, R. 2008. Tracking the genocide in Darfur: Population displacement as recorded by remote sensing. Genocide Studies Working Paper No. 36. New Haven, CT: Genocide Studies Program, Yale University.

Scoones, I., ed. 1996. *Living with uncertainty: New directions in pastoral development in Africa*. Brighton, UK: Institute of Development Studies, University of Sussex.

———. 1998. Sustainable rural livelihoods: A framework for analysis. IDS Working Paper No. 72. Brighton, UK: Institute of Development Studies, University of Sussex.

Shazali, S., and A. G. M. Ahmed. 1999. Pastoral land tenure and agricultural expansion: Sudan and the Horn of Africa. http://pubs.iied.org/pdfs/7403IIED.pdf.

Siddig, E. F. A., K. El-Harizi, and B. Prato. 2007. *Managing conflict over natural resources in Greater Kordofan, Sudan: Some recurrent patterns and governance implications.* IFPRI Discussion Paper No. 00711. Washington D.C.: International Food Policy Research Institute. www.ifpri.org/sites/default/files/publications/ifpridp00711.pdf.

Solesbury, W. 2003. Sustainable livelihoods: A case study of the evolution of DFID policy. Working Paper No. 217. London: Overseas Development Institute.

Sorensen, L. W. 2015. The power of economic data: A case study from Rwanda. In *Governance, natural resources, and post-conflict peacebuilding*, ed. C. Bruch, C. Muffett, and S. S. Nichols. London: Earthscan.

Srey, C., and J. Schweithelm. 2015. Forest resources in Cambodia's transition to peace: Lessons for peacebuilding. In *Livelihoods, natural resources, and post-conflict peacebuilding*, ed. H. Young and L. Goldman. London: Earthscan.

Stewart, J. G. 2011. *Corporate war crimes: Prosecuting the pillage of natural resources.* New York: Open Society Foundations. www.opensocietyfoundations.org/reports/corporate-war-crimes-prosecuting-pillage-natural-resources.

Stites, E., and D. Akabwai. 2009. Changing roles, shifting risks: Livelihood impacts of disarmament in Karamoja, Uganda. Medford, MA: Feinstein International Center, Tufts University.

Stites, E., S. Lautze, D. Mazurana, and A. Anic. 2005. *Coping with war, coping with peace: Livelihood adaptation in Bosnia Herzegovina, 1989–2004.* Medford, MA: Feinstein International Center, Tufts University. http://fic.tufts.edu/assets/Coping-With-War.pdf.

Stites, E. H. 2013. Identity reconfigured: Karimojong male youth, violence and livelihoods. Ph.D. diss., Tufts University.

Talbott, K., J. Waugh, and D. Batson. 2013. A U.S. Asian-Pacific pivot point: Burma's natural resources. *Prism* 4 (3): 111–125. http://cco.dodlive.mil/files/2012/08/PRISM_4-3.pdf.

Tanik, A., D. Z. Seker, I. Ozturk, and C. Tavsan. 2008. GIS based sectoral conflict analysis in a coastal district of Turkey. *International Archives of the Photogrammetry, Remote Sensing and Spatial Information Sciences* 37 (Part B8): 665–668. www.isprs.org/proceedings/XXXVII/congress/8_pdf/6_WG-VIII-6/03a.pdf.

Themnér, L., and P. Wallensteen. 2013. Armed conflict, 1946–2012. *Journal of Peace Research* 50 (4): 509–521.

Timilsina, A. R. 2007. Getting the policies right: The prioritization and sequencing of policies in post-conflict countries. Santa Monica, CA: RAND Corporation. www.rand.org/pubs/rgs_dissertations/RGSD222.html.

UCDP (Uppsala Conflict Data Program). 2014. Data publications. www.pcr.uu.se/research/ucdp/publications/data_publications/.

UCDP (Uppsala Conflict Data Program) and PRIO (Peace Research Institute Oslo). 2013. *UCDP/PRIO armed conflict dataset codebook.* Version 4-2013. www.pcr.uu.se/digitalAssets/124/124920_1codebook_ucdp_prio-armed-conflict-dataset-v4_2013.pdf.

UN (United Nations) and IASC (Inter-Agency Standing Committee). 2008. *Civil-military guidelines and reference for complex emergencies.* New York: United Nations Office for the Coordination of Humanitarian Affairs. www.refworld.org/docid/47da82a72.html.

UNCTA (United Nations Country Team in Afghanistan). 2013. *Natural resource management and peacebuilding in Afghanistan.* Nairobi, Kenya: United Nations Environment Programme. www.unep.org/disastersandconflicts/portals/155/countries/Afghanistan/pdf/UNEP_Afghanistan_NRM.pdf.

UNDG (United Nations Development Group). 2013. Natural resource management in transition settings. New York. www.un.org/en/land-natural-resources-conflict/pdfs/UNDG-ECHA_NRM_guidance_Jan2013.pdf.

UNDP (United Nations Development Programme). 2005. *Promotion of sustainable livelihoods.* Kabul, Afghanistan.

UNEP (United Nations Environment Programme). 2007. *Sudan: Post-conflict environmental assessment.* Nairobi, Kenya. http://postconflict.unep.ch/publications/UNEP_Sudan.pdf.

———. 2008. *Destitution, distortion and deforestation: The impact of conflict on the timber and woodfuel trade in Darfur.* Geneva, Switzerland; Khartoum, Sudan. http://postconflict.unep.ch/publications/darfur_timber.pdf.

———. 2009. *From conflict to peacebuilding: The role of natural resources and the environment.* Nairobi, Kenya. http://postconflict.unep.ch/publications/pcdmb_policy_01.pdf.

———. 2013a. *Pastoralism in practice: Monitoring livestock mobility in contemporary Sudan*. Nairobi, Kenya. http://reliefweb.int/sites/reliefweb.int/files/resources/Pastoralism-in-Practice-final.pdf.

———. 2013b. *Standing wealth: Pastoralist livestock production and local livelihoods in Sudan*. Nairobi, Kenya. www.unep.org/disastersandconflicts/Portals/155/countries/sudan/pdf/Livelihood/TUFTS_1339_Standing_Wealth_5_online.pdf.

———. 2014. *Relationships and resources: Environmental governance for peacebuilding and resilient livelihoods in Sudan*. Nairobi, Kenya. http://postconflict.unep.ch/publications/UNEP_Sudan_RnR.pdf.

UNEP (United Nations Environment Programme), FAO (Food and Agriculture Organization of the United Nations), and UNFF (United Nations Forum on Forests). 2009. *Vital forest graphics*. Nairobi, Kenya: United Nations Environment Programme. www.unep.org/vitalforest/Report/VFG_full_report.pdf.

UNEP (United Nations Environment Programme), International Organization for Migration, United Nations Office for the Coordination of Humanitarian Affairs, United Nations University Institute for Environment and Human Security, and Permanent Interstate Committee for Drought Control in the Sahel. 2011. *Livelihood security: Climate change, migration and conflict in the Sahel*. Geneva, Switzerland: UNEP. www.unep.org/pdf/UNEP_Sahel_EN.pdf.

UNEP (United Nations Environment Programme) and UNDP (United Nations Development Programme). 2013. *The role of natural resources in disarmament, demobilization and reintegration: Addressing risks and seizing opportunities*. Nairobi, Kenya; New York. http://postconflict.unep.ch/publications/UNEP_UNDP_NRM_DDR.pdf.

UNEP (United Nations Environment Programme), United Nations Entity for Gender Equality and the Empowerment of Women, United Nations Peacebuilding Support Office, and United Nations Development Programme. 2013. *Women and natural resources: Unlocking the peacebuilding potential*. Nairobi, Kenya. http://postconflict.unep.ch/publications/UNEP_UN-Women_PBSO_UNDP_gender_NRM_peacebuilding_report.pdf.

Unruh, J., and R. C. Williams. 2013. Lesson learned in land tenure and natural resource management in post-conflict societies. In *Land and post-conflict peacebuilding*, ed. J. Unruh and R. C. Williams. London: Earthscan.

UNSC (United Nations Security Council). 2013. Report of the Monitoring Group on Somalia and Eritrea pursuant to Security Council Resolution 2060 (2012): Somalia. S/2013/413. July 12. www.un.org/ga/search/view_doc.asp?symbol=S/2013/413.

Waldman, M. 2008. Community peacebuilding in Afghanistan: The case for a national strategy. Oxford, UK: Oxfam International. www.comw.org/warreport/fulltext/0802waldman.pdf.

Walters, J. T. 2015. A peace park in the Balkans: Cross-border cooperation and livelihood creation through coordinated environmental conservation. In *Livelihoods, natural resources, and post-conflict peacebuilding*, ed. H. Young and L. Goldman. London: Earthscan.

Webersik, C., and A. Crawford. 2015. Commerce in the chaos: Bananas, charcoal, fisheries, and conflict in Somalia. In *Livelihoods, natural resources, and post-conflict peacebuilding*, ed. H. Young and L. Goldman. London: Earthscan.

Westrik, C. 2015. Transboundary protected areas: Opportunities and challenges. In *Livelihoods, natural resources, and post-conflict peacebuilding*, ed. H. Young and L. Goldman. London: Earthscan.

Williams, R. 2013. Title through possession or position? Respect for housing, land, and property rights in Cambodia. In *Land and post-conflict peacebuilding*, ed. J. Unruh and R. C. Williams. London: Earthscan.

World Bank. 2014. Agriculture, value added (% of GDP). http://data.worldbank.org/indicator/NV.AGR.TOTL.ZS.

Young, H. 2009. Pastoralism, power and choice. In *Environment and conflict in Africa: Reflections on Darfur*, ed. M. Leroy. Addis Ababa, Ethiopia: University for Peace.

Young, H., E. Bontrager, R. Krystalli, and A. Marshak. 2014. *Eastern Chad and West Darfur: An analysis of conflict and livelihood linkages*. Medford, MA: Concern Worldwide / World Agroforestry Centre / El Massar / Tufts University.

Young, H., and D. Maxwell. 2013. Participation, political economy and protection: Food aid governance in Darfur, Sudan. *Disasters* 37 (4): 555–578.

Young, H., A. E. K. Osman, M. Buchanan-Smith, B. Bromwich, K. Moore, and S. Ballou. 2007. *Sharpening the strategic focus of livelihoods programming in the Darfur region:. A report of four livelihoods workshops in the Darfur region (June 30 to July 11, 2007).* Medford, MA: Feinstein International Center, Tufts University. http://fic.tufts.edu/assets/8nau6d0uugqce0wq8fe.pdf.

Young, H., A. M. Osman, A. Abusin, M. Asher, and O. Egemi. 2009. Livelihoods, power and choice: The vulnerability of the Northern Rizaygat, Darfur. Medford, MA: Feinstein International Center, Tufts University.

Young, H., A. M. Osman, Y. Aklilu, R. Dale, B. Badri, and A. J. A. Fuddle. 2005. Darfur—Livelihoods under siege. Medford, MA: Feinstein International Famine Center, Tufts University. http://fic.tufts.edu/assets/Young-Darfur-Livelihoods-Under-Seige.pdf.

Young, H., A. Rahim, A. Mohamed, and M. Fitzpatrick. 2012. *Pastoralism and pastoralists in Sudan: A stakeholder mapping and survey*. Medford, MA: Feinstein International Center, Tufts University / SOS Sahel / UNEP Sudan. www.fao.org/fileadmin/user_upload/drought/docs/Pastoralism-and-Pastoralists-in-Sudan-LB3-HY2.pdf.

Zulu, L. C., and R. B. Richardson. 2012. Charcoal, livelihoods, and poverty reduction: Evidence from sub-Saharan Africa. *Energy for Sustainable Development* 17 (2): 127–137. http://dx.doi.org/10.1016/j.esd.2012.07.007.

APPENDIX 1
List of abbreviations

ACC: Afghan Conservation Corps
ACR: Colombian High Council for Reintegration (Alta Consejería Presidencial para la Reintegración)
ADB: Asian Development Bank
ADF: Allied Democratic Forces (Uganda)
Afmet: Africa fisheries management
AMM: Aceh Monitoring Mission
ANDS: Afghanistan National Development Strategy
ARD: Agricultural and Rural Development (Sector Strategy) (Afghanistan)
AREU: Afghanistan Research and Evaluation Unit
ARMM: Autonomous Region in Muslim Mindanao (Philippines)
AUC: United Self-Defense Groups of Colombia (Autodefensas Unidas de Colombia)
AU-IBAR: Africa Union-InterAfrican Bureau for Animal Resources
AWF: African Wildlife Foundation
BINP: Bwindi Impenetrable National Park (Uganda)
CBNRM: community-based natural resource management
CEWARN: Conflict Early Warning and Response Network
COOPI: Cooperazione Internazionale
DDR: disarmament, demobilization, and reintegration
DENR: Department of Environment and Natural Resources (Massim, Philippines)
DMZ: demilitarized zone
DNFFB: National Directorate of Forestry and Wildlife (Direcção Nacional de Florestas e Fauna Bravia) (Mozambique)
DRC: Democratic Republic of the Congo
EcoGov: Environmental Governance (Project) (Philippines)
EEZ: exclusive economic zone
EITI: Extractive Industries Transparency Initiative
ELN: National Liberation Army (Ejército de Liberación Nacional) (Colombia)
EU: European Union
E.U.: Empresa Unipersonal, Pradera Verde (Colombian BioTrade company)

FAO: Food and Agriculture Organization of the United Nations
FARC: Revolutionary Armed Forces of Colombia (Fuerzas Armadas Revolucionarias de Colombia)
FESS: Foundation for Environmental Security and Sustainability (Sierra Leone)
FEWS-Net: Famine Early Warning System-Network
FMC: forest management committees (Afghanistan)
FRELIMO: Liberation Front of Mozambique (Frente de Libertação de Moçambique)
GAM: Free Aceh Movement (Gerakan Aceh Merdeka)
GDP: gross domestic product
GIZ: Germany Society for International Cooperation (Deutsche Gesellschaft für Internationale Zusammenarbeit)
GOI: Government of Indonesia
GPH: Government of the Republic of the Philippines
GTZ: German Technical Cooperation (Deutsche Gesellschaft für Technische Zusammenarbeit)
ICC: indigenous cultural committee
ICCN: Congolese Institute for Nature Conservation (Institut Congolais pour la Conservation de la Nature)
IDDRS: Integrated Disarmament, Demobilization and Reintegration Standards
IGAD: Intergovernmental Authority on Development
INPFC: International North Pacific Fisheries Convention
IP: indigenous people
ISAF: International Security Assistance Force
IUCN: international Union for Conservation of Nature
IUU: illegal, unreported, and unregulated fishing
IWC: International Whaling Commission
KPCS: Kimberley Process Certification Scheme
LGU: local government unit
MAIL: Ministry of Agriculture, Irrigation and Livestock (Afghanistan)
MGNP: Mgahinga Gorilla National Park (Uganda)
MILF: Moro Islamic Liberation Front (Philippines)
MNLF: Moro National Liberation Front (Philippines)
MOU: memorandum of understanding
MPA: marine protected area
MSY: maximum sustainable yield
NEPA: National Environmental Protection Agency (Afghanistan)
NGO: nongovernmental organization
NPA: New People's Army (Mindanao, Philippines)
NRP Toolkit: *Natural Resources for Peacebuilding and Statebuilding: A Toolkit for Analysis and Programing*
ONUMOZ: United Nations Mission in Mozambique
PCDMB: Post-Conflict and Disaster Management Branch (United Nations Environment Programme)
PCNA: post-conflict needs assessment

PCNRM: post-conflict natural resource management
PNV: Volcanoes National Park (Parc National des Volcans) (Rwanda)
PNVi: Virunga National Park (Parc National des Virunga) (Democratic Republic of the Congo)
PRSP: poverty reduction strategy paper
REDD: Reducing Emissions from Deforestation and Degradation
RENAMO: Mozambican National Resistance (Resistência Nacional Moçambicana)
RUF: Revolutionary United Front (Sierra Leone)
SALEH: Sustainable Agricultural Livelihoods in Eastern Hazarajat (Afghanistan)
SCAP: Supreme Commander for Allied Powers
SLST: Sierra Leone Selection Trust
SME: small and medium-sized enterprise
SNC: Supreme National Council (Cambodian Interim Government)
SNV: Dutch Development Organization
TNI: Indonesian Military Forces (Tentara National Indonesia)
UN: United Nations
UNAMA: United Nations Assistance Mission in Afghanistan
UNCTAD: United Nations Conference on Trade and Development
UNDAF: United Nations Development Assistant Framework
UNDP: United Nations Development Programme
UNEP: United Nations Environment Programme
UNESCO: United Nations Educational, Scientific and Cultural Organization
UNSC: United Nations Security Council
UNTAC: United Nations Transitional Authority in Cambodia
UPDF: Uganda People's Defense Forces
USAID: United States Agency for International Development
WCPA: World Commission on Protected Areas (International Union for Conservation of Nature)
YRTEP: Youth Reintegration Training and Education for Peace (Sierra Leone)

APPENDIX 2
Author biographies

Oliver Agoncillo is the team leader for the U.S. Agency for International Development/Philippines' Natural Resources and Biodiversity Program; the program focuses on improving the governance and resilience of coastal marine and forest resources in order to achieve economic growth and sustainable development. He currently manages the US$24 million five-year Biodiversity and Watersheds Improved for Stronger Economy and Ecosystem Resilience Program, which covers seven key biodiversity areas in the Philippines. Agoncillo's areas of expertise include program development, management, and evaluation; participatory research; policy advocacy; civil society and community development; and natural resource management. He has a master's degree in environmental management and development (supported by an award from the Australian government) from the Australian National University, and a master's degree in social development (supported by an award from the Ford Foundation) from the Ateneo de Manila University, in the Philippines.

Liz Alden Wily is a land tenure specialist who works as a researcher, practitioner, and independent policy advisor for governments and aid agencies, addressing land and forest tenure issues. She has thirty-five years of experience in fifteen countries in Africa and Asia. Alden Wily established the first minority land rights program in Africa (in Botswana); played a lead role in the institution of community ownership as the basis of forest conservation and governance in Tanzania; and has developed innovative, community-based land tenure and natural resource management strategies in a number of countries, including Afghanistan, Liberia, Nepal, and Sudan. Alden Wily's primary commitment is to the recognition of customary or indigenous property rights, with a focus on collective tenure as it affects forests, rangelands, and wetlands. She has published extensively on land law and governance issues in agrarian economies. Alden Wily holds a Ph.D. in political economy from the University of East Anglia.

Belinda Bowling is a country director for Marie Stopes International, a United Kingdom–based nonprofit organization working on issues related to maternal and child health, and currently operates out of Zimbabwe and previously in Papua

New Guinea. Bowling has more than a decade of experience in the field of environmental law and policy in developing countries. Before joining Marie Stopes International, she served as program manager for the Capacity Building and Institutional Development Programme for Environmental Management in Afghanistan, a program of the United Nations Environment Programme, and was a widely recognized expert in environmental law and international conventions. Bowling also has experience working in both the public and private sectors as an environmental attorney and legislative and policy consultant, primarily in southern Africa. She holds a B.A., an LL.B., and an LL.M. in marine and environmental law from the University of Cape Town.

Glaucia Boyer is a policy specialist at the Bureau for Crisis Prevention and Recovery, United Nations Development Programme; she also coleads the UNDP–UNEP (United Nations Development Programme–United Nations Environment Programme) Joint Initiative on Natural Resource Management and Disarmament, Demobilization, and Reintegration (DDR). Boyer has worked for the United Nations in various capacities since 1994 and has supported DDR programs in Angola, Burundi, the Central African Republic, the Democratic Republic of the Congo, Indonesia, Niger, the Republic of Congo, Rwanda, Sri Lanka, and Sudan. She has a law degree from the University of São Paulo and a Ph.D. from the Graduate Institute of International Studies, in Geneva.

Cynthia Brady is a senior conflict advisor for the Bureau for Democracy, Conflict and Humanitarian Assistance in the Office of Conflict Management and Mitigation (CMM) of the U.S. Agency for International Development (USAID). She is the agency's technical lead on environment, natural resources, and conflict. Her recent applied research has focused on climate change, water resources, and food security. Brady also leads CMM's Field Support Team, managing the office's direct support for USAID's overseas missions. Brady's primary responsibilities include identifying and analyzing sources of conflict and instability; supporting early responses to address the causes and consequences of fragility and violent conflict; and integrating conflict mitigation and management into USAID's analyses, strategies, and programs. Previously, Brady served as a foreign affairs officer for the U.S. Department of State. She has also worked for the United Nations and the Organization for Security and Cooperation in Europe. Brady holds a master's degree in international affairs from the Fletcher School of Law and Diplomacy, Tufts University, and a bachelor's degree in political science from Denison University.

Maria Zita Butardo-Toribio is a partnerships specialist in a project (funded by the Asian Development Bank) that focuses on facilitating responses to climate change in Asia and the Pacific. Previously, she was a senior policy specialist for the Philippine Environmental Governance Project Phase II, a program funded by the U.S. Agency for International Development. Butardo-Toribio has more than twenty years of multidisciplinary and interdisciplinary research experience in the environment and natural resource field, and has participated in development projects involving upland, forest, coastal, and urban ecosystems. She holds a master's degree and a Ph.D., both in environmental science, from the University of the Philippines Los Baños.

Alec Crawford is an associate with the Environment, Conflict and Peacebuilding program at the International Institute for Sustainable Development. He also works closely with the Environmental Cooperation for Peacebuilding program of the United Nations Environment Programme. His work focuses on understanding the linkages among natural resources, environmental change, conflict, and peacebuilding. In particular, his work focuses on understanding the links between climate change and the risk of violent conflict in Africa and the Middle East; on conflict-sensitive conservation in Central, East, and West Africa; and on greening peacekeeping operations. He holds a bachelor of commerce degree from Queen's University, Canada, and a master's degree in environment and development from the London School of Economics.

Buenaventura Dolom was the forest sector team leader for the Philippine Environmental Governance Project, a program funded by the U.S. Agency for International Development; he has more than twenty years of experience planning and implementing resource management projects at the national and community levels and has worked with local nongovernmental organizations, national government agencies, local government units, and civil society organizations. Dolom holds a master's degree in forestry, with an emphasis on social forestry, from the University of the Philippines Los Baños.

Lisa Goldman is a senior attorney and counsel at the Environmental Law Institute (ELI). Her projects include initiatives on international climate change adaptation and biodiversity protection; forest sector reform in Liberia; post-conflict natural resource management; transboundary environmental impact assessment; and constitutional environmental law. She graduated from Stanford University with a major in human biology, received her J.D. from the University of Pennsylvania Law School, and received an LL.M. from the Georgetown University Law Center. Before joining ELI, Goldman spent two years as a graduate fellow at Georgetown's Institute for Public Representation and clerked for the Honorable Robert J. Timlin, U.S. District Judge for the Central District of California. Goldman also served in the Peace Corps, working on natural resource management and community development projects in Niger.

Arthur Green is the chair of the Department of Geography and Earth & Environmental Science at Okanagan College in British Columbia, Canada. He is an educator, researcher, and consultant with experience in Central America, sub-Saharan Africa, and southeast Asia. He worked as a forestry extension agent for two years in Cameroon and has done extensive consulting for international organizations on agroforestry and natural resource management. His research interests include human-environment interaction, political ecology, food security, and access to property in post-conflict and post-disaster situations. His research on post-conflict property management was featured in an official event at the Rio+20 United Nations Conference on Sustainable Development. Green holds a Ph.D. in geography from McGill University, where he was a McGill Major Fellow and a United States–Indonesia Society (USINDO) Sumitro Fellow.

Lorena Jaramillo Castro, an economist specializing in sustainable development, currently serves as an economic affairs officer in the Trade, Environment, Climate Change and Sustainable Development Branch of the United Nations Conference on Trade and Development. Since 2001, she has developed and implemented initiatives for the sustainable trade and sourcing of biodiversity-based products and services—both at the international level and as the director of Ecuador's national Sustainable BioTrade Programme. Jaramillo Castro has also worked at the Climate Change Training Programme of the United Nations Institute for Training and Research, and has conducted training in Africa and Asia. She has written several articles and papers on sustainable development, value chain development, business engagement, biodiversity, and trade, and has also conducted an online course on biotrade and value chain development. Jaramillo Castro is a graduate of the Pontificia Universidad Católica del Ecuador and holds an M.B.A. from HEC (Section des Hautes Études Commerciales), University of Geneva.

Benjamin Jones is an associate in the Global Disputes practice of Jones Day, and is the executive editor of the *World Arbitration and Mediation Review*. He was previously the editor in chief of the *Berkeley Journal of International Law*.

Andrew Keili, a mining engineer by profession, is an executive director of Construction, Engineering, Manufacturing and Technical Services (CEMMATS) Group Ltd., a leading engineering, environmental, and project management consultancy in Sierra Leone. He has more than thirty years of experience working for private industry and parastatals, and in consulting practice. He has had considerable involvement in the formulation and review of government policies and legislation in the mining, environmental, and infrastructure sectors and in sustainable development in Sierra Leone, where he has also spearheaded several environmental and social impact assessments in the mining sector. Keili is a member of several business and professional organizations in Sierra Leone and has written extensively on Sierra Leone's mining sector.

Annette Lanjouw is a vice president for the Strategic Initiatives and Great Apes Program at the Arcus Foundation. A behavioral ecologist with twenty-four years of experience in ape conservation, she has focused primarily on apes in Central Africa, including the bonobo and the Eastern chimpanzee in the Democratic Republic of the Congo (DRC), and the mountain gorilla on the border of DRC, Rwanda, and Uganda.

Jeremy Lind is a research fellow at the Institute of Development Studies (IDS), University of Sussex. His research, which focuses on northeast Africa, examines livelihood dynamics in conflict areas, the relationship between vulnerability and violence, and the difficulties of delivering aid in conflict-affected areas. Before joining IDS, Lind was a lecturer in human geography at the University of Sussex, where he led and contributed to a range of undergraduate and graduate courses relating to the environment, conflict, and development. He coedited (with Andy Catley and Ian Scoones) *Pastoralism and Development in Africa: Dynamic Change at the Margins* (Routledge and Earthscan, 2012); coauthored (with Jude Howell) *Counter-Terrorism, Aid and Civil Society: Before and After the War on Terror* (Palgrave, 2009); coedited (with Jude Howell) *Civil Society under Strain: The War on Terror Regime, Civil Society and Aid Post-9/11* (Kumarian Press, 2009); and coedited (with Kathryn Sturman) *Scarcity and Surfeit: The Ecology of Africa's Conflicts* (Institute of Security Studies, 2002).

Miko Maekawa is a lecturer at the Graduate School of Human Sciences at Osaka University, and previously was an assistant professor for the Wisdom of Water (Suntory) Corporate Sponsored Research Program at the University of Tokyo. She was a program officer in the China office of the United Nations Development Programme (UNDP) (2000–2003), a planning specialist at UNDP headquarters (2003–2005), the assistant resident representative heading the Sustainable Livelihoods Unit of the UNDP office in Rwanda (2005–2006), and the secretary-general of the Against Malaria Foundation Japan (2010). Maekawa has managed a wide range of environmental projects on climate change mitigation, biodiversity conservation, and environmental mainstreaming, and has also worked extensively on aid coordination. During her tenure at UNDP Rwanda, Maekawa served as the cochair of the Environment and Land Use Management Sector Working Group for the formulation of Rwanda's Economic Development and Poverty Reduction Strategy, 2008–2012. Maekawa holds an M.Sc. in environment and development from the University of East Anglia and a Ph.D. in international studies from the University of Tokyo. Her Ph.D. dissertation was titled "Aid Coordination, Competition and Cooperation among UN Organizations for Better Development Results."

Casimiro V. Olvida is a watershed management specialist for the Alcantara Group. He also provides consultancy services for the Philippine Department of Environment and Natural Resources, including conducting watershed characterization and vulnerability assessments; preparing and implementing forest land use plans with local government units; and preparing integrated watershed and river basin management plans, such as the Integrated Ecosystem Management Plan at project sites in watersheds covered by the National Program Support to Environment and Natural Resources Management Project, a World Bank–funded project. Previously, he served as the Mindanao uplands and governance specialist for the Philippine Environmental Governance Project, a program funded by the U.S. Agency for International Development (USAID). He also served as the watershed management specialist for the Southern Mindanao Integrated Coastal Zone Management Project, a program of the Japan Bank for International

Cooperation, and as the project development officer for USAID's SWIFT (Support with Implementing Fast Transition) project, which provided emergency livelihoods assistance to former Moro National Liberation Front combatants in conflict-affected regions of Mindanao. Olvida holds a B.S. and M.S. in forestry from the College of Forestry and Natural Resources, University of the Philippines Los Baños.

Matthew F. Pritchard is a doctoral student in the Department of Geography at McGill University; he also holds degrees in geography and international development from institutions in Canada, the United Kingdom, and the United States. His doctoral research examines the evolution of land tenure systems and natural resource management within the complex and legally pluralistic environments of post-conflict countries. His general research interests include land reform, legal pluralism, forced migration, post-conflict development, natural resource management, and political ecology. In addition to his current work in South Sudan and the Democratic Republic of the Congo, Pritchard has undertaken extensive research in Burundi, Cambodia, and Rwanda.

Blake D. Ratner is the program leader for governance at the WorldFish Center, a member of the Consultative Group on International Agricultural Research; previously, he served for five years as the WorldFish Center regional director in Phnom Penh, Cambodia. In 1995, as a consultant for the World Bank, he worked on the design of the first rural development project developed by the Bank and the post–United Nations Transitional Authority in Cambodia coalition government, which focused on agricultural rehabilitation; in 1996, he consulted on the Bank's first effort to assist with the demobilization and reintegration of former combatants in the country. Ratner's recent articles on resource conflict, collaboration, accountability, and equity in environmental decision making have appeared in *Ecology and Society, Development Policy Review*; *Journal of Environmental Management*; *International Journal of the Commons*; *Human Organization, Human Rights Dialogue*; *Population Research and Policy Review*; and *Society and Natural Resources*. Ratner holds a Ph.D. from Cornell University.

Michael Renner is a senior researcher at the Worldwatch Institute. Before joining Worldwatch Institute in 1987, Renner was a Corliss Lamont Fellow in Economic Conversion at Columbia University and a research associate at the World Policy Institute. Since the early 1990s, his work has focused on the linkages between the environment, resources, and conflict. In 2007, he coauthored (with Zoë Chafe) a report examining the opportunities for peacemaking in the wake of natural disasters in Aceh, Indonesia; Kashmir, India; and Sri Lanka. In 2010 and 2011, he carried out a project on water, climate change, and peacebuilding opportunities in the Greater Himalayas for the Norwegian Peacebuilding Centre. Renner has served on the board of the Global Policy Forum and is a senior advisor to the Institute for Environmental Security. He graduated cum laude with a master's degree in international relations from the University of Amsterdam.

Alan Roe is a research leader with the National Field Research Centre for Environmental Conservation in Oman and an adjunct research fellow at the School for Environmental Research, Charles Darwin University. Since completing his Ph.D., an investigation of pastoral systems in Jordan, Roe has held a postdoctoral research fellowship at the University of Glasgow and has served as senior research manager for natural resource management at the Afghanistan Research and Evaluation Unit. In Afghanistan, he designed and led multidisciplinary research projects on behalf of both the European Commission and the World Bank. Roe also works on natural resource management issues in northern Australia, and currently works with the National Field Research Centre for Environmental Conservation in Oman.

Eugène Rutagarama is the director of the International Gorilla Conservation Programme (IGCP), where he works on all aspects of regional program design, management, and technical support for the mountain gorilla and habitat conservation efforts of the IGCP. Rutagarama has more than twenty years of conservation experience in the African Great Lakes region, including particular expertise in wildlife and park management, training, program coordination, contingency planning, emergency programming, and team building. Rutagarama was awarded the Jean Paul Getty Prize in 1996 and the Goldman Environmental Prize in 2001, and was recognized as a CNN Hero in 2007. He holds a bachelor's degree in zoology and animal biology from the University of Burundi, and a master's degree in applied ecology and conservation from the University of East Anglia.

Harry N. Scheiber is the Riesenfeld Chair Professor of Law and History, emeritus, at the School of Law, University of California, Berkeley (UC Berkeley). He is director of the Law of the Sea Institute and is past director of the Sho Sato Program in Japanese and US Law, both in the School of Law, UC Berkeley. Previously he served as associate dean and as chair of the UC Berkeley Jurisprudence and Social Policy doctoral program. For many years a member and then chair of the California Sea Grant Program, he has taught and conducted research programs at UC Berkeley on ocean resources and international law since 1981. Scheiber has written extensively on Japanese-U.S. relations in ocean resource management, including monographs in the journal *Ecology Law Quarterly* and a book, *Inter-Allied Conflicts and Ocean Law, 1945–53: The Allied Command's Revival of Japanese Whaling and Marine Fisheries* (Institute of European and American Studies, Academia Sinica, 2001), and is now completing a major historical study of the quest for sustainable development in the marine fisheries and the origins of modern ocean law. He has published over 200 articles in journals of law, economics, history, and marine studies, including articles on the Convention on Biological Diversity and Law of the Sea, on fisheries oceanography history, and on the crisis of the International Whaling Commission. Among his other recent work in ocean resources and law are the books *Law of the Sea: The Common Heritage and Emerging Challenges* (Martinus Nijhoff, 2000), *Bringing New Law to Ocean Waters* (Brill Academic Publishers, 2004; coedited with David

D. Caron), *The Oceans in the Nuclear Age: Legacies and Risks* (Martinus Nijhoff Publishers, 2010; coedited with David D. Caron); and *Regions, Institutions and the Law of the Sea* (Martinus Nijhoff, 2013; coedited with Jin-Hyun Paik). He has also written widely in the fields of economic and legal history of the United States; and he is editor and contributing author of a series of books and journal symposia on Japanese law in comparative perspective. His doctorate was earned at Cornell University, and he was awarded an honorary D.Jur. from Uppsala University, Sweden. Scheiber is an elected fellow of the American Academy of Arts and Sciences, and has twice been a Guggenheim Fellow and a fellow at the Center for Advanced Study in Behavioral Sciences at Stanford.

Jim Schweithelm is the principal of Forest Mountain Consulting, which specializes in issues related to forests and climate change in Asia. In the course of three decades of experience in natural resource management, Schweithelm has provided technical services to a number of international development agencies and nongovernmental organizations; led a three-year project (funded by the U.S. Agency for International Development) that analyzed forest conflict in Asia; and led the design of large Reducing Emissions from Deforestation and Forest Degradation in Developing Countries projects in Indonesia for the Australian Agency for International Development and the Nature Conservancy. Schweithelm holds a bachelor's degree in engineering from the United States Military Academy at West Point; a master's degree in natural resource policy and planning from Cornell University; and a Ph.D. in geography from the University of Hawaii, where he was affiliated with the East-West Center.

Douglas Sharp is a J.D. student at Stanford Law School. In 2010, he was a research and publications intern at the Environmental Law Institute, where his work focused on the intersection of policy, economics, and the environment in the context of post-conflict natural resource management. Previously, he was a James B. Angell Scholar at the Gerald R. Ford School of Public Policy, University of Michigan, where he earned a B.A. in public policy, with a focus on environmental policy. While at the University of Michigan, Sharp was a leader of a student group dedicated to raising awareness of social and ecological issues associated with the coffee industry.

Srey Chanthy is a consultant for the Canadian Cooperation Office in Cambodia, a project support unit of the Canadian International Development Agency. From 1992 to 1997, he served in the planning sections of various departments within Cambodia's Ministry of Agriculture, Forestry and Fisheries, where his work involved sector analysis, policy formation, planning and programming, and negotiation with bilateral and multilateral institutions. He has since worked as an independent development consultant for donor agencies and nongovernmental organizations, with a focus on agriculture and land sector reforms. Srey is a founding member of the Agri-Business Institute of Cambodia, the Asian Institute of Technology Alumni Association of Cambodia, and the Cambodian Economic

Association. He received a bachelor's degree from Cambodia's Royal University of Agriculture, and a master's degree from the Asian Institute of Technology.

Adrienne M. Stork is an environmental advisor for the United Nations Environment Programme in Haiti. Stork's work focuses on post-crisis protected areas management, renewable energy, livelihoods, and value chain development. She has a background in conservation and community development, including incentive-based conservation mechanisms, which she gained by working for the United Nations Development Programme, the Environmental Defense Fund and the U.S. National Marine Protected Areas Center; she also has field experience in locations throughout Africa, Asia, and Latin America. Stork holds an M.A. in international environmental policy from the Monterey Institute of International Studies.

Bocar Thiam was the chief of party for the Property Rights and Artisanal Diamond Development Project in Liberia, a U.S. government–funded program that was implemented by Tetra Tech ARD. A social scientist who specializes in natural resource management in sub-Saharan Africa, Thiam has more than fifteen years of experience in land tenure and property rights; public participation in natural resource management; natural resource policy development; environmental and socioeconomic impact assessments; knowledge management; and the Kimberley Process Certification Scheme, as it pertains to alluvial diamond mining. Thiam has worked on projects and programs funded by the U.S. government, United Nations agencies, and the private sector.

J. Todd Walters is the founder and executive director of International Peace Park Expeditions, which applies experiential learning within transboundary protected areas to foster an interdisciplinary approach to leadership and collaboration, to build a network dedicated to the advancement of cross-border environmental collaboration, and to support community participation in local development. Walters holds a master's degree in international peace and conflict resolution from the School of International Service at American University, where his research focused on international peace parks and environmental peacebuilding. While at American University, he received the Petra Kelley Memorial Award for activism on environmental and peace issues. Walters is a National Outdoor Leadership School–certified adventure guide and has led expeditions in dozens of locations around the globe. Published works by Walters include, "Environmental Peacebuilding: Extending the Framework for Collaboration," "The Social-Ecological Aspects of Conducting a Transboundary Peace and Conflict Impact Assessment in Waterton-Glacier International Peace Park," and the entry "Experiential Peacebuilding" for the Oxford International Encyclopedia of Peace.

Christian Webersik is an associate professor at the Department of Development Studies, University of Agder. In 2007, Webersik joined the United Nations University–Institute of Advanced Studies as a postdoctoral fellow to research links between drought and political violence. Before that, he worked briefly for the Bureau for Crisis Prevention and Recovery of the United Nations Development Programme (UNDP) and was a postdoctoral fellow at Columbia University's Earth Institute. In the course of his career, Webersik has worked with UNDP, the Office of the United Nations High Commissioner for Refugees, and the United Nations Office for the Coordination of Humanitarian Affairs. His main areas of interest are human interaction with the environment, the role of environmental factors in armed conflict, and the impact of natural hazards on well-being and livelihoods. He holds a D.Phil. in political science from Oxford University, where he studied the political economy of war and the role of natural resources in conflict in Somalia.

Carol Westrik is an art historian with a specialty in cultural landscapes and has recently done research at the Vrije Universiteit, in Amsterdam. She also has her own consultancy as a heritage advisor. Her current research focuses on World Heritage sites and on the role of heritage in conflict-affected areas. Her latest publications are linked to World Heritage sites and associated issues in the Netherlands. Westrik has a Ph.D. in post-war reconstruction and development from York University; her doctoral work focused on contested landscapes as a tool for peace.

Helen Young is a research director at the Feinstein International Center and a professor at the Friedman School of Nutrition Science and Policy, Tufts University. Since 2004, she has directed the Darfur Livelihoods Program at the Feinstein International Center, which has become a Sudan-wide, research-based network of local, national, and international actors focusing on livelihoods, conflict, and the environment. For more than twenty-five years, Young has combined practical field experience with writing; undertaking action research; and producing best-practice guidelines, training packages, minimum standards, and sectoral strategies and policies. Young has written more than fifty peer-reviewed articles, books, book chapters, reports, and conference papers—and, since 1998, has been the coeditor of the journal *Disasters*.

Asif Zaidi is operations manager for the Post-Conflict and Disaster Management Branch of the United Nations Environment Programme (UNEP). He has more than two decades of experience in international development and environmental management in Afghanistan, Iran, Pakistan, and Tajikistan and has worked for the Aga Khan Development Network, the International Union for Conservation of Nature, and the government of Iran. Before assuming his current post, in Geneva, Switzerland, he spent more than four years as program manager for UNEP in Afghanistan. Zaidi is qualified as a medical doctor, holds a master's degree in public health from Leeds University, and has studied at the Yale University School of Forestry and Environmental Studies and at the Cranfield University School of Management.

APPENDIX 3

Table of contents for *Post-Conflict Peacebuilding and Natural Resource Management*

This book is one of a set of six edited books on post-conflict peacebuilding and natural resource management, all published by Earthscan. Following is the table of contents for the full set. Titles and authors are subject to change.

Forest user groups and peacebuilding in Nepal
Tina Sanio and Binod Chapagain

Lurking beneath the surface: Oil, environmental degradation, and armed conflict in Sudan
Luke A. Patey

Part 6: Lessons learned

Building or spoiling peace? Lessons from the management of high-value natural resources
Siri Aas Rustad, Päivi Lujala, and Philippe Le Billon

ASSESSING AND RESTORING NATURAL RESOURCES IN POST-CONFLICT PEACEBUILDING
Edited by David Jensen and Steve Lonergan

Foreword
Klaus Töpfer

Placing environment and natural resource risks, impacts, and opportunities on the post-conflict peacebuilding agenda
David Jensen and Steve Lonergan

Part 1: Post-conflict environmental assessments

Introduction

Evaluating the impact of UNEP's post-conflict environmental assessments
David Jensen

Environment and peacebuilding in war-torn societies: Lessons from the UN Environment Programme's experience with post-conflict assessment
Ken Conca and Jennifer Wallace

Medical and environmental intelligence in peace and crisis-management operations
Birgitta Liljedahl, Annica Waleij, Björn Sandström, and Louise Simonsson

Thinking back-end: Improving post-conflict analysis through consulting, adapting to change, and scenario building
Alexander Carius and Achim Maas

Part 2: Remediation of environmental hot spots

Introduction

Salting the Earth: Environmental health challenges in post-conflict reconstruction
Chad Briggs and Inka Weissbecker

GOVERNANCE, NATURAL RESOURCES, AND POST-CONFLICT PEACEBUILDING

Edited by Carl Bruch, Carroll Muffett, and Sandra S. Nichols

Index

NOTE: Page numbers followed by *f* indicate figures; those with *t* indicate tables.